Contents

KU-036-339

Programming Data

Off-Air

Directory

Index

CHRISTIE'S

Entertainment Memorabilia

Auctions 2004
Vintage Film Posters
16 September
Film & Entertainment
Memorabilia
14 December

Enquiries
Sarah Hodgson
+44 (0)20 7752 3281

Catalogues
+44 (0)20 7389 2820

South Kensington
85 Old Brompton Road
London, SW7 3LD

View catalogues and
leave bids online at
christies.com

Breakfast At Tiffany's
1961, Paramount, a rare double-sided U.S.
one-sheet cinema poster
Sold for £13,145 March 2004

Film Distributors' Association *presents*

www.launchingfilms.com

*Featuring the essential guide to UK
film distribution, weekly release schedule,
industry talking points and more*

"Extremely user-friendly, incredibly informative"
"Great...so professional"
"It's the business"

On screens everywhere now

Foreword

About this book

Welcome to the first *BFI Television Handbook – the Essential Guide to UK TV*. The first? As it happens, yes. Though the *BFI Film and Television Handbook* has become an annual fixture, the industries have become so extended, so diverse, it seemed to make less and less sense to try combining film and TV in one set of covers. Television in particular seemed short-changed in the old format, so now we have two books for the two industries.

The book's purpose is to engage readers from the ranks of professionals, serious followers and fans of UK TV, students and tutors in many sectors of education and readers from other interested industries and professions. The format is intended to provide a wide range of content: from broad industry statistics and a selection of significant industry contact details, to overviews of TV activity by channel and by genre, with commentary and opinion on format and content developments as well a taster of 'off-air' culture devoted to TV. Our ambitions have been to be broad in both content and readership.

The BFI Television Handbook begins with a broad statistical overview, and then puts the industry policy and various channels under the microscope before an extensive overview of programming trends. (See the list of Contents for further elaboration.) How should the book be read? The book can be read in sequence if you like but we expect most people to hop from section to section. Most material is self-contained and chapters can be read as stand-alone sections. That said it is intended that out of this mosaic, readers can form a picture of a complex whole with most of the important contemporary strands of UK TV being touched upon along the way.

As regards timing, the majority of the book's chapters reflect on an entire year. Note the year in question is a 'broadcasting' year which gears up in September after the annual debating showcase of the Edinburgh Television festival at the end of August. Though in one section, 'Looking Ahead', there is a conscious look to the immediate future, the book's focus and purpose is to look at the immediate past from the autumn of 2003 to the summer of 2004.

One of the problems tackling TV is its sheer pace of development which has contributed to the relative lack of academic engagement with the contemporary industry and inhibited much in the way of considered industry reflection. Moving on keeps moving on. And who individually can keep tabs on all but a tiny fraction of traditional and multichannel programming in a year? In this context there was little alternative but to engage many hands from the worlds of journalism, the public sector, librarianship, universities and television itself to try and capture this picture in perpetual motion. The various specialists may not sing with one voice but we think that *en masse* they offer a formidable critical chorus on a contemporary industry that probably doesn't often have the most considered public reflection on its activities (although right now Ofcom might dispute that).

Of course the views expressed here are not those of the BFI but always of the many contributors, all of whom selflessly got behind the 'project' and offered up their knowledge and views for a wider public. Of course there will be gaps: so apologies to religious programming, for inattention to reflection on the output of the English regions and for not delving too far into TV celebrity culture which we feel is covered extensively elsewhere. For any inaccuracies we would of course appreciate notification.

Ultimately the book was driven by a passionate conviction by BFI staff, the book's editor and our contributors, that there was more of a serious nature to say about contemporary UK television than was readily available to the wider public. We hope you agree that this book takes a good step in that direction.

A unique Cinema and TV Studio

35 seats in a spacious auditorium with raked seating

A large variety of stylised reception rooms

Compatible with all video formats and 35mm presentations

Contact Joe Bateman
Direct line: 020 7170 9134
joeb@thehospital.co.uk
www.thehospital.co.uk

THE HOSPITAL

24 ENDELL STREET
LONDON WC2H 9HQ

Acknowledgments

Obviously a book like this is a logistical puzzle that can only be solved by a group effort. Thanks must of course go to our named contributing writers for their submissions and their patience when events moved on just prior to our publication deadlines (moving on keeps moving on indeed) and revisions – and revisions of revisions – were required. A little special credit too, is reserved for contributors who responded at the publishing equivalent of 'two minutes to midnight': they were Luke Hockley, Alby James, Andrea Millwood Hargrave and Janice Turner.

Thanks are due to the sub-editors, who took charge of their allocated sections: to Phil Wickham for compiling our Statistics section; to Tise Vahimagi for his unstinting work on Programming Data (and for all those lengthy conversations on the exact title of the current *Poirot* films); and to Information Services Manager Peter Todd for overseeing the activities of BFI Information Services staff in assembling our Directory.

Advice and guidance also came from the *BFI Film Handbook* Editor Eddie Dyja and Dick Fiddy. Dick's 1985 *Television Yearbook* has been on my bookshelf for many a year and acted as a fantastic inspiration for this book – his practical advice was much appreciated. Thanks are due to the sometimes unsung heroes without whom and all that: Tess Forbes, Susanna Goodson, Matt Ker, Erinna Mettler, Ian O'Sullivan, David Reeve and Phil Wickham (again) in Information Services and also Ayesha Khan, Anastasia Kerameos, Emma Smart and Eddie Dyja (again) in the BFI Library for researching the majority of our Directory material. Also, huge thanks go to Claire Milburn in marketing, Ronnie Hackston for advertising and to Tom Cabot in production – who we have to thank for getting this book to you as paper and ink – and also to Jonathan Tilston for his assistance in his brief stay with the BFI.

I'd also like to extend my personal thanks to various bods only too happy to help out a desperate editor with interviews and info – Richard Marson at *Blue Peter*, Tim Beddows at Network, Steve Rogers, Graham Kibble-White, Steven Moffat, Tom Spilsbury and in particular Paul Moore for never considering any minor request to be too much trouble.

I would like to suggest that this was all my idea, a project inspired by the constant frustration any TV historian feels when faced with researching the 90s, without recourse to the wonderful old BBC and ITV/IBA yearbooks of record which were published annually in the 60s, 70s and 80s. I can claim no such thing however, as the *BFI TV Handbook* has come about only due to the vision and dogged determination of former BFI Head of Publishing Andrew Lockett. Andrew left the BFI halfway through this project for commercial publishing pastures anew but he has continued to devote incredible amounts of his spare time to ensuring that the project stayed on track. I am hugely grateful to Andrew for believing I could edit this title and I hope his faith was not misplaced.

Lastly, huge thanks to Barrie MacDonald – his input is credited throughout this book but he has also worked tirelessly without credit to keep us all straight on factual matters in the past year. Barrie provided the index to this book, as he did on so many of the classic ITV/IBA yearbooks – we hope readers will detect a not so indirect link to that fine publishing heritage.

Dr Alistair D. McGown

new television studies titles from wallflower press
www.wallflowerpress.co.uk

Big Brother International
Formats, Critics and Publics

edited by Ernest Mathijs and Janet Jones
foreword by John Corner

£15.99 pbk   1–904764–18–5
£45.00 hbk   1–904764–19–3

November 2004

Big Brother is one of the key cultural phenomena to mark the move into the twenty-first century. Both scandal and commercial hit, it has revolutionised television practice, changing the status of live multimedia events and challenging cultural theory. This book tells the story of its international impact. It chronicles many of the most striking moments of the show's global career, putting these events in perspective by linking them to their respective cultural contexts and media audiences. This unique collection includes essays on *Big Brother* Africa, Argentina, Australia, Belgium, Brazil, France, Germany, Italy, the Netherlands, South Africa, Turkey, the UK, Uruguay and the US, and thus constitutes an important step in understanding contemporary global media culture.

Reality TV
Realism and Revelation

Anita Biressi and Heather Nunn

£15.99 pbk   1–903364–04–5
£45.00 hbk   1–903364–05–3

November 2004

Reality television has little to do with reality and everything to do with television form and content. This book takes the reality television phenomenon to be a significant movement within documentary and factual programming. It analyses new and hybrid genres including observational documentaries, talk shows, game shows, docu-soaps, dramatic reconstructions, law and order programming and 24/7 formats such as *Big Brother* and *Survivor*. These programmes are both popular with audiences and heavily debated in the media; they are at the centre of heated discussions about tabloidisation, media ethics, voyeurism and the representation of the real. Through detailed case studies this book breaks new ground by linking together two major themes: the production of realism and its relationship to revelation.

wallflower press • 4th *floor 26 shacklewell lane* • *london e8 2ez* • t: 020 7690 0115 • e: *info@wallflowerpress.co.uk*

Robbery, cookery and two great Danes.

Masterfully directed and winner of Un Certain Regard Jury Award at Cannes, this is an intimate, absorbing and powerful drama set on the streets of Tehran.

Offering delightfully droll observations on national misunderstandings, Bent Hamer's Kitchen Stories is a comedy not to be missed.

A fascinating, visually stunning look at the human condition, and the creativity it engenders. A must-see for any dedicated fan of film-making.

PREDICTABLY UNPREDICTABLE FILMS

Available now from selected stores

That Was The Year

Dick Fiddy
with Alistair McGown

What a year it's been. Presented here is a calendar of the key moments in one of most eventful periods in the recent history of British television.

July 2003

18 Sky News sack reporter James Forlong after it transpires that he 'faked' a news report of a cruise missile firing, using library footage.

23 Italian State TV chief Lucia Annunziata says she will quit if a new bill is passed giving more media control to Prime Minister Silvio Berlusconi.

August 2003

29 Survey by Human Capital media research firm finds that Saturday night is now the least watched evening of TV in the UK.

31 Anna Kournikova ends her short career as a sports reporter for the USA Network

September 2003

2 BBC veteran all-round sports commentator and presenter Peter West dies, aged 83.

3 Survey publishes stating that one in three under-sixes watch between two and six hours of TV a day

3 ITN reveal their Top 20 footage requests. The top 5 are: 1) Moon Landing, 2) JFK Assassination, 3) 9/11, 4) Princess Diana Funeral, 5) 1966 World Cup

4 Five announce first full year profit

5 Battersea Arts Centre (originators of *Jerry Springer – The Opera*) announces new production, *Newsnight – The Opera.*

5 Britain's poor showing at the World Athletics Championships is blamed for BBC 1's lowest-ever peak viewing figures.

6 Illusionist David Blaine begins forty-four day fast in glass box suspended over London, an event covered heavily by Sky.

9 Daily Telegraph announces *Beebwatch*, a new series monitoring BBC bias.

14 Victoria Baths gets the winning votes in BBC 2's *Restoration* series, which pitches historic structures against each other to win money for restoration.

21 Children are more affected by violence in the news than violence in TV soaps or dramas, states a report commissioned by the ITC, BBC, Broadcasting Standards Commission (BSC) and the British Board of Film Classification (BBFC).

23 BSkyB chief executive Tony Ball is to step down from the post.

24 Graham Norton lands a two-year multi-million pound deal with the US's Comedy Central channel to make a US version of his hit Channel 4 show.

25 Study (by Strathclyde University scientists for the Food Standards Agency) states that TV advertising encourages unhealthy eating in children and probably plays a key role in obesity.

25 BBC announces that a new series of *Doctor Who* is being planned.

29 Dirty Den (Leslie Grantham) returns to *EastEnders* after an absence of fourteen years. 17 million viewers watch the return as Den confronts his daughter Sharon with the words 'Hello Princess'.

Den Watts (Leslie Grantham) back from the dead in *EastEnders*

October 2003

2 ITV announces it will drop *News at Ten* and move bulletin to 10.30 p.m.

5 *Coronation Street* airs its first gay kiss in its forty-three year history when Todd Grimshaw (Bruno Langley) kisses his girlfriend's brother Nick Tilsley (Adam Rickitt)

6 Survey (by BSC and ITC) concerned with sex in soap operas says viewers voted in favour of retaining the watershed.

6 Renowned 'mentalist' Derren Brown presents controversial 'Russian Roulette' routine on Channel 4.

6 James Forlong – the journalist who faked a Sky News item – is found dead. Suicide is suspected.

7 Merger of media giants Carlton and Granada approved, paving the way for ITV plc. UTV, Scottish, Grampian and Channel remain independent.

8 BBC announces multi-million pound deal to screen series of Hollywood films including *Calendar Girls* and *Chicago*.

15 The DVD release of the second series of Peter Kay's *Phoenix Nights* becomes the fastest-ever selling of a TV series in the UK, breaking the record held previously by *The Office*.

21 Michael Green, Chairman of Carlton Group, bows to shareholder pressure and stands down.

21 BBC 1 airs a covertly made documentary *The Secret Policeman* – reporter Mark Daly goes undercover as a trainee officer and reveals racist attitudes prevalent among new recruits in the Greater Manchester Force. There is initial hostile reaction to Daly's 'deception' from government figures but within weeks six officers featured in the programme have either been suspended or have resigned from the force.

Coronation Street

22 Thameslink (Bedford to Gatwick service) trial-runs on-board TV service (TNX) consisting of bite-size news and magazine programmes.

25 Meg Ryan makes a controversial appearance on the *Parkinson* show, seemingly uncomfortable with *Parkinson* and his line of questioning, making for excruciating but fascinating TV.

30 ITV announces it's pulling *Man Versus Beast* from the schedules (due to air Saturday 1 November). ITV deny the cancellation was due to animal rights protests and instead claim it was merely a scheduling decision.

Michael Green, ex-Carlton boss

Derren Brown plays *Russian Roulette*

There's Something About Miriam

30 Sky One announce new reality show *There's Something About Miriam*, filmed in the summer in Ibiza by Brighter Pictures. Six men vie for the attentions of the beautiful Miriam only to find out finally that Miriam is a transsexual. Contestants who took part in the show threaten to sue.

31 Sky One announces it is postponing *There's Something About Miriam*.

November 2003

4 Final episode of Channel 4 soap *Brookside* airs, attracting 1.9 million viewers. The series had begun in 1982.

4 Thirty-year-old James Murdoch (son of Rupert) takes over as chief executive at BSkyB.

12 Greek TV station Mega is fined 100,000 Euros for airing footage of two men kissing. Greek TV critic Popi Diamamdakaou says that the fine is hypocritical after shots of Britney Spears kissing Madonna at the last MTV Awards were repeatedly shown.

23 Bosnian TV station TV Pink (Serbian-owned) has announced it will screen Granada's *Prime Suspect 6* – which concerns the murder of a Bosnian refugee – over Christmas and the New year.

24 At the International Emmy Awards, BBC Director General Greg Dyke attacks US TV news coverage of the Iraq war.

December 2003

12 BBC poach Graham Norton from Channel 4 in a multi-million dollar 'golden handcuffs' deal.

16 Sky News fined £50,000 over James Forlong's faked news item.

20 Michelle McManus wins *Pop Idol* – a result criticised in many circles as Michelle is claimed, by some, to be a poor role model due to her excess weight.

23 The ITC's final annual report criticises ITV for failing to compete 'as strongly as it could' with the BBC. The report praised ITV drama but said the current affairs series *Tonight with Trevor McDonald* was 'uneven in range and quality'.

27 Combined ratings of BBC and ITV over Christmas are less than 50 per cent for the first time ever.

28 Veteran TV presenter/comedian Bob Monkhouse dies.

30 Channel 4's audience share has fallen below 10 per cent for the first time in a decade (BARB). The fall comes amid accusations that the channel relies too much on reality and property programmes.

January 2004

1 Norwegian singer Kurt Nilsen is named *World Idol* after an international TV contest with other *Pop Idol* winners.

9 BBC suspend *Kilroy* programme following the response to a Robert Kilroy-

Silk newspaper article attacking Arabs. The Friday edition goes ahead but the show is replaced from Monday.

9 Sky One air a *Simpsons* episode featuring a special guest appearance from Prime Minister Tony Blair.

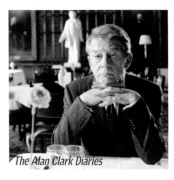
The Alan Clark Diaries

13 BBC is accused of 'hiding away' arts and cultural programming on new digital channel BBC 4. The row has come to a head following the BBC's heavy advertising for *The Alan Clark Diaries* which is only available on the minority digital channel.

15 Afghanistan re-instates a ban on women appearing on TV in reaction to complaints following the broadcast of a twenty year-old clip of a woman singing without a headscarf.

15 Embarrassment reigns in Spain when, live on TV, leading Spanish politician José Bono – unaware that his comments are being picked up by a TV crew – refers to Tony Blair as a 'complete dickhead' ('un gilipollas integral').

16 Robert Kilroy-Silk quits as presenter of his BBC discussion show following the suspension of the series.

GREG DYKE RESIGNS
Greg Dyke leaves Broadcasting House

16 *The Alan Clark Diaries* attract record audiences for BBC 4 (836,000 viewers).

26 Ricky Gervais and his series *The Office* unexpectedly win two Golden Globe Awards at the ceremony in Los Angeles. An American version of the show is in the works.

27 70s athlete David Bedford wins ruling against new directory inquiries provider 118-118 for spoofing his image in their series of TV adverts.

28 The Hutton Report is finally published. It criticises the BBC but exonerates Tony Blair from any blame. BBC Chairman Gavyn Davies quits in response.

28 In Italy critics claim RAI has banned two journalists because they are unpopular with the government of media tycoon Silvio Berlusconi.

29 More Hutton fall-out as Greg Dyke resigns as BBC DG.

30 Andrew Gilligan – the reporter whose story provoked the Hutton inquiry – resigns from the BBC.

February 2004

2 ITV plc floats on the stock exchange. ITV rebranding is rolled out in merged Carlton and Granada regions and the ITV News identity is established.

2 Moral outrage in the US when singer Janet Jackson bares one of her breasts during a routine in the Super Bowl entertainment extravaganza. The ensuing hysterical reaction to the 'wardrobe malfunction' even affects the upcoming Oscar ceremony which will now not be televised 'live' for the first time.

4 A study of America's most watched TV shows ever is published. No less than two stateside performances by The Beatles are in the Top 5. The Top 5 are:
1) *M*A*S*H* finale 1983 (105.9 million viewers)
2) Beatles on *The Ed Sullivan Show* 9 February 1964 (73 million)
3) Beatles on Ed Sullivan 16 February 1964 (70.7 million)
4) Super Bowl XVI 1982 (85.2 million)
5 *Dallas* – Who Shot JR 1980 (83 million).
Survey was based on percentage of population watching rather than viewing figures.

5 John Lydon walks out of ITV's *I'm A Celebrity … Get Me Out Of Here.*

9 Former Atomic Kitten star Kerry McFadden wins *I'm A Celebrity ... Get Me Out Of Here.*

15 BBC announces that *The Two Ronnies* show is to return to screens after a seventeen-year absence.

22 *Sex and the City* final episode airs in the US (see March for UK airdate).

25 US viewers in LA watching a police chase live, witness the felon being shot dead in a hail of police bullets.

25 At the Royal Television Society journalistic awards ITN takes the top award for its coverage of the Iraq war.

26 Rumours circulate that Channel 4 and Five could be planning a merger after discussions about combining sales operations are opened up into other areas.

27 Journalists from Central TV protest against ITV's decision (following the Carlton/Granada merger) to close the Nottingham Studios.

Michael Grade arrives at the BBC

March 2004

2 BBC announces it will put coverage of the upcoming Olympic games and Glastonbury Festival live on the internet.

3 Anglia TV Weather presenter Sara Thornton, stumbles over her script and utters a string of swear words on air. Anglia later explains that a rehearsal tape has been broadcast in error.

5 NBC faces criticism for airing *Princess Diana: The Secret Tapes,* hitherto unseen tapes of Princess Diana talking candidly about her marriage problems.

5 OFSTED chief David Bell praises *Buffy The Vampire Slayer* and says more such shows of female empowerment 'would help to ensure that the superior achievements of girls in school and university were mirrored later in careers'.

9 Sky News sign a £40 million deal with Five to replace ITN as the channel's news provider.

19 *Sex and the City* final episode airs in the UK on Channel 4, attracting 4.1 million viewers.

20 Actor Christopher Eccleston is announced as the lead in the BBC's upcoming *Doctor Who* series.

28 BBC 2's search to find Britain's favourite sitcom ends in triumph for *Only Fools and Horses,* which beats second placed *Blackadder* and third placed *Vicar of Dibley.*

29 BBC 2 Controller Jane Root announces she is leaving the BBC to work for the Discovery Channel in the US.

April 2004

2 Michael Grade appointed new Chairman of the BBC. He will take up the post on 17 May.

13 Former *Blue Peter* presenter Caron Keating dies of breast cancer at forty-one.

19 Australian soap *Neighbours* makes its US debut on the cable channel Oxygen.

20 BBC 2 celebrates its fortieth anniversary.

21 Soccer pundit Ron Atkinson resigns from ITV after racist comments about Chelsea footballer Marcel Desailly are broadcast. The insulting comment was heard on some Middle East channels broadcasting a live feed after ITV went off-air following Chelsea's 3-1 loss to Monaco in a Champions League semi-final first leg.

May 2004

6 In the US, the final episode of *Friends* airs to an audience of over 50 million.

8 Michael Parkinson presents his last BBC chat show, with Bruce Forsyth as his main guest. Parkinson has signed a new deal with ITV.

14 Roly Keating, Controller of digital channel BBC 4, is announced as successor to Jane Root as Controller of BBC 2.

15 *The Eurovision Song Contest* brings more disappointment for the UK – British entrant James Fox scores twenty-nine points and sixteenth place amid increasingly partisan voting. BBC commentator Terry Wogan registers his dismay at voting bias: 'Someone has got to stop this. The European Broadcasting Union has to take a hand.'

17 Michael Grade takes his seat as Chairman of the BBC Board of Governors.

17 SMG officially announces it is to sell Scottish TV's Cowcaddens studio site to

Derren Brown: Séance

developers and move to new riverside premises on Pacific Quay, next door to BBC Scotland's future home. It aims to open the new site in Autumn 2006.

17 *EastEnders* records a new low of 6.4 million viewers for its Tuesday episode (not including the omnibus figures), up against both a one-hour *Emmerdale* special and good summer weather.

20 Richard and Judy sign a deal worth £6.5 million to keep their daily 5 p.m. show on Channel 4 for the next three years – reports suggest Nigel Pickard tried to take them and the show to the same slot on ITV1.

21 The BBC appoint Channel 4 Chief Executive Mark Thompson as new Director General.

24 Following a lengthy period of rumour, the BBC confirms actress Billie Piper will play Rose Tyler, new assistant to Christopher Eccleston's *Doctor Who*.

24 Setanta Sport announces that its newly acquired Scottish Premier League package of thirty-eight live matches will cost digital football fans a monthly subscription of £12.99. Their four-year contract follows two years of 'free' football from BBC 1 Scotland.

27 The Commons Health Select Committee publishes a report aimed at tackling increasing child obesity levels – among various recommendations is a call

to crackdown on junk food TV advertising aimed at children and it's particularly keen to see endorsements of unhealthy food by sports stars banned.

27 BBC 1 England and Wales air a Party Political Broadcast by the British National Party (BBC 1 Scotland showed it the previous day), but Five refuses to air a different BNP broadcast supplied to them, containing what they feel are unsubstantiated claims of rape of a white teenager by Asian youths which may break broadcasting codes by inciting racial hatred. The BNP complies with Five's requested edits – the final broadcast version has almost its entire soundtrack obscured.

27 Channel 4 airs the last ever episode of *Friends*. With advertisers paying double the regular £50,000 ad rate they are rewarded with a viewing audience of 9.64 million. *Big Brother 5* benefits as it opens the same night with 6.7 million.

31 Channel 4 screens *Derren Brown: Séance* – Ofcom receive 208 complaints and Channel 4 497 complaints. While most were received before the show aired (such complaints are usually ignored) this makes it the third most complained about programme since the first ITC records, 'beaten' only by the TV showing of *The Last Temptation of Christ* and the *Brass Eye Special*. If they'd actually waited to watch all would have been explained ...

 Emma makes her point – *Big Brother 5*

June 2004

1 Jane Root takes up her post as general manager at the Discovery Channel in the US; Roly Keating steps in as acting controller until he begins his post full time on 21 June.

6 Freelance cameraman Simon Cumbers is killed in Riyadh in a drive-by shooting while covering terrorist events in Saudi Arabia for the BBC. The BBC's Security Correspondent Frank Gardner is seriously wounded in the attack. By early July, Gardner is in a British hospital, making a slow but steady recovery.

10 BSkyB makes the first announcement of its 'Freesat' offering, intended to plug a recognised gap in the digital switchover strategy and compete with Freeview. Initial indications are that a one-off fee of £150 will give viewers up to 200 channels without subscription from the Autumn – the boxes used will be capable of being upgraded to Sky subscription packages at a later date.

14 England's Euro 2004 match against France attracts 17.6 million viewers to ITV1 (reaching a peak of 20.7 million at 9.30 p.m.). This makes it ITV1's most watched programme of the year thus far, beating the 16 February edition of *Coronation Street*, which had scored 16.3 million.

14 Channel 4's head of specialist factual, Janice Hadlow, is confirmed as the controller of BBC 4.

17 A violent confrontation breaks out in the *Big Brother* house at around 1.30 a.m. and for the first time in the series' (UK) history, security has to intervene as the live feeds on Channel 4, E4 and the web are taken off the air for several hours. The Hertfordshire police answer worried viewers' calls and launch their own investigation. More than 200 viewer complaints are received within days, prompting Ofcom to fast track a review into the incident.

24 England go out of Euro 2004, losing to host nation Portugal on penalties. This dramatic national event draws a huge average of 20.6 million (73.6 per cent) throughout the match with the penalty shoot-out hitting a colossal peak of 24.7 million viewers. The BBC claims this is the highest figure ever recorded for a televised BBC sports event.

29 The BBC takes the first steps towards Charter Renewal by publishing its *Building Public Value* manifesto. The document tackles many of the key questions aimed at the corporation. It defends the BBC's right to the licence fee; pledges to drop ratings-chasing, derivative shows; advocates moving parts of the corporation to Manchester and creating a new Central region based in Milton Keynes; gives its continued backing to promoting take-up of digital services; suggests public value testing of any proposed new services and confirms there will be governance reform.

July 2004

6 *EastEnders* earns another disastrous overnight rating, again up against a one-hour *Emmerdale* on ITV1 – 6.3 million compared with Emmerdale's 6.9 million. Yorkshire Television begins to make noises about plans to make *Emmerdale* Britain's second soap.

13 The BBC publishes its Annual Report for 2003-4, set to become one of its most closely scrutinised in years. Commercial rivals predictably look beyond the spin to ask if the reach of the new digital services in particular offers a valuable return for such considerable investment.

17 The DCMS publishes the results of its research into what more than 5000 licence payers think of the BBC. *What You Said About the BBC* reveals that 85 per cent of respondents have little idea of how the BBC is run, many complain about derivative programmes and a lack of 'cutting edge' but there is general support for the licence fee when alternatives are suggested to those questioned.

20 Five men are arrested in the week following *The Secret Agent*, BBC 1's undercover exposé of racism in the British National Party. The arrests are instigated by scenes of activists seemingly confessing to race hate crimes.

20 Bookmakers pay out after conceding that, finally, two *Big Brother* housemates have had sex on the programme. Stuart Wilson and Michelle Bass appeared to do the deed while hidden under a table, with the soundtrack providing the strongest suggestion yet of the 'Big Brother Bonk' so eagerly anticipated by the tabloids. The scenes, from the early hours of the previous morning, are aired on tonight's highlights programme – overnights calculate 5.8 million viewers are watching (30.7 per cent share) with the 'sex' scenes at the programme's climax drawing 6.3 million (34 per cent).

22 BBC Director of News Richard Sambrook is to be moved to a new position in the World Service and Global News division, to be replaced by Radio Four Controller Helen Boaden.

22 Ofcom publishes the findings of a study into the effects of TV snack advertising on growing child obesity levels in the UK. They find sufficient empirical evidence to conclude that TV advertising has only a 'modest' direct effect on children's food choices as well

Mark Thompson and Michael Grade launch the *Building Public Value* document

as possibly a substantial amount of indirect effects. Factors such as children's own taste preferences, price, familiarity, peer pressure, parental choice, healthiness and convenience are thought be more important influences on diet. The report makes no recommendation – that is for the DCMS to decide – but an outright ban of snack advertising on children's TV now looks less likely.

22 Brighter Pictures, makers of *There's Something About Miriam*, announce another controversial programme idea, *Make me a Mum*. In what Brighter describe as a science show investigating fertility, a group of men will be vetted to find the most suitable sperm donor for a childless woman. It's not known whether the show will air in the US, UK or both.

23 Tessa Jowell sets about formulating a realistic timetable for digital switchover. 2012 now looks more likely for total switchover rather than 2010. The cost of the exercise may be up to £1 billion.

26 TV chef Gordon Ramsay and indie producer Optomen sign an exclusive three-year deal with Channel 4. Disappointed will be ITV, who had

planned a second series of reality show *Hell's Kitchen* for Ramsay.

26 A seven-day EPG is rolled out on capable Freeview boxes, replacing the old 'Now and Next' system. The service is initially available on the Crystal Palace, Waltham, Sandy Heath, Oxford, Tacolneston, Bluebell Hill, Fenton, Caradon Hill and Rowridge transmitters.

28 Ofcom imposes its first fine on a broadcaster. Satellite channel XplicitXXX, is fined £50,000 for accidentally broadcasting their porn shows unencrypted on Sky Digital between 8.30 and 10 p.m. on 8 April.

29 Michael Grade makes his first appointments to the BBC Board of Governors – leading corporate lawyer Anthony Salz is appointed vice chairman to replace Lord Ryder and Richard Tait, Professor of Journalism at Cardiff University and former ITN editor-in-chief, also joins.

With acknowledgment to *Broadcast* magazine, www.bbc.co.uk, www.digitalspy.co.uk and *The Guardian* among other sources.

Looking Ahead: 2004–5

Alistair D. McGown

If a week is a long time in politics, then a year in television must be a lifetime. Back in September 2003 Greg Dyke was still the BBC's Director General, Carlton and Granada were separate ITV power blocs, *Big Brother* looked to have run its course with a moribund fourth series and there were fewer digital than analogue viewers watching at home.

The run-in between the BBC and the government over *that* radio two-way seems to have run its course – at least as far as the BBC is concerned. When new DG Mark Thompson took to the stage at the Edinburgh Television Festival on Sunday 29 August he seemed unconcerned with the headlines delegates had woken to find in that morning's *Observer*. Greg Dyke was giving his side of the Hutton story in extracts from his forthcoming book *Inside Story* – Alastair Campbell was labelled 'a deranged, vindictive bastard', while the board of governors were accused of having acted like 'frightened rabbits'. The book will be published on 20 September with a Channel 4 documentary to follow soon after.

The BBC, it seems, has moved on and now finds itself, oddly, in perhaps a stronger position than before Hutton. The government's appointment of Michael Grade as BBC Chairman – a politically-neutral, lifelong television man – was seen by many as an olive branch. With Thompson, a longstanding BBC man with extensive recent experience in commercial television at Channel 4,

Building Public Value is a rod for the BBC's own back and no doubt on occasions in 2004-5 it will also readily serve as a stick which its enemies will use to beat it.

at Grade's side it seems the right men were in place to tackle the initial findings of Ofcom's Public Service Review and re-examine the BBC's core values. The Hutton affair, not for the first time in the Corporation's history, illustrated that the dual role of the Governors as defenders and inquisitors of the BBC's activities was at best fraught and at worst untenable – if the affair leads at last to a radical, meaningful restructure of the governing mechanism, the BBC may yet have cause to be thankful for their slap on the wrist.

Grade and Thompson claim their *Building Public Value* manifesto is not intended as a cynical charter renewal strategy aimed at sealing a continuation of the licence fee from 2006 – more than that, it is a response to the recent proclamations of the DCMS and Ofcom and, above all, an increasingly digital broadcasting market. The document's more far-reaching promises include moves to decentralise the BBC, with new or extended production and broadcast facilities in the likes of Bristol, Birmingham, Milton Keynes, Glasgow and possibly a genuine second power base in Manchester. Peter Salmon is currently undertaking this facilities review and his verdict is expected in late December. The manner and extent to which resources, services and commissioning powers might be moved out of London are guaranteed to be a talking point in 2005.

As far as television is concerned, Thompson has vowed to 'eliminate derivative programmes from the schedules'. Critics will watch closely to see if talk of 'quality and originality' and 'excellence [that] is not elitist' can go beyond mere spin. It's tempting to see the Autumn 2004 BBC 1 and BBC 2 schedules as the first fruits of this new refocus on Public Service Broadcasting but as BBC 1 Controller Lorraine Heggessey reminds us, it would usually take two years for such a policy change to yield concrete results.

The BBC's autumn schedule brochures

Certainly, there's plenty of 'typically BBC' fare among the forthcoming schedules. On BBC 1, Michael Palin's epic travelogue *Himalaya*, two years' in the making, will no doubt please all those who 'never watch television except for David Attenborough', as will *Bear – Spy in the Wood*, a six-part natural history series tracing the lives of species of bear all over the world. Popular approaches to education and factual, in the lucrative vein of *Walking With Dinosaurs*, come in the shape of *Space Odyssey*, a spectacular CGI-aided trip round the solar system and, on BBC 2, *The Future is Wild*, a speculative look at the future evolution of wildlife on earth.

This season's period drama centrepiece is Elizabeth Gaskell's *North and South*, a love story set among dark, satanic mills; while bosses must be hoping that quirky contemporary drama serial *Blackpool*, set among a seedy clubland world in the Vegas of the North and starring *State of Play*'s David Morrissey, will become this season's must-see critical favourite.

An apparent contemporary climate of fear and fascination is reflected in *Dirty War*, a dramatised account of a terrorist attack on London made in conjunction with the Current Affairs department, perhaps a successor of sorts to *The War Game* and *Threads*. Making terrorist disaster sexy is the rather stoic and corny Fox/BBC 2 co-production *The Grid*, while the channel also offers a post-9/11 game show variant *Crisis Command* alongside the BBC 2/3 co-commission *Spy*. Slick espionage thriller *Spooks* returns to BBC 1 for its third series.

Most importantly, the BBC will attempt to build public value with altruistic, public-spirited event programming that aims higher than the cruelty with premium phone lines attached on offer elsewhere. *Fat Nation* studies a Birmingham street's eating and exercise habits with the aim of getting Britain fitter but could yet descend into docusoap voyeurism. BBC 2 tries to get people interested in genealogy with the ten-part *Who Do You Think You Are?* – the format's lack of an artificial 'vote' perhaps demonstrates how Roly Keating's BBC 2 may differ from that of his predecessor Jane Root. A key entertainment show for BBC 1 will be *Hard Spell*, a spelling bee contest for 11-14s.

Hard Spell may well feature, flying the flag for respectable populism, in the Saturday evening schedules. 2004 hit *Strictly Come Dancing* will return in 2004-5; *Johnny and Denise – Passport to Paradise* probably won't. It's hard to reconcile *Building Public Value*'s tenets with a virtually all-year-round run of *Casualty* (and its weekday sister

Panini's official *Doctor Who Magazine* was thrilled to welcome Christopher Eccleston as the ninth Doctor, now due to debut on BBC 1 in Spring 2005

show *Holby City*) but the Saturday schedules from Spring 2005 look set for Russell T. Davies' brave, modern reworking of *Doctor Who*. Christopher Eccleston is an intense ninth Doctor, dressed down in jeans and leather jacket, with Billie Piper cast as his streetwise companion Rose. Senior BBC executives have realised that after a decade in the wilderness, the sci-fi show, enthusiastically and fiscally-backed, could be the unifying family hit BBC 1 craves. Bruce Forsyth, *Doctor Who* and the Daleks, *Match of the Day* ... there's a familiar ring to it. How recent purchase Graham Norton fits in is a source of conjecture.

Building Public Value is a rod for the BBC's own back and no doubt on occasions in 2004-5 it will also readily serve as a stick which its enemies will use to beat it. Makeover show *Changing Rooms* is the first major casualty of the new era and while there's no need for the BBC to don dull sackcloth and ashes, further moves into distinctive programming will be welcomed by critics. Whether viewers will appreciate such changes remains to be seen. If BBC 1 axes exhausted Australian soap *Neighbours* in the year to come we'll know they really mean it.

Richard Armitage and Daniela Denby-Ashe star in BBC 1 period drama *North and South*

Louis Walsh, Sharon Osbourne and Simon Cowell in *The X Factor* will be a fixture of ITV Saturday nights this autumn

ITV's future will be shaped by Phase Three of Ofcom's Public Service Review guidelines, due late September 2004 and also expected to recommend Channel 4's future funding modes.

ITV's Controller Nigel Pickard now regards BBC 1 more as a qualitative yardstick and not so much a head to head rival – in this multichannel age there are rivals all on sides. He sees ITV1's Autumn schedule as majoring in dramatic events – whether that be in written fictions or the Reality of *I'm a Celebrity* series four. Advance publicity suggests that ITV is getting its money up there on screen, with a slate of big-name, big-budget drama series and serials forthcoming.

There's Corrie and *Emmerdale* as ever, *Heartbeat* and *The Royal*, *Rosemary and Thyme*, *Taggart*, *Foyle's War*, *Midsomer Murders* and *Poirot* while the (ostensibly) new fare seems a collection of similarly reassuring surefire hits: ensemble firefighting drama *Steel River Blues* has already launched as an effective carbon copy of the much-loved *London's Burning*, relocated to the North East; Geraldine McEwan is the latest incarnation of Christie's *Miss Marple*; Martin Clunes is a cynical big city GP all at sea in a beautiful, sleepy Cornish village as *Doc Martin*. Further ahead, January 2005 looks set for Mr Television, David Jason, to return in a new role as an ex-con in *Diamond Geezers*.

If Mark Thompson promises that there will be 'risk in everything we do' at the BBC, ITV1's (valid) mission seems merely to please the crowds. If the rumours are true, 2005 may even see Kevin 'Leeeewis!' Whately return to ITV1 in a Morse-less *Inspector Morse*.

There are some signs of creativity in ITV1's drama output to be fair – three-part comedy drama anthology *Trapped* opened well with Caroline Quentin in 'Von Trapped!'. What the audience expected to be a daft, camp comedy about Maria, a woman with a *Sound of Music* fixation, featured a subtext about the trials of Maria's gender-swapping lesbian daughter. Martin Clunes (him again!) and Richard Wilson will star in the remaining instalments. ITV1 will also deviate from the conventional and the criminal to tread on BBC territory with *Dirty, Filthy Love*, a play about

Tourette's syndrome and obsessive compulsive disorder, and Stephen Fry stars in costume drama *Tom Brown's Schooldays*.

Like much of the drama slate, Simon Cowell's *The X Factor* seems unlikely to innovate, but Cowell hopes that the backstories of the older contestants (there is no upper age limit, unlike the twenty-five ceiling of *Pop Idol*) will engage viewers – its opening week served up toe-curling moments that everyone's talking about. Speaking of toes, Sarah Ferguson is among those rumoured to be signed up for *I'm a Celebrity*, back on ITV1 and ITV2 this Autumn (only seven months after its last run). A new reality event is *Press Ganged*, a month-long endurance test for two teams crewing a 19th Century sea vessel.

What will really shape ITV's imminent future will be the delivery of Phase Three of Ofcom's Public Service Review. Pickard and his colleagues stand beside the likes of *The South Bank Show* but resent the prescriptive guidelines they are forced to work within as regards arts, religious, regional and children's programmes. Will these guidelines be relaxed, or will ITV's PSB spectrum licence payments be reduced as due reward? The report is due in late September 2004.

That report will also have a serious influence on the direction of Channel 4 – it's expected to recommend the channel's future funding modes. The station is suffering a minor identity crisis in the wake of the loss of Graham Norton, *Friends*, *Sex and the City* and *Frasier*, not to mention the fumbled handling of the *Big Brother 5* fight. The autumn schedules hint at little in the way of clear focus – although the 5 November launch of *The Simpsons* is a statement of intent – but there are undoubtedly highlights in store, ranging from insane comedy *Green Wing* to David Starkey's history epic *Monarchy*. US co-production drama *NY-LON* looks all a bit aspirational and shallow but will draw fans. The channel also looks set to continue to major in primetime property shows (you have been warned). It may be a case of Channel 4 waiting to sort out the funding base first

– advertising, trust fund or PSB top-slicing – and then realigning remit and programming to match.

Five have of course been euphemistically drawn into Channel 4's future via loud whispers of the possible merger of the two. There's little doubt that without some kind of fairly radical repositioning sometime soon, both channels stand to become the biggest losers after digital switchover, when a position high up the EPG is no longer guaranteed in a more level playing field.

Five seems keen to chase the affluent 16-34 audience at present, an over-served audience, and a stronger identity – and programmes – are what's needed. Controller Dan Chambers is backing reality launch *The Farm* to be a hit, based on the central premise that viewers want to watch Paul Daniels, Debbie Magee and their ilk scrape sheep shit for a fortnight. Five's *Cosmetic Surgery Live!* has booked its place in TV Hell after just a few shows. Twin glamour models aimed for identical boob jobs and came into the studio Live! to bare their new assets Live! to appreciative coos from host Vanessa Feltz. Like the models' breasts, Chambers' hopes that such fare – Live! or no – can build share are surely over-inflated.

Real inroads could be made by serious money acquisition *Joey*, the *Friends* spin-off starring Matt le Blanc – bought for a rumoured £4-500,000 an episode. Some industry bods reckon Five paid over the odds but the demographic that came to Channel 4 for *Friends* could put Five on the map. Chambers sees the show – and another US acquisition, *Two and a Half Men* with Charlie Sheen – as central in building a platform for new British comedy material that will result from a partnership deal with Paramount Comedy UK. *Joey* should air from January-February 2005 but for now Five will be relying on returning popular tabloid strands like *The Curse of ...* and *Greatest ... Moments* and new shows *Boxing Academy* and *Pet Plastic Surgery*. You heard right.

Channel 4's unhinged hospital sitcom *Green Wing*

If *Joey* attracts the demographic that came to Channel 4 for *Friends*, it'll put Five on the map.

All of the above sees the terrestrial big boys adapting to the digital landscape, ever-mindful of share being slowly chipped away as digital take-up grows. Eyes will focus on the digital home percentages Ofcom will publish through 2004-5. There's no real major change in multichannel – Sky One for example is making moves to regain share by buying big in the US but has plans to move upmarket – though as it becomes available in more homes the share of non-analogue viewing may creep ever upwards.

If all the activity outlined here is predicated by the new technology, commentators will be closely observing the next years' innovations. ITV embraces the digital broadcast future, with ITV3 launching 1 November on Freeview (Sky will carry it soon after). ITV3 will air recent archive drama hits such as *Morse* and *A Touch of Frost*. ITV CEO Charles Allen indicated at Edinburgh that he was aiming at a family of five ITV channels, including a children's service – this latter idea appeared dead in the water only weeks before but perhaps new partnerships are being sourced.

Sky's free satellite service is to launch imminently, providing a one-off-payment BSkyB rival to Freeview; the BBC admits it's looking to launch its own satellite version of the DTT Freeview service. The first experimental steps towards digital switchover will take place with tests in several Welsh towns in late 2004 – the trial's outcomes will be eagerly awaited by the industry.

The BBC will also continue to test the water in broadband delivery of programme content to PCs – its interactive Media Player (iMP) will allow home users to access selected BBC TV output via their desktops. Policy makers will monitor how the Sky+ personal video recorder is changing viewing habits – already programme-makers seem to have a renewed enthusiasm for live event shows that demand to be viewed as they happen.

Otherwise, who can say where television broadcasting will be in a year's time? The last twelve months show how volatile the industry is right now. We only hope that we at the *BFI TV Handbook* will be back with you in autumn 2005 to run the rule over another unpredictable year.

Statistical Overview

Phil Wickham

2003–4 has proved a momentous period in broadcasting history with revolutionary changes in technology, institutions and audiences. The impact and implications of change are discussed throughout the book but this statistics section aims to give you the hard data to judge its nature and extent. This process is not without its problems, however. For one thing the revolution shows no sign of flagging, and inevitably data is constantly changing.

There have probably been an extra few Freeview subscribers and changes in channel share since you started reading this. It is best therefore to consider these figures as a snapshot in time. This was the point when the British TV industry finally changed from the near duopoly that had been sustained by a mass audience for nearly fifty years, to a majority digital market where business and audience identities have become much more fluid. Figures cover the calendar year 2003, following on from the last *BFI Film and TV Handbook* and, where possible, the first half, or quarter of 2004.

The other main difficulty has been the availability of information. Sadly, despite all the hopes for freedom of information and the information highway, obtaining statistics on British TV has become harder in the twelve years that I have been putting figures together for our handbooks. Companies and organisations now tend to communicate a few limited facts and hold back material that they

deem their own. However the more people know, the better their understanding of media business and culture will be. Ofcom only effectively started operating on 1 January 2004, so a system to disseminate much more data widely about the industry will come – although the quicker more information is on their website the better. In the end though figures we wanted have largely come through and we appreciate Ofcom's help in making this possible. Occasionally a sum has proved elusive, but I hope you will agree, a nearly complete picture is better than no picture at all.

Table 1: TV Homes 2004

Number of TV Households 1st half 2004	24.67 m
TV Licences in Force	24.5 m
Licence fee income	£2,798 m
Pay Per View Enabled Households 2003	8.039 m
Pay Per View 'Plugging in' Households 2003	7.235 m
UK Pay Per View Revenue 2003	132.40 Euros
UK TiVo Subscribers 2003	1.2 m
Sky + Subscribers	0.3 m
TV Homes with Teletext	78%
TV Homes with Widescreen TV	33%
TV Homes with Stereo TV	44%
TV Homes with Flat Plasma TV	4%

Source: BBC/Screen Digest/Ofcom/Sky

Table 2: Trends in TV Viewing

		4-15s	16-34s	35-54s	55+
Average Daily Hrs Viewing '03	3.72				
Terrestrial Viewers		3.4	1.9	3.2	3.2	4.6
Multichannel Viewers		3.8	2.5	4.1	4.1	5.0

Number of TV Households 2003: 24.62 million

Average Daily Hours Viewing (1st half 2004): 3.82

Source: Ofcom/BARB

Table 3: Household Ownership of Media Hardware in the UK %

Year	% Satellite Receiver	DVD Player	Video Recorder	Home PC	Internet Access	Mobile Phone
1985			30	13	0	0
1990			61	17	0	N/A
1994-5			76	N/A	0	N/A
1995-6			79	N/A	0	N/A
1996-7	19		82	27	0	17
1997-8	26		84	29	0	21
1998-9	28		86	33	10	27
1999-2000	32		85	38	19	44
2000-1	40		86	44	33	47
2001-2	43	25.7	87	50	40	65
2002-3	46	32	90	55	45	70
2003-4	53	45	85	54	53	75
	inc. Digital/Cable					

Source: ONS/Screen Digest

Television Homes

Tables 1-5

These first tables show how the experience of television is changing in this country. After years of being relatively static the number of TV Homes is creeping up (and continues to do so in the first half of 2004) and so is the amount of time spent watching TV. (2). Table 2 also makes it clear why this is happening -across all ages people in multichannel households watch more television than those still in analogue only homes. More 'choice', at least when it comes to channels means it takes up more of our time. This year has seen the crucial tipping point when more than half of TV homes have some kind of multichannel option, squeezing past the 50% barrier at the end of 2003 and already 53% by the end of March 2004 (4). Sky and cable (5) saw small rises in customers but the motor behind this increase has been the astonishing success of Freeview, the digital terrestrial platform. Freeview's simplicity and cheap price has attracted customers happy with a limited spectrum of quality channels and keen to avoid commitments to contracts. Digital terrestrial has reached out to many initially reluctant to climb aboard the digital revolution -the challenge is to see if that can be extended to the 40% plus yet to be convinced by it in time for the government's planned analogue switch-off in 2010. Ofcom, the BBC, and other analysts are persuading them that 2012 is more realistic.

Home Entertainment technologies are clearly now standard items in most homes (3) but there is also caution and selectivity in what people acquire for their homes and actually chose to use. Pay per view, for instance, has over 8 million enabled homes but less actually bother to 'plug in'. Most use PPV as a video rental alternative, not as television as such – dour football matches proving less than alluring. Similarly TiVo and equivalents have yet to really take off here; perhaps people finally feel they have got to grips with their video recorders (1). This may all change but simplicity of function, time efficiency, and a cheap price, are the watchwords of the British consumer.

Table 4

Multichannel Numbers 2003

Number of TV Households (millions)		24.617
Number of Multichannel TV Households (millions)		12.66

Operator	Analogue (millions)	Digital (millions)	Total	% of all TV homes	%increase on 2002
BSkyB		6.893	6.893	28.9	9.41
ADSL		0.009	0.009	0.04	
Freeview		3.287	3.287	11.9	*130.54
Other Free to Air		0.211	0.211	0.8	
Cable	0.978	2.325	3.303	13.4	-13.02
Total	0.978	12.361	13.39	54.2	21.97
% of TV homes	4.2	50.2	54.4		
% increase on 2002	-23.31	28.22	21.97		

Source: Ofcom

Multichannel Numbers Q1 2004

Operator	Analogue (Millions)	Digital (Millions)	Total	% of all TV Homes	%inc. on 2003 Q4
BSkyB		6.956	6.956	29.1	0.9
ADSL		0.009	0.009	0.04	-2.6
Freeview		3.929	3.929	14.1	19.5
Other Free to Air		0.231	0.231		9.5
Cable	0.916	2.409	3.325	13.5	1.0
Total	0.916	13.072	13.989	56.7	4.9
% of TV Homes	3.7	53	56.7		
% Increase on Q4 '03	-6.3	5.7	4.9		

Ofcom subtract 15% from Free to View figures to take account of second sets.

Source: OFCOM

Table 5: Cable homes Passed and Connected by Operator

Operator	2003	Q1 2004
NTL		
Homes Passed and Marketed	7,779,755	7,861,100
Total Residential Subscribers	2,867,885	2,923,200
TV Homes Connected	2,022,055	2,048,900
Digital TV Homes Connected	1,329,213	1,371,000
TV Penetration Rate (%)	26	26
TELEWEST BROADBAND		
Homes Passed and Marketed	4,674,764	4,678,182
Total Residential Subscribers	1,730,438	1,742,144
TV Homes Connected	1,272,064	1,285,797
Digital TV Homes Connected	1,029,759	987,873
TV Penetration Rate (%)	27	28

Channel Share

Tables 6-8

The multichannel effect is also apparent when we look at channel performance over the last year (6). The terrestrial channels share is declining in the face of new television, although 2004 has so far managed to arrest this fall somewhat, helped by big audiences for event programming, like the Euro 2004 football tournament and *I'm a Celebrity ... Get me out of Here!*. Underlying figures show this fight back may be short-lived though - look at the figures by age in multichannel households, with children (and very nearly the 16-34 age group) spending more than half their viewing time with non-terrestrial channels (6). Differences in demographic composition of channels, even in terrestrial only homes, are also marked (8). ITV1 has a larger majority of women viewers, Channel 4 does well in the 16-34 bracket and over two-thirds of Five's audience are from the C2DE social group. Partly this reflects the demographics of some programmes they produce (8) but this becomes a self-perpetuating trend, leading to channels branding themselves for a particular audience, aping the principles, if not the extent, of multichannel broadcasting.

In 2001 BBC 1 stole ahead of ITV1 for the first time in years. Across all viewing BBC 1 still lead, but this is only maintained by the BBC's command of daytime; when it comes to peak hours ITV1 have regained their advantage. Political challenges to the BBC have altered the corporation's perspective, so fighting this particular share war is no longer the agenda. ITV1 is likely to resume the mantle of 'Britain's favourite button' sooner rather than later, similarly share lead over Channel 4 is no longer the prime motivator for BBC 2. Meanwhile Five continues its canny rise upwards.

What BBC executives are much more concerned about officially are the figures for reach (7). This is the proportion of the population who tune in for at least 15 minutes a week. BBC 1's figure is still very healthy, although they will note the smaller reach in multichannel homes and consider how to at least hold off further decline. ITV1 has taken the initial big drop in share to multichannel and will have to work hard to bring those viewers back. (6).

Table 6: Channel Share 2003

All Homes	2003 % Share	1st Q 2004	1st Half 2004
BBC 1	25.6	24.8	24.8
ITV1	23.5	23.9	23.3
BBC 2	10.9	10.9	10.3
Channel 4	9.7	9.4	9.8
Five	6.6	6.7	6.8
Non-terrestrial Channels	26.5	24.3	25

Multichannel Homes	2003 % Share	1st Half 2004	% change since 1998
ITV1	19.32	19.39	-26
BBC 1	19.25	19.19	-14
BBC 2	6.95	6.98	17
Channel 4/S4C	6.87	7.10	-1
Five	4.75	5.14	79
Sky One	2.9	2.46	
UKTV Gold	2.03	1.35	
Sky Sports 1	1.84	1.73	
ITV2	1.57	1.65	
E4	1.2	1.1	
CBeebies	1.2	1.3	
Sky News	1.1	0.6	
UKTV Style	0.8	0.6	
Hallmark	0.8	0.9	
BBC 3	0.7	0.6	
BBC 4	0.2	0.2	

Peak Share (%)	2003	1st Q 04	1st Half 04
BBC 1	27.01	26.1	26.5
ITV1	28.46	32.9	31.5
BBC 2	10.74	8.8	8.6
Channel 4	9.21	8.6	9.0
Five	6.30	6.0	6.2
Non-Terrestrial Channels	18.29	17.6	

Channel Share by Age Group 2003 In Multichannel Households (%)	Children	Age 16-34	Age 35-54	Age 55+
BBC 1	15	16	20	24
ITV1	15	17	20	23
BBC 2	6	5	7	10
Channel 4	5	8	7	7
Five	4	4	5	5
Non-Terrestrial Channels	56	49	41	31

ABC1 Channel Share 2003	
BBC 1	27.26
ITV1	22.18
BBC 2	11.61
Channel 4	10.69
Five	5.30
Non-Terrestrial Channels	22.96

Source: BARB/Channel 4

Table 7: Fifteen Minute Weekly Reach in Multichannel Households 2003-4

Channel	% All Homes	Multichannel Homes
BBC 1	83.7	79.8
BBC 2	67	57.3
ITV1	78.9	75.3
Channel 4	62.1	54.8
Five	43.2	41.8
All Sky Channels	29	53
UKTV	18.4	33.3
BBC 3	7	12.6
BBC 4	2.1	3.7

Source: BBC/BARB

Period covered is 1/4/03 – 31/3/04

Table 8: TV Audience Composition 2003

Audience Composition of Channels in Terrestrial Analogue Households 2003

% of audience	BBC 1	BBC 2	ITV1	C4/S4C	Five	All Terrestrial
Men	41	47	39	44	44	42
Women	59	53	61	56	56	58
Age 4-15	7	9	6	6	7	7
Age 16-34	15	15	17	23	19	17
Age 35-54	24	24	25	27	27	25
Age 55+	54	52	52	44	47	51
ABC1	40	42	34	41	31	38
C2DE	60	58	66	59	69	62

Audience Composition of selected programmes 2003

% of Audience	A Touch of Frost	The Simpsons	Friends	Property Ladder	Weakest Link	Wife Swap
Children	4	29	11	6	6	8
16-34	10	29	45	27	12	33
35-54	26	28	30	39	24	37
55+	59	14	24	28	58	23

Adult Digital Multichannel Audience Composition

	%
Age 16-34	40
Age 35-54	37
Age 55+	23
ABC1	49
C2DE	51

Source: Ofcom/BARB

Programming

Tables 9-12

Programming – hours, costs and regulations – inform the schedules we see and the operations of the business. The price of producing good programmes, maintaining profits and keeping up with rivals is high -as the thousands of broadcasting workers that lost their jobs this year will testify. The total programme costs are climbing steadily upwards and reflect the different priorities of the channels - look at Sky's vast outlay on sport or ITV1's 67% spend on new commissions (9).

We have included an interesting table here published by *Broadcast* that estimates the value of particular programmes based on notional advertising rates according to ratings and audience composition (12), which may clarify the thinking behind television money.

The quotas table (10) has an elegiac feel - Ofcom is gradually denuding itself of its powers to dictate aspects of the programming schedule and following lobbying by ITV and others the picture next year is likely to be very different. Ofcom paved the way for these changes with their report into attitudes to public service television. Likewise the programming hours still reflect this fading culture (11),

Table 9: TV Programme Costs 2003

	£m Total	Acquisitions	Commissions	Sport
BBC 1	797	64	172	130
BBC 2	366	38	75	92
BBC TV Total	1400	110	323	222
ITV1	806	40	207	167
GMTV1	35	1	9	n/a
Channel 4	449	66	376	40.6
Five	158	36	100	41
Total Terrestrial	2,611	245	939	441
Sky	1528	Unavailable	Unavailable	653
Total Multichannel*	1606			

* Excluding BBC Digital channels

BBC Figures refer to Financial year 2003-4. Figures for all other channels refer to calendar year 2003.

Source: Ofcom/BBC/Sky

Table 10: Quotas

	BBC Terrestrial	BBC Digital	ITV1	C4	Five
Independent Production (% hours)	25% across all channels	25%	25%	25%	25%
Total original production (% hours)	70%	BBC 3 80% BBC 4 70%	65%	60%	51%
Regional production (% hours)	25%	25%	33%	30%	10%
News & Weather (hours per week)	BBC 1 – 26h 28m	None	7h	4h	9h
Current Affairs	7h	None	1h 30m	4h	2h 30m
Religion	BBC 1 – 1h 30m BBC 2 – 35m	None	2h	1h	1h
Children's	BBC 1 – 7h 40m BBC 2 – 1h 55m	2 dedicated digital channels	10h	None	10h 56m
Education	None	None	1h 45m	7h	3h
Arts	BBC 1 – 50m BBC 2 – 3h 50m	45m	30m	None	30m
Regional Programmes	126h 12m	None	8h 30m	None	None

All figures include repeats except for Independent Production Quotas. h = hours; m = minutes

Source: Ofcom/BBC/Five

Table 11: Annual Programming Output by Hours

	Channel BBC 1	BBC 2	BBC Digital Channels	ITV1 (inc GMTV)	C4	Five	Multichannel*
Original Production	6964	6913	14800	5495	6183	3979	97,501
In-House Production	4809	2381	n/a	3278	n/a	51	n/a
Acquisitions	1617	2006	2414	759	4160	2891	135,970
Independent Productions	890	856	n/a	1067	3823	4242	67,330
Sport	504	864	65	599	1041	1460	41,483
News & Current Affairs	2830	698	17,768	1649	572	829	21,456
Entertainment	685	876	1262	1111	2382	546	119,991
Drama	961	412	406	1059	906	1596	n/a
Children's	809	1301	7466	1015	538	1424	46,594
Arts & Music	66	317	1381	37	140	31	n/a
Factual & Learning	1697	1180	1650	1556	1586	699	83240
Religion	87	41	43	109	55	53	n/a
Education	n/a	1696	824	154	1426	214	n/a

*Multichannel excluding BBC Digital Channels

BBC figures refer to Financial year 2003-4. All other channel's figures refer to calendar year 2003.

Original Production is defined as channel-originated material including repeats.

Source: Ofcom/BBC

although it will be interesting to see if when quotas go, Five, for example, keep up their Arts output having discovered an aptitude for it. Traditionally the British mass audience like American stories on the big screen but prefer the local and familiar at home - acquisitions budgets are therefore more important to the smaller commercial channels who aim to build fan bases for the best US shows. The quota for independent television is another area of constant debate, particularly as the BBC failed to meet its target in 2002-3. Producers call for a big increase in an overall quota 'floor', ITV call for it to be scrapped altogether.

Table 12: Programme Value

Real and notional (i.e. BBC) values for programmes based on potential advertising rates

Programme Title	Channel	Real/Potential Value
Coronation Street	ITV1	£73,809
Emmerdale	ITV1	£62,738
The Bill	ITV1	£55,357
Bad Girls	ITV1	£55,357
Eurovision Song Contest	BBC 1*	£55,357
EastEnders	BBC 1*	£47,976
Have I Got News For You	BBC 1*	£44,286
Big Brother	C4	£40,595
The Weakest Link	BBC 2*	£29,524
Crimewatch UK	BBC 1*	£29,524

* Based on potential cost of 30 second advertising slot from analysis of ratings and demographics of the programmes

Source: Mediacom/*Broadcast*

Table 13: Top 50 Programmes of 2003   Source:BARB

Pos	Title	Channel	Tx Date	Viewers (m)
1	Coronation Street	ITV1	24-Feb	19.40
2	EastEnders	BBC 1	29-Sep	16.70
3	Tonight with Trevor McDonald: Millionaire – A Major Fraud	ITV1	21-Apr	16.10
4	Only Fools and Horses	BBC 1	21-Dec	15.50
5	Tonight with Trevor McDonald: Living with Michael Jackson	ITV1	3-Feb	15.30
6	Heartbeat	ITV1	12-Jan	12.80
7	I'm a Celebrity ...	ITV1	12-May	12.70
8	Billy Elliot	BBC 1	1-Jan	12.60
9	Rugby World Cup Final	ITV1	22-Nov	12.30
10	A Touch of Frost	ITV1	3-Mar	12.20
11	The Royal	ITV1	19-Jan	12.00
12	Emmerdale	ITV1	10-Feb	11.90
13	Comic Relief	BBC 1	14-Mar	11.80
14	Rosemary & Thyme	ITV1	31-Aug	11.10
15	Pop Idol Final	ITV1	20-Dec	10.90
16	Cold Feet	ITV1	16-Mar	10.70
17	Prime Suspect 6	ITV1	9-Nov	10.50
18	UEFA Champions League: Man Utd V Real Madrid	ITV1	23-Apr	10.50
19	Children in Need	BBC 1	21-Nov	10.50
20	The Bill	ITV1	30-Oct	10.50
21	Ten O'Clock News	BBC 1	21-Nov	10.30
22	Antiques Roadshow	BBC 1	9-Feb	10.23
23	My Family	BBC 1	4-Apr	10.16
24	Coronation Street Xmas Crackers	ITV1	29-Dec	10.14
25	Pompeii – The Last Day	BBC 1	20-Oct	10.09
26	Midsomer Murders	ITV1	2-Nov	10.01
27	Casualty	BBC 1	1-Mar	10.01
28	Jonathan Creek	BBC 1	8-Mar	9.90
29	Holby City	BBC 1	16-Dec	9.82
30	It'll be Alright on the Night	ITV1	31-Aug	9.79
31	Foyle's War	ITV1	7-Dec	9.74
32	The Booze Cruise	ITV1	7-Sep	9.70
33	Cast Away	BBC 1	29-Dec	9.60
34	William and Mary	ITV1	27-Apr	9.56
35	Creature Comforts	ITV1	26-Oct	9.53
36	Celebrity Driving School	BBC 1	28-Feb	9.53
37	Match of the Day: England v Turkey	BBC 1	2-Apr	9.33
38	The Sixth Sense	ITV1	2-Feb	9.26
39	Monarch of the Glen	BBC 1	28-Sep	9.20
40	The British Soap Awards	ITV1	14-May	9.19
41	The Return	ITV1	30-Dec	9.14
42	UEFA Champions League: Man Utd v Juventus	ITV1	19-Feb	9.02
43	Ant & Dec's Saturday Night Takeaway	ITV1	8-Mar	8.98
44	Blue Murder	ITV1	18-May	8.88
45	The Lost Prince	BBC 1	26-Jan	8.86
46	Indiana Jones & The Last Crusade	BBC 1	26-May	8.79
47	UEFA Champions League: Man Utd v Juventus	ITV1	8-Apr	8.74
48	The National Lottery – Midweek Draws	BBC 1	12-Mar	8.66
49	Danielle Cable – Eyewitness	ITV1	14-Apr	8.59
50	The Royal Variety Performance	ITV1	26-Nov	8.56

Table 14: Top 50 Programmes 01/01/2004 - 04/07/04

Pos	Title	Channel	Tx Date	Viewers (m)
1	Euro 2004: England v Portugal	BBC 1	24-Jun	20.66
2	Euro 2004:England v Croatia	BBC 1	21-Jun	18.28
3	Euro 2004: England v France	ITV1	13-Jun	17.60
4	Coronation Street	ITV1	16-Feb	16.33
5	I'm a Celebrity ... Get Me Out Of Here	ITV1	9-Feb	14.99
6	EastEnders	BBC 1	1-Jan	14.58
7	Euro 2004: England v Switzerland	ITV1	17-Jun	14.31
8	A Touch of Frost	ITV1	22-Feb	12.97
9	Emmerdale	ITV1	2-Jan	11.76
10	Heartbeat	ITV1	22-Feb	11.12
11	Euro 2004 Final: Portugal v Greece	BBC 1	4-Jul	10.85
12	Life Begins	ITV1	16-Feb	10.45
13	Midsomer Murders	ITV1	25-Jan	10.24
14	Casualty	BBC 1	17-Jan	10.11
15	Friends	C4	28-May	9.64
16	ITV News	ITV1	17-Jun	9.52
17	The Bill	ITV1	15-Jan	9.42
18	The Royal	ITV1	4-Jan	9.39
19	Strictly Come Dancing	BBC 1	3-Jul	9.28
20	My Family	BBC 1	19-Mar	9.17
21	Stars in Their Eyes Final	ITV1	13-Mar	9.14
22	Ant & Dec's Saturday Night Takeway	ITV1	13-Mar	9.09
23	Auf Wiedersehen Pet	BBC 1	4-Jan	9.07
24	William and Mary	ITV1	7-Mar	9.06
25	The British Soap Awards	ITV1	12-May	9.01
26	What Women Want	BBC 1	1-Jan	8.94
27	Antiques Roadshow	BBC 1	18-Jan	8.86
28	Wall of Silence	ITV1	12-Jan	8.84
29	Dalziel and Pascoe	BBC 1	3-Jan	8.83
30	Euro 2004: Spain v Portugal	BBC 1	20-Jun	8.78
31	Fat Friends	ITV1	28-Jan	8.69
32	Unbreakable	ITV1	15-Feb	8.68
33	Hell's Kitchen	ITV1	24-May	8.64
34	Grand National	BBC 1	3-Apr	8.53
35	Holby City	BBC 1	6-Jan	8.52
36	Jonathan Creek	BBC 1	21-Feb	8.45
37	Donovan	ITV1	5-Jan	8.41
38	Eurovision Song Contest	BBC 1	15-May	8.38
39	National Lottery: Jet Set	BBC 1	21-Feb	8.29
40	Euro 2004: Czech Republic v Germany	ITV1	23-Jun	8.28
41	The Second Quest	ITV1	5-Apr	8.28
42	Bad Girls	ITV1	21-Apr	8.25
43	Euro 2004: Portugal v Holland	BBC 1	30-Jun	8.24
45	National Lottery – In It to Win It	BBC 1	29-May	8.24
46	Poirot: Death on the Nile	ITV1	12-Apr	8.15
47	Euro 2004: Czech Republic v Greece	ITV1	1-Jul	8.19
48	Euro 2004: Germany v Holland	BBC 1	15-Jun	7.95
49	Ten O'Clock News	BBC 1	21-Jun	7.90
50	Ronnie Barker – A Tribute	BBC 1	7-Mar	7.82

Source: BARB

Table 15: BBC 2, Channel 4 and Five Top 50 2003

Pos	Title	Channel	Tx Date	Viewers (m)
1	Big Brother	C4	23-May	7.05
2	Wife Swap	C4	21-Oct	6.90
3	Celebrity Wife Swap	C4	11-Nov	6.43
4	Comic Relief	BBC 2	14-Mar	6.01
5	Little Voice	BBC 2	2-Jan	5.80
6	Boy Who Gave Birth to His Twin	C4	8-Dec	5.41
7	Top Gear	BBC 2	7-Dec	5.40
8	Kennedy Assasination	BBC 2	23-Nov	5.30
9	World Snooker Final	BBC 2	5-May	5.28
10	Taken	BBC 2	11-Jan	5.23
11	Wild Child	C4	15-Dec	5.07
12	How Clean is Your House?	C4	12-Nov	5.06
13	Match of the Day Live: Liverpool v Celtic	BBC 2	20-Mar	5.04
14	The Weakest Link	BBC 2	3-Jan	5.04
15	Friends	C4	13-Jun	4.98
16	Relocation, Relocation	C4	18-Mar	4.90
17	Miracle on 34th Street	Five	7-Dec	4.85
18	Wife Swap Changed Our Marriage	C4	30-Sep	4.85
19	The Natural World	BBC 2	26-Jan	4.84
20	My Best Friend's Wedding	C4	5-Jan	4.77
21	Location, Location, Location	C4	17-Jun	4.73
22	Property Ladder	C4	14-Jan	4.63
23	Grand Designs	C4	12-Feb	4.62
24	UEFA Cup: Celtic v Liverpool	Five	13-Mar	4.61
25	When Michael Portillo Became a Single Mum	BBC 2	15-Oct	4.60
26	Cutting Edge:Bad Behaviour	C4	22-Jul	4.55
27	Living the Dream	BBC 2	25-Feb	4.51
28	The Queen's Lost Uncle	C4	9-Nov	4.51
29	Grand Designs Revisited	C4	8-Oct	4.40
30	Location, Location Revisited	C4	12-Nov	4.40
31	How to be a Gardener	BBC 2	6-Feb	4.37
32	Erin Brockovich	Five	10-Mar	4.28
33	Seven Wonders of the Industrial World	BBC 2	16-Oct	4.27
34	The Simpsons	BBC 2	19-Dec	4.25
35	Million Pound Property Experiment	BBC 2	17-Dec	4.21
36	A Place in the Sun	C4	25-Feb	4.21
37	No Going Back	C4	4-Sep	4.19
38	Horizon: The Big Chill	BBC 2	13-Nov	4.12
39	Return to Jamie's Kitchen	C4	16-Oct	4.11
40	Gladiator	Five	19-Oct	4.10
41	Terminator 2: Judgment Day	Five	27-Jul	4.10
42	Louis and the Brothel	BBC 2	9-Nov	4.08
43	Newsnight – Blair on Iraq	BBC 2	6-Feb	4.08
44	The Real Heather Mills	C4	7-May	4.08
45	Concorde: The End of the Dream	BBC 2	24-Oct	4.06
46	What Are You Staring At?	BBC 2	6-Aug	4.06
47	The Day Britain Stopped	BBC 2	13-May	4.05
48	The Matrix	Five	21-May	4.02
49	Neighbours	BBC 2	9-Apr	4.00
50	Selling Houses	C4	1-Apr	3.98

Source: BARB

Table 16: BBC 2, Channel 4 and Five Top 50 01/01/04-04/07/04

Pos	Title	Channel	Tx Date	Viewers (m)
1	Friends	C4	28-May	9.64
2	Big Brother	C4	28-May	7.23
3	Grand Designs	C4	3-Mar	5.88
4	Wife Swap	C4	29-Jun	5.60
5	Ramsay's Kitchen Nightmares	C4	11-May	5.58
6	Britain's Best Sitcoms: The Final	BBC 2	27-Mar	5.45
7	Relocation, Relocation	C4	7-Jan	5.41
8	The Boy Whose Skin Fell Off	C4	25-Mar	4.75
9	Sex and the City	C4	19-Mar	4.71
10	Dunkirk	BBC 2	18-Feb	4.62
11	The Weakest Link	BBC 2	30-Jan	4.61
12	Gardener's World	BBC 2	27-Feb	4.57
13	Have I Got Bruce For You	BBC 2	1-Jan	4.47
14	Property Ladder	C4	13-Jan	4.11
15	You are What You Eat	C4	29-Jun	4.09
16	Brat Camp	C4	16-Mar	4.05
17	CSI: Crime Scene Investigation	Five	13-Apr	3.99
18	How to be a Gardener	BBC 2	6-Mar	3.90
19	Crufts 2004	BBC 2	7-Mar	3.88
20	Snooker	BBC 2	2-May	3.88
21	The Simpsons	BBC 2	5-Jan	3.87
22	How Clean is Your House?	C4	26-May	3.85
23	Jimmy's Farm	BBC 2	26-May	3.82
24	Property Chain	C4	3-Mar	3.81
25	Nile	BBC 2	27-Feb	3.80
26	Sex and the City Farewell	C4	19-Mar	3.79
27	The RHS Chelsea Flower Show	BBC 2	25-May	3.78
28	Will and Grace	C4	18-Jun	3.77
29	Hawking	BBC 2	13-Apr	3.74
30	Horizon: The Atkins Diet	BBC 2	22-Jan	3.74
31	Independence Day	Five	8-Jan	3.73
32	Secret Intersex	C4	5-Apr	3.70
33	Swordfish	C4	30-May	3.70
34	Ten Years Younger	C4	26-May	3.69
35	Room 101 (with Bruce Forsyth)	BBC 2	1-Jan	3.67
36	The Vicar of Dibley	BBC 2	13-Mar	3.67
37	Dispatches: Third Class Post	C4	29-Apr	3.66
38	ER	C4	4-Mar	3.64
39	Honey I Ruined the House	C4	23-Jun	3.59
40	Charlie's Angels	C4	21-Mar	3.57
41	Riddle of the Elephant Man	C4	5-Jan	3.53
42	Newcastle Utd v Olympique Marseilles	Five	6-May	3.48
43	The Games	C4	18-Apr	3.47
44	Britain Goes Wild with Bill Oddie	BBC 2	10-Jun	3.46
45	Crouching Tiger, Hidden Dragon	C4	4-Apr	3.45
46	Ghost	Five	19-Jan	3.44
47	Mercury Rising	Five	9-May	3.41
48	World Darts Final	BBC 2	11-Jan	3.41
49	Sleepy Hollow	C4	2-May	3.39
50	Top Gear	BBC 2	6-Jun	3.39

Source: BARB

Table 17: Top 20 Factual 01/01/2003-30/06/2004   Source: BARB

Documentaries, Factual Entertainment, News

Pos	Title	Tx Date	Producer/B'caster	Viewers (m)
1	Tonight w/ Trevor McDonald: Millionaire Special	4/21/03	Granada/ITV	16.10
2	Tonight w/ Trevor McDonald: Michael Jackson	2/3/03	Granada/ITV	15.32
3	Ten O'Clock News	11/21/03	BBC	10.30
4	Antiques Roadshow	2/9/03	BBC	10.23
5	Pompeii – The Last Day	10/20/03	BBC	10.09
6	Celebrity Driving School	2/28/03	BBC	9.53
7	Hell's Kitchen	5/25/04	ITV	8.64
8	DIY SOS	2/6/03	BBC	8.23
9	BBC News and Weather	1/12/03	BBC	8.11
10	Spoilt Rotten	2/27/03	Yorkshire/ITV	7.98
11	Airline	11/14/03	LWT/ITV	7.85
12	Ground Force America	7/21/03	Endemol/BBC	7.85
13	Neighbours From Hell	6/4/03	Granada/ITV	7.73
14	Watchdog	9/30/03	BBC	7.70
15	Rogue Traders	1/30/03	BBC	7.65
16	Holiday Airport: Lanzarote	3/17/03	LWT/ITV	7.65
17	Victoria Wood's Big Fat Documentary	1/9/04	BBC	7.39
18	Holiday Showdown	10/30/04	RDF/ITV	7.32
19	Big Brother	5/28/04	Endemol/C4	7.23
20	Big Cat Week	1/9/04	BBC	7.10

Table 18: Top 20 Entertainment 01/01/03-04/07/04

Comedy/Light Entertainment/game Shows

Pos	Title	Tx Date	Producer/B'caster	Viewers (m)
1	Only Fools and Horses	12/25/03	BBC	16.37
2	I'm a Celebrity ... Get me out of Here!	2/9/04	LWT/ITV	14.99
3	Comic Relief	3/14/03	BBC	11.74
4	Pop Idol	12/20/03	Thames/ITV	11.04
5	Children in Need	11/21/03	BBC	10.48
6	My Family	4/4/03	DLT/Rude Boy/BBC	10.16
7	It'll be Alright on the Night	8/31/03	Granada/ITV	9.79
8	Friends	5/28/04	Warner Bros TV/C4	9.64
9	Stars in Their Eyes	3/13/04	Granada/ITV	9.14
10	Creature Comforts	10/26/03	Aardman/ITV	9.53
11	Strictly Come Dancing	7/3/04	BBC	9.28
12	The British Soap Awards	5/14/03	Carlton/ITV	9.19
13	Ant & Dec's Saturday Night Takeaway	3/13/04	Granada/ITV	9.09
14	The National Lottery – Midweek Draws	3/12/03	BBC	8.66
15	The Royal Variety Performance	11/26/03	Granada/ITV	8.56
16	Who Wants to be a Millionaire?	12/2/03	Celador/ITV	8.54
17	The Eurovision Song Contest	5/15/04	BBC	8.38
18	The National Lottery – Jet Set	2/21/04	BBC	8.29
19	The National Lottery – In It to Win It	5/29/04	BBC	8.24
20	Des O'Connor Comedy Tonight	8/25/03	LWT/ITV	8.15

Source: BARB

Programmes

Tables 13-23

The extensive list of ratings tables here cover a long period (1st January 2003 to the 4th July 2004, so we take in the end of Euro 2004) and tell interesting stories. The first half of 2004 (14) show that terrestrial TV can still get a mass audience for shared events, but football and the Jungle apart, a decline is noticeable compared to 2003 (13).

Fewer shows are making the 8 million mark and old favourites like *The Bill* and *Heartbeat* are shedding millions. It's a similar story on the minority channels (15, 16) where occasional big audiences on Channel 4 (the end of *Friends* or some of their 'considerably richer than you' or 'she's no better than she ought be' programming) are offset by a decline in the number of shows that break the 4 million audience barrier. Reality shows prevail, except on Five, which bring the numbers in for US imports and blockbuster films.

Table 19: Top 20 Original Drama 01/01/03-04/07/04

Pos	Title	Tx Date	Producer/B'caster	Viewers (m)
1	Coronation Street	2/24/03	Granada/ITV	19.43
2	EastEnders	9/29/03	BBC	16.66
3	A Touch of Frost	2/22/04	Yorkshire/ITV	12.97
4	Heartbeat	1/12/03	Yorkshire/ITV	12.84
5	The Royal	1/19/03	Yorkshire/ITV	12.24
6	Emmerdale	2/10/03	Yorkshire/ITV	11.88
7	Rosemary and Thyme	8/31/03	Carnival Films/ITV	11.08
8	Cold Feet	3/16/03	Granada/ITV	10.69
9	Prime Suspect 6	11/9/03	Granada/ITV	10.50
10	Life Begins	2/16/04	Granada/ITV	10.45
11	The Bill	10/30/03	Thames/ITV	10.41
12	Midsomer Murders	1/25/04	Bentley Prods/ITV	10.28
13	Casualty	1/17/04	BBC	10.11
14	Jonathan Creek	3/8/03	BBC	9.90
15	Holby City	12/16/03	BBC	9.82
16	Foyle's War	12/7/03	Greenlit/ITV	9.74
17	The Booze Cruise	9/7/03	Yorkshire/ITV	9.70
18	William and Mary	4/27/03	Granada/ITV	9.56
19	Monarch of the Glen	9/28/03	Ecosse Prodns/BBC	9.20
20	The Return	12/30/03	Sally Head/Octagon/ITV	9.14

Source: BARB

Table 20: Top 10 Sports programmes 01/01/03 - 04/07/04

Pos	Title	Tx Date	Channel	Viewers (m)
1	Euro 2004: England v Portugal	6/24/04	BBC 1	20.66
2	Euro 2004: England v Croatia	6/21/04	BBC 1	18.28
3	Euro 2004: England v France	6/13/04	ITV1	17.60
4	Euro 2004: England v Switzerland	6/17/04	ITV1	14.31
5	Rugby World Cup Final: England v Australia	11/22/03	ITV1	12.30
6	Euro 2004 Final: Portugal v Greece	7/4/04	BBC 1	10.85
7	Champions League: Manchester United v Real Madrid	4/23/03	ITV1	10.50
8	Match of the Day: England v Turkey	4/2/03	BBC 1	9.33
9	Champions League: Manchester United v Juventus	2/19/03	ITV1	9.02
10	Champions League: Manchester United v Juventus	4/8/03	ITV1	8.74

Source: BARB

Table 21: Top 10 Children's Programmes 01/01/03 – 04/07/04

Pos	Title	Tx Date	Channel	Viewers (m)
1	Sleeping Beauty Uncovered	22/12/03	BBC 1	1.25
2	The Story of Tracy Beaker	28/1/03; 9/1/03	BBC 1	1.04
3	Cave Girl	28/1/2003	BBC 1	1.00
4	Grange Hill	28/1/03	BBC 1	0.99
5	Newsround	25/11/03	BBC 1	0.97
6	SMArt	16/12/03	BBC 1	0.96
7	The Face at the Window	21/1/03	BBC 1	0.94
8	Tracy Beaker's Movie of Me	22/2/04	BBC 1	0.93
9	The Queen's Nose	16/12/03	BBC 1	0.89
10	Blue Peter	12/12/03	BBC 1	0.87

Source: BARB

Note: BARB do not publish ratings for animated Children's programmes

Table 22: Top 10 most complained about TV Programmes 2003-4

Pos	Title	Channel	Nature of Complaint	Number	Outcome
1	Derren Brown's Séance	C4	Use of séance and the 'paranormal'.	644	Not Upheld
2	UEFA Champions League trailer	ITV	Encouraging poor behaviour in children	223	Upheld
3	Big Brother	C4	Brawl between housemates	215	Not Yet Adjudicated
4	The Missing Chink	C4	Alleged racist language of title	191	Upheld in part
5	Panorama: London Under Attack	BBC 1	Causing unnecessary alarm	140	Not Yet Adjudicated
6	Derren Brown: Russian Roulette	C4	Premise of live 'Russian Roulette'	c. 130	Not Upheld
7	Dumb Foreigners	ITV1	Use of Scottish flag in title sequence	129	Not Yet Adjudicated
8	I'm a Celebrity ...	ITV1	John Lydon swearing	96	Resolved
9	Coronation Street	ITV1	Depiction of gay relationship	89	Not Upheld
10	TV Trailer for BBC radio comedy	BBC	Scene of Johnny Vegas in fridge thought to be dangerous for children	51	Upheld

Period Covered is July 2003-June 2004. Figures are collated from reported complaints to Ofcom and the appropriate broadcaster.

Source: Ofcom/BBC

Table 23: Top Ten most complained about programmes since 1991

Pos	Title	Channel	Nature of Complaint	Number	Outcome	Year
1	The Last Temptation of Christ	C4	Blasphemy	1554	Not Upheld	1995
2	Brass Eye	C4	Comedic treatment of paedophilia	992	Upheld in Part	2001
3	Derren Brown's Séance	C4	Use of Séance and the 'paranormal'	644	Not yet Adjudicated	2004
4	Spitting Image	ITV	Use of image of God	341	Upheld in Part	1992
5	Champions League Trailer	ITV	Encouraging poor behaviour in children	223	Upheld	2003
6	Big Brother	C4	Brawl between housemates	215	Not yet Adjudicated	2004
7	The Missing Chink	C4	Alleged racist language	191	Upheld in Part	2003
8	Living with Michael Jackson	ITV	Alleged bias	171	Not Upheld	2003
9	The Bill	ITV	Gay scenes	170	Not Upheld	2002
10	Queer as Folk	C4	Gay scenes	163	Not Upheld	1999

Our **genre charts** (17-21) largely speak for themselves, continuing trends of the last few years such as the BBC's domination of children's programmes and the sad ratings decline of much talent based entertainment programming. Drama still shows that it delivers big audiences for its large spend.

The **complaints lists** (22-23) are an interesting indication of social mores. The relatively relaxed reaction to John Lydon swearing suggests a pretty unshockable audience - no Superbowl style furore on this side of the pond. However complaints as a whole are rising due to e-mail and campaigns from religious and political groups are becoming very organised, very early - 'thousands' complained about *Popetown*, a satirical comedy nowhere near broadcast.

Table 24: Overseas Trade and the UK TV Industry 2002

	1998	1999	2000	2001	2002
	(£million)				
Exports	444	440	551	673	684
Imports	692	843	767	1007	1237
Balance of Trade	-248	-403	-216	-334	-553

Source: ONS

British TV Exports 2002 and 2003

	2002 ($m)	2003 ($m)	% Change
Television programmes	333	371	12
Licensing	176	239	35
Video/DVD	117	128	9
Co-Production	84	115	38
Format sales	39	63	62
Commission	5	4	-14
TOTAL	754	921	22

Source: BTDA

Table 25

International transactions of the British TV Industry 2002 by Geographical Area

Area	Exports (£millions)	Imports	Balance of Trade
EU	214	300	-86
EFTA	43	96	-53
Other Europe	93	29	64
Total Europe	350	428	-79
Africa	14	4	10
USA	194	742	-549
Other Americas	38	15	23
Asia	49	17	32
Australasia	38	30	8
World Total	684	1237	-553

Source: ONS

British TV Sales by Territory 2002 and 2003

Territory	2002 ($m)	2003 ($m)	% change
USA	284	399	41
Canada	30	31	2
Germany	44	68	53
France	40	50	25
Spain	23	32	38
Italy	18	25	34
Scandinavia	27	36	33
Rest of Western Europe	73	69	-6
Eastern Europe	19	18	-1
Australasia	73	76	4
Latin America	23	16	-31
Asia	59	62	4
Other territories	39	39	0
TOTAL	754	921	22

Source: BTDA

Sales

(Tables 24, 25)
I have included two official sources of information for TV imports and exports. The Office of National Statistics figures for 2002 (24, 25) follow from previous handbooks and give an idea of the balance of trade between imports and exports and our relationship with different overseas territories.

The minus column is surprisingly high in 2002 but 2003 was more respectable. The British Television Distributors Association data has fuller and more current figures for sales (24-26) and shows us how much programmes are selling. Sure enough, factual scoops and murders in attractive locations are the order of the day.

Table 26

Top Ten Selling UK TV Programmes 2003

Pos	Title	Countries Sold to	Distributor
1	Living with Michael Jackson	120+	Granada International
2	Ancient Greek Olympics	80	Carlton International
3	Innovations	80	Carlton International
4	Hornblower	73	Granada International
5	Prime Suspect	58	Granada International
6	Walking with Dinosaurs	47	BBC Worldwide
7	The Natural World	46	BBC Worldwide
8	A Touch of Frost	41	Granada International
9	Popstars	40	Target International
10	Norah Jones in New Orleans	32	Eagle Star

Top Ten Selling UK TV Programmes 1998-2003

Pos	Title	Countries Sold to	Distributor
1	Inspector Morse	200+	Carlton International
2	Midsomer Murders	164	All3Media
3	Frenchman's Creek	150+	Carlton International
4	Bob the Builder	142	Hit Entertainment
5	Living with Michael Jackson	120+	Granada International
6	Teletubbies	120	BBC Worldwide
7	The Brit Awards	120	Eagle Star
8	Pingu	107	Hit Entertainment
9	Hornblower	102	Granada International
10	Poirot	100	Granada International

Source: BTDA

Advertising

Tables 27, 28

After the advertising recession at the start of this decade 2003 saw a modest, if steady, improvement as overall revenue increased (27). Advertisers have started to realise the power they hold in a competitive commercial market and ITV1 have been the first to feel the pressure on ratings and prices. Now they have new markets to experiment in and have plenty of choices on where to place their products. Rather more people seem inclined to complain about adverts than programmes, perhaps mindful that the only context is cash (28).

Table 27: TV Advertising Revenue 2003

	£m	Share %	Sponsorship (£m)	Share %
ITV	1484	45	35	35
Channel 4	625.5	19	17	17
Five	249	8	7	7
GMTV	58	2	3	3
Total terrestrial	2,416.5	74	62	62
Sky	284	8	n/a	n/a
Others	580	18	n/a	n/a
Total Non-Terrestrial	860	26	39	39
Total Net Revenue	3,280.5	100	101	100

Source: ITV/C4/Five/Advertising Association

Table 28: Top 10 most complained about TV Adverts since 1993

Pos	Brand	Advert	Nature of Complaint	No. of Complaints	Outcome	Year
1	Wrigley's X-cite	Man regurgitating dog	Poor taste & too frightening	860	Upheld	2003
2	Mr.Kipling's Cakes	Visceral Nativity Play	Blasphemy & poor taste	797	Resolved	2003
3	Levi's	Kevin the hamster	Alleged cruelty to animals	544	Upheld	1998
4	Red Devil	Vinnie Jones luring robin to its death	Distasteful and cruel to animals	390	Not Upheld	2000
5	Velvet Toilet Tissue	'Love your Bum'	Indecency & distasteful	322	Not Upheld	2003
6	Take a Break	Meals on Wheels. Old lady left hungry while home help reads mag	Cruelty to old people	318	Upheld	2003
7	Pot Noodle	'Slag of all Snacks'	Indecent	310	Upheld	2002
8	Freeserve	Nudists	Indecent	228	Not Upheld	2001
9	Fosters	Crocodile bites head off bungee jumper	Distasteful & frightening	184	Not Upheld	2003
10	Dulux	'Paint matching'	Distasteful	158	Upheld/ Guidance	2000

Source: ITC/Ofcom

Companies

Table 29
Our list of the top 50 independent production companies comes from *Broadcast* and is based on turnover, with an indication of the hours they have produced.

A few well-established producers and conglomerates dominate the big money - interestingly many have been around for some time and been able to both establish a reputation in particular product genres and develop the business to make the most of their productions, especially through sales. Now the Communications Act has given independents more power over their rights profits are set to rise further. Location has proved a hot issue because of rather cynical interpretations of Ofcom regulations on the percentage of hours produced outside the M25. 'Provincial' offices in Guildford and Amersham are hardly the spirit of the agreement.

NB Table 29. Source: *Broadcast*. Ranked by turnover for UK business including overseas sales. From 2003 or last available financial year.

Table 29: Top 50 Independent Production Companies in UK Television 2004

Pos	Company	Turnover (£m)	Total Hours (2003)	Location
1	HIT Entertainment	169	180	
2	talkbackTHAMES	131	3737	London/Amersham
3	All3Media (inc. North One/Bentley/Cactus/Assembly)	93	663	London
4	Endemol UK (inc. Initial, Brighter Pictures)	90	8929	London
5	TWI	72.5	1651	London
6	The Television Corporation (inc. Mentorn, Sunset & Vine, Folio, VTV, Music Box)	68.3	2700	London/Glasgow/Oxford/Otley
7	RDF Media	45.3	384	London
8	Tiger Aspect Productions	43.6	133	London
9	Celador	42.95	360	London
10	Mersey TV	38	411	Liverpool
11	Lion Television	22	210	London
12	19TV	22	140	London
13	Princess Productions	20	793	London
14	Company Pictures	19.6	24	London
15	Wall to Wall	18.32	81.5	London
16	Zenith Entertainment	18.15	241	London/Newcastle
17	Hat Trick Productions	18	53.66	London
18	So TV	16.8	529	London
19	Kudos	14.2	11.5	London
20	Shed Productions	14.2	48	London
21	Avalon TV	13	484	London
22	Ten Alps (incorporating Brook Lapping)	13	64.5	London
23	September Films	12.7	135	London
24	Ecosse Films	12	21	London
25	Tinopolis	12	677.75	Llanelli
26	Principal Films	11.46	35	London
27	Box TV	10.5	12	London
28	Zeal TV	10.2	30	London
29	Shine	10	225.5	London
30	Ideal World	9.94	62	Glasgow/London
31	Wark Clements	9.4	49.8	Glasgow
32	Red Productions	9	20.45	Manchester
33	Greenlit Productions	8.69	8	London
34	Two Four Productions	8.6	150	Plymouth
35	Coastal Productions	8.5	6	Newcastle
36	12 Yard Productions	8.2	71.5	London
37	Prospect Pictures	8.1	522	London
38	DLT Entertainment	8	20	London
39	Ragdoll	7.4	697	Pinewood
40	Optomen	7	61	London
41	Baby Cow Productions	6.7	14.75	Brighton
42	Aardman Animations	6.5	2	Bristol
43	Carnival Films	6.4	392	London
44	The Comedy Unit	6.28	25.5	Glasgow
45	Windfall Films	6.17	19	London
46	Flashback TV	6	424	London/Bristol
47	UMTV	6	207	London
48	At It Productions	6	195.5	London
49	Diverse	6	28.5	London
50	World's End	6	25	London

Table 30 (pt I): UK TV Films Premiered January 2003-June 2004

Title	TX Date	Writer	Director
BBC1			
The Afternoon Play: Turkish Delight	27-Jan-2003	Rowan Joffe	Adrian Bean
The Afternoon Play: Coming Up for Air	28-Jan-2003	Matthew Parkhill	Dominic Keavey
The Afternoon Play: The Real Arnie Griffin	29-Jan-2003	Jeff Povey	Nigel Havers
The Afternoon Play: Heroes and Villains	30-Jan-2003	Lesley Clare O'Neill	Unavailable
The Afternoon Play: Girls Weekend	31-Jan-2003	Jane English	Unavailable
Murder In Mind: Favours	2-Feb-2003	J.C.Wilsher	Frank W Smith
Murder in Mind: Stalkers	16-Feb-2003	Gregory Evans	Gerry Poulson
Murder in Mind: Suicide	22-Feb-2003	Ann-Marie di Mambro	Tania Diez
New Tricks (Pilot)	27-Mar-2004	Roy Mitchell	Graham Theakston
Murder in Mind: Contract	3-Apr-2003	Guy Burt	Adrian Bean
Murder in Mind: Landlord	11-May-2003	Simon Sharkey	David Thacker
Murder in Mind:Justice	19-Jun-2003	Eric Deacon	Alrick Riley
Murder in Mind: Cornershop	29-Jun-2003	Stephen Leather	Menhaj Huda
Canterbury Tales: The Miller's Tale	11-Sep-2003	Peter Bowker	John McKay
Canterbury Tales: The Wife of Bath's Tale	18-Sep-2003	Sally Wainwright	Andy de Emmony
Canterbury Tales: The Knight's Tale	25-Sep-2003	Tony Marchant	Marc Munden
Canterbury Tales: The Sea Captain's Tale	2-Oct-2003	Avie Luthra	John McKay
Canterbury Tales: The Pardoner's Tale	9-Oct-2004	Tony Grounds	Andy de Emmony
Colosseum – Rome's Arena of Death	13-Oct-2003	Unavailable	Tilman Remme
Canterbury Tales: The Man of Law's Tale	16-Oct-2003	Olivia Hetreed	Julian Jarrold
Pompeii – The Last Day	20-Oct-2003	Edward Canfor-Dumas	Peter Nicholson
Holy Cross	10-Nov-2003	Terry Cafolla	Mark Brozel
Oliver Cromwell: Warts and All	24-Nov-2003	Ronald Frame	Unavailable
Frankenstein: Birth of a Monster	7-Dec-2003	Unavailable	Unavailable
The Young Visiters	26-Dec-2003	Patrick Barlow^	David Yates
Carrie's War	1-Jan-2004	Michael Crompton^	Coky Giedroyc
The Afternoon Play: Venus and Mars	26-Jan-2004	Johanna Baldwin	Nick Jones
Afternoon Play: Sons, Daughters & Lovers	27-Jan-2004	Matthew Parkhill	Matthew Parkhill
The Afternoon Play: Drive	28-Jan-2004	Pete Lawson	John Greening
The Afternoon Play: Viva Las Blackpool	29-Jan-2004	Damian Fitzsimmons	Sarah Lancashire
The Afternoon Play: Glasgow Dreams	30-Jan-2004	Shan Khan	Christopher Timothy
The Deputy	23-Feb-2004	Richard Stoneman	Patrick Lau
Pat and Mo	1-Apr-2004	Susan Boyd	Michael Owen Morris
England Expects	5-Apr-2004	Frank Deasy	Tony Smith
The Legend of the Tamworth Two	12-Apr-2004	Jed Mercurio	Metin Huseyin
May 33rd	21-Apr-2004	Guy Hibbert	David Attwood
Wren: The Man Who Built Britain	25-Apr-2004	Laura Lamson	Unavailable
The Two Loves of Anthony Trollope	2-May-2004	Unavailable	Richard Downes
D-Day	6-Jun-2004	Unavailable	Richard Dale

* Denotes prior release at cinemas
^ Denotes adaptation from literary source

Source: BFI/BBC

Table 30 (pt II): UK TV Films Premiered January 2003-June 2004

Title	TX Date	Writer	Director
BBC2			
Wild About Harry*	15-Jan-2003	Colin Bateman	Declan Lowney
Witchcraze	29-Jan-2003	Mark Hayhurst	James Kent
Among Giants*	1-Jan-2003	Simon Beaufoy	Sam Miller
Newton: The Dark Heretic	1-Mar-2003	Unavailable	Malcolm Neaum
Devil's Words – the Battle for an English Bible	17-Mar-2003	Peter Ackroyd	Tim Niel
This Little Life	19-Mar-2003	Rosemary Kay	Sarah Gavron
Rehab	26-Mar-2004	Rona Munro	Antonia Bird
The Other Boleyn Girl	28-Mar-2003	Philippa Lowthorpe^	Philippa Lowthorpe
Killing Hitler	30-Mar-2003	Jeremy Lovering	Jeremy Lovering
The Day Britain Stopped	13-May-2003	Simon Finch & Gabriel Range	Gabriel Range
Peter in Paradise	6-Jun-2003	Gwyneth Hughes	Mary MacMurray
George Orwell – A Life in Pictures	14-Jun-2003	Unavailable	Chris Durlacher
Love Again	26-Jul-2003	Richard Cottan	Susanna White
Copenhagen	30-Aug-2003	Michael Frayn & Howard Davies^	Howard Davies
Eroica	4-Oct-2003	Nick Dear	Simon Cellan Jones
Indian Dream	22-Oct-2003	Avie Luthra	Roger Goldby
The Private Life of Samuel Pepys	16-Dec-2003	Guy Jenkin	Oliver Parker
Iris*	20-Dec-2003	Richard Eyre & Charles Wood^	Richard Eyre
Bella and the Boys	15-Feb-2004	Brian Hill	Brian Hill
Morvern Callar*	7-Mar-2004	Lynne Ramsay^	Lynne Ramsay
Happy Now	13-Mar-2004	Belinda Bauer	Phillipa Collie-Cousins
Skaggerak	20-Mar-2004	Soren Kragh-Jacobsen & Anders Jensen	Soren Kragh-Jacobsen
In This World*	28-Mar-2004	Tony Grisoni	Michael Winterbottom
The Claim*	30-Mar-2004	Frank Cottrell Boyce^	Michael Winterbottom
Hawking	13-Apr-2004	Peter Moffat	Philip Martin
Every Time You Look At Me	14-Apr-2004	Lizzie Mickery	Alrick Riley
Date Rape: Sex and Lies	8-Jun-2004	Jeremy Lovering	Jeremy Lovering
The Elgin Marbles	26-Jun-2004	Unavailable	Unavailable

* Denotes prior release at cinemas   ^ Denotes adaptation from literary source

TV Films Premiered

Table 30

And lastly ... following on from previous handbooks here is a database of eighteen months of self-contained TV films or documentaries with a significant acted element that are an hour or over. Fittingly this shows how good British television can still be and highlights some of the creative talent we should be proud of. The single play is transformed, not dead yet and the success of ambitious ventures like *The Canterbury Tales* and *Omagh* is something to celebrate.

Acknowledgments

Statistics section compiled and edited by **Phil Wickham**. Phil is an Information Officer at the BFI National Library. He also writes and lectures extensively on British television and film.

Many thanks to those who helped Phil with the compilation of these figures, especially Nick Collins, Mark Bunting and Janet Lowther at Ofcom, Michelle Waldron at BTDA and Richard Webster at Five. *Broadcast* magazine remains, as always, an essential resource. Matt Ker in the BFI Information Service offered valued advice.

Table 30 (pt III): UK TV Films Premiered January 2003–June 2004

Title	TX Date	Writer	Director
ITV1			
Pollyanna	1-Jan-2003	Simon Nye^	Sarah Harding
Unconditional Love	20-Jan-2003	Chris Lang	Ferdinand Fairfax
Loving You	24-Feb-2003	Matthew Hall	Jean Stewart
Lucky Jim	11-Apr-2003	Jack Rosenthal^	Robin Sheppard
Danielle Cable: Eyewitness	14-Apr-2003	Terry Winsor/Kate Brooke	Adrian Shergold
Watermelon	16-Apr-2003	Colin Bateman^	Kieron J Walsh
The Booze Cruise	7-Sep-2003	Brian Levinson/Paul Minett	Paul Seed
Carla	15-Sep-2003	Barbara Machin	Diarmud Lawrence
Boudica	28-Sep-2003	Andrew Davies	Bill Anderson
Sparkling Cyanide	5-Oct-2003	Laura Lamson^	Tristam Powell
Real Crime: Lady Jane	14-Oct-2003	James Strong	James Strong
Gifted	29-Oct-2003	Kay Mellor	Douglas MacKinnon
Reversals	19-Nov-2003	Tim Loane	David Evans
Poirot: Five Little Pigs	14-Dec-2003	Kevin Elyot^	Paul Unwin
The Crooked Man	17-Dec-2003	Shaun McKenna^	David Drury
Promoted to Glory	21-Dec-2003	Rob Heyland	Richard Spence
Poirot: Sad Cypress	26-Dec-2003	David Pirie^	David Moore
Late Night Shopping*	26-Dec-2003	Jack Lothian	Saul Metzstein
The Return	30-Dec-2003	Kate O' Riordan	Dermot Boyd
The Brides in the Bath	31-Dec-2003	Glenn Chandler	Harry Bradbeer
Wall of Silence	12-Jan-2004	Neil McKay	Chris Menual
The Second Quest	5-Apr-2004	Douglas Livingstone	David Jason
Poirot: Death on the Nile	12-Apr-2004	Kevin Elyot^	Andy Wilson
Channel 4			
Sexy Beast*	30-Mar-2003	Louis Mellis/David Scinto	Jonathan Glazer
Twelfth Night	5-May-2003	Andrew Bannerman/Tim Supple^	Tim Supple
The Death of Klinghoffer	25-May-2003	John Adams	Penny Woolcock
The Deal	28-Sep-2003	Peter Morgan	Stephen Frears
Pornography – The Musical	21-Oct-2003	Simon Armitage	Brian Hill
Pleasureland	16-Nov-2003	Helen Blakeman	Brian Percival
Galileo's Daughter	22-Dec-2003	Unavailable	David Axelrod
Jack and the Beanstalk	24-Dec-2003	Unavailable	Brian Henson
The Illustrated Mum	31-Dec-2003	Debbie Isitt^	Cilla Ware
Pissed on the Job	14-Jan-2004	Unavailable	Paul Wilmshurst
Comfortably Numb	25-Jan-2004	Leo Regan	Leo Regan
The Badness of King George IV	28-Feb-2004	Unavailable	Tim Kirby
Room to Rent*	7-Mar-2004	Khalid El Hagar	Khaled El Hagar
Gangster No.1*	17-Apr-2004	Louis Mellis/David Scinto^	Paul McGuigan
Croupier*	18-May-2004	Paul Mayersberg	Mike Hodges
Omagh	27-May-2004	Paul Greengrass/Guy Hibbert	Pete Travis
Five			
Hear the Silence	15-Dec-2003	Timothy Prager	Tim Fywell

* Denotes prior release at cinemas
^ Denotes adaptation from literary source

Source: bfi/BBC

bfi Publishing
New and forthcoming titles

BFI FILM HANDBOOK

BFI Film Handbook 2005
Edited By
Eddie Dyja

£23.99

BFI WORLD DIRECTORS

Wong Kar-Wai
Stephen Teo

£13.99

The Matrix
Joshua Clover

The Thin Red Line
Michel Chion

BFI FILM CLASSICS & BFI MODERN CLASSICS

£8.99

Viridiana
Gary Indiana

if...
Mark Sinker

TELEVISION STUDIES

Selling Television
British Television in the Global Marketplace
Jeanette Steemers
£15.99

European Television Industries
Petros Iosifidis, Jeanette Steemers,
Mark Wheeler
£14.99

Serial Television
Big Drama on the Small Screen
Edited by Glen Creeber
£15.99

Contemporary World Television
Edited by John Sinclair
£15.99

 **Publishing**

Available from all good booksellers
For more information please phone 020 7957 4789 or visit
www.bfi.org.uk/books
e-mail: publishing@bfi.org.uk

BBC 1

Phil Wickham

It is much more than a TV channel. BBC 1 is a cultural symbol and a political football, constantly at the heart of raging national debates. Publicly funded but popular, BBC 1 is on the frontline of the intense political pressure that dogs the corporation these days; either lambasted for populism or jeered at for poor ratings.

In 2001 BBC 1 overhauled ITV to take the position of 'Britain's favourite button' and has maintained this share lead ever since. Admittedly terrestrial share is falling in the face of multichannel advance, and the position is now achieved through daytime rather than peak domination, but it is still an impressive feat. Ratings victory came from Greg Dyke's strategy to invest in programming, implemented by his appointee as Controller of BBC 1, Lorraine Heggessey. Now Dyke has been forced out following the Hutton enquiry, change is in the air after judicial admonishments, Mark Thompson's appointment as his replacement, charter renewal, and a resurgent ITV.

In recent years the cry from many quarters has been that the BBC, BBC 1 in particular, has been 'dumbing down'. This is characterised as a greedy chase for ratings and profitable spin-offs at the expense of its public service obligations. In this environment, critics argue, the licence fee becomes an unacceptable imposition on the population, used to create corporate profits. But how true is this when we look at the programmes BBC 1 has screened in 2003-4?

There is some damning evidence to back up these criticisms. Reliance has grown on endless runs of popular dramas like *Holby City*, and four weekly episodes of *EastEnders*, inevitably diluting their strengths, and their popularity (*EastEnders* sunk to almost seven million one night in May). Other popular dramas have looked distinctly formulaic, or occasionally downright cynical. Look at *Merseybeat*, or *Born and Bred*, a brazen attempt to recreate the homely success of ITV's *Heartbeat*. Other once charming shows like *Monarch of the Glen* and, sad to say, *Auf Weidersehen Pet*, have outstayed their welcome but carry on regardless.

Comedy, once the crowning glory of the channel, has largely been displaced or is approached with panic. The uprooting of the subtle and clever *Trevor's World of Sport* from the schedules was one of the year's low points. Light entertainment looks somewhat tired – yes, *They Think It's all Over* is still running – and Saturday night variety, despite the successful return of *Bruce Forsyth*, strikes an uneasy balance between the old and the new. The ratings success of family hit *Strictly Come Dancing* is the first sign of recovery; the abject failure of *Johnny and Denise – Passport to Paradise* is a step back.

Oddly, given Heggessey's own background in documentaries, factual programming has also had weaknesses. The *Panorama* specials on the Kelly affair and the BBC itself are obvious, if indulgent, exceptions but much other material covers old

Above: Crime caper *Hustle* – 'great fun'.
Right: 'traditionally-BBC' costume epic *Charles II*

ground or invariably feature the ubiquitous Dr Robert Winston. There are other stories, presenters and styles out there.

Above all there is still too much from the fag end of reality programming. The genre that made the last decade is now very near the bottom of the barrel and much of BBC 1's output feels a bit desperate. What's the point of say, *Perfect Holiday*, *A Life of Grime* (in its eighth series!) or *Fame Academy*? They fail in both Reithian terms and as fun mass entertainment, as ratings testify. When the new Grade-Thompson leadership say they want to 'eliminate derivative and cynical programming' let's hope they start here.

On top of this are the relentless trails and corporate branding idents that detract from the BBC's selling point of no commercials. Yes, the BBC is in the marketplace for viewers but it can be like being cornered by a double-glazing salesman. Self-promotion ranges from the excessively didactic – such as the film where BBC stars rip off masks to reveal each other – to the merely mystifying – the interminable dancers between programmes.

The inevitable 'but' in the face of this outweighs the negative evidence however. BBC 1 still does brave and astonishing things and does them well. Despite ratings disappointments much drama output is fabulous. This success is wide-ranging from traditionally 'BBC' costume epics like *Charles II – The Power and the Passion* and *He Knew He Was Right* to careful contemporary tragicomedy like *Bedtime*, or indeed the low rated but brilliantly acted *Family Business*. The updated versions of *The Canterbury Tales* thrillingly made the ancient modern. When we need dramatic comment on the events that are shaping our society, BBC 1 delivers in spades with *Holy Cross*, *Passer By* or *England Expects*. Talented people with something to say still find a place on the channel and can access an audience of millions. There was also a welcome return to intelligent but entertaining popular drama series with the highly implausible, but great fun, *Hustle* and *New Tricks*. All this and they are still prepared to do *The Afternoon Play* too. Popular factual did still challenge on occasion, especially with human-interest series *ONE Life* and some episodes of Alan Yentob's arts series *Imagine*.

Importantly, BBC 1 also does familiar and comfortable things well. To a greater extent than anyone else BBC 1 creates our cultural signposts. There is comforting permanence in much of the schedule – *Blue Peter*, *Top of the Pops*, *Antiques Roadshow* – that we can all comprehend. The news and sport also

The nature of BBC1's place at the heart of national life will always lead to controversy, particularly when its commercial critics are so politically powerful

have this unifying quality and remain of a higher standard than their competitors.

BBC 1's place at the heart of national life will always create controversy, particularly when its commercial critics are so politically powerful. Thus Heggessey has to fire fight rows that can erupt overnight. This year saw daytime stalwart Kilroy toppled by its host's bigotry, and allegations of bias from all political perspectives. The stakes are high as charter renewal and Ofcom's public service broadcasting review unfolds. Mark Thompson's return raises some questions after aspects of his Channel 4 reign, not to mention his opening speech promising cutbacks after claiming in his previous incarnation that the BBC was 'awash in a Jacuzzi of cash'.

2004 started a shift to more obviously public service programmes – what *Broadcast* magazine cynically called 'a cynical charter strategy' – but this is all to the good. July's manifesto 'Building Public Value' strives to make the balance between share and programme quality the right one. Michael Grade understands that this justifies BBC 1's continued importance.

Phil Wickham is an Information Officer at the BFI National Library.

Right: Natasha Kaplinsky and Brendan Love won *Strictly Come Dancing* – and the final won BBC 1 8.1 million viewers

BBC 2

Forty years after its birth BBC 2 finds itself at the crossroads. Controller Jane Root left for the U.S. in May and BBC 4 chief Roly Keating will take the channel forward into in the somewhat hazy new multichannel universe.

Root succeeded in maintaining an impressive channel share of 11 per cent and oversaw undoubted triumphs, such as *The Office*. BBC 2 is currently a frustrating paradox however – it shows the best programmes of any terrestrial channel, with an RTS award to prove it, but there is a nagging feeling that it could be so much better still. Change at the top may be no bad thing, and Keating's heavyweight credentials (Editor of *The Late Show*, *Bookmark*, BBC 4 and all) feel very timely.

Greg Dyke once said that he was 'not sure what BBC 2 was for', which should stop us getting too sentimental about the great man's departure. It should be obvious. BBC 2 is for anyone with an enquiring mind. It has a privileged position in the national culture, enabling programme makers to challenge us. As Channel 4 has declined by aiming so much of its output to a specific imagined viewer, probably a twenty-five-year-old ad executive in Clapham, so BBC 2 started down the same road, albeit to an older, more suburban, target - perhaps the ad executive's mum. It is vital for broadcasting in Britain that the station retains a broad appeal. This means a mixed schedule for different audiences, and this should not equate to mainstream any more than intelligent should equate to elitist.

There are worrying signs that the channel's strengths are being sapped by the relationship with the digital channels. Many of BBC 2's best shows are either edgy comedy courtesy of BBC 3, reruns of BBC 4 documentaries tucked after *Newsnight*, US imports like *Buffy* or *The Simpsons* and repeats of 70s sitcom hits. Other output can look limp and occasionally condescending in comparison. BBC 2 is more culpable of 'dumbing down' than BBC 1 because its responsibilities to make us think increase our demands.

Any good idea is flogged mercilessly until it loses all appeal. The idea of interactive event TV with expert champions worked well in 2002's *Great Britons*, and had a discernible point in *Restoration* (which returned for a second run in July 2004), but got in the way of the subject in *Britain's Best Sitcoms* and proved ridiculous in the frankly patronising *The Big Read*. These exercises in sham democracy are all too eloquent, if unintentional, a judgment on contemporary Britain and Keating has rightly damned them with faint praise.

Some documentaries disappointed, especially when rehashing over-familiar history and science subjects without new insights. Apparent fear of archive footage and talking heads sometimes make us feel like the victims of trendy teachers who think we might get bored without perpetual gimmickry. Five's sudden enthusiasm for arts and history documentaries seems to have caught BBC 2, the natural home of such fare, by surprise and they need to up their game accordingly.

Drama has been squeezed out, largely on cost grounds. There has been disappointingly little contemporary work this year in comparison to 2002-3. Instead costume biopics prevail, such as *Byron*, *Eroica*, or Jimmy McGovern's overblown

Roly Keating

Coupling - the signature BBC 2 sitcom found its fourth series premiered on BBC 3

Gunpowder, Treason and Plot. Extra money has now been promised to invest in new talent and to fund big projects from more established writers, essential from the station that brought us *Boys from the Blackstuff* and *Our Friends in the North.* Hopefully summer's eagerly anticipated *The Long Firm* could herald a new dawn.

The area that has worked well is drama-documentary, although here again there has been a tendency to over-egg the pudding. *Dunkirk* and *Seven Wonders of the Industrial World* are deserved critical and ratings triumphs, making the subject real and relevant to new generations without talking down to them. Attempts to move this into contemporary debates have not worked as well. Following the excellent and frightening *The Day Britain Stopped*, the series *If ...* ventured into silly scaremongering. Its editor Peter Barron's move back to being in charge of *Newsnight* shows the sudden fluid boundaries between news, documentary and drama.

In the last months of her reign Root signalled a welcome change of direction. After undignified ratings chasing in the last few years there is a damascene conversion on the importance of appreciation indices. These unpublished figures measure how much those watching actually enjoyed and engaged with a programme. Surely this should be the key factor for a channel like BBC 2, not mere numbers, especially as recent reports suggest an appreciation downturn. Symbolically Root scrapped two series emblematic of its problems, *Living the Dream* and *SAS: Are You Tough Enough?* The former was a bandwagon jumping exercise on Channel 4's golden property show trail and the latter was as sad as its title suggests. These are the kinds of projects that might fail the new 'public value' tests the BBC are set to install under Michael Grade – such tests could protect BBC 2's integrity.

BBC 2 has the best programmes of any terrestrial channel but there is a nagging feeling that it could be so much better still

Disappointments apart, BBC 2 can still shine, proven by two examinations of our recent past. *Who Killed PC Blakelock?* and *The Miner's Strike* show it at its inspiring best. The comedy is still great (though more needs to be originated by BBC 2 itself), *Newsnight* excels, and shows like *Grumpy Old Men* bring up talking points about society in a fun and pertinent way. Not everything has to be edgy – gardening, cooking and snooker have always been part of BBC 2 and are still done well.

Jane Root has said 'ambition is rewarded on BBC 2' but it hasn't always felt that way in 2003-4. Keating now has the best job in television with a corporate promise of 'quality and innovation' to ensure its cutting edge identity in the BBC's branding stampede, rather than just be a vehicle to show others achievements or lifestyle leisure viewing for the moneyed middle classes with the occasional public service sop. It will be fascinating to see if this can be achieved and a decent share maintained, especially as BBC 2 will likely lose its advantage over Channel 4 when *The Simpsons* transfers there in the autumn. Its availability to all and remit to engage is why BBC 2 is still important and why we should expect so much.

INDUSTRY IN FOCUS

April marked BBC 2's fortieth birthday

Benedict Cumberbatch as *Hawking*

Griff Rhys Jones hosts *Restoration*

BBC 3 & BBC 4

Alistair D. McGown

Developing digital services

Among the nostalgia which attended the fortieth Anniversary of BBC 2 in April was a useful lesson. While driven by the technological and economical imperatives of piloting the 625-line and colour services – to grumblings from those needing new sets and aerials – the channel foundered in its search for an identity and cultural purpose for at least a year, until David Attenborough replaced Michael Peacock as channel controller and set about revising the schedules. History echoes the challenge facing BBC 3 and BBC 4 today. The technological impetus is there but the channels are meeting and forming cultural remits with mixed fortunes as they bed in; BBC 4 has been on air since 2 March 2002, BBC 3 since 9 February 2003.

BBC 3 – 'Innovative and diverse'?

Eighteen months after launch BBC 3 continues to struggle with a dichotomous remit for informative youth entertainment that provokes hatred in commercial rivals. Controller Stuart Murphy complained to *Broadcast* in February; 'When we don't get big audiences people say: "How can the BBC spend [£97 million a year] on a channel that doesn't rate?" and when we do get good numbers they say, "How can the BBC spend public money taking away our commercial audience?"' BBC 3's remit is, even after the DCMS-imposed redrafts that held up its inception by a year, still as much defined by its production quotas and methods as by its fuzzy mission statement. 2003's goals were 'to engage a demanding audience of young adults with ambitious, stylish programming ... a mixed schedule of news, current affairs, education, music, arts, science ... high quality, innovative drama and entertainment'.

With its stated target demographic of 25-34s, BBC 3 seems not to be chasing the 18-24s – the current taste for trash TV among yoof (*Dirty Sanchez*, *The Osbournes*, *Jackass*, the ever more extreme *Big Brother*) sits uneasily with the aforementioned corporation-wide PSB agenda. BBC 3 is sometimes hampered by its onerous responsibilities – it may reflect the life of urban youth in a tough documentary series like January's *Tower Block Dreams* but such urban youths are likely to be watching *World Famous For Dicking Around* rather than such worthy – but to them dull – fare. Similarly well-intentioned but not gripping was child behaviour adult education series *Little Angels* (later seen, oddly, surrendering to *Emmerdale* on BBC1 in 7 p.m. slots).

Above: monkey business with Julian and Noel – *The Mighty Boosh*. Right: Julia Davis wrote and starred in black comedy *Nighty Night* (with Angus Deayton and Rebecca Front)

Life swap social experiment *Who Rules the Roost?* recast working parents as housewives and househusbands but studiously and responsibly avoided the engineered and nastily obvious conflicts of *Wife Swap* – thus also avoiding high ratings. Other reality series similarly lacked the watchable cruelty of a *Hell's Kitchen* – *The Other Boat Race* was populated by warm, funny Oxbridge alumni like Konnie Huq, Richard Herring and Emma Kennedy and the resulting lack of rampant celebrity egotism mixed with a positive vibe sank the show. The trick of making instructive programmes that can connect with hip young audiences continues to elude BBC 3 – Channel 4's *Ramsay's Kitchen Nightmares* perhaps shows the way they should go.

Unlike multichannel rivals E4 or MTV, BBC 3 cannot do 'extreme' – mixing in the 'informative' would seem fraudulent. *Body Hits* achieves the mix fairly successfully, looking into the science and health issues surrounding drinking and sex and all those other things The Kids get up to. Sexual health clinic series *Sex, Warts and All* had originally been a straight catalogue of STDs with a minimum of gross out material but follow up *SWAA: Down Under* was an Antipodean *Eurotrash*; voyeuristic nudity with a clap pamphlet thrown in. It's at the point when you're watching attractive young women making peeing videos that you really begin to question BBC 3's nebulous remit. This is the same remit that also encourages the big name, low budget series *From Bard to Verse* – famous actors reading passages from Shakespeare. Diverse, or just plain schizophrenic?

BBC 3 continues to struggle with a dichotomous remit for informative youth entertainment that provokes hatred in commercial rivals.

An almost unending stream of cutting edge comedy series has made inroads to forging BBC 3's identity. *Grass, Fifteen Storeys High, The Mighty Boosh, Catterick, Monkey Dust* and, particularly, *Little Britain* have received glowing notices, awards and even begun to attract decent audiences – *Little Britain*'s outstanding first series drew almost half a million to the channel. Wayne Garvie, of the BBC Entertainment Group, believed; 'If BBC 3 didn't exist nor would [these shows] and there would be a blank space in our lives'. Is this the really the case, or has BBC 2 merely hived off almost all of its comedy output? Conversely, for example, why was BBC 2's animated satire *I Am Not An Animal* not on BBC 3? The BBC 3 premiere run of series four of established BBC 2 hit *Coupling* further muddied the waters. Some might call for the BBC 2/3 co-commissioning process that begat many of these hits to be made transparent; others will just get on and enjoy the shows.

Above: *Date Rape: Sex and Lies* was a rare example of single drama on BBC 3. Right: inconsequential but amusing chat – and copious amounts of fag smoke - filled *The Smoking Room* (yes, that *is* Paula Wilcox with Nadine Marshall)

A self-imposed 100 per cent regional quota means all BBC 3 drama is now made outside of the M25. *Burn It*, stories of Manchester friends hitting thirty, seemed well tailored to the channel's target audience even if it's not quite yet hit the cult heights of BBC 2 classic *This Life* (surely the kind of hit BBC 3 is aiming for). Gory medical drama *Bodies* has drawn some good reviews and, perhaps more importantly, would not sit easily on BBC 1 or BBC 2.

BBC 3 had been a concerted effort to give new focus to the vague digital offering from the ONdigital/ITV Digital days, BBC Choice, a rather aimless spin-off channel. Another vestige of BBC 3's origins in BBC Choice was removed when daily entertainment bulletin *Liquid News* was axed in April, after being shunted out to a graveyard slot to die a quiet death (where it spent its last few weeks' on air, rather wonderfully, heaping abuse on Stuart Murphy!). Never a ratings hit, this agreeable peak time alternative was crucially seen as contrary to the BBC 3 mission. Surely a misreading, as *Liquid News* often refreshingly mocked the celebrity world fawned to by the commercial stations. It was *Liquid News* who quizzed S Club about money wrangles with their record company in May 2003, prompting the group's PR woman to terminate the interview. Perhaps *Liquid News* was just too expensive – the low-powered quiz *Headjam* must be far cheaper to produce.

Celebdaq, the TV version of the successful celebrity futures trading website, was expected to fill the gap left by *Liquid News'* passing but an ironic revamp with Joe Mace and Jenny Éclair failed to reverse the ratings decline and it too was canned. Similar whimsical irony permeated Johnny Vaughan's downsized chat-show *Live At Johnny's*, now based in a fake shed set reminiscent of *Why Don't You ...?* and featuring Dickie Davies as sports reporter. The increased presence of the divine Lauren Laverne – memorably seen having drinking races with a ten-year-old boy – was a plus but the show flopped when regularly pitted against *EastEnders*, a programme apparently quite popular with 25-34s.

BBC 3 still has timeshifted 10 p.m. *EastEnders* to bring viewers to the channel and overspill live coverage of a Newcastle UEFA cup game drew a sizeable 0.95 million in March, hitting number three in BARB's weekly multichannel only chart. Hipper, youth-oriented spin-offs of BBC 1 hits such as the *Eurovision Song Contest* and *Fame Academy* have also done well for the channel (although a youth version of *Strictly Come Dancing* was taking the point too far). Probably only the hours of extra coverage of music from the Glastonbury Festival carried by BBC 3 at the end of June really provide the perfect symbiosis of complementary coverage and audience remit. Even so, more needs to be done to make BBC 2 and BBC 3 Glastonbury schedules genuinely complement each other – nirvana in theory, the reality is often a channel-flicking nightmare! BBC 3's remit, loose as it is, severely limits the 'turn over now for more of ...' approach that's quickly made ITV2 a multichannel hit. Rightly forced to work much harder for its audience, if anything its remit is to innovate and explore and it is slowly but surely grasping that nettle.

BBC 4 – Still building 'a place to think'?

It's unmistakeably a niche channel but the BBC's Ofcom-prompted renewed interest in PSB values is likely to shield BBC 4 from many outside pressures. If anything can take BBC 4 off-mission ('television's most intellectually and culturally enriching channel ... providing real alternatives' as stated in early 2003) it could be BBC 2's renewed interest in such values. As of June, ex-BBC 4 controller Roly Keating will guide BBC 2's future with, one imagines, a refocus on documentary and drama, away from light lifestyle. It will be interesting to see how the two channels remain distinct, with former Channel 4 controller of specialist factual Janice Hadlow now at the helm of BBC 4.

Broadcast's Philip Reevel jocularly likened the channel to an outrageously subsidised public utility costing fortunes per viewer, noting most programmes rate in the tens of thousands. It's true that BBC 4 can sometimes pander to the narrowest of niche audiences, particularly in the Arts, but this can be celebrated as a positive – *The Alchemists of Sound*, bar the odd whimsical indulgence, was, for any cult devotee of the BBC Radiophonic Workshop, simply one of the greatest television programmes ever made. BBC 4 has blazed a trail in this direction, reclaiming the television archives from the clips shows to rerun an unrivalled selection of shows, supplemented by intelligent, meticulous archive-based programmes merging social history and television retrospective, usually under the *Time Shift* banner. June's *Summer in the 60s* has been television's finest ever archive theme season.

As far as new programmes go, drama in particular is curtailed by lower budgets (BBC 4 received a budget boost of £10 million for 2004-5 but the increased total of £40m is still someway

June saw much of BBC 4's airtime given over to a fantastic archive TV season of documentaries and repeats – Summer in the 60s

below BBC 3's £97 million). Viewed optimistically, this has rekindled creative ingenuity and risk-taking in a form that now often indulges in spectacle and sensation on mainstream channels. *The Alan Clark Diaries* became the breakthrough series that put BBC 4 on the map in January via the channel's best ever viewing figures (0.87 million and a 7.3 per cent share in multichannel homes for episode one, reckoned BARB, although the final episode had dropped to 0.15 million, perhaps as viewers realised a BBC 2 rerun was imminent) and a subsequent outcry by digital desisters. It's hoped that via such controversy digital refuseniks will eventually come on board (as *The Forsyte Saga* and its ilk drove BBC 2 uptake in the 60s). Only certain kinds of drama can be made on BBC 4 budgets – even the relatively lavish *Alan Clark Diaries* was made with much recourse to archive BBC news footage and voiceover passages of the MP's journals from lead actor John Hurt. Hurt nonetheless publicly complained about the tight conditions under which the series was made.

A highlight in the single drama form was October's *Home*, starring Anthony Sher – a J. G. Ballard short story about a man who retreats from the world to try living isolated indoors. This frightening allegory of a descent into madness and, eventually, murder indicated how resourceful BBC 4 must be. Shot as a low-grade video diary within a real house with a minimal cast and a ready script, something very worthwhile came out of such tight parameters. BBC 3's *Date Rape* also deserves a mention for utilising a low budget to spin an ambiguous tale of sexual perspectives, relying heavily on the device of a radio phone-in (a voiceover from Simon Pegg as an exploitative DJ). Elsewhere, BBC 4 does as best it can with taped versions of stage plays such as *Hotel in Amsterdam* or *Three Sisters*.

The uniqueness of such single plays was echoed in the unique stories spun by several diverting single documentaries sharing a coincidental WWII link: *The Guinea Pig Club*, about the pioneering reconstructive surgery carried out on a band of badly burned fighter pilots; *The Island*, a visit to a weapons research bunker now abandoned in a National Trust conservation area; and *Imber*,

INDUSTRY IN FOCUS

> *The Alan Clark Diaries* put BBC 4 on the map in January via the channel's best ever viewing figures and a subsequent outcry by digital desisters – such controversies may eventually bring digital refuseniks on board.

England's Lost Village, the tale of a town 'killed' by the Ministry of Defence when evacuated and commandeered for combat practice, never to be repopulated. *The National Trust* documentary series drew good figures, boosted by an opening episode (which scored 0.35 million and 2.6 per cent share) about conflict between the Trust and nudists over a stretch of English beach.

Those who complain there's never anything on should switch to BBC 4 once in a while – they should be pleasantly surprised.

John Hurt starred as the wayward Tory MP in *The Alan Clark Diaries*

ITV1 & ITV2

Steve Bryant

t was events off-screen which dominated ITV's year, with the passage of the Communications Act finally paving the way for the merger between Granada and Carlton, unifying all but the Scottish, Northern Irish and Channel Island companies of the ITV Network into a single entity. In the event, it was seen by many analysts as more of a takeover of ITV by Granada than a merger of two equal partners – what was undeniable was that prior to merger the staffing levels of each were in the ratio 72:28 in Granada's favour and the companies' ITV output was of a similar ratio. The regional structure and Network Centre still remain, while other areas of activity are rationalised.

The merger brought to an end a long period of uncertainty and instability at Britain's leading commercial network, with the failure of ITV Digital and the slump in advertising revenue both adding to the air of despondency and demanding the clearest of solutions. At the same time, programming problems such as the scheduling of Premiership football and the failure of high profile offerings such as *Survivor* had exacerbated the problems. At ITV, however, there are no problems so bad that a few big ratings hits won't solve and, having, it seems, come to terms with the fact that they will never again command the automatically high audience shares they once took for granted,

the past year can be regarded as a fairly successful one on-screen.

Most of the greatest successes in terms of audiences and impact came from returning light-entertainment and reality formats, particularly those fronted by Ant and Dec. Once again, it was *Pop Idol*, *I'm A Celebrity ... Get Me Out of Here!* and *Ant and Dec's Saturday Night Takeaway*, the first two supplemented by expanded coverage on ITV2, which provided the backbone of the output. The Geordie duo are now such a vital part of ITV's strategy that they almost carry the channel's fortunes on their backs. The recruitment of Michael Parkinson from the BBC may ease the burden a little.

A great deal of effort and expenditure has been put into ITV's drama output over the past twelve months, with a great deal of new material ending up on the screen, but not a great deal of variety of tone or content. The percentage of drama related to crime and the police seems to have been higher than ever, with a massive number of titles, some new, some returning; *Murder in Suburbia*, *Wire in the Blood*, *Donovan*, *The Last Detective*, *The Crooked Man*, *Taggart*, *Midsomer Murders*, *Amnesia*, *Foyle's War* and the stalwart *The Bill* to name just some of them. There were also some new episodes of *A Touch of Frost* and *Poirot* for good

Helen Mirren was back as Tennison in *Prime Suspect 6*

Comedy drama *Life Begins*, starring Caroline Quentin, drew a huge average of 10 million to ITV

measure, and even the major historical drama of the Autumn season, *Henry VIII*, looked like a gangster story, with Ray Winstone in the lead. The pick of ITV's drama output also came from the crime genre, though: the long-awaited return of Helen Mirren as Jane Tennison in *Prime Suspect 6: The Last Witness*, cleverly complemented with a showing of the first in the series on ITV2, as if to demonstrate that ITV's commitment to quality and innovation in drama still stands.

There were some successes away from the crime scene as well. *Footballers' Wives* continued to generate the most publicity and audiences, as well as demanding and receiving a general suspension of critical analysis, while *Between the Sheets* and *William and Mary* look like established hits. There was great anticipation generated by Mike Bullen's follow up to the phenomenal success of *Cold Feet*, with many doubting whether he could produce anything else of similar quality. In the event, *Life Begins*, starring Caroline Quentin as an abandoned wife struggling to re-build her life proved that Bullen has plenty more to offer and retained its high audiences throughout its first series. Recently, many series on all channels have faded after a promising start but *Life Begins* opened with 10.5 million and never fell below 9.5 million for the rest of its run – these were serious figures by any standards and in many ways this was ITV's most unassuming hit of the year. A second series is in production for 2005.

Possibly the most challenging new drama of the year also had a *Cold Feet* connection through its star, James Nesbitt. Nesbitt had already proved his ability to tackle darker roles, though, and it was no surprise that *Wall of Silence*, in which he played a father dealing with the murder of his son, was a powerful and affecting piece.

In continuing drama, *Coronation Street* was generally felt to have had an outstanding year, and was very much to the fore when the awards season came around.

Comedy proved to be a continuing problem for ITV, however. Having declared an intention to beef up their later evening output, far too many of their offerings were ill-judged in terms of the audience expectations of the channel and suffered accordingly. It really cannot have been a

This camera-shy duo were all over ITV in 2003-4 with no fewer than three hit shows

The trend towards even greater commercialism and populism on ITV is already irreversibly set.

surprise that Reeves and Mortimer would not work well on ITV. They remain probably the most innovative forces at work in British TV comedy over the last fifteen years, but their natural home is on Channel 4 or BBC2. So, even filling *The All-Star Comedy Show* with more mainstream talents, performing Vic and Bob's scripts, could not save it from looking terribly out of place on the main commercial network.

Frank Skinner is a different proposition. He is an established face of ITV and repeats of *The Frank Skinner Show* are a staple of ITV2, but it has long been clear that his strength lies in his impromptu comic abilities, as in his chat show and *Fantasy Football*, which returned to ITV for the Euro 2004 Championships. So his sitcom, *Shane*, which critics judged to have been little more than a vehicle for Skinner's jokes, suffered from panic re-scheduling after its initial failure to impress.

Other attempts to beef up ITV's comedy output by buying in some of the outstanding talents developed on the BBC, which can be judged to have failed in the particular environs of ITV, included *The Impressionable Jon Culshaw*, in which the *Dead Ringers* star foundered without his cohorts, and *The Director's Commentary*, an ingenious idea from Rob Brydon which was totally unsuited to the leading mainstream channel.

55

The highlight of ITV's sports coverage in the past year was the Rugby World Cup, with England's success bringing in not only substantial audiences, but large numbers of the very people advertisers have long been known to cherish most – the ABC1 males. Champions League football also benefited from the presence and progress of four Premier League teams, and also from the ability to schedule simultaneous games on ITV2. Indeed, there was plenty of coverage to satisfy both ITV and Sky Sports, who share the UK transmission rights. Only *The Premiership* continued to disappoint, so there was little to upset ITV in the loss of the rights to the BBC. ITV's signing of Michael Parkinson, in what looks like a straight swap, is probably a shrewd move.

In terms of factual programming, ITV's flagship *Tonight With Trevor McDonald* maintained an impressive range of coverage of a mainly domestic agenda, occasionally tipping over into tabloid excess with programmes like the special, *Our Daughter Holly*, which added little to the coverage of the Soham murders by interviewing, at length, the parents of one of the victims and made uncomfortable viewing. John Pilger produced his annual polemic, this time tackling US policy in Afghanistan and Iraq in *Breaking the Silence: Truth and Lies in the War on Terror*. His conscience-salving presence may in future be confined mainly to the ITV News Channel, for which he will make a series of pieces. The main

historical documentary of the year was a three-parter on the life of Churchill, which contained little in the way of new material, but satisfied the main criterion of the genre in dealing with the Second World War.

ITV2 developed little during the year, continuing to schedule complementary and additional material to the main channel, such as *Behind the Scenes at the BAFTAs*, and plenty of repeats, but little in the way of original programming. One of ITV's biggest innovations of the year, however, and certainly a great airtime filler on both channels, was the *24 Hour Quiz*. The announcement of the arrival of ITV3 later in 2004 may change things, though, as it is likely to feature recent archive material (*Inspector Morse* and *A Touch of Frost* seem the most likely candidates) and may thus free up ITV2 to develop some original programming.

The future shape of ITV programming may well be influenced by the outcome of Ofcom's review of Public Service Broadcasting. ITV has already let it be known that it would like to be freed from its obligations to provide religious and arts programmes, so the future could be bleak for Melvyn Bragg. Whatever the result, though, the trend towards even greater commercialism and populism is already irreversibly set.

Steve Bryant is Keeper of Television at the National Film and Television Archive.

Romance between Jordan and 'insaniac' Peter André fuelled tabloid coverage of Series 3 of *I'm a Celebrity*

Michael Kitchen and Honeysuckle Weeks are the stars investigating wartime crime in ITV1's Sunday night favourite *Foyle's War*

Channel 4

Michael Darlow

Channel 4, which started transmissions on Tuesday, 2 November 1982, was conceived out of the idealism of the 60s, but born into post-Falklands War Thatcherism.

The channel was a potentially uneasy compromise between the desire of radical younger programme makers for a channel where they could give rein to their creativity freed from the constraints of the BBC and ITV, and of a Conservative 1979 election manifesto pledge to give the ITV companies a second, advertiser funded channel. Set up as an independent corporation, regulated by ITV regulator, the IBA, and run by its own board, Channel 4 was charged with providing programmes not provided by the BBC or ITV, but funded out of subscriptions paid by the ITV companies in return for selling the channel's advertising airtime. It was not to produce its own programmes but acquire them from outside suppliers, including 'a substantial proportion' from independent producers.

The contradictions inherent in its foundation soon became evident . There were rows about its programmes (charged with catering 'for tastes and interests not generally catered for' elsewhere and 'innovation and experiment in the form and content of programmes'), when the channel initially came under repeated attack from both the nation's self-appointed moral guardians and the popular press for going too far and disappointed programme makers and social progressives for not going far enough.

Although the quality of its programmes was uneven the channel's unorthodoxy built its audience, especially among the young. Full of surprises, minorities and the unexpected, led by its inspirational first Chief Executive, Jeremy Isaacs, the channel became a place where people confronted new programme forms and ideas.

Michael Grade took over from Isaacs in 1988 and ended what he dubbed the channel's 'amateur status', increasing audience numbers but reducing originality and risk taking. He successfully saved Channel 4 from being privatised in the 1990 Broadcasting Act and won it the right to sell its own advertising while remaining a public corporation.

By the time Michael Jackson (who had started his career in 1979 as a campaigner for the fourth channel) succeeded Grade in 1997, Channel 4 faced a growing number of little-regulated commercial competitors. Fearing that advertising revenue

Mark Thompson assured critics Channel 4 would plug British TV's 'creative deficit'. Yet by the time he left for the BBC, attention-seeking trivialities still proliferated.

would not sustain its future, Jackson initiated a new drive for popular audiences and was attacked for 'attention seeking and sensation'.

When Mark Thompson succeeded Jackson in 2002 he assured critics that Channel 4 would plug British television's 'creative deficit'. Yet by summer 2004, when he left to become Director-General of the BBC, attention-seeking trivialities still proliferated. Autumn 2003 had seen Derren Brown playing Russian roulette with what was billed as a live bullet and a teenage version of *Big Brother* promoted from a daytime educational slot to peak time in the knowledge that participants had been recorded having sex on camera. Days later Thompson, admitting that Channel 4 had 'sometimes been guilty' of 'cynical' programming, promised to cut the amount of pointless sex.

However, 2004 brought a new reality show, *Shattered*, where contestants were deprived of sleep for a week, more *Wife Swap*, *Boss Swap*, makeover shows, no less than six property shows in the hours between 8pm and 10pm in one week in February, and in March, when the last *Sex and the City* aired, an entire evening (from 20.30 to

Ramsay's Kitchen Nightmares – ep 1 took us to a nightmare kitchen in West Yorkshire

02.55) of U.S. imports, apart from Graham Norton in what looked like a pilot for his U.S. career.

Summer produced yet another massive dose of *Big Brother*. Billed as '*Big Brother* gets evil', it appeared constructed to be more attention-seeking than ever. The housemates were show-offs, misfits, the prejudiced and people whose self-obsession seemed matched only by their desire to become famous – 'I desperately want to be a C-list celebrity, so for God's sake don't throw me out of here!' A mix of black, white, gay, straight and one (undisclosed) trans-sexual (How brave! Ho, ho!!) promised sexual shenanigans, conflict and attendant tabloid headlines. These duly came a couple of weeks later with a late-night brawl, viewers summoning the police and audiences obligingly hitting five million.

Against this kind of thing must be set the opera *The Death of Klinghoffer*, Paul Abbott's widely (over-?) praised *Shameless* and Rodrigo Vazquez's moving account of the killing of an American peace activist in Gaza, *Death of an Idealist*. But would

had held exploratory merger talks with Five. Shortly after, Thompson publicly resuscitated the idea of ownership passing to an independent trust, with the remit enshrined in perpetuity in its trust deed (an arrangement similar to the Scott Trust and *The Guardian*).

In January Ofcom appointed Luke Johnson as Channel 4's new Chairman, stressing that he is 'a well-known and successful entrepreneur'. Johnson built his fortune from a string of food outlets and once nominated Rupert Murdoch as his business hero but he too rejects privatisation: 'It would ruin what it does ... If it were privatised it would destroy its remit and purpose'. However, in July 2004, in his first really significant move as Chairman, he appointed Andy Duncan, the BBC's Director of Communications and Marketing, as the new Chief Executive. Duncan is the first person to lead the channel without a background in programme making. Previously Duncan was best known as being the man behind Freeview and for selling us products like Flora, PG Tips and Batchelors

Derren Brown debunked the myth of the *Séance*; Jimmy Corkhill ranted as *Brookside* closed; US sitcom *Frasier* also bowed out

Vazquez's documentary have been awarded its exemplary 8 p.m. slot had a vital England Euro 2004 match not been on BBC1 at the same time?

Thompson did little to 'plug the creative deficit' but presided over a big change in programme executives and cut costs. Channel 4 now employs 130 staff less than in 2002, profits have tripled and the programme budget has increased to a record £457m. Although increased competition has reduced audience share a little, its share of advertising holds up.

Nevertheless, concerns remain about survival in the longer term. One suggestion, mooted by Ofcom and backed by senior people at Channel 4, is that part of the BBC licence fee might fund public service programmes on other channels. Like its predecessors, Channel 4's Board rejects privatisation. Thompson reiterated Michael Grade's arguments of a decade ago – as a privatised channel, almost certainly a part of a larger media empire, it would increasingly, whether it wanted to or not, come to put profits before its remit. However, in late February it emerged that, apparently with Ofcom's tacit approval, Channel 4

Supernoodles. Johnson assures us Duncan will be 'a great champion of Channel 4's public service mission and its unique brand of creativity'. The head of *Big Brother* producer Endemol, Peter Bazalgette, called Duncan's appointment 'really imaginative', adding that Duncan is a 'fantastic brand manager'. So what price the channel's founding values, sorry 'brand', now?

In the first stage of its public service broadcasting review, published in April, Ofcom stressed that Channel 4 'will have a critical part to play, especially given the public desire for originality and innovation'. A good indication of the new top team's fitness to play that role will be what they do about trashy, popular hits like *Big Brother* and replacing hit acquisitions *Friends* and *Sex and the City*. Will they spend time and some of the increased profits on creating worthy home grown replacements or will they opt for more of the same and a new U.S. spending spree?

Michael Darlow was a leading campaigner for the creation of Channel 4 in the 70s. His book **Independents Struggle** *was published in 2004.*

Five

Christine Fanthome

INDUSTRY IN FOCUS

In her first year as Five's Chief Executive, Jane Lighting has overseen the channel's transition from what she describes as 'a spotty teenager' to 'a grown up' and 'part of the establishment.' She ascribes this shift in perspective to a change in the company's financial situation, noting: 'Last year was the first year we made a profit – a modest one, but a profit nevertheless'. This prompted Lighting to define new objectives and identify and implement strategies to achieve them. Lighting introduced 'cross-functional working' designed to promote greater interaction between creative and commercial personnel, and supervised a strategic review which looked at coverage, programming, the commercial prospects for raising secondary revenue through merchandising, distribution and telephony, interactive and gaming possibilities, and digital and multi-channel opportunities.

Five was the only terrestrial broadcaster to increase its audience share in 2003, achieving an overall average of 6.5 per cent for the year. In the first half of 2004 this has edged up towards 7 per cent. Films such as *Miracle on 34th Street*, *Erin Brockovich*, *Gladiator*, *Terminator 2* and *The Matrix* accounted for many of the top rated programmes for 2003. These also included live soccer, such as the Celtic v Liverpool UEFA Cup match; overseas acquisitions like *America's Finest*, *CSI*, *Law & Order* and spin offs; and documentaries like *The Michael Jackson Interview*, *The Funniest Ads In The World* and *The Curse of Blue Peter*. Other key programming included *House Doctor*, *Home and Away* and *Britain's Finest*.

Following Kevin Lygo's departure to Channel Four, Dan Chambers became Five's Director of Programmes in October 2003. Chambers had previously been Five's Controller of Factual Programming and initiated many of the projects he is currently overseeing in his new role. He has made several programme changes in order not only to increase share but to alter the demographics of the channel's audience, which in 2003 tended to be relatively old and downmarket. As Chambers explained to me, he has maintained the commitment to arts programming in peak time but also introduced a new science strand with *Five Big Science Ideas*, featuring Stephen Hawking, Richard Dawkins and other eminent scientists, and *Five Great Scientists*, which focused on Aristotle, Darwin, Einstein, Galileo and Newton; 'We'd had a big success with the arts – big critical success rather than ratings success. We'd had ratings success and some critical success with history, and then science seemed to be the third genre, the third upmarket genre, that we hadn't really tapped into.'

Five was the only terrestrial broadcaster to increase audience share in 2003, achieving 6.5 per cent. In the first half of 2004 it edged towards 7 per cent. Films such as *Gladiator* and *The Matrix* accounted for many of the top rated programmes.

Rik Waller, Jade Goody, Maureen off of *Driving School* ... how could it fail? *Back to Reality* was not the hit Five had hoped for

Series like *Dream Holiday Home* help Five compete with the leisure and lifestyle shows on offer from Channel 4

Jane Lighting confirmed the aim and importance of attracting a younger, more upmarket audience and developing the channel's image to its future advantage. 'We have actually been more specific about our targets. It was about getting the right focus in terms of the commercial audiences we really needed to deal with, and to seriously improve the profile of the channel. Everyone talks about 16-34s and ABCs; we are doing just the same.'

Chambers also decided to scale up Five's leisure and lifestyle output and to 'be more ambitious with our entertainments projects', allocating the budget to fewer shows so that they will attract new viewers. These changes have yet to appear on screen, and the top rated programming for the first half of 2004 remains generically unchanged: films (like *Independence Day* and *Miss Congeniality*), soccer matches (Liverpool vs Levski Sofia) and *America's Finest*. New highly rated programming includes the *Britain's Worst* franchise, *Comedy Heroes*, and single documentaries such as *ABBA's Biggest Secret*. The second half of 2004 will include films *Legally Blonde*, *Planet of the Apes* and *Kiss of the Dragon*, and new series *Plastic Surgery Live* which will reflect the 'noisy' image of the Five brand.

There have also been ratings disappointments. *Back to Reality*, in which twelve people from previous reality shows were united under one roof in what Five publicity billed as 'the ultimate reality show', was universally panned by critics and attracted only about a million viewers per episode. However, it enabled Five to embrace interactivity for the first time by running a second channel 24/7 on the Sky platform, and although Chambers admits that 'the brand of the channel took a bit of a knocking for three weeks', the programmes successfully delivered a younger audience, part of which has been retained.

A perennial issue for Five is reach, which is around 55 per cent of the total audience each week. To improve coverage, four new transmitters have been activated – in Brighton, Reigate, Tunbridge Wells and Hastings. In order to win new viewers, there has also been a change in marketing strategy. Chambers confirms that rather than singling out between twelve and twenty shows for promotion each year, the plan since the beginning of 2004 has been to promote only the major programmes, reckoning that 'you reach more people, those shows do better, and it's much more of a statement about the channel'.

Not surprisingly, there is continuing press speculation about Five's future. One line of thought is that if it is to survive and compete with the bigger channels it needs a partner, and an intermittent rumour hints at a takeover by BSkyB. This began when Dawn Airey, Lighting's predecessor, left to join BSkyB, and was both fuelled in the spring of 2004 by the announcement that BSkyB would supply news to Five from January 2005 when Five's contract with ITN expired, and by the defection to BSkyB of Five's Deputy Chief Executive and Director of Sales, Nick Milligan.

New to 2004 was the rumour that Channel 4 and Five may merge. This has been the subject of several newspaper articles, and indeed, the Chief Executive of Five's majority shareholder, RTL, confirmed to *The Guardian* in March; 'We spoke to Channel 4, as we speak to other players on an informal basis, but nothing's decided yet'. Whilst emphasising her determination to take Five forward, Lighting remains non-committal about how this will be achieved. 'We have talked to Sky about all sorts of things; we have talked to Channel 4 about all sorts of things; we have talked to multichannel about all sorts of things. We are exploring strategic options for ourselves in terms of how we can expand Five and importantly develop a family of multi-channel channels.'

In today's volatile environment, change seems inevitable: it is just its timing and nature that are unknown.

Dr Christine Fanthome is a freelance consultant and lecturer. She is the author of **Channel 5 – the Early Years** *(2003: University of Luton Press). Original quotes in this article are from an interview Dr Fanthome conducted with Dan Chambers and Jane Lighting in May 2004.*

Globalisation Strategies Jeanette Steemers

In terms of global television, Britain's strongest player continues to be the BBC. Its wholly-owned commercial arm, BBC Worldwide, operates a raft of international channels and is the largest exporter of British television programmes. With turnover of £658 million in 2002-3 from programme sales, commercial channels and the exploitation of ancillary rights, BBC Worldwide accounted for 54 per cent of Britain's total television export revenues in 2002.

Channel BBC America, wholly owned by BBC Worldwide, was available in 34.5 million US homes in 2003 and has proved a showcase for British programming, notably spoof docusoap, *The Office*, which was awarded two U.S. Golden Globes at the start of 2004. BBC Prime, launched in 1995, focuses largely on the pan-European market. Broadcast in English it was available in 11.5 million homes in 2003. BBC World, a global 24-hour English language news service, started in 1995 and was available in 253 million homes in 2003. BBC Food was launched across Europe in 2003.

As part of a long-running joint venture with Discovery Communications Inc, BBC Worldwide operates the jointly owned commercial factual channels, Animal Planet (available in 188.4 million homes in Asia, Latin America, Europe, the US, Canada and Japan) and People and Arts (available in 13.5 million homes in Latin America). The company has also established joint venture channels with local partners in its other English-speaking markets of Canada (BBC Kids, BBC Canada), Australia and New Zealand (UK TV).

During the course of 2003-4 the BBC's position of global pre-eminence was challenged. First the 2003 Communications Act led to the merger of the two ITV franchises, Carlton and Granada. Their international operations, Granada International and Carlton International, were brought together at the start of 2004, creating an international sales arm with an estimated turnover of £139 million. In theory the merger will give ITV plc the scale thought necessary to participate on the global stage, creating one of the largest commercial broadcasters and content providers in Europe.

Granada International is now a more formidable global operator with an international production base, grounded largely on the exploitation and production of non-scripted formats in the US by its Los Angeles-based production entity, Granada America, which merged with Carlton's US-based

Granada and Carlton's international sales arms merged to create a powerful new vendor, unveiled at March 2004's Mipcom event

TV movie business at the end of 2003. Productions include *American Princess* for the NBC network, *I'm A Celebrity ... Get Me Out of Here!* for ABC, and *Airline* for cable channel, A&E. Unlike BBC Worldwide however it has no international channel presence. Also, following changes in ownership rules in the 2003 Communications Act, general consensus warns that sooner or later ITV may be absorbed by a US corporation, with Viacom and Time Warner both cropping up in press reports. A U.S. take-over might put a brake on ITV's global aspirations if it became part of a larger US-based and globally integrated corporation.

The second threat to BBC dominance came when the Communications Act heralded changes for the independent production sector. Codes of practice, approved in January 2004 by the new regulatory body, Ofcom, allow independent producers to retain control of secondary, international and ancillary rights to their programmes, giving them greater opportunities to generate profits from international sales, consumer products, DVD and video. Broadcaster-distributors like BBC Worldwide and Channel 4 International no longer get automatic access to the secondary and ancillary rights of independent commissions. In a report commissioned for producers association, Pact, it was estimated that Channel 4 and the BBC would lose £36 million through the loss of rights and payments for re-runs.

The new terms of trade make some independent production companies more attractive investment propositions, particularly if their properties can be exploited internationally. An influx of city money is anticipated based on the exploitation of these assets, and further mergers and acquisitions are predicted among the larger independent companies to create scale and presence.

INDUSTRY IN FOCUS

March 2003 saw Hat Trick sell a 45 per cent stake to the venture capital firm, Kleinwort Capital although plans to buy drama producers Shed for £20 million were later shelved. Shed was attractive because it retained rights to its programmes through licensed deals with the ITV Network. In August 2003 the production business of Chrysalis TV (*Midsomer Murders, Ultimate Force*), since renamed All3media, was sold for £51 million to former Granada executives, with capital from Bridgepoint and MBI. All3media bought Lion Television in June 2004 and by July looked poised to seal a deal with Company Pictures (*Shameless*).

Growing confidence has led some independents to set up shop in America to market formats, produce locally and secure co-production funding. In 2003 almost 94 per cent of British co-production revenues ($108 million) came from the U.S. The holy grail for most remains a primetime sale to one of the US networks (ABC, Fox, CBS, NBC). Prominent is RDF Media, whose Los Angeles production outpost now generates a significant proportion of the company's £45.3 million turnover. Key properties include *Junkyard Wars* (a US version of Channel 4's *Scrapheap Challenge*) for cable channel TLC, and a version of *Wife Swap* for the US network, ABC, set to air in 2004. Other indies with a US production presence include Tiger Aspect Productions and Lion Television. By February 2004 Lion Television, with turnover of £22 million, had more than forty hours in US production, accounting for almost 40 per cent of its turnover.

Children's specialist, HIT Entertainment remains the largest British independent in the US market. In 2002-3 64 per cent of its £168.9 million turnover was generated in the US, largely from consumer products and home entertainment, based on the enduring success of pre-school brands *Bob the Builder*, *Thomas the Tank Engine* and *Barney*. The latter is produced at HIT's studios in Dallas. At the start of 2004 HIT announced it was looking to launch a dedicated pre-school channel in the US market. This would guarantee access to US screens, and offer a potential platform for lucrative DVD and consumer products sales.

In terms of globalisation strategies, Britain is now seeing a gradual shift with a small number of independent producers taking on a more active role on the global stage, given their newly granted ability to retain rights.

Jeanette Steemers is Principal Lecturer in the School of Media and Cultural Production at De Montfort University in Leicester.

A Corporate History of ITV

Barrie MacDonald

ITV: from regional companies to ITV plc

The consolidation of ITV in the past decade changed it from a federation of fifteen separately owned and independent regional television companies to a virtual duopoly owned by Carlton Communications and Granada Media Group. After the Communications Act 2003 removed the final barriers to single ownership of ITV, the long-expected merger of Carlton and Granada to form a single company took place. So at this crucial point for ITV, and as it approaches its fiftieth anniversary in 2005, it's appropriate to reflect on its origins, development and regionality, as well as the events of the past year.

Origins

Commercial television in Britain was established by the Television Act 1954, breaking the BBC's thirty-year monopoly on broadcasting. The Act provided for Independent Television (ITV) to be set up and regulated by a public body, the Independent Television Authority (ITA). Five days after the legislation reached the Statute Book, on 4 August 1954, the ITA was appointed, and only fifty-nine weeks later ITV started on Thursday 22 September 1955. Between those dates the foundations of policies for setting up and regulating ITV were laid, the extensive transmitter network begun, and the first programme contractors appointed and on air.

Laying the foundations

The Act had provided a framework, delegating to the ITA the responsibility for creating the necessary policies and procedures. ITA Chairman Sir Kenneth Clark and DG Sir Robert Fraser designed a federal structure of independently owned and separate local television stations (based on an American model) linked together for the supply of programmes, the result being the distinctive ITV system of a national television channel with a strong regional base and character.

This provided a benevolent form of cross-subsidy, where the larger (and richer) companies produced most of the peaktime programming for the whole network, enabling the smaller stations to broadcast the same high quality and popular programmes as the others via affiliation. Each company produced its own local news and local interest programmes for their region. ITV has always been independent of public funds, unlike the BBC, being financed through advertising (and later sponsorship) revenues, with no funding from the licence fee or government.

Franchises, contracts and licences

1954-1968 1st and 2nd Contract Periods
For the first franchise awards the ITA appointed Associated-Rediffusion to the London weekday contract; Associated Television (ATV) to London weekends and the Midlands weekdays; Granada Television to weekdays in the North of England (both West and East); and ABC Television to the weekend service in the Midlands and North. This original weekday/weekend split now only remains, nominally, in the London area. The other remaining franchises were appointed for seven-day services.

Between 1955 and 1962 programme contractors were appointed to the rest of the country (see Table 1) with the last to go on air 14 September 1962 – Wales West & North (WWN). It took seven years to complete the nationwide ITA transmitter network.

ITV began transmission on 22 September 1955, when Associated-Rediffusion and Associated Television jointly opened the London area service. The first ITV companies jointly established Independent Television News (ITN) to provide their news service. These first ITV programme contracts, whether entered into in 1955 or as late as 1962, all ended simultaneously on 29 July 1964.

In the second contract period, 1964-68, all fourteen original, surviving ITV companies were re-appointed with contracts to end July 1967, later extended by one year to July 1968.

1968-1981 3rd Contract Period
For the third contract period the ITA offered one new franchise area, dividing the North of England region into two separate seven-day contracts for Lancashire and Yorkshire. It also made the Midlands a seven-day contract, as well as the two Northern franchises. A new company, HTV (Harlech Television), took over in Wales, and in London Thames Television and London Weekend Television were appointed (Thames was created via an ITA-enforced merger of Rediffusion and ABC Television). The Midlands seven-day service went to ATV, Granada was awarded Lancashire and the neighbouring franchise to a new company,

Yorkshire Television. Originally intended to last six years, franchises were extended to 31 December 1981.

1982-1992 4th Contract Period
For the fourth period from January 1982, the IBA offered contracts to two new companies, the South and South East of England to TVS (Television South) and South West England to TSW (Television South West). The contract for the new East and West Midlands dual region was awarded to ATV, but required them to entirely restructure and relocate their studios within the region; ATV took the name Central Independent Television. TV-am was awarded the first national breakfast-time television contract. The contracts, due to end on 31 December 1989, were extended under the terms of the Broadcasting Act 1987 to 31 December 1992, to allow time for new legislation.

1993-2002 5th Contract Period
The fifth franchise round in 1991 was radically different, as the Broadcasting Act 1990 had introduced a new licensing and regulatory regime for commercial television. A new regulator, the Independent Television Commission (ITC), was created to license and regulate all commercial television whether terrestrial, cable or satellite. The Act introduced a new licensing system for television, whereby licences were awarded by competitive tender to applicants who submitted the highest bid after passing quality threshold and sustainability tests.

Four new groups were appointed: Carlton in London (weekdays); Westcountry in South West England; Meridian in the South of England; and Sunrise (later GMTV) for the breakfast-time service. The Channel Three licences took effect from 1 January 1993, for a ten-year period (until 31 December 2002) in the first instance, though renewal for a further ten years was possible from 1 January 1999. All ITV companies agreed new ITC terms and renewed their licences.

During this period ITV had a notable failure with digital television, when DTT service, ITV Digital, went into administration. The Broadcasting Act 1996 had provided for the licensing of digital terrestrial television (DTT) by the ITC. Jointly owned by Carlton and Granada, ONdigital launched 15 November 1998 and re-branded itself as ITV Digital in 2001, but closed in 2002 with a loss of £1.2 billion for its owners.

INDUSTRY IN FOCUS

After the Communications Act 2003 removed the final barriers to single ownership of ITV, the long-expected merger of Carlton and Granada to form a single company took place.

Consolidation

Soon after the new Licences came into force the consolidation of ITV began, with an agreed take over of Tyne Tees Television by Yorkshire Television in 1992, but it was the end of the moratorium on TV takeovers in January 1994, and the relaxation of the ownership rules by the Broadcasting Act 1996, that started the succession of takeovers that ended the decade with Carlton and Granada having a near duopoly of ownership of ITV (see Tables 2 & 3). The Communications Act 2003 finally paved the way for a single-owned ITV.

Serious merger negotiations between Granada and Carlton had begun in 2002, and by October 2003 the Competition Commission had approved the arrangements, but required rules to protect the advertisers from unfair or discriminatory practices in airtime sales. ITV plc now controls ninety per cent of ITV advertising. Carlton and Granada announced agreement of the rules and acceptance by the Secretary of State on 14 November 2003. However, in October, Carlton Communications Chairman, Michael Green was forced to stand down as ITV Chairman-designate through shareholder pressure, partly over his handling of ITV Digital and subsequent losses. A new Chairman of ITV plc, Sir Peter Burt, formerly Chief Executive of the Bank of Scotland, was appointed. Shares in ITV plc floated on the Stock Exchange from 2 February 2004.

There has been criticism that it was more of a takeover than a merger, Granada effectively taking over the channel and most of the key jobs. Granada had 6,500 employees while Carlton had 2,000, making it a 72:28 merger, considered by the City to be a takeover. However, in reality Granada was by far the larger company, and contained most of the strengths of ITV. Certainly, jobs have been lost in the cost-cutting exercise to meet a target of £100m cost saving, including up to 400 jobs in the Midlands at Central, the closure of its Nottingham studios and Meridian axing half its 350-strong workforce in Southampton. Media trade unions, BECTU and NUJ, lobbied Parliament on 23 March to protest over merged-ITV's plans to dismantle regional production, and over 100 MPs, as well as local authorities, have expressed their concern at the Nottingham studios closure. Later in June, Central workers handed in a 20,000-signature petition to the Prime Minister calling on him to save the region's television studios

There is also the question of the remaining ITV companies not included in the merger – Scottish Television and Grampian Television owned by Scottish Media Group (SMG), Ulster Television, Channel Television and GMTV. ITV plc owns eleven of the fifteen regional Channel 3 licences, and 16.9 per cent of SMG. ITV enhanced its ownership in GMTV from fifty per cent to seventy-five per cent by buying SMG's stake for £31m , and is considering a similar offer to the Walt Disney Company for the remaining twenty-five per cent. SMG, however, unhappy at the appropriation of the ITV 'brand' for the corporate identity of ITV plc, is considering court action.

After its first unsuccessful move into digital television with the ITV Digital platform, ITV is now trying again by building a family of advertising-financed digital channels with ITV News, ITV2, and the soon-to-be launched ITV3. The company announced in June that it was to invest an extra £36m a year in the ITV2 programme budget and would launch ITV3 – a new channel for mature audiences – in Autumn 2004.

*Barrie MacDonald was formerly the Librarian of the Independent Television Commission and its predecessor the IBA, from 1979 to 2001. He is the author of **Broadcasting in the United Kingdom: a guide to information sources** (Cassell, 2nd rev ed 1994). He is completing an electronic archive of key policy decisions from 1990 to 2003 for the ITC, and administrative histories of the ITA/IBA and the ITC for the records management staffs of the ITC/Ofcom.*

Table 1: ITV Companies, 1955-2003

ITV/Channel 3 Licence	Company	On-air	Off-air
Channel Islands	Channel Television	1.9.62	
England			
The Borders	Border Television	1.9.61	
East of England	Anglia Television	27.10.59	
London (Weekday)	A-R – Associated Rediffusion^	22.9.59	29.7.68
	Thames Television	30.7.68	31.12.92
	Carlton Television	1.1.93	
London (Weekend)	ATV – Associated Television	24.9.55	28.7.68
	LWT – London Weekend Television	2.8.68	
Midlands	ATV – Associated Television (Weekdays)	17.2.56	29.7.68
(East & West Midlands	ABC Television (Weekends)	18.2.56	28.7.68
from 1982)	# Associated Television	30.7.68	31.12.81
	+ Central Television	1.1.82	
North-East	Tyne Tees Television	15.1.59	
North of England	Granada Television (Weekdays)	3.5.56	29.7.68
(later North-West England)	ABC Television (Weekends)	5.5.56	28.7.68
	# Granada Television	30.7.68	
South & South East	Southern Television	30.8.58	31.12.81
	TVS – Television South	1.1.82	31.12.92
	Meridian Broadcasting	1.1.93	
South-West	Westward Television	29.4.61	11.8.81
	TSW – Television South West	12.8.81	31.12.92
	Westcountry Television	1.1.93	
Yorkshire	Yorkshire Television	29.7.68	
Northern Ireland	Ulster Television	31.10.59	
Scotland			
Central Scotland	STV – Scottish Television	31.8.57	
North	Grampian Television	30.9.61	
Wales			
Wales & West of England	TWW	14.1.58	3.3.68
	HTV – Harlech	4.3.68	
West & North Wales	* Wales (West & North) Television [Teledu Cymru]	14.9.62	26.1.64
National Breakfast-time	TV-am	1.2.83	31.12.92
	GMTV	1.1.93	

Note: ^ Associated Rediffusion became just 'Rediffusion' in Autumn 1964 due to ownership restructure
   # ATV and Granada became seven-day contractors in 1968.
   * Wales West & North and its franchise area were absorbed by TWW
   + ATV restructured as Central Independent Television under instructions of the IBA

INDUSTRY IN FOCUS

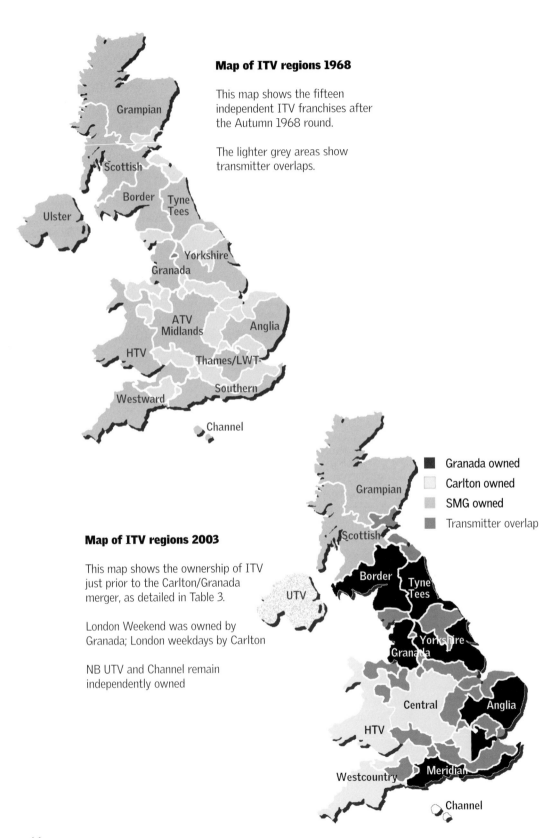

Map of ITV regions 1968

This map shows the fifteen independent ITV franchises after the Autumn 1968 round.

The lighter grey areas show transmitter overlaps.

Grampian

Scottish

Border

Tyne Tees

Ulster

Yorkshire

Granada

ATV Midlands

Anglia

HTV

Thames/LWT

Southern

Westward

Channel

Map of ITV regions 2003

This map shows the ownership of ITV just prior to the Carlton/Granada merger, as detailed in Table 3.

London Weekend was owned by Granada; London weekdays by Carlton

NB UTV and Channel remain independently owned

Granada owned

Carlton owned

SMG owned

Transmitter overlap

Grampian

Scottish

Border

Tyne Tees

UTV

Yorkshire

Granada

Central

Anglia

HTV

Westcountry

Meridian

Channel

Table 2: Takeovers in ITV, 1992-2003

Year	Original Licensee	Region	New Parent Company
1992	Tyne Tees Television	North-East England	Yorkshire Television
1994	Central Television	East & West Midlands	Carlton
	Anglia Television	East of England	MAI (later UN&M)
	London Weekend Television	London (Weekend)	Granada
1996	Westcountry Television	South-West England	Carlton
1997	Grampian Television	North of Scotland	Scottish Television
	Yorkshire Television/Tyne Tees	Yorkshire/North-East England	Granada
	HTV	Wales & the West of England	UN&M
2000	Border Television	The Borders	Capital Radio Group
	Anglia Television	East of England	Granada
	Meridian Broadcasting	South & South East England	Granada
	HTV	Wales & the West of England	Carlton
2001	Border Television	The Borders	Granada
	Channel Television	Channel Islands	Iliffe News & Media

Table 3: Ownership of ITV by 2003

	Parent Company	Original Licensee	Licence
	Carlton	Carlton Television	London (Weekday)
		Central Television	Midlands
		HTV	Wales & the West of England
		Westcountry Television	South-West England
'Merged ITV': Carlton/Granada merged to form ITV plc 2 February 2004	Granada	Anglia Television	East of England
		Border Television	The Borders
		Granada Television	North-West England
		London Weekend Television	London (Weekend)
		Meridian Broadcasting	South & South-East England
		Tyne Tees Television	North-East England
		Yorkshire Television	Yorkshire
	Scottish Media Group	Grampian Television	North of Scotland
		Scottish Television	Central Scotland
	'Independent'	Channel Television	Channel Islands
		UTV (was 'Ulster')	Northern Ireland
		GMTV	National Breakfast-time

Nations: Wales

Jamie Medhurst

It's been a year of anniversaries: in November Sianel Pedwar Cymru (S4C) turned twenty-one, the Crawford Committee's report which led to the channel's establishment was thirty years old and February 2004 saw the fortieth anniversary of BBC Wales. Is there still much to celebrate in Welsh broadcasting?

The short answer is 'yes'. The three main broadcasters in Wales, BBC Wales, ITV Wales and S4C, have continued to reflect and engage with the nation on a number of levels. This is becoming increasingly important in post-devolutionary times and in the age of the globalised television market. The broadcasters now have to maintain their position and role as national (as opposed to regional) bodies in an age where the audiences they serve have more choice in terms of what they watch. The opening statement of S4C's 2004 Review notes that when the channel was formed in 1982, everybody knew (or thought they knew) what a television channel was. This is no longer the case.

BBC Wales continued to produce award-winning drama in the shape of *Belonging* (described by the Corporation as 'soap with an attitude') which won the award for Best Drama Series in the 2004 Celtic Film and Television Festival. It also won fourteen Baftas at the Bafta Cymru Awards Ceremony in April 2004. The BBC continued to provide ten hours per week of programming for S4C in the Welsh language although the flagship Welsh programme, the soap opera *Pobol y Cwm* saw a decline in audience numbers and criticism for its storylines. The Corporation ventured into new territory by establishing a new 'Capture Wales' digital storytelling project in English and in Welsh and it continued to develop its digital 2W service on BBC 2, using the animated 70s character Ivor the Engine to promote the service. For many, this channel provides the English-language equivalent of S4C, although the debate over national provision for non-Welsh speakers continues. Two other

The Welsh broadcasters have continued to reflect and engage with the nation on several levels.

notable events were the loss of television rights to live Football Association of Wales matches to Sky Television, and the news that BBC Wales' Drama Department was to resurrect *Doctor Who* (the series began shooting in July 2004 in Cardiff).

ITV Wales had a tougher year. The creation of ITV plc has raised doubts amongst many (not least Plaid Cymru, the Welsh Nationalist Party) as to the national identity and national role of the commercial broadcaster. There were also fears over job losses and the curtailing of programme budgets. Yet the company still produces ten hours per week of English-language programming across a variety of genres and provides Welsh-language programming input to S4C, including the ever-popular *Cefn Gwlad* series and the award-wining current affairs programme *Y Byd ar Bedwar*. Despite fears over the broadcaster's national role, in June 2004, the company announced a major re-structuring which led to the creation of ITV Wales and ITV West, a clear division between two regions hitherto served by one company. ITV Wales will now have its own Managing Director and management, the first time that this has happened since ITV arrived in Wales in 1958.

The broadcasting industry in Wales plays an active and vital role in the nation's political, social, economic and cultural life. This is particularly true in the case of S4C where, as the Chair of the S4C Authority noted in February, 'the Fourth Channel in Wales was the broadcasting solution to a particular combination of political and social issues.' The channel continues to play a key role in the Welsh economy (during 2002, for example, 97 per cent of the programme budget was spent in

Will and Vanessa; Ceri and Robbie; Steve and Ruth Lewis – all characters from popular BBC Wales drama serial *Belonging*

Wales). Politically, there are debates as to whom the channel should be answerable – the Welsh Assembly or Westminster. It is currently the latter and the the S4C Authority has asked the DCMS to conduct a major review of the channel as it enters the multichannel age. There are calls, for example, for S4C to maximise the potential of its three channels, S4C Analogue, S4C Digital and S4C2. One suggestion would see S4C2 (currently showing live Assembly proceedings) become a channel for younger audiences with the analogue channel becoming S4C1, serving the ageing indigenous Welsh-speaking population. One channel for many audiences is becoming increasingly problematic.

With digital penetration higher in Wales than in any other nation/region in the UK (at around 60 per cent of homes), it's worth noting May's Government announcement of a pilot of analogue switch-off for 350 homes in the Llansteffan area (near Carmarthen, south west Wales). The experiment hasn't yet begun, but during 2005 a clearer picture of Wales' digital future will emerge.

Jamie Medhurst is degree scheme co-ordinator and lecturer in film and television studies at the University of Wales Aberystwyth.

INDUSTRY IN FOCUS

Ofcom's PSB review and the English regions

The *Communications Act 2003* requirement for the main terrestrial public service channels – BBC 1, BBC 2, ITV1, Channel 4, S4C and Five – to deliver programmes that should reflect the lives and concerns of different communities in the UK, differs little from the provision in the *Television Act 1954*, which established Independent Television, calling for programmes 'to contain a suitable proportion of material calculated to appeal to regional tastes and outlook'. This fifty-year consensus is now about to be challenged by the *Ofcom review of public service television broadcasting.*

Phase 1 of the review, *Is television special?*, published in April, found that overall the hours of regional programming broadcast and expenditure on regional programmes rose between 1998 and 2002. But the UK nations fared better than the English regions, and the total number of hours of programming on ITV1 fell. Cutbacks by ITV1, whose total regional hours fell by 8 per cent from an average of 171 hours per week in 1998 to 157 hours in 2002, were partly as a result of an agreement with the ITC to enable them to focus investment on fewer hours of better-resourced and scheduled output. However, the overall stability of regional programming has been due to a 23 per cent increase in BBC output. The BBC has been more successful in attracting audiences to some regional programmes.

The large-scale audience survey commissioned by Ofcom found that regional programming received mixed reviews: many people felt it was important, but there was evidence that audiences did not engage with much regional programming other than regional news. Generally, 65 per cent of those surveyed supported programmes that reflected the needs and concerns of different regional communities within the UK. Most felt that regional news, regional current affairs and other regional programmes were relatively more important to society than to them personally. In Scotland, Wales and Northern Ireland people still watch and value a range of national programming, with significant support for local production and Gaelic and Welsh language services. However, in the English regions there appears less support for regional programmes other than news. And, some felt that 'regional' news was not 'local' enough. In fact both viewers and broadcasters appear uncertain about the role of non-news programmes for the English regions.

Considering the citizen, as distinct from the consumer, Ofcom believes programming must 'reflect and strengthen our cultural identity through high quality UK, national and regional programming'. It proposes a new framework of PSB, defined in terms of its purposes and characteristics, one of which is its underpinning an informed society, reflecting and strengthening its cultural identity.

At present, it seems to Ofcom that a large number of regional programmes are providing low benefits at relatively high costs. Among the many questions it raises are: should we expect the BBC and ITV1 to provide them to the same degree, or would other media do the job more effectively; and is it more important for the regions to be properly reflected in network programming than for programmes to be made that are specific to each regional audience? Phase 2 will investigate the importance of national and regional programming, including consideration of how it is delivered, comparing models of national and regional delivery. The review, due to be completed by the end of the year, may result in a radical shake-up in the nations and regions.

Barrie MacDonald

Nations: Scotland

Jane Sillars

The complexity of how devolved Scotland is woven into the rest of the UK broadcasting system plays out on screen and institutionally; and Scotland's national political and cultural distinctiveness continues to pose problems for policy and regulatory systems alike. The blurriness of the picture can be seen in the division of political responsibilities; while cultural activity generally and specific areas such as Gaelic language provision have been devolved to the Scottish parliament, control over broadcasting remains with Westminster.

As old public service requirements are reworked, lobbying around the new Communications Bill has attempted to bring into focus the interests of Scottish industry and audience within a rapidly globalising media market. A Summit Group established by Scotland's Screen Industries has begun a campaign for Scotland to receive a production quota, set at 9 per cent to reflect its population share of the UK. This would require a marked increase from terrestrial broadcasters. Ofcom has responded to lobbying by appointing a Scottish advisory committee and director in 2004.

An early challenge may well be Scotland's relation to the new ITV, as its original regional structure has effectively disappeared. The Scottish Media Group, owners of Scottish Television and Grampian (Border Television, the third, part-Scottish franchise, now forms part of the new ITV plc), along with UTV have so far resisted

incorporation. This means that SMG forms the largest independent player outside ITV plc. However despite their status as a relative goliath in the Scottish media scene (somewhat shrunk after the divestment of their newspaper and other holdings) they remain minnows on the UK television scene. This has led some analysts to predict that the fall of their television holdings to ITV is a question of 'when, rather than if'. While SMG continues to produce substantial Scottish opt-out programming in news and sport (with a recent £5 million investment in Grampian's newsroom), its wider penetration of the new ITV national UK network remains at issue. As hardy perennial *Taggart* slogs on as the UK's longest running detective drama, the search for another network and overseas hit continues. Scottish had acquired the rights to adapt more of Ian Rankin's *Rebus*, but the series was cancelled by the network in 2004, having met the muted response common to much contemporary ITV drama.

BBC Scotland has also undergone a year of change with the departure in April of its controller, the thoughtful and well-respected John McCormick. New controller, Ken McQuarrie, is an experienced BBC Scotland hand and former head of programmes. The appointment suggests some degree of continuity within the organisation over coming years (as insiders had predicted was required post-Hutton), as well as an ongoing commitment to programme making, both opt-out

A new series of sitcom *Still Game* is big news in Scotland – in May it made the cover of the Scottish *Radio Times*

The wedding of Ray (Paul Samson) and Roisin (Joyce Falconer) was a major event in Scottish soap *River City*. It's not always as tacky as this.

and network. Both men have found themselves in the news, as BBC Scotland found itself snarled up in the ongoing Fraser Inquiry into the building of the new Scottish parliament, over the refusal to hand over interview tapes about the project.

On the production side, BBC Scotland continues to produce a substantial slate of opt-out programming and contributes across network scheduling. Recent strength in the field of factual programming is reflected in the success of *Restoration*, a noted hit in 2003, which returns from independent producer Endemol for BBC Scotland in 2004. Children's television (as with Scottish Television) continues to be a network strength, with pre-school sensation *Balamory* also making an economic impact in the nascent field of toddler tourism. In comedy there are high hopes that the engaging comedy *Still Game* will repeat the success of *Rab C. Nesbitt* as it too moves from opt-out to network. In Scotland, its third BBC 1 series bowed out on 1.1 million viewers, a 49 per cent share.

In drama, the opt-out Scottish soap opera *River City* has begun to steady its ship a little after a markedly shaky start. The series premiered in September 2002 to an audience high of 0.76 million but had fallen to a low of 0.19 million by November. A year later audiences had climbed to a steady 0.5 million. The massive investment in the project, usually quoted as £10 million, as well as the huge front-loading of the spend, particularly in the construction of an extensive urban set, has meant the BBC has little choice but to stand by its gamble. After an initially brutal turnover of both on-screen characters and off-screen producers and writers there is a sense that it may be finding its feet and an audience. The cost of the project can also be calculated by the relative paucity of Scottish produced drama elsewhere and perhaps too in the respectively high networked visibility of comically regressive tosh like *Monarch of the Glen*. In much network drama (*1,000 Acres of Sky*) and notably in lifestyle programming (*Get a New Life* et al) Scotland remains to be seen as a place to escape to.

More varied representations of highland Scotland do appear in the Gaelic programming which continues to be supported by government block grant to the Gaelic Media Service. However, this agency currently has no impact on the programming strategy of those terrestrial broadcasters (BBC Scotland, Scottish Television and Grampian) that carry the programming it commissions. This has led to frustration amongst Gaelic lobbyists and producers, who see Gaelic programming as increasingly relegated to the margins of the schedules. The answer for many, including the Gaelic Broadcasting Task Force set up by the Scottish Executive, lies in the establishment of a dedicated Gaelic channel on all digital platforms. This would of course require a massive hike in funding and one which would appear to require Westminster and further Holyrood backing.

Channel 4 continues to support the establishment of a stronger production base within Scotland through the work of its Nations and Regions office in research and business development. (The contribution of its commissioning editors is seen by Scottish producers, as ever, as more questionable.) For many years the bulk of the independent sector in Scotland operated as something like a cottage industry of small-scale producers. The increasing commercialisation and internationalisation of television generally and the desire for format-led, long-running returning series (on all channels, but with particular relevance on Channel 4 given Scotland's lack of an equivalent to S4C) has led to a chill wind blowing around this artisan mode of television production. Public funding, particularly through Scottish Screen, retains importance to the development of new talent and the creation of challenging one-off drama and documentary, for strands such as Scottish Television and Grampian's *New Found Land* and *This Scotland*.

The most successful independents have responded creatively to these changes, chief among them Wark Clements and Ideal World. (Indeed Ideal World's *Location, Location, Location* sums up certain trends in current television: lifestyle-driven; relatively cheap to produce; able to return and generate spin-off programming; and, like *Restoration*, while produced for a Scottish company, not contributing visibly Scottish representations on screen.) Their merger in April 2004 is big news within the Scottish production sector. Their respective strengths across a range of channels, genres and programming and their substantial combined size (the new company IWC Media is now thought to be the second largest indie outside London) could provide not only a counterweight to South-Eastern pull, but a significant contribution to the maintenance of a sustainable infrastructure for Scottish production. Of course that economic pull may well have other consequences.

Jane Sillars is a Teaching Fellow in Film & Media Studies at the University of Stirling

Nations: N. Ireland

Martin McLoone

Both of Northern Ireland's main local broadcasters, BBC NI and UTV, this year reported continued strong growth and performance in a small but highly competitive market.

UTV, especially, has continued to buck the trend as far as the rest of the ITV network is concerned and has developed a marketing strategy that has prepared it for life on the margins of ITV plc. The company's television advertising last year increased by 2.1 per cent compared to a decrease of 3.4 per cent for ITV, nudging its share of the total ITV advertising market up to 2.36 per cent. UTV, in other words, has successfully weathered the deep recession in the advertising industry that precipitated the crisis in ITV. How it has done so is extremely interesting.

First, UTV long ago re-branded itself as an 'all-Ireland' broadcaster ('UTV' rather than 'Ulster') and went after the substantial advertising market in the booming economy of the Republic of Ireland. UTV, in other words, rode the 'Celtic Tiger' to good effect so that now the Irish marketplace accounts for over half of its total advertising revenue. About 70 per cent of homes in the Irish republic can receive UTV (all the main affluent urban areas) and remarkably enough, the company

> **UTV (no longer 'Ulster') long ago re-branded itself as an 'all-Ireland' broadcaster and went after the advertising market in the booming economy of the Republic of Ireland**

achieved an impressive 12.9 per cent share of the Republic's peaktime audience (second only to the Irish public service broadcaster, RTÉ).

In addition, UTV has expanded its operations across other media, again with an emphasis on the Irish republic. In its pursuit of the lucrative advertising market in the south of Ireland, it now owns radio stations in Cork, Limerick and Dublin (and has also applied for a licence to operate a new commercial radio station in Belfast). It has expanded its on-line operations and UTV Internet launched its 'Clicksilver' broadband service, again with a focus on the market in the south (price: EUR 29.99). There has been much speculation that the smaller ITV franchises in the UK (UTV, Channel and the SMG in Scotland) might merge to consolidate a certain amount of clout in dealing

Pulling Moves – the BBC 1 NI drama also aired nationally on BBC 3

with the centre but UTV's all-Ireland focus and its relatively powerful market presence in Ireland rather suggests that the company is better placed than most to exist on the margins.

The UTV strategy has had an impact on the kind of programmes it makes and the way in which it addresses its now trans-border audience. Although it still addresses the Northern Ireland audience first, increasingly its mode of address is 'all-Ireland' and its local programming – largely popular news and current affairs strands and rather light-hearted documentaries – reflects a non-contentious blandness. UTV certainly is popular in its homebase of Northern Ireland and its early evening news programme, *UTV Live*, consistently beats that of BBC NI, *Newsline*, sometimes by a factor of 2:1. However, UTV is often criticised for being successful by 'not making programmes' and its main commercial advantage is that it relays the mainstream network programmes of ITV plc to good effect. Thus *Coronation Street* is always ahead of *EastEnders* in Northern Ireland (though part of the reason for this is that UTV consistently programmes a popular local programme, like the quirky and sentimental travelogue *Lesser Spotted Ulster*, opposite *EastEnders*). UTV does not, however, make its own drama (too expensive and too risky) so that all local drama from Northern Ireland is made by the BBC.

The BBC's local output looks very similar to UTV's in many ways – an emphasis on local news and documentary strands, a concentration on human interest stories and reality documentary, a great deal of nostalgia and sentimentality – but BBC NI makes a more concentrated local contribution (it also operates two local radio stations, Radio Ulster and Radio Foyle) and has produced the edgier and more challenging programming. The provision of local drama is one of BBC NI's strengths. The satirical sit-com *Give My Head Peace* continues to attract a huge local audience. The programme itself is in its ninth season and inevitably, its blast at the sectarian culture that underpins Northern Ireland's troubled politics is less edgy and adventurous than previously. Nonetheless, it is an important part of local television culture and its success has seen a few spin-off dramas result. The same team was responsible for six-part comedy drama *I Fought the Law* about a group of young Belfast lawyers and later in the year, BBC NI provided the satirical 'lads' drama *Pulling Moves*.

The most interesting and potentially the most controversial drama of the year was BBC NI's *Holy Cross*. This very emotional drama was co-produced with RTÉ and looked at the sectarian tensions in the Ardoyne area of North Belfast in 2001. In the end, the drama was critically well-received, attracting a sizeable network audience and going on to win three FIPA D'ors at the Biarritz Festival International de Programmes Audiovisuels as well as the feature length drama award at the Celtic Film Festival.

UTV does not make its own drama (too expensive and too risky) so that all local drama from Northern Ireland is made by the BBC.

Over the last decade, BBC NI's drama department has succeeded in establishing its presence on the BBC network in a series of well-executed and sometimes controversial ways so that today it is expected that the Belfast office originate drama for the network that is not necessarily about Northern Ireland itself. This year's big drama production was *Gunpowder, Treason and Plot*, a complex co-production deal which originated in Belfast but did not actually get made there nor contribute much to the local Northern Ireland film and television industry. Nonetheless, the fact that BBC NI can operate on these two levels – the relevance and immediacy of *Holy Cross* and *Give My Head Peace* as well as the prestige of *Gunpowder Treason and Plot* – suggests that its relationship to the local, the regional and the national is in a healthier state than it has ever been.

The BBC's Charter renewal strategy, released in June in the document *Building Public Value*, emphasises its commitment to increased local and regional programming. The Corporation's Head of Regions and Nations is former Controller of BBC NI, Pat Loughrey and it remains to be seen how this regional remit will develop in his former region as the BBC re-consolidates after the traumas of the Hutton Report.

Martin McLoone is Professor of Media Studies at the Centre for Media Research, School of Media & Performing Arts, University of Ulster. His publications include **Broadcasting in a Divided Community: 70 Years of the BBC in Northern Ireland** *(Institute of Irish Studies: 1996).*

INDUSTRY IN FOCUS

Multichannel Platforms · Barrie MacDonald

By the end of the first quarter of 2004 53 per cent of all TV viewers had multichannel television, with access to dozens or possibly hundreds of channels through cable, satellite, and terrestrial digital services.

Cable: Local Delivery Services and Programme Channels

Cable television is a subscription-based service usually offered as a package with telephone and internet connection, and delivered to the home via underground cable systems. Cable has developed slowly in the UK, still only reaching 3.3 million homes by 2004, and cable companies have yet to complete the conversion of all their former analogue customers to digital television.

Cable was the earliest multichannel platform in Britain, with origins as far back as the 1920s, as a way of relaying radio broadcasts to homes in areas of poor reception, via community or master aerials linked to underground cable networks. 'Wired television' began in the 1950s. An experiment in the 1970s created community cable stations to provide additional local interest channels. But the real kick-start for multichannel television came from the Cable and Broadcasting Act 1984, which provided for broadband cable systems, using new fibre optic technology, and established a new public body to set up and regulate cable, the Cable Authority. The Broadcasting Act 1990 replaced it with the Independent Television Commission (ITC) to regulate television across all platforms – terrestrial, cable and satellite.

Cable systems and programme services currently operating were licensed firstly by the Cable Authority, and then the ITC up to 2003. The Communications Act 2003 merged the ITC, Oftel and Radiocomunications Agency into Ofcom, and abolished the licensing of local delivery services, implementing EU Directives on electronic communications networks and repealing parts of the earlier Telecommunications Act 1984.

Programme channels provided to cable systems nationally, community cable services and video-on-demand services carried over a telephone network required a Licensable Programme Services (LPS) licence. LPS licences were available virtually on demand, provided that the service was compatible with the law, and the licensee was not a disqualified person. They had to comply with the *ITC Programme Code, ITC Advertising Standards Code*, and the *ITC Sponsorship Code*. The LPS (and STS) licensing system was replaced by the Communications Act 2003. Television Licensable Content Services (TLCS) licences for analogue or digital programme services distributed through electronic communications networks are available on demand from Ofcom, with unlimited duration unless either surrendered or revoked.

Consolidation of cable ownership in the 1990s made the ntl Group Ltd and Telewest Communications the two dominant operators, both companies reporting heavy losses as they tried to convert customers from analogue to digital, prompting major financial restructuring The ntl Group, owned by American shareholders, emerged from US Chapter 11 bankruptcy protection in 2003 to instigate rationalisation, including axing 1,500 jobs, in order to compete against BSkyB in pay-TV and BT in telephony provision. It achieved its first quarterly operating profit in over ten years, of £2.2 million in March 2004. Telewest reduced its continuing losses in March 2004, with increased revenues from broadband internet balancing losses from television and telecoms, and announced a restructuring programme. Telewest, through its content division Flextech, is a major provider of multichannel programme services.

Satellite Television Service

Originally, provision of satellite television in Britain was to have been through Direct Broadcasting by Satellite (DBS), direct-to-home transmission from a UK satellite. The Independent Broadcasting Authority, under the Cable and Broadcasting Act 1984, awarded the UK's five DBS licences to British Satellite Broadcasting (BSB), which planned to transmit from the Marcopolo satellite in the UK orbital position. BSB launched its five-channel service in 1990. However, Sky had already begun transmitting a four-channel service in February 1989, using the existing Astra satellite on a Luxembourg orbital position. On 2 November 1990 BSB merged with Sky Television to form British Sky Broadcasting (BSkyB), eventually broadcasting a single set of programme services from Astra, thus effectively ending DBS in the UK.

BSkyB is today the market leader in the provision of satellite services, a vertically integrated business controlling both the platform and broadcasts, which had 7.3 million subscribers by March 2004. Sky went into profit in 2003, for the first time since 1998, finally overcoming huge debts incurred launching Sky Digital. So successful had Sky been in converting its existing analogue subscribers to digital, it was able to turn off its analogue pay TV services in 2001. To attract new subscribers and retain existing ones, BSkyB launched a personal video technology, Sky+ in 2001, which marketed together with their commitment to introduce High Definition Television (HDTV) broadcasts by 2006 may give it an advantage over the DTT platform.

By the end of 2003 Sky Television faced fresh challenges, with a new Chief Executive, a threat from Europe to overturn its deal for live Premiership football and increased competition. James Murdoch, son of BSkyB's largest shareholder Rupert Murdoch, took over from Tony Ball as Chief Executive in November 2003. The European Commission investigation of the tendering process for the Sky-Premier League deal for 2004-2007 required Sky to sub-lease some Premiership games to other broadcasters. BSkyB held onto all its 138 live games until 2007 however, after it rejected rival bids for the tendered package of games as too low. The Commission conceded BSkyB's right to reject low bids, but made clear that the next contract period bidding must be fully competitive with at least two broadcasters able to share the games.

Sky channels, particularly Sky One, have been declining the past couple of years, and by April 2004 they had dipped to an 11.8 per cent share of all multichannel viewing. In September 2002 Dawn Airey had been recruited from Five to be Managing Director of Sky Networks, responsible for all channels except sport. She brought a popular programming policy, made some high profile buy-ins – *24*, *Nip/Tuck*, *Tarzan and Jane*, and *Mr Personality* (hosted by Monica Lewinsky) – and a promise to try out independent producers. Critics say Sky One still lacks much overall identity or personality as a channel. The challenge is to develop more Sky One-branded programmes and win back viewers from its multichannel rivals. To compete with MTV, Sky entered music television for the first time by launching three new youth music channels in summer 2003 – The Amp, Flaunt and Scuzz. Then, in a major coup in March 2004, Sky News won a five-year contract to provide Five's lunch-time and evening news bulletins.

Ofcom's April 2004 digital switchover review identified the problems of consumer takeup and warned that a million households will be unable to receive digital terrestrial television by the switchover date

Digital Television Services

By the end of 2003, 50 per cent of all TV households had digital television, an considerable achievement in only just over five years since the launch of digital TV.

The impetus for the development of Digital Terrestrial Television (DTT) services came from the Broadcasting Act 1996. The Government was anxious to gain the benefits for the UK of pioneer developments in digital technology, but also to achieve an early switch off of analogue television. The Act enabled the ITC to license digital networks (multiplexes) for the provision of digital terrestrial television programme and other services, including interactive and internet services. Of the six multiplexes, one was reserved for the BBC, and one for ITV, Channel 4 and teletext services (awarded to Digital 3 and 4 Ltd). Of the remaining four, multiplex A was awarded to S4C Digital Networks Ltd for Channel 5, S4C, and Gaelic language programming in Scotland, and multiplexes B, C and D were awarded on 24 June 1997 to British Digital Broadcasting (BDB), jointly owned by Carlton and Granada.

BDB launched its service under the brand name ONdigital in November 1998, offering digital terrestrial subscription services. Finding it difficult in the marketplace, ONdigital was re-branded ITV Digital in 2001, but eventually went into administration on 27 March 2002, temporarily putting in doubt the future of the DTT platform. However, the ITC quickly re-tendered the DTT licences, and awarded them to the BBC and Crown Castle. Freeview, a partnership between the BBC, BSkyB and Crown Castle, began on 30 October 2002, offering free access for only the cost of a set top box costing less than £100. Freeview, now offering over thirty channels, has proved a success, partly because of heavy BBC promotion of its BBC3 and BBC 4 channels. By the end of 2003 it had over three million viewers and accounts for 24 per cent of all digital homes. Sky, threatened by its success, have kept their mainstream channels off Freeview, in an attempt to drive viewers to their own service.

Sky Digital, which launched in October 1998, provided free-to-air terrestrial channels and subscription or pay satellite channels. Sky had invested £2 billion in digital. Despite the price increases in basic and top-end premium packages, Sky Digital continued to increase the number and range of channels, and grow their subscriber base. Its initial rapid growth was through converting its existing analogue subscribers to digital. By its fifth anniversary Sky Digital had over 7 million subscribers, and it now accounts for 55 per cent of all digital homes. However, the surprise success of Freeview recently resulted in a drop in the net growth in new subscribers to Sky's pay-TV services, and brought pressure on BSkyB management from shareholders. BSkyB had been happy to be a partner in Freeview as long as it wasn't a threat to its own premium services. Consequently, Sky's Chief Executive, James Murdoch, announced at the beginning of June that it would offer a no-subscription satellite package of up to 200 channels with a set-top receiver and dish at a one-off cost of £150 - dubbed 'Freesat' - in Autumn 2004. Though appearing to turn the pay-TV company into a free-to-air service for the first time in its fifteen-year history, the company's long-term aim must be to eventually upgrade those viewers to some form of pay-TV.

Cable digital services from ntl and Telewest were launched in 1999. They have been less successful in attracting new subscribers, and slower to convert their existing analogue customers to digital. Cable digital accounts for 25 per cent of all multichannel homes, and 19 per cent of all digital homes.

The government target for switching over from analogue to digital transmission is 2006 to 2010. Ofcom's April 2004 digital switchover review identified the problems of consumer takeup, warned that a million households will be unable to receive digital terrestrial television by the switchover date, and recommended that they should be offered a free-to-air satellite service by broadcasters. BSkyB's recent 'Freesat' initiative should certainly please both Ofcom and the Government. The BBC suggested that the chances of achieving the target date would be greatly improved by financial assistance to poorer viewers. Tessa Jowell, Culture Secretary, asked the Treasury to provide £300 million to help fund the proposed switch. The switch would be worth £2 billion to the Government from the sale of the analogue spectrum to mobile communications.

BSkyB
Luke Hockley

Its fifteenth year has been a busy one for BSkyB. The Murdoch dynasty has been further consolidated by the appointment of James Murdoch (Rupert Murdoch's son) as the new chief executive on 3 November 3 2003. He replaced Tony Ball (former CE) and bought with him pay-tv experience from his time as chief executive of Hong Kong Star TV – News Corporation's Asian satellite broadcaster. The appointment was not without controversy. Attempting to allay fears, BSkyB appointed two new non-executive directors and in so doing put non-executives in the majority on the board.

Another key change in personnel had come earlier in the year when Dawn Airey was appointed to run Sky Networks in January 2003. Previously she had been responsible for running Channel 5 where there was general agreement that she had done an excellent job in getting the channel 6.55 per cent of the UK audience share. The move seems to have had its troubles with Airey admitting that it took a good nine months to settle in and come to terms with running a multichannel business. While Sky One remains a key part of her portfolio she is keen to correct the common assumption that this is all her role covers. In fact she also has responsibility for Sky Movies, the music channels, Sky News and airtime sales.

In the current year the style of programming on BSkyB has remained broadly similar to previous years. The loss of *Friends* and *ER* to E4 does slightly diminish the channel's boast that it provides the best of American programming – although it has recently purchased *24*, *Cold Case* and *Nip/Tuck*. The two thousand scheduled movies a year (mostly American product) on Sky Movies brings the channel into direct competition with DVD rental and sales. Here Airey has introduced a couple of innovations including complementary scheduling and multiple start times. Sky One shows such as *There's Something About Miriam* (produced by Endemol's subsidiary Brighter Pictures; a reality TV programme where six men unwittingly date a transsexual) and *How Gay are You?* leave the impression however that the future for BSkyB is avowedly tabloid rather than broadsheet. In terms of audience share Sky One convincingly retained its lead with 2.90 per cent against its nearest rival, UKTV Gold who managed 2.03 per cent. However, this performance was not up to the previous year where Sky flagship's channel had a 3.79 per cent share – a loss of 0.89 per cent for the current year.

Launched in April 2003, the BSkyB music channels (Flaunt, Scuzz and The Amp) have achieved just a 4 per cent share of viewers. This contrasts with the 36 per cent share of the seven EMAP music channels and with 56 per cent for the MTV channels. After only six months Sky's head of music, Lester Mordue, left the company. In a round of musical chairs, he was replaced by Jo Wallace from Channel 4 where she commissioned music and teen programming. In turn, Wallace has recently been moved to oversee all original programming on Sky One. Chiara Cipriani (currently head of commercial and interactive) will replace Ms Wallace.

It might appear that BSkyB are supporting the Government in its preparations to switch off the analogue TV signal but the development of 'freesat' makes good long-term business sense

The first significant business announcement of the year came in August 2003 with the reporting of BSkyB's first annual pre-tax profit in five years. The £260 million profit was matched with a growth in turnover of 15 per cent to £3.19 billion. This marked a considerable change to the previous year where there had been a loss of £22 million. In part, the rise in turnover was due to an aggressive acquisitions policy of film rights. It also came from a campaign in which customers were persuaded to switch from analogue to digital dishes. BSkyB, in which Rupert Murdoch's News Corporation has a 36 per cent controlling stake, also continued to add subscribers during the fourth quarter of the year, despite the successful launch of BBC-backed digital terrestrial service Freeview in October 2002.

In June 2004 BSkyB announced an ambitious and aggressive plan to roll out a subscription-free digital television package this Autumn, one offering two hundred television and radio channels for a once only payment of £150. Previously, the direct buying of dishes had not been promoted by BSkyB as it is not as profitable as selling subscription packages. This new tactic seems to indicate a concern about the success of Freeview. Freeview is currently watched in 3.5 million homes across Britain, although BSkyB retain the dominant market position with 7.3 million

The deception at the heart of *There's Something About Miriam* may have delayed transmission but also brought Sky One a great deal of attention.

subscribers as of May 2004. The BSkyB 'freesat' package offers 115 television channels, eighty-one radio channels and thirteen interactive services including BBCi and Sky Active. This contrasts with the subscription package, which currently offers up to 455 television channels, eighty radio stations, movie channels and coverage of major sporting events. However, the free service is guaranteed for just twenty-four months. In terms of coverage BSkyB have an advantage as the Sky satellite footprint covers all of Britain and can therefore be received by the 27 per cent of households currently unable to receive Freeview.

It might appear that BSkyB are supporting the Government in its preparations to switch off the analogue TV signal (by 2010 at the latest) but this development also makes good long-term business sense. The report, Digital Terrestrial TV: Prospects in the Enlarged EU, forecasts that when BSkyB's planned 'freesat' digital service is taken into account, 89 to 90 per cent of UK households will have gone digital by 2009.

Looking at the future, BSkyB has flagged a commitment to high-definition television (HDTV) and is developing a premium package of channels in HDTV format. HDTV, delivers substantially superior picture quality over standard-definition television and is the preferred format for a growing number of US television productions across a range of genres including news, sport, drama, and entertainment. The premium service is expected to launch in 2006, with a set of dedicated HD channels and selected events produced in HD format.

With a clear commitment to new television technology and the aggressive launch of a 'freesat' service the future looks bright for BSkyB if slightly more complicated than in the past few highly successful years.

Luke Hockley is Head of Media at the University of Sunderland.

Multichannel Overview

Paul McDonald

The tipping point of acceptance of multichannel services was reached in November 2003, by which time 51 per cent (or 28.7 million) of viewers in the UK were able to receive digital services – by the end of the first quarter of 2004 it had risen to 53 per cent. While the main terrestrial broadcasters together continued to retain the majority audience share in multichannel homes for the year from January to November, other channels raised their collective share to 43 per cent, compared to 41.5 the previous year. Of these channels, Sky One convincingly retained its lead with 2.90 per cent against nearest rival UKTV Gold's total share of 2.03 per cent. Nevertheless, this performance masked a fall compared to the Sky flagship's 3.79 per cent share the previous year, a loss of 0.89 per cent, the largest by any channel in the UK during the year. ITV2 achieved the biggest gain after raising its share from 1.13 to 1.57 per cent.

Discovery retained its position at the forefront of factual programming during 2003, with a 0.7 per cent total share of multichannel homes. Competing against new arrivals like UKTV People and UKTV Documentary (created out of the old UK Horizons, with populist fare such as *Robot Wars* on People and more serious topics on Documentary), Discovery gained a major advantage with the £8

million co-production and output deal signed between Discovery Networks Europe and Channel 4 in mid-January 2003, which gave the factual channel first-look for the non-terrestrial rights to Channel 4's factual output. With the deal, Discovery also secured first option as UK partner for factual co-productions. Beating rival bids from UKTV History, The History Channel and National Geographic, the deal gave Discovery a major advantage over its competitors. Part of the acquired programming went towards strengthening Discovery's Home and Leisure channel (0.68 per cent share in 2003) against competition from UKTV Style (total 1.08 per cent share in 2003) and UKTV Bright Ideas.

While Discovery continues to hold the highest ratings in the factual category, with strong brand recognition and a weekly audience of 3.5 million adults in the UK, over the last two years the channel has worked at creating a stronger British identity by investing in original programming. This has included broadening the channel's appeal by taking an infotainment direction through the introduction of new celebrity fronted shows in early 2004, including *Bloody Britain* fronted by Rory McGrath. This investment has led Discovery to claim itself the largest commissioner in the multichannel market, with some commission

Kate Adie hosted *War Women* for UK History

Antix Productions' *Most Haunted.* Live 'event' editions in particular draw strong audiences to Living TV

prices rumoured to be near those paid by terrestrial broadcasters. Nearly a year after it debuted, UKTV History also made its first original series commission in September 2003 with *War Women* from Eagle Media Productions.

In children's television, during 2003 the BBC's CBeebies and CBBC both registered gains in audience share. Cartoon Network's Boomerang and Viacom's Nick Jr (under fours) and Nicktoons (5-8 year olds) also saw gains, however the share for Nickelodeon's main channel declined. At the start of 2003, Disney claimed their subscription only channel was taken up by over half of multichannel homes in the UK. There soon followed indications that Disney intended to create a stronger UK identity for the channel. Previously, all Disney's output was produced in-house, but in March 2003, they announced a new 'open door' policy for independent commissioning of programmes for the British versions of the Disney Channel, Disney Playhouse and Toon Disney. In July 2003, the first external order was made, with the commissioning of *Inside Clyde* from Talent Television, a game show investigating the human body, broadcast from January 2004.

After their launch in April 2003, BSkyB Networks' three new music channels, Flaunt, Scuzz and The Amp, were failing to make any major impact on the music television market. By July 2003, the new channels combined were attracting only 4 per cent share of 16-34 year olds in digital Sky homes, compared to the 56 per cent share of

Even though multichannel audience may have increased, the major question remains whether UK broadcasting can in the long term sustain the number of digital channels currently airing.

MTV's eight channels and the 36 per cent share of EMAP's seven channels. EMAP has maintained all-promo video programming, while MTV has expanded its identity beyond its foundations in music TV by investing in original programming. Back in February 2003 MTV formed a unit for developing UK hits in the style of *The Osbournes* and *Jackass*, seeing itself as now competing against entertainment channels E4 and Sky One.

Since it was launched on Sky in December 2002, Classic FM has enjoyed an unrivalled place in the market, and has worked towards making a distinctive mark by encouraging emerging and independent film companies to make footage for the channel, alongside that supplied by major labels like Sony. With nearly twenty channels now competing for the relatively small music television audience, new arrivals such as the Sky channels cannot be seen to fill any gap in the market, and so the expectation must be that some channels will go to the wall. At the very least, this could involve the

Talent Television's *Inside Clyde*, a UK origination for the Disney Channel

Game show *Fort Boyard* – shot in France for Challenge TV

Peter Powers is the star of *Street Hypnosis,* a Comedy Unit production for Bravo

three major groups closing individual channels while moving into new territory if classical proves a successful niche, but could also ultimately result in one group leaving the market altogether.

Even though the multichannel audience may have increased, the major question remains whether UK broadcasting can in the long term sustain the number of digital channels currently airing. Channels are routinely closing. During 2003, the Granada/Boot venture Wellbeing, along with Carlton Cinema and p-rock, were just some of the channels to close. A deflated advertising market has contributed to making multichannel television a risky environment, alongside the expenses of start-up costs and payments for playout, satellite uplinks, EPG listing and licence fees. With the trend in recent years being for broadcasters to create a bouquet of channels to produce various sub-brands, it is unclear if this strategy actually results in broadcasters increasing their overall audience share or in cannibalising their own audiences. A crucial issue for the future is therefore if this sector of the television market will be subject to 'digital Darwinism'.

Paul McDonald is Director of the Centre for Research in Film and Audiovisual Cultures at the University of Surrey Roehampton.

It is unclear if broadcasters' bouquets of sub-brand channels actually increase overall audience share or merely cannibalise their own audiences.

Indies
Michael Darlow

Conventional wisdom has it that independent production remains an unalloyed good thing, bringing innovation, new talent and new jobs.

It really took off with the launch of Channel 4 as a publisher/broadcaster in 1982. From a handful in 1980, the number of independents rapidly grew to many hundreds. As numbers grew, pressure mounted for new outlets, leading to the '25% Campaign', and eventually, with the 1990 Broadcasting Act, to the BBC and ITV companies having to commission 25 per cent of programmes from independents.

Today one in three new programmes are made by independents and the sector's turnover is more than £1,400 million (up £400 million on last year). In the early days most production companies were small and the producers who owned them saw themselves primarily as programme makers rather than businessmen. Even today the vast majority of independents remain small, making four or less programmes a year. The majority of output hours – perhaps as much as half of total UK independent output – are produced by just a handful of companies, the likes of Endemol, The Television Corporation and TWI (another giant producer, talkbackThames, is a subsidiary of Fremantle and as such is usually disqualified from any survey of independent activity).

The 2003 Communications Act perpetuated the 25 per cent quota and led in January 2004 to Ofcom introducing a new code to govern terms of trade between broadcasters and independents, giving producers greater control over rights in their programmes.

On the day in July 2003 that the Communications Act received the Royal assent, Hat Trick's founders announced that they had sold a 45 per cent stake to a venture capital firm for £23 million. In March 2004 came news came news that Hat Trick was looking to use some of its new cash to increase its drama output and make acquisitions among other independents – a £20 million merger between Hat Trick and *Footballers' Wives* and *Bad Girls* producer Shed was announced but the deal amicably fell through at the end of June. Also in March, the birth of Scotland's first 'super-indie' from the merger of Ideal World and Wark Clements went through more successfully and the new company, IWC Media, is expected to have a turnover of £19m and staff of fifty.

Phil Redmond, creator of *Brookside*, which ended twenty-one years on Channel 4 in November 2003, has announced plans to sell his and his wife's interest in the company for £30 million. Groups of smaller independents are getting together to sell rights or share resources and many are looking for ways to expand, setting up sales arms and trying to maximise returns from the exploitation of programme rights. In February 2004 Channel 4 and Pact announced a scheme to put eleven independents through a crash course on how to break into the American market.

News that the BBC had again fallen 4 per cent short of the 25 per cent independent quota prompted the Culture Secretary, Tessa Jowell, to warn that in future the BBC, or any other broadcaster which failed to meet the quota, could be fined by Ofcom. The BBC claims to have failed to meet the quota because some large suppliers have recently been disqualified under rules limiting the financial stake held by a broadcaster in an independent but that, following a successful campaign orchestrated by Pact to have the rules changed, it would comfortably fulfil its quota. It looks, therefore, as if Pact's campaign may lead to fewer programme commissions over all.

Pact's John McVay has suggested that the BBC should more or less cease to produce programmes and become a publisher-broadcaster. Early in 2004 it emerged that Ofcom is considering increasing the quota to 50 per cent prior to scaling it down to zero. Channel 4 and others have pushed similar proposals, arguing that the BBC should be made to set up a separate commissioning arm and commission all its programmes, in-house or from outsiders, purely on merit. SMG (holder of the ITV franchises in Scotland) proposes that it should be treated as an independent outside Scotland, while Granada's production arm claims to 'feel like an indie' and that the independent quota should be scrapped altogether. Just where all this will end remains unclear, but it is hard to believe that inflicting serious damage on BBC in-house production will actually benefit viewers or improve the quality of programmes.

The Government has said repeatedly that its principal aims in the Communications Act were economic and that it wanted to stimulate the creation of businesses capable of succeeding in the international market place. So it's hardly surprising that the independents most likely to benefit are the bigger, business orientated companies, producing high volume, internationally saleable product, not the smaller, more personal producers who make

The majority of output hours – perhaps as much as half of total UK independent output – are produced by just a handful of companies, the likes of Endemol, The Television Corp and TWI

mainly one-offs or short series tailored to British audiences. The boss of one large independent has described his company as 'like a large rights factory. Our production side creates products that we can sell. How and where we vend them is driven by what the markets are like at any time.' Yet such attitudes remain alien to the way in which most of the hundreds of smaller independents see themselves and the programmes they make.

Although in 2003 Channel 4 alone still commissioned programmes from over 300 independents, smaller independents are finding it hard to survive because broadcasters increasingly deal with only a few larger producers. Some producers, like the award winning co-operative Teliesyn, may decide to close rather than turn out the safe programmes increasingly favoured by broadcasters. Even some large, highly respected companies are running into trouble. In January 2004 Uden Associates, which last year produced over 260 hours of programming, went into administration. The longer term outlook for many others looks hardly more promising. Pact's Television Vice Chairman said in February 2004; 'It's very difficult to sustain an argument that says that having 600 tiny independents is the way to deliver the best programmes to viewers. There's always room for boutique suppliers but there should be forty to fifty of them. At the moment we've got 600. That is crackers.'

Whether a concentration of independents into fewer bigger companies, their eyes fixed firmly on foreign markets and the bottom line, will really benefit the quality of British broadcasting seems questionable. Twenty years ago it was the range of small, creative, highly motivated programme maker-independents that was essential to making Channel 4 a ground-breaking success and established the independents' reputation for innovation which, rightly or wrongly, endures.

*Michael Darlow led the independents' negotiations for the 25 per cent in the 80s. His book **Independents Struggle** was published in 2004.*

Ofcom

Barrie MacDonald

Ofcom – the Office of Communications – officially took up its statutory duties on 29 December 2003, a new unified regulator responsible for a £44 billion communications industry, replacing a plethora of sector-specific regulators for the communications sector. This article charts the origins and evolution of the single-regulator concept, and Ofcom's first few months in action.

Early days in office

Ofcom Chief Executive Stephen Carter believes that the regulator has a duty to help 'develop and nurture the independent production sector'. In January Ofcom agreed new codes of practice with the broadcasters for their dealings with the independents, providing a fairer system whereby programme rights are retained by the production company, not the broadcaster, unless otherwise negotiated.

As part of its supervision of broadcasting standards, complaints handling will be an important part of Ofcom's work. Its Contact Centre anticipates 250,000 calls, emails and letters a year. An early test case was John Lydon's foul-mouthed exit from ITV's *I'm A Celebrity ... Get Me Out of Here!*, which brought many complaints from viewers, but no censure from the regulator because it was a live unscripted programme and after the watershed. ITV issued an apology. However,

Driving digital switchover:
a report to the Secretary of State

5th April 2004

Ofcom
OFFICE OF COMMUNICATIONS

As a major priority in its first year, Parliament charged Ofcom with reviewing the effectiveness of public service broadcasting (PSB) to answer two questions: how well are the main channels delivering on PSB objectives, and what needs to be done to maintain and strengthen them up to digital switchover?

Channel 4's *Little Friends*, featuring child actors using bad language in sexual sketches, was dropped after Ofcom's intervention.

On 5 April, in its review of digital switchover, Ofcom warned that a million households will be unable to receive digital terrestrial television in 2010, when the government wants to switch off the analogue signal, and recommended that those people should offered a free-to-air satellite service by broadcasters.

As a major priority in its first year, Parliament had charged Ofcom with reviewing the effectiveness of public service television broadcasting (PSB) to answer two questions: how well are the main channels delivering on PSB objectives, and what needs to be done to maintain and strengthen PSB up to the point of digital switchover. The challenge would be to meet the objectives for PSB in a world that is radically different from when they were first drawn up. The Ofcom review of PSB will be published in three phases to be completed by December 2004.

Phase One, *Is television special?*, published on 21 April, reported on the extent to which the BBC, ITV, Channel 4 (and S4C in Wales), and Five, taken together have fulfilled the purpose of PSB, and what the public gets for £4 billion of spending annually. To assist Ofcom in its task, it conducted a large-scale audience survey. The survey found the public appreciated and valued television, and that though viewers saw TV primarily as a form of entertainment they also believed it should support wider social values. Multichannel viewers watch less public-service programmes, but nonetheless are likely to see such programmes as a good idea.

Ofcom structure.

The main decision making body is the Ofcom Board, made up of executive members, including the Chief Executive, and part-time members, including the Chairman. The Chairman and the non-executive members are appointed by the Secretary of State for Culture Media and Sport and the Secretary of State for Trade and Industry acting together.

Ofcom has a number of committees and advisory bodies that either have been given delegated powers by the Board or offer advice to it. These bodies include the Consumer Panel, the Content Board, Advisory Committees for the Nations, the Advisory Committee on Older and Disabled People, and a Spectrum Advisory Board.

The **Consumer Panel** gives advice, supported by independent research, to Ofcom on the interests and concerns of consumers in the broadcasting and telecommunications sectors – small businesses, rural consumers, the elderly, people with disabilities or who are on low incomes or otherwise disadvantaged.

The **Content Board** is a committee of the main Ofcom Board, with delegated and advisory responsibilities for a wide range of content issues, predominantly in broadcasting. It is Ofcom's primary forum for the regulation of television and radio quality and standards. It considers content issues in three 'tiers':

- **Tier 1** negative content regulation, matters principally concerning harm and offence, accuracy and impartiality, fairness and privacy
- **Tier 2** quantitative matters, such as quotas for independent production, regional production and EU/UK origination programming
- **Tier 3** covers public service broadcasters, with particular responsibility for ITV, Channel 4 and Five

The Content Board has thirteen members, appointed by Ofcom, and is chaired by the Deputy Chairman, Richard Hooper.

The **Advisory Committees for the Nations** are four separate advisory committees for Scotland, Wales, Northern Ireland and the English Regions, each chosen by open public process.

The **Spectrum Advisory Board** offers independent advice to Ofcom on spectrum management issues.

Regulatory Style

Ofcom proposes regulating through a set of clearly articulated principles and stated policy objectives, with intervention where there is a specific statutory duty. Chief Executive Stephen Carter has said 'Ofcom will operate with a bias against intervention, but a willingness to intervene firmly where required'. The aim is to operate the least intrusive regulatory mechanisms, ensuring that any interventions are evidence-based, proportionate, consistent, accountable and transparent in both deliberation and outcome. To achieve these ends Ofcom will regularly undertake market research, and consult with consumers.

Principle Duties

as set out in the Communications Act are:

- to ensure optimal use of the electro-magnetic spectrum
- to ensure that a wide range of electronic communications services are available
- to ensure a wide range of television and radio services of high quality and wide appeal
- to maintain plurality in the provision of broadcasting
- to apply adequate protection for audiences against offensive and harmful material
- to adequately protect audiences against unfairness and infringement of privacy

Annual Plan

Ofcom is required to publish an Annual Plan for public scrutiny. In its first annual plan for its first full year of operation from 1 April 2004, its purpose is to:

- set out Ofcom's strategic priorities and plans for its first full year of operation
- ensure transparency and accountability of Ofcom's work to its stakeholders
- provide Ofcom staff with a guide to the organisation's work and priorities
- enable the Ofcom Board, the Content Board and management teams to manage and monitor progress

Priorities

Ofcom's priorities in the first year are:

- a far-reaching review of public service television broadcasting
- a strategic study of the UK telecommunications sector
- consultation on proposals to allow the trading of rights to use radio spectrum.

INDUSTRY IN FOCUS

Ofcom moved into its new offices at Riverside House at the close of 2003

Viewers also placed a high value on accurate, impartial news, and regard drama, soap operas and sports coverage as of benefit to society as a whole, whereas arts, religion and some regional programming were less widely valued. Ed Richards, Ofcom Senior Partner, said 'Viewers have made it clear that public service broadcasting matters'. The review concluded that PSB should in future be defined in terms of its purposes and its characteristics, in underpinning an informed society and cultural identity with programming of quality, innovation and wide availability. Ofcom should focus regulatory intervention on those PSB characteristics to which viewers give the highest social value. It placed importance on the BBC being the standard-setter for delivering the highest quality PSB, but also reaffirmed Channel 4's critical role. The Ofcom review will complement and inform the Government's BBC Charter Review under Lord Burns.

After its first 100 days there was criticism of the sheer scale of Ofcom's operation and its annual budget of £164 million (with start-up costs of £52 million), currently running at 27 per cent more than the costs of the former five regulators it replaced.

Conclusion

After its first 100 days there was criticism of the sheer scale of Ofcom's operation, and its annual budget of £164 million (with start-up costs of £52 million), currently running at 27 per cent more than the costs of the former five regulators, though its 800 staff is a reduction of 400 in manpower. However, with over 260 statutory tasks, many of them once only, Ofcom justifies its cost to the licensees. A review of how the cost of ITV licences are calculated may result in a fall in licence charges. Complaints from licensees are not only over paying extra for regulation, but about 'consultationitis', with over forty different Ofcom consultations in progress.

Ofcom possesses tremendous power through influence with Government and patronage. Its first major appointment – of maverick businessman and restaurant entrepreneur Luke Johnson as Channel 4 Chairman in January 2004 – came as a surprise. Ofcom's role as a competition regulator, particularly in ensuring Lord Puttnam's all important plurality test to be applied to mergers, will be tested if an eventual American takeover of ITV plc emerges, or a purchaser for Five. As a tidying up exercise in rationalising regulation across the media, some inconsistencies still remain under Ofcom – the BBC, the internet and newspapers. Its first full year in action will be a testing time for Ofcom, its licensees and public acceptance.

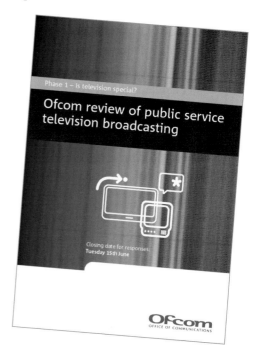

Phase 1 – Is television special?

Ofcom review of public service television broadcasting

Closing date for responses: Tuesday 15th June

Ofcom
OFFICE OF COMMUNICATIONS

Milestones in the evolution of Ofcom

1990 *Broadcasting Act 1990* introduces new sector regulators for television and radio, the Independent Television Commission (ITC) and the Radio Authority, and a new franchise auction and licensing system from 1991.

1994 British Media Industry Group (BMIG) submission to a review of cross-media ownership, set up by Peter Brooke, Secretary of State for National Heritage in January 1994, claims that new-media developments are being hampered by the UK regulatory framework.

Government White Paper *The future of the BBC* (Cmnd 2621) recognises 'that new technologies are emerging and boundaries between broadcasting, telecommunications and other media are becoming blurred'. The National Consumer Council suggests 'there may be a case for a single regulator of broadcasting'

July 1994: The 21st Century Media Conference in, marks the coming together of Labour and big media companies. Mo Mowlam, Shadow Heritage Secretary, calls for a 'rationalised regulatory structure to meet the challenges of the new market place'.

1995 *Communicating Britain's Future*, the report of a Labour Party forum on the information superhighway set up by Tony Blair under Chairman Chris Smith, makes a firm commitment to combine telecommunications regulator, Oftel, with the commercial television regulator, the ITC.

1996 *New media, new policies*, edited by Richard Collins and Cristina Murroni, the influential report of the Labour-supported centre-left think-tank, the Institute for Public Policy Research (IPPR) calls for 'replacing existing regulatory agencies with a single regulator, 'Ofcom', working with self-regulatory bodies'. Ofcom could be independent of government, bringing carriage and content regulation together.

1997 **11 February:** ITC calls for a single regulator in its evidence to the National Heritage Committee inquiry *The BBC and the Future of Broadcasting*.

1 May: General Election: Labour Party manifesto, *New Labour: Because Britain Deserves Better* states 'the regulatory framework ... should reflect the realities of a far more open and competitive economy'.

1998 21 July: Government Green Paper: *Regulating Communications*.

2000 **12 December:** Government White Paper, *A New Future for Communications* (Cm 5010), outlines a new regulatory framework: 'We will create a new regulator, an Office of Communications (Ofcom), with the expertise and the vision to understand the converging communications landscape'.

2001 **28 March:** Memorandum of Understanding between the five regulators (ITC, Radio Authority, BSC, Oftel, and the Radiocommunications Agency) on arrangements for closer working and co-operation.

12 October: Towers Perrin scoping study lays the foundations of Ofcom.

2002 **19 March:** *Office of Communications Act 2002* enables preparatory establishment of Ofcom.

7 May: *Draft Communications Bill* published: scrutiny by a Parliamentary Joint Committee (Chairman: Lord Puttnam)

25 July: David Currie (Lord Currie of Marylebone) appointed Ofcom Chairman.

25 September: Ofcom Board appointed.

29 October: Government accept 120 of the recommendations of the Joint Committee.

20 November: Communications Bill published.

2003 **21 January:** Stephen Carter appointed Ofcom Chief Executive.

February: Ofcom Executive Management Board formed to run the implementation process through to establishment of Ofcom.

17 July: Communications Act 2003 receives Royal Assent.

December: final move to Riverside House headquarters.

28 December: ITC (and other legacy regulators) wound up.

29 December: Ofcom assumes full statutory duties.

Trade Policy

Richard E. Collins

The UK's international trade in television

In 2002, the most recent period for which data is available, the UK TV industry's international trade deficit was a record £553m.

This might imply that trade deficits are bad things. Perhaps they are if considered in strictly economic terms (although there would not be much international trade if every country sought to have a positive balance of trade in every area!) but the growth in opportunities for UK TV viewers to see more material from other countries, which rising imports provide, might be seen as a very positive change. Whatever the state of the TV trade balance, trade in television is almost never considered solely as an economic question and television (and film) trade is one of the most fraught areas of international trade policy.

In November 2001 proponents of the 'cultural exception' – the exemption of film, television and other cultural commodities from international free trade regimes – secured a UNESCO *Declaration on Cultural Diversity*. Articles 8 and 10 of the Declaration provide grounds for resisting international free trade in cultural (including television) goods and services. Article 8 draws 'particular attention ... to the diversity of the supply of creative work ... and to the specificity of cultural goods and services which, as vectors of identity, values and meaning, must not be treated as mere commodities or consumer goods' and Article 10 argues that 'In the face of current imbalances in flows and exchanges of cultural goods and services at the global level, it is necessary to reinforce international co-operation and solidarity aimed at enabling all countries, especially developing countries and countries in transition, to establish cultural industries that are viable and competitive at national and international level'. Both articles

> **Whatever the state of the TV trade balance, trade in television is almost never considered solely as an economic question and television trade is one of the most fraught areas of international trade policy**

clearly point towards legitimisation of public subsidies for television production and national exhibition quotas and thus to measures which, if applied, would be likely to reduce volumes of international trade in television resulting both in fewer imports and fewer exports.

Proponents of the 'cultural exception', led by Canada and the EU, have locked horns many times with US-led free traders among whom, thus far, the UK has usually been numbered. The UK has been cool towards international movements to manage trade in television, both in international trade negotiations and the current EU review of the *Television Without Frontiers* Directive (which requires EU broadcasters 'where practicable' to schedule at least 50 per cent of European programmes – with some exceptions such as news and sport). The last completed World Trade Organisation (WTO) trade round, the Uruguay Round, effectively ended in a tacit agreement to decide not to decide on trade in audio-visual services, including television. The hiatus in negotiations in the current WTO Doha Round means that the effect of the Declaration on Cultural Diversity is far from clear. If the Doha Round progresses, the 'cultural exception' is likely to again be a key point of difference between the USA and the EU.

The UK does not fall neatly into either camp for reasons that the trade statistics cited above make clear. As the European Audiovisual Observatory (EAO Press Release 28/1/03 can be seen at http://www.obs.coe.int/about/oea/pr/a02vol5.html on 16/2/04) comments of UK television: 'Programmes and films originating in the UK are clearly those most programmed on television channels in Western Europe,' and 'Among the five principal markets in Europe, UK channels are the most heavily dependent on American-originated material – 88 per cent of fiction programming imported into the UK and 93 per cent of feature films are either entirely American or American co-productions'. Unlike the rest of the EU, the UK is a successful television exporter. Unlike the USA, the UK imports a lot of television – so much it's now consistently in deficit.

The worsening of UK trade performance in television between 2000 and 2002 followed a trend established in the 90s when, after consistently positive trade balances in the 80s, the UK international television trade account first fell

UK television trades 2002

Figures given in £ million
(figures rounded and do not include television services)

	Exports	Imports	Export/Import Balance	% Change in trade balance +/-2000/2002
USA	194	742	-549	-95%
EU	214	300	-86	-458%
Rest of World	276	195	+81	+21%
World	684	1237	-553	-294%

Source: ONS 2003. International service transactions of the film and television industries, 2002 published 30/10/03

into deficit. The 90s produced, quite simply, an increase in UK consumption (as satellite and cable channels came on stream) beyond what domestic production and financial capacity could supply. In the 1990s the UK shared the general global experience of an adverse trade balance in television and increasing penetration of the domestic market by US programmes. But unlike most of the rest of the world, the UK both successfully exports programmes (including to the USA) and hosts services targeted on overseas markets (e.g. satellite-delivered commercial channels for Scandinavian viewers such as MTV Nordic and Fox Kids Scandinavia).

But, defining trade flows, not least the UK balance of trade in television and the rules under which international trade is conducted, necessitates agreement on what TV is. Hitherto, a clear distinction has been made between trade in goods and trades in services. Trade in goods comes under the remit of the General Agreement on Tariffs and Trade (GATT), and trade in services under the General Agreement on Trade in Services (GATS). Film has been treated as goods because film is a tangible object, whereas TV has been treated as a service without a similar tangible object. This distinction obviously started to break down with the end of live TV and the 'tangible-isation' of television via video tape and DVD, while the digitalisation of film, e.g. the distribution of movies to theatres via satellite, accelerates that process. Accordingly, existing boundary problems of definition in recording trade flows are likely to grow (Should a particular trade be recorded as a film or television trade? Co-productions, depending on the nature of the agreement, might be recorded as an import or an export.)

> **Defining trade flows, not least the UK balance of trade in television and the rules under which international trade is conducted, necessitates agreement on what TV is.**

Finally, it's important to recognise that the value of exports and imports (and the relative importance of trading partners) changes as international exchange rates shift. Most international audio-visual trades are dollar trades and so the trade volumes and balances reported by the ONS are particularly strongly skewed by changes in the Pound/Dollar exchange rate though the importance of the EU as a trading partner means the Pound/Euro exchange rate is now also very important. Between 2001 and 2002 the value of the Pound rose, relative to the US Dollar, by c.4 per cent – meaning that the value of dollar denominated exports and the cost of dollar imports both fell. In the same period the Pound fell, relative to the Euro, by c.1.25 per cent, meaning that the value of Euro denominated exports and the cost of Euro imports rose.

Richard Collins is Professor of Media Studies at the Open University. His most recent book is **The Consequences of Convergence: Media and Identity in Contemporary Europe** *(Intellect:2002).*

INDUSTRY IN FOCUS

Censure & Censorship
Julian Petley

Censure has largely replaced censorship as the means by which controversial programming is, if not banned, then certainly discouraged. This kind of flak comes from various sources – the government, as in the Gilligan/Kelly affair, or David Blunkett branding the BBC's investigation of police racism, *The Secret Policeman*, 'a covert stunt to get attention'; the press, as in the Murdoch papers' endless war against the BBC, or the *Mail*'s obsession with broadcast sex and violence; and, finally, the medium's own regulators.

Until the end of 2003 there were three regulators: the Independent Television Commission (ITC), the Broadcasting Standards Commission (BSC), and the BBC Programme Complaints Unit. At the start of 2004 the first two were merged into Ofcom which continues to operate the programme codes of its predecessors until it devises new ones. As BBC programme standards fell within the BSC's remit, so too they come under Ofcom's jurisdiction.

Much of the regulatory work carried out by such bodies is uncontroversial, even laudable. Few people, presumably, would want to defend the use of the f-word or of graphic images of sex or violence before the watershed; such incidents, which usually happen by mistake and on the minority multichannels, account for a significant number of complaints from viewers and consequent reprimands by the regulators. Not all censuring of pre-watershed programmes is quite so clear-cut however. For instance, on 4 January 2004, ITV showed Schwarzenegger film *Kindergarten Cop* at 16.45; over thirty edits had been made to render it suitable for the timeslot, although the BBFC had passed the film at '12' with one brief cut. Ofcom censured the screening because the ITC *Programme Code* advises that no '12' rated version of a film should start before 20.00, a rule some may find surprising and unnecessarily restrictive.

The watershed was also a problem for two episodes of *EastEnders*, 9 and 11 December 2003. These concerned the rape of Little Mo, and attracted six complaints to Ofcom. In its response to the regulator the BBC admitted that one of the episodes 'was a degree more adult in tone than was appropriate for its scheduling and the expectations of its large family audience' and Ofcom, censuring the programme for breaching the above code, agreed, stating that 'the nature and tone of the programme was unsuitable for broadcast at this time'. On the other hand, it could be argued that *EastEnders* is renowned for its tough subjects and that these two episodes would thus not have unduly shocked its usual audience.

A post-watershed slot, however, doesn't mean that anything goes. Thus a violent scene near the beginning of a *Wire in the Blood* episode (ITV1 26 February 2004) was censured by Ofcom, even though the programme was preceded by a warning. Ofcom observed that the first series had been censured by the ITC and reiterated its predecessor's point that 'there is an expectation that any programme starting immediately after the 9 p.m. watershed will not swiftly include stronger material, more suited to later in the schedule'.

Some things, though, are unacceptable at any time. Hence the BSC considered that *My Night with Julia* (Channel 4, 30 July 2003), in which the film's director recorded his night with a Moscow prostitute, had 'exceeded acceptable limits', and upheld the complaints of four viewers who condemned it as 'exploitative of the contributor, voyeuristic and degrading'. Ofcom also censured *Little Friends* (episodes of which were broadcast late night between October 2003 and January 2004 on both Channel 4 and E4). The programmes involved young actors tricking members of the public and celebrities in which often involved swearing and sexual innuendo, and Ofcom ruled that parts of the programmes breached the *Code*'s provisions on general offensiveness.

Similarly, a scene in *Trouble at the Top* (BBC 2, 25 March 2004) in which a stressed chef uttered the words 'Jesus f***ing Christ' was found to have contravened the *Code*, even though the programme started at 21.50 and was preceded by a warning; furthermore, the phrase occurred some way in. And was it *that* much more offensive than 'Jesus shitting Christ', which emerged unscathed from an Ofcom examination of the previous night's *Footballers' Wives*? Or John Lydon calling the viewers who'd failed to vote him out of *I'm a Celebrity ... Get Me out of Here!* (3 February 2004) 'f***ing c****'? This elicited ninety-six complaints from viewers. ITV had warned viewers at the start of the programme that it might contain strong language, presenters Ant and Dec had apologised twice for Lydon's outburst and ITV immediately installed a seven-second delay on the live satellite feed and given the production team a further briefing on *Code* compliance – because of these measures Ofcom took no further action.

One of the ITC's final acts of censure concerned the series *Sex Court*, originally made for the encrypted Playboy Channel but shown on the un-encrypted Living TV in June 2003. This attracted a complaint from Mediawatch-UK, successor to the National Viewers and Listeners Association, and presumably not representative of the series' intended audience. Although broadcast between 23.00 and 24.00, the ITC identified several scenes which raised serious taste and decency issues and which, 'in their explicitness and duration on screen, went beyond what was acceptable on an unencrypted service'. The regulator concluded that 'the case well illustrates that sex series made for encrypted channels are not easily transferable to open channel viewing and require a degree of editing beyond the removal or blurring of obviously explicit and inappropriate images'. It remains to be seen, however, whether Ofcom will allow BBFC R18-rated material even on encrypted channels.

The ITC was similarly critical of *Free Sex TV*, broadcast by Friendly TV, unencrypted, on 14 July 2003 from 23.00 – 03.00. As well as breaching the *Programme Code*'s taste and decency provisions, it also fell foul of its rules forbidding programmes giving undue prominence to commercial websites. Additionally it broke the ITC *Advertising Code* by advertising premium rate services of a sexually explicit nature, and by not clearly separating advertising from programming. Friendly TV has since encountered similar problems with Ofcom.

In today's commercial television environment the question of maintaining boundaries between advertising/sponsorship and programming – something which most people would presumably find desirable – increasingly preoccupies the regulators. An edition of *GMTV News* (ITV1, 19 June 2003) featuring the launch of a new Harry Potter book breached the ITC *Programme Code* provision that forbids programmes from giving undue prominence to commercial products or services; another offender was an item on Fox News, 30 August 2003, ostensibly about the many uses of tomatoes but in fact entirely about one particular tomato seed company. Fox News also fell foul of Ofcom on 7 November 2003 for featuring the actress Susan Licci and her Youthful Essence beauty products. This piece, Ofcom decided, was 'nothing more than an advert'.

Many wonder how Fox News' political agenda squares with Ofcom's requirements for 'due impartiality' in news programming. Perhaps Ofcom is simply awaiting a detailed complaint before making a pronouncement, but meanwhile it's interesting to note that an edition of *The Big Story: My Word* on 28 January 2004 attracted twenty-four complaints when the programme anchor, John Gibson, lambasted the BBC after the Hutton Enquiry. He charged the BBC for a 'frothing-at-the-mouth anti-Americanism that was obsessive, irrational and dishonest' and that it 'felt entitled to lie and, when caught lying, felt entitled to defend its lying reporters and executives'. Although this is a 'personal view' slot, Ofcom pointed out all factually-based shows should be characterised by a 'respect for the truth', and that even in 'personal view' programmes, the opinions expressed, however partial, should not 'rest upon false evidence' and should respect facts. Further, programmes which contain damaging critiques of individuals or institutions should offer those criticised a chance to respond. In Ofcom's view, Gibson did none of these, and Fox News was censured under three sections of the *Code*.

Murdoch's Sky News earned the year's most serious rebuke when, on 19 November 2003, the ITC Sanctions Sub Committee fined it £50,000 for an item on 31 March 2003, purporting to show a Cruise missile being fired at Iraq by HMS Splendid. However, the latter was in dock at the time that it was supposedly firing the missile, and the shot in question came from library footage. The item thus breached ITC regulations concerning accuracy and dramatised reconstructions. Tragically, this episode, which first came to light in a programme in the BBC 2 series *Fighting the War* (20 July 2003), resulted in the suicide of the reporter on the item, James Forlong, a suicide which many journalists blamed on the pressures of today's hyper-competitive broadcast news environment.

Julian Petley is joint chair of the Campaign for Press and Broadcasting Freedom.

'Go on ... say something outrageous ...'. John Lydon duly complies.

INDUSTRY IN FOCUS

TV & Parliament

Barrie MacDonald

Television and media issues in Parliament

Probably the most far-reaching measure concerning broadcasting on the Parliamentary calendar in the past year has been the Communications Act 2003. The bill began its Parliamentary passage with its first reading in the Commons on 19 November 2002, and took many months of Parliamentary scrutiny, nineteen days of full debates in Commons and Lords, twenty-six sittings of the Standing Committee, and over 500 amendments for consideration before reaching Royal Assent on 17 July 2003.

This latest staging post in broadcasting deregulation aimed to unify the regulation of broadcasting and telecommunications, and to introduce lighter-touch regulation, particularly in relaxing the media ownership rules. Opposition to the bill came from the Lords in particular, as well as some Labour MPs, over deregulatory aspects and concerns for any terrestrial television channel being taken over wholly or partially by newspaper groups. The Lords secured amendments which aimed to protect media companies in the case of takeovers by introducing a 'public interest test'. Another major concession made sure that Ofcom considered 'citizens' rights as well as 'consumers'. An important measure to come out of the Parliamentary scrutiny was a definition of public service broadcasting, of the key services and programme strands to be judged across the public service broadcasters. Parliament, and particularly the Lords, had a very constructive role in this key piece of legislation.

On 28 January 2004 there was a short debate following the Prime Minister's statement on Lord Hutton's report into the circumstances of the death of weapons expert, David Kelly. 'The report's findings about the BBC speak for themselves,' said

---

Michael Howard, Leader of the Opposition: 'The Hutton report's findings about the BBC speak for themselves. We have long argued that the board of governors cannot both run and regulate the BBC'

Michael Howard, Leader of the Opposition, 'We have long argued that the board of governors cannot both run and regulate the BBC'. A full Commons debate on 4 February, opened by the Prime Minister, generally agreed that the most far-reaching repercussions of the Hutton report had been for the Corporation. Michael Howard called for a role for Ofcom in handling complaints about the BBC but felt that 'Hutton must not be used to undermine the independence of the BBC'.

Television coverage of Parliament

Television often struggles to make Parliament and politics interesting to viewers, particularly a younger generation which doesn't even exercise its vote. Recent BBC research found that the five new programmes commissioned in 2003 as a result of a wide-ranging review of BBC political output, partly to attract younger viewers, which included two short-lived series *Weekend* (BBC 2) and *The Sharp End* (BBC 1), as well as replacing the Sunday lunchtime show *On The Record* with *The Politics Show* (BBC 1), failed to boost younger audiences. However, the controversy surrounding the Iraq War and subsequent Hutton Inquiry into the death of David Kelly, have made television coverage of the debates in Parliament unusually exciting this year.

Prime Minister's Questions in the House of Commons on Wednesdays, the weekly gladiatorial combat between Prime Minister and Leader of the Opposition and other MPs, is occasionally televised live, but mostly edited into news bulletins. It has been considerably enlivened since the election of a new Tory Leader, Michael Howard, in 2003: a barrister by profession, like Tony Blair, he relishes the debate with the Prime Minister.

BBC Parliament, airing on Sky Digital and in quarter screen on Freeview, provides valuable news and comments on Parliamentary activities, as well as access to transcripts of programmes and advance schedules, on the BBC News website (www.news.bbc.co.uk).

Regular coverage and analysis of the work of Parliament is provided by several weekly current affairs programmes. *Question Time* (BBC 1) continues to field panels of politicians and public figures, under the magisterial gaze of Chairman David Dimbleby, to respond to a studio audience's

Television often struggles to make Parliament and politics interesting to viewers, particularly a younger generation which doesn't even exercise its vote.

questions. Also including interviews and filmed reports are *Jonathan Dimbleby* (ITV1), *The Politics Show* (BBC 1), and *Tonight with Trevor McDonald* (ITV1). *Panorama* (BBC 1), the veteran current affairs programme which continues to make quality single-subject programmes on political issues, produced a widely acclaimed special edition, 'The Fight to the Death', on the Government's battle with the BBC over the David Kelly affair, on 21 January 2004. Perhaps the most entertaining programme on politics is *This Week* (BBC 1), in which Andrew Neil chairs a lively discussion between two armchair pundits, normally MPs Diane Abbott and Michael Portillo, about the week in Parliament. From the same production team, *The Daily Politics* (BBC 2) presents political and Parliamentary stories of the day, with reports from BBC correspondent Guto Harri and extended on Wednesdays to include Prime Minister's Questions.

The cut and thrust of Parliament can also make good drama programmes. BBC 4's *The Alan Clark Diaries*, dramatised with John Hurt as Clark, gave an insight into Parliamentary life under Margaret Thatcher, just as Channel 4's *The Deal* did for Labour in opposition from 1992 to 1997, and the alleged Tony Blair and Gordon Brown pact over the Party leadership. Most compulsive of all was Paul Abbott's conspiracy thriller, *State of Play* (BBC), a gripping view of the imagined pressures and deceptions of political and Parliamentary life.

Housing Need
The revised projections are based on a new approach to "plan, monitor and manage" which the Government says is more flexible than the "predict and provide" system

Publications

The select committees of Parliament are an important part of its ongoing scrutiny.

The **Culture, Media and Sport Committee** examined several media issues in the past year:
Privacy and Media Intrusion (Report: Session 2002-03: HC 458 I/II);
BBC Report and Accounts, 2002-2003 (Report: Session 2002-03: HC 984);
The ITV Merger (Report: Session 2003-04: HC 74);
Ofcom: Preparation and Handover (Report: Session 2003-04: HC 132);
Broadcasting in Transition (Report: Session 2003-04: HC 380 & HC 585);
BBC Charter Renewal (Session 2003-04: HC 598)

The **Trade and Industry Select Committee** examined Broadband in the UK, and published The UK Broadband Market (Session 2003-04: HC 321 I/II).

The **Broadcasting Select Committee** examined The Rules for Coverage (televising the Chamber, Westminster Hall, Select and Standing Committees), as part of general policy on improving access to and understanding of Parliament (Report: Session 2002-03: HC 786). The report was debated in the Commons on 5 February 2004.

Early Day Motions, the MPs favourite way of letting off steam on issues they care about, or have vested interests in, continue to be a useful barometer of Parliamentary opinion. Among the media issues tabled and attracting signatories have been:

'The BBC and the Hutton Report' (EDM 508);
'The BBC and the Government' (EDM 513);
'The Prime Minster and the appointment of the new BBC Chairman' (EDM 515);
'The BBC and Public Service Broadcasting' (EDM 519).

Employment Issues

Kate O'Connor

The Communications Act; BBC Charter renewal; the establishment of Ofcom; the Hutton enquiry; mergers, established and potential; never ending advances in technology, these are changing times for the television industry ... but what's new? Change is one of the few ever present constants in broadcasting and one of the many reasons why skills, training and company development are an imperative in such a dynamic, fast moving industry.

The importance to the television industry of having a workforce equipped with the skills and talent needed to meet the changing needs of businesses can never be overstated. Future growth and competitiveness depend upon the people in the industry and their ability to excel regardless of the changes to the landscape. But the project based nature of the industry and freelance working patterns pose particular challenges. In recent years the industry has however put skills firmly at the top of its agenda, demonstrating a renewed commitment to the development of its people. Working together, through Skillset, TV is addressing productivity issues and targeting collective investment, which bodes well for the industry's future.

The Freelance Training Fund demonstrates that the industry now recognises that freelances are its lifeblood and their skills are paramount to future sustainability and growth.

Skillset itself has not escaped the changing tides. We've been championing the issue of skills in the audio visual industries for more than ten years in which time we've been under many guises – a lead body; an industry training organisation; a national training organisation, before, becoming, in 2001, one of the first organisations to receive their Sector Skills Council licence from Government. This position not only gave us more scope and funding, it also gave us more clout with a renewed partnership, in the truest sense, with government as the voice of employers on skills. Now we are one of four pathfinders working on developing a Sector Skills Agreements bringing industry and public investment in training and education into closer alignment.

As the Sector Skills Council for the Audio Visual Industries, Skillset covers television, radio, film, video, interactive media and photo imaging, working with the industry to address skills, talent and company development issues that threaten competitiveness. Through our extensive research programme – consisting of an annual Census of employers across the audio visual sectors; a biennial Workforce Survey of employees and freelancers; sector specific projects; and qualitative research consulting with panels and forums made up of industry practitioners – Skillset is able to profile the industry and its workforce, charting trends and helping to identify existing and emerging skills gaps and shortages. This is pivotal in targeting efforts and resources in the right direction where the industry needs it most.

Some of these research findings make for fascinating reading. Skillset's biennial Workforce Survey questioned nearly 2000 employees and freelancers working in the audio visual industries over spring and summer 2003. The results show that we currently have a very young workforce – 62 per cent are aged under 35 with just 8per cent aged over 50; that 39 per cent are women; 6 per cent are ethnic minorities; and that 82 per cent are based in England – 47 per cent in London. The survey also found that despite a highly qualified workforce – 66 per cent of whom are educated to degree level compared to 16 per cent of the UK as a whole – almost two thirds reported training needs. Nine out of ten who sought training reported barriers to receiving it including availability of information and cost of courses – not advantageous in an industry at the cutting edge of technology where the ability to upskill is a necessity. Changes in technology will continue apace, the advent of high definition for example, will be a significant learning curve for the majority of the post production industry and in an increasingly competitive multichannel digital age, where technology is becoming cheaper and more accessible, the need for individuals to be multi skilled will also increase. To meet these challenges it is crucial that we enable our workforce to continually develop and also crucial we have managers and leaders that recognise this.

The Freelance Training Fund is a prime example

of the commitment broadcasters are making to the future of the industries' workforce. The fund, which ITV, BBC, Channel, PACT / IPTF contribute to annually, is managed by Skillset and invested in training courses for the freelance workforce in priority areas. It demonstrates that the industry now recognises that freelances are its lifeblood and their skills are paramount to future sustainability and growth. Over £5 million has been invested in the fund over the last five years, enabling thousands of practitioners to access skills development at a fraction of the cost.

Further evidence of changing attitudes can be seen in the launch of National Skills Day at this year's Broadcast Production Show. It is a day devoted to highlighting the importance of skills to the industry. The first National Skills Day will take place on 19 May 2005 with employers, training providers and trade associations across the UK staging activities to provide access to and promote the skills development across all areas, from management and leadership through to craft skills.

Whilst it is a much needed and long overdue initiative, the concept would have been unheard of just a few years ago but it now boasts the solid support of joint partners Skillset, BBC, Channel 4, ITV, Five, *Broadcast* magazine, BECTU and Pact. It also casts a spotlight on the audio visual industries, presenting an example to other sectors in the UK.

There is also the Communications Act 2003 – the furthest reaching legislation relating to our industry for more than a decade – which made training a Tier One responsibility on all broadcasters. In January 2003 Skillset was asked by the Secretary of State for Culture, Media and Sport to set up a formal task force to report to Ofcom on how best to implement the training remit of the Act. The Taskforce reported in Autumn 2003. The Ofcom Board welcomed the report and established a Co-regulatory Design Group to look at taking forward proposals around a new do-regulatory structure supported by the industry, Ofcom and Skillset. Reports on people development in each company, agreeing and supporting industry wide action plans, developing common definitions for training, the monitoring and publishing of training activity across the industry and pooled investment for freelances are expected outcomes of the new proposed approach. A new TV Skills Strategy Committee has been established to identify where the industry needs to work together to raise its game. There is of course some commonality but also distinct differences in modern television – terrestrial, multichannel and

Skillset's biennial employment census provides a detailed picture of the television industry workforce

independent television production will all be looked at in detail.

These are indeed changing times but with the level of support and very real commitment to skills continuing to grow, the industry's ability to adapt and capitalise on those changes also grows. There couldn't be a more positive and encouraging sign in the face of the challenges of tomorrow.

Kate O'Connor is Executive Director and Deputy CEO of Skillset, the Sector Skills Council for the Audio Visual Industries. Skillset's website is at http://www.skillset.org

TV's Diverse Labour Force Janice Turner

Television is one of the most important cultural institutions of our society. It is therefore imperative that it reflects the multicultural society in which we live, both in front of and behind the camera.

Progress towards achieving a truly diverse labour force in television was patchy in 2003. On the one hand, the BBC, Channel 4 and Five all increased the percentage of black and minority ethnic staff. But on the other, the Skillset Workforce Survey for 2003 reports that overall employment of ethnic minority workers actually declined slightly from the previous year (6 per cent, down from 8 per cent).

The BBC achieved its target of 10 per cent of its total workforce of over 20,000 and 4 per cent of senior management coming from ethnic minorities by December 2003. The BBC states that this was through sustained recruitment efforts as well as improved monitoring. The corporation's new targets are 12.5 per cent across all staff and 7 per cent for senior staff by the end of 2007.

Channel 4 reported that its ethnic minority workforce increased from 9.8 per cent to 12 per cent of staff in 2003. Five reports an increase from 10.4 per cent to 13.8 per cent. 2003 data for ITV was unavailable, but fallout from the merger of Granada and Carlton, such as plans to slash programme making capacity with heavy job losses in the Central (Midlands) franchise in 2004, would be expected to hit black workers. In 2002 Central employed 39 (5 per cent) minority ethnic staff, the highest number in ITV outside the London franchises.

The Skillset survey warns against comparing audiovisual employment statistics with the 11 per cent ethnic minority national workforce. Much of the audiovisual industry is located in London and the south east where the ethnic minority workforce is much higher – 38 per cent in London. Skillset states that the proportion of ethnic minorities in the industry would therefore be expected to be greater than the UK average. It is not. It is important that diversity within broadcasting organisations is reflected at all levels and within key departments, including programme making and management.

Contradiction

The apparent contradiction between the broadcasters' diversity figures and the Skillset survey may be explained by the inclusion of freelances only in the latter data. This indicates there has not been the same focus on diversity in connection with freelance employment.

A new study was undertaken in 2004 by independent producers' association Pact and the UK Film Council to explore whether ethnic minority-led film and TV companies face 'ghettoisation' – being limited to making programmes for or about minority communities – and barriers to growth.

And the Cultural Diversity Network reports that following Channel 4's commitment in 2003 to increase the number of commissions of black and Asian-owned companies, there was an 86 per cent increase over the following year.

Other initiatives in 2003 included:
• the BBC's writing initiatives to encourage ethnic minority writers.
• Channel 4's sponsoring of four ethnic minority trainees to work in various departments on the production *Second Generation*.
• Channel 4's trainee deputy commissioning editor programme giving three professionals from ethnic minority backgrounds a year's experience.

A particularly positive development in 2003 was a new partnership developed between the industry and the union BECTU. The union's event, *Move on Up*, in November 2003 was backed by the government, the TUC and Skillset. The union scheduled 530 one-to-one meetings between 230 ethnic minority professionals and almost 100 key executives from the terrestrial broadcasters especially the BBC, plus the UK Film Council and others. The aim was that in the long term these contacts would result in jobs or commissions.

But the union and the industry has a long way to go before real diversity is achieved: Skillset reports that in 2003 representation of ethnic minorities in the audiovisual industry was highest among cinema cleaners and box office/kiosk and attendant staff.

Janice Turner is Editor of **Stage, Screen & Radio** *magazine (the journal of the Broadcasting Entertainment Cinematograph & Theatre Union) and organiser of the BECTU Black Members' Committee*

The Global TV Bazaar

Jeanette Steemers

INDUSTRY IN FOCUS

Britain remains the second largest exporter of television programmes after the US, based largely on the English language, which gives it preferential access to the wealthy American, Canadian and Australian markets. According to the British Television Distributors Association (BTDA), revenues from television programme exports totalled $921 million in 2003. The US buys the most, accounting for over 43 per cent of sales in 2003 ($399 million). Western Europe (led by Germany on 7.4 per cent), accounts for a further 30 per cent ($280 million).

Export revenues from video/DVD, co-production, formats/local production and licensing are still lower than revenues from programme sales, but their growth underlines the increasing importance of trading rights up front, local programming and the exploitation of ancillary rights.

There continues to be a shift in the type of sales. Programme sales accounted for 40 per cent of exports in 2003 ($371 million), down from 75 per cent in 1998. Revenues from sales of completed programmes rose by 12 per cent in 2003, compared to a decline of over 5 per cent in 2002, because of improved economic conditions. Export revenues from video/DVD (13.9 per cent, $239 million), co-production (12.5 per cent, $115 million), formats/local production (6.8 per cent, $63 million) and licensing (26 per cent, $239 million) are still lower than revenues from programme sales, but their growth underlines the increasing importance of trading rights up front, local programming and the exploitation of ancillary rights. Significantly format sales and local production, while growing, are still modest by comparison with sales of finished product, and largely based on a small number of major hits.

Sales of scripted formats to the US continue to attract press interest, but Britain has not delivered a scripted format success on US network television since the early 1980s (*Three's Company* on ABC,

based on Thames' *Man About the House*). A format based on Channel Four's gay drama, *Queer as Folk* has run on pay channel, Showtime, for four seasons. A US version of the BBC2 situation comedy *Coupling* was launched on the NBC network in September 2003 but was pulled after just four episodes of the intended run of ten, when it failed to attract a sufficiently large audience in a highly competitive marketplace. A US version of Hat Trick's *The Kumars at No. 42*, retooled with a Mexican family *The Ortegas*, was axed by the Fox network in September 2003 soon after launch. In 2004 hopes rest on a successful US adaptation of the BBC's spoof docusoap *The Office* (now subtitled *An American Workplace*) for Fox – initial reaction to its pilot episode is rumoured to have been dreadful but nonetheless Fox is committed to making a run of six. The reputation of this series was sealed at the start of 2004, when the British original, aired in the States by BBC America, received two Golden Globes, including one for best comedy series.

Unscripted factual, entertainment and reality formats have been much more successful in North America, as evidenced by Granada USA, which shifted the focus of its US production operation away from scripted to unscripted formats in 2003. Notable successes have been achieved both on network television and on cable, building on earlier

Mentorn Scotland's reality life-swap show *Take My Mother-In-Law* aired on ITV1 last year but the format was sold to Germany's RTL2 in 2004.

The most effective operators are not just selling formats but are also marketing their technical expertise and know-how in making complex shows.

British successes including *Who Wants to Be a Millionaire?* (Celador for ABC) and *The Weakest Link* (BBC Worldwide for NBC). The list of independent players with serious track records is not long but includes Mentorn (The Television Corporation), RDF Media, Fremantle, Lion Television, Tiger Aspect, Hat Trick and Wall to Wall. All have sought to maximise revenues through involvement in the US production of their formats. The most effective operators are not just selling formats but are also marketing their technical expertise and know-how in making complex shows.

For example, in August 2003 Granada secured a deal with cable channel A&E to make a US version of its docusoap *Airline* (10 x 30), on top of a six part commission to produce the reality-game format *American Princess* for the NBC network. In October it secured a pilot with Fox for the light entertainment vehicle, *Saturday Night Takeaway*. Cable channel, TLC, took a further forty episodes of the BBC format *What not to Wear* in August 2003. In 2003 RDF Media secured format production deals for *My Best Friend's Wedding* with cable channel, Lifetime Television, and with the ABC network for *Wife Swap*, following a successful second airing of *Faking It* on TLC. However, *Banzai*, RDF's irreverent Japanese game show format struggled on Fox. In March 2004 Talkback's *How Clean Is Your House?* was acquired by Lifetime Television, to be produced by Talkback parent, Fremantle Media. In September 2003 Lion Television secured a second run on PBS (Public Broadcasting System) for *The History Detectives*, but its gay-themed format for Fox, *Playing it Straight*, where a woman seeks to identify a straight suitor, was pulled from the schedules in April 2004 shortly after launch. Following the success of its summer 2003 reality hit *Paradise Hotel* on Fox, Mentorn launched *Forever Eden* in March 2004, a $20 million 'never-ending reality show', a living soap where characters compete to remain in a luxurious Jamaican resort. After poor initial ratings it lost its place in the schedule to baseball in April. Fox bosses insisted the series will return ... sometime.

Factual entertainment formats have also made a mark in other territories. RDF Media sold its *Wife Swap* format to Germany (RTL), Australia (Nine), Denmark (TV3), the Netherlands (RTL4) and France (M6). Granada sold and produced *I'm a Celebrity...Get Me Out of Here* for Germany's RTL. This launched in January 2004 securing record audiences in the 14-49 demographic. Talkback's *How Clean is Your House* format was sold in October 2003 to Fremantle's German subsidiary UFA Entertainment for RTL 2 as well as to Dutch commercial channel, RTL 4. The TV Corporation sold the format of *Take My Mother-in-Law* to Germany's RTL 2 in January 2004. Italian commercial channel Canale 5 agreed to do a local pilot of Hat Trick's *The Kumars at Number 42* in February 2004, and Dutch public broadcaster, Ned 3/NPS decided to make a second series based on the same format.

Further afield, Lion Television linked up with Hong Kong based Phoenix Satellite Television in November 2003 to produce historical and cultural programmes for the Chinese market as well as programming about China for the rest of the world. In March 2004 Chorion entered a deal with the Beijing-based Foreign Language Teaching and Research Press (FLTRP) to negotiate the sale of its CGI animated series *Make Way for Noddy*_to Chinese television for use as a basic learning and language skills aid.

Britain remains a substantial exporter of television programmes and formats but the declining share of revenues from sales of finished programmes underlines the growing importance of licensing, formats, video and co-production for a small number of British properties.

*Jeanette Steemers is Principal Lecturer in the School of Media and Cultural Production at De Montfort University in Leicester. Her publications include **Selling Television: British Television in the Global Marketplace** (BFI: 2004), **The European Television Industries** (Co-Author, BFI: 2005) and **Changing Channels: The Prospects for Television in a Digital World** (University of Luton Press: 1998, Editor). She is also co-editor of **Convergence: The Journal of Research into New Media Technologies**.*

Technology on Trial

Paul McDonald

Digital Television Platforms

Since BSkyB went all-digital back in 1998, the way has seemed clear for DST to continue its domination of the pay television sector. Cable operators NTL and Telewest have carried major debt burdens while undertaking their own moves towards attracting subscribers for digital packages. After Granada and Carlton's ITV Digital (formally ONdigital) venture folded in April 2002, after attracting only 1.2 million subscribers, broadcasters reasonably believed there could be no short or long term future for DTT in Britain.

By early 2003, however, rumours of DTT's demise appeared exaggerated, as Freeview rapidly attracted new users. A joint venture between the BBC, BSkyB and transmission operator Crown Castle International, Freeview was launched on 30 October 2002, available through either a separate digital receiver box or integrated digital television (IDTV) plugged into a conventional TV aerial. Freeview was also accessible to viewers who'd retained the old ITV Digital decoders.

In its first few months, it became clear Freeview was attracting a larger base of customers than ITV's DTT venture. Within the first four months, an estimated 500,000 receivers were sold, over 30,000 units per week. In comparison, during its first four months, ONdigital was selling 7,000 units per week and was only shifting 11,000 units per week at the height of sales. When those Freeview units were combined with the remaining owners of the ITV boxes, by the end of February 2003 it was estimated Freeview was reaching 1.4m homes, already surpassing the total ever take-up of ITV Digital. After attracting 1m customers by June 2003, Freeview became the fastest adopted item of consumer electronics technology in British history and on its first anniversary was believed to have 2.1 million customers. By April 2004, Freeview was in 3.5 million homes, carrying twenty-five news, entertainment, documentary, kids, music and shopping television channels, plus interactive and text services, and twenty-one radio stations. All the major high street electronics retailers were selling boxes from various manufacturers, with prices starting at around £59.99.

Freeview's adoption is having a significant impact on the multichannel sector and is raising many questions about the digital future. Freeview has attracted many 'digital virgins' previously reluctant to subscribe to any of the pay digital services already available. This suggests that digital television has discovered an untapped market for viewers wanting the greater choice of multichannel delivery but unprepared to pay for it. Freeview's free service has departed from the pay DTT model of ITV Digital, which aimed to compete directly with BSkyB and the cable providers. Cabot Communication forecast that by 2005, Freeview users will exceed satellite subscribers, a situation which may raise questions over BSkyB's future commitment in the venture.

Freeview is undoubtedly now a major plank in government plans for analogue switch-off. Back in September 1999, then media secretary Chris Smith announced that ninety-five per cent digital take-up was regarded as the threshold that would justify analogue switch-off, with 2006-10 marked as the target window by which to achieve this. Since then, all digital platforms have failed to demonstrate the levels of growth that would fulfil such predications. The government's 'digital tsar', Barry Cox, deputy chairman of Channel 4 and chairman of the Digital Television Stakeholders Group, has in the past stated that he regards 2014 to be a more realistic target. If the digital revolution therefore seemed to be waning, the rapid expansion of Freeview's installed base of users may not only signal a revisitalising of the DTT platform but also of the whole DTV enterprise.

INDUSTRY IN FOCUS

The BBC used these cuddly puppet monkeys to promote the Freeview digital TV service. Good grief - don't they remember what happened the last time someone tried that?

Top Up TV offered a mini-subscription package on a 'free' platform

As the price of DTT receivers falls, then at least in the near future, Freeview is likely to provide the model for competitors to imitate, and in the summer BSkyB finally announced their 'Freesat' package (see pages 76-77) by way of competition. Top Up TV, a new venture managed by former Sky executives and backed by US venture capital company Access Industries, was launched 31 March 2004 as a premium package costing £7.99pcm for ten channels including E4, Discovery, UKTV Gold, Cartoon Network and TCM. Initially available only to customers with Freeview receivers bearing a smartcard facility, i.e. the old ITV Digital boxes, manufacturer Thomson later developed new slot boxes supporting the service. The BBC raised concerns that a pay service on the free DTT platform could confuse customers, hampering the take-up of Freeview. Top Up were later rapped by Ofcom for misleading advertising; their ads claimed to offer a ten-channel package but some services were only available for parts of the day. Potentially, Top Up, Freesat or any similar venture will raise questions in the future over whether Freeview is really free.

In February 2004, the BBC, ITV, NTL and the Digital Stakeholders Group lobbied government to fix a date for switch-off in order to establish a timetable for technical work, with 2007 proposed as a preferred date. Plans for implementing the change included staggering the closure of analogue signals by separate channels, starting with BBC 2 and followed by BBC 1 then Channel 4 and ITV. The DCMS stated they refused to be swayed by industry pressure on the matter. Ofcom added to the debate in April with the publication of its report *Driving Digital Switchover*. In the report, Ofcom made twenty-three recommendations to government, including reiterating the call for a definite timetable for switch-off, the need for a public information campaign, the need for a free digital satellite service and the possible establishment of an independent body, 'SwitchCo', to oversee the changes.

Other Ways of Viewing

Alongside digital delivery, the digital video recorder or Personal Video Recorder (PVR) continues to raise questions about the future of television viewing. When TiVO first introduced PVRs to the UK in October 2000, they promised viewers the opportunity to create *a la carte* television through the capability for pre-programming the recorder's hard drive to record shows tailored to personalised tastes, a facility promoted as allowing the viewer to create his or her own personal television channel.

Sky+ followed in 2001, with an integrated PVR and satellite receiver unit, promoted with the line 'Create Your Own Channel'. However, after attracting just 35,000 subscribers in three years, TiVO pulled out of the UK in January 2003 to concentrate on its North American market, where the majority of the global total of 510,000 PVR users is located. At that time, Sky+ had only 38,000 subscribers – by late 2003, 105,000 boxes had been sold. Sales were dramatically boosted after a £20 million television marketing campaign, with Sky reporting subscriptions exceeding 250,000 by early 2004.

The Personal Video Recorder (PVR) continues to raise questions about the future of television viewing.

A BBC research trial of homes in Hull equipped with video-on-demand (VoD) and PVRs revealed PVR users were watching more television but time-shifting 70 per cent of their viewing and choosing to skip through shows and commercial breaks. Sky+ research also confirmed an increase in viewing from twenty-three to twenty-seven hours per week, together with a multiplying of the number of channels watched, but with 60 per cent of programmes still watched live and 70 per cent of adverts fast-forwarded. While the PVR is a technology clearly intended to pass choice on to the consumer, it has raised industry concerns. PVRs have intensified the belief among advertisers that alternative methods of promotion, such as product placement and sponsored programmes or break bumpers, are required to serve their clients' interests. Fast forwarding is also seen to dislodge linearity of viewing, with BBC research showing viewers watching just the first few set-up minutes of *Changing Rooms* before forwarding onto the final make-over revelation, while Celador have noted viewers passing over the first few easy questions on *Who Wants to Be a Millionaire?*. Other implications include the loss of channel identity or recognition as viewers make choices at programme level only, together with the possibility that broadcasters may look towards producing more programming where the full impact is conditional on the live experience. A major anxiety is that the vast majority of medium- and low-rating programming filling the schedules will be decimated as viewers select only the most popular shows to record and watch later. If so, the PVR may result in viewers having the capability to choose but only from a reduced number of options.

Broadcasters are also looking to partnerships with mobile phone operators towards diversifying platforms for their content, with text messaging or voting also providing new revenue opportunities. For the second series of *Pop Idol* in August 2003, Fremantle Media (co-owner of the format with 19TV) announced a partnership with O2 that launched a range of mobile services, including text voting, picture messaging, news alerts and downloads. With text voting and messaging emerging as the most popular modes of interaction, game or reality shows as the main categories for mobile spin-offs.

The industry keenly anticipates 2.5G and 3G networks to deliver mobile video. During September 2003, MTV Networks Europe announced a deal with the 3 network for mobile packages of music news, live performances and video clips from shows like *Jackass* and *Dirty Sanchez*. By March 2004, 3 had launched 'Today on 3' as the first live video mobile news and entertainment channel in the UK, with clips from Sky Sports, ITN and MTV.

Broadband is also attracting interest as a new channel for content. In February 2004, Discovery Networks International launched a dedicated premium pay-per-view or subscription service with two channels: Discovery Select carries science, history and nature programming, while Discovery Home & Leisure presents lifestyle programming. The BBC meanwhile announced plans for the broadband relay of the Glastonbury music festival and Athens Olympics during summer 2004 (see right). Both would act as an acid test of how far off the imagined idyll of convergence really is.

Paul McDonald is Director of the Centre for Research in Film and Audiovisual Cultures at the University of Surrey Roehampton.

BBC Broadband

The BBC's eagerly-awaited Glastonbury 'broadband' coverage was a nice add-on, very much in line with the BBC's PSB aims of providing access to the arts and culture, but ultimately showed that broadcasters are still far short of the envisaged 'future' of video-on-demand.

Glastonbury broadband offered a slightly improved, faster bitrate version of the services available to dial up browsers. UK Music fans could access the full sets (each about an hour or so long) of four of the bands performing each day including Franz Ferdinand, Belle and Sebastian and Goldfrapp (i.e. four bands per day over the three days of the festival making a total of twelve sets). Sets were streamed live while the acts were onstage and after the fact.

What broadband viewers got was a tiny postage stamp screen of low frame rate 'action' and sub-MP3 sound, marginally better and with fewer stops and starts than the regular 56K streams. When people talk of convergence and 'TV via broadband' they usually dream of MPEG files that can be downloaded, burned to VCD or DVD and then viewed at or near PAL picture quality, or at least viewed full screen on the average monitor. Such dreamers would be disappointed with the Glastonbury service! Such a system does presently exist of course but only via bootleg file sharing servers, usually trading in new blockbuster movies and cult US TV shows.

It is expected that August's Olympic broadband services from the BBC will be along similar lines to those available at Glastonbury.

The next generation of service will come via the BBC's imminent interactive media player (iMP), testing August 2004, which will allow users to view programmes up to a week after broadcast. A laudable idea but far short, one suspects, of watching the real thing. **AMcG**

News & Current Affairs
Steve Bryant

Newsgathering and journalism itself was the focus of the biggest news story of the year: the Hutton Enquiry into the suicide of government weapons expert Dr David Kelly, following his naming as the source for a contested BBC radio story about the reasons for going to war with Iraq. Throughout the process of evidence gathering (unfortunately not televised, much to the disappointment of the twenty-four-hour news channels), the debate on BBC newsgathering procedures and the role of the Board of Governors was the most prominent aspect. Although the Report was widely leaked in advance, the announcement of its findings, with virtually all the blame laid at the BBC's door, still came as a major shock to the broadcasting community.

The BBC's own coverage of the enquiry and the report was exemplary throughout. Reporters could occasionally be seen restraining themselves from calling the BBC 'we' or 'us', much as they had

to become apparent after Dyke's successor, Mark Thompson, took up his job, at about the same time as the Corporation's internal report on the journalistic and editorial lessons of Hutton, carried out by Ron Neil at the request of acting DG Mark Byford, was delivered. Amongst the innovations announced by the BBC in its wake was a 'journalism academy', in which new BBC News staff could learn from the experience of old hands like John Simpson, and an improved complaints system, to manifest itself through the questioning of news executives on a weekly access programme on BBC News 24. Byford himself was appointed by Thompson to head the BBC's new Journalism Board.

The aftermath of the Iraq War in general also continued to provide the main news stories throughout the year, with the maltreatment of Iraqi prisoners a particularly prominent running story. Coverage of the war and its aftermath

ITV's *Lunchtime News* launched a dynamic new-look 'News Wall', perhaps slightly reminiscent of *The Day Today*?

difficulty with using the term 'the British' during the Falkands War, but, generally, the impression of impartiality was complete. A *Panorama* special, transmitted just before the findings were made public, was especially critical of the Corporation. The mood changed after the publication of the Report, though, and particularly after the resignation of Greg Dyke as Director General and the formal apology issued by the BBC. Prominence was then given to those who declared the Report excessively one-sided and the Government did not hurry to complain. The resignation of Alistair Campbell as the Prime Minister's press secretary at the beginning of the enquiry only began to deliver a less strained relationship between government and broadcasters after the initial Hutton fuss had died down, though.

For the BBC, the long-term consequences began

dominated the awards ceremonies of early 2005 and the high death toll of those sent to cover it provided a sobering theme. With important developments in Europe and an American Presidential election year also commanding attention, this meant that the foreign agenda was more to the fore than usual, even on ITV. BBC 4 News continued to set the standard for foreign reporting, though, with Hilary Andersson's reports particularly prominent.

The most eye-catching development in news presentation was the almost universal trend towards making newscasters stand up. Both the BBC *Six o'Clock News* and *Channel 4 News* went down this path, usually with one presenter seated handing over to another on their feet, but the most startling manifestation of the trend was the makeover of the lunchtime ITN bulletin on ITV (part of a general new look for ITV's bulletins and the ITV News Channel), with a sloping set and low angled shots giving the standing presenter a multitude of opportunities to strike authoritative poses. The leggy Katie Derham proved particularly adept in this regard. Sir Trevor McDonald usually remained firmly seated for the late evening bulletin, though.

The piece of investigative journalism which caused the biggest stir and gained the greatest plaudits was *The Secret Policeman*, transmitted on BBC 1 in October 2003, in which reporter Mark Daly went undercover as a police recruit and used secret filming to expose disturbing levels of racism amongst his fellow trainees. The result was a public outcry, an early end to several careers in the police and a hatful of awards for the programme.

While *Tonight with Trevor McDonald* (ITV) continued to lead the pack on the coverage of domestic stories, BBC 1's *The Real Story with Fiona Bruce* proved a worthy rival in the presenter's-name-in-the-title stakes. The report on cot death was particularly noteworthy. The regular coverage of domestic politics outside news bulletins and *Newsnight* was left almost entirely to the BBC's *The Daily Politics*, with Andrew Neil. That other BBC attempt to make political coverage more appealing to an increasingly apathetic audience, the Sunday lunchtime *The Politics Show* continued to make little impact. The most insightful discussions on political matters are now mostly confined to the twenty-four-hour news channels.

Polemic was provided by John Pilger's annual special on ITV, *Breaking the Silence: Truth and Lies in the War on Terror*, which looked at the background to American policy in Afghanistan and

The BBC's own coverage of the Hutton enquiry and the report was exemplary throughout. Reporters could occasionally be seen restraining themselves from calling the BBC 'we' or 'us' but, generally, the impression of impartiality was complete

Iraq. Pilger's pieces are passionately argued and well researched, but seem increasingly like a sop to the kind of committed journalism which is now confined mainly to broadsheet newspapers.

Sky News continued to go from strength to strength, winning the News Channel of the Year Award at the Royal Television Society Journalism awards. The channel was particularly adept at devising ways of covering judicial proceedings through a combination of actors and journalists and this proved its value by allowing fast and convincing coverage of the evidence to the Hutton Enquiry. Apart from its editorial successes, in March 2004 it succeeded in wresting the contract to supply the main news bulletins to Five from ITN, although Kirsty Young, firmly established as Five's star face, will continue to present. As Sky's morning *Sunrise* bulletin was already a fixture of the Five schedule, this was no real surprise, though the exposure that Sky News will now receive on a terrestrial platform can be considered a highly significant development.

PROGRAMMING

The photogenic Fiona Bruce is one of the faces of BBC News, also fronting her own investigative reports series

Political Events

WMD, Kelly and the Hutton Inquiry

Throughout 2003-4, the political story dominating the UK's television news coverage concerned the dispute between the BBC and the government about the motivations for entering the War in Iraq. The Blair government's former Director of Communication Alastair Campbell launched a blistering attack on the BBC about those allegations, which arose from its news reports suggesting the government had 'sexed up' two dossiers concerning the Iraqi's 'Weapons of Mass Destruction' (WMD).

This dispute was to have tragic consequences as it led to the suicide of a Ministry of Defence (MoD) scientist Dr David Kelly, who had leaked information to the BBC's Defence correspondent Andrew Gilligan. Gilligan had reported on Radio Four's Today Programme on 29 May 2003 during the 6.07 a.m. broadcast that government spin-doctors had 'sexed up' two controversial dossiers outlining Saddam Hussein's capability to employ WMDs. They were accused of inserting a claim that Iraq could deploy WMDs in forty-five minutes into the first dossier, published in September 2002.

Although the story had initiated on radio, Gilligan's position was supplemented by two more circumspect television reports made by the *Ten o'Clock News'* Gavin Hewitt and by *Newsnight's* Science Editor Susan Watts, who had also interviewed Kelly. At the centre of the public debate

credible, denied he had attempted to exaggerate the forty-five minute claim and had abided by the Joint Intelligence Committee (JIC) concerning Saddam's military capacity.

Then Campbell spun the focus away from his actions to the veracity of the BBC's reporting. He contended the BBC had pursued a campaign to undermine the government because it was critical of Blair's stance against Iraq. Thus, he argued the corporation's News and Current Affairs departments had decided to mislead the public by rubbishing the government's case for going to war. On completing his cross-examination, he called on the BBC to apologise for its coverage.

In response, the BBC's Head of News and Current Affairs Richard Sambrook wrote a detailed letter to Campbell's refuting his charges of bias and unreliable reporting. The dispute escalated when an unannounced Campbell angrily appeared on *Channel 4 News* on 27 June 2003 accusing Sambrook of writing a letter full of 'weasel words'. He restated that the BBC must admit it had made a mistake and should issue an apology.

Subsequently, the BBC Board of Governors, chaired by Gavyn Davies, met with Director-General Greg Dyke to discuss whether the BBC should provide an apology. They decided to support Sambrook by stating that proper journalistic practices had been employed and commenting that Gilligan's anonymous source was reliable. For reasons of confidentiality, the BBC refused to name

Key figures who took to the stand as events broke; Greg Dyke, Acting Chairman Lord Ryder and the new Acting DG Mark Byford

stood the House of Commons' Foreign Affairs Select Committee, which was chaired by Labour MP Donald Anderson. In a surprising turn of events, Campbell agreed to appear in front of the committee and the televised proceedings, stating he wanted to set the record straight about his role in 'sexing up' the government's claims concerning WMDs. He was examined on 25 June 2003 and apologised for the errors within the second dossier. However, he contended the first dossier remained

the source and Dyke asked Campbell 'to bury the hatchet' and let both sides 'agree to disagree'. However, the MoD began, with the apparent backing of Downing Street, an investigation to discover who had been responsible for the leak. On 8 July 2003, it announced an official had come forward to admit to his superiors that he had met Gilligan on 22 May 2003 at the Charing Cross Hotel. Instead of being the senior intelligence official Gilligan claimed, the source was named as

MoD weapons' expert Dr. David Kelly who was summoned to give evidence to the Foreign Affairs Select Committee on 15 July 2003. In this session, he denied he had been Gilligan's main source and, while the MPs agreed with his version of events, the Labour MP Andrew MacKinlay tormented him about being a 'fall guy'.

Moreover, Kelly fitted the description given by the MoD in its briefings to the press and by Gilligan in a follow-up Mail on Sunday article explicitly naming Campbell as being responsible for inserting the forty-five minute claim. In the meantime, Gilligan's confidence over whether the government's spin doctors had 'sexed up' the first dossier had waned at a private Foreign Affairs Select Committee session. He was recalled to face the MPs for a further grilling about his source behind close doors on 16 July 2003. At the very moment of Gilligan's cross-examination, Kelly left his Oxfordshire home and was reported to have gone missing. His body was discovered on 18 July 2003 and he had apparently committed suicide by slashing his wrists. Alternatively, his death was seen as his final admission of being Gilligan's source or as that a crown official he had feared the consequences of his public exposure.

The BBC announced that Kelly had been Gilligan's main source on 19 July 2003. The corporation's journalistic practices, the reliability of its reporting and the governors' unconditional support of Gilligan were criticised in a number of quarters, including Peter Mandelson in a series of television and radio interviews. It was reported that Dyke and Davies could have named the source, perhaps stopping Kelly's suicide, in a peace

Lord Hutton's report reflected the narrowness of his brief. He damned the BBC's reporting and editorial strategies, stated Andrew Gilligan's notes were unreliable and exaggerated and he was also highly critical of the BBC Governors and Dyke's failure as Editor-in-Chief.

BBC's reporting practices and for the heads of Dyke and Davies. From governmental opponents, most especially the Associated Newspapers group, accusations were made over the role of MoD and Defence Secretary Geoff Hoon in 'outing' Kelly. Elsewhere, Campbell and Downing Street's macho 'attack-dog culture' was criticised, and questions were raised about his role in the crisis.

A judicial inquiry headed by former Law lord Lord Hutton began its investigation on 1 August 2003 into the forms of government spinning and those BBC journalistic practices which were cited as being causal to Kelly's death. The Hutton inquiry took four months to investigate the events and unearthed volumes of information concerning governmental intervention, the close relationship between Campbell and John Scarlett, chair of the JIC, and a vast range of detail on the Gilligan report and the BBC's editorial processes. When his report was issued in 28 January 2004, it, however,

PROGRAMMING

Spontaneous protests at TV centre; Dyke arrives to say his goodbyes; BBC journo Nick Higham pushes his way through the crowd

offering made by the government. Further, Gilligan's credibility diminished as the now deceased Kelly had disputed the reporter's version of events. Moreover, as Kelly had not been such a senior official, Gilligan was accused of 'sexing up' the information he had received from Kelly, most especially with regard to his assertion concerning Campbell's insertion of the forty-five minute claim.

From New Labourites and the Murdoch press, calls were extended for an investigation of the

reflected the narrowness of his brief. Hutton damned the BBC's reporting and editorial strategies, most especially stating that Gilligan's notes of his meeting with Kelly were unreliable and he had exaggerated the story on the initial 6.07 broadcast. He also was highly critical of the BBC Board of Governors and Dyke's failure as the Editor-in-Chief to check the veracity of the story. Conversely, he exonerated the government and Campbell so completely, that many public opinion polls reflected the belief that the report had been a 'whitewash.'

In his ensuing press conference and within televised interviews, Campbell called for the heads of Davies and Dyke and in these extraordinary circumstances both the Chairman and Director-General were forced to resign. Dyke's apparent sacking on 29 January 2004 by an enfeebled Board of Governors led by acting chair Lord Ryder and the BBC's unreserved apology to the government was seen to have undermined the corporation's political independence. Ironically, the most commercial of DGs, who had been accused of 'dumbing down' televised news, became a martyr because of his decision to protect the BBC's editorial autonomy. Dyke's popularity with his workforce and the News and Current Affairs Departments was evident in an immediate series of demonstrations and walkouts by the BBC staff. Subsequently, Dyke made it clear that he did not want to resign and was critical of what he saw as a politically compliant Board of Governors.

In the aftermath, the Deputy DG Mark Byford was promoted to Acting DG. His interregnum has been controversial and his investigation into the credence of the BBC's reporting strategies has undermined his internal position with his senior managers. Further, it was announced on 2 April 2004, that former the Head of BBC programming and Chief Executive of Channel 4, Michael Grade, had been appointed as the BBC's new Chairman. Grade's antipathy to Byford, whose main ally is Grade's old enemy and former DG Lord Birt, was a poorly kept secret – on 21 May, just four days after Grade took up his Chairman's post, he appointed Mark Thompson as his deputy.

Promises of the creation of a BBC journalism academy of excellence and, finally, on 22 July the move sideways of BBC Director of News Richard Sambrook to a new position in the World Service and Global News division, to be replaced by Radio Four Controller Helen Boaden, seem to mark the end of the affair as far as the BBC is concerned.

Overall, this political controversy, while not being entirely unique in terms of the history of governmental relations with the BBC, has had major consequences for the corporation's reporting strategies, its political independence and the role of the Board of Governors. Finally, it may have a significant impact upon the future of the corporation as it enters into negotiations for Charter Renewal.

Mark Wheeler is Lecturer in Politics at London Metropolitan University

Iraq in the News
Andrew Hoskins

The media event that was the '2003 Iraq War' still appears without end, as with the conflict itself. The continuing dominance of war news over the past year is reflected in how quickly the networks can engage their 'visioning machines' (to borrow from Paul Virilio) to deliver instant virtual views of the sporadic attacks across Iraq or the siege of Falluja in April. Sky News regularly employs 'Defence Expert' Francis Tusa, with their 'SkyStrater' enabling him to effortlessly draw over maps of the region like a virtual General.

Western television, which had done much to cultivate the myth of Saddam Hussein and relentlessly demonized him since the late 1980s, provided viewers with the spectacle of the gloating announcement of his capture from Paul Bremer: 'Ladies and gentlemen, we got him'. BBC 1, ITV1 and all the news networks carried this conference live on the 15 December. Preceding this, television had continued to recycle the stock images of the former Iraqi President (some dating back to 1990) which made the disjuncture of the stills of a broken man who had emerged from a hole in the ground, all the greater.

This point was not lost on the Americans, who displayed two stills of Saddam on screens at their press conference. One showed Saddam in his olive-green uniform and beret and was labelled 'HISTORICAL', the other depicted him in white tee-shirt and jacket and minus his beard taken after his 'medical examination' and was labelled 'CURRENT'. These simplistic representations of 'before' and 'after' played to a domestic audience accustomed to a diet of dichotomies when it comes to televising war. However, the problem with suddenly humanising Saddam is that this undermined the very image-driven narrative used to gather support for the final military campaign against him. Change the image, change the story.

The sustained gravitas of the news from Iraq has seemed at odds with the trend towards tabloid presentation, a dumbing down of style. On screen, brevity and movement have become the predominate framing devices as television news has merged the tabloid front page headline and by-line, with a busy computer desktop. This year, BBC News 24's banners have grown larger and brighter as they have adopted the tabloid-top red of Sky News and on occasion the rolling text along the bottom of the screen. The huge headline banner, the breaking news icon, the five- or six-word byline summary reduce the news to instant fragments. It is no wonder that Neil Postman's *Amusing Ourselves to Death* (1987), a critique of the disconnected and entertainment-driven nature of television news, is back in print.

Despite the news flow from Iraq, it has not been sufficient to slow the relentless increase in competition for news viewers. The pursuit of audience share over the course of the evening led ITV to allow its former flagship *News at Ten* to roam its schedule rather than to anchor it. On 2 February, the 'News at When?' taunts finally ended with the new weekday 'fixed' slot of the ITV News at 10.30 p.m. This day also marked another phase in the trend towards bigger, brighter, and briefer news. The 're-launch' of both of the ITV evening bulletins introduced viewers to a greater cinematic take on events, even outdoing Sky News' 'video wall', and making the BBC's big screen look positively puny. Presenters are dwarfed against a blue background that is filled with moving images and graphics. The absence of most of the 'newsroom' environment clutter that fills News 24 and Sky's sets produced a purer cinematic effect – image is everything.

Other attempts to shore-up audience share over the year include the more frequent shift of the continuity announcer into programmes, rather than appearing between them. Chris Tarrant is probably the most visible of these as he attempts to persuade the *Who Wants To Be A Millionaire?* audience to stick around for the news, or maybe switch over to ITV2. The repeats of *Inspector Morse* running on ITV, for example, have had their end credits truncated and windowed to allow us to hear a preview of the latest atrocity story from Baghdad that follows.

The Sunday BBC1 Evening News has often linked directly into *Panorama*, a programme also diminished by its schedule moves. However, the former flagship of BBC current affairs underwent something of a renaissance over the past year, peaking with its pre-emption of the Hutton Report. Broadcast on 21 January, its use of dramatised reconstructions to illustrate the circumstances surrounding the death of Dr David Kelly, was a real coup for the Corporation. Unfortunately, it was soon forgotten in its own chaotic response to the real Hutton Report.

The BBC began by treating 28 January, the day of the Hutton statement, almost like a State occasion with Huw Edwards anchoring a simulcast News Special on BBC 1 and News 24. The sense of occasion at the BBC, however, soon unwound, as the day wore on. Nick Higham, the BBC's Media Correspondent had the unenviable job of holding a mirror up to the chaos that ensued, wandering amongst his seemingly hyperreal colleagues at Broadcasting House, very much like a host of a bad reality TV game show. He admitted that the BBC reports were contradicting themselves on a moment-to-moment basis, yet the 'self-flagellation', to cite Martin Bell, went on.

The BBC began by treating 28 January, the day of the Hutton statement, almost like a State occasion with Huw Edwards anchoring a simulcast News Special on BBC 1 and News 24.

That evening's *Newsnight* hoisted the white flag further both in contrast and in competition to Radio Four's Today programme, from where the Iraqi dossier 'sexed up' allegations had been launched. Jeremy Paxman opened the programme standing up as though to signify the enormity of events and was strangely resigned in an interview with a vindicated Alistair Campbell (even holding up his hands at one point) and admitted that the Corporation had 'spent the afternoon running around like headless chickens without a head'.

Thursday witnessed the new Acting Chair of the Board of Governors live 'unreserved' apology, and backlash, and the populist circus that enveloped the departure of Greg Dyke. Friday's *Newsnight* carried a remarkable ten minute interview of new Acting DG Mark Byford gritting his teeth as Gavin Estler managed to hit his target both ways in that firstly, getting an apology out of the BBC was like pulling teeth, and, secondly, when it did arrive it was widely perceived as grovelling and damaging. Two days later a new Channel 4 satirical series of *Bremner, Bird and Fortune* was launched with a spoof of Lord Ryder involving an imitation of a BBC announcer apologising for everyone and everything, and a white towel. For the BBC, at least, it was a year to forget.

*Andrew Hoskins is Senior Lecturer in Media and Communication at Swansea University and the author of **Televising War: From Vietnam to Iraq** (Continuum, 2004).*

PROGRAMMING

Arts

Amy Sargeant

2003-4 was, as ever, shaped by a calendar of events and awards ceremonies. While ITV covered *The Brit Awards* and *The National Television Awards*, the BBC transmitted the *37th Country Music Awards* and the BAFTAs. The announcement of the Booker Prize (termed 'posh bingo' by former contender Julian Barnes) was presented by *Newsnight*'s Kirsty Wark on BBC 2 and the BBC-backed Samuel Johnson Prize (for non-fiction) was carried by Channel 4. The Turner Prize was carried by Channel 4 alongside the documentary *Twenty Years of the Turner Prize* (including interviews with artists and critics), both fronted by Matthew Collings (who, in turn, used the occasion as an opportunity to promote his Channel 4 series, *Matt's Old Masters*).

Referring to the proliferation of 'clip shows' (a cheap format pioneered by Channel 4 – one of which in July posed the question *Who Killed Saturday Night TV?* and debated the demise of

Waldemar Januszczak hosted
Every Picture Tells a Story for Five

Saturday-night viewing) *The Observer* claimed: 'It's Official. British Television has gone list mad,' and announced BBC 2's *Britain's Best Sitcom*. Audience participation (as in 2002's *Great Britons*) was enlisted in the selection of the winner of *Restoration* (the Victoria Baths, Manchester) and *The Big Read* (which occupied no less than thirteen weeks of the BBC's Autumn schedule), the finale presented by a literary panel including Booker chair Jonathan Carey and the ubiquitous Lisa Jardine. Not surprisingly (a result encouraged by the 'dramatisations' constructed for the series itself) the winner was J.R.R. Tolkien's recently filmed *The Lord of the Rings*. However, the series did promote the sale of the books short-listed. Further intervention in Brit Lit has been seen in *End of Story* (a BBC 3 and BBC Talent initiative, launched on BBC 2).

Other annual and seasonal offerings included coverage of Glyndebourne and the Last Night of the Proms (simultaneously on radio and television). BBC terrestrial channels carried broadcasts from Glastonbury and Reading and BBC 4 covered the London Jazz Festival. *The Nutcracker*, choreographed by Matthew Bourne (a regular Christmas treat), more jumps than jetees, was introduced by Dawn French (recalling a previous French and Saunders appearance with prima ballerina Darcy Bussell) and Christmas 2003 also witnessed a more staid and traditional Russian production of *Swan Lake*.

The BBC (as competitors have frequently noted) found itself in an advantageous position with regard to cross-channel scheduling and promotion. A BBC 4 documentary about the late, great alto Kathleen Ferrier was accompanied by readings on Radio Four from her diaries; the second series of *Restoration* is being advertised on Radio Four's *The Archers*. Daisy Goodwin introduced *Essential Poems for Britain* (on BBC 2) while poet Simon Armitage (with former acclaimed commissions from BBC Radio and television) contributed to Channel 4's uncelebrated *Pornography: the Musical*. The BBC 'Summer of Opera' included radio items, a documentary on Benjamin Britten and a new production for television of *The Turn of the Screw*. David Hare's stageplay *The Permanent Way* transferred to both radio and television, as did John Cage's *4' 33" for large orchestra*, transmitted from the Barbican (a novel rendition of the work, of which the composer could but approve). BBC 4's *Summer in the Sixties* season included documentaries on the brilliant but doomed Vivian Stanshall ('a national treasure', commented Neil Innes, alongside other new interviews and archival footage of the Bonzo Dog Doodah Band's television appearances), Leonard Cohen and Bob Dylan and *I Hate the '60s* (a reference to previous years' clip shows). Meanwhile, classic films transmitted by BBC's terrestrial channels provided a broader context. Melvyn Bragg's radio series *The Use of English* transferred to Channel 4 and *The Seven Ages of Britain* was re-presented for Channel 4 by archaeologist Bettany Hughes. Bragg's ITV *South Bank Show* plugged Germaine Greer's book, *The Boy*.

In February 2004, the BBC announced an £8 million line-up of topical arts programming in prime time (equating to fifty hours' output over eighteen months) to combat criticisms that it had neglected high culture; *The Big Read*, *Restoration* and *Rolf on Art* were considered too low-brow. There were also objections to the 'shunting' of drama and arts from BBC 2 to BBC 4 ('Everyone Needs a Place to Think ...', but apparently not a place we could all share). Tessa Jowell complained at the preponderance of make-over shows while architects objected to *Restoration*'s support for conservation over new building. Channel 4's *Grand Designs*, meanwhile, often showed the public doing without architects altogether (for better or worse).

But there were still exemplary one-off documentaries, including BBC 1's *Wren: The Man Who Built Britain* and BBC 2's dramadocs *The Genius of Mozart* and *Eroica* (devoted to Beethoven's Ninth Symphony). The long-running *Arena* series produced biographies of Harold Pinter and Alec Guinness; Channel 4 provided *Brits go to Hollywood* (a two-parter concerning the careers of David Niven and Hugh Grant) and *J-Lo: Behind the Behind*. The *South Bank Show* carried a profile of The Dance Theatre of Harlem and *Dice Life*, on Channel 4, was an imaginative collaboration between Mick Jones, formerly of The Clash, cult author Luke Rhinehart and choreography. Dance has also been well-served by 'insiders' the Ballet Boyz (for Channel 4) and Deborah Bull (for BBC 2 – in a considered combination of science and art). Five offered *Great Artists with Tim Marlow* and the *Artsworld* series (including the entertaining spoof, 'Original Schtick'), BBC 2 *The Private Life of a Masterpiece* and the welcome return of Robert Hughes with *The New Shock of the New*. Channel 4 serialised *The Voice* (excellent) and *The Art Show* (including

In April 2004 Ofcom reported that only 6 per cent of the potential audience regard Arts and Classical Music programmes as important

film-makers, puppeteers, artists – such as Tom Phillips' portrait of the director of the NPG – and TV itself in 'How to Watch Television').

In April 2004 Ofcom reported that only 6 per cent of the potential audience regard Arts and Classical Music programmes as important, although customers and patrons seemingly like their being available (like corner shops) even when they are not actually using them. Whether the BBC will fulfill its Charter obligations with more Deborah Bull and considered *Arena* profiles, more talk shows (in which supposed experts talk willingly outside their area of expertise) or more Nick Knowles capers in *Historyonics* remains to be seen. However, while television continues to cannibalise its own archives, it seems as well to look for new Art between the programmes as in them. The graphics for *The Big Read* often merited more attention than the tiresome, endless, self-satisfied presentations and BBC 1's distinctive red idents (sometimes keyed to concurrent series or seasons) enthusiastically display a range of dance styles, from *Come Dancing* to trapeze to Capora.

Amy Sargeant is Lecturer in the History of Film and Visual Media at Birkbeck College. She is the co-editor of British Historical Cinema (Routledge: 2002).

Were the bookworm animations used as part of *The Big Read* better than the programmes themselves?

Documentary

Stella Bruzzi

After docusoaps and alongside Reality TV, television documentary has diversified – if not fragmented – and eclecticism has dominated. Since the success in the 1990s of docusoaps, documentary has drifted away from its traditional affiliation to sobriety, to the extent that Andrew Billen in *The Times* argued that Peter Dale, Commissioning Editor for Documentaries at Channel 4, 'knows' that *Wife Swap* isn't 'a real documentary ... it has a documentary element, but it has sitcom, soap opera and game show elements too'.

The traditional documentary has been displaced, but it has not disappeared. BBC 4 produced several documentaries that would meet Billen's criteria for the 'real documentary', such as *The National Trust*, which resembled BBC series of old and which was repeated on BBC 2. An award-winning documentary in the investigative style was BBC 1's *The Secret Policeman* a film that used hidden cameras to expose widespread racism within the Greater Manchester Police. This investigative style, an established format, was used again for BBC 2's *Police Protecting Children*.

This year also saw new series of two long-standing docusoaps, *Airline* and *Airport*, but otherwise documentary output was notable for clustering around a set of repeated styles and subjects: formatted series, a predilection for reconstruction, an attachment to crisis and confrontation and a voyeuristic preoccupation with freakishness.

Of the formatted series, RDF's *Wife Swap* and *Faking It* were the most enduring. Both had new series and the former spawned spin-offs and imitations. In January 2004, a series of *Boss*

Mark Daly went undercover to reveal racist attitudes in the police force for BBC 1's *The Secret Policeman*

Swap began, and there was the one-off *Celebrity Wife Swap*, featuring Jade Goody and Major Charles Ingram. A more serious copycat programme was BBC 2's *When Michael Portillo Became a Single Mum*, in which the Conservative MP looked after a brood of four Liverpudlian children on a tight budget for a week.

Documentary has always been intrigued by crisis, but recently this has become an obsession. Undoubtedly influenced by docusoaps, series as diverse as *Property People, Risking it All* and *Ramsay's Kitchen Nightmares* revolved around fear, crisis and the potential for failure. Each episode of *Property People*, a series featuring a chain of north London estate agents, was far more interested in those agents who were in crisis. Likewise, *Risking it All* had as its premise a couple relinquishing their jobs and sinking their fortunes into a speculative entrepreneurial venture. The second episode, 'Harvey Fashion', focused on a couple opening a women's fashion boutique; relations soon become strained and the potential for financial failure is consistently highlighted. The second series of *Ramsay's Kitchen Nightmares* is similarly structured around an imminent crisis, as the confrontational chef Gordon Ramsay is brought in to see if he can save a restaurant in danger of going under.

The group of 'freak' obsessed documentaries was similarly homogenous. From programmes about obesity (*America's Fattest City*; *Victoria Wood's Big Fat Documentary*) to the sensationalist *My Foetus* and the voyeuristic longer running BBC 1 series *ONE Life*, which began in September 2003, what was evident was a questionable preoccupation with the sort of disfigurement or lifestyle that would make most onlookers gawp. This attachment to the grotesque reached its apotheosis with Channel 4's *Bodyshock: The Man Who Ate His Lover*, about the German cannibal Armin Meiwes who ate his internet lover Bernd Brandes – here the mother-obsessed Meiwes was depicted as a latter day Norman Bates.

Maybe fearing that fact is rarely this dramatic, the year produced an overwhelming number of films that mixed traditional documentary methods (the use of archive and interviews) alongside dramatised reconstruction. Despite Janice Hadlow (Channel 4 Commissioning Editor for History until June 2004 and the very mother of historical reconstruction), warning on *Happy Birthday BBC2* that filmmakers ventured into reconstruction at their peril, documentaries have become obsessed with it. Reconstruction can perform a liberating function, particularly to a historical subject for which no archive is handily available. This year there have been too many examples of gratuitous reconstruction. BBC 2's *The Miner's Strike*, which interviewed some wonderfully articulate ex-miners, still felt the need to reconstruct the events these talking heads had so vividly just recounted; similarly, in BBC 2's *The Four Minute Mile* – for which authentic archive of Bannister's record-breaking run existed and was used – the producers felt the necessity to re-enact the closing moments of the 1954 race.

In documentaries about murders, heists etc. or historical events that took place before the advent of photography, reconstruction served a more valid purpose. In *Brinks Mat: The Greatest Heist*, reconstructions of the 1983 robbery were intercut with the original police reconstruction, interviews and archive to recreate the largest heist in UK history. Other documentaries about modern day subjects that included reconstruction were ITV1's *Real Crime: Lady Jane* about the assistant to Sarah Ferguson convicted of killing her boyfriend and BBC 2's *Who Killed PC Blakelock?* which re-examined the Tottenham riots of 1985.

The largest group to use reconstruction were historical documentaries, films that signal the end of the presenter-led history jaunt, perhaps. What distinguishes documentaries such as *Oliver Cromwell: Warts and All*, *Timewatch: Through Hell for Hitler* or *Lawrence of Arabia: The Battle*

Documentary has always been intrigued by crisis, but recently this has become an obsession.

for the Arab World from docudramas is the placement of their reconstructions alongside more classic documentary elements such as interviews, voiceover and archive. Other series such as *The Divine Michelangelo* and *Leonardo's Dream Machines* (repeated in April 2004), which use reconstruction dramatically and literally – in the former, replicas of Michelangelo's David and his pieta were made, while in the latter machines were made and tested using Leonardo's original drawings.

The most stylistically ambitious reconstruction-based series was BBC 2's *Dunkirk*. Based on eyewitness accounts, the three parts interwove black and white archive with reconstructed colour footage, all filmed in a highly contemporary style (restless camera, crisp editing and CGI). Put alongside each other in much the same way as Oliver Stone had done in *JFK*, the archive sequences become energetic, dramatic renditions of the British salvage operation. Whether or not reconstruction will save or kill or the traditional documentary, remains to be seen.

Stella Bruzzi is Professor of Film Studies at Royal Holloway, University of London.

PROGRAMMING

BBC 2's *Dunkirk*

Cultural Diversity

Alby James

It may have been the public spat between Channel 4 and excluded Black and Asian programme-makers in the summer of 2002, or the pressure from outgoing regulator the Broadcasting Standards Commission (with its regular research outcomes showing general dissatisfaction with culturally diverse programming among both audiences and programme-makers) or that the Cultural Diversity Network that all major broadcasters have subscribed to has helped their managers to accept and appreciate the opportunities that a more culturally diverse broadcasting environment could offer for innovation, audience reach and satisfaction. Whatever the key factor, it seems that cultural diversity is finally on the agenda of the controllers and commissioning editors of the main television channels. This led to some marked achievements in reflections of minority community interests and culturally diverse programming during this year, let down, unfortunately, by one dreadful turkey.

The turkey was the BBC's first all black sitcom, *The Crouches*. Starting at the beginning of the autumn 2003 schedules, the BBC clearly had high hopes for the series but what a misjudgment this was. Here was a family of two generations of Black Brits and a third generation of long-time immigrants in a Jamaican grandma and Trinidadian grandpa (Mona Hammond and Rudolph Walker, known from their roles in *EastEnders*) playing characters in situations that seemed a throwback to the 70s. The whole thing was so patronising and unfunny, it was embarrassing. When we learned it had been scripted by *Rab C. Nesbitt* creator, Ian Pattison, it was obvious why the makers had gotten it so wrong. It was as if the previous milestones of black writers writing about their own communities for TV

The Crouches

drama and comedy had not already been passed and so black writers couldn't be trusted. What about BBC 2's successful comedy drama series *Babyfather* scripted by Avril Russell, Sharon Foster and Roy Williams? What about the experienced Michael Abensetts, whose television writing career started with *Empire Road* (BBC 2 1978-79)? What about Trix Worrall and Joan Hooley who scripted six series of *Desmond's* for Channel 4 (1989-94)? Still, Lorraine Heggessey is giving *The Crouches* a second chance. The producers have engaged Jamaican-born writer Liselle Kayla to write alongside Pattison for series two. Kayla, has a track record writing for *EastEnders, Rude Girls, The Real McCoy* and sitcom *Us Girls* so maybe they'll have better luck next time but the impression remains that BBC 1's head honchos still lack confidence in black writers.

The BBC has been markedly more successful with its other experiences of culturally diverse programming. British-Asian comedy in the form of *The Kumars at No. 42* has been reproduced with their specifically relevant immigrant groups in America, Australia, Germany, Israel and The Netherlands. It's an ingenious formula which captures both the mainstream audience seeking gossip and insights into celebs and the minority audience that loves to see exaggerations of characters from home getting one-up on these celebs. No wonder it has become a phenomenon.

Generally, though, on the basis that programming for a culturally diverse society is welcomed when it gives a sense of belonging and equality of opportunity to all people within the nations of the United Kingdom, that it should foster a better understanding of different cultures and allow people from minority communities and their countries of origin to see themselves portrayed honestly and fairly, there is evidence that all mainstream channels are now attempting to offer this. BBC 1's *Canterbury Tales* was one good example of this, utilising a mix of ethnic actors, writers and settings among the six episodes. Channel 4 did far better this year with documentary series like *The Hajj*, about a pilgrimage to Mecca, and superb investigations of the news and the war in Iraq on flagship programme *Channel 4 News*, among others. New drama wasn't so hot but the integration of Black and Asian people in a range of programming was much better than previously. ITV1 has also performed better in this area and Trevor McDonald and Trisha have continued to be great front people while ITV Sport, especially, has pulled its finger out.

The channel that has performed best in the cultural diversity arena has been BBC 4. From documentary *The Bushmen's Last Dance* to the World Cinema seasons to the relaunched BBC World News to the series about the rise of black players in English football, *Black Flash*, to *The Black and White Minstrel Show Revisited*, the channel has excelled in the attention given to all aspects of diverse programming. What we seek now is the same commitment for popular programming on the other channels. When audiences from the UK's ethnic communities start watching the full range of prime time television again in large numbers – that will be when cultural diversity on TV has really been achieved.

Alby James is a writer and director and is head of screenwriting and external developments at Leeds Metropolitan University.

Cultural Diversity in the Policy Environment

Andrea Millwood Hargrave

Amid recent events such as the passing of the Communications Act and the creation of Ofcom, the issue of cultural diversity remains firmly on the policy agenda.

Research published by broadcasters and content regulators in 2002 highlighted significant shortcomings in the way broadcasters provided for various minority communities. The study had considered representations of minority ethnic groups, the numbers actually represented on screen and audience attitudes towards such representations. It found that representation of people from minority ethnic groups was patchy, particularly in certain programme genres. Audience attitudes towards the representations, especially those of audiences within minority communities, were mixed with some praise for the way in which depictions had changed over time. There was however, a call for far greater representation across all genres and the younger people interviewed wanted a greater presence in mainstream programming. In addition, the study looked at the employment opportunities open in the media industries for people from diverse ethnic groups.

The study also sought to define 'multicultural programming' and made interesting distinctions between multicultural, monocultural and cross-cultural programming. These are useful, particularly when one considers the public service nature of such programming.

Following this research, and taking advantage of the Communcations Act going through, the Broadcasting Standards Commission facilitated meetings of an informal group of policy makers, regulators and programme makers under the chairmanship of Baroness Prashar. This group examined in detail the agenda for the incoming Ofcom Content Board in this area. Through this group, and with the active support of many peers in the House of Lords, an amendment was made to the Act (Part 1, Section 3.4.1) so that Ofcom should give due regard to 'the different interests of ... the different ethnic communities within the United Kingdom' as part of its general duties.

These events did not happen in isolation. The television industry had itself established the Cultural Diversity Network earlier in 2000. This Network of television broadcasters was formed in response to research undertaken by Carlton Television, the driving force behind its formation. Their research had shown that mainstream television broadcasters were losing viewers from the Black and Asian communities to cable and satellite channels. In order to change this and to ensure fair representation of minority ethnic groups in mainstream broadcasting (on screen and within the industry), the Network set itself the task of sharing expertise, resources and models of good practice in many areas. These include initiatives such as raising awareness of how minority communities are depicted on-screen and industry training schemes. Non-commercially sensitive research is shared and there is an endeavour to set up an industry-wide system for collecting data about on-screen representation. All data feeds into the Network, which regularly meets and organises events across the country to spread information about its work .

In addition to the Network the Broadcasting Standards Commission had been asked by the Government, post 9/11, to bring together a meeting of Muslim organisations and UK media representatives to discuss the way in which those events had been portrayed and continued to be depicted. Meetings held under the chairmanship of Lord Dubs resulted in the publication in 2002 of guidelines for such portrayals to be distributed under separate covers through the organisations within their communities.

These initiatives and the amendment to the Act firmly place the representation of minority ethnic groups on the agenda of broadcasters, whether they have direct public service requirements or not. The BBC's document Building Public Value placed issues of diversity centrally within the BBC's strategy into the future. DG Mark Thompson cautioned against tokenism or the irrelevance of portrayal criticised in 2002's research, recognising that: 'Modern diversity isn't about political correctness or narrow categories. It's about a public who are eager to discover and celebrate their identity and to fully realise themselves.'

It remains to be seen how the industry and the policy makers and regulatory authorities will address the issues of diversity in an increasingly fragmented and competitive broadcasting environment. The initiatives and requirements already in place, of which these are some notable examples, should give impetus to an area that has a strong social, cultural and commercial imperative in any case.

Andrea Millwood Hargrave, former Director of Research at the BSC/ITC, is an independent advisor on media policy research issues.

PROGRAMMING

Daytime

Alistair D. McGown

There's not a daytime ratings war – just a battle that dictates who wins the war for overall share. It's long been acknowledged that while ITV1 regularly beats BBC 1 in peak evening hours, BBC 1's impressive performance between 9 a.m. and 6 p.m. makes it Britain's most watched channel across all broadcast hours.

BARB figures indicate that in 2003 BBC 1 took 31.4 per cent share between 9 a.m. and 3.30 p.m. to ITV1's 20.9 per cent. It's a landscape of varying fortunes over the day – between 9.30 a.m. and 6 p.m BBC 1 took 25 per cent while ITV1 took just 16.1 per cent (even BBC 2 took 14.3 per cent for the same period while combined multichannel took 27.6 per cent). The first quarter of 2004 saw ITV1 regain ever so slightly across 9–3.30, shaving BBC1's 2003 10.5 percentage point lead to 9.8.

The day sees broad areas of conflict. Mornings are largely even, with ITV1's *Trisha* performing strongly with the female audience and BBC 1 later taking a slight percentage point or two lead over ITV1's breezy *This Morning* magazine. Early afternoon, BBC 1 storms ahead with a soap double of *Neighbours* and homegrown drama *Doctors*. ITV1 goes with children's programmes between 3.15 p.m. and 5 p.m., with BBC 1 following suit shortly afterwards. BBC 2 then demonstrates its role as the foot soldier in this battle – the strong showing of *Ready Steady Cook* (3-3.5 million in the Winter months) and *The Weakest Link* (3.5-4 million) keeps ITV1's performance flat between 4.30 and 6 p.m. The 5-6 p.m. zone most concerns ITV bosses – the desperate reality/quiz hybrid *24-*

Hour Quiz lacked all tension and flopped in this slot in February-March, like Carlton's revived *Crossroads* before it. Overlong reality/makeover/lifestyle/soap hybrid *Building the Dream* also failed to build much of a following. *Heartbeat* repeats are being used to plug the summer gap, facilitated by a 50 per cent reduction in Equity payments to actors for repeats aired 4-6 p.m.

Daytime TV made the headlines this year. Robert Kilroy-Silk's anti-Arab comments in his newspaper column led to his suspension from the BBC and then the pulling of his 9.30 a.m. *Kilroy* discussion show in January. His production company, Kilroy TV, were magnanimously offered the contract for a replacement, but *Now You're Talking* wasn't renewed beyond Summer 2004, and Kilroy TV looks set to close.

Trisha, always the trashier human interest variant of the two studio talk-ins, continues to pull high figures in opposition but June produced a twist. Trisha Goddard formed indie Town House with former Granada daytime executive Malcolm Allsop – with ITV rules preventing Trisha being outsourced, could it be that the BBC might buy a new Trisha-fronted talk show when her ITV contract expires? If so, the grubbier, more exploitative leanings would inevitably be curbed.

Also in the news, Richard and Judy re-signed with C4 in May, in a deal that runs until December 2007. Clearly the pair had also been courted by ITV1, keen for the regular two million plus viewers (sometimes more) they deliver between 5 and 6 p.m. Incoming Channel 4 daytime chief Adam MacDonald, who had taken the post late March, passed this early test with flying colours.

Another executive swap happened at ITV1 mid-May. Liam Hamilton, ITV1's daytime controller, left to oversee ITV's fiftieth birthday programming, a resulting restructure making CITV's Steven Andrew controller of all off-peak ITV1 output, with an incoming daytime editor beneath him. Liam Hamilton had earlier promised/warned of a new daytime soap project so we'll see if this notion is forgotten in the reshuffle. Dianne Nelmes became director of Granada daytime, Siubhan Richmond replacing her as executive producer of *This Morning*.

The £43,000 per half hour episode cost of BBC medical drama *Doctors* is astronomical compared with a more typical £15-45,000 an hour elsewhere. Doctors has to be a particular kind of soap to enable it to achieve anything like the economies of

Today With Des & Mel with ... Des and Mel

BBC 1's impressive daytime performance helps make it Britain's most watched channel

Christopher Timothy and Diane Keen star as Mac and Julia McGuire in BBC Birmingham's daytime soap *Doctors*

scale of the high volume series surrounding it (its crews shoot sixteen minutes of tape daily). Ensemble background stories develop slowly amid otherwise standalone episodes. Despite a wider modern daytime audience makeup taking in home workers, most controllers still aim shows primarily at women and *Doctors* is timeslotted to appeal to mums taking a break before heading off on the school run. Its storylines generally head in feminine directions, with the medical centre as the focus of human interest character stories. A worthwhile effort (though the acting from non-regulars varies greatly), the throughput is uniformly impressive.

BBC Birmingham's *Doctors* team produced a week-long second run of single dramas under *The Afternoon Play* banner in January. Such atypical big gestures are intended to draw attention to the daytime schedules and here we are discussing it, so the ploy obviously works. Peaktime stars mucked in (Robson Green, Michael French and Jamie Theakston; Sarah Lancashire directed the 'Viva Las Blackpool!' instalment). Majoring in light romcom this was very much aimed at the school run mums.

Mersey TV launched *The Courtroom* in June, a useful bridge between *Countdown* and *Richard and Judy* on Channel 4. New production approaches brought costs way down – its single standing set is shot using remote controlled cameras, giving the overall feel of a radio drama with pictures (not necessarily a bad thing). Essentially a retread of *Crown Court*, ITV daytime staple from 1972-84, *The Courtroom* drops its predecessors' three-part storylines for standalones and while its story codas suggest the 'true-life' dramas used by *Crown Court* its scripts are in fact completely fictional. Early episodes promise plenty of twists per half-hour.

Drama's relative rarity in daytime is logical – the form has limited appeal for floating viewers. The live magazine, influenced by talk radio, makes ideal, intermittent background viewing. *This Morning*'s varied menu of short items, taking in makeovers, agony aunts and the occasional eyebrow-raiser (road-testing vibrators) has proved durable, though there has been an over-reliance on plugging ITV1 of late, the last half hour often given over to Granada tie-ins with *Pop Idol*, *I'm a Celebrity ...* or *Hell's Kitchen*. Relative newcomer *Today With Des and Mel* is already a magazine

fixture. It has its faults (big-name guestlists are too often shored up by Des' tired old club comedian mates and when not speaking Melanie Sykes can seem transfixed by the autocue) but it's engaging, light and eminently watchable.

Occasional lows among the world's least worst daytime schedules included *Love 2 Shop*, a pre-Christmas orgy of commercialism dragging together C-listers, music PAs, camp makeovers and a staff *Pop Idol*-style singing contest under one shopping mall roof; episodes of *Trisha* can still be unenlightening and sensationalist.

Daytime has rightly lost much of its earlier reputation as what comic Rob Newman called 'the death of the soul between 9 and 5'. Galling however is the samey-ness of the me-too makeover-auction-interiors shows. *Bargain Hunt* forsook a two-dimensional version of David Dickinson to peaktime and continues with the less charismatic Tim Wonnacott. Copycat mark 'em up antiques shows proliferate, all looking for a hybridised twist. The vogue is working in human stories, a sob story or life goal that can utilise money raised by a sale. Newcomer *Star Sale* is merely *Cash in the Attic* gone *Through the Keyhole* with a camp host.

Some short run premium series attracted cherry-picking timeshifters. Back-to-basics big-name rock interview show *Jeremy Vine Meets ...* was a highlight (although first guest Bob Geldof was a big clue to how the show came about – his indie Ten Alps produced the show!) as was a second run of congenial TV-nostalgia coffee morning *Stars Reunited*. Heavier fare came from the BBC again, with week-long investigations into such topics as bullying and crime proving surprisingly popular.

The schedules currently lack revolutions (like *Light Lunch* in the mid-90s) but are generally far better produced than we should rightly expect of this high volume, low budget arena.

Acquisitions

Dick Fiddy

There was a time when US imports made a sizeable impact on UK audiences. Back in the 50s and 60s it wasn't unusual for shows like *Wagon Train*, *77 Sunset Strip*, *The Man from UNCLE* and many others to appear regularly in the week's top 20 charts. In the 70s a show like *Kojak* could attract many millions, but US shows have rarely made such impact since *Dallas* in the 80s. Now US imports are used to drive demand for non-terrestrial channels or carefully chosen to suit the branding of an individual station. This was a watershed year for such programming as some of the biggest hitters in the field finally bowed out: *Buffy The Vampire Slayer*, *Angel*, *Sex and the City*, *Frasier* and *Friends* have all left the building.

With such gaps opening up, the frenzied shopping around for the next hits have thrown channels into competition and seen prices rise. Channel 4 paid heavy to get *The Simpsons*, gambling that it would be a proven audience winner for its demographic. Its controller of acquisitions June Dromgoole admitted (in *Broadcast*) that American imports are an important part of the channel's schedule. Over at Sky One, bad luck has resulted in many of its latest acquisitions already being cancelled in the US

including *Jake 2.0*, *The Handler*, *Tarzan* and *Fearless*. However the two series that they especially hyped *Nip/Tuck* and *24* (series three) have performed well for the channel. Desperate to seek out new equally strong product, the channel has hired Rebecca Segal (former BBC vice-president of acquisitions in LA) to strengthen their acquisition team. The value that BSkyB puts on these shows is evident from their relentless cross channel self promotion (although there was a classic example of Sky One shooting themselves in the foot earlier in the year accidentally trailing the next week's 'story so far' promo shortly before a new episode of *24* – the promo showed all the highlights of the upcoming episode thereby rendering the episode totally anti-climatic).

So much for the business, what about the programmes? The *CSI* dramas have proved highly successful for Five and with *CSI: New York* about to roll off the assembly line the franchise seems robustly healthy. Class comedies *Scrubs* and *Malcolm in the Middle* (both showing on Sky One prior to terrestrial transmission) continue to impress, though new US comedy hits are proving harder to find (one reason for this is the slew of family-oriented comedies made in the US after 9/11 – these traditionally fail to score in the UK). *ER* and *Will and Grace* are dependable Channel 4 fodder as is the *Law and Order* franchise for Five. The fantasy genre looks set to suffer in the wake of the *Buffy* and *Angel* bow-outs as the new shows *Jake 2.0* (updated *Six Million Dollar Man*), *Tru Calling* (a murderous spin on *Groundhog Day*), *Tarzan* and (new-ish) *Mutant X* (*X-Men* lite) seem distinctly second class. Those suffering withdrawal symptoms after the demise of *Dawson's Creek* were probably delighted by the arrival of *The O.C.* on E4, though the programme itself is currently at the centre of a $10 million lawsuit with two writers accusing show creator Josh Schwartz of 'stealing their ideas'.

Screenings of US versions of shows originated in the UK (like *American Idol* on ITV2 and *Big Brother USA* on E4) have opened up new areas of exploitation with audiences familiar with the shows' formats and happy to watch the different variations on the theme. The preponderance of US TV shows on UK TV also make it easier to appreciate many of the small screen stars who turn up on the US's flagship chat shows *David Letterman* (ITV2) and *Jay Leno* (Ftn and CNBC)

Kath and Kim is one of the more inventive Australian series to appear recently - it airs regularly on Ftn

This was a watershed year for acquisitions as some of the biggest hitters in the field finally bowed out: *Buffy The Vampire Slayer, Angel, Sex and the City, Frasier* and *Friends* have all left the building.

both screening in the UK shortly after their US transmissions. The BBC picked up *Kingdom Hospital*, the Stephen King adaptation of Lars von Trier's startling *Kingdom* series, the original of which (a rare Danish import) had also shown on the BBC. The US version (a flop for ABC) had its moments but just couldn't match the eerie 'otherness' of its precursor.

And what of non-US imports? Well there's the endless Australian soaps (*Neighbours* on BBC1, *Home and Away* and *Sons and Daughters* on Five), though a more imaginative acquisition from down under is the feisty mother/daughter sitcom *Kath and Kim* on Ftn. Various documentaries from all sources turn up on the non-fiction channels but the bulk of non-US import productions on offer is from the East with anime and various children's animated series mostly from Japan and animation superstate Korea. Such cartoon series (many of which are co-productions, with the animators working in the East) fill the schedules of The Cartoon Network, Nickelodeon, MTV, The Sci-fi Channel and their ilk. The digital revolution has also opened up the airwaves for totally foreign language channels (Hindi, Italian, French etc) running homegrown programming without subtitles.

As the TV landscape expands so we should expect to see more import programming – especially from the US. The sheer volume of episodes-per-title plus the relative cheapness (in some cases) of the product make it an easy choice for those with schedules to fill and limited funds. Niche channels can also provide a home for programming that perhaps wouldn't work too well on mixed-programming channels (like ITV1), thus run-of-the-mill fantasy series play well on The Sci-fi Channel, just as middle-of-the-road sitcoms can sit happily on Paramount Comedy.

The competitive nature of US television ensures that the programmes keep rolling off the assembly line, though UK TV acquisition chiefs are finding balancing things tricky, anxious to snap up

programmes early before their competitors but wary of obtaining shows that are cancelled just weeks into their US runs. Channel 4 in particular must be looking with some trepidation to a *Friends*-free future. In the weeks leading up to their transmission of the last ever *Friends*, the channel milked its comedy cash cow to an unprecedented degree, cramming the schedules of both Channel 4 and E4 with hours upon hours of *Friends* episodes, most showing for the umpteenth time. The channel will be hoping the US's longest-running sitcom *The Simpsons* (at fifteen seasons and counting*) will be able to fill a *huge* gap.

Dick Fiddy is television consultant to the BFI.

*Although lasting a year longer than previous record holder *The Adventures of Ozzie and Harriet*, *The Simpsons* (335 episodes so far) still has a way to go to overtake the episode haul of the former (435 episodes).

CSI: Crime Scene Investigation is a signature show for Five, regularly boosting its share. The show also airs on Living TV.

Advertising

Martin Hart

In the summer of 2003, UK television advertising was battered by one of the worst advertising recessions ever. Nevertheless, UK television advertising remained high in the public consciousness. A change of regulator, individual advertisements attracting record complaints, a whole new sector of advertising, growing concern about advertising to children, effects of the ITV merger and some stunning creative work were some of the issues that marked the year 2003/4.

The shift from the ITC to Ofcom will bring big changes to the regulation of television advertising – it could arguably prove to be the most significant event since the start of commercial television in 1955. During the year, Ofcom consulted on a proposal to transfer the regulation of broadcast advertising to a co-regulatory body. This would bring broadcast advertising under the auspices of the existing self-regulator for non-broadcast advertising, the Advertising Standards Authority. In May 2004, Ofcom announced that co-regulation would go ahead from November, subject to some modifications to the original proposal, including the creation of an independently chaired Advertising Advisory Committee, to provide lay and expert input to the broadcast advertising code-making process. 2004 will therefore go down in history as the final year in which television advertising was directly regulated by a statutory regulator.

The shift from ITC to Ofcom will bring big changes to the regulation of TV advertising – it could prove to be the most significant event since the start of commercial television in 1955.

The end of the ITC provided an opportunity to reflect on the most complained about ads since 1993. The winner was 2003's 'dog breath' ad for Wrigley's X-cite (860 complaints). The ad featured a young man, clearly the worse for drink, regurgitating a large shaggy dog. This comfortably overtook the previous holder, 1998's Levi's 'Kevin', featuring a dead hamster (a mere 544 complaints).

But one advertisement crossed both regulators and almost stole Wrigley's crown. An advertisement for Mr Kipling Mince Pies featured a nativity scene with the unexpected punch line 'It's a girl'. No fewer than 797 complaints were received and the advertiser voluntarily pulled the commercial. Ofcom used the case to try a new form of regulatory solution – 'case resolved' – and took no further action.

The new sector of advertising came about from Oftel's decision to deregulate the market for directory enquiries services. An estimated £70 million was spent as a number of new entrants took the opportunity to promote themselves. The most successful on television was 'The Number 118 118'. Using a pair of 70s style runners, 118 118's advertising ensured The Number was the best known of the plethora of new entrants to the market and, despite some bad press over its call centre operations, easily emerged as market leader. The party spirit was only slightly dampened by the action of runner David Bedford in successfully appealing to Ofcom over the use of his caricature in the advertisements. Although Ofcom allowed the advertisements to continue, they resumed with changes to the images of the runners featured (who were given slightly neater hair and had their running vests replaced with beige jumpsuits).

The main product-related issue of the year was undoubtedly an increasing debate about food (or specifically, unhealthy food) advertising to children. As *Marketing* magazine described it, 'Food became the new tobacco in 2003'. The Food Standards Agency undertook an extensive literature review that led it to conclude that advertising had a significant influence on children's preferences and diet. In response, culture secretary Tessa Jowell asked Ofcom to review its advertising code but stopped short of seeking new curbs on advertising junk food to children. However, she urged the advertising industry to play its part in tackling the issue of obesity – the number of obese children in

Avoid Dog Breath ... Ofcom certainly did, by upholding complaints made against this Wrigley's X-cite advert

the UK has doubled over the past twenty years. Earlier in the year, Debra Shipley MP proposed a private member's bill calling for a ban on food and drink advertising to children. Ofcom has been undertaking its own research and initial findings published in summer 2004 seem to indicate Ofcom will not consider an outright ban necessary.

In March, it was the turn of alcohol to come under the advertising spotlight as a Cabinet Office report urged Ofcom to tighten the rules on the advertising of alcohol. Support for such a move also came from the Portman Group, the drinks

The pessimism of twelve months ago is replaced by considerable optimism – advertising growth of over 3 per cent is predicted, due to factors such as the Olympics, Euro 2004 football and US Presidential elections.

Honda's intricate 'cog' campaign won it the accolade of *Campaign*'s Advertiser of the Year

industry's own watchdog, who expressed concern that television advertising was not being regulated with the same degree of strictness as the self regulatory bodies.

The ITV merger surprised many in the advertising industry when the Competition Commission agreed the plan without requiring ITV to sell off their sales houses. Indeed, many were surprised by the few strings attached to the merger at all. A remedy was devised – the Contract Rights Renewal – which was designed to protect advertisers and media buyers in their negotiations with ITV. As a further safeguard, David Connolly was appointed as Adjudicator to resolve individual disputes. There was also speculation that the merger would lead to a further consolidation of advertising sales houses, with combinations of Channel 4, Five and Sky talked about most often.

In the creative arena, *Campaign*'s Advertiser of the Year was Honda, with its 'cog' campaign which it described as 'one of the most eloquent expressions of a company's confidence about its product and positioning'. The ad, involving eighty-five individual motor parts, required 606 takes and cost almost £1 million – the success of the campaign was measured with a 10 per cent rise in sales.

In television sponsorship, one of the most talked about relationships was the Five series *Dinner Doctors*, advertiser-supplied by Heinz in the summer of 2003. The series examined ways for households to make use of convenience foods in preparing healthy and nutritious meals for their

families. Many observers felt the interests of sponsor and programme content were too close for regulatory comfort but the ITC, regulator at the time, did not intervene.

Looking back, the pessimism of twelve months ago is replaced by considerable optimism. Both Zenith Optimedia (one of the largest media buyers) and the World Advertising Research Centre predict advertising growth of 3.5 per cent and 3.2 per cent respectively for the UK, pointing to factors as diverse as the Olympics, the Euro 2004 football tournament and US Presidential elections as growth factors. There is also an expectation in the advertising industry that a combination of Ofcom's review of Public Service Broadcasting and the BBC Charter review will lead to a shift in public service obligations to the BBC and allow commercial public service broadcasters more scope to maximise their revenue. To top it all, apparent scandal has failed to dent the appeal of England captain David Beckham who has reportedly clinched a record breaking £40 million deal to become the worldwide advertising face of Gillette, making him the highest paid British advertising star of all time. The advertising recession, it seems, has come to an end.

Martin Hart is Policy Manager in the Content and Standards group at Ofcom. In 2003 he was an employee of the ITC. Views expressed in this article are the author's own and do not necessarily reflect Ofcom policy.

PROGRAMMING

Archives & Restoration

Steve Bryant

The phenomenal growth of the DVD market, together with an even greater number of archive-based programmes on-air in the past year, has thrown the spotlight onto television archives as never before. Channel 4's 'list' programmes (100 Greatest TV Moments from Hell etc) and the BBC's public votes (*Britain's Favourite Sitcom*) have provided masses of airtime for clip material from the vaults, as has BBC 4, which cleverly schedules complete archive programmes as complementary output in the context of new programming.

Indeed, it was BBC 4 that made a programme about television archiving, rather than just using the archive material to illustrate the past. This was *Time Shift: Missing, Believed Wiped* which looked at the recovery of programmes, missing from the official archives, thought lost – basing it on the British Film Institute's initiative of the same name and the BBC's Treasure Hunt, which famously recovered two lost episodes of *Dad's Army* ('The Battle of Godfrey's Cottage' and 'Operation Kilt'). The programme, transmitted over the Christmas and New Year period together with a selection of recovered programmes, concentrated on comedy, focusing on the BFI's recovery of episodes of *The Complete and Utter History of Britain* and its restoration of *At Last the 1948 Show*, as well as the BBC successes and the contribution of private collectors.

Much of the archive material put out on DVD dates from the era of two inch Quad videotape recording, which has frequently necessitated transfer from the original recordings, even though

---

Now that Carlton is part of Granada, the centralisation of the archiving of current (and some past) ITV companies is almost complete.

---

an earlier transfer to a more modern format may have been made. The National Film and Television Archive completed its Heritage Lottery Fund project to transfer ITV Quad tapes in August 2003. Among the total of 36,000 tapes processed was part of the ATV collection, bought three years ago by Carlton International. As Carlton acquired that collection towards the end of the project, there was not time to include all the tapes contained in it, so the company has been funding the NFTVA to continue the transfer programme. At the same time, it has initiated an award-winning conservation project to make its archival film holdings accessible. Now that Carlton is part of Granada, the centralisation of the archiving of current (and

BBC 4's *Missing Believed Wiped* season showcased previously lost comedy items and highlighted the preservation efforts of the NFTVA and fans alike. Terry Jones visited the NFTVA to watch recovered material from his *Complete and Utter History of Britain*

The BFI's own annual Missing, Believed Wiped event, which showcases the latest recoveries in front of a loyal NFT audience every Autumn, contained a number of interesting items, the undoubted highlight of which was a twenty minute tape, found at BBC Television Centre, of the emergency news bulletin put out from Alexandra Palace on the ill-fated opening night of BBC 2 in 1964, when TV Centre itself was shut down by a power cut. Unintentionally hilarious, the recording was also used in BBC 2's programming celebrating their own fortieth anniversary in April 2004.

some past) ITV companies is almost complete.

After many years of anticipation and preparation, television archives in general now seem to be taking the leap into the digital future. No preservation programme can now be considered without a full digitisation strategy and the rapid move towards fully digital transmission is forcing archives to embrace digital asset management technology as the only future. It is significant that the job title of the new Head of the BBC Information and Archives department is actually Head of Media Management. Channel 4 are also well advanced down this road and the National Film and Television Archive proposes to replace its off-air recording system with digital capture and file management. All of which will place greater emphasis on the migration of legacy collections and the retention of skills to ensure their preservation.

Digital and web-based systems are already dominant in the area of archive sales. ITN have long been the leader in this field, as well as providing representation for other companies, particularly from the ITV system. In January 2004 this pre-eminence was reinforced when ITN took over extract sales for the entire Granada Media catalogue, including material from Anglia, Border, HTV, LWT, Meridian, Tyne Tees and Yorkshire as well as Granada itself. The inclusion of Anglia in the Granada portfolio means the inclusion, also, of the impressive *Survival* catalogue. ITN described this, at the time, as 'the UK's biggest archive representation agreement of all time' and the subsequent ITV merger seems set to make it even bigger. The collection catalogue can be browsed online at www.itnarchive.com

Archives have also been at the centre of the political debates in broadcasting. The Edinburgh International Television Festival heard a plea from Culture Secretary Tessa Jowell for greater use of Archives, followed almost immediately by Greg Dyke's announcement of the BBC Creative Archive

Out of the Archives

The archive TV fan's dream is a specialist channel exploiting both the ITV and BBC archives and carefully chosen imports. Episodes would be unedited and shown in the right order. Pieces could be contextualised, the scene set, important contemporary references explained, with programme makers introducing screenings. It would be the broadcast equivalent of a DVD, complete with best possible picture and sound quality and pertinent extras

This is a pipe dream. Such a channel would be hugely costly, with material difficult to clear. The deals made with unions already mean that actors and writers get minuscule amounts for satellite and digital screenings – only even more draconian measures could make this channel cost effective. Obviously, without these deals we wouldn't be able to have any nostalgia channels and the archives would remain virtually completely unused as a huge and costly white elephant. If such a channel seems far off, until then we have BBC 4.

BBC 4 has made giant strides in the area of retrospective television, resurrecting single plays, dedicating seasons to individual programme makers or themes, exploiting the archive profusely with its media history strand Time Shift and – perhaps most importantly – showing a willingness to broadcast black and white programmes. December 2003's *Missing Believed Wiped* night, consisted of a documentary about the quest to unearth programmes awol from the official archives and the transmission of some of the shows which had been recovered – mostly due to the BFI's Missing Believed Wiped initiative and the BBC's sister project Treasure Hunt.

2004 saw BBC4's most ambitious season so far, *Summer in the Sixties*, which aired weekends in June and featured classic drama (Dennis Potter's Nigel Barton plays, *The Prisoner*) alongside sitcoms (*Likely Lads, Till Death Us Do Part*), chat shows (*Dee Time, Face to Face*), panel shows (*Call My Bluff*) and specially made documentaries on the decade (including *Sport in the Sixties, The Black and White Minstrel Show ... Revisited*). An attempt to undermine the notion of the 60s being a 'golden age' for TV (Mark Lawson's *The Truth About Sixties TV*) was lost amidst the kaleidoscope of programming that seemed to suggest the reverse. Minor carping aside (occasional playout errors meaning vintage programmes shown in widescreen; the omnipresence of the BBC4 logo on the screen) this was the most comprehensive trawl of the archives since Channel 4's *TV Heaven* more than a decade earlier.

Archive programming appeared on other channels of course but, with very few exceptions, scant imagination was demonstrated. UKTV Gold and Plus (formerly Granada Plus) were probably the brand leaders and while Plus should receive kudos for re-running the classic US sitcom *The Dick Van Dyke Show*, the channel needs to have its wrist slapped over its cavalier treatment of vintage UK sitcom *Please, Sir!*, the first series of which featured forty-five minute episodes. Plus repeats in 2003 re-edited them into a thirty-minute slot, thereby cutting over 30 per cent and rendering plots incomprehensible. Such treatment is all too typical.

Dick Fiddy

Summer in the 60s was another BBC 4 archive season. Writer Nigel Kneale and actor Gerald Harper contributed to the documentary *Time Shift: Fantasy Sixties*

initiative to make sections of the Corporation's holdings freely available for all to re-use on-line. The idea survived Dyke's departure as Director-General and has become a plank in the BBC's Charter renewal proposals and is due in Autumn 2004, though it seems certain that copyright issues will restrict the content available to factual material, particularly natural history footage. In the commercial field, the BBC has launched its Motion Gallery clips download project, aimed at exploiting the predicted explosion in 3G and 4G mobile technologies but this is not to be confused with the charter renewal-driven Creative Archive.

In terms of the national collection, there was a re-enforcement of the statutory provision for a National Television Archive with the inclusion in the Communications Act of a transfer of the responsibility to oversee the funding of the operation from the ITC to Ofcom and an extension of that responsibility to Channel 4, as well as ITV and Five. The archiving of the expanding satellite sector, however, remains outside the scope of the national provision and subject to the extreme commercial pressures of its business environment.

On the international front, the International Federation of Television Archives (FIAT/IFTA) held its annual conference in Brussels, where the theme was television history, in acknowledgement of the fact that the two host broadcasters (RTBF and VRT) were celebrating their fiftieth anniversaries, along with several other European television companies. The tenth annual FIAT/IFTA award for the best use of archive material in a new television programme was won by a Russian production. The Federation of Commercial Audiovisual Libraries (FOCAL International) meanwhile organised their first awards ceremony at the London Television Centre and gave awards in a variety of categories, including factual productions, advertising, pop promos, content libraries and electronic publishing. This only proves the large variety of outlets for re-use of material from moving image archives.

Steve Bryant is Keeper of Television at the National Film and Television Archive.

Making Use of Regional Archives

Regional television is not all about local news and current affairs. Regional slots complement the network schedules with local variations of popular formats such as consumer, lifestyle, gardening, cookery and quiz programmes. In the past year the people and places of the regions were well represented in history programmes.

Recent years have seen the growth of archive-based programmes across the country. ITV franchises Anglia, Border, Granada, Tyne Tees and Yorkshire all made their own versions of *The Way We Were* telling the stories of family life in their regions through home movies and collaborations with local archives. Westcountry revisited stories making the headlines over the past forty years in *Whatever Happened to ...* while Central trawled through their television archive with *TV Gold*. On a larger scale Scottish Television's *The Sea Kings* explored the history of Celtic Britain and Ireland, Meridian's *Making of England* the history of Wessex and *A Promised Land* the past sixty years in Wales. BBC Scotland meanwhile recently produced another series of local history reminiscences in *Scotland on Film*, delving into the archives of Scottish Screen.

The history of local industry was celebrated. Central paid tribute to famous food and drink brands of the region, such as Marmite and HP sauce, with two series of *A Taste for Success*. Wales raised a glass to the *Great Beers of Wales*. Ulster's *Trains, Boats and Planes* provided a nostalgic looked at transport in the region. Border looked back at the history of nuclear energy in *Critical Times*. Broadcast by both Westcountry and West of England *Brunel – the Little Giant* followed the route of the Isambard Kingdom Brunel's Great Western Railway to learn more about the engineer.

Kathleen Luckey, BFI

Soap

Gary Gillatt

Soap operas – or Continuing Dramas, as BAFTA more formally identified them for their 2004 TV Awards – remain a powerful weapon in the armoury of TV schedulers. The success of a soap has a profound effect upon its channel, delivering viewers early in the evening who, if all goes well, will be inherited by the programmes that follow. The recent trend has been to increase soap output, guaranteeing a bankable audience share. BBC 1's *EastEnders* gained a fourth weekly episode in 2002, ITV1's *Emmerdale* has been broadcast five nights weekly since 2000, a move that its stablemate *Coronation Street* has only resisted by screening two of its five weekly episodes on a Monday. This policy is not without risk, however, and if a soap falls out of favour, either terminally (the case with Channel 4's *Brookside*) or temporarily (*EastEnders'* much-publicised Spring 2004 slump), channel executives get nervous. A subtle side-effect of this increased output is that cast members are more rapidly exhausted by the punishing schedule – and the days have now passed when viewers can expect to follow a character grow from youth to middle age.

Coronation Street performed strongly throughout the year, delivering memorable storylines and showpiece confrontations. Still riding high in 2003 from its powerful Richard Hillman 'Norman Bates with a briefcase' multiple murder storyline, the soap didn't pause for breath, delivering its finely-tuned mix of family drama and droll northern comedy. A masterclass in plotting and scripting, the series knows exactly how to deliver on the promises of its storylines, spinning out the drama just long enough – and never a day too long – to obtain the most explosive, crowd-pleasing results. True to the show's proud history of strong female characters, the year's most memorable

During an already difficult Spring, *EastEnders* was dealt a further blow in May 2004, losing a head-to-head battle with an hour-long *Emmerdale*.

moments have featured confrontations between battleaxes, young and old. Even the climax of the series' first ever gay storyline – charting young Todd Grimshaw's realisation of his homosexuality, and eventual rejection of his fiancée – was played out in a round of hellcat slapping and hair-pulling on the Weatherfield cobbles between Todd's mother, Eileen, and his almost mother-in-law, Gail Platt.

Some of *EastEnders* defining moments this year occurred off screen rather than on; the soap failing to secure so much as a nomination in its category at the 2004 BAFTAs and the webcam confessions of Leslie Grantham whipping the tabloids into a frenzy, and prompting reported insurrection in the Elstree green room.

During an already difficult Spring, a further blow came on 18 May 2004 when, after a head-to-head

PROGRAMMING

When Den Watts returned to his extended family in *EastEnders* in September 2003 it seemed the show could do no wrong – but a year later it is struggling to reassert itself as the nation's top soap

ratings battle with an hour-long edition of *Emmerdale*, the rural soap trounced its ailing competitor – *Emmerdale* claiming a 47 per cent audience share to *EastEnders*' 36 per cent – a fact gleefully celebrated in a Yorkshire TV press release the following morning. Ironically, on 9 June 2004, ITV chief executive Charles Allen told the Commons culture, media and sport select committee: 'I don't think it can be in the public interest when the main channels are targeting exactly the same demographics at the same time.' His point is justified, but Allen's shareholders can certainly take comfort that ITV1's soap operas are flourishing under such competitive scheduling. *Coronation Street* managed to squeeze three episodes into one evening prior to Euro 2004 disruption – was this a shape of things to come from the aggressively commercial ITV?

The reasons for *Emmerdale*'s recent renaissance and *EastEnders*' doubtless temporary tumble can be traced to one root cause – quality of storylining, or the lack of it. The northern soap has rewarded viewer loyalty by remaining true to its characters, and allowing plot to develop naturally from their carefully established personalities, while its East End cousin has, rather perversely, taken to forcing its characters into behaviour that viewers simply cannot accept as true or – within the accepted constraints of a daily melodrama – realistic. In

those ratings-reversal May episodes, *Emmerdale* reaped the rewards of a simple love-triangle plot – between brothers Robert and Andy Sugden, and Andy's wife Katie – which had been simmering for months. Viewers had been given time to understand and empathise for all three players, and the final confrontation would engage anyone who seen even the smallest episode in the development of the story.

Meanwhile, over on BBC 1, *EastEnders*' were selling a love triangle of their own. Kat, the otherwise devoted wife to hangdog pub landlord Alfie, had spent a night with her former fiancé Andy Hunter. She did this to raise money to pay off Graham, who had been roughed-up by Kat's dad after raping Kat's sister, but was willing to drop the charges in return for £10,000. This may all seem, at first glance, to be standard soap fare, but this plot required the much-loved Kat Moon, and those privy to her decisions, to act completely out-of-character on at least two separate occasions. And would the 'us against the world' Slaters *really* pay off someone who had attacked one of their own? *EastEnders* may have spun itself a smug *Indecent Proposal* pastiche, but it had to sacrifice the 'reality' of one of its best-loved characters in the process – and viewer loyalty into the bargain. And this is far from being the only example of the series' careless disregard for consistency in 2004: Zoe

Shelley's date from the brewery turned out to be something of a mummy's boy – and he looked a lot like Peter Kay in a ginger wig too.

Slater was a lesbian for two minutes; Mark Fowler's passing was bungled, Todd Carty being allowed to leave for duty on *The Bill* without shooting the deathbed scenes we had been waiting since 1991 to see – Mark's death was mere 'noises off'. The soap's abstruse plotting became a favoured target for mockery from BBC 2's satirical sketch show, *Dead Ringers*, who reminded us that Sonia has now fallen in love with the young man who ran over and killed her previous sweetheart.

Events on Channel 4 in late 2003 stand as stark testimony to what can happen when a soap loses the plot. On 4 November, sometime Liverpudlian bad boy Jimmy Corkhill marked the demise of Channel 4's *Brookside* with a flick of a paintbrush. Adding a 'D' the end of the iconic sign 'BROOKSIDE CLOSE', Jimmy signalled the residents' surrender to a scheme that would see the cul-de-sac demolished to allow the building of an incinerator. *Brookside* itself was fed to the flames on the orders of Channel 4 chief executive Michael Jackson, after ratings for the sensationalist soap had slumped from a onetime high of 8 million to around 500,000 – the show having already 'celebrated' it's twentieth birthday in November 2002 by being dumped into a graveyard slot around 11.00 p.m. The final episode also saw drug dealer, Jack Michaelson, hanged from his bedroom window by a marauding lynch mob. This cheeky Spoonerism surely stands as *Brookside* creator Phil Redmond's final impudent gesture to his Channel 4 executive.

Some comfort came for Redmond's Mersey Television when, in the same month as *Brookside*'s cancellation, the company's teen soap for Channel 4, *Hollyoaks*, was granted a fifth weekly episode. Following the lives of energetic young adults and a small selection of befuddled parents in a fictional suburb of Chester, the series has always found much mileage in charting the frenetic love lives of its well-groomed principal characters, with an epic two-and-a-half hour omnibus edition proving perfect 'hangover television' for those of its target audience – and others old enough to know better – still hiding under a duvet on Sunday mornings. The soap's principle storyline of 2003/2004 was effectively a re-heat of *Coronation Street*'s most successful recent plot, as a serial killer stalked the streets of Chester. In a self-referential twist, the *Hollyoaks* murderer's favoured prey was young, blonde women – a cheeky wink to those who had criticised the series for its policy of casting identikit peroxide 'babes'. While the unlucky Dan Hunter found himself framed for the murders, the real culprit, Toby Mills, fell to his death at the climax of

Events on Channel 4 in November 2003 stand as stark testimony to what can happen when a soap loses the plot. Jimmy Corkhill marked the demise of *Brookside* with a flick of a paintbrush.

a *Hollyoaks After Hours* episode. This second string of programmes, running irregularly since 2000, allows the series to tackle what Mersey Television describes as 'more adult-orientated issues' in a late-night timeslot (as well as feature Caprice starring as a group sex fiend, for example). It's surely more than a coincidence that this format also allows a greater acreage of young flesh to be displayed, cementing *Hollyoaks*' symbiotic relationship with the lads' magazine business – its principal female stars being no strangers to the pages of *Loaded* and the like.

Elsewhere, other continuing dramas continued to do good business. ITV1's *The Bill*, and BBC1's *Holby City* and *Casualty* both earned BAFTA nominations, due reward for the careful concentration with which these crime and medical series weave soap opera strands into a broader tapestry of stunt-fuelled '999' drama. Five's low-budget soap, *Family Affairs*, gained strength from a cast cull and careful revamp at the hands of incoming executive producer Paul Marquess (*Brookside*, *The Bill*), and performed strongly in its quiet way. *Family Affairs*' quirkiest gimmick of 2004 was an 'interactive plot', allowing viewers to phone in and decide which of two suitors should win the heart of indecisive ladies' man Marc MacKenzie. In adopting the methodology of the leading interactive reality TV shows, such as *Big Brother* and *Pop Idol*, *Family Affairs* was making a deferential nod to the most powerful threat to the soaps in the battle for the hearts and minds of the nation. With unplotted 'reality' claiming more of the TV schedule than ever, viewers are now quick to notice when they are being manipulated by soap storyliners and script writers. And as *EastEnders* has found, those viewers will vote swiftly and decisively with their remote controls – so the message to producers is clear: Keep It Real.

*Gary Gillatt is a staff writer at **Inside Soap** magazine.*

PROGRAMMING

Series and Serials

Glen Creeber

Many critics today appear to place British serial drama into two distinct groups – the shallow and the serious. Those who insist that the contemporary drama serial is forever being reduced to soap opera point to the continued success of shows like *Footballers' Wives* (ITV1), *Bad Girls* (ITV1), and *Cutting It* (BBC 1) as proof that sensational melodrama seems to be the current flavour of the month. In contrast are serials such as *Second Generation* (Channel Four), *D-Day: The Untold Story* (BBC2) and *Prime Suspect: The Last Witness* (ITV1) that still arguably manage to retain an element of 'serious' realism in a television world seemingly populated by cheating spouses, murderous wives and drug addicted prison guards.

Shallow or not, there is certainly a strain of contemporary melodrama that appears to be thriving on British television at the moment. Most notably we saw the return of ITV's *Footballers' Wives*. Although the first series was little more than a pale imitation of Sky One's *Dream Team* (itself currently in its seventh 'season') and its ratings were disappointing, it seemed to strike the national zeitgeist with a surprising bang. Even Germaine Greer was provoked enough to share her comments about the show with the readers of *The Guardian*. Produced by Shed productions, the third series took all the most successful elements of the first (glamour, melodrama and sex) but just

notched it all up a gear whilst also adding celebrity guest appearances from the likes of glamour model Jordan, a Thailand setting and, of course, a dildo. It certainly seemed to boost the ratings, producing the sort of kitsch, ironic and talked about serial drama that ITV must produce if it is to both distinguish itself from the BBC while also stealing its audience.

With *Bad Girls* already a long running hit (now into series five), Shed are clearly on a roll. In their latest bid to remain at the top of their game they've taken the evil and manipulative Tanya Turner (Zöe Lucker) out of *Footballers' Wives* and transferred the character to *Bad Girls*. It is an inspired idea and one that will continue to make the company a powerful force in British television drama for years to come.

At the other end of the generic spectrum *Second Generation* was a contemporary two part serial that dramatised the internal struggles of a modern Asian family in Britain. Written by Neil Biswas (co-writer of 2001's *In a Land of Plenty*) and directed by newcomer Jon Sen it failed to really make much of an impact on the critics or its target audience. While there was lots of Asian dub (one of the main characters was a DJ) to remind ourselves that this really was contemporary multicultural Britain, it seemed surprisingly familiar and predictable territory not helped by its cumbersome and rather heavy-handed allusions to *King Lear*. Meanwhile

Footballers' Wives: you should have seen this photo in colour. *Orange* it was.

D-Day was clearly the BBC's attempt to counteract Steven Spielberg's Americanised version of the Second World War while seemingly borrowing the same stylised realism that typified HBO's earlier *Band of Brothers*. It was an admirable attempt but perhaps its drama documentary techniques (most notably a rather heavy-handed narration) was a little too educational in both tone and feel to attract the sort of popular interest and discussion that the BBC might have liked.

More successful was the sixth in the *Prime Suspect* series that has remarkably reinvented itself yet again while sticking pretty close to the original formula that made it so popular in the first place. Having tackled sexism, homosexuality, racism, paedophilia, drug addiction and male prostitution in the past, the crime serial now turned its attention to the sensitive issue of asylum seekers. When the body of a young Bosnian woman is found, with evidence of torture, Tennison takes personal charge of the case, her investigation leading to Serbian war criminals eager to silence the 'last witness'. Peter Berry's story might equally be remembered for the way it sensitively dealt with the ageing process of Helen Mirren's Supt Jane Tennison. Pushed towards early retirement, she seemed to be facing up to prejudice about her years with the same obstinate tenacity with which she once faced sexual discrimination. Unlike *Second Generation* and *D-Day*, which both did rather poorly in the ratings, *Prime Suspect* continues to gain glowing reviews while also remaining incredibly popular with audiences. Unsurprisingly *Prime Suspect 7* is currently in production.

However, in between these two extreme generic spectrums came the drama serial that seemed to successfully balance the worthy with the stylish and the ironic. Channel Four's new medical series *No Angels* was clearly not aiming to be *King Lear* but was nevertheless fresh, innovative and hugely enjoyable. More critically acclaimed was *Shameless*, a new seven-part serial created by writer Paul Abbott (*Touching Evil*, *Reckless*, *Linda Green*, *State of Play* and *Clocking Off*) that has already been commissioned for a second series. Set on a run down council estate in Manchester and revolving around a motherless, dysfunctional working-class family with an alcoholic father, its subject matter would seem to have come straight out of the 'golden age' of British social realism. However, its funny, classy and up-beat script and direction suggests that British television drama need not fall into only two distinct generic camps. The winner of the Dennis Potter Award for writing at

The funny, classy and up-beat script and direction of *Shameless* suggests that in television drama the 'serious' and the 'shallow' need not always be mutually exclusive.

April's BAFTAs, Abbott's work (like the drama of Kay Mellor, who provided *Between the Sheets* in 2003, and Russell T. Davies, author of the forthcoming *Mine All Mine* and producer of 2005's revival of *Doctor Who*) continues to suggest that the 'serious' and the 'shallow' need not always be mutually exclusive. Although last year proves that the British TV serial can still do both remarkably well, it perhaps excels when it skillfully and sometimes surprisingly manages to combine the two.

Dr Glen Creeber is a Senior Lecturer in the Department of Theatre, Film & Television, University of Wales, Aberystwyth. He has edited titles including **The Television Genre Book** *(BFI: 2001),* **50 Key Television Programmes** *(Arnold: 2004) and* **Serial Fictions: Television Drama from Roots to Sex and the City** *(BFI: 2004).*

Shameless

Single Drama

Lez Cooke

Since the 'golden age' of the single play in the 60s and 70s the single or one-off drama has been an endangered species on British television, superseded by the greater ratings potential of series and serials. Evolving during the 70s into the television film the form enjoyed a new lease of life in the 80s with the advent of Channel 4's *Film on Four* and the BBC's *Screen One* and *Screen Two*, while the more traditional television play survived in anthology series such as *Theatre Night*, *The Play on One* and *Performance*. While such anthologies no longer exist, 2003-4 has seen a small but interesting collection of single dramas transmitted on all the major channels, and with the advent of BBC 4 there has been a revival of the traditional studio-based drama with stage plays such as *Justifying War*, about the Hutton enquiry, and John Osborne's *Hotel In Amsterdam* being restaged for television, while *Three Sisters* even saw a return to the televised theatre play, complete with live audience.

For its award categories BAFTA classifies a single drama as one which is 'transmitted and concluded on one night only' which includes dramas scheduled in two parts either side of the main evening news, such as *England Expects*, in which Steven Mackintosh gave a chilling performance as a racist security guard, but excludes two-part dramas transmitted over two nights, such as *Passer By* in which James Nesbitt featured as a man racked with guilt for not intervening when he witnesses a woman being harrassed by two men on a late-night train. However in terms of length (two hours), structure and its single-issue nature, *Passer By* is a single drama in every respect except its scheduling, whereas other two-part dramas can be three or four hours in length, too long for a conventional single drama (gone are the days of three-hour dramas such as *Artemis 81*).

Passer By was trailed as a new drama by Tony Marchant, one of British television's most original writers, underlining the 'authored' nature of many single dramas – Marchant's contribution to the *Canterbury Tales* anthology series, 'The Miller's Tale', was similarly highlighted. Other well-known writers responsible for single dramas this year include Andrew Davies (*Boudica*), Kay Mellor (*Gifted*) and Sally Wainwright (*Canterbury Tales*: 'The Wife of Bath'), as well as a multi-talented newcomer, Kwame Kwei-Armah, an actor in *Casualty* whose National Theatre play *Elmina's Kitchen* was restaged for television by BBC4.

These 'authored' dramas reaffirm single drama as a writer's medium, yet directors and producers have always had an important role to play and two 'golden age' figures were responsible for two of the best single dramas screened this year. The BAFTA-winning *The Deal*, about the relationship between Tony Blair and Gordon Brown prior to Blair assuming the New Labour leadership, was directed by Stephen Frears, who cut his directorial teeth on the television play in the 70s and 80s, while *Promoted To Glory* was produced by erstwhile

Left to Right: Lia Williams as a girl whose ritual abuse has caused mental illness in *May 33rd*; Steven Mackintosh as a racist security guard in *England Expects*; Billie Piper and Dennis Waterman in *Canterbury Tales*: 'The Miller's Tale'

Social and political issues continue to be the mainstay of single drama

James Nesbitt stars as a man who stands back rather than get involved, in two-part BBC 1 drama *Passer By*

Dennis Potter collaborator Kenith Trodd and there was more than a hint of Potter in this tale of a homeless drunk (Ken Stott) who falls for a Salvation Army captain (Lesley Manville) and decides to sober up, only for an unexpected twist to be revealed at the end.

Single dramas often provide more challenging roles for actors. In addition to Steven Mackintosh's compelling performance in *England Expects* and James Nesbitt's roles in 'The Miller's Tale', *Wall of Silence* and *Passer By*, Julie Walters has been prominent this year, excelling as a recovering alcoholic in the psychological drama *The Return* and winning the BAFTA for Best Actress for her role in 'The Wife of Bath'. There has also been a trend for actors to turn director with David Morrissey, who played Gordon Brown in *The Deal*, going behind the camera to direct *Passer By*, David Jason directing *The Second Quest*, and Sarah Lancashire and Christopher Timothy both directing a BBC *Afternoon Play* each.

As during the 'golden age', social and political issues continue to be the mainstay of single drama. In addition to *Passer By*, *Wall of Silence*, *The Deal* and *Justifying War*, BBC2 chipped in with *Bella and the Boys*, a drama about children in care, and *Every Time You Look At Me*, about attitudes towards disability, while Five contributed *Hear the Silence*, an unashamedly partisan drama attributing an increase in autism in young children to the MMR vaccine. With *Gifted* dealing with a date-rape scandal, *Holy Cross* dramatising sectarian conflict in Northern Ireland, *England Expects* addressing racism and *Pissed On The Job*, *Comfortably Numb* and *May 33rd* exploring alcoholism, drugs and sexual abuse. Many of these dramas were either based on actual events or used drama-doc techniques to explore their subject.

What with historical dramas such as *Boudica*, the mid-20th century history of *Copenhagen* (about the meeting of two physicists whose work led to the atomic bomb), the recent history of *Justifying War* and the modern reworkings of Chaucer's *Canterbury Tales*, not to mention *The Legend of the Tamworth Two*, a family drama for Easter loosely based on the real-life story of two escaped pigs, single drama has been a significant presence on British television in the past year.

*Lez Cooke is the author of **British Television Drama: A History** (BFI: 2003)*

PROGRAMMING

Billie Piper surprised many critics with her strong performance as a girl in care in *Bella and the Boys*

Crime Drama

Alan Barnes

What was the most controversial crime drama on British television over 2003–4? Lynda La Plante's umpteenth *Trial and Retribution*, all severed screens and split appendages? *Cracker* wannabe *Wire in the Blood*, with its deeply unsympathetic, quietly demented forensic psychologist lead and its cast of nearly-but-not-quite supporting crims – a Hindley type seeking out long-forgotten child graves in one; a Shipman-like killer on the wards in another? Or maybe *The Last Witness*, the first *Prime Suspect* in seven years, which took Bosnian war crimes for its backdrop and a deeply scary optician for its baddie?

None of the above, of course, albeit not for the want of trying. *Rosemary and Thyme*, a jolly corpses-and-coppicing vehicle for Felicity Kendal (as ex-University of Malmesbury horticulturalist Rosemary Boxer) and Pam Ferris (as ex-married ex-policewoman Laura Thyme) attracted end-of-civilisation-as-we-know-it notices: 'You see, you're supposed to sit and identify with this Complan *Cagney & Lacey*, the elasticated, comfy-fit *Thelma & Louise*, as they do a bit of digging and detecting,' wrote *The Sunday Times*' A. A. Gill. 'It was desperate, sort of *Ground Force*-meets-*A Touch of Frost* in drag.' It was also by far and away the most successful drama launch of the year full stop, the first episode winning 11.1 million viewers – a 44 per cent share of the available audience (BARB). 'It's dodgy stuff, that digitalis,' as Laura Thyme would tell you.

What, then, does *Rosemary and Thyme* (and if

What does the success of *Rosemary and Thyme* tell us? That the most influential crime show of the last decade may not have been *Prime Suspect* nor *Cracker* but *Midsomer Murders*?

its heroes' names sound contrived, that's as nothing to its villains – step forward Delia Kettle, the so-called 'Witch of Withersedge') tell us about the state of the genre? That the most influential television crime show of the last decade may not have been *Prime Suspect*, nor *The Cops*, nor *Cracker* – but *Midsomer Murders*, after all? Certainly, the evergreen *Midsomer* (six new episodes of which saw John Nettles' DCI Tom Barnaby joined by a fresh sidekick, John Hopkins as Sergeant Dan Scott) was in ITV1 drama controller Nick Elliott's mind at the time of the development of *Murder in Suburbia*, which featured Caroline Catz (ex-*The Vice*) as DI Kate 'Ash' Ashurst and the ubiquitous Lisa Faulkner as DS Emma 'Scribbs' Scribbins: 'Two-thirds of our audience lives in suburbia, at the end of the Tube line ... I want to make suburbia the star of this show, in the same way that a sleepy countryside village is the star of *Midsomer Murders*.' Cue storylines about school discos for fortysomethings, wife-swapping (of course) and a DIY enthusiast found battered with his own hammer.

Undemanding, yes. But if literary crime has always been a populist genre, why should television crime make any great claim to such abstract values as worth and verisimilitude? By such tokens, *The Last Detective* ought to be feted for its sheer ordinariness, Peter Davison's sarcastically-nicknamed plodding copper 'Dangerous' Davies embodying the virtues of the also-ran. ITV1's two other new launches were altogether more portentous in tone – but *Family* (Martin Kemp as the head of the Cutler clan, a dubious East End *Sopranos*) would be shunted to a graveyard slot two-thirds of the way through its six-part run; and the styled-to-within-an-inch-of-its-life *Murder City* (Amanda Donohoe as DCI Susan Alembic and Kris Marshall as her borderline-autistic associate, DS Luke Stone) struggled in its slot against BBC 1's altogether more

New Tricks – a successful new crime series on BBC 1

Ash and Scribbs uncovered *Murder in Suburbia*

traditional *Inspector Lynley Mysteries*, despite a few devilishly clever conceits in its plotting (a killer precisely times a so-called 'critical path' past twenty-seven constantly turning CCTV cameras).

The 'new unreality' was no guarantor of success, however. *Sparkling Cyanide*, with Pauline Collins and Oliver Ford Davies as husband-and-wife government spooks, was the car crash of the year, updating a minor Agatha Christie potboiler to a world of 'tox screens' and 'data encryption' populated by Premiership footballers and the Minister for Culture, Media and Sport. ITV1's other one-offs and mini-series included no less than four 'did-they-or-didn't-they?' psychological thrillers about maybe-murderers suffering memory loss in the space of just four months, making this the most worn-out premise of the moment: Julie Walters was alcoholic Lizzie Hunt, wondering whether or not she was rightly convicted for the murder of her husband in *The Return*; Tom Conti was narcoleptic ex-police forensic scientist *Donovan*, who may or may not have autographed murder scenes in blood; John Hannah was DS Mackenzie Stone, who may or may not have done in his missing missus in *Amnesia*; and Jonathan Cake was forgetful CID man Jason Shepherd, researching his own apparent corruption in *Fallen*. None kept us guessing like Paul Abbott's blackly comic *Alibi*, which had Michael Kitchen as a cuckolded husband (or cold killer?) persuading part-time waitress (or cynical blackmailer?) Sophie Okonedo to cover up the manslaughter of his wife's lover.

BBC 1, meanwhile, poached P. D. James' Commander Adam Dalgleish from the long-defunct Anglia and reincarnated him in the form of Martin Shaw, doing his best to look rugged amid the cloistered histrionics of *Death in Holy Orders*. They gave him a love interest, too, not something associated with the stringy Roy Marsden, his predecessor in the role. Efforts were made to add weight to *Dalziel and Pascoe*, what with an episode about a murdered docusoap star and a shaggy dog

story about a spectral hound – but of BBC 1's returning series, only *Waking the Dead* and *Murphy's Law* retained any real bite (the former with, for example, a very weird two-parter seemingly inspired by legends of the making of cult film *Performance*; the latter with a closing episode about a victim support group which turns to revenge killing as therapy). *New Tricks*, in which Supt Sandra Pullman (Amanda Redman) heads a squad of has-been coppers charged with re-examining old cases, was given a six-part series following a successful pilot – and proved significantly better than its premise, Alun Armstrong putting in a noteworthy performance as an obsessive fuelled by a sense of personal injustice.

At least BBC 2's choice to adapt the 1960s gangland novel *The Long Firm* this Summer suggests that there might be more to the crime genre than the ongoing adventures of maverick cops. Should their commissioning executives be prepared to explore the further fringes, BBC 2 or Channel 4 might do well by adapting David Peace's so-called 'Red Riding Quartet', a wilfully unforgiving epic of police corruption which takes the Yorkshire Ripper killings for its backdrop, or perhaps the creepy, alternative serial killer thrillers of Mark Billingham. Certainly, a counterweight is needed to the dependable unrealities of the genre mainstream. After all, 2003 was the year that a covertly-recorded expose of probationary constables spouting racist cant (*The Secret Policeman*) caused deep discomfort at the Home Office. Where was there for fiction to reflect the drama of the fact?

Alan Barnes is the author of **Sherlock Holmes on Screen** *(Reynolds & Hearn: 2001). A former editor of* **Doctor Who Magazine**, *he now edits* **Judge Dredd Megazine** *for Rebellion.*

Waking the Dead – its summer 2004 run scored big audiences of around 8 million

PROGRAMMING

Sci-fi & Fantasy

Gary Gillatt

Derren Brown: Séance hoaxed its participants and viewers

While programme makers in the UK have fallen out of love with science fiction and fantasy based dramas, viewers retain an affection for the genre.

Most Haunted: a serious investigation of the paranormal, factual history or just plain old horror telefantasy dressed up in post-reality togs?

There was a time when homegrown science fiction and fantasy was a familiar fixture of British television. The *Quatermass* serials remain perhaps the most vividly remembered television drama of the 50s. The 60s brought us such iconic, era-defining series as *The Avengers* and *The Prisoner*. The 70s delivered the more sinister, apocalyptic *Doomwatch*, *Survivors* and *Blake's 7*. Outstripping them all, the BBC's time-travelling adventure serial *Doctor Who* debuted in 1963 and ran for twenty-six years.

The taste for such imaginative fare seemed to diminish during the more pragmatic, world-weary 80s; even *Doctor Who* fell by the wayside in the dying days of that decade. The years since have been a barren time for those who prefer their drama not to focus on the troubled private lives of policeman, doctors, lawyers or the inhabitants of picture postcard villages in the north of England.

This year's only bone fide fantasy drama was BBC 1's short run of lightly supernatural chillers, *Sea Of Souls*. Written by David Kane and produced by Phil Collinson for BBC Scotland, *Sea Of Souls* comprised three stories, each with a pair of hour-long episodes. All took inspiration from a different aspect of parapsychology. The series was touted by the press as a 'British X Files', in reference to the hit US drama that saw FBI agents investigate a wide range of Fortean fare, from alien abduction to the Bermuda Triangle. However, while *Sea Of Souls* employed such outré dramatic hooks as black magic and reincarnation, these were kept low in the mix, as the series played familiar murder mystery plots – including a pretty standard 'evil twin' storyline that wouldn't have looked out of place in an episode of *Taggart* or *Columbo*. In fact, while the series' lead characters – the lugubrious Professor Douglas Monagahan (Bill Paterson) and his handsome young assistants, Megan (Archie Panjabi) and Andrew Gemmill (Peter McDonald) – would dither briefly in their lab discussing matters extra-sensory, it was never long before they were out on the streets solving a murder, and together struck a silhouette identical to that of the crime-fighting team of early *Taggart*. It seems that by not overloading their series with assorted ghosts, ghouls, and things that go 'bump' out of primetime, the team behind *Sea Of Souls* produced the UK's first mass-appeal fantasy hit in years, and a second series has been confirmed for 2005.

To truly embrace the spirit world on British TV,

you have to leave the humdrum terrestrial domain far behind. One channel that is far from embarrassed to be associated with the paranormal – and all its associated eccentrics – is LivingTV. Its ghost-hunting *Most Haunted* has become a cult hit, with around half a million tuning in regularly to see host Yvette Fielding scared out of her slingbacks in a variety of brooding castles and mouldering country houses. Each episode, Fielding, generally accompanied by spiritualist medium Derek Acorah, investigates the history of a different haunted house and tries to stir up some camera-friendly poltergeist activity.

Of course, if the team had ever managed to capture proof of an afterlife on tape, then it might receive slightly more coverage than a late-night hour on cable TV, but these game ghostbusters do their best to convince us that their footsteps are dogged by the uncanny and the unearthly. The cameraman will often draw our attention to floating 'orbs' of supernatural energy (though the sceptical may only see light catching motes of dust close to the lens), while Fielding can be relied upon to scream at the slightest creak or squeak from whichever Elizabethan doorframe she is leaning against. Acorah makes the best contribution to the narrative, by 'reading' the history of old murder weapons or cutlery ('I sense a young girl called Sarah, perhaps a chambermaid ... There was a maid here called Susan ... Yes, Susan – that's right.').

Whether you treat *Most Haunted* as a serious investigation of the paranormal or merely a modern way of telling a good ghost story, the series remains entertaining, its success marked by such spin-offs as live specials and a copycat celebrity version: *I'm Famous And Frightened!* Further, the televisual sleights-of-hand it employs to convince us that unknowable forces are at work have been co-opted by more mainstream programming, most notably in Derren Brown's *Séance* – in which the TV mind reader sought to uncover the truth behind Ouija Boards and the like, while all the time seeking to keep his audience shivering with talk of possession and conversations with the dead.

While programme makers in the UK have fallen out of love with science fiction and fantasy based dramas, viewers retain an affection for the genre. The majority of all time highest-grossing motion pictures feature spaceships, spells, mutants or monsters, and the public's enthusiasm for escapist entertainment remains as clear as ever. But SF is very expensive to produce, so British TV tends to buy second or third hand, with US series like various *Star Trek*s and *Buffy The Vampire Slayer* attracting loyal audiences to Sky One and BBC 2.

Sea of Souls – story one guest-starred Siobhan Redmond as supernatural twins

It seems odd, therefore, that perhaps the BBC's most lavish drama commission for 2005 should be a revival of *Doctor Who*, starring Christopher Eccleston in the title role. In a TV age where few risks are taken, there's a certain discontinuity in BBC 1's sudden enthusiasm for this most whimsical of fantasy series, given that other recent dalliances with the genre – *Strange*, *Randall And Hopkirk (Deceased)* – hardly set the world alight. The chief creative force behind the new *Doctor Who* is *Queer As Folk* and *The Second Coming* creator Russell T. Davies. This talented and critically-acclaimed writer carries a life-long passion for *Doctor Who*, and his involvement would prove a key factor in the BBC's decision to revive this series after so long. Furthermore, it's probable that the channel isn't even considering *Doctor Who* as a brave step into the world of TV fantasy at all. The show remains a 'brand' strongly identified with Auntie Beeb's glory days as the nation's favourite broadcaster, so the return of *Doctor Who* fits in more closely the recent trend for the BBC to take inspiration from its own archive; the 2004 revival of *(Strictly) Come Dancing* and 2005's planned return for *The Two Ronnies* standing as other examples.

Should the new mega-budget, star cast *Doctor Who* be a hit, it might well inspire a wealth of new home-grown fantasy and science fiction drama. Whether this will be original and ground-breaking material – thrilling a generation the way *Quatermass* or *The Avengers* did – or merely further revivals and pastiche, remains to be seen.

*Gary Gillatt is a staff writer at **Inside Soap** magazine. He is a former editor of **Starburst** and **Doctor Who Magazine**.*

Costume & Historical

Sarah Cardwell

Costume dramas and literary adaptations

This was a disappointing year for fans of costume dramas and literary adaptations with barely any classic-novel adaptations – no Austen, Dickens or Eliot. Even prolific adapter Andrew Davies only turned out one adaptation: of Anthony Trollope's novel *He Knew He Was Right* (though he also produced the historical drama *Boudica* this year).

At his best, Davies is unmatched in his flair for reshaping his sources with an attitude of sympathetic irony towards them. *He Knew He Was Right* benefited from this approach. It could have become a somewhat heavy handed melodrama, but Davies's tongue-in-cheek re-presentation endowed the rather thin storyline and two-dimensional characters with humour and warmth. The result was not as innovative or startling as some of his more recent work, and failed to attain the level of complexity, style and dark humour found in his 2001 adaptation of Trollope's *The Way We Live Now*, but the serial was an entertaining, amusing instance of television that stretches the conventions of naturalism without breaking them entirely.

In some ways, the programme constituted a return to the old-fashioned Sunday family serial, though scheduled at 9 p.m. The relative absence of Davies was compensated for to some degree by a short season of work on BBC 4 in December, including a new interview with the man himself.

The Christmas period, usually fecund with big-budget classic-novel adaptations, produced just one such programme – ITV's *The Mayor of Casterbridge*, made several years ago and gathering dust on a shelf ever since, waiting for an appropriate broadcast slot. Perhaps indicative of this lengthy hiatus, the programme was competently produced, with an emphasis upon the 'authenticity' of its locations, costumes and the thick Dorset accents of its cast but little of the stylistic innovation visible in other recent adaptations.

The BBC broke with tradition, offering *The Young Visiters*, adapted from nine-year-old

author Daisy Ashford's Victorian novel. This used its source cleverly, retaining elements of the exuberant style and childlike tone of the book, primarily through the expert direction of David Yates (responsible for the aforementioned *The Way We Live Now*). Wonderfully exaggerated and yet sympathetic performances from the cast, especially Jim Broadbent as the hapless Alfred Salteena, complemented excessive qualities elsewhere (the ridiculously large egg balancing on top of Ethel's eggcup at breakfast; the embellished costumes; the intense colours). The plot progressed at a rattling pace, ideal for young viewers, and the programme integrated musical qualities (a dominant musical score; extras who broke spontaneously into song; choreographed groups of servants, farmhands and office workers; rhythmic visual repetitions), conveying a sense of old fashioned all-round entertainment. This was charming festive family television, of a kind that is particularly hard to produce nowadays.

Another significant literary adaptation saw *The Canterbury Tales*, updated to the present day. The programmes bore very little relation to the source texts that inspired them, instead utilising the bare bones of Chaucer's tales to create essentially modern stories. The sense of connection created by the interrelation between the stories in Chaucer's text was lost; rather, the six episodes were completely independent, making use of television's single play format.

The year may have witnessed some successful attempts to open up the breadth of source texts beyond the usual suspects of the nineteenth-century 'great' authors but also displayed a paucity of engaging literary adaptations and/or period dramas. Perhaps 2004-5 will see a return to the kind of courageous, quality programming we have come to expect from the genre in recent years.

Historical dramas

There's been a strong emphasis this year upon famous, charismatic individuals, and with the exception of *Eroica*, focusing on Beethoven and his third symphony, there was a

Rufus Sewell was *Charles II*

predominant focus on characters with strong British connotations. There were several dramas based on British rulers and royalty, as well as British artists, scientists and legendary figures. Presented larger-than-life they were endowed with semi-legendary status, whether programmes were based in historical accounts or extensively fictionalised.

Andrew Davies ventured into the historical drama genre with *Boudica*, boasting a cast of thousands (constituted primarily of Romanians, who cost only one tenth of the usual Equity rate paid to British actors), and starring Alex Kingston. Davies made no claims for historical accuracy, citing a fragment from Tacitus's account of Boudica's exploits as inspiration, and focusing on her as a mythic figure; moments of mysticism contributed to the sense that this was a fantastical, fabulous tale rather than a realistic one.

Other programmes based on the well-documented lives of more recent figures exhibited a similar emphasis on the charismatic individuals 'behind' the official roles, and moved beyond the kinds of historical reconstruction found in drama documentaries and documentary dramas towards lively presentations of engaging protagonists. The choice of big-name, home-grown stars was important: Ray Winstone played an intense, 'rough diamond' as *Henry VIII* and Rufus Sewell offered an enchanting performance as a seductive yet flawed Charles II, in *Charles II: The power and the passion* (a title expressing perfectly the approach taken this year).

A discernible trend saw greater experimentation in terms of visual style. Extensive use of hand-held cameras, direct address, stylised camerawork and editing – along with the use of stars – created an appealing, glossy, cinematic feel. Yet these dramas also managed mostly to retain a sense of television's power to offer intimate insights into characters' lives, and simultaneously claim a level of emotional truthfulness that made for powerful, engaging drama. The viewer was shown the 'real' people behind the legends and given access to their messy personal and political lives.

In this way, the emphasis in historical dramas this year was most definitely upon drama, rather than history. The programmes were not primarily educative in their aims, and there was a sense of popularising the genre, both through the choice of popular, mythic figures (*Henry VIII*, *Charles II*, *Samuel Pepys*, *Byron*), and through the casting choices of popular stars like Winstone and Sewell, and Steve Coogan, wonderfully cast as the licentious Samuel Pepys (this trend was also

With charter renewal due 2006, the BBC may decide to put aside entertaining historical dramas in favour of more didactic, 'serious' docudramas or documentaries

discernible in the related genre of documentary drama, with Simon Callow as Galileo in *Galileo's Daughter* and Prunella Scales as Queen Victoria in *Looking for Victoria*).

Such developments are not evidence of 'dumbing down'; instead, they rightly highlight the distinction between historical dramas and most other historical genres. The emphasis on the intimate portrait of highly visible individuals, the dramatic licence taken with their stories and the attention paid to creative camerawork, scripting and editing places these programmes firmly within a consolidated genre of 'quality drama', distinguishing them from other history-based programmes (including, this year, *Ancient Egyptians*, *Pompeii*, *Looking for Victoria* and *Churchill*). The latter fit more readily within the categories of documentary drama or drama documentary, more dependent upon dramatic reconstructions, and with didactic, educative aims.

One might also suggest that excessive emphasis on British 'heroes' or well-known 'characters' provided a sense of national specificity and emphasis, in a year when the characteristically British classic-novel adaptation was thin on the ground. It will be interesting to see whether both the 'dramatic' trends and the reaffirmed focus on British individuals will be sustained next year. Broader institutional and political factors may prove influential: the BBC faces its charter renewal in 2006, and with this will undoubtedly come a renewed focus on public service broadcasting (PSB) values. This may affect programming choices, with the BBC deciding to put aside entertaining historical dramas in favour of more didactic, 'serious' docudramas or documentaries that more manifestly fulfil a PSB remit of educating, informing and entertaining.

*Dr Sarah Cardwell is Lecturer in Film and Television Studies at the University of Kent and the author of **Adaptation Revisited: Television and the Classic Novel** (MUP: 2002) and **Andrew Davies** (MUP: 2004).*

PROGRAMMING

Docudrama

Stella Bruzzi

Docudramas are back in vogue and early in 2004 the BBC created a new role to oversee the development of docudramas, the first incumbent being current affairs producer Tom Giles. Having been thought worthy, serious and often politically motivated (Granada's *Who Bombed Birmingham?* in 1990 for example) they have now acquired entertainment value. The spaces these docudramas occupy in the schedules, the diversification of their subject matter and their production values are the most important factors in this renewal of interest. Docudramas tend to be put out at times reserved traditionally for documentary; a series such as *Ancient Egyptians* – transmitted on Channel 4 at 9 p.m.– occupied a slot which has at other times been reserved for documentary strands such as *Dispatches*.

Ancient Egyptians differed markedly from a standard *Dispatches* (April's 'Third Class Mail', for instance, in which an undercover reporter infiltrated the Royal Mail's sorting rooms). Firstly, *Ancient Egyptians* cost £6 million and employed Oscar-winning outfit The Mill (which worked on *Gladiator*) to produce its special effects and so resembles drama rather than documentary. Secondly, like the BBC's phenomenally successful

> **A glossier style has become the norm for docudramas. What has also become the norm is a relaxed – some might say dubious – detachment from factual accuracy.**

Walking With Dinosaurs, the series' relation to historical authenticity is ambiguous – the dialogue and scenarios are fabricated, although creatively based on fact. After previous recent successes such as *Bloody Sunday* (Granada Film, 2002) or *Small Pox 2002*, this glossier style has become the norm for docudramas. What has also become the norm is this relaxed – some might say dubious – detachment from factual accuracy. Two sorts of docudramas were produced during the year: those that dramatised a specific historical event (and so used dramatic licence within a more confined context) and those, like *Ancient Egyptians*, that fictionalised either a general or a hypothetical factual issue.

Phil Davis and James Nesbitt starred in the true life ITV1 docudrama *Wall of Silence*

During the last year, other docudramas that fell into the latter category included Channel 4's *Comfortably Numb*, Five's *Hear the Silence* and the BBC 2 series *If ...* . *Comfortably Numb* gave a fictionalised account of a rehabilitation clinic in which actors played the two main parts, whilst real doctors and patients assumed the secondary roles in a series of realistic, ad-libbed scenes. One argument mobilised in the press for such an approach was that drama is able to show things that documentary could not (although there have been factual series that have taken a hard and graphic look at drug abuse, which mitigates against this).

Hear the Silence was a gripping, moving and highly watchable film about the case of Dr Andrew Wakefield and the MMR crisis his beliefs precipitated (that in certain cases the MMR vaccine caused bowel disorders and autism in the children to whom it was administered). The film's apparent bias towards Wakefield received sustained criticism in the press and *Hear the Silence* broke a cardinal rule of traditional docudrama by taking such a subjective position and siding, if not wholly with Wakefield, then with the mothers (particularly Juliet Stephenson's character) who believed their children had been damaged by the vaccine. Author Timothy Prager confirmed this bias when commenting in *Broadcast* that he intentionally sought to put the mothers' case across because 'I had a horrible feeling that they were being silenced'.

Like *Comfortably Numb, Hear the Silence* is part of a new docudrama drama style; it is based on a topical (and sensitive) issue and mingles conventional generic elements such as real characters (Wakefield, for example) with fictionalised representative figures (the mothers) that offer composite as opposed to authenticated individual portraits. *If ...* took this a step further as it dabbled in 'projective current affairs' as the series' editor Peter Barron has termed it and dramatised potentially cataclysmic but so far hypothetical future crises such as the UK's looming energy crisis when it becomes dependent upon imported gas supplies.

By contrast, docudramas such as ITV 1's *Wall of Silence* and BBC 1's *In Denial of Murder* were more focused on a single historical event, and so appeared more conventional. Both were written by Neil MacKay who, after having scripted previous docudramas such as *This is Personal,* about the 'Yorkshire Ripper', and *Innocents*, about the Bristol babies heart scandal, has become the writer

> **One argument mobilised for a docudrama approach was that drama is able to show things that documentary could not.**

now most readily associated with the genre. Both of this year's docudramas conformed to a classic generic model; they both took as their subject a murder case that, for some, had produced an unsatisfactory initial verdict.

Wall of Silence dramatised the murder on the Osprey Estate in Rotherhithe, London in August 1997 of Jamie Robe; it began with Jamie being beaten to death by a gang of youths from the estate and showed witnesses to the scene not doing anything at the time and largely refusing to assist the police in their subsequent investigations. The protagonists are Jamie's father Stuart (James Nesbitt) and the tenacious inspector (played by Phil Davis) who eventually helps Stuart in his aim to see three of the four accused jailed for murder. *Wall of Silence* unambiguously supported the case of Stuart Robe, whose protracted, personalised fight for justice proved its emotional core; it also conformed to the rules of traditional docudramas as it included only real people (for instance the MP Simon Hughes, who actively helped the police investigation, is named).

In Denial of Murder was more equivocal in its approach to its subject matter. This two-part docudrama reconstructed the 1990s' investigation by a local newspaper reporter, Don Hale, into the murder of Wendy Sewell in Bakewell cemetery in 1973. Hale believed there had been a miscarriage of justice and campaigned for the release of Stephen Downing, the man initially convicted of Sewell's murder. By the end of the film, however, Downing's innocence is far from certain and *In Denial of Murder* concludes by intimating that maybe Hale had been duped.

Wall of Silence and *In Denial of Murder* share a classic docudrama style; their acting is earnest, there are no flashy special effects, the filming style is unobtrusive and the historical reconstructions go for stolid authenticity. This is a far cry from the grandiosity of the hypothetical docudramas, but one suspects that, with all the main channels, those more bombastic docudramas will predominate.

Stella Bruzzi is Professor of Film Studies at Royal Holloway, University of London.

PROGRAMMING

135

Comedy

Phil Wickham

Comedy at the Cutting Edge

Comedy currently occupies a paradoxical position in British television. Classic shows and great comics help define TV and our national identity. At the same time ratings pressure, institutional change, and new viewing habits are changing the experience for industry and audiences alike.

A new type of comedy has become the dominant mode over the last decade, reflecting this new landscape. This 'new comedy' is often edgier in content, experimental in form, and broadcast on minority or digital channels. Sitcom has been revitalised. The best programmes have moved the genre on, leaving behind studio sets, audience laughter, and the traditional construction of the comic situation so instead of returning to the status quo at the end of each episode there is often now a complex, unfolding narrative.

Christmas saw two special concluding episodes of *The Office*, probably the most definitive new comedy and certainly the most popular. Seven million viewers on BBC 1 said goodbye to the workers of Slough paper firm Wernham Hogg. The show speaks to our soul, triumphantly bringing out the full comic horror of modern Britain. Writers Ricky Gervais and Stephen Merchant ended on very satisfying grace notes. David Brent, an iconic

With *The Office Christmas Specials* we sadly said goodbye to the staff of Wernham-Hogg

figure for our age with his desperate bonhomie and rampant insecurities, gets a glimmer of hope for redemption and a nation roared their approval as Tim and Dawn, the Thames Valley Romeo and Juliet, finally, awkwardly, get together at last. The success of *The Office*, with its record breaking DVD sales, reassures us that there can still be an audience for great work, however challenging. Its sensational Golden Globe wins bestow national confidence and self-respect.

Plenty of other excellent material from this new tradition of free-form, darkish-hearted sitcom appeared this year to show the well had not run dry. *Early Doors*, from *Royle Family* creator Craig Cash, is a perfect comic gem first shown in May 2003 but repeated (and recommissioned for a second series) in our time period. Set entirely in a Manchester pub it has many of the attributes of classic 60s or 70s sitcoms, but the 'new comedy' style allows it room to breathe, exploring subtler character traits for both comic and poignant effect. The sumptuous photography creates an atmosphere that's like a cross between *Are You Being Served?* and the films of Terence Davies – and I mean that in a very good way. Repeats remain vital to TV comedy in organically building up an audience by word of mouth.

Grass also uses beautiful photography to bring out its leisurely narrative about Billy Bleach's (Simon Day's cockney bar bore character in *The Fast Show*) move to Norfolk on the witness protection scheme. Its plot was echoed by Reeves and Mortimer's sitcom *Catterick* but *Grass* is more successful in making it funny, character and acting rather getting in the way of what Vic and Bob do best.

Peep Show sees Channel 4's youth obsessions finally come good. It mixes stylistic quirks, notably a device where we see the action through particular characters' eyes, with a hilarious dissection of the love-hate relationship between flatmates Mark and Jez. Interestingly it is the character comedy that really grips, proving that what always works best in British comedy is deluded losers.

The best critically received new sitcom of the year was Julia Davis' *Nighty Night*, which plunged British comedy further down its long journey to dark despair with jokes about cancer, multiple sclerosis and pathological cruelty. Davis, performing the lead role of evil hairdresser Jill as well as writing, is an important talent and there are some splendid black comedy moments, though ultimately its relentless misanthropy proves somewhat wearing.

There now seems to be nothing that can't be done in sitcom form. Beckett style meanderings in a high-rise council block in Kennington? Yes! Sean Lock's *Fifteen Storeys High* manages to be both absurdly and realistically funny. A tightly plotted comic satire about contemporary consumerism featuring a celeb-obsessed rat and a Eurosceptic sparrow? Yes! The extraordinary animated parable *I Am Not An Animal*, about a vivisection experiment gone wrong.

The skill of 'new comedy' practitioners was also evident in sketch shows, which had their best year since *The Fast Show*. Matt Lucas and David Walliams' *Little Britain* fulfilled the vital function of the sketch show, which is to have the catchphrases screamed across offices and playgrounds the next morning. Characters like Dafydd, 'the only gay in the village' and wayward teen Vicky Pollard hit the zeitgeist in the way such shows should. Subtler but equally funny, *The Catherine Tate Show* explored a range of female archetypes from belligerent youth to foul mouthed grandmother.

The good news is that broadcasters and production companies such as talkbackThames, Tiger Aspect, and Steve Coogan's outfit Baby Cow, are recognising and nurturing these new talents. Freer forms leave more room for exploring new ideas. Comedy is also becoming less of a boys club with female performers like Davis, Tate and Ronni Ancona at the head of the new wave. Screening on minority or digital channels protects the work from the ratings hothouse – many shows mentioned here have debuted on BBC 3 and built up an audience by word of mouth to achieve ratings success (like *Little Britain*) or critical acclaim.

However there are problems with this direction. Comedy is not just a niche brand aimed at the young and wealthy. Comedy has become the main selling point of BBC 3, but

> **'New comedy' has become the dominant mode over the last decade, often edgier in content, experimental in form, and broadcast on minority or digital channels. Sitcom has been revitalised.**

there are limitations as well as opportunities. Nearly fifty percent cannot access digital, so budgets are reduced and material is expected to suit the channel's young, metropolitan target audience. Channel 4 is embarrassingly desperate for youth's disposable income to sate slavering advertisers. Much of their 'comedy' output, the welcome return of the ever reliable *Black Books* apart, spills over into other genres to entice this demographic like the reality style *My New Best Friend* or game show *Distraction*. This cult of youth favours the dark, the cruel, the hip or the raucous – fine if it means some of the shows detailed earlier but grim if it means BBC 3's woeful *Cyderdelic* or the worst bits of Channel 4's *Bo' Selecta!*. There is more to comedy than swearing and Posh and Becks gags ... honestly.

Vicky Pollard and her long-suffering teacher were just two of the characters living in *Little Britain*

PROGRAMMING

Comedy in the Mainstream

Comedy is a high-risk business, needing time and money to develop an audience while they get used to characters, situations, and performers. In a new TV world demanding instant gratification and quick results its future is threatened. These harsh economic facts and new talent's success in altering many of our expectations of TV comedy, raise questions over the future of the genre on mainstream channels. This is worrying because to preserve its impact on society, comedy needs to engage with a mass audience and cut across demographics.

Proof of the continued popularity and importance of comedy to British society came in the BBC 2 poll for *Britain's Best Sitcoms* (see box-out, right). Over one and a half million votes cast and audiences of nearly six million for the programmes make one proud to be part of the British public, hard to forgive though the top three positions of *Blackadder* (if only in my house) and *The Vicar of Dibley* (in lots of peoples' houses) may be.

The prevailing feeling in broadcasting seems to be fear that mass appeal can no longer be achieved and this nervousness infects many programmes. Many mainstream sitcoms are too self-conscious and uneasy in tone, sometimes leading to crassness, predictability and a whiff of desperation. So on BBC 1 we get *My Hero*, a children's show on in primetime, *Eyes Down*, a sort of cut-price *Phoenix Nights*, *All About Me* an American style multicultural warmedy that could put progressive

Amanda Holden and Jamie Theakston in *Mad About Alice* failed to replicate the success of *My Family*

> ## The prevailing feeling in broadcasting seems to be fear that mass appeal can no longer be achieved and this nervousness infects many programmes.

politics back years, the badly misjudged black Londoners series *The Crouches*, the semaphoring of creaking gags in *Mad About Alice*, and the flogging of the very dead horse that is *Absolutely Fabulous*, once fresh and funny, sadly now just shouting in search of a joke.

It is not all the broadcasters fault though – reviewers have written off traditional comedy to such an extent that any mainstream sitcom is automatically savaged, perpetuating an aura of defeat. This can be desperately unfair; witness the hostile reception for two Simon Nye scripted shows, the quirky *Wild West* and the simple but effective *Hardware*, both well acted, well written and often very funny. In this context the huge ratings success of *My Family* (up to nine million viewers) is important. Slick and slightly shallow though the show may be, it is also funny and popular. Such success may stop British TV from completely throwing the baby out with the bathwater – new and old sitcom can co-exist. The end of *Friends* and *Frasier*, may also limit the damaging received wisdom that American is better.

Direct satire in any comic form also seems in a poor state – bizarre given the available material. The tendency is either go for earnest but unfunny, like Rory Bremner, or for the Oxbridge backslapping dressed up as criticism that characterises *Have I Got News For You* at its weakest, exemplified by the sitcom *Absolute Power* which is as cynical as those it purports to mock. Impressionist Jon Culshaw has some telling Blair moments but top mimic Alistair McGowan prefers to stay safely with showbiz. The one satire that scores real blows is the very broad and traditional Northern Ireland sitcom *Give My Head Peace*, shown outside the province for the first time, which builds ferocious political attacks around funny characters and situations.

Fear of mainstream comedy also creates a void where comedians once were. Stand up just doesn't effectively translate to screen anymore and the same old faces – Jasper Carrott and Jim Davidson – in rehashed specials compensates not at all. Lenny Henry tries hard but to little

Retro-Comedy

Familiarity, it seems, breeds content. This year the BBC mounted a campaign to find *Britain's Best Sitcom*. It was no surprise to find that the Top Ten were all BBC shows (though Channel 4's *Father Ted* at number 11 nearly gatecrashed the party), and it was less of a surprise to note that all of the Top Ten had enjoyed many repeats since their first transmission. Third was *The Vicar of Dibley*, a series that seems to have been omnipresent in the schedules since its debut in 1994, despite the fact that only sixteen episodes have been made. This constant repetition has moved the series up in the public consciousness – most TV pundits were surprised at *Dibley* finishing so high but in the last year alone thirteen episodes have been shown on BBC 1. *Only Fools and Horses* was top and that was represented by thirty-five

episodes on BBC1 this year. So are these shows so popular because they are repeated so much – or are they repeated so much because they are so popular?

When the BBC resurrect vintage comedies they seem to only pick from a pool of about ten titles. (*Only Fools and Horses, Fawlty Towers, Dad's Army, The Good Life, 'Allo 'Allo, Some Mother's Do 'ave 'em*), while ITV, Channel 4 and Five ignore the (UK) genre altogether.

The antipathy towards black and white means that many classic series have scant chance of resurrection but even many shows that were made in colour and have much to recommend them, still never surface because of a Catch 22. As the shows aren't repeated they don't get a chance to become familiar to a new generation; and because they're not familiar, they don't get repeated. Thus many series remain ignored – classics like *Chance In A Million* (Simon Callow and Brenda Blethyn in an early Channel 4 series about a man beset by bizarre coincidences), *I Didn't Know You Cared* (Peter Tinniswood's TV tales of his beloved Brandon family), Mel Smith's bittersweet *Colin's Sandwich* (male menopause comedy), LWT's *Six Dates With Barker* (anthology comedy showcasing Ronnie Barker's talents); and Jack Rosenthal's *The Dustbinmen* (earthy sitcom whose first series was number one in the ratings, beating *Coronation Street*).

Dick Fiddy

effect. There is no earthly reason why Peter Kay, the great comic talent of the age, who packs out venues and sells DVDs by the tonne, could not dominate primetime yet it does not happen. We see what we are missing in Bob Monkhouse's brilliant deathbed documentary *Behind the Laughter*, shrewdly analysing the comic genius of his contemporaries, Morecambe, Cooper and the rest. Frank Skinner and Graham Norton hardly suffice.

Comedy slips into other genres very stealthily from *Coronation Street* to *I'm a Celebrity* to *Friday Night with Jonathan Ross* but a firm place for itself in the mainstream schedule is necessary. In these difficult times strangely we salute ITV1 where, despite the fierce commercial pressures placed on the most mainstream channel of them all, Head of Comedy Sioned Wiliam has built a slate of diverse and funny shows in post-2200 slots ranging from *Harry Hill's TV Burp* to Rob Brydon's *Director's Commentary*. This kind of

commitment and the plethora of British talent give hope for the comic future but it will require broadcasters to keep their nerve.

Quiz & Game Shows

Graham Kibble-White

The last twelve months have been largely unmemorable for the genre, with no particular standout shows or calamitous follies. Instead the familiar parade of faces dishing out those big and not-so big money prizes have been bringing us business as usual.

Over the last six years *Who Wants to be a Millionaire?* has been afforded the position at the head of the quiz show table. However, ITV1's former ratings Exocet is clearly in decline, with its run commencing 30 August continuing to shed viewers, despite various tweaks to the format. On 10 September *The Guardian* reported: 'The twist of bringing back former million pound winners to partner celebrities ... did little to halt *Who Wants to be a Millionaire?*'s ratings slide ... the hour-long quiz show had [only] 5.2 million viewers.' Even a jackpot winner on 24 April 2004 attracted just 6.2 million, far short of the series' highs.

While BBC1's The National Lottery variants Jetset and Winning Lines have continued to prove reliable if unspectacular fodder, *Celebrities Under Pressure* and *The Vault* were less successful for ITV, leaving *Ant and Dec's Saturday Night Takeaway*, a modern mixed variety show relying heavily on game and quiz items, as the one programme that looks set to upset Chris Tarrant's

seating arrangements, attracting regular audiences around the 7 million mark.

Ofcom's review of public service television broadcasting, tasked with examining the value of PSB programming to both the public and the commercial broadcasters, chose to see quiz and game shows as simply entertainment, outwith their remit. Nonetheless, away from mainstream expectations, the year's output showed how game shows can actually contribute something of 'societal importance' to the schedules. BBC 2's *Time Commanders*, fronted by Eddie Mair, featured teams re-enacting historical conflicts via computer-generated battlefields. History lessons came alongside strategies, as experts chipped in with public-service driven facts about the real events being restaged. *Bill Oddie's History Hunt* sported a similar educational vein as the eponymous Oddie set contestants off on a daily treasure hunt around British towns to discover which historical figure once lived in the environs.

There is a fast emerging trend for 'event' based shows, which are already more pervasive than the admittedly limited sub-genre of public service formats, and arguably inspired by the success of the BBC's *Test the Nation*. This interactive quiz, which lets viewers use 'red button' technology to participate in the game, has continued to attract upwards of 6 million viewers when pushed back into service on four subsequent occasions.

Another such BBC 1 programme has been *Come and Have a Go If You Think You're Smart Enough* on Saturday nights. A weekly quiz hosted by Nicky Campbell it, again, allowed viewers at home to compete with studio-based teams but this time for a cash prize. A neat concept, it didn't catch the public's imagination and the show was subsequently seen as a key contributor to a week in April when BBC 1 recorded a 22.2 per cent audience share – the lowest in its history.

Similarly, ITV1 were keen to improve our driving skills in *The Great British Driving Test – Men vs Women*, a ninety-minute one-off that packaged driving tips into a light entertainment format (for those who really want to know, the programme 'proved' men are better behind the wheel).

ITV1's *24-Hour Quiz* was less based on interactivity, but still packaged as an event. Hosted by a perspiring Shaun Williamson, it was an uneasy hybrid of a general knowledge quiz and reality show – the contestants being recorded

BBC 2's *The Sack Race* – the semi-scripted 'Reality' style game show ran into legal problems which interrupted its run

Shaun Williamson hosted reality-quiz hybrid *24-Hour Quiz* on ITV1. Contestants lived in the 'quiz pod' and played non-stop – but the quiz itself seemed like an afterthought

around the clock, with their potential successors 'auditioned' live on the programme – and similarly proved a ratings flop, with its peak teatime edition getting around the 1 million mark. A late-night version boasted some impromptu nudity, to no great audience upswing, while a final celebrity week, involving Richard Blackwood and Cheryl Baker among others, also failed to improve its fortune.

These last twelve months have probably seen more success in creating and sustaining 'lo-fi' quiz formats. The no-frills approach of *Grand Slam* (Channel 4), *19 Keys* (Five) and *Fifteen To One* replacement, *Beat the Nation* (Channel 4) have provided a range of undemanding programmes, all boasting a neat underlying concept. At the same time *Countdown* continues to remain a core part of Channel 4's output, moved forward to 3.15 p.m. on weekday afternoons in 2003 to buoy up that part of the schedule and recommissioned for at least another two years.

Another new show that proved to be equally straightforward was BBC 1's *Didn't They Do Well?* which although essaying a unique format wherein questions were posited via clips from old quiz shows retained the reassuring feel of BBC quizzes of yore thanks to host Bruce Forsyth. When he declared in the first edition that, 'There will be a Brucie Bonus - where I go, my Bonuses go,' viewers knew they were in familiar territory.

The flipside of this rather stoic fare has been the introduction of more anarchic programmes. Sky One's *Little Monsters* saw adults take on a series of humiliating challenges 'created' and overseen by children, while *Distraction* on Channel 4 proved a surprise hit as comedian Jimmy Carr challenged contestants to answer general knowledge questions while also engaging in – yes – humiliating challenges. Slightly more problematic was BBC 2's abortive *The Sack Race* which challenged two aspiring comedians (not 'regular members of the public' as the pre-publicity implied) to get themselves fired from a job before the end of their first day. This was pulled from its Monday night slot after just one episode citing 'unforeseen production problems', returning a month later in a less favourable Saturday late night spot.

Certainly, none of this last batch could sensibly be said to contribute anything of societal importance to viewers, but if we jump to a higher altitude and look down on this last year, it's fair to say that while the landscape offers up nothing sensational in peaks and troughs, there's still a commendable diversity to behold. And, yes, while we wouldn't want to claim that the quiz show is specifically rattling a sabre for social action, somewhere between Richard Whiteley ad-libbing bad puns and Jimmy Carr cajoling contestants to participate in wheelbarrow races with naked pensioners must surely come the odd bit of 'relevant' and socially beneficial programming.

Graham Kibble-White is the Press Association's Deputy TV Editor and the creator of www.offthetelly.co.uk

PROGRAMMING

'Where I go, my Brucie bonuses go!' We were on familiar ground with BBC 1's cut and paste game show *Didn't They Do Well?*

141

Lifestyle

Helen Wheatley

L ifestyle in its various forms has continued to dominate the television schedules over the past year, despite a growing uneasiness regarding its place within public service broadcasting. Ofcom's consultation on PSB noted that while lifestyle or makeover shows continue to attract large numbers of viewers, it would seem that watching the genre on television has also become a rather guilty pleasure.

Viewers canvassed by the report complained that as a genre, 'makeover television' is formulaic and has blocked innovation elsewhere in the television schedules, even while it remains compelling viewing. While the much-berated formats of reality TV and makeover shows continue to do well in terms of viewing figures, viewers feel strongly that this type of programming is derivative, and that more could be done to create original programming. In relation to this, it is telling that Jane Root's much-publicised promise to eradicate lifestyle from BBC 2 has actually just meant a shifting of BBC 2's more successful lifestyle shows (*Saturday Kitchen*, *What Not to Wear*) to BBC 1.

Correlating with the soaring rise in property values, the property programme dominated the lifestyle slots during the year, which saw the aspirational narratives of lifestyle 'step up a gear'. Property programmes like *Property Ladder (Revisited)*, *Grand Designs*, *The Million Pound Property Experiment*, *The Property Chain*,

Alistair and Ann host *House Doctor* for Five

Trading Up, *Location, Location, Location*, and its sister programme *Relocation, Relocation* signalled a shift in the genre from narratives of personal growth to financial growth. *Property Ladder* (and its *Revisited* repeat) for example, featured an often-exasperated Sarah Beeny advising the programme's participants on how best to extract the maximum resale or rental value from their property (with many episodes centring around the tensions created when Beeny's 'clients' ignore her advice, thus failing to meet the full market potential on their sale/rental).

In *Property Ladder*, as in contemporaneous makeover shows like Channel 4's *Selling Houses* (itself derivative of Five's *House Doctor*), *taste* is what is at stake of course, or rather the eradication of personal, local, and especially lower class tastes in favour of a bland, middle class, middle age, middle-England version of style (located in the oatmeal coloured walls and stainless steel accessories of each property's makeover). The *frisson* at the centre of these programmes is found within the moment in which the participant is confronted with the 'truth' of their bad taste (either through the candid comments of potential buyers via video footage of an open house day, or through brutally frank confrontation by programme's resident expert), a moment which bears testament to Pierre Bourdieu's suggestion that 'aesthetic intolerance can be terribly violent'. What remains to be seen however is whether this genre can survive a potential slump in property prices in the coming year, or whether the cheaper end of lifestyle television (cookery, gardening) will make a return to our screens.

The other major development in the lifestyle genre in the 2003-4 period has been what might be termed the 'queering' of lifestyle television, whereby a shift in expertise has attempted to confirm the notion that gay men are the arbiters of all that is stylish and tasteful. In programmes such as Bravo's highly successful US import *Queer Eye for the Straight Guy* (Living TV's most expensive programme investment, recently remade for the domestic market as *Queer Eye for the Straight Guy UK*) and Channel 4's *Queer Eye/Wife Swap/Living with the Enemy* hybrid *Fairy Godfathers*, teams of gay men train errant scruffy straight men to be, in the words of *Fairy Godfathers* 'a little more gay'. By which they mean more concerned with their personal hygiene, sense of style and more 'in tune' with their emotions and those of their partners. To take *Queer Eye for the Straight Guy* as the indicative and originating example of this turn in lifestyle, the series sees the 'fab five' – Carson Kressley (Fashion), Kyan Douglas (Grooming), Ted Allen (Food and Wine), Thom Filicia (Design) and Jai Rodriguez (Culture) – descend on their straight subject for a day of lifestyle transformation in which they ritually trash his slobbish looks and habits and then rebuild his home, body and behaviour before delivering him back to his longsuffering partner a 'changed man'.

The show is characterised by a complicated system of looks whereby straight regards gay with some trepidation, constantly giggling with the 'is he looking at me in *that* way' tension; in turn, the fab five seem to take great pleasure in playfully suggesting a desiring look, offering flirtatious touches and smiles. Interestingly, the show has proved phenomenally successful with a mainly female fanbase, to the extent that a series of *Queer Eye for the Straight Girl* has been commissioned to further appeal to its key demographic. However, whether this show will have the same appeal is uncertain.

As such a visible space of negotiation between queer and straight culture, these lifestyle programmes are bound to prompt a good deal of debate in relation to questions of representation. They offer a complex viewing experience often challenging the casual homophobia of their subject but then reinforcing a strict divide between gay and straight, represented in the title sequence of *Queer Eye for the Straight Guy* (UK and US) by street signs pointing (in opposite directions) to 'Gay Street' and 'Straight Street'. This image suggests that the lifestyle programme is designated as a crossroads or interstitial space in which gay and straight meet and playfully flirt, only to safely go their separate ways at the end of each programme.

As Colin and Nick zoom off into the night in their Mini Coopers in the conclusion to *Fairy Godfathers*, or as the 'fab five' of *Queer Eye* sit in their 'own' stylish apartment at the end of the show to watch the reunion of their straight subjects with their wives or girlfriends on TV, we are reminded that there is only room in the straight world for these queer experts as temporary 'helper figures', situating them outside of dominant culture whilst figuring them as essential to its success. Here the public visibility serves always and only as an opposite to straightness, as something which is brought in during an 'encounter moment' at the beginning of each episode and must be banished to regain equilibrium by the end.

> **Ofcom's PSB consultation noted that while lifestyle or makeover shows continue to attract viewers, it would seem that watching this genre has become a rather guilty pleasure.**

Other notable developments in 2003-4 included the rather worrying cycle of 'extreme' makeover programmes including *Extreme Makeovers* (Living TV), *Ten Years Younger* (Channel 4), and *I Want a Famous Face* (MTV) in which the subjects undergo surgery in order to radically change their appearance (and, it is implied, live a better and happier life). Holiday programme/reality TV hybrids *Holiday Showdown* (ITV) and *Perfect Holiday* (BBC 1) signalled another marked transformation in the genre, asking viewers to decide whether the subjects 'deserved' their holidays, rather than the traditional consumer-led holiday programming (hopefully the news that BBC 1 boss Lorraine Heggessey has ordered a radical revamp of the channel's long-running *Holiday* programme due to flagging viewing figures will not mean that the show takes its lead from these hybrid programmes).

Meanwhile, on multi-channel television, channels such as UKTV Style, Discovery Home and Leisure, UKTV Food, and UKTV Bright Ideas continued to soak up seemingly endless hours of television with reruns from a growing back catalogue of lifestyle programming. With a constant stream of lifestyle programming available almost round the clock, it seems unlikely that Ofcom's findings will have any real impact other than to prolong the debate over the value of makeover television.

Queer Eye UK

PROGRAMMING

Reality & Event TV

Janet Jones

This year, lawyers have been kept busy trying to define the indefinable, as Reality and Event TV creators moved to protect their intellectual property – not easy given the constant state of flux that defines the genres' slippery boundaries. With the increase in the perceived format value protectionist instincts surfaced as Endemol (*Big Brother's* creators) tried to halt the production of Five's *Back to Reality.* Unmistakably derivative, *Back To Reality* trained eighty cameras on a handful of D-list celebrities incarcerated in a house waiting to be voted out by the viewing public.

It transpired that lawyers were less damaging than the viewing public itself: the show haemorrhaged one million viewers in its first two weeks. *Big Brother's* creator Jon De Mol chose this time to announce that unless UK producers were more innovative and less derivative in their Reality creations then the European river of gold would quickly flow over the Atlantic where the Americans are poised to 'wipe us from the map'.

Yet, the old standards provided the big successes of 2003/4. These capitalised on a few key, tried and tested ingredients of 'nowness', 'liveness' and 'audience interactivity'. A case in point, *I'm A Celebrity … Get Me Out of Here!* (ITV1) proved once again its ability to dominate tabloid headlines through crafty casting, romance between glamour model Jordan and pop has-been Peter André provided the tabloid fuel that can often make the difference between a middling reality show and a bona fide hit. Ex-Sex Pistol John Lydon also helped up the ante, with his anarchic, if not unpredictable, walkout. A huge 14.99 million watched the final, beating last year's 12.73 million. A fourth series is being hastily prepared for Autumn 2004.

As testimony to the establishment, if not elevation, of the genre, 2003-4 saw the coining of a new neologism, *irritainment,* to describe shows that are both annoying and compulsively watchable. The granddaddy of all irritainment returned in the Summer of 2004.

The theme of season five, 'Big Brother Gets Evil' seriously backfired on producers, Endemol, who were accused of deliberately cultivating an atmosphere that encouraged sex, fights and cruelty. The Hampshire Police and Ofcom both got involved after housemate, Emma threatened to kill fellow housemate Victor. A more claustrophobic house with a cast of sexual extroverts and gaming rules that encouraged duplicity all surely

contributed to the violence that became known, infamously, as 'Day 20'. Many critics questioned how, in such a relatively short time, *Big Brother* could have mutated from a relatively benign social experiment into what one reviewer termed a 'squalid little study in barbarism'.

Despite the lure of teenage sex, the taped rather than live nature of October's *Teen Big Brother* lost it some of its edge, and this pre-recorded slice of Reality attracted more column inches than viewers.

Issues of taste and decency surfaced once more in the rush for ratings. Sky One's *There's Something About Miriam* pushed the moral boundaries – tricking six young men into courting a pre-operative transsexual. Major cash payments had to be made to the contributors as inducements to allow the final show to air.

Despite ongoing taste anxiety, raunchiness was not the main feature of this year's crop which instead tended to stick to the tried-and-tested themes – *you can't escape,* and *it's going to hurt. Shattered* (Channel 4) exploited pain and boredom in a most creative way with a seven day experiment in sleep deprivation. Underneath its gruelling veneer, it contained a useful health warning, demonstrating the effects of exhaustion on everything from driving skills to libidos. There were a number of series that used psychology as a hook. *Who Rules the Roost* (BBC 3) made working parents give up their jobs to see what life is like bringing up their own kids full time. *My Week in the Real World* (BBC 2) saw MP Clare Short struggling teach in a South London Comprehensive School, and *The Carrot or the Stick* (Channel 4) tested which method of military training is most effective: barbaric abuse or friendly encouragement.

There was continued competition and a little sparring backstage in the pursuit to be crowned king of the Reality TV production circuit. Steve Lambert, creator of *Boss Swap* and *Wife Swap* heavily criticised what he saw as poor replicas maintaining that there is a definite art behind each success story. 'It isn't all blindingly simple – get two couples who are like chalk and cheese, switch on the cameras and wait for the fireworks.' It doesn't always work. 'Just look at the ITV show *Take my Mother In Law –* insufficient dramatic upheaval. It has to be transformational. It has to say something about the human condition.' *Ramsay's Kitchen Nightmares,* a strong new addition to Channel 4's reality range, must have

Tessa Jowell appeared to give broadcasters the sign they were hoping for, acknowledging that 'reality TV does indeed qualify as PSB'.

Big Brother 5: Day 20 – nothing more than a 'squalid study in barbarism'?

done just that. Following on from the successes of *Wife Swap*, *How Clean is Your House?* and *Brat Camp*, it won over its audience with a *Trouble Shooter* style chef providing unwelcome advice to cooks in provincial restaurants. Its final episode drew 5.6 million viewers and reached Number 30 in the week's ratings chart. The recipe of cooking and reality TV was also successful in the pits of *Hell's Kitchen* (ITV1) which employed Angus Deayton to watch as celebrities suffered under Gordon Ramsay's cruel kitchen watch.

The Event TV highlight of the year had to be *Derren Brown plays Russian Roulette Live* (Channel 4). It certainly won the critics' award for best title and gave the nation an opportunity to talk about just how far a programme could go to attract an audience. Many hailed it as pure 'white knuckle TV' others as macabre voyeurism. His later *Séance* drew hundreds of concerned complaints from Christian viewers in advance of transmission but the show turned out to be a clever hoax that debunked hokey occult spiritualism. We also had to endure forty days and forty nights of David Blaine's superb publicity stunt. To some, his public starvation as he towered over the Thames in a little glass box was seen as the ultimate test of human endurance, to others it was an obscenity.

On a more cerebral note, the pull of the public service remit gave rise to a few highbrow success stories including *The Big Read* (BBC 2), *Test The Nation* (BBC 1) and *End of Story* (BBC 2/3). These populist intellectual formats built on the success of last year's *Restoration* (BBC 2) and cumulatively these programmes have established a healthy sub-genre in the niche event category.

Finally, 2004 was the year that culture secretary Tessa Jowell at last gave broadcasters the U-turn they were hoping for and acknowledged that 'reality TV does indeed qualify as Public Service Broadcasting'. Why? Because it attracts audiences, and that, she claimed, is an important part of a healthy PSB system.

So what competition have British producers to be worried about as they look across the pond into next year? Fox Network has been genre-busting with its new hybridisation of soap and reality formats to create *Forever Eden*. It's a bit like *El Dorado*, but with real people who have been transplanted from their ordinary lives onto a luxury resort, where they can spend their days on the beach and in the bar. What's unusual about this new hybrid is that it is potentially open-ended, like a real soap opera. After a stuttering start the show was pre-empted by sports events and while Fox are committed to paying for twenty-six episodes it seems this attempt to create ongoing, living soap has failed. Another series tipped to grace our screens is *Starting Over,* a fusion of *Big Brother* and *Trisha,* with life coaches attempting to get the lives of six desperate women back on track. This one's a hybrid between reality, makeover and soap.

Despite the many Jeremiahs predicting the end of the formatted factual, 2003-4 won't be remembered as the year the genre died. Predictions for next year inevitably centre around the continued aggressive exploitation of multi-media and interactive formats and the innovative trans Atlantic competition. At least the lawyers will have another busy year.

*A former BBC broadcast journalist, Janet Jones regularly presents on BBC Radio Wales. She recently conducted a three-year study of reality TV audiences and is co-editor with Ernest Mathijs of **Big Brother International: Format, Critics and Publics** (Wallflower Press: 2004).*

PROGRAMMING

Music

Kevin J. Donnelly

ast year saw the continued fragmentation of pop music on television into 'youth' and late night 'serious' or 'adult' pop/rock music. Television coverage of popular music is merely a reaction to the divergence of music consumers into ageing adult record buyers and young music fans. The download culture of the latter fits multichannel music television with its quick access, instant gratification and short shelf-life. Schedules generally have shunted all but the most unchallenging pop into the margins of television, and the growth of dedicated music television channels has led to there being less music on terrestrial television than there was a couple of years ago.

The world's longest-running TV pop show, *Top of the Pops*, was revamped under the direction of ex-children's television presenter Andi Peters (who replaced the outgoing Chris Cowey). It had a new set, news reports and interview sections, a

Fearne Cotton hosted a Saturday morning kids' version of *Top of the Pops* – and later joined Tim Kash on the peaktime BBC 1 show

top of the pops™
S A T U R D A Y

permanent presenter, and became a live broadcast rather than being recorded. This rethink helped arrest the alarming slide in figures in the short term (which had halved since the mid-1990s), but wasn't a resounding success. In all likelihood, another revamp, or return to earlier formats will happen sooner or later and indeed the sole presenter idea seems to have been dropped within six months, with rotation of co-presenters looking to be the established norm. *Top of the Pops* is unlikely to lose its place as the pre-eminent pop music show on British television, especially after the successful sale of its franchise abroad, but rumours persist that it might be shunted from BBC 1 to BBC 3 and consternation over the wisdom of scheduling it opposite ITV's *Coronation Street* – hardly the best way to conserve fragile viewing figures.

Top of the Pops has successfully diverged into both the 'youth' market (in its Saturday morning version) and the 'adult'/'retro' market (with its early evening *Top of the Pops 2*). TOTP 2 continues to be cheap and relatively successful with its mix of archive footage from yesteryear and in recent months has factored in personal reminiscences of celebrity presenters. Reeves and Mortimer, Phill Jupitus and Jack Dee have been among recent hosts. There was some exciting archive footage, such as Queen performing 'Killer Queen' from 1974, with a black-fingernailed and fur-coated Freddy Mercury, The Smiths and The Jam. After several years on air however the programme is running short of notable material, particularly from the monochrome 60s – only four full *TOTP* from that decade survive. The Jimi Hendrix Experience performing 'Voodoo Chile' was taken from *A Happening for Lulu* in 1969 and the show could surely benefit from searching wider into the BBC music and variety archive, looking to *Crackerjack*, *The Basil Brush Show* or *Cheggers Plays Pop*.

The most popular television pop programme was doubtless *Pop Idol*, which had a significant impact on ITV's Saturday evening schedules. In *Pop Idol – The Finale*, Michelle McManus was overall winner (with 10.3 million votes). An international version, *World Idol*, was won by Norway's Kurt Nilsen (a plumber in his mid-twenties, married with a child), while UK representative Will Young made a poor showing. Further variations on this format included opera version, *Operatunity*, and a longer running Welsh version called *Just Up Your Street*, taking the format back to its *New Faces* roots.

The success of *Pop Idol* complemented another ITV1 Saturday evening perennial, *Stars in Their Eyes* and its offspring *Stars in their Eyes Kids*. The diminutive show's first contestants were four mid-teen girls and one ten-year old boy who did a remarkable Kurt Cobain impression, singing *Smells Like Teen Spirit* – although he was not yet a teenager! This was a timely reminder of the anniversary of Cobain's death, commemorated by the *MTV2 Nirvana Weekend* which included Cobain's widow Courtney Love as presenter from Saturday at midnight onwards.

There were no surprises in the UK's annual Eurovision choice (*Eurovision – Making Your Mind Up*), which was won convincingly by a *Fame Academy* failure. Yet the striking thing about *The Junior Eurovision Song Contest* was that many of the youngsters were inspired by more 'serious' music than by boy and girl bands and *Pop Idols*. This irony was lost on a schedule that sandwiched it between two hours of *Pop Idol*! Eurovision itself was won by Ukraine's Ruslana, with their stage show seemingly inspired by *Conan the Barbarian*. The paucity of notable songs was less remarkable than countries appearing to vote for their immediate neighbours (as compere Terry Wogan drolly noted).

The Brits turned out to be a clarion call for adult pop/rock, the antithesis of *Pop Idol* television and its diet of pop music aimed at ten-year-olds. Presenter Cat Deeley declared, 'Booze is back! Rock'n'roll is back!' A retro sense dominated, most notably in the multiple success of glam rockers The Darkness. Even teen idols Busted performed The Undertones' 'Teenage Kicks' (from the late 70s), while there was duet performance of The Cure's 'The Lovecats' (from the 80s) by Jamie Cullum and Katie Melua. To cap it, Duran Duran were given an award for 'outstanding contribution to music', over twenty years after their first hit single. While their artistic value might be moot, their retro value was beyond doubt.

The interest in retro music, fuelled by back catalogue sales, led to plenty of retrospectives and documentaries, both aimed at the casual consumer and the more serious or minority music fan, from lid-blower *The Truth About Take That* to *The South Bank Show*'s video diary by jazz pianist and singer Jamie Cullum. BBC 4 had a range of music documentaries aimed at minority and older music fans, such as *Ian Dury: My Life*, *Gram Parsons: Fallen Angel* and *EmmyLou Harris: From a Deeper Well* (the latter followed by an archive episode of *The Old Grey Whistle Test* from 1977). BBC 4 is lagging far behind print – magazines such as *Q* and *Mojo* have specialised in hefty retrospectives and discographies of such cult acts for years – but it's a case of better late than never that such artists are receiving due attention.

Schedules generally have shunted all but the most unchallenging pop into the margins of television, and the growth of dedicated music television channels has led to there being less music on terrestrial television than a few years ago.

Getting good bands performing live was the aim of *The Carling New Kings of Rock'n'Roll*, which included The Vines and Elbow. This night slot is far from new, but Channel 4's '4Music' after midnight on Wednesdays was the only dedicated zone for music on terrestrial television. Yet Channel 4's recent migration towards the mainstream has meant that almost all its music programmes are now in the margin of the schedules. Any sense of public service in terms of minority music – or even simply adult-oriented pop music – is confined largely to Four's single late night slot and BBC 4. Even the dedicated cable channels are disappointing in their range, with MTV diversifying into lifestyle and reality shows that displace their concentration on music.

These are not good times for music on television, with little exciting or innovative over the past year. While television is proving less effective as a means to sell pop music, pop music has become more useful as a means of selling television. The *Pop Stars/Pop Idol* franchise not only dominated ratings and brought in copious phone-in money, but also formed the new foundation of ITV's Saturday evening schedules. ITV1 is set to launch its Autumn 2004 Saturday schedule with Simon Cowell and his new *Idol* variant for all age groups, *The X Factor* ...

Kevin J. Donnelly is a lecturer in the department of Theatre, Film and Television at the University of Wales, Aberystwtyth. He is the author of **Pop Music in British Cinema** *(BFI: 2001) and editor of* **Film Music** *(Edinburgh University Press: 2001).*

PROGRAMMING

Talk Shows

Helen Wheatley

Talk

The big news of the talk show year was Robert Kilroy-Silk's disgrace and sacking. Following his anti-Arab comments in the *Sunday Express*, Kilroy was asked to give up fronting his eponymous early morning talk show (with the BBC dumping twenty-five editions of the programme which had already been recorded at a cost of £625,000). In order to fulfil its contract, the BBC agreed to let the Kilroy TV Company make another talk show for the reduced *Kilroy* slot, with the Nicky Campbell/Nadia Sawalha/Sian Williams fronted *Now You're Talking* taking over in March 2004.

The programme, overseen by Paul Woolwich (one of the BBC's most experienced journalist executives), attempted to differentiate itself from its ITV rival, *Trisha*, on the grounds of its commitment to a public service ethos, with a much greater emphasis on 'edginess and topicality' expected from the programme. What was delivered, however, was a thirty-minute show based entirely on the *Kilroy* format, without the

Live at Johnny's – ironic shed-based chat and gags from Johnny Vaughan and Lauren Laverne on BBC 3

pull of a single, identifying face and name to hold it together. Losing viewers to an increasingly trashy, Jerry Springer-esque *Trisha* (another blow for public service broadcasting?), the BBC has decided to remove the morning talk show from the slot completely and will rethink the way in which it delivers news/current affairs in its daytime slots. Kilroy's production company looks set to close, with the man himself relaunching his political career.

On multi-channel television, the most striking innovation of the talk show format continues to be what might be described as the 'paranormal turn' on Living TV, whereby the audience participation talk show has been transformed into television séance, with presenters passing on messages to audience members from their dead friends and relatives. Following a ruling by the Independent Television Commission in summer 2003, Living TV continued to broadcast US import *Crossing Over with John Edwards* and its UK-produced counterpart *The 6ixth Sense with Colin Fry*, despite the fact that both shows come very close to flouting the ITC Programme Code, which states that 'actual demonstrations of exorcisms and occult practices ... are not acceptable in factual programming, except in the context of a legitimate investigation'.

On the strength that additional 'safeguards of scepticism' were put in place, in the form of disclaimers at the beginning and end of each show, Living TV were given the go-ahead by the ITC, though there is still a good deal of uneasiness about the place of such talk (to the dead) shows within British broadcasting. On the one hand they claim to provide a clear public service to those who take part in the programme, who are shown towards the end of each episode testifying to the fact that they have taken great comfort from their participation in the show. On the other hand however, sceptics will say that this paranormal talk show turn represents the duping of vulnerable audiences at its very worst, harking back to the moral panics about psychics and mediums at the turn of the last century. Ofcom will need to police such formats to ensure that existing ITC guidelines are still adequate, as the genre becomes more visible and expands further.

Chat

Meanwhile, the late night chat stalwarts were back again this year, with both *Friday Night with Jonathan Ross* and *Parkinson* returning to BBC1 in the autumn with no real change to their formats. The 'big two' were also joined on BBC 3 by a slightly downsized Johnny Vaughan in *Live at Johnny's*, a show set in a faux shed to suggest the matey-homeliness which suits Vaughan better than the suit-behind-a-desk of his original BBC 3 show, and by another US Graham Norton show, *NY Graham Norton*, his last for Channel Four.

Indeed, this year will be remembered as one of big transfers, with the move of Graham Norton from Channel 4 to the BBC in a lucrative two year deal suggesting that Norton's near-the-knuckle comedy and interviewing techniques will inevitably be toned down for a Saturday night primetime family audience. BBC 1 have pointed out that Norton will not initially fill the hole in the schedules left by Michael Parkinson's defection to ITV; the chat show stalwart left the BBC over a disagreement about scheduling, with his show facing a move to 9 p.m. to accommodate the return of *Match of the Day*.

Perhaps Parkinson's day as the 'king of chat' is over, given his recent record of soft, 'gentlemanly' interviewing which doesn't sit easily in an era of what has been described as 'tabloid culture'. With a viewership which has grown to expect salacious

This year will be remembered as one of big transfers, with the move of Graham Norton from Channel 4 to the BBC. BBC 1 have pointed out that Norton will not fill the hole in the schedules left by Michael Parkinson's defection to ITV.

personal detail as standard in any encounter with 'celebrities', *Parkinson's* polite, restrained interviewing style may seem a little old fashioned. However, this may also be his appeal, in that he carries with him a pre-multichannel heritage of old-school broadcasting which ITV1 will be pleased to have a piece of. It will be interesting to see whether effectively swapping the late night Saturday schedules of BBC1 and ITV1 will mean a simultaneous swapping of viewing figures.

Dr Helen Wheatley is a Postdoctoral Research Fellow at the Centre for Television Drama Studies, Department of Film, Theatre & Television, University of Reading. Her book **Gothic Television** *will be published by Manchester University Press in 2005.*

The 6ixth Sense With Colin Fry – controversial paranormal talk show on Living TV

Parky's defection to ITV1 from BBC 1 Saturday late nights generated headlines

PROGRAMMING

Children's

Alistair D. McGown

BBC

Licence fee income means CBBC has circumvented the financial problems suffered by commercial rivals in recent years, letting them concentrate purely and simply on *programmes*. Dorothy Prior took charge of output on 17 February 2003, inheriting from predecessor Nigel Pickard a largely robust schedule and with two digital channels, CBeebies for toddlers and CBBC for six-to-twelve-year-olds, launched 2002.

CBBC offers a range of quality programmes that ITV simply cannot match. *SMart* was among the most popular shows – with features on art history, artist biography and reports on community art projects, *SMart* is more than just a 'makes' show. Such high-minded topics engage the audience with a soundtrack of Avril Lavigne and Busted, while guests like Harry Hill and Vic Reeves also joined in this year.

Newsround is another programme to demonstrate the BBC's PSB remit (see Panel p.155) and it enjoys large figures due to pre-echo won preceding Australian soap *Neighbours* at 5.35 p.m. This is a win-win situation for the BBC though, as the repositioning of *Newsround* to 5.25 from 5.00 p.m. can be said to have delivered high audiences to news programming. Public Service Reviews should see the Aussie soap removed from the BBC schedules and *Newsround*'s BBC 1 ratings will inevitably suffer. The brand is uniquely strong however and extends far outwith the BBC 1 5.25 bulletin, now supplemented by a genuine news website and updated bulletins throughout the day on the CBBC channel.

In homegrown drama and comedy genres, the long-running 'brands' dominated the schedules through familiarity but most had something different to offer in 2003-4. *Grange Hill* had a make or break year. Having left BBC Elstree last year to return to Phil Redmond and Mersey

TV for a back-to-basics reboot that majored in comic japes, it was a question of whether the show could age up with its new core audience. The answer was a resounding yes, with excellent storylines including a girl's crush on her teacher prompting lesbian taunts, a recalcitrant pupil (shades of Danny Kendall) driving a teacher to minor assault and a brother and sister whose father was suffering from mental illness. Series 27 finally closed on the discovery of Tucker Jenkins' archive pants in an unearthed time capsule.

The Story of Tracy Beaker, set in a children's home, mixes citizenship issues and comedy – it's consistently popular and indeed stripped and stacked repeats form the backbone of the CBBC channel. Stroppy tomboy antics have matured into slightly more complex stories and February 2004 saw a feature length episode *The Movie of Me*. This filled its extended runtime well with the story of Tracy meeting her natural mother. After four seasons teenage actress Dani Harmer is clearly not long for this series if it's to remain credible with the target audience and this has predicated an unseemly rush to shoot as many episodes as possible – twenty-six aired within six months.

Pubescent soap *Byker Grove* continues to pull big audiences but this run was indistinguishable from any other. Pacy direction from Graeme Harper enlivened an action episode set in Blackpool's Pleasure Beach but the script had little time for character or resolution of issues.

A seventh series of *The Queen's Nose* bravely rebooted the cast and setting to great effect – allied to stronger plotting this overhaul undoubtedly revitalised the series. Another fantasy was *Intergalactic Kitchen*, a well-made sci-fi sitcom featuring a family and their kitchen blasted into space. The rather more serious *Powers* owed a clear debt to telepathic forerunners like *The Tomorrow People* – sometimes overly complex or downright daft plots were carried off with dramatic conviction and a slick production style harking back to the eccentric Home Counties milieu of *The Avengers*. Here's hoping for a sequel run.

The short-run serial looks set to go the way of the single play, forsaken in the rush to volume series production, but Childsplay's *Feather Boy* belied the medium's uncertain future. This involving tale transferred intact from its printed source, with a smiling bully who was at times surprisingly friendly, at times spiteful, making life hell for

Dick and Dom – chaos for Saturday mornings

Norbert No Bottle. Exploring themes like terminal illness and suicide, this was gripping stuff.

Following the dominance of Ant and Dec's *SM:TV Live* and the misfire of the BBC's vapid, tragically hip *The Saturday Show* Mk I, *Dick and Dom in Da Bungalow* came to BBC 1 in September 2003 from the CBBC channel and reinstalled the Beeb as the Saturday morning favourite. Instantly there were parental complaints, as rowdy kids went crazy with gunge and mess and, in the first episode, dogs were made to lick dog food off vases (in the game 'Vase-Licking Puppies').

The show soon dropped the gratuitously grotty without losing its insane humour. *Da Bungalow* is one of the first shows to let children be themselves and go wild rather than appear as mediated living props cheering on cue. Dick and Dom have the rare knack of acting like big kids while slipping in naughty and surreal references for the oldies – there were guest spots (mostly mute cameos) for such luminaries as Tony Hart, Trevor and Simon, Pat Sharp and the Chuckle Brothers and thrash metal versions of the *Jim'll Fix It* and *Bertha* themes. With a low budget and tiny set it relies on comic invention and sheer energy – this lifelong TISWAS fan believes kids' TV has never seen *anything* like the genuine chaos witnessed in the last few editions of *Da Bungalow*.

Bungalow's summer replacement, *The Saturday Show* Mk III, looks forced and contrived in comparison. *The Mysti Show* joined it – a curious hybrid of *Sabrina*-influenced glossy sitcom with (faux) live magazine format. The direction is laboured and tricksy, a de-interlaced film look robbing studio items of any spontaneous energy. If reversioned as twenty-two-minute sitcom episodes, *Mysti* could sell well abroad or in the digital market.

Da Bungalow piloted extensively on the CBBC channel before transferring to BBC 1 (a CBBC-only Sunday edition continues); ironic gameshow *The Tiny and Mr Duk Show* may follow in its footsteps. By providing this testbed, CBBC has extended its remit beyond providing an advert-free, non-US-owned children's digital offering. CBBC still lags behind CBeebies but its rating performance has improved since launch to tie with Boomerang as most popular children's channel (non pre-school viewers) with 3.5 per cent share by November 2003. CBeebies is the most watched of all children's channels, with 6.8 per cent of all children's digital viewing.

CBBC offers a range of quality programmes that ITV simply cannot match.

These channels are part of the cycle driving DTT take-up and reaping the rewards in audience increase as a result. While it can seem odd when CBBC airs a new show – such as the reality/celebrity influenced football-coaching show *Beckham's Hotshots* – against CBBC output on BBC1, this acknowledges the modern TV landscape. You need to give yourself a chance of increasing your reach when people flick over from your terrestrial parent.

BARB ratings published in *Broadcast* showed *Sleeping Beauty: Uncovered* way out in front as the highest-rated show of the period 2003-4. The success of this panto, at heart a celebration of the CBBC family, really cements the BBC as the home of children's TV.

Drama serial *Feather Boy*

Fantasy series *Powers*

CITV

CITV spent this season in limbo, while the Carlton/Granada merger rumbled on. Controller Steven Andrew (installed 28 February 2003) has benefited directly from the merger and 2003's £33.5 million budget increased to £40 million for 2004. A slew of new shows, many from the combined ITV production arm, will air from the autumn. Andrew believes that if his department is to invest in making its own shows he requires changes in Ofcom rules, enabling ITV to profit from merchandise revenues and secondary sales (as BBC Worldwide does).

Increased in-house output was also seen as necessary to fuel a CITV digital channel. Andrew had gone as far as to say that 'No kids strategy is complete without us being able to play in the multichannel world ... we can't not do this and ultimately survive as a kids player'. ITV Controller Nigel Pickard admitted ITV1's children's line-up was now 'a minnow in a sea of twenty channels'. Then, suddenly, in June 2004 it was all off. A hinted-at partnership with a US-owned broadcaster had seemed a shoo-in, with Disney and Nickelodeon openly named but CITV conceded defeat, suggesting that CITV take branded slots on either of these multichannels. Interestingly this deal seems to be two-way, which will mean a US-owned multichannel brand offering on CITV's airwaves – the beginning of the end?

Political debate of child obesity and the effect of 'junk food' advertising on TV continues. Steven Andrew claimed a snack advertising ban would lose CITV £10-12m a year – a third of its budget. Labour MP Debra Shipley put physical health before the cultural diet – 'Sorry, but I don't care if children's TV becomes wall-to-wall cartoons [if] the alternative is children being bombarded with messages portraying products that will make them obese'. Such opinion, if mobilised, will spell the end for quality commercial TV for children.

Ofcom's PSB Reviews may help decide whether a children's service is sustainable in a commercial framework. Ofcom's *Measuring Public Service Broadcasting* report of April 2004 calculated that running children's programmes costs ITV around £27 million a year in lost ad revenue so Ofcom must decide whether such opportunity cost will be paid back to ITV in the form of subsidies.

There is clear potential crossover between this issue and digital switchover. Should CITV ever get a channel up and running ahead of digital switchover in 2006-8 it is tempting to imagine ITV1 dropping children's programmes between

Ofcom's PSB Reviews may help decide whether a children's service is sustainable in a commercial framework.

3.15 and 5 p.m. in favour of more recognisably 'daytime' fare, relying on the 'ITV Kids' channel for their children's service. Whether a 'CITV Channel' is now truly in the dead file remains to be seen.

Programming has had a hiatus feel – the second series of excellent tween drama *Girls in Love* failed to appear, but Nigel Pickard's cancellation order was rescinded and it'll return late 2004. Pre-school puppet series *Ripley and Scuff* (from indie The Children's Company) was axed but could its 2003 BAFTA award mean a similar repeal? CITV's only genuine ratings hit has been *My Parents Are Aliens*, an outrageous comedy which always manages to say something about kids' lives by poking fun at some of their more trivial hang ups. This ratings juggernaut is over-relied upon – daily summer repeats nonetheless leapt into the published weekly Top 10s. The biggest compliment it can be paid is that it's the only series CBBC would steal from CITV.

Production powerhouse The Foundation, based at Maidstone Studios, oversees much CITV output (also producing CBBCs *The Basil Brush Show*). Spoofy game show *Globo Loco* remains genuinely inventive and its crazy games format was extended to create Saturday morning show *Ministry of Mayhem*, which began in January. A 2003 fourth quarter run of *SM:TV Gold* compilations gave Dick and Dom a head start, with the *Ministry* struggling to establish itself. Only a few items on the show need the vast space of the Maidstone Studios – elsewhere there are tight shots on the presenters sitting in a small bunker room. The presenters are all very experienced but there's little unrehearsed chemistry as yet – some spontaneity is creeping in, mostly between Mulhern and Peter Cocks as wacky German scientist Dr Helmut Undgoggles. The 'Ministry' theme (Is it a spy organisation?) is not carried through all items and stylings, hinting it's reached the screen in a hurry.

Whether in-house or outsourced, CITV presently specialises in transatlantic fare. Such material can fall between two stools – *24 Seven*'s glossy but vapid second series ended up buried in Saturday afternoon slots last year. 2003's much-hyped *Star*, about a boy movie star attending a normal school, was dropped from its prime afternoon slot halfway

Ministry of Mayhem

My Parents Are Aliens

through the series. A good cast and strong, satirical writing seemed fudged in production.

Most consciously international was 'girls' series *The Sleepover Club*. Wark Clements' Richard Langridge explained it had been a conscious decision to set Rose Impey's British books in Australia to 'make it more transatlantic'. Already selling well abroad, whether its squeaky clean sunniness brings much to CITV is less certain. Also worth noting was the additional input of US producer Josh Selig of Little Airplane Productions into a second series of pre-school animation *Engie Benjy* (voiced by Ant and Dec). Granada Kids appointed Selig to create 'pre-school shows which will appeal to US as well as British audiences' and hopes his name will lead to extra sales overseas.

Less calculating than any of these, fun factual series *The Yuk Show* deserves a mention. Teaching the science of grottiness, features on farts predominate but it's unlikely to set any international sales records.

An hour-long quadruple bill of US cartoon *Jimmy Neutron* on 11 March 2004 marked a new nadir for CITV. Hopefully the new post-merger commission slate can banish such lowpoints. Asian comedy diary *My Life as A Popat*, talking dog comedy *Barking*, the adventures of an 18th Century boy highwayman in *Help! I'm an Outlaw* and a sci-fi cloning thriller all sound hugely promising. These shows must deliver – autumn 2004 is make or break for the future of children's programmes on ITV.

Other Commercial Channels

Five continues to be a cheap and cheerful morning window of acquisitions but worth a mention is *Chinese Breakaway*. An informative

and hilarious reality travelogue, it followed Peter Duncan and family trekking their way through China and aired over the Christmas holidays. July saw Five make a bold first move into live Saturday morning entertainment with *No Girls Allowed*.

Chinese Breakaway

Channel 4 is sticking with more consciously 'youth' fare and sorties into children's territory tend to disappear without a dedicated schedule to support them. *The Illustrated Mum*, a drama based on Jacqueline Wilson's novel, aired as a Christmas movie. This heartbreaking tale starred Michelle Collins as an alcoholic goodtime girl struggling to meet her responsibilities as a mother and first aired as part of schools strand 4 Learning.

Multichannel now extends to twenty-four dedicated children's channels including CBBC and CBeebies – the rest still tend to be US-owned and run samey animations from US/Japan/Korea. The success of the BBC digital channels has not made them raise their game as yet but still their offerings chip away at the share of BBC1 and ITV.

Alistair D. McGown is author (with Mark Docherty) of **The Hill & Beyond: Children's TV Drama – an Encyclopedia** *(BFI:2003)*

PROGRAMMING

CBBC = PSB?

Hopefully Ofcom's ongoing PSB review will question the basic assumption that all children's television is by blanket definition PSB and run the rule over particular programmes as they will for adult schedules. The best of children's programmes have long denied such narrow definitions, entertaining while opening up ideas, facts and experiences to the young viewers. Current BBC output looks in good shape to undergo close scrutiny.

Wide-ranging magazine *Blue Peter* retains a strong sense of its traditions thanks to Editor – and unofficial show historian – Richard Marson. *Blue Peter* still covers calendar events better than anyone – its bonfire night and Christmas editions evoke the spirit of those events. The *Blue Peter Goes Forth* edition (BBC 1 28/1/04) added a dash of 2004 dynamism to the classic template, with animal features (cute penguins), daring feats (climbing to the top of the Forth Road Bridge) and riding horses, dressed in historical costume (Liz Barker as Mary Queen of Scots).

The programme has undergone 'brand expansion' to encompass a 'let your hair down' Friday edition of pop bands and wacky games. It's also moved into comedy drama with the regular series of beautifully made, tongue-in-cheek adventure romps *The Quest*. 'Some of our 'brand extensions' are re-inventions of the wheel,' Marson argues, 'As TV output has expanded, on the whole range and choice have narrowed. I think part of our role in the digital age will be to provide space for a huge variety of material that no longer has a home elsewhere but which children find relevant and absorbing'. The team receive 2000 emails a week from viewers and these help deliver what the audience wants; 'Forty years on, viewers still tend to vote for makes and cooks, animals and sports and adventure and this is at the core of what we do. Every programme maker we employ should ask themselves: "What is the one glittering piece of knowledge a viewer will retain from watching this item?" Children say they like us "because you tell us stuff".'

Despite this connection with the audience, autumn 2004 premieres a stripped strategy responding to the multichannel challenge. 'We go five times a week from September. This has been carefully planned for the last year – the last thing I want to do is spread the jam too thin or kill the presenters or production team. We'll return to a two month summer break every year rather than running fifty-two weeks. Two shows will remain live in studio, another will be on location in the UK or overseas. Another will be a compilation, the fifth a repeat or extended re-version of a presenter challenge. We'll air Monday-Wednesday-Friday on CBBC1 and five times a week on the CBBC channel (at different times). We'll no doubt adapt and evolve but this is the way forward.'

Is *Blue Peter*, along with *Panorama* or *Newsnight*, a raven in the PSB Tower of the BBC? 'Yes, it encapsulates everything that the BBC is about – it's PSB in its purest form. It is there for its audience and not afraid to stretch and challenge them. We seek to promote aspirations, understanding and active citizenship. Not just pompous hot air but real principles ... its fate is intrinsically linked with that of the BBC. No other modern commercial organisation would bankroll and support such a programme. It is our job on the programme to work as hard as we can to respond to the very many challenges we face to survive as a player in the years to come.'

Serious Desert attempted to splice together the wildlife travelogue of the still popular *Really Wild Show* with Reality TV. A sequel to *Serious Jungle* (*Serious Arctic* is due October 2004), it took a selected bunch of auditioning thirteen- to fifteen-year-olds to work in a Namibian desert reserve for endangered black rhino. The fall-outs amid teambuilding exercises are hilarious, informative and compelling, with the promise of adolescent romance too. At the core though remains *RWS*-style information, explaining the local environment, indigenous wildlife and the plight of the rhino. *Serious Desert* shames its adult influence *I'm A Celebrity ... Get Me Out of Here!* which humiliates celebrity egos by making them eat the 'disgusting' local insect life. One wonders how anyone can really equate all Reality TV with genuine PSB. **Alistair McGown**

The *Blue Peter* team get dressed for *The Quest*

Youth/Teen TV

Glyn Davis

Channel 4's *Teen Big Brother: The Experiment* garnered notable press attention when it aired in October, for one key reason: it was the first British *Big Brother* in which two of the contestants had sex inside the house. Interest was stoked further by the revelation that the 'teen' variant of the Endemol franchise was originally commissioned by Heather Rabbatts, the head of 4 Learning, for broadcast to a schools and colleges demographic: a supposedly 'educational' piece of programming, it seemed, had been tarnished by the force of unharnessed adolescent libidos.

Following the under-the-duvet coupling of Tommy and Jade, the programme was re-edited for a post-watershed audience, and ran over five consecutive weekday nights at 10 p.m. And yet, despite the predictably sensationalist tabloid coverage (such as *The Sun*'s 'Bonk on Big Bruv' headline), *Teen Big Brother* attained relatively low ratings, with the 'sex episode' netting only 1.9 million viewers. The winner of the programme was gay Irish hairdresser Paul, who took housemate Caroline on a £30,000 round-the-world trip – a journey filmed by Channel 4, and due to be broadcast shortly.

According to Rabbatts, *Teen Big Brother* signalled the beginning of a new attempt by Channel 4 to capture the fourteen-to-nineteen age group: as she said in interview, 'we're trying to create innovative programming about stuff you didn't learn at school but should have.' Whether a similar impulse to engage this demographic lay behind 4's 'Adult at 14' season is unclear. Running over a week in November, with all of the programmes aired after 9 p.m., the strand incorporated documentaries, a one-off drama, and an opinion piece on the age of consent. Among the documentaries was *Kids on Porn*: devoid of

> **According to 4Learning's Heather Rabbatts, *Teen Big Brother* signalled the beginning of a new attempt by Channel 4 to capture the 14-to-19 age group.**

narrative, and padded with extraneous visual effects, it presented footage of technologically adept teenagers downloading videos and watching DVDs, discussing their use of hardcore material, and deconstructing the realism of porn. Although lacking any major revelations, the programme suggested that teenage boys consume more pornography than girls, that parents may be more uncomfortable talking about porn than their offspring and that adolescents who use pornography may have limited basic sexual knowledge (one boy claimed that pornography was obviously fake, because *real* women don't masturbate).

PROGRAMMING

Teenage angst and awakening in Kudos' film for Channel 4's 'Adult at 14' season: *Pleasureland*

Channel 4's branding strategies, promotion and programming position it as the most significant channel in relation to youth and teen programming.

The drama, *Pleasureland*, bore similarities to the American MTV-produced theatrical release *Thirteen*. Both focused on teenage girls hitting puberty, experimenting with sex and drugs, experiencing peer pressure, and struggling to find their own identities. Although the content of *Pleasureland* was markedly tamer than that of *Thirteen*, it shared with the latter an overly swift resolution, the main teenage girl in each fiction overcoming her growing pains and achieving re-integration within the family unit. Making limited use of its coastal setting, *Pleasureland* did contain some solid acting, most notably from Katie Lyon as the lead, fourteen-year-old Joanna Mosscroft, and – in a well-cast cameo – *Brookside*'s Philip Olivier as a student with whom Joanna has sex. Finally, the 'television essay' – entitled *Sex Before 16* – was written and presented by the journalist and critic Miranda Sawyer. Drawing attention to upcoming repressive and punitive changes in British legislation regarding the age of consent, Sawyer spoke to children and teenagers, health workers, doctors and lawyers, ultimately positing that the age of consent should be twelve, not sixteen.

Channel4.com complemented the 'Adult at 14' programmes with a raft of online materials (helplines and contacts, linked internet resources, video clips, and so on) accessed through its 'health' pages. These seemed to imply an educational impulse behind the season; from the typefaces and language used, a youth audience was evidently being assumed. Yet the content and scheduling of the season was not so clear-cut. The tidy ending of *Pleasureland*, for instance, could have acted as a palliative, reassuring anxious parents; one of the documentaries, *Lovestruck*, was screened at 11.50 p.m. That this season could have played to audiences other than actual teenagers is indicative of a wider problem raised when discussing British television's youth and teenage programming: in the battle for ratings, channels blur the intended demographic for particular shows, hoping to attract wider catchments.

This blurring can be identified in operation on numerous digital, cable and satellite channels: BBC 3, ITV2, and pop video channels such as The Hits and TMF are all mainly marketed as 'youthful' channels, if not solely for youth audiences. However, I would argue that Channel 4's bold, savvy branding strategies and promotional campaigns, taken in tandem with its devotion to producing original shows about (and/or for) adolescents, positions it as the most significant British television channel in relation to youth and teen programming.

Indeed, the fudging of the 'teenage' category is perhaps seen most clearly with Channel 4's T4 strand. Although T4 programming screens on weekday mornings during the school holidays, and begins early on Sundays – a schedule which implies a youthful audience – the past year has seen T4 spread into Saturday daytimes, and extend its Sunday running time until late afternoon/early evening. Regular hosts June Sarpong and Vernon Kay have been joined by two new co-presenters: cute-and-chunky Anthony Crank, and 'New Lad' Welshman Steve Jones. In terms of schedule, T4's expansion has relied heavily on repeats (*Friends*, *Will and Grace*), US reality TV imports (*The Simple Life*, *Newlyweds*, *Joe Millionaire*), and the Sunday morning *Hollyoaks* omnibus (the teen soap has recently expanded to five episodes a week, stripped across weekdays, and plays to a regular audience of 5 million viewers).

Whilst these programmes are not without their pleasures, the hidden gem in the T4 schedule is *Popworld*. A weekly, hour-long music show with studio performances, interviews, and promo videos, hosts Simon Amstell and Miquita Oliver make the most of their cheap set and early position in the Sunday timetable with sparky banter, salacious nuggets of gossip, and a refreshingly irreverent tone (Amstell, interviewing bland boyband 24-7: 'Which one of you is the gay one?').

The latest addition to the T4 roster is the US 'quality' teen show *The O.C.*, which follows the exploits and adventures of Ryan Atwood, a working-class adolescent adopted by the wealthy (but politically liberal) Cohen family, living in a gated California community. Notable for the production input of Hollywood directors McG and Doug Liman, it's watchable but far from compelling. Still, with *Buffy the Vampire Slayer* and *Dawson's Creek* both having reached their conclusions this year, *The O.C.* fills a void for British fans of US teen television – whatever their actual age.

*Glyn Davis is a lecturer in Screen History and Theory at Edinburgh College of Art; he is the co-editor (with Kay Dickinson) of **Teen TV: Genre, Consumption and Identity** (BFI: 2004).*

Sport

Garry Whannel

Nineteen years ago, when Virgin published the most recent comprehensive television yearbook, football in England was at a low ebb and one of the big stories of the television sport year was athletics and the Mary Decker v Zola Budd race. In recent years, though, football has reigned unchallenged as the major television sport. It is the only sport to earn regular peaktime slots, with *The Champions League* (ITV1 and ITV2), and the biggest regular sports audience was regularly won by *Match of The Day* (BBC 1), typically between 5-8 million.

However there is a discrepancy between the macho competition for rights, which sees payments soar ever upwards and the relatively unspectacular performance of football as an audience winner. *The Premiership* (ITV) dipped below 4 million on several occasions, while Sky's football audience, even after all these years of subscription growth, rarely tops 2 million; pay per view audiences lurk in the low hundred thousands.

By contrast, ITV's Formula One coverage has won audiences of 3-4 million and even its seriously dull qualifying days have been watched by around 1.5 million, audiences that compare well with those for Sky Football. The two great national triumphs, the Rugby World Cup victory and the successful cricket tour of the West Indies, provided some marvellous television moments, but neither sport is capable of producing regular large audiences.

The European Commission spent much of the year casting a beady eye over the football deals worth £1.02 billion that gave Sky 137 matches per season for the next three years (cynics might wonder why Murdoch and his papers are spearheading the anti-European campaign). By 2004, pressure from the Commission had caused Sky to respond by dividing its football portfolio and offering a range of subsidiary rights for auction. The options on offer failed to appeal to potential buyers and no bids reached the reserve price. Indeed some suggested the offer was structured to deter rather than attract. Sky retained all its football rights, whilst the European Commission, distinctly unimpressed, is pursuing the issue, by insisting on a restructuring of the rights acquisition process in the next round.

For horse racing, the most fascinating speculation has taken place off-course. The establishment of attheraces eventually put paid to The Racing Channel. More than 80 per cent of

Britain's sixty racing tracks signed up with attheraces but the interactive betting element failed to produce the requisite revenue stream. By March, attheraces had to be restructured, and is now owned by Sky and Arena Leisure. A new company, The Horse Racing Channel, has emerged however, with backing from around thirty courses. It is unlikely that both can survive and, ridden by that lean and mean jockey, Sky, attheraces looks the best bet.

The European Commission cast a beady eye over the football deals worth £1.02 billion that gave Sky 137 matches per season for the next three years

This year's boat race, the last on BBC, produced that rarest of things, a close finish but can the race deliver for ITV? This year's race was seen by 5. 7 million, with over 7 million watching in 2003 but in 2002 only 3.6m viewed. ITV have acquired the rights for five years, for around £2 million, with the greater scope for sponsorship prominence a significant factor for the organisers. ITV are probably banking on the potential appeal of a gender balanced audience, over half of whom could be in the ABC1 category. The Boat Race is no longer on the list of Category A restricted events, which

Mark Lawrenson, Gary Lineker, Alan Hansen and Peter Schmeichel were the BBC's team at Euro 2004

PROGRAMMING

Euro 2004

Martin Kelner

Like the England team itself, the television coverage of Euro 2004 struggled to get past the quarter final stage. Championship TV it was not.

Long before the tournament was over, the BBC's relentless advertising campaign in the weeks leading up to it – 'The Beautiful Game presented by the Past Masters' – was looking like a case for the Advertising Standards Authority or the Truth Commission or whoever regulates these things.

Their chief commentator, John Motson – the blessed Motty – could, I suppose, lay claim to being a Past Master, but while his is still the voice of football, especially for a lay audience, he is in the veteran stage of his career, and as is the way of the world, has lost half a yard of pace.

I knew he was in trouble when – from the vantage point of my sofa, sadly more than a thousand miles from Lisbon – I was still able to identify Igor Tudor as the Croatian scorer before Motty managed it.

In another match he confused Sol Campbell with another of England's black players, a gaffe which might have taken him into Ron Atkinson territory, were it not for the fact that he was also guilty of confusing Edgar Davids with Ruud Van Nistelrooy, proving his howlers took no notice of race, creed or colour.

Back in the studio, cheery crisp salesman Gary Lineker and his panel seemed relaxed enough – Alan Hansen veered dangerously towards the comatose at times – but favoured banter over analysis to a degree that did not find favour with football aficionados if my electronic mailbag is anything to go by.

A common theme of correspondence to my column at *The Guardian* was that analysis on foreign TV channels – Johann Cruyff in Holland, Eamon Dunphy and Liam Brady in the Republic of Ireland, Arsene Wenger on French TV – was of a different order to that offered to the domestic audience.

The specialist subject of regular BBC panellists, the two Peters – Schmeichel and Reid – was, in the memorable words of John Cleese, the 'bleedin' obvious', with Reid 'revealing' at one point that Wayne Rooney was 'a very, very good player, who could become a great player'. (Something there we might have missed, unless we happened to have seen any English newspaper at all during the first two weeks of the tournament.)

The position of Ian Wright, who probably attracted more opprobrium than any other pundit in letters to *The Guardian*, was more defensible in my view, since he did not pretend to any great expertise, and appeared to be there primarily as a cheerleader for England and as a spot of light entertainment for football agnostics. But, all in all, not a triumph for the BBC other than in audience terms.

Nor did ITV have any reason to look smug. They always seem to go into big football occasions with A Big Idea, that sounds great sounds great round the table at some planning meeting but turns out to be a real dog on air.

Gazza, for instance, was their keynote signing for the 2002 World Cup, but appeared to be going through one of his personal crises at the time, was often incoherent on air, and was given the heave-ho at the first available opportunity.

When they launched *The Premiership*, they goofed again, airing it at teatime, a decision that was ill-advised for a number of reasons, and was later reversed. The so-called tactics truck, in which Andy Townsend (one of the better pundits, as it happens) sat in an outside broadcast van spooling through match footage with coaches or players, was a gimmick also junked at a comparatively early stage.

ITV's big mistake at Euro 2004 was throwing the affable and highly respected Bobby Robson into the heat of battle alongside Clive Tyldesley in the commentary box. Robbo is undoubtedly an astute coach, but speed of thought may not be his strong point, and often he was commenting on action in one penalty box when the play had moved on into the other. Again, ITV had to backtrack, and Townsend and Robbo were wisely encouraged to swap seats.

One thing Euro 2004 did prove, though, despite all these shortcomings, is that there is undoubtedly a massive audience for top class football. But maybe there is a new and better way to televise it.

Manchester United fan and former nightclub manager and music supreme Tony Wilson suggested as much, making the very valid point that the old commentator-analyst-panel format goes back more than thirty years. With Sky showing more Premiership matches than ever this season, the BBC having recaptured the rights to highlights, and ITV televising Coca-Cola Championship action, the opportunities are certainly there to freshen up TV footy in time for the 2006 World Cup. As long as nobody suggests bringing back the tactics truck.

*Martin Kelner is a sports columnist for **The Guardian**, and presents a football phone-in on BBC Radio Leeds. His first book, **When Will I Be Famous?** is published by BBC Books. His website is at www.martinkelner.com*

means in theory it could be acquired by BSkyB but don't hold your breath on this one.

The more egalitarian London Marathon (BBC1) has now firmly established itself as a new shared national ritual, in the way that the Boat Race used to be. BBC's coverage of the World Athletics Championship meanwhile dominated the sports scene in late August, but its audiences of between 2-5 million tended to reduce BBC1's primetime audience share.

In October it was announced that the Arab channel Al Jazeera was launching a sports channel. In November, England achieved a great victory in The Rugby Union World Cup, watched by huge numbers in homes and bars throughout the country. The resultant euphoria and media scrum should not however trigger unrealistic expectations of what is in the end a minority sport, played at genuine elite level by less than a dozen nations, and played at school by only 4 per cent of boys.

In December the BBC announced the results of a poll to list the top 100 sporting moments. Interestingly England's 1966 World Cup win came only seventh (probably reflecting the age range of the respondents), and only one of the top five was an English triumph. Ali v Foreman was voted top, nine of the top twenty featured football and two athletics, with nine other sports represented.

Sports Review of the Year (BBC 1) continues to suffer from the BBC's loss of sporting dominance, having to deal with great moments for which it is not the rights holder, and being watched by a modest 6.6 million. Even at this level, though, it outperforms the majority of television sport.

In April Big Ron Atkinson's racist remarks during a football broadcast were beamed around the Middle East. Unlike some – Anne Winterton and Robert Kilroy-Silk come to mind – Atkinson had the grace to acknowledge the offence, apologise, and resign. Several black footballers condemned the remark, some of them as much in sorrow as in anger, given Atkinson's previous record of support for black players. October 2004 will see BBC 1 air a documentary (by Welsh indie Aspect) in which Atkinson examines both the attitudes of himself and the wider public towards race.

So where are the channels going with their sport strategies? BBC lost one champion of sport in departing Director-General Greg Dyke, only to gain another in the incoming Chairman, Michael Grade. The return of *Match of the Day* with Premiership Football highlights should prove that this is the most solid regular established slot for TV

The alternate Scottish edition of *Radio Times* suggested Scots could support, er, Sweden. And what were Rangers fans supposed to do?

football. The BBC still retains many of its crown jewels, but a digital sport channel must be a tempting option. It would give more breadth, allow the BBC to extend its coverage of time intensive events like snooker, tennis and athletics and provide a platform for regaining cricket rights.

For ITV *The Champions League* can produce occasional giant audiences, and the Formula One Motor Racing has been a success, but the cherry picking strategy has, in the wake of the acquisition of The Boat Race taken on the appearance of impulse buying. Despite having livened up the coverage of cricket with valuable technical innovations, Channel 4 could go cool on cricket in the same way that it did on athletics, and their sport policy has yet to regain the focus and prominence given it by its first commissioning editor, Adrian Metcalfe.

So football is currently king. Sky has what appears to be an unassailable link with Premiership Football that gives a solid base and has advanced to more than 7 million subscribers, largely on the back of its sports rights, but must be secretly frustrated that so much of its football is still watched by less than two million. It is less clear how further significant growth might be achieved.

*Garry Whannel is Director of the Centre for International Media Analysis, University of Luton and author of **Media Sport Stars: Masculinities and Moralities** (Routledge: 2001).*

PROGRAMMING

Programme Data

Tise Vahimagi with Alistair McGown

This compiled programme data gives details, wherever possible, of programmes mentioned in the Programming articles, with subjects and genres covered in the same order as the original articles. The data has been compiled by Tise Vahimagi with the assistance of Alistair McGown. Thanks are also due to those contributors who supplied basic data for their relevant programmes areas – special thanks are due to Phil Wickham, Lez Cooke, Alan Barnes, Kevin J. Donnelly, Graham Kibble-White, Barrie MacDonald and Stella Bruzzi.

We have endeavoured to produce as full details as possible but inevitably, in these days of indies, multichannel and volume production it becomes increasingly difficult to track down every detail. Our apologies for such omissions. We gratefully acknowledge that *Radio Times* and www.trilt.ac.uk have been invaluable research resources in the preparation of this index.

Key

Programme Title

Series number; number of episodes
Production company; Broadcaster tx (transmission) date

Pres: Presenter
Narr: Narrator
Wr: Writer
Scr: single or adapted Screenplay
Scr Ed: Script Editor
Dir: Director
Pr: Producer
Ser Pr: Series Producer
Ed: Series Editor
Exec Pr: Executive Producer
ntx: programme not transmitted

BBC3

Bodies
Hospital drama
Series 1; 6 episodes
Hat Trick; BBC3 tx 23/5/04-27/6/04
Cast: Max Beesley, Karen Bryson, Neve McIntosh, Susan Lynch, Patrick Baladi, Keith Allen
Wr/Pr: Jed Mercurio (from his novel)
Dir: John Strickland

Burn It
Series 2; 11 episodes
Red Productions/BBC; BBC3 tx 8/9/03-10/11/03
Youth drama
Cast: William Ash, Melanie Brown, Chris Coghill, Lisa Faulkner, Kieran O'Brien, Marsha Thomason
Wr: Matt Greenhalgh
Dir: Adam Rowley
Pr: Tom Sherry

Celebdaq
Entertainment news
BBC3: Continuous tx (Fri) from 14/2/03-16/1/04
Pres: Patrick O'Connell, Libby Potter
Revamp 'pilot' series; 8 episodes; 8/3/04-18/3/04 (Mon-Thu)
Pres: Jenny Éclair, Joe Mace

Date Rape: Sex and Lies
Single drama
Blast! Films; BBC3 tx 20/2/04 (BBC2 tx 8/6/04)
Cast: Keeley Hawes, Stuart Laing, Stacey Roca, Johann Myers, James Hillier, Simon Pegg
Wr/Dir: Jeremy Lovering
Pr: Madonna Baptiste

From Bard to Verse
Arts (Shakespeare readings)
Series 1; 8 episodes
Baby Cow; BBC3 tx 5-8/4/04; 13-15-16-19/4/04
Pres: Johnny Vegas, Ronni Ancona, Simon Pegg, David Walliams, Anthony Head, Meera Syal

Liquid News
Entertainment news
BBC; BBC3 tx 9/2/03-1/4/04
Pres: Claudia Winkleman, Patrick O'Connell, Colin Paterson, Mark Frith, Julia Morris, Jo Whiley
Reporters: Steph West, Tom Brook, Alex Stanger, Clare McDonnell, Dasha Pushkova, Emma Jones, Gareth Davies, Jane Goddard, Jeff Moody, Manoush Zomorodi, Max Flint, Naina Parmar Chauhan, Rebecca Lovell, Ruth Liptrot, Sam Singh, Tamzin Sylvester, Tim Muffett, Vanessa Langford
Ed: Chris Wilson

Little Angels
Factual
Series 1; 4 episodes
BBC3 tx 9-10-12-16/2/04; BBC1 tx 8/6/04-29/6/04
Narr: Jo Whiley, Dr Tanya Byron
Ser Pr: Sacha Baveystock
Exec Pr: Jill Fullerton-Smith

Live At Johnny's
See TALK SHOWS

The Mighty Boosh
See COMEDY

The Other Boat Race
Reality
6 editions
BBC; BBC3 tx 22-27/3/04
Participants: Anna Botting, Richard Herring, Konnie Huq, Stephanie Cook, Jonathan Aitken, Edward Stourton, Helen Atkinson-Wood, Emma Kennedy, Toby Young, Steve Redgrave, Gillian Lindsay, Greg Searle, Jan Ravens, Kit Hesketh-Harvey, Grub Smith

Sex, Warts and All Down Under
Factual
9 editions
BBC3 tx 17-20/2/04; 24-28/2/04
Narr: Gill Mills

The Smoking Room
See COMEDY

Three's a Crowd
Reality/Dating Show
Series 1; 5 episodes
BBC3 tx 16-20/2/04 (Mon-Fri)
Pres: Claudia Winkleman

Tower Block Dreams
Documentary
3 editions
Raw TV; BBC3 tx 8/1/04-22/1/04

Who Rules the Roost?
Reality/Factual
Series 1; 8 editions
Ricochet Digital; BBC3 tx 22/2/04-
11/4/04
Exec Pr: Nick Southgate

BBC4

The Alan Clark Diaries
Political Drama Serial
6 episodes
BBC; BBC4 tx 15/1/04-19/2/04 (BBC2 tx
17/3/04-22/4/04)
Cast: John Hurt, Jenny Agutter, Victoria
Smurfit, Julia Davis
Scr/Dir: Jon Jones (from book by Alan
Clark)
Pr: Kate Lewis
Exec Pr: Laura Mackie, Philippa Giles,
Richard Fell

The Alchemists of Sound
Archive/Documentary (history of BBC
Radiophonic Workshop)
Associated-Rediffusion TV; BBC4 tx
19/10/03
Narr: Oliver Postgate
Dir: Roger Pomphrey
Pr: John Warburton
Exec Pr: Victor Lewis-Smith, Graham Pass

Elmina's Kitchen
See SINGLE DRAMA

The Guinea Pig Club
Documentary/History Factual
BBC/TLC; BBC4 tx 16/3/04
Narr: Geraldine James
Dir: Karen Kelly
Pr: Tamara Bodenham
Exec Pr: Anne Laking

Home
Single Drama
BBC; BBC4 tx 6/10/03
Cast: Anthony Sher, Matilda Ziegler,
Deborah Findlay, Guy Henry, Keith Allen
Scr/Dir: Richard Curson Smith (from
story by J.G. Ballard)
Pr: Richard Fell

Hotel in Amsterdam
See SINGLE DRAMA

Imber – England's Lost Village
Documentary/History Factual
Artangel Media/CTVC; BBC4 tx 10/5/04
Dir: Mark Kidel
Pr: Annie McGeoch
Exec Pr: Nick Stuart, Michael Morris,
Rodney Wilson

The Island
Documentary/History Factual
Seventh House Films; BBC4 tx 4/12/03
Pres: Andrew Motion
Pr/Dir: Clive Dunn
Exec Pr: Nick Ware

The National Trust
See DOCUMENTARY

Three Sisters
See SINGLE DRAMA

Wales

Belonging
Drama serial
Series 5; 8 episodes
BBC Wales; BBC 1 Wales tx 5/5/04-
23/6/04
Cast: Charles Dale, Donna Edwards, Eve
Myles, William Thomas, Beth Morris, Alun
Raglan, Di Botcher
Wr: Jason Sutton, Catrin Clarke, Alex
Carolan, Janys Chambers
Dir: Rhys Powys
Pr: Sophie Fante

Pobol y Cwm
Soap opera (on air since 1974)
BBC Wales; S4C tx 5 episodes weekly
(Mon-Fri)
Cast: Nia Caron, Donna Edwards, Sue
Roderick, Andrew Teilo, Dewi Rhys

Williams, Siw Hughes, Rhys ap Hywel,
Lisa Victoria, Rhys ap William, Shelley
Rees
Dir: Rhiannon Rees
Pr: Bethan Jones

Scotland

River City
Soap opera (first ep. tx 24/9/02)
Continuing; 2 weekly episodes
BBC Scotland; BBC 1 Scotland tx 2
episodes weekly (Tue-Thur)
Cast: Lorraine McIntosh, Gordon
Kennedy, Jenni Keenan Green, Allison
McKenzie, Stephen Purdon, Gordon
McCorkell, Deirdre Davis, AnnMarie
Fulton, Joyce Falconer, Paul Samson, Libby
McArthur, Morag Calder, Johnny Beattie
Wr (in 2004): Mark Cairns, Martin
Brocklebank, Patrick Harkins, Vivien
Adam, James McCreadie, Fergus Mitchell,
James Doherty, Pia Ashberry, Stephen
McAteer, David Young, Aileen Ritchie,
David Robertson, Marc Pye, Paul F Logue,
Jack Dickson, James McIntyre, David
Young, Des Dillon
Dir: (in 2004) Fiona Walton, Brian
Horsburgh, Mike Alexander, Garth Tucker,
Bill McLeod, Phillip Wood, Norman Stone
Pr: Sandra MacIver, Jim Shields, Paula
MacGee

Sea of Souls
See SCI-FI & FANTASY

Still Game
Sitcom
Series 3; 6 episodes
The Comedy Unit; BBC 1 Scotland tx
7/5/04-11/6/04
Cast: Ford Kiernan, Greg Hemphill, Paul
Riley, Mark Cox, Jane McCarry, Sanjeev
Kohli, Gavin Mitchell
Wr: Ford Kiernan, Greg Hemphill
Dir/Pr: Michael Hines

PROGRAMMING DATA

Northern Ireland

Lesser Spotted Ulster
Factual
11 episodes
Westway Films; UTV tx 6/1/04-30/3/04
Pres: Joe Mahon

Give My Head Peace
See COMEDY

Gunpowder, Treason and Plot
See HISTORICAL DRAMA

Holy Cross
See SINGLE DRAMA

I Fought the Law
Series 1; 6 episodes
BBC1 NI tx 30/9/03-6/11/03
Cast: Paul Loughran, Katherine Igoe, Billy Carter, Seeta Indrani, Kieran Lagan, Jonjo O'Neill
Creators: Tim McGarry, Michael McDowell, Damon Quinn

Pulling Moves
Series 1; 10 episodes
BBC NI; BBC3 tx 5/3/04-2/4/04 (BBC1 NI tx 31/5/04-13/7/04)
Cast: Simon Delaney, Ciaran McMenamin, Kevin Elliott, Ciaran Nolan
Wr: Pearse Elliott
Dir: Brian Kirk
Pr: Grainne Marmion

Parliament & Politics

The Daily Politics
BBC2 tx 9/9/03-22/7/04
(three editions weekly Tue-Wed-Thur)
Pres: Andrew Neil, Daisy Sampson
Dir: Claire Bellis
Ed: John McAndrew, John Rigby, Jamie Donald
Prog Ed: Natasha Shallice
NB: occasionally replaced by Scottish Questions Live and Holyrood Live, BBC2 Scotland

Jonathan Dimbleby
ITV1 tx 28/9/03-18/7/04
Chairman: Jonathan Dimbleby
Ed: David Sayer

Exec Pr: Alexander Gardiner

Panorama
BBC; BBC1 tx semi-regular runs Sunday evenings, continuing from 28/9/03 (regularly on air since 1953)
Pr: Darren Kemp, Fiona Gough
Ed: Mike Robinson

Question Time
BBC1 tx 25/9/03-8/7/04
Chairman: David Dimbleby
Ed: Nick Pisani
Exec Pr: George Carey

The Politics Show
BBC1 tx 14/9/03-18/7/04
Chairman: Jeremy Vine
Ed: James Stephenson

This Week
BBC1 tx 11/9/03-22/7/04
Pres: Andrew Neil, Diane Abbott, Michael Portillo
Pr: Natasha Shallice, Caroline Taylor
Ed: Jamie Donald

Arts

Arena
BBC2 tx; occasional one-off episodes
Ed: Anthony Wall

'Imagine Imagine'
BBC2 tx 20/9/03
Dir/Pr: Frederick Baker

'Dylan Thomas – From Grave To Cradle'
BBC2 tx 22/11/03
Dir: Anthony Wall

'Buffalo Bill's Wild West: How the Myth Was Made'
BBC2 tx 19/12/03
Pr: Mary Dickinson

'Alec Guinness, a Secret Man'
BBC2 tx 29/12/03
Dir/Pr: David Thompson

'Pavarotti – The Last Tenor'
BBC2 tx 29/5/04
Narr: Ian McKellen
Pr: Erica Banks, Adam Sweeting

Art Safari
Series 1; 4 editions
BBC4 tx 28/9/03-19/10/03
Pres: Ben Lewis

The Art Show
Series 2; 12 editions
Various producers; Channel 4 tx 14/11/03-19/12/03; 8/1/04-30/1/04
Dir: Bernadette O'Brien, Jacques Peretti, Paul Tickell, Charlie Booker, Neil Crombie, Bruno Wolheim, Emma Davies
Pr: Chloe Thomas, Mike Lerner
Ser Pr: Jacques Peretti

Before the Booker
Series 2; 6 editions
BBC4 tx 16/2/04-29/3/04
Pres: Clive Anderson

The Big Read
9 editions/21 books presented
BBC; BBC2 tx 18/10/03-13/12/03
Host: Clive Anderson
Pres: Meera Syal, Benedict Allen, William Hague, Ruby Wax, Phill Jupitus, Clare Short, John Humphrys, Sanjeev Baskhar, Arabella Weir, Ray Mears, Alistair McGowan, John Sergeant, David Dimbleby, Alan Titchmarsh, Jo Brand, Fay Ripley, Bill Oddie, Ronni Ancona, Simon Schama, Sandi Toksvig, Lorraine Kelly
Dir: Rupert Miles, Deep Sehgal, Francis Whately, Georgina Harvey, James Runcie, Merryn Threadgould, Richard Valentine
Pr: Peter Higgins, John Holdsworth, Alastair Laurence, Ben Southwell, Geoff Dunlop, Sally Thomson
Ser Pr: Mary Sackville West, Michael Poole
Exec Pr: Mark Harrison

The Divine Michelangelo
2 parts
BBC; BBC1 tx 29/2/04 & 7/3/04
Cast: Stephen Noonan
Ser Pr: Tim Dunn
Exec Pr: Kim Thomas

Every Picture Tells a Story
Series 1; 8 editions
Five tx 10/12/03-19/12/03 (twice weekly); 12/8/04-2/9/04
Pres: Waldemar Januszczak
Dir: James Bluemel
Pr: Mike Lerner

Frankenstein: Birth of a Monster

BBC1 tx 7/12/03
Narr: Robert Winston
Cast: Lucy Davenport, Oliver Chris, David
Schofield, Harriet Walter, Clive Merrison,
Ronan Vibert
Pr: Mary Downes
Exec Pr: Kim Thomas

Great Artists with Tim Marlow

aka Great Artists 2 with Tim Marlow
Series 2; 12 editions
Seventh Art Productions; Five tx 18/9/03-
30/10/03; 15/1/04-5/2/04; 19/2/04
Pres: Tim Marlow
Dir: Phil Grabsky, Andrew Hutton, Ben
Harding
Pr: Phil Grabsky

Handel's Water Music

BBC2 tx 8/5/04
Pres: Peter Ackroyd
Dir: Trevor Hampton, Fergus O'Brien
Pr: Suzy Klein

Imagine

Series 2; 6 editions
BBC; BBC1 tx 12/11/03-18/12/03
Pres: Alan Yentob
Dir: Rupert Edwards, Vanessa Frances,
Sarah Aspinall, Rebecca Frayn, John
Needham, Roger Parsons
Pr: Vanessa Frances, Sarah Aspinall,
Rebecca Frayn, John Needham, Ian
MacMillan
Ser Pr: Ian MacMillan
Exec Pr: Alan Yentob
Series 3; 6 editions
BBC; BBC1 tx 2/6/04-7/7/04
Pres: Alan Yentob
Dir: Ian MacMillan, James Nutt, Ben
McPherson, Margy Kinmouth
Pr: William Feaver, Sarah Aspinall, Ben
McPherson
Ser Pr: Ian MacMillan

Matt's Old Masters

4 editions
World of Wonder; Channel 4 tx 23/11/03-
21/12/03
Pres: Matthew Collings
Dir: Chris Rodley
Pr: Sarah Mortimer
Exec Pr: Fenton Bailey, Randy Barbato

Matthew Bourne's Nutcracker!

BBC1 tx 21/12/03 (BBC2 in Scotland)
Intro: Dawn French
Dir: Ross MacGibbon
Pr: Simon Flind

The Private Life of a Masterpiece

Series 2; 5 editions
BBC2 tx 18/1/04-23/2/04
Pr: Bob Bentley, Mick Gold, Judith
Winnan, John Bush, Ian Jones
Ed: Jeremy Bugler
Series 3; 5 episodes
BBC2 tx 17/4/04-22/5/04
Narr: Sam West
Pr: Bob Bentley, Mick Gold, Lucie
Donahue, Judith Winnan, Michael Burke
Ed: Jeremy Bugler

Restoration

Endemol UK for BBC Scotland
Series 1; 11 editions
BBC2 tx 8/8/03-14/9/03 (twice weekly
Fri-Tue; final Sun)
Pres: Griff Rhys Jones, Marianne Suhr,
Ptolemy Dean
Pr: Minoo Bhatia, Victoria Watson, Simon
Mansfield, Jonathan Barker
Ed: Simon Shaw
Exec Pr: Nikki Cheetham, Annette Clarke,
Andrea Miller
Series 2; 8 editions
BBC2 tx 13/7/04-8/8/04 (twice weekly
Tue-Sun)
Dir: Alex Rudzinski
Pr: Andrew Thompson, Paul Coueslant,
Kate Scholefield, Jonathan Barker, Sarah
Barclay, Robert Pendlebury, Tim Usborne
Ed: Katie Boyd

The South Bank Show

LWT; 19 occasional editions shown on
ITV1 between 31/8/03-22/8/04
Pres: Melvyn Bragg
Pr: Archie Powell, Mathew Tucker,
Christopher Walker, Bob Bee, Gerald Fox,
David Thomas, Aurora Gunn, Susan Shaw,
Matt Cain

Turner Prize 2003

Channel 4 tx 7/12/03
Pres: Matthew Collings, Patricia Bickers,
Alain de Botton, Mike Figgis, Oliver James
Dir: Rik Lander
Pr: Linda Zuck

Turner Prize People's Poll

4 editions
Channel 4 tx 1-4/12/03
Dir: Rik Lander
Pr: Linda Zuck

Vincent: The Full Story

3 editions
ZCZ; Channel 4 tx 16-30/5/04
Pres: Waldemar Januszcak
Dir: Mark James
Pr: Mike Lerner

Wren: The Man Who Built Britain

BBC1 tx 25/4/04
Pres: Michael Buerk
Cast: Hugh Bonneville, Stephen Mangan,
Julian Wadham, Oliver Ford Davies
Wr: Laura Lamson
Dir/Pr: Julian Birkett

Documentary

America's Fattest City

Granada TV; Channel 4 tx 4/1/04
Dir: Mark Jones
Exec Pr: Sarah Murch

Bodyshock: The Man Who Ate His Lover

Mentorn; Channel 4 tx 1/3/04
Dir/Pr: Srik Narayanan
Exec Pr: Nick Curwin

Brinks Mat: The Greatest Heist

2 parts
Blast! Films; Channel 4 tx 24/11/03 &
1/12/03
Cast: Russell Levy, Cavan Clerkin, Roland
Manookian, Jonny Phillips, Rupert
Procter; Steven Mackintosh (nar)
Dir: Bruce Goodison
Pr: Mark Hayhurst

The Divine Michelangelo

See ARTS

Dunkirk

3 parts
BBC; BBC2 tx 18-19-20/2/04
Cast: Simon Russell Beale, Clive Brunt,
Phil Cornwell, Benedict Cumberbatch,
Ricci Harnett, Nicholas Jones
Narr: Timothy Dalton

PROGRAMMING DATA

Scr: Neil McKay, Lisa Osborne, Alex Holmes
Dir: Alex Holmes
Pr: Rob Warr

The Four Minute Mile
BBC2 tx 21/4/04
Pr: Carl Hindmarch
Exec Pr: Richard Bradley, Bill Locke

Lawrence of Arabia: The Battle for the Arab World
2 parts
Lion Television/PBS; BBC2 tx
6 & 13/12/03
Dir/Pr: James Hawes
Exec Pr: Nick Catliff, Carol Sennett

The Miners' Strike
BBC2 tx 27/1/04
Pr: Steve Condie
Exec Pr: Fiona Stourton

My Foetus
Bivouac; Channel 4 tx 20/4/04
Dir/Pr: Julia Black

The National Trust
10 editions (BBC4 5 editions)
Oxford Film and Television; BBC2 tx
14/1/04-16/3/04 (BBC4 tx 16/11/03-
14/12/03)
Dir: Patrick Forbes
Pr: Claire Kavanagh

Oliver Cromwell: Warts and All
BBC1 tx 24/11/03
Cast: Jim Carter, Martin Turner, Hazel Ellerby, Tim Frances, Gideon Turner, Steve Elder, Jeffrey Daunton
Scr: Ronald Frame
Dir/Pr: Andrew Thompson
Exec Pr: Neil McDonald

ONE Life
7 parts
BBC; BBC1 tx 24/9/03-5/11/03
Dir/Pr: Min Clough, Benetta Adamson, Jenny Crowther, Nicholas O'Dwyer, Mags Gavan, Brian Woods, Jeremy Wales, Annie Kossoff
Ed: Todd Austin

Police Protecting Children
3 editions
BBC; BBC2 tx 23 & 30/3/04 (pt.3 ntx)
Pr: Ben Rumney
Ser Pr: Bob Long

Property People
6 editions
BBC; BBC2 tx 7/1/04-11/2/04
Narr: Martin Freeman
Dir: Jennie Cosgrove, Anthony Wonke, Victoria Taylor
Pr: Anthony Wonke
Ser Pr: Cassie Braban

Real Crime: Lady Jane
Granada TV; ITV1 tx 14/10/03
Cast: Kaye Wragge, Tim Wallers, Deborah McLaren
Scr/Dir: James Strong
Pr: Miranda Peters

Risking It All
5 parts
Ricochet South; Channel 4 tx 21/4/04-
19/5/04
Dir/Pr: Marcus Sulley, Livia Russell
Exec Pr: Joanna Head, Nick Powell

The Secret Policeman
BBC; BBC1 tx 21/10/03
Reporter: Mark Daly
Exec Pr: Simon Ford

Timewatch: Through Hell for Hitler
BBC/MS Films; BBC2 tx 5/12/03
Cast: Ben Silverstone
Dir/Pr: Jonathan Hacker
Ed: John Farren

Victoria Wood's Big Fat Documentary
2 parts
Liberty Bell; BBC1 tx 9 & 16/1/04
Pres: Victoria Wood
Pr: Judith Holder, Ben Warwick

When Michael Portillo Became a Single Mum
BBC; BBC2 tx 15/10/03
Ser Pr: Alison Cahn, Charlotte Desai

Who Killed PC Blakelock?
Films of Record Production; BBC2 tx
2/3/04
Dir: Jonathan Jones
Exec Pr: Roger Graef, Fiona Stourton

Diversity

Time Shift: The Black and White Minstrel Show Revisited
Documentary/TV history
BBC Bristol; BBC4 tx 6/6/04
Dir/Pr: Stephanie Wessell
Ser Pr: Kate Broome
Exec Pr: Michael Poole

Black Flash: a Century of Black Footballers
Documentary/sporting history
BBC History; BBC 4 tx 21/9/03
Dir/Pr: Geoff Small

Earth Summit: The Bushmen's Last Dance
Documentary/politics
BBC 4 rpt tx 19/7/03 (first tx 29/8/02)
Dir: James Smith

The Crouches
See COMEDY

Elmina's Kitchen
See SINGLE DRAMA

The Kumars at No. 42
See COMEDY

Second Generation
See DRAMA SERIES

Daytime

The Afternoon Play
See SINGLE DRAMA

Antiques Auction
Series 1; 36 editions
ITV1 tx 10/5/04-25/6/04 (Mon-Fri)
Pres: Lynda Bellingham
Pr: Debbie Gaunt
Ser Pr: Janet Frawley

Bargain Hunt (daytime editions)
BBC Bristol
40 editions; BBC1 tx 1/9/03-24/10/03
(Mon-Fri)
5 editions; BBC1 tx 5/1/04-9/1/04
(Mon-Fri)
Bargain Hunt Live!; 5 editions; BBC1 tx
22/3/04-26/3/04 (Mon-Fri)
5 editions; BBC1 tx 19/4/04-23/4/04
(Mon-Fri)
Pres: Tim Wonnacott
Ser Pr: Pete Smith

Big Strong Boys
50 editions
BBC1 tx 10/11/03-12/12/03; 12/1/04-
13/2/04 (Mon-Fri)
Pres: Craig Phillips, Stewart Castledine,
Debra Veal

Britain's Secret Shame – Bullying
Series 1; 5 editions
BBC1 tx 19-23/4/04
Pres: Sally Magnusson

Building the Dream
Series 1; 143 editions
Zeal Television; ITV1 tx 4/4/04 (Sun) then
5/4/04-2/7/04 (Mon-Fri)
Pres: Linda Barker

Call My Bluff
14 editions
BBC Birmingham; BBC1 tx 1-18/6/04
(Mon-Fri)
Pres: Fiona Bruce, Rod Liddle, Alan Coren
Pr: Veronica Butt

Car Booty
Series 1; 5 editions
BBC1 tx 26/4/04-30/4/04
Pres: Lorne Spicer

Cash in the Attic
Leopard Films
Series 2; 30 editions; BBC1 tx 10/11/03-
19/12/03 (Mon-Fri)
Series 3; 30 editions; BBC1 tx 5/1/04-
30/1/04; 9/2/04-13/2/04 (Mon-Fri)
Series 4; 15 editions; BBC1 tx 10/5/04-
28/5/04 (Mon-Fri)
Pres: Alistair Appleton, Paul Hayes
Ser Pr: Bernard Periatambee

City Hospital
38 editions
Topical TV; BBC1 tx 5/4/04-28/5/04 [not
12/4/04] (Mon-Fri)
Pres: Matthew Kelly, Nadia Sawalha,
Roger Black, Rageh Omaar
Dir: Sue Robinson
Ed: Peter Hayton

Countdown
Yorkshire TV; Channel 4 tx [from
2/11/82]-continuing (Mon-Fri)
Pres: Richard Whiteley, Carol Vorderman

The Courtroom
Series 1; 23 episodes
Campus Manor Productions/Mersey TV;
Channel 4 tx 21/6/04-21/7/04 (Mon-Fri)
Cast: Terrence Hardiman, Derren Nesbitt,
Alison Pargeter, Judith Barker, Daryl
Fishwick, Charles Foster, Christopher
Ravenscroft, Terence Harvey, Malcolm
Stoddard
Wr: Maurice Bessman, Richard Burke,
Judith Clucas, Heather Robson, Andy
Lynch, Barry Woodward, Arthur Ellison,
Neil Jones, Steve Lawson, Richard Burke,
William Franklyn
Scr Ed: Laura McCann
Dir: Chris Corcoran, Craig Lines, Chris
Jury, Michael Kerrigan, Jeff Naylor
Pr: David Hanson
Exec Pr: Phil Redmond

Doctors
Continuing; 186 episodes (to 14/6/04)
BBC Birmingham; BBC1 tx 1/9/03-
19/12/03; 5/1/04-24/1/04; 3/2/04-
19/3/04; 5/4/04-14/6/04
Cast: Christopher Timothy, Diane Keen,
Maggie Cronin, Corinne Wicks, Natalie J.
Robb
Scr Pr: Peter E. Lloyd
Scr Ed: Terry Barker
Pr: Rosalynd Ward, Carol Harding
Ser Pr: Beverley Dartnell
Exec Pr: Mal Young

Everything Must Go
(and **EMG: Under the Hammer**)
Hotbed Media
Series 3; 40 editions; ITV1 tx 8/9/03-
10/10/03 (Mon-Fri)
EMG: Under the Hammer
ITV1 tx 13/10/03-24/10/03 (Mon-Fri)

Series 4; 30 editions; ITV1 tx 9/2/04-
13/2/04; 8/3/04-19/3/04 (Mon-Fri)
EMG: Under the Hammer
ITV1 tx 16/2/04-5/3/04 (some not shown
in Scottish region)
Pres: Clayton Riches, Adrienne Lawler
Ser Pr: Amanda Lowe (EMG)
Exec Pr: Johannah Dyer (EMG)

Flesh and Blood
Series 1; 5 editions
BBC1 tx 17/5/04-21/5/04
Pres: Sally Magnusson

Home From Home
Series 3; 10 editions
Maverick Television; Channel 4 tx 2/6/04-
18/6/04 (Mon-Fri)
Pr: Jennie Sandford
Ser Pr: Claire Hobbs

Homes Under the Hammer
20 editions
BBC1 tx 17/11/03-12/12/03
Ser Pr: Melanie Eriksen

House Invaders
BBC1 tx 1/9/03-9/10/03 (Mon-Fri)
and 45 editions; BBC1 tx 1/3/04-24/6/04
(Mon-Fri)
Pres: Anna Ryder Richardson

Jeremy Vine Meets ...
Series 1; 5 editions
Ten Alps; BBC1 tx 10-14/5/04
Pres: Jeremy Vine (interviews with Bob
Geldof, Lionel Richie, Sting, Debbie Harry,
Elvis Costello)
Dir/Pr: Niall MacCormick
Exec Pr: Sam Cash, Gilly Hall

Kilroy
(Originally as **Day to Day** from 11/86; as
Kilroy from 1987)
Series 15; (some editions scrapped
untransmitted; Robert Kilroy-Silk
suspended by BBC 9/1/04)
Kilroy Television Company; BBC1 tx
1/9/03-9/1/04 (Mon-Fri)
Pres: Robert Kilroy-Silk
Exec Ed: David O'Keefe

PROGRAMMING DATA

Love 2 Shop

Series 1; 43 editions
Chameleon Television; ITV1 tx 27/10/03-24/12/03 (Mon-Fri)
Pres: Jenny Powell

Money Spinners

Series 1; 10 editions
Leopard Films; BBC1 tx 22/3/04-2/4/04 (Mon-Fri)
Pres: Lorne Spicer
Ser Pr: Nick Rigg
Ed: Bernard Periatambee
Exec Pr: James Burstall, Katherine Parsons

Now You're Talking!

Series 1; 63 editions
Kilroy Television Company;
BBC1 tx 15/3/04-15/6/04 (Mon-Fri)
Pres: Nadia Sawalha, Nicky Campbell, Sian Williams
Exec Pr: David O'Keefe
Exec Ed: Paul Woolwich

OK! TV

Series 1; 5 editions
Carlton; ITV1 tx 16-20/2/04
Pres: Ronan Keating

A Place in the Sun

Freeform; Channel 4 tx 15/9/03-12/12/03; 5/1/04-6/2/04 (Mon-Fri)
Pres: Amanda Lamb, Zilpah Hartley, Bella Crane
Dir/Pr: Craig Brooks, Angela Norris, Eliot Fletcher, Paul Denchfield

Ready Steady Cook

Series 13; 120 editions
Endemol UK; BBC2 tx
Pres: Ainsley Harriot
Exec Pr: Linda Clifford

Richard and Judy

Series 3
Cactus TV; Channel 4 tx 15/9/03-21/7/04 (Mon-Fri)
Pres: Richard Madeley, Judy Finnigan
Exec Pr: Amanda Ross
Ed: Cillian de Buitlear

60-Minute Makeover

Series 1; 33 editions
Granada TV; ITV1 tx 19/4/04-4/6/04

(Mon-Fri)
Pres: Claire Sweeney
Ser Pr: Rachel Bloomfield
Exec Pr: Sarah Caplin

Stars Reunited

Series 2 (same shooting block as Series 1); 5 editions ('Allo 'Allo, Bread, Z Cars, TOTP, Nationwide)
Liberty Bell; BBC1 tx 5-9/1/04
Pres: Dale Winton
Dir: Pati Marr
Ser Pr: Mary Ramsay

The Terry and Gaby Show

UMTV; Five tx 2/6/03-26/3/04 (Mon-Fri)
Pres: Terry Wogan, Gaby Roslin, Johnny Ball, Danny Baker
Ser Pr: James Winter
Exec Pr: Chris Evans

This Morning

Granada TV; ITV1 tx 8/9/03-16/7/04 (Mon-Fri) (will return September 2004)
Pres: Phillip Schofield, Fern Britton (guest presenters include John Suchet, Brian Capron, Ross Kelly, Gloria Hunniford, Lorraine Kelly)
Dir: Martin Lord
Ed: Siubhan Richmond
Exec Pr: James Hunt

Through the Keyhole

30 editions
David Paradine Productions; BBC1 tx 1/3/04-9/4/04 (Mon-Fri)
Pres: David Frost, Catherine Gee

Today With Des and Mel

Series 2; 140 editions
Carlton Television; ITV1 tx 8/9/03-19/12/03; 19/1/04-16/4/04 (Mon-Fri)
Pres: Des O'Connor, Melanie Sykes (guest presenters include Paul O'Grady, Gabby Logan)
Dir: Alasdair MacMillan
Pr: Zoe Tait
Ser Pr: Robert Gray
Ser Ed: Elizabeth Murphy
Exec Pr: Colin Fay, Mark Wells

Trisha

Anglia TV; ITV1 tx-continuing
Pres: Trisha Goddard
Ed: Lucy Garbutt

24-Hour Quiz

See QUIZ & GAME SHOWS

Up Your Street

Series 1; 33 editions
Maverick Television; Channel 4 tx 13/4/04-27/5/04 (Mon-Fri)
Pres: Simon O'Brien
Ser Pr: Melissa Feather
Exec Pr: Niall Fraser

The Weakest Link (daytime editions)

BBC; BBC2 tx (Mon-Fri) continuing since August 2000
Pres: Anne Robinson
Pr: Alexandra McLeod
Ser Pr: Andy Rowe

The Wright Stuff

Princess Productions; Five tx 1/9/03-continuing
Pres: Matthew Wright
Ed: Johnny McCune

Soap

Brookside

Mersey TV; Channel 4 tx weekly 2/11/82-4/11/03 (series' run ends with 90-minute eps, shown late-night)
Main Cast: Dean Sullivan, Sarah White, Vince Earl, Tiffany Chapman, Philip Olivier, Suzanne Collins, Paul Duckworth, with Claire Sweeney, Paul Usher
Senior Pr: David Hanson
Exec Pr: Phil Redmond

Casualty

BBC; BBC1 tx 1 episode weekly (Sat) 13/9/03-5/6/04 (extra ep Sun 14/9/04); 17/7/04-continuing
Main Cast: Kelly Harrison, Christopher Colquhoun, Simon MacCorkindale, James Redmond, Sarah Manners, Maxwell Caulfield, Kwame Kwei-Armah, Suzanne Packer, Loo Brealey, Ian Bleasdale, Julia Hills, Christine Stephen-Daly, Matthew Wait
Pr: Pippa Brill, Steve Lightfoot, Lowri Glain, Sue Howells, Sophie Anwar

Coronation Street

Granada; ITV1 tx 5 episodes weekly (Mon(x2)-Wed-Fri-Sun)
Main Cast: William Roache, Anne Kirkbride, Kate Ford, Suranne Jones, Simon Gregson, Beverley Callard, David Neilson, Julie Hesmondhalgh, Johnny Briggs, Barbara Knox, Sue Nicholls, Helen Worth, Sean Wilson, Adam Rickitt, Sally Whittaker, Michael Le Vell, Bill Tarmey, Liz Dawn, Alan Halsall, Sam Aston, Jennie McAlpine, Sally Lindsay, Keith Duffy, Shobna Gulati, Jimmi Harkishin, Bruce Jones, Vicky Entwistle, Jane Danson, Wendi Peters, Tina O'Brien, Bruno Langley, Bradley Walsh, John Savident, Steven Arnold, Julia Haworth
Pr: Kieran Roberts, Tony Wood

EastEnders

BBC; BBC1 tx 4 episodes weekly (Mon-Tue-Thu-Fri) with omnibus repeat Sun
Main Cast: Leslie Grantham, Letitia Dean, Nigel Harman, Scarlett Johnson, Tracy-Ann Oberman, Wendy Richard, Ian Lavender, James Alexandrou, Natalie Cassidy, Adam Woodyatt, June Brown, John Bardon, Pam St Clement, Shane Richie, Jessie Wallace, Christopher Parker, Hilda Braid, Michael Higgs, Kim Medcalf, Michelle Ryan, Kacey Ainsworth, Elaine Lordan, Laila Morse, Derek Martin, Ricky Groves, Perry Fenwick, Gary Beadle, Jill Halfpenny, Brooke Kinsella, Nabil Elouahabi, Ray Panthaki (written out in 2003-4 – Steve McFadden, Lucy Benjamin, Shaun Williamson, Hannah Waterman, Charlie Brooks, Sid Owen)
Pr: Rumu Sen-Gupta, Colin Wratten, Sue Butterworth, Nicholas Prosser, Mark Sendell, Nicky Cotton, Jamie Annett, Jo Johnson, Jonathan Phillips
Exec Pr: Louise Berridge

Emmerdale

Yorkshire TV; ITV1 tx 6 episodes weekly (Mon-Fri + Sun)
Main Cast: Clive Hornby, Christopher Chittell, Elizabeth Estensen, Patrick Mower, Emma Atkins, Leah Bracknell, Mark Charnock, Billy Hartman, Steve Halliwell, Jeff Hordley, Lucy Pargeter, Jane Cox, James Hooton, Andy Devine, Kelvin Fletcher, Sammy Winward, Lorraine Chase, Shirley Stelfox, Deena

Payne, Carolyn Pickles, Charlie Hardwick, Patsy Kensit
Pr: Kathleen Beedles, Steve Frost, Tim Key

Family Affairs

talkbackTHAMES; Five tx 5 episodes weekly (Mon-Fri)
Main Cast: Nicola Duffett, Gareth Hale, Rosie Powell, David Easter, Kazia Pelka, Anna Acton, Carol Starks, Sam Barriscale, Joshua Copstick, Ann Marcuson, Christopher Mills, Leon Ockenden
Pr: Stephen Moore, Susan Breen

Holby City

BBC; BBC1 tx 1 episode weekly (Wed)
Main Cast: Hugh Quarshie, Patricia Potter, Art Malik, Noah Huntley, Luisa Bradshaw-White, Tina Hobley, Sharon Maughan, Mark Moraghan, Jaye Jacobs, David Bedella, Amanda Mealing, Ian Aspinall, Verona Joseph
Pr: Sharon Hughff, Chris Ballantyne, Emma Kingsman-Lloyd, Michael Offer, Huw Kennair Jones

Hollyoaks

See YOUTH/TEEN

River City

See SCOTLAND

Pobol y Cwm

See WALES

Drama Series & Serials

The Alan Clark Diaries

See BBC4

Auf Wiedersehen, Pet

(BBC) Series 4; 6 episodes
BBC/Ziji Productions; BBC1 tx 4/1/04-8/2/04
Cast: Tim Healy, Kevin Whately, Timothy Spall, Jimmy Nail, Christopher Fairbank, Pat Roach, Noel Clarke
Wr: Dick Clement & Ian La Fresnais
Dir: Maurice Phillips, David Innes Edwards
Pr: Chrissy Skinns

Bad Girls

Series 6; 12 episodes
Shed Productions; ITV1 tx 14/4/04-19/5/04; 2-23/8/04 (break for Euro 2004)
Cast: Eva Pope, Dannielle Brent, Antonia Okonma, Jack Ellis, Helen Fraser, Charlotte Lucas, Tristan Sturrock, Tracey Wilkinson, Kika Mirylees, Victoria Alcock, Stephanie Beacham, Amanda Barrie and Zoe Lucker (crossover with **Footballers' Wives**)
Wr: Di Burrows, Paul Mousley, Jane Marlow, Helen Eatock, Phil Ford
Dir: Nigel Douglas, Ian Knox, Julian Holmes, Ian White
Pr: Cameron Roach

Between the Sheets

Series 1; 6 episodes
Rollem; ITV1 tx 17/11/03-22/12/03
Cast: Brenda Blethyn, Alun Armstrong, Liz Smith, Julie Graham, James Thornton, Gaynor Faye
Wr: Kay Mellor
Dir: Robin Sheppard, Jane Prowse
Pr: Yvonne Francas

Born and Bred

Series 3; 9 episodes
BBC; BBC1 tx 29/2/04-25/4/04
Cast: Michael French, James Bolam, Jenna Russell, Maggie Steed, Tracey Childs, John Henshaw, Sam Hudson, Naomi Radcliffe, Clive Swift, Peter Gunn
Wr: Chris Chibnall, Dan Sefton, Nick Warburton, Gaby Chiappe
Dir: Simon Massey, Rob Evans, David Tucker, Paul Harrison
Pr: Chris Clough

The Brief

Series 1; 4 episodes
Carlton; ITV1 tx 25/4/04-16/5/04
Cast: Alan Davies, Cherie Lunghi, Zara Turner, Linda Bassett, Christopher Fulford
Wr: Dusty Hughes
Dir: Jack Gold, Stuart Orme, Sandy Johnson
Pr: Chris Burt
Exec Pr: Ted Childs

PROGRAMMING DATA

Cutting It

Series 3; 6 episodes
BBC; BBC1 tx 27/4/04-1/6/04
Cast: Sarah Parrish, Jason Merrells, Ben Daniels, Angela Griffin, Sian Reeves, Lucy Gaskell
Wr: Debbie Horsfield
Dir: John Alexander, Euros Lyn, Catherine Morshead
Pr: Diederick Santer, Debbie Horsfield

Down to Earth

Series 4; 8 episodes
BBC1 tx 4/1/04-22/2/04
Cast: Angela Griffin, Ian Kelsey, Denise Welch, Ricky Tomlinson, Elizabeth Bennett, Ram John Holder, Inga Brooksby
Wr: Peter Gibbs, Jane Hollowood, Susan Wilkins, Joe Fraser, Stuart Morris
Dir: Simon Meyers, Simon Massey, Dominic Keavey
Pr: Sharon Houlihan

Dream Team

Series 7; 32 episodes
Hewland International; Sky One tx 28/9/03-16/5/04
Cast: Chucky Venis, Michael Ryan, Alan Stocks, Cheryl Mackie, Tim Smith, Neil Newton, Terry Kiely, Rachel Brady, Jake Lloyd, Ricky Whittle, Terence Maynard
Wr: Harry Hewland, Jesse O'Mahoney, Ellen Taylor, Rachel Flowerday, Ben Harris, Jane Hewland, Andrew Hunt

Family Business

Series 1; 6 episodes
Tiger Aspect/BBC; BBC1 tx 11/2/04-17/3/04
Cast: Jamie Foreman, Elizabeth Berrington, Abbie Nichols, Michael Tucek, Trevor Peacock, Meg Wynn Owen
Wr: Tony Grounds, Chris Dunlop
Dir: Tom Shankland, Sarah Harding
Pr: Barney Reisz

Footballers' Wives

Series 3; 9 episodes
Shed Productions; ITV1 tx 11/2/04-7/4/04
Cast: Zoe Lucker, Gary Lucy, Jesse Birdsall, Ben Price, Laila Rouass, Jamie Davis, Sarah Barrand, Gillian Taylforth, Marcel McCalla, Alison Newman, John Forgeham

Wr: Liz Lake, Guy Picot, Harriet Warner
Dir: Jim Loach, Laurence Moody, Rob Bangura, Dominic Santana, Julie Edwards
Pr: Sean O'Connor

Foyle's War

Series 2; 4 episodes
Greenlit Productions; ITV1 tx 16/11/03-7/12/03
Cast: Michael Kitchen, Honeysuckle Weeks, Anthony Howell
Wr: Anthony Horowitz, Michael Hall, Michael Russell
Dir: Giles Foster, Jeremy Silbertson
Pr: Jill Green, Simon Passmore

Heartbeat

Series 14; 25 episodes
Yorkshire TV; ITV1 tx 7/9/03-9/11/03; 22/2/04-6/6/04
Cast: Derek Fowlds, Tricia Penrose, Geoffrey Hughes, Peter Benson, Duncan Bell, William Simons, Mark Jordon
Wr: John Flanagan, Andrew McCulloch, Brian Finch, Peter Gibbs, Susan Wilkins, Candy Denman, Neil McKay, Richard Monks, Jane Hollowood, Peter Mills, Duncan Gould, Johnny Byrne
Dir: Paul Walker, Jonas Grimas, Andrew Morgan, Frank W. Smith, Noreen Kershaw, Adrian Bean, Judith Dine, Gerry Mill, Matt Bloom, Declan O'Dwyer, Pip Short
Pr: Gerry Mill

Island at War

Series 1; 6 episodes
Granada; ITV1 tx 11/7/04-15/8/04
Cast: James Wilby, Clare Holman, Philip Glenister, Saskia Reeves, Julian Wadham, Joanne Froggatt, Samantha Robinson, Owen Teale, Julia Ford, Sean Ward, Ann Rye, Amy Ginsburg Harvey
Wr: Stephen Mallatratt
Dir: Thaddeus O'Sullivan, Peter Lydon
Pr: John Rushton

Life Begins

Series 1; 6 episodes
Granada; ITV1 tx 16/2/04-22/3/04
Cast: Caroline Quentin, Alexander Armstrong, Frank Finlay, Anne Reid, Claire Skinner
Wr: Mike Bullen, John Forte
Dir: Catherine Morehead, Charles Palmer
Pr: John Chapman

Making Waves

Series 1; 6 episodes (1-3 only tx)
Carlton; ITV1 tx 7-14/7/04 (4th ep cancelled; ntx. Series was scheduled to run to 11/8/04)
Cast: Alex Ferns, Emily Hamilton, Ian Bartholomew, Steve Speirs, Paul Chequer, Lee Boardman, Darren Morfitt, Joanna Page
Wr: Terry Cafola, Damian Wayling, Niall Leonard
Dir: Matthew Evans
Pr: Philip Shelley
Exec Pr: Ted Childs

Monarch of the Glen

Series 5; 10 episodes + special
Ecosse Films/BBC Scotland; BBC1 tx 28/9/03-30/11/03
Monarch of the Glen Hogmanay Special; BBC1 tx 28/12/03
Cast: Susan Hampshire, Alastair Mackenzie, Dawn Steele, Hamish Clark, Alexander Morton, Julian Fellowes
Wr: Niall Leonard, Mark Holloway, Andrew Taft, Leslie Stewart, Jeremy Front, John Martin Johnson, Michael Chaplin (+Hogmanay Special)
Dir: Richard Signy, Robert Knights (+Hogmanay Special), Ian Knox, Brian Kelly
Pr: Stephen Garwood

No Angels

Series 1; 10 episodes
World Productions; Channel 4 tx 2/3/04-4/5/04
Cast: Louise Delamere, Jo Joyner, Sunetra Sarker, Kaye Wragg, Derek Riddell, James Frost, Francis Magee
Wr: Toby Whithouse, Jane English, Kate Gartside, Sarah Phelps, Chris Dunlop, Ben Richards
Dir: Minkie Spiro, Julian Holmes, Clara Glynn, Julie Anne Robinson
Pr: Helen Gregory

P.O.W.

Series 1; 6 episodes
Company Pictures; ITV1 tx 10/10/03-14/11/03
Cast: James D'Arcy, Joe Absolom, Patrick Baladi, Anatole Taubman, Ewan Stewart, Craig Heaney
Wr: Matthew Graham, Stephen Davis,

Chris Lang, Clive Dawson, Tom Grieves
Dir: John Strickland, Roger Gartland
Pr: Victoria Fea

Prime Suspect 6
See CRIME

The Royal
Series 3; 14 episodes + special
Yorkshire TV; ITV1 tx 16/11/03-15/2/04
The Royal Christmas Special; ITV1 tx
21/12/03
Cast: Wendy Craig, Michael Starke,
Robert Daws, Amy Robbins, Zoie Kennedy,
Andy Wear, Michelle Hardwick
Wr: Sarah Bagshaw, Deborah Cook, Mark
Holloway, Andrew McCulloch & John
Flanagan, Jane Hollowood (Christmas
Special), Nick Saltrese, Patrick Melanaphy
Dir: Adrian Bean, Tim Dowd (+Christmas
Special), Paul Duane, John Greening,
Graeme Harper
Pr: Ken Horn

Second Generation
2 episodes
Oxford Film and Television; Channel 4 tx
14 & 15/9/03
Cast: Om Puri, Parminder Nagra,
Christopher Simpson, Anupam Kher,
Amita Dhiri, Rita Woolf, Roshan Seth
Wr: Neil Biswas
Dir: Jon Sen
Pr: Catherine Wearing

Shameless
Series 1; 7 episodes
Company Pictures; Channel 4 tx 13/1/04-
24/2/04 (E4 tx 13/1/04-17/2/04)
Cast: David Threlfall, Anne-Marie Duff,
Jody Latham, Gerard Kearns, James
McAvoy, Maxine Peake, Dean Lennox
Kelly, Maggie O'Neill
Wr: Paul Abbott, Danny Brocklehurst,
Carmel Morgan
Dir: Mark Mylod, Jonny Campbell,
Dearbhla Walsh
Pr: Emma Burge

Single
Series 1; 6 episodes
Tiger Aspect; ITV1 tx 25/10/03-4/12/03
Cast: Michelle Collins, Brendan Coyle,
Ophelia Lovibond, Robert Lowe, Alastair
Galbraith, Morwenna Banks

Wr: Peter Bowker
Dir: Dominic Brigstocke, Rebecca Frayn
Pr: Amanda Davis

Sweet Medicine
Series 1; 10 episodes
Carlton; ITV1 tx 4/9/03-23/10/03;
26/10/03-2/11/03
Cast: Patricia Hodge, Jason Merrells,
Gillian Kearney, Oliver Chris, Oliver
Milburn, Lucy Cohu
Wr: Nick Collins, Michael Jenner & Colin
Bytheway, Michael Aitkens, Matthew
Bardsley
Dir: John Woods, Douglas Mackinnon, Tim
Leandro, Jim Loach, David Holroyd, Terry
McDonough
Pr: Claire Phillips

Where the Heart Is
Series 8; 8 episodes
Anglia TV; ITV1 tx 11/7/04-29/8/04
Cast: Lesley Dunlop, Philip Middlemiss,
Brian Capron, Jamie Davis, Jenny Platt,
Adam Paul Harvey, Andrew Paul, Katy
Clayton, Samantha Giles, Keith Barron,
Holly Grainger, Julian Jones Lewis, Kerrie
Taylor, Katie Riddoch, Christian Cooke,
Roger Lloyd Pack, Heather Bleasdale, Tom
Chadbon
Wr: Cecily Hobbs, Sian Evans, Matt
Parker, Nicola Baldwin
Dir: Emma Bodger, Paul Walker, Moira
Armstrong
Pr: Ian Hopkins

William and Mary
Series 2; 6 episodes
Meridian TV; ITV1 tx 7/3/04-11/4/04
Cast: Martin Clunes, Julie Graham, Cheryl
Campbell, Michael Begley, Claire Hackett,
James Greene
Wr: Mick Ford
Dir: Matthew Evans, Nick Laughland,
Coky Giedroyc
Pr: Trevor Hopkins

Single Drama

The Afternoon Play
Series 2; 5 episodes
BBC Birmingham; BBC1 tx 26/1/04-
2/2/04
Ser Pr: Will Trotter

'Venus and Mars' (26/1/04)
Cast: Robson Green, Tina Hobley, Patrick
Baladi
Scr: Johanna Baldwin
Dir: Nick Jones

'Sons, Daughters and Lovers' (27/1/04)
Cast: Michael French, Liam Garrigan,
Caroline Langrishe
Scr/Dir: Matthew Parkhill

'Drive' (29/1/04 rescheduled from
28/1/04)
Cast: Kaye Wragg, Jamie Theakston, Jean
Alexander
Scr: Pete Lawson
Dir: John Greening

'Viva Las Blackpool' (30/1/04)
Cast: Paula Wilcox, Denise Black, Noreen
Kershaw
Scr: Damian Fitzsimmons
Dir: Sarah Lancashire

'Glasgow Dreams' (2/2/04)
Cast: James Young, Rashid Karapiet,
Shabana Baksh
Scr: Shan Khan
Dir: Christopher Timothy

Bella and the Boys
Century Films; BBC2 tx 15/2/04
Cast: Tom Burke, Freddie Cunliffe, Billie
Piper, Jane Lapotaire
Scr/Dir: Brian Hill
Pr: Katie Bailiff
Exec Pr: Judy Counihan

Canterbury Tales
6 episodes
Ziji Productions/BBC; BBC1 tx 11/9/03-
16/10/03
Pr: Kate Bartlett

'The Miller's Tale' (11/9/03)
Cast: James Nesbitt, Billie Piper, Dennis
Waterman, Kenny Doughty
Scr: Peter Bowker
Dir: John McKay

'The Wife of Bath' (18/9/03)
Cast: Julie Walters, Paul Nicholls, Pascale
Burgess, Bill Night
Scr: Sally Wainwright
Dir: Andy De Emmon

Single Drama

'The Knight's Tale' (25/9/03)
Cast: Chiwetel Ejiofor, John Simm, Keeley Hawes, Bill Paterson
Scr: Tony Marchant
Dir: Marc Munden

'The Sea Captain's Tale' (2/10/03)
Cast: Om Puri, Indira Varma, Nitin Chandra Ganatra, Usha Patel
Scr: Avie Luthra
Dir: John McKay

'The Pardoner's Tale' (9/10/03)
Cast: Jonny Lee Miller, Sally Whittaker, Ben Bennett, William Beck
Scr: Tony Grounds
Dir: Andy De Emmony

'The Man of Law's Tale' (16/10/03)
Cast: Nikki Amuka-Bird, Andrew Lincoln, Adam Kotz, Rakie Ayola
Scr: Olivia Hetreed
Dir: Julian Jarrold

Carla
RDF Television; ITV1 tx 15/9/03
Cast: Lesley Sharp, Helen McCrory, Iain Glen, Shaun Dingwall
Scr: Barbara Machin (from novel by Joanna Hines)
Dir: Diarmuid Lawrence
Pr: Alison Jackson

Carrie's War
BBC Wales; BBC1 tx 1/1/04
Cast: Alun Armstrong, Keeley Fawcett, Geraldine McEwan, Pauline Quirke, Lesley Sharp
Scr: Michael Crompton (from novel by Nina Bawden)
Dir: Coky Giedroyc
Pr: Bill Boyes

Copenhagen
BBC; BBC4 tx 23/8/03 (BBC2 tx 30/8/03)
Cast: Stephen Rea, Daniel Craig, Francesca Annis
Scr/Dir: Howard Davies (from play by Michael Frayn)
Pr: Richard Fell

Date Rape: Sex and Lies
See BBC3

The Deputy
BBC; BBC1 tx 23/2/04
Cast: Warren Clarke, Jack Dee, Dervla Kirwan, Diane Keen
Scr: Richard Stoneman
Dir: Patrick Lau
Pr: Ann Tricklebank

Dose
BBC Wales; BBC Wales tx 25/3/03 (BBC3 tx 15/9/03)
Cast: Lewis Owen, Kate Jarman
Scr: Irvine Welsh, Dean Cavanagh
Pr: Peter Watkins-Hughes

Elmina's Kitchen
BBC; BBC4 tx 21/1/04
Cast: Paterson Joseph, Shaun Parkes, George Harris, Oscar James, Dona Croll, Emmanuel Idowu
Scr: Kwame Kwei Armah
Dir: Angus Jackson
Pr: Sally Stokes

England Expects
BBC Scotland; BBC1 tx 5/4/04
Cast: Steven Mackintosh, Keith Barron, Susan Vidler, Camille Coduri, Sadie Thompson
Scr: Frank Deasy
Dir: Tony Smith
Pr: Ruth Caleb

Every Time You Look At Me
BBC; BBC2 tx 14/4/04
Cast: Mat Fraser, Lisa Hammond, Lindsey Coulson, Lorraine Pilkington
Scr: Lizzie Mickery
Dir: Alrick Riley
Pr: Ewan Marshall

Gifted
Rollem; ITV1 tx 29/10/03
Cast: Claire Goose, Christine Tremarco, Kenny Doughty, Kay Mellor, David Hayman
Scr: Kay Mellor
Dir: Douglas MacKinnon
Pr: Pippa Cross

Hotel in Amsterdam
BBC; BBC4 tx 9/3/04
Cast: Tom Hollander, Susannah Harker, Olivia Williams, Anthony Calf, Adrian Bower
Scr: John Osborne (his 1968 play)

Dir: Julian Jarrold
Pr: Richard Fell

Justifying War – Scenes from the Hutton Inquiry
Tricycle Theatre; BBC4 tx 8/1/04
Cast: David Michaels, David Fleeshman, William Chubb, James Woolley
Dir: Nicolas Kent, Charlotte Westenra
Ed: Richard Norton-Taylor, Nicolas Kent

The Legend of the Tamworth Two
Impossible Pictures/Box TV Productions; BBC1 tx 12/4/04
Cast: Kevin Whately, Emma Pierson, Gerard Horan, Darren Boyd
Scr: Jed Mercurio
Dir: Metin Huseyin
Pr: Matthew Bird, Lynn Horsford

May 33rd
Endor; BBC1 tx 21/4/04
Cast: Lia Williams, Soren Byder, Mali Harries, Wesley Nelson, Annabelle Apsion
Scr: Guy Hibbert
Dir: David Attwood
Pr: Hilary Bevan Jones

Passer By
2 episodes
BBC; BBC1 tx 28 & 29/3/04
Cast: James Nesbitt, Siobhan Finneran, Emily Bruni, Benjamin Smith, Bryan Dick
Scr: Tony Marchant
Dir: David Morrissey
Pr: David Snodin

Promoted to Glory
Thames Television; ITV1 tx 21/12/03
Cast: Ken Stott, Lesley Manville, Kevin Whately, Adrian Scarborough
Scr: Rob Heyland
Dir: Richard Spence
Pr: Kenith Trodd

The Return
Sally Head Productions/Octagon Films; ITV1 tx 30/12/03
Cast: Julie Walters, Neil Dudgeon, Ger Ryan, Glen Barry
Scr: Kate O'Riordan
Dir: Dermot Boyd
Pr: Keith Thompson

Reversals

Box TV Productions; ITV1 tx 19/11/03
Cast: Sarah Parish, Marc Warren, Anthony Head, Indira Varma
Scr: Tim Loane
Dir: David Evans
Pr: Jake Lushington

The Second Quest

Yorkshire Television; ITV1 tx 5/4/04
Cast: David Jason, Roy Hudd, Hywel Bennett, Greg Faulkner, Max Wrottesley, Jim Sturgess
Scr: Douglas Livingstone
Dir: David Jason
Pr: David Reynolds

Three Sisters

BBC4; BBC4 tx 7/2/04
Cast: Kristin Scott Thomas, Robert Bathurst, James Fleet, Douglas Hodge
Scr: Christopher Hampton (from play by Anton Chekhov)
Dir: Michael Blakemore
Pr: Howard Panter (stage)

Crime Drama

55 Degrees North

Series 1; 6 episodes
Zenith North for BBC Scotland; BBC 1 tx 6/7/04 – 10/8/04
Cast: Don Gilet, Dervla Kirwan, Andrew Dunn, Christian Rodska, George Harris
Wr: Timothy Prager
Dir: Andy de Emmony, Brian Kelly, Roberta Bangura
Pr: Jo Wright
Exec Pr: Barbara McKissack, Adrian Bate

Agatha Christie – Poirot: Death on the Nile

Agatha Christie (Chorion)/LWT/A&E Network; ITV1 tx 12/4/04
Cast: David Suchet, James Fox, Emma Malin, J.J. Field, Emily Blunt, Judy Parfitt, Frances de la Tour, Barbara Flynn
Scr: Kevin Elyot (from novel by Agatha Christie)
Dir: Andy Wilson
Pr: Margaret Mitchell

Agatha Christie – Poirot: Five Little Pigs

Agatha Christie (Chorion)/LWT/A&E Network; ITV1 tx 14/12/03
Cast: David Suchet, Rachael Stirling, Aidan Gillen, Toby Stephens, Marc Warren, Aimee Mullins, Julie Cox, Gemma Jones
Scr: Kevin Elyot (from novel by Agatha Christie)
Dir: Paul Unwin
Pr: Margaret Mitchell

Agatha Christie – Poirot: Sad Cypress

Agatha Christie (Chorion)/LWT/A&E Network; ITV1 tx 26/12/03
Cast: David Suchet, Elisabeth Dermot Walsh, Rupert Penry-Jones, Kelly Reilly, Paul McGann, Phyllis Logan, Marion O'Dwyer, Diana Quick
Wr: David Pirie (from novel by Agatha Christie)
Dir: David Moore
Pr: Margaret Mitchell

Alibi

2 episodes
AKA Pictures/Wark Clements; ITV1 tx 25 & 26/8/03
Cast: Michael Kitchen, Sophie Okonedo, Phyllis Logan, Hilary Maclean, Adam Kotz
Wr: Paul Abbott
Dir: David Richards
Pr: Judith Hackett

Amnesia

2 episodes
Ecosse Films; ITV1 tx 29 & 30/3/04
Cast: John Hannah, Brendan Coyle, Anthony Calf, Jemma Redgrave, Patrick Malahide, Beatriz Batarda
Wr: Chris Lang
Dir: Nick Laughland
Pr: Jeremy Guilt

Dalziel & Pascoe

Series 8; 4 episodes
BBC 1 tx 3/1/04-24/1/04
Cast: Warren Clarke, Colin Buchanan
Wr: Stan Hey, Tony McHale, Elizabeth-Anne Wheal, Bill Gallagher
Dir: Patrick Lau, David Wheatley, Colin Buchanan, Paul Marcus
Pr: Ann Tricklebank

Donovan

Pilot; 2 episodes
Granada TV; ITV1 tx 5 & 6/1/04
Cast: Tom Conti, Samantha Bond, Malcolm Scates, Indira Varma, Daniel Pape
Wr: Mike Cullen
Dir: Simon Delaney
Pr: Spencer Campbell

Fallen

2 episodes
Granada TV; ITV1 tx 26 & 27/4/04
Cast: Jonathan Cake, Simone Lahbib, Kerrie Taylor, Gary Love, David Gant, William Beck, Barry Aird, Gary Powell
Wr: Steve Griffiths
Dir: Omar Madha
Pr: Matthew Read

Family

Series 1; 6 episodes
Granada TV; ITV1 tx 29/9/03-12/11/03
Cast: Martin Kemp, Jamie Forman, David Calder, Simone Lahbib, Camille Coduri, Linda Marlowe, Sally Dexter
Wr: Roger Smith, Tim Vaughan
Dir: David Drury
Pr: Rebecca Edwards
Exec Pr: Michele Buck, Tim Vaughan

The Inspector Lynley Mysteries

Series 3; 4 episodes
BBC; BBC 1 tx 4/3/04-25/3/04
Cast: Nathaniel Parker, Sharon Small, Lesley Vickerage
Wr: Ann-Marie Di Mambro, Kevin Clarke, Simon Booker
Dir: Sebastian Graham-Jones, Brian Stirner, Alrick Riley
Pr: Jenny Robins

The Last Detective

Series 2; 4 episodes
Granada TV; ITV1 tx 13/2/04-5/3/04
Cast: Peter Davison, Sean Hughes, Rob Spendlove, Charles De'Ath, Billy Geraghty, Emma Amos
Wr: Richard Harris, Russell Lewis, Michael Aitkens, Russell Lewis, Tim Vaughan
Dir: Ferdinand Fairfax, Moira Armstrong, Gavin Millar, David Tucker
Pr: Deirdre Keir

PROGRAMMING DATA

The Long Firm
4 episodes
BBC/BBC America; BBC2 tx 7/7/04-28/7/04 (BBC4 tx from ep 2: 7/7/04-21/7/04)
Cast: Mark Strong, Derek Jacobi, Lena Headey, Joe Absolom, Phil Daniels, Shaun Dingwall, George Costigan, Judy Parfitt, Tracie Bennett
Wr: Joe Penhall (from novel by Jake Arnott)
Dir: Bille Eltringham
Pr: Liza Marshall

Midsomer Murders
Occasional series (broadcast from 22/3/98); 33 episodes (to 29/2/04)
Bentley Productions/A&E Network; ITV1 tx 2/11/03-29/2/04
Cast: John Nettles, Daniel Casey, Jane Wymark, Laura Howard
Wr: Michael Russell, Peter Hammond, Isabelle Grey, Elizabeth-Anne Wheal, Andrew Payne, Jeff Dodds
Dir: Sarah Hellings, Peter Smith, Richard Holthouse
Pr: Brian True-May

Murder City
Series 1; 6 episodes
Granada TV; ITV1 tx 18/3/04-22/4/04
Cast: Amanda Donohoe, Kris Marshall, Geff Francis, Connor McIntyre, Laura Main, Tim Woodward
Wr: Robert Murphy
Dir: Sam Miller, Ashley Pearce, Richard Spence
Pr: David Boulter, Tony Dennis

Murder in Suburbia
Series 1; 6 episodes
Carlton; ITV1 tx 13/3/04-17/4/04
Cast: Caroline Catz, Lisa Faulkner, Jeremy Sheffield
Wr: Nick Collins, John Flanagan & Andy McCulloch, Michael Aitkens
Dir: Edward Bennett, David Innes Edwards, Douglas MacKinnon
Pr: Joy Spink

Murphy's Law
Series 2; 6 episodes
Tiger Aspect/BBC Northern Ireland; BBC 1 tx 10/5/04-14/6/04

Cast: James Nesbitt, Del Synnott, Sarah Berger, Mark Benton
Wr: Colin Bateman, Tony McHale, Stephen Brady
Dir: Brian Kirk, Ed Fraiman, Phillip John
Pr: Jemma Rodgers

New Tricks
Series 1; 6 episodes
Wall to Wall Television; BBC 1 tx 1/4/04-6/5/04
Cast: Alun Armstrong, James Bolam, Amanda Redman, Dennis Waterman, Chike Okonkwo, Susan Jameson
Wr: Simon Block, Nick Fisher, Roy Mitchell
Dir: Paul Seed, Jamie Payne, Jon East
Pr: Gina Cronk

P.D. James's Death in Holy Orders
2 episodes
BBC; BBC 1 tx 23 & 24/8/03
Cast: Martin Shaw, Robert Hardy, Janie Dee, Alan Howard, Jeff Rawle, Jesse Spencer
Scr: Robert Jones (from novel by P.D. James)
Dir: Jonny Campbell
Pr: Margaret Enefer

Prime Suspect – The Last Witness
Story 6; 2 episodes
Granada TV/WGBH (Boston)/CBC; ITV1 tx 9 & 10/11/03
Cast: Helen Mirren, Ben Miles, Barnaby Kay, Robert Pugh, Mark Strong, Tony Pritchard, Tanya Moodie, Sam Hazeldine
Wr: Peter Berry
Dir: Tom Hooper
Pr: David Boulter

The Return
See SINGLE DRAMA

Rosemary & Thyme
Series 1; 6 episodes
Carnival Films; ITV1 tx 31/8/03-3/10/03
Cast: Felicity Kendal, Pam Ferris
Wr: Clive Exton, Clive Exton & Isabelle Grey, David Joss Buckley, Chris Fewtrell, Simon Brett & Peter Spence
Dir: Brian Farnham, Tom Clegg
Pr: Brian Eastman

Sparkling Cyanide
Company Pictures/Chorion; ITV1 tx 5/10/03
Cast: Pauline Collins, Oliver Ford Davies, Kenneth Cranham, Jonathan Firth, Susan Hampshire, Clare Holman, James Wilby
Scr: Laura Lamson (from novel by Agatha Christie)
Dir: Tristram Powell
Pr: Suzan Harrison

Trial and Retribution - Suspicion
2 episodes
La Plante Productions; ITV1 tx 1 & 2/9/03
Cast: David Hayman, Victoria Smurfit, Charles Dance, Ben Cross, Georgia Mackenzie
Wr: Lynda La Plante
Dir: Charles Beeson
Pr: Peter McAleese

Waking the Dead
Series 3; 8 episodes
BBC; BBC 1 tx 14/9/03-6/10/03
Wr: Ed Whitmore, Simon Mirren, Stephen Davis
Dir: Robert Bierman, Andy Hay, David Thacker, Betsan Morris Evans
Series 4; 12 episodes (6 x 2-part stories)
BBC; BBC 1 tx 11/7/04 – 16/8/04 (twice weekly)
Wr: Tony McHale, Stephen Davis, Ed Whitmore, Andy Hay & John Milne, Doug Milburn
Dir: Andy Hay, Suri Krishnamma, Ben Bolt, Philippa Langdale
Cast: Trevor Eve, Sue Johnston, Holly Aird, Claire Goose, Wil Johnson
Pr: Richard Burrell
Exec Pr: Alexei de Keyser

Wire in the Blood
Series 2; 4 episodes
Coastal Productions; ITV1 tx 12/2/04-4/3/04
Cast: Robson Green, Hermione Norris, Tom Chadbon, Alan Stocks, Mark Letheren, Emma Handy
Wr: Niall Leonard, Jeff Povey, Alan Whiting
Dir: Andrew Grieve, Nick Laughland, Terry McDonough`
Pr: Phil Leach

Sci-Fi & Fantasy

Derren Brown: Séance

Objective Productions; Channel 4 tx
31/5/04
Pres: Derren Brown
Dir: Stefan Stuckert
Pr: Debbie Young
Ser Pr: Anthony Owen
Editor: Dan MacDonald
Exec Pr: Derren Brown, Andrew O'Connor

Most Haunted

Series 3; 10 editions
Antix; Living TV tx 7/10/03-9/12/03
Series 4; 12 editions
Antix; Living TV tx 23/3/04-8/6/04
Pres: Yvette Fielding, Derek Acorah, Phil
Whyman, Richard Felix, Gwen Acorah
Dir: Karl Beattie
Pr: Yvette Fielding, Karl Beattie

Most Haunted Live

Live at Halloween
1 edition
Antix; Living TV tx 31/10/03
Summer Solstice
3 editions
Antix; Living TV tx 19-21/6/04

Sea of Souls

Series 1; 6 episodes (3 x 2-part stories)
BBC Scotland/Sony Pictures Television
International; BBC 1 tx 2/2/04 – 17/2/04
(twice weekly)
Cast: Bill Paterson, Archie Panjabi, Peter
McDonald
Wr: David Kane
Dir: James Hawes, Nick Willing, Richard
Laxton
Pr: Phil Collinson
Exec Pr: Barbara McKissack, Nadine
Marsh-Edwards, Dean Hargrove

Costume Drama

The Canterbury Tales

See SINGLE DRAMA

He Knew He Was Right

4 episodes
BBC Wales/Deep Indigo
Productions/WGBH Boston; BBC1 tx
18/4/04-9/5/04

Cast: Bill Nighy, Laura Fraser, Anna
Massey, Oliver Dimsdale, Jane Lapotaire,
Geoffrey Palmer, Geraldine James
Wr: Andrew Davies (from novel by
Anthony Trollope)
Dir: Tom Vaughan
Pr: Nigel Stafford-Clark

The Mayor of Casterbridge

2 episodes
Sally Head Productions; ITV1 tx 28 &
29/12/03
Cast: Ciaran Hinds, Juliet Aubrey, Jodhi
May, James Purefoy, Polly Walker
Wr: Ted Whitehead (from novel by
Thomas Hardy)
Dir: David Thacker
Pr: Georgina Lowe

The Young Visiters

BBC; BBC1 tx 26/12/03
Cast: Jim Broadbent, Hugh Laurie,
Lyndsey Marshall, Bill Nighy, Geoffrey
Palmer
Wr: Patrick Barlow (from novel by Daisy
Ashford)
Dir: David Yates
Pr: Christopher Hall

Historical Drama

Boudica

Box TV Productions/MediaPro
Pictures/WGBH Boston; ITV1 tx 28/9/03
Cast: Alex Kingston, Steven Waddington,
Emily Blunt, Leanne Rowe, Ben Faulks,
Hugo Speer, Jack Shepherd
Scr: Andrew Davies
Dir: Bill Anderson
Pr: Matthew Bird

Byron

2 episodes
BBC Drama/BBC Arts; BBC2 tx
27 & 28/9/03
Cast: Jonny Lee Miller, Natasha Little,
Vanessa Redgrave, Oliver Dimsdale, Sally
Hawkins
Wr: Nick Dear
Dir: Julian Farino
Pr: Ruth Baumgarten

Charles II: The Power & The Passion

4 episodes
BBC/A&E Network; BBC1 tx 16/11/03-
7/12/03
Cast: Rufus Sewell, Helen McCrory, Diana
Rigg, Shirley Henderson, Martin Freeman
Wr: Adrian Hodges
Dir: Joe Wright
Pr: Kate Harwood

Eroica

BBC; BBC2 tx 4/10/03
Cast: Ian Hart, Tim Pigott-Smith, Frank
Finlay, Claire Skinner, Anton Lesser,
Robert Glenister, Jack Davenport
Wr: Nick Dear
Dir: Simon Cellan Jones
Pr: Liza Marshall

Henry VIII

2 episodes
Granada Television/WGBH
Boston/Powercorp/CBC/Australian
Broadcasting Commission; ITV1 tx 12 &
19/10/03
Cast: Ray Winstone, David Suchet, Helena
Bonham-Carter, Emilia Fox, Sean Bean,
Joss Ackland
Wr: Pete Morgan
Dir: Pete Travis
Pr: Francis Hopkinson

The Private Life of Samuel Pepys

Baby Cow Productions/BBC; BBC2 tx
16/12/03
Cast: Steve Coogan, Lou Doillon, Tim
Pigott-Smith, Nathaniel Parker
Wr: Guy Jenkin
Dir: Oliver Parker
Pr: Ben McPherson

Docudrama

Ancient Egyptians

4 editions
Wall to Wall; Channel 4 tx 13/11/03-
4/12/03
Dir: Tony Mitchell
Pr: Ben Goold

PROGRAMMING DATA

Comfortably Numb
Kudos; Channel 4 tx 25/1/04
Wr/Dir/Pr: Leo Regan
Exec Pr: Jane Featherstone

Hear the Silence
Zenith North; Five tx 15/12/03
Cast: Juliet Stevenson, Hugh Bonneville, Jamie Martin, Andrew Woodall, Adie Allen
Wr: Timothy Prager
Dir: Tim Fywell
Pr: Adrian Bate

Holy Cross
BBC Northern Ireland/RTE; BBC1 tx 10/11/04
Cast: Zara Turner, Bronagh Gallagher, Colum Convey, Patrick O'Kane, Louise Doran
Wr: Terry Cafolla
Dir: Mark Brozel
Pr: Robert Cooper, Jonathan Curling

If ...
5 editions
BBC; BBC2 tx 10/3/04-7/4/04
Cast: John Vine (pt.1), Colin McFarlane (pt.2)
Dir: Ben Fox, Mary Downes
Pr: Dai Richards, Jill Marshall, Ursula Macfarlane, Richard Curson Smith

In Denial of Murder
2 episodes
Hat Trick/BBC; BBC1 tx 29/2/04 & 7/3/04
Cast: Stephen Tompkinson, Caroline Catz, Jason Watkins, Steve Jackson, Wayne Foskett, David Troughton
Wr: Neil McKay
Dir: David Richards
Pr: Mary McMurray

Omagh
Tiger Aspect/Hell's Kitchen International/Izenda; Channel 4 tx 27/5/04
Cast: Stuart Graham, Peter Balance, Gerard McSorley, Michele Forbes, Pauline Hutton
Wr: Guy Hibbert, Paul Greengrass
Dir: Pete Travis
Pr: Ed Guiney, Paul Greengrass

Pissed on the Job
Betty; Channel 4 tx 14/1/04
Dir/Pr: Paul Wilmshurst
Exec Pr: Liz Warner

Wall of Silence
Granada TV; ITV1 tx 12/1/04
Cast: James Nesbitt, Phil Davis, Sophie Stanton, Calum Callaghan, Freddie Cunliffe
Wr: Neil McKay
Dir: Christopher Menaul
Pr: Saurabh Kakkar

Comedy

Absolute Power
Series 1; 6 episodes
BBC; BBC2 tx 10/11/03-15/12/03
Cast: Stephen Fry, John Bird, James Lance, Zoe Telford
Wr: Guy Andrews, Scott Cherry, Mark Lawson, Andrew Rattenbury
Dir: John Morton
Pr: Paul Schlesinger

Absolutely Fabulous
Series 5; 7 episodes
French and Saunders Productions/BBC/Comedy Central; BBC1 tx 17/10/03-24/12/03
Cast: Jennifer Saunders, Joanna Lumley, Julia Sawalha, June Whitfield, Jane Horrocks
Wr: Jennifer Saunders
Dir: Dewi Humphries
Pr: Jo Sargent

All About Me
Series 2; 8 episodes
Celador; BBC1 tx 17/10/03-12/12/04
Cast: Jasper Carrott, Nina Wadia, Ryan Cartwright, Natalia Keery Fisher, Jamil Dhillon
Wr: Steven Knight, Tanika Gupta, Geoff Rowley, John Phelps, Paul Alexander
Dir/Pr: Richard Boden

Behind the Laughter
2 editions
BBC; BBC1 tx 13/10/03-20/10/03
Wr/Participant: Bob Monkhouse
Pr: Mark Turnbull
Exec Pr: Karen Steyn

Black Books
Series 3; 6 episodes
Assembly Film & Television; Channel 4 tx 11/3/04-15/4/04
Cast: Dylan Moran, Bill Bailey, Tamsin Greig
Wr: Dylan Moran, Andy Riley, Kevin Cecil
Dir: Dennis Martin
Pr: Nira Park

Bo' Selecta!
(aka Bo' Selecta! Vol. 3)
talkbackTHAMES
Series 3; 9 episodes; Channel 4 tx 18/6/04-13/8/04
Pres: 'Avid Merrion'
Wr/Cast: Leigh Francis
Pr: Spencer Millman
Exec Pr: Sally Debonnaire

Bremner, Bird and Fortune
Series 5; 6 episodes
Vera Productions; Channel 4 tx 1/2/04-7/3/04
Cast: Rory Bremner, John Bird, John Fortune
Wr: cast plus Geoff Atkinson, John Langdon
Dir: Steve Connelly, Chris Fox
Pr: Geoff Atkinson

Britain's Best Sitcom
12 programmes
BBC; BBC2 tx 10/1/04-27/3/04
Pres: Jonathan Ross, John Sergeant, Jack Dee, Ulrika Jonsson, Armando Ianucci, Rowland Rivron, Johnny Vaughan, David Dickinson, Clarissa Dickson Wright, Carol Vorderman, Phill Jupitus
Pr: Will Bryant, Shirley Hunt, Stephen McGinn, Cybele Rowbottom, Alex Hardcastle with Garry Hughes, Matt O'Casey, Mark Turnbull, Elaine Shepherd, Stephen Franklin, Gerard Barry, Andrew Nicholson, Karina Brennan, Norman Hull
Exec Pr: Ricky Kelehar

The Catherine Tate Show
Series 1; 6 episodes
Tiger Aspect; BBC2 tx 16/2/04-22/3/04
Cast: Catherine Tate, Jonathan McGuinness, Ella Kenion, Michael Brandon
Wr: Catherine Tate, Darren Litten
Dir: Gordon Anderson
Pr: Geoffrey Perkins

Coupling

Series 4; 6 episodes
Hartswood Films; BBC3 tx 10/5/04-
14/6/04 (BBC2 tx 5/7/04-9/8/04)
Cast: Jack Davenport, Sarah Alexander,
Gina Bellman, Ben Miles, Kate Isitt,
Richard Mylan
Wr: Steven Moffat
Dir: Martin Dennis
Pr: Sue Vertue

The Crouches

Series 1; 6 episodes
BBC; BBC1 tx 9/9/03-14/10/03
Cast: Robbie Gee, Jo Martin, Rudolph
Walker, Mona Hammond, Akemnji
Ndifornyen, Ony Uhiara, Danny John-Jules,
Don Warrington
Wr: Ian Pattison
Dir: Nick Wood
Pr: Stephen McCrum, Carlton Dixon

Cyderdelic

Series 1; 6 episodes
BBC3 tx16/2/04-21/3/04
Wr/Cast: Marc Wootton, Barry
Castagnola, Liam Woodman
Narr: John Peel
Dir: Terry Johnson, Roger Pomphrey

The Director's Commentary

Series 1; 7 episodes
Jones the Film; ITV1 tx 28/1/04-17/3/04
Cast: Rob Brydon
Wr: Rob Brydon & Paul Duddridge
Pr: Miles Ross

Distraction

talkbackTHAMES
Series 1; 8 episodes; Channel 4 tx
31/10/03-19/12/03
Series 2; 8 episodes; Channel 4 tx
16/4/04-11/6/04
Pres: Jimmy Carr
Dir: Pati Marr (S1)
Ser Pr: Simon London

Early Doors

Series 1; 6 episodes
Ovation Entertainment; BBC2 tx 12/5/03-
16/6/03
Cast: Craig Cash, Phil Mealey, John
Henshaw, Rita May
Wr: Craig Cash, Phil Mealey

Dir: Adrian Shergold
Pr: Lucy Ansbro, John Rushton

Eyes Down

Series 1; 8 episodes
BBC; BBC1 tx 15/8/03-3/10/03
Cast: Paul O'Grady, Tony Maudsley,
Sheridan Smith, Neil Fitzmaurice, Rosie
Cavaliero, Edna Dore
Wr: Angela Clarke
Scr Ed: Paul Mayhew-Archer
Dir: Christine Gernon
Pr: Rosemary McGowan

Fifteen Storeys High

Series 2; 6 episodes
BBC; BBC3 tx 12/2/04-18/3/04 (BBC2 tx
16/5/04-20/6/04)
Cast: Sean Lock, Benedict Wong
Wr: Sean Lock, Mark Jones, Martin
Trenaman
Dir: Mark Nunneley
Pr: Phil Bowker

Give My Head Peace

(continuing)
BBC Northern Ireland; BBC2 tx 28/2/04-
20/3/04 (4 episodes)
Cast: Tim McGarry, Damon Quinn, Olivia
Nash, Martin Reid, Michael McDowell,
Alexandra Ford
Wr: Tim McGarry, Damon Quinn, Michael
McDowell
Dir: Michael McDowell, Tom Poole, Martin
Shardlow, David G. Croft
Pr: Damon Quinn, Martin Shardlow, Colin
Lewis

Grass

Series 1; 8 episodes
BBC; BBC3 tx 8/9/03-27/10/03 (BBC2 tx
17/1/04-6/3/04)
Cast: Simon Day, Robert Wilfort, Philip
Jackson, Tristan Gemmill, Josephine
Butler
Wr: Simon Day & Andrew Collins
Dir: Martin Dennis
Pr: Alex Walsh-Taylor

Hardware

Series 2; 6 episodes
talkbackTHAMES; ITV1 tx 7/3/04-11/4/04
Cast: Martin Freeman, Peter
Serafinowicz, Ken Morley, Susan Earl,
Ryan Cartwright, Ella Kenion

Wr: Simon Nye
Dir: Ben Kellett
Pr: Margot Gavan Duffy

Harry Hill's TV Burp

Avalon TV/Channel TV
Series 2; 8 episodes; ITV1 tx 30/10/03-
18/12/03
Series 3; 7 episodes; ITV1 tx 20/2/04-
2/4/04
Pres: Harry Hill
Dir: Peter Orton
Pr: Nick Symons
Exec Pr: Richard Allen-Turner, Jon Thoday

Have I Got News For You?

Hat Trick Productions
Series 26; 9 episodes; BBC1 tx 17/10/03-
19/12/03
Series 27; 8 episodes; BBC1 tx 16/4/04-
4/6/04
Cast: Ian Hislop, Paul Merton
Dir: Paul Wheeler (S26/S27)
Pr: Rebecca Papworth (S27)
Ser Pr: Nick Martin (S26/S27)

The Kumars at No. 42

Series 4; 6 episodes and Christmas
Special
Hat Trick; BBC2 tx 15/9/03-20/10/03
and 22/12/03
Cast: Sanjeev Bhaskar, Meera Syal, Indira
Joshi, Vincent Ebrahim
Wr: Richard Pinto, Sharat Sardana,
Sanjeev Bhaskar
Pr: Anil Gupta, Richard Pinto, Sharat
Sardana
Exec Pr: Jimmy Mulville, Denise
O'Donoghue

Little Britain

Series 1; 8 episodes
BBC; BBC3 tx 16/9/03-4/11/03 (BBC2 tx
1/12/03-19/1/04)
Cast: Matt Lucas, David Walliams,
Anthony Head, Tom Baker, Mollie Sugden
Wr: Matt Lucas, David Walliams
Scr Ed: Mark Gatiss
Dir: Steve Bendelack
Pr: Myfanwy Moore

PROGRAMMING DATA

Mad About Alice

Series 1; 6 episodes
Tandem Entertainment; BBC1 tx 23/1/04-27/2/04
Cast: Amanda Holden, Jamie Theakston, John Gordon-Sinclair, Debra Stephenson
Wr: Paul Waite
Dir: Gareth Carrivick
Pr: Sue Birbeck

My Family

Series 5; 13 episodes
DLT Entertainment/Rude Boy Productions/BBC; BBC1 tx 19/3/04-18/6/04
Cast: Robert Lindsay, Zoë Wanamaker, Daniela Denby-Ashe, Gabriel Thomson, Siobhan Hayes
Wr: Ian Brown, James Hendrie, Andrea Solomons, Jim and Steve Armogida, Darin Henry, James Cary, Sophie Hetherington
Dir: Dewi Humphreys
Pr: John Bartlett

My Hero

Series 4; 10 episodes
Big Bear Films; BBC1 tx 8/8/03-10/10/03
Cast: Ardal O'Hanlon, Emily Joyce, Hugh Dennis, Lou Hirsch, Geraldine McNulty
Wr: Paul Mayhew-Archer, James Cary, Paul Mendelson, Trevelyan Evans, Pete Sinclair, Gary Lawson, John Phelps
Dir: John Stroud
Pr: Jamie Rix, John Stroud

My New Best Friend

Series 1; 6 episodes
Tiger Aspect; Channel 4 tx 8/8/03-12/9/03
Cast: Marc Wootton
Dir: Misha Manson-Smith
Pr: Mobashir Dar

Nighty Night

Series 1; 6 episodes
Baby Cow Productions; BBC3 tx 6/1/04-10/2/04 (BBC2 tx 15/3/04-19/4/04)
Cast: Julia Davis, Angus Deayton, Rebecca Front, Kevin Eldon, Ruth Jones, Mark Gatiss
Wr: Julia Davis
Dir: Tony Dow
Pr: Alison MacPhail, Ted Dowd

The Office Christmas Special

2 episodes
BBC; BBC1 tx 26 & 27/12/03
Cast: Ricky Gervais, Martin Freeman, Mackenzie Crook, Lucy Davis
Wr/Dir: Ricky Gervais, Stephen Merchant
Pr: Ash Atalla

Peep Show

Series 1; 6 episodes
Objective Productions; Channel 4 tx 19/9/03-24/10/03
Cast: David Mitchell, Robert Webb, Matt King, Olivia Coleman, Elizabeth Marmur
Wr: Sam Bain, Jesse Armstrong
Dir: Jeremy Wooding
Ser Pr: Phil Clarke

The Smoking Room

Series 1; 8 episodes
BBC; BBC3 tx 29/6/04-17/8/04
Cast: Robert Webb, Paula Wilcox, Nadine Marshall, Leslie Schofield, Jeremy Swift, Emma Kennedy, Debbie Chazen, Fraser Ayres, Selina Griffiths, Siobhan Redmond
Wr: Brian Dooley
Dir: Gareth Carrivick
Pr: Peter Thornton
Exec Pr: Sophie Clarke-Jervoise, Micheal Jacob

Still Game

See SCOTLAND

Vic and Bob in Catterick

Series 1; 6 episodes
Channel X/Pett Productions; BBC3 tx 15/2/04-21/3/04
Cast: Vic Reeves, Bob Mortimer, Matt Lucas, Tim Healy, Charlie Higson, Reece Shearsmith, Morwenna Banks
Wr: Vic Reeves, Bob Mortimer
Dir: Matt Lipsey
Pr: Lisa Clarke

Wild West

Series 2; 6 episodes
BBC; BBC1 (not Scotland) tx 12/3/04-13/4/04
Cast: Dawn French, Catherine Tate, David Bradley, Stewart Wright, Sean Foley, Richard Mylan
Wr: Simon Nye
Dir: Juliet May
Pr: Jacinta Peel

Quiz & Game Shows

Ant and Dec's Saturday Night Takeaway

Series 3; 6 editions
Granada; ITV1 tx 13/3/04-17/4/04
Pres: Ant McPartlin, Declan Donnelly
Dir: Chris Power
Pr: James Sunderland

Beat the Nation

Series 1; 70 editions
Endemol UK; Channel 4 tx 5/1/04-2/7/04 (Mon-Fri)
Pres: Graeme Garden, Tim Brooke-Taylor
Ser Pr: Richard Hague
Exec Pr: Richard Osman, Tim Hincks

Bill Oddie's History Hunt (working title: History Hunters)

Series 1; 5 editions
BBC Bristol; BBC1 tx 13-17/10/03 (Mon-Fri)
Pres: Bill Oddie, Tessa Dunlop
Ser Pr: Ian Pye
Exec Pr: Jane Lomas

Celebrities Under Pressure

Series 2; 4 editions
Granada TV; ITV1 tx 10/1/04-31/1/04
Pres: Melanie Sykes
Dir: Sue McMahon
Pr: Lee Connolly

Come and Have a Go ... If You Think You're Smart Enough

Series 1; 6 editions
Tailor-Made Films/BBC/The Chatterbox Partnership; BBC1 tx 3/4/04-6/5/04
Pres: Nicky Campbell
Dir: Simon Staffurth
Ser Pr: Jo Street

Countdown

Series (continuing, from 2/11/82)
Yorkshire Television; Channel 4 tx (Mon-Fri)
Pres: Richard Whiteley, Carol Vorderman

Didn't They Do Well?

Series 1; 10 editions
BBC; BBC1 tx 15/1/04-18/3/04
Pres: Bruce Forsyth
Dir: Alex Rudzinski
Ser Pr: Andy Rowe

Distraction

See COMEDY

Grand Slam

Series 1; 15 editions
Monkey; Channel 4 tx 6/6/03-12/9/03
Pres: Carol Vorderman, James Richardson
Dir: John F.D. Northover
Ser Pr: Steve Pinhay

The Great British Driving Test: Men v Women

Carlton; ITV1 tx 19/1/04
Participants: Michael Le Vell, Sean Wilson, Deena Payne, Nicola Wheeler
Dir: Sue McMahon
Pr: Iestyn Williams
Exec Pr: Mark Wells

Little Monsters

Series 1; 10 editions
Princess Productions; Sky One tx 4/9/03-6/11/03

The National Lottery: Jet Set

Series 4; 19 editions
BBC; BBC1 tx 20/12/03-24/4/04
Pres: Eamonn Holmes
Dir: John L. Spencer
Ser Pr: Michael Mannes

The National Lottery: Winning Lines

Series 5; 14 editions
BBC; BBC1 tx 19/7/03-18/10/03
Pres: Phillip Schofield
Dir: Patricia Mordecai
Pr: Colman Hutchinson, Jane O'Brien
Exec Pr: Colman Hutchinson

19 Keys

Series 1; 5 editions
Objective TV/Crook; Five tx 10/11/03-9/12/03 (Mon-Fri)
Pres: Richard Bacon
Dir: Sian Hamilton
Pr: Chris O'Dell
Exec Pr: Matt Crook, Andrew O'Connor

The Sack Race

Series 1; 8 editions
BBC; BBC2 tx 12/1/04; run aborted after first edition, returning 20/2/04-2/4/04
Cr: Hugh Rycroft
Dir: Guy Templeton

Ser Pr: Mike Agnew
Consultant Pr: Mob Dar

Test the Nation

4 editions
Talent Television; BBC1 tx 6/9/03; 22/12/03; 20/3/04; 22/5/04
Pres: Anne Robinson, Phillip Schofield
Dir: Julian Smith, Simon Staffurth
Pr: Caroline Taylor, Jean Davison
Ser Pr: Jane O'Brien
Ser Ed: Alexandra Henderson
Exec Pr: Jon Beazley, John Kaye Cooper

Time Commanders

Series 1; 10 editions
Lion Television; BBC2 tx 4/9/03-23/10/03 (Thu); 19 & 26/3/04 (Fri)
Pres: Eddie Mair
Ser Pr: Ludo Graham
Exec Pr: Cassian Harrison, Adam MacDonald

24-Hour Quiz

Series 1; 104 editions
Endemol UK; ITV1 tx 16/2/04-2/4/04 (Mon-Fri)
Pres: Shaun Williamson (daytime), Matt Brown (late night)
Ser Pr: Dee Todd, Lorna-Dawn Creanor
Exec Pr: Elaine Hackett

The Vault

Series 1; Carlton TV; 9 editions; ITV1 tx 28/6/03-23/8/03
Series 2; Granada TV/King World Productions; 15 editions; ITV1 tx 11/5/04-24/8/04
Pres: Melanie Sykes, Gabby Logan (from 6/7/04)
Dir: Patricia Mordecai
Pr: Claire Thomas
Exec Pr: Mark Wells

Who Wants To Be a Millionaire?

Series 15; 48 editions
Celador; ITV1 tx 30/8/03-5/6/04
Pres: Chris Tarrant
Dir: Ian Hamilton, Jonathan Bullen, Paul Kirage, Claire Michel, Patricia Mordecai
Pr: David Briggs, Damon Pattison

Lifestyle

Extreme Makeover

(US: ABC tx special/pilot 11/12/02 + S1 tx 23/4/03-21/5/03; S2 tx 18/9/03-26/11/03)
Lighthearted Entertainment
Series 1; 6 editions; Living TV tx 15/1/04-19/2/04
Series 2; 10 editions; Living TV tx 6/5/04-15/7/04
Pr: Peter Steen
Exec Pr: Howard Schultz

Fairy Godfathers

Series 1; 3 editions
RDF Media; Channel 4 tx 29/4/04-13/5/04
Pres: Colin Wolfenden, Nick Bagrie
Dir: Spencer Kelly, Nancy Bornat, Jessica Orr
Pr: Spencer Kelly, Nancy Bornat
Exec Pr: Stephen Lambert

Grand Designs

Series 6; 8 editions
TalkBack; Channel 4 tx 21/1/04-10/3/04
Pres: Kevin McCloud
Dir: Emma Bowen, Martin Morrison, Christian Trumble
Ser Pr: Amy Joyce, Helen Simpson
Ser Ed: John Silver

Holiday 2003/4

BBC; BBC1 tx 20/10/03-15/12/03; 12/1/04-22/3/04
Pres: Craig Doyle, Russell Amerasekera, Sankha Guha, Ginny Buckley, Simon Calder, Jennifer Cox
Ser Pr: Gary Broadhurst
Ed: John Comerford
Exec Pr: Owen Gay

Holiday Showdown

Series 1; 8 editions
RDF Media; ITV1 tx 30/10/03-18/12/03
Dir/Pr: Ros Ponder, Emily Shields, Robert Wilkins
Ser Pr: Nick Shearman
Exec Pr: Grant Mansfield

PROGRAMMING DATA

House Doctor
Series 6; 13 editions
TalkBack; Five tx 24/7/03-23/10/03
Pres: Ann Maurice, Alistair Appleton
Dir: Vanessa Williams
Ser Pr: Isabelle Gunner
Exec Pr: Andrew Anderson

I Want a Famous Face
(US: MTV tx 15/3/04-19/4/04)
Series 1; 7 editions
MTV (UK) tx 12/4/04-24/5/04

Location, Location, Location
(first 6 episodes use subtitle **First-Time Buyers**)
11 editions
Ideal World; Channel 4 tx 22/6/04-
31/8/04
Pres: Kirstie Allsopp, Phil Spencer
Dir: Richard Crawford, Kathryn Ross
Ser Dir: Andrew Jackson
Ser Pr: Sarah Walmsley

Location, Location, Location Revisited
Series 7; 5 editions
Ideal World; Channel 4 tx 12/11/03-
10/12/03
Pres: Kirstie Allsopp, Phil Spencer
Dir: Loran-Dawn Creanor
Ser Pr: Annette Gordon

The Million Pound Property Experiment
Series 1: 8 editions
BBC Birmingham; BBC2 tx 5/11/03-
23/12/03
Pres: Colin McAllister, Justin Ryan
Dir: Mike Taylor
Pr: Ann Banks, Jane Merkin
Exec Pr: Paul Wooding

Perfect Holiday
Series 1; 8 editions
BBC1 tx 14/1/04-3/3/04 (some editions
shown Mondays in Scotland)
Pres: Russell Amerasekera, Simon Calder,
Jennifer Cox, Jamie Bowden, Mary Johns
Pr: Lucy Hooper
Ser Pr: Karen Brown
Exec Pr: Jannine Waddell

The Property Chain
Series 1; 4 editions
Maverick Television; Channel 4 tx
2-23/3/04
Pres: Kirstie Allsopp
Dir: Jim Sayer, Simon Horton, Claire Walls
Pr: Jim Sayer
Ser Pr: Simon Wood

Property Ladder
Series 3; 12 editions
talkbackTHAMES; Channel 4 tx 23/9/03-
21/10/03; 11/11/03-2/12/03; 6/1/04-
20/1/04
Pres: Sarah Beeny
Dir: Lucie Donahue, Claire Hobday,
Graham Sherrington, Ruairi Fallon, Kate
Drysdale; revised rpt dir: Ed St Giles,
Jenny Freilich
Ser Pr: Charlie Bunce
Exec Pr: John Silver, Daisy Goodwin
(**Property Ladder Revisited**: revised rpts,
shown 28/10/03, 4/11/03, 9/12/03,
16/12/03; 20/1/04-3/2/04)

Queer Eye for the Straight Guy
(US series; Series 1; 25 editions; Bravo tx
15/7/03-20/4/04)
Scout Productions; Living TV tx 6/11/03-
Pres: Ted Allen, Kyan Douglas, Thom
Filicia, Carson Kressley, Jai Rodriguez
Pr: Craig H. Shepherd
Exec Pr: David Collins, Michael Williams,
Francis Berwick, Amy Introcaso-Davis,
Christian Barcellos

Queer Eye for the Straight Guy UK
Series 1; 16 editions
Making Time/NBC; Living TV tx 6/5/04-
14/7/04
Pres: Tristan Eves, Peyton, Jason
Gardiner, Dane Bailey, Julian Bennett
Dir/Pr: Simon Harries

Relocation Relocation
Series 2; 14 editions
Ideal World; Channel 4 tx 7/1/04-7/4/04
Pres: Kirstie Allsopp, Phil Spencer
Dir: Andrew Jackson, Lynda Maher, Chris
Webster, Martin O'Connell
Pr: Jane McGoldrick
Ser Pr: Fiona O'Sullivan
Exec Pr: Hamish Barbour, Katie Boyd

Saturday Brunch
BBC1 tx 19/6/04-4/9/04
9 editions
Crew as **Saturday Kitchen** below

Saturday Kitchen
(also as **Saturday Kitchen Live** from
30/11/02)
Series 2; 33 editions
Prospect Pictures; BBC2 tx 13/9/03-
5/6/04
Pres: Anthony Worrall Thompson, Keith
Floyd, James Martin
Pr: Lucy Lomas, Michael Connock
Ser Ed: Elaine Bancroft
Exec Pr: Barry Lynch

Selling Houses
Series 3; 10 editions
Ricochet South; Channel 4 tx 6/4/04-
8/6/04
Dir: Dan Roland, Alice Barnett, Liz Dyson,
Jane Gerber
Ser Pr: Sue Dulay

10 Years Younger
Series 1; 8 editions
Maverick Television; Channel 4 tx
28/4/04-16/6/04
Pres: Nicky Hambleton-Jones
Dir/Pr: David Smith, Marisa Merry
Ser Pr: Colette Foster
Exec Pr: Alexandra Fraser

Trading Up
Series 1; 49 editions
BBC1 tx 13/10/03-24/10/03; 17/11/03-
28/11/03; 8/12/03-12/12/03;12/1/04-
6/2/04; 4/5/04-7/5/04 (Mon-Fri)
Pres: Justin Ryan, Colin McAllister

What Not To Wear
Series 3; 6 editions
BBC2 tx 5/11/03-10/12/03
Pres: Trinny Woodall, Susannah
Constantine
Dir: Jane Gerber, Nicola Silk, Scott
Tankard
Ser Pr: Kaye Godleman

Reality & Event

Back to Reality
Princess Productions; Five tx 15/2/04-5/3/04 (daily)
Pres: Richard Bacon, Tess Daly
Dir: Alex Rudzinski
Ed: Justin Gorman
Ser Pr: Madeleine Knight
Exec Pr: Henrietta Conrad, Sebastian Scott

Big Brother
Series 5
Endemol UK Productions; Channel 4 tx 28/5/04-6/8/04 (daily)
Live feeds on E4
Pres: Davina McCall
Dir: Tony Gregory, Rob Armstrong, Rob Tavernier, Ben Hardy, Kate Douglas-Walker
Asst Pr: Dawn McVeigh
Pr: Sarah Clarke
Ser Pr: Simon Welton
Ed: David Williams, Rebecca de Young
Exec Pr: Shirley Jones

Also **Big Brother's Efourum** tx
E4/Channel 4 31/5/04-6/8/04 (three times weekly Mon-Wed-Fri)
Pres: Russell Brand
Ser Pr: Dan Whitehead
Exec Pr: Chris Brogden

Big Brother's Little Brother tx
E4/Channel 4 28/5/04-8/8/04 (daily except Saturday)
Pres: Dermot O'Leary
Ser Pr: Anna Reid
Exec Pr: Chris Brogden

See also **Teen Big Brother: The Experiment** in YOUTH/TEEN

The Carrot or the Stick
Series 1; 3 editions
RDF Media; Channel 4 tx 26/2/04-11/3/04
Dir: Matt Reid, Ed Wardle
Exec Pr: Stephen Lambert

Hell's Kitchen
Series 1
LWT/Granada; ITV1 tx 23/5/04-6/6/04 (daily)

Pres: Angus Deayton, Gordon Ramsay
Ser Pr: Rachel Arnold
Exec Pr: Natalka Znak, Richard Cowles

Also: daily highlights and extended coverage on **Hell's Kitchen: Extra Portions** ITV2 tx 23/5/04-6/604
Pres: Mark Durden-Smith

I'm A Celebrity ... Get Me Out of Here!
Series 3
LWT/Granada; ITV1 tx 26/1/04-9/2/04 (daily)
Pres: Anthony McPartlin, Declan Donnelly
Dir: Chris Power, John Leahy
Pr: Des Daniels, David Mapstone, Craig Pickles, Jo Scarratt, Marty Benson, Jane Beacon, Jo Inglott, Katie McAfee, Shelley Rigg, Christopher Lore
Prog Pr: Beth Dicks
Ser Pr: Richard Arnold
Exec Pr: Natalka Znak, Richard Cowles, Jim Allen

Also: daily highlights and extended coverage on **I'm A Celebrity ... Get Me Out of Here! Now!** ITV2 tx 26/1/04-9/2/04
Pres: Mark Durden-Smith, Tara Palmer-Tomkinson

Ramsay's Kitchen Nightmares
Series 1; 4 editions
Optomen; Channel 4 tx 27/4/04-18/5/04
Pres: Gordon Ramsay
Dir: Christine Hall
Exec Pr: Pat Llewellyn

Shattered
Endemol UK; Channel 4 tx 4-10/1/04 (daily, with additional coverage on E4)
Pres: Dermot O'Leary
Ed: Izzie Pick
Exec Pr: Phil Edgar Jones

Take My Mother-in-Law
Series 1; 3 editions
Mentorn Scotland/The Television Corporation; ITV1 tx 18/11/03-2/12/03
Dir: Guy O'Sullivan, Ceri Rowlands, Michelle Fobler
Ser Pr: Virginia Hill

That'll Teach 'Em
Twenty Twenty
Series 1; 5 editions
Channel 4 tx 5/8/03-2/9/03
Dir: Dan Berbridge, Kate O'Driscoll, Chloe Solomon, Suzanne Foster
Ser Pr: Jamie Isaacs, Simon Rockell
Exec Pr: Ros Franey, Claudia Milne
Series 2; 5 editions
Channel 4 tx 17/8/04-
Dir: Simon Unwin
Ser Pr: Simon Rockell

Wife Swap
RDF Media
Series 2; 6 editions
Channel 4 tx 30/9/03-4/11/03
Dir: Vicky Hamburger, Bridget Deane, Sarah Spencer, Laurence Turnbull, Simon Davies, James Dawson
Ser Pr: Jenny Crowther
Exec Pr: Stephen Lambert
Celebrity Wife Swap: When Jade met the Major
1 edition special; Channel 4 tx 11/11/03
With: Jade Goody, Charles Ingram, Diana Ingram, Jeff Brazier
Dir: Jonathan Smith
Series 3; 5 editions
Channel 4 tx 29/6/04-27/7/04
Dir: Stef Wagstaffe, Danny Horan, Karen Plumb, Tim Quicke
Exec Pr: Jenny Crowther

Music

The Brit Awards 2004
Brits TV; ITV1 tx 17/2/04
Pres: Cat Deeley
Dir: Hamish Hamilton
Pr: Guy Freeman

Busted: Christmas for Everyone
Blaze Television/Zenith Entertainment; ITV1 tx 23/12/03
Cast: Busted (James Bourne, Matt Jay, Charlie Simpson), Brian Capron, Pete Waterman
Dir/Pr: Adam Kaleta
Exec Pr: Conor McAnally

PROGRAMMING DATA

Ear Candy
Series 1; 30 editions
Remedy Productions; Channel 4 tx
20/11/03-18/12/03; 8/1/04-25/3/04
Pres: Colin Murray, Megan Arellanes
Dir/Pr: Huse
Ser Pr: Toby Dormer

Eurovision – Making Your Mind Up
BBC; BBC1 tx 28/2/04
Pres: Terry Wogan, Gaby Roslin
Dir: Richard Valentine
Pr: Barrie Kelly, Dominic Smith
Exec Pr: Bea Ballard, Kevin Bishop

Eurovision Song Contest 2004
Turkish tx by Tiscali/EBU; BBC1 tx
15/5/04
UK commentary: Terry Wogan
Dir: Sven Stojanovic
Pr: Muhsin Yildirim

Gram Parsons: Fallen Angel
Spothouse/BBC; BBC4 tx 9/4/04
Pr: Gandulf Hennig, Sid Griffin

Junior Eurovision Song Contest
Carlton; ITV1 tx 6/9/03 (British final) &
15/11/03 (Grand final)
Pres: Mark Durden-Smith, Tara Palmer-
Tomkinson
Dir: Ian Hamilton
Pr: Sue Andrew
Exec Pr: Mark Wells

Just Up Your Street
Series 6; 6 editions
Alfresco/BBC Wales; BBC1 Wales tx
23/1/04-27/2/04
Pres: Owen Money, Sarra Elgan

MTV2 Nirvana Weekend
MTV; MTV2 tx 3-4/4/04
Includes rpt of **MTV Unplugged**
performance, **Nirvana Live and Loud**
Pres include: Courtney Love

The New Kings of Rock 'n' Roll
(aka **Carling Live New Kings of Rock 'n'**
Roll)
Series 1; 6 editions
Fired Up TV; Channel 4 tx 3-5/4/04
Pres: Edith Bowman
Dir: Helen Downing, Paul Shyvers
Pr: Jim Parsons

Operatunity: The Winners' Story
Special
Diverse; Channel 4 tx 16/12/03
Dir/Pr: Michael Waldman
Exec Pr: Roy Ackerman

Pop Idol
Series 2; 27 editions
talkbackTHAMES; ITV1 tx 9/8/03-
20/12/03
Pres: Ant McPartlin, Declan Donnelly
Ser Pr: Claire Horton
Exec Pr: Simon Fuller, Richard Holloway

The South Bank Show: 'Jamie Cullum'
LWT; ITV1 tx 22/2/04
Pres: Melvyn Bragg
Dir/Pr: Matthew Tucker

Stars In Their Eyes Kids
Series 1; 10 editions
Granada TV; ITV1 tx 20/3/04-15/5/04
Pres: Cat Deeley
Dir: Chris Power, Simon Staffurth, Sue
McMahon
Pr: Simon Marsh
Exec Pr: Heather Coogan, Jeff Thacker

[The All-New] Top of the Pops
(continuing series, from 1/1/64)
BBC; relaunch edition BBC1 tx 28/11/03
Pres: Tim Kash, with Fearne Cotton from
28/5/04 (Reggie Yates from June)
Exec Pr: Andi Peters

Top of the Pops 2
Series [from 17/9/94-]
BBC; BBC2 tx weekly (some editions ntx
in Scotland)
Pres (voice): Steve Wright
Guest Pres: include Vic Reeves & Bob
Mortimer (9-13/2/04), Phill Jupitus
(16-20/2/04), Jack Dee (4-6/3/04)
Pr: Mark Hagen

The Truth About Take That
Shine Productions; Channel 4 tx 11/4/04
Dir/Pr: Jaine Green

Talk Shows

Friday Night with Jonathan Ross
Open Mike
Series 5; 15 editions; BBC1 tx 12/9/03-
19/12/03
Series 6; 14 editions; BBC1 tx 12/3/04-
11/6/04
Pres: Jonathan Ross
Pr: Suzi Aplin
Exec Pr: Addison Cresswell

Kilroy
See DAYTIME

Live at Johnny's
Series 1; 30 editions
World's End TV; BBC3 tx 16/2/04-
26/3/04 (Mon-Fri)
Pres: Johnny Vaughan, Lauren Laverne,
Dickie Davies
Wr: Giles Boden, Mark Hurst, Richard
Turner
Dir: Phil Chilvers, Nick Cory-Wright
Pr: Chris Heath
Ser Pr: Ben Rigden
Exec Pr: Gregor Cameron

Now You're Talking
See DAYTIME

NY Graham Norton
Series 1; 10 editions
So Television; Channel 4 tx 30/1/04-
2/4/04
Pres: Graham Norton
Pr: Graham Stuart
Ser Pr: Jon Magnusson

Parkinson
BBC
Series 11; 10 editions; BBC1 tx 20/9/03-
29/11/03
Series 12; 10 editions; BBC1 tx 21/2/04-
8/5/04
Dir: Stuart McDonald
Pr: Danny Dignan
Exec Pr: Beatrice Ballard

Trisha
See DAYTIME

Children's

Art Attack

(continuing since 1990)
10 editions
Media Merchants/HIT Entertainment;
ITV1 tx 10/9/03-17/12/03
Pres: Neil Buchanan

The Basil Brush Show

Series 2; 13 episodes
The Foundation/Entertainment
Rights/CBBC; BBC1 tx 21/11/2003-
1/1/04
Cast: Christopher Pizzey, Michael Hayes,
Georgina Leonidas, Ajay Chhabra, Tisha
Martin, Michael Winsor
Wr: Ged Allen, Peter Cocks, Danny Robins
Dir: Michael Kerrigan
Exec Pr: Vanessa Hill, Ged Allen, Anne
Gilchrist, Mike Heap, Jane Smith

Beckham's Hotshots

Series 1; 10 editions
CBBC; CBBC tx 23/2/04-5/3/04
(Mon-Fri)
Pres: Reggie Yates
Exec Pr: Reem Nouss

Blue Peter

BBC Television/CBBC; BBC1 tx continuing
Run ended for summer break 28/6/04
Pres: Konnie Huq (from 1/98), Simon
Thomas (from 1/99), Matt Baker (from
6/99), Liz Barker (from 6/2000)
Dir: Martin Williams, Jeanette Goulbourn,
Chris Godwin, Debbie Martin, Catherine
Gildea, Helen Scott, Emma Clark
Pr: Anne Dixon, Matt Gyves, Gavin
Woods, Catherine Gildea, Jon Donaldson
Ser Pr: Kez Margrie
Ed: Richard Marson

Blue Peter: The Quest 4 – Masters of Time

Series 4; 7 episodes
CBBC; BBC1 tx 31/10/03-12/12/03 (in
Friday BP editions)
Wr: David Agnew
Dir: Emma Clark

Byker Grove

Series 15; 20 episodes
Zenith North for CBBC Scotland; BBC1 tx
9/9/03-13/11/03

Cast: Jade Turnbull, Alex Beebe, Dominic
Beebe, Nicholas Nancarrow, Anne Orwin,
Rachael Lee
Wr: Brian B. Thompson, Keith Temple,
Jayne Kirkham, Tom Ogden, David Young,
Malorie Blackman, Robert Rigby, Barry
Purchese, Helen Eatock
Scr Ed: Bryan Johnson
Dir: Graeme Harper, Craig Lines
Pr: Edward Pugh
Exec Pr: Julian Scott

Chinese Breakaway

Series 1; 5 editions
Here's One I Made Earlier; Five tx
22-26/12/03 (Mon-Fri)
Pres: Peter Duncan and the Duncan family
Dir: Peter Duncan
Pr: John Snelgrove

Dick and Dom in da Bungalow

Series 1 (first BBC1 run; previous runs on
CBBC channel, 19/4/03-29/6/03); 30
editions
CBBC; BBC1 tx 20/9/03-10/4/04 (Sunday
editions on CBBC 21/9/03-11/4/04)
Pres: Richard McCourt, Dominic Wood
with Dave Chapman
Dir: Simon Hepworth
Pr: Steve Ryde
Exec Pr: Anne Gilchrist

Feather Boy

6 episodes
Childsplay; BBC1 tx 16/3/04-1/4/04
(twice weekly, Tue-Thu); feature-length
revised rpt BBC1 tx 30/5/04
Cast: Thomas Sangster, Aaron Johnson,
Sheila Hancock, Lindsey Coulson
Wr/Pr: Peter Tabern (from novel by Nicky
Singer)
Dir: Dermot Boyd
Exec Pr: Elaine Sperber

Globo Loco

Series 2; 13 episodes
Foundation Television; ITV1 tx 6/5/04-
29/7/04
Pres: Stephen Mulhern
Dir: Michael Kerrigan
Pr: Caroline Coleman
Exec Pr: Ged Allen

Grange Hill

Series 27; 20 episodes
Mersey TV; BBC1 tx 6/1/04-11/3/04
(twice weekly, Tue-Thu)
Cast: Chris Perry-Metcalf, Lucas Lindo,
Chris Crookall, Kirsten Cassidy, Kacey
Barnfield, Daniella Fray, John Joseph,
Amanda Fahy, Reeve Noi, Thomas Hudson,
Lauren Bunney, Stuart Organ
Wr: Kaddy Benyon, Sarah Daniels, Neil
Jones, Kay Stonham, Matthew Evans,
Richard Burke, Si Spencer
Scr Ed: Laura McCann, Kathy Harris
Dir: Paul Murphy, Jill Robertson, David
Andrews, Chris Corcoran, Shani Grewal,
Peter Hoar, David Richardson, Murilo
Pasta
Pr: Karl Dolan, Jo Hallows
Exec Pr: Phil Redmond, Elaine Sperber

The Illustrated Mum

Granada Kids; C4 tx 31/12/03 (first
shown as part of 4Learning 5/12/03)
Cast: Michelle Collins, Alice Connor, Holly
Grainger
Wr: Debbie Isitt (from the book by
Jacqueline Wilson)
Dir: Cilla Ware
Pr: Julia Ouston
Exec Pr: Anne Brogan

Intergalactic Kitchen

Series 1; 13 episodes
BBC Scotland; BBC1 tx 9/1/04-2/4/04
Cast: Lloyd Bailie, Luke Mackie, Helen
McAlpine, Joshua Manning, Linzi
Campbell, Emma Ballantine
Wr: Frank Rodgers, Moray Hunter, Robyn
Charteris, Mark Robertson, David Cairns,
Rhiannon Tise
Scr Ed: David Cairns
Dir: Martin Burt, Shiona McCubbin
Pr: Nigel R. Smith
Exec Pr: Simon Parsons

Ministry of Mayhem

Series 1; 52 editions (a year)
Foundation TV/Carlton; ITV1 tx 10/1/04-
continuing
Pres: Stephen Mulhern, Holly Willoughby,
Michael Underwood
Cast: Peter Cocks, Laura & Jessica Tilli,
Ray Griffiths
Scr Sup: Dianne Leutner
Dir: Liz Clare, Paul Walker

PROGRAMMING DATA

Pr: Steve Kidgell
Ser Pr: Vanessa Hill
Exec Pr: David Mercer, Ged Allen

My Parents Are Aliens
Series 5; 13 episodes
Granada Kids; ITV1 tx 22/10/03-3/12/03
(twice weekly, Mon/Wed)
Cast: Tony Gardner, Carla Mendonca,
Danielle McCormack, Alex Kew, Charlotte
Francis
Wr: Andy Watts, Paul Alexander, Brian
Lynch, Connal Orton, Paul Rose, Joe
Williams, Holly Lyons
Scr Ed: David Collier
Dir: Dominic MacDonald, Chris Bernard
Pr: Chris Bernard
Exec Pr: Anne Brogan, Andy Watts

The Mysti Show
Series 1
Mystical Productions/CBBC; BBC1 tx
17/4/04-5/6/04 (BBC2 tx from 12/6/04-
continuing until approx September)
Cast: Laura Aikman, Oliver Mason, Ashley
Campbell, Eva Alexander, Yasmin Paige,
David Sterne
Wr: Gail Renard
Dir: Angelo Abela, Stephen Wolfenden,
Alli Jeronimus
Pr: Michael Connock
Ser Pr: Debbie Gray
Exec Pr: Anne Gilchrist, David Wong

Powers
Series 1; 13 episodes
CBBC; BBC1 tx 7/1/04-31/3/04
Cast: Adam Jessop, Amy Yamazaki,
Rupert Holliday-Evans, Mandana Jones
Wr: Jim Eldridge, Stephen Hallett,
Christopher Wicking, Carolyn Sally Jones,
John Jackson
Scr Ed: Kathy Harris
Dir: Emma Bodger, Brian Farnham
Pr: Chris Le Grys
Exec Pr: Jesse Cleverly

The Queen's Nose
Series 7; 6 episodes
Film & General Productions; BBC1 tx
11/11/03-16/12/03
Cast: Jordan Metcalfe, Lucinda Dryzek,
Juliet Cowan
Wr: Graham Alborough, Phil Hughes, Dan
Anthony, Jesse Armstrong & Sam Bain

Dir: David Skynner
Pr: Davina Belling & Clive Parsons

The Really Wild Show
Series 17; 13 editions
BBC Bristol; BBC1 tx 6/4/04-13/7/04
Pres: Michaela Strachan, Nick Baker, Eils
Hewitt, Steve Backshall
Dir: Katja Anton, Vanessa Coates, Jerry
Short, Roger Webb
Pr: Reema Lorford
Exec Ed: Vyv Simson

The Saturday Show
Series 2
CBBC; BBC1 tx 17/4/04-5/6/04 then
BBC2 from 12/6/04-4/9/04
Pres: Angellica Bell, Simon Grant, Jake
Humphrey
Dir: John Smith, Grigor Stirling
Pr: Yvonne Gordon, Donald MacInnes
Dev Pr: Jonathan Rippon
Ser Pr: Peter Mulryan
Exec Pr: Colin Nobbs

Serious Desert
Series 2; 6 editions
CBBC; CBBC tx 20-24/10/03 (BBC1 tx
29/12/03-2/1/04)

Short Change
Series 10; 13 editions
CBBC; BBC1 tx 8/4/04-15/7/04
Pres: Angellica Bell, Ortis, Rhodri Owen
Dir: Natalie Barb, Louise Wilson
Pr: Moray London, Carolyn Clancy
Exec Pr: Reem Nouss

Sleeping Beauty: Uncovered
Christmas special
CBBC; BBC1 tx 22/12/03
Cast: Fearne Cotton, Kirsten O'Brien,
Barney Harwood, Ortis, Angellica Bell,
Simon Thomas, Dick & Dom, Mark
Speight, Konnie Huq, Matt Baker
Wr: Ben Ward & Richard Webb
Dir: Dermot Canterbury
Pr: Christina Brown
Exec Pr: Sue Morgan

The Sleepover Club
Series 1; 26 episodes
Wark Clements/Burberry
Productions/Rialto Films; ITV1 tx 5/1/04-
5/4/04 (twice weekly, Mon/Wed to

4/2/04 then Mon)
Cast: Caitlin Stasey, Ashleigh Chisholm,
Eliza Taylor-Cotter, Basia A'Hern, Hannah
Wang
Wr: Chris Kunz, David Hannam, Jo
Horsburgh, Kirsty Fisher, Louise Le Nay,
David Phillips, Rose Impey, Marieke Hardy,
Meg Mappin (based on the books by Rose
Impey)
Scr Sup: Karen Mansfield
Scr Ed: Kirsty Fisher
Dir: Arnie Custo, Catherine Millar, Michael
Pattinson, Kate Woods
Pr: Jan Tyrrell
Exec Pr: Andrew Rowley, Ewan Burnett

SMart
Series 10; 11 episodes
CBBC; BBC1 tx 18/11/03-26/12/03 (twice
weekly, Tue/Thu)
Pres: Mark Speight, Kirsten O'Brien
Dir: James Morgan, Victoria Harrison
Pr: Caroline Norris
Exec Pr: Anne Gilchrist

Spook Squad
Series 1; 13 episodes
CBBC Scotland; BBC1 tx 6/1/04-30/3/04
Cast: Andrew Pepper, Ford Kiernan
Dir: Carys Edwards
Pr: Fiona White

Star
Series 1; 12 episodes shown (1 held over)
Tiger Aspect/MTV Networks; ITV1 tx
18/9/03-23/10/03; unscheduled tx 27-
31/10/04; 23/12/03
Cast: Nicholas Hoult, Gregg Chillin,
Hannah Tointon, Julia Hills, Mark Williams
Wr: Jenny LeCoat, Mark Grant, Moray
Hunter
Dir: Angelo Abela
Pr: Philippa Catt

The Story of Tracy Beaker
Series 3; 13 episodes
CBBC; BBC1 tx 25/9/03-18/12/03
Series 4; 13 episodes
CBBC; BBC1 tx 8/1/04-1/4/04
Special: **Tracy Beaker's The Movie of Me**
CBBC; BBC1 tx 22/2/04
Cast: Dani Harmer, Lisa Coleman,
Montanna Thompson, Ben Hanson

Wr: Mary Morris (+The Movie), Laura Summers, Gary Parker, Othniel Smith, Simon Nicholson, Abigail Abban Mensah, Holly Lyons, Marvin Close, Andy Walker, Ariane Sherine, Dan Anthony
Dir: Joss Agnew (The Movie)
Pr: Jane Steventon (The Movie)

The Yuk Show
Series 1; 10 editions
Top TV Productions; ITV1 tx 17/3/04-19/5/04
Pres: Jamie Rickers, Naomi Wilkinson

Youth/Teen

Adult at 14: Kids on Porn
Maverick TV; Channel 4 tx 18/11/03
Dir/Pr: Jamie O'Leary

Adult at 14: Pleasureland
Kudos Productions; Channel 4 tx 16/11/03
Cast: Katie Lyon, Tara Wells, Leah Whittaker, Claire Bailey, Claire Hackett
Wr: Helen Blakeman
Dir: Brian Percival
Pr: Natasha Dack
Exec Pr: Jane Featherstone

Adult at 14: Sex Before 16 – Why The Law is Failing
Juniper Productions; Channel 4 tx 16/11/03
Wr/Pres: Miranda Sawyer
Pr: Jenny Williams
Exec Pr: Samir Shah

Hollyoaks
Mersey TV; Channel 4 tx 5 weekly episodes (Mon-Fri) with Sunday omnibus repeat
After Hours specials; 4 episodes; Channel 4 tx 5-8/7/04
Main Cast: Marcus Patric, Helen Noble, Nick Pickard, Sarah Baxendale, Andy McNair, Alex Carter, Gemma Atkinson, Darren Bransford, Sarah Lawrence, John Graham Davies, Stuart Manning, Sarah Dunn, Richard Calkin
Ser Pr: Jo Hallows

The O.C.
(US series; Season 1; 27 episodes; Fox Network tx 5/8/03-5/5/04)
Hypnotic Pictures/Wonderland Sound and Vision/Warner Bros Television; 14 episodes; Channel 4 tx 7/3/04-6/6/04

Cast: Peter Gallagher, Benjamin McKenzie, Kelly Rowan, Adam Brody, Mischa Barton, Tate Donovan, Rachel Bilson, Chris Carmack, Melinda Clarke
Cr/Exec Pr: Josh Schwartz
Exec Pr: Doug Liman, McG, Bob DeLaurentis, Dave Bartis

Popworld
Series continuing
At It Productions; Channel 4 tx [from 21/1/01]
Pres: Simon Amstel, Miquita Oliver
Dir: Chris Fouracre
Ser Pr: Richard Cook

Teen Big Brother: The Experiment
Series 1; 5 editions
Endemol Entertainment UK; Channel 4 tx 13-17/10/03
Pres: Dermot O'Leary
Ser Pr: Lorna-Dawn Creanor
Exec Pr: Elaine Hackett

PROGRAMMING DATA

Books

Andrew Lockett & Barrie MacDonald

Off-Air

This section provides a miscellaneous overview of some varied, related topics that do not fit easily into our main categories.

We review recent activity in publishing; this section provides reference listings of TV-related books published since Autumn 2003, a mini-directory of television journals and a look at fan publishing in the online age.

There's also a timely assessment of the healthy market in television, especially archive television, currently being released on DVD.

On a sadder note, the section ends with an Obituaries listing – a remembrance of those working in the television industry who passed away in the last twelve months.

Academic & Industry

The following are a selection of recent books on television, published on industry matters or of specific educational or academic interest. They reflect a predominantly UK content focus.

Allen, Robert C & Hill, Annette (editors)
The Television Studies Reader
London: Routledge 2003.
656p. ISBN 041528348
This massive anthology of previously published materials reflects cultural studies preoccupations (no history, little textual analysis) and will amply serve advanced university courses on television studies in the UK and US. The selection is encouragingly up to date for a collection such as this and includes UK materials and contributors.

Bell, Emily, and Alden, Chris
Media Directory
London: Guardian Books, 2003.
433p. ISBN 184354041X
For many years *The Guardian Media Guide* has been an indispensable reference guide to the press and broadcasting, for journalists, media professionals, researchers and students. Now relaunched as the *Media Directory*, it has expanded its coverage and includes *Media Guardian* analysis of media news and events.

Bignall, Jonathan
An Introduction to Television Studies
London: Routledge 2003.
352p. ISBN 0415261139
A well-designed overview of the subject that is geared to introductory courses on television. This able and solid overview offers few surprises but includes recent case studies on the likes of *Sex and the City*.

Creeber, Glen (editor)
Fifty Key Television Programmes
London: Hodder Arnold 2004
288p. ISBN 0340809434

Fifty short quality essays by specialists on fifty television programmes with British material well represented. A book that really does what 'it says on the tin'. Many teachers and students will find the pedagogical pointers handy though general readers might wish the space had been devoted to longer coverage of the programmes themselves.

Curran, James and Seaton, Jean
Power Without Responsibility: the press, broadcasting and new media in Britain
London: Routledge, 6th ed. 2003.
459p. ISBN 0415243904
Standard, authoritative textbook on British media, considerably updated for this sixth edition to cover the *Communications Act 2003* and Ofcom, and including three new chapters on the Internet and new media.

Darlow, Michael
Independents Struggle: the programme makers who took on the TV establishment
London: Quartet Books 2004
670p. ISBN 074381559
An engaged and engaging first-hand account of the events that led to the creation of Channel 4 and the expansion of independent television during the Thatcher years and beyond. Personalities and politics and the links between the two are highlighted in a lively 'alternative' history of recent British Television.

Dunn, Kate
Do Not Adjust Your Set: the early days of live television
London: John Murray, 2003
240p. ISBN 0719554802
The early days of live television are recalled by veteran actors, directors and technicians, in this entertaining oral history. Such distinguished actors as Eileen Atkins, Nigel Hawthorne and George Baker, recall the inadequate rehearsal time, the technical difficulties in the studios and the terror of being 'On

Air' to nationwide audiences without being able to stop or do retakes. Pioneering live drama such as *Dixon of Dock Green*, *Armchair Theatre* and *Z Cars* is affectionately remembered, as is the work of live television's legendary directors - Michael Barry, Sydney Newman and Rudolf Cartier.

Fanthome, Christine
Channel 5: the early years
Luton: University of Luton Press, 2003
220p. ISBN 18602089 5
Channel 5 began in March 1997, the first terrestrial television channel to be launched against multi-channel competition. Despite initial disadvantages of having incomplete coverage of the UK, an extensive retuning exercise and public service obligations, it succeeded. Operating on a fraction of the financial resources of BBC1 or ITV it acquired low-cost but innovative programmes, and by 2002 had reached a respectable 6.4% audience share. The author, a former Thames Television reporter, now media consultant, interviewed Dawn Airey, Greg Dyke, David Elstein and Kevin Lygo amongst others, and has written a valuable history and analysis.

Finch, John (editor)
Granada Television: the first generation
Manchester: Manchester University Press, 2003
294p. ISBN 0 7190 6515 1
Granada Television was one of the earliest ITV companies, going on air in May 1956. Sidney Bernstein, its pioneering co-founder, established a distinctive identity synonymous with their northern base – 'Granadaland' – and the most socially conscious of the ITV companies. These written memoirs by over seventy Granada veterans, including Sir Denis Forman, David Plowright, John Birt and Jack Rosenthal are a testament to its climate of creative activity. Julia Hallam has written an excellent historical introduction on ITV, and it contains a chronology and biographical notes.

Freedman, Des
Television Policies of the Labour Party, 1951-2001
224p. London: Frank Cass, 2003
ISBN 0-7146-5455-8
Anthony Smith comments in his foreword, 'Labour governments were in power for only 15 of the 50 years covered by this book, and in these years enacted none of the historical measures which shaped the forms and impact of television ...'. Critics accuse the Labour leadership of being conservative (with a small c), more accepting of the status quo. This valuable book examines these debates, from early opposition to commercial television to New Labour embracing the role of the market, competition and globalisation.

Hilmes, Michele (editor)
The Television History Book
London: BFI Publishing, 2003
163p. ISBN 0851709877
This cross-cultural and trans-national approach to the history of television in the United Kingdom and the United States contains articles by British and American media scholars giving an overview of technologies, institutions, policies, programming and audiences. British topics include: technical developments by Brian Winston; pre-war origins of public service broadcasting by Glen Creeber; aspects of Channel 4 by Sylvia Harvey and John Ellis; television in the 60s and 70s, particularly in Wales, by Jamie Medhurst; and the question of television dumbing down in the 1990s by Rachel Moseley.

Holmes, Su & Jermyn, Deborah (editor)
Understanding Reality Television
London: Routledge, 2004
320p. ISBN 0415317959
For a number of years the hot topic in the academic world has been reality television. Numerous new articles reflect on what it all means with *Big Brother* and *The Osbournes* featuring heavily.

Hoskins, Andrew
Televising War: From Vietnam to Iraq
London: Continuum
208p. ISBN 0826473054
A very timely look at changes in war

reporting on television that succeeds in registering the considerable distance travelled since Vietnam.

Jenkins, Milly
Creative Careers: TV
London: Trotman
224p. ISBN 0856609013
This book is part of a series on media vocations published in association with Channel 4. It offers a very accessible introduction and down-to-earth insights on working in television and what specific careers in the industry can offer.

Miller, Toby
Spyscreen: Espionage on film and TV from the 1930s to the 1960s
Oxford: Oxford University Press, 2003
230p. ISBN 0198159528
Written by the author of the definitive study of *The Avengers*, this volume looks at a period of British television and film history of enduring interest. Its provocative readings (from critical angles such as cultural imperialism to gender studies) include analyses of TV shows *The Prisoner*, *The Man From Uncle* and others though it is a real pity the publishers have yet to issue a paperback of this book on a topic with such wide appeal.

Sandvoss, Cornell
A Game of Two Halves: Football, television fandom & globalisation
London: Comedia/ Routledge 2003
224p. ISBN 0415314852
Is it possible not to notice football on the small screen? This study examines the relationship between football and television, and takes it very seriously indeed, arguing (not unreasonably) that football now plays a major role in national-identity formation in the age of globalisation.

Seymour-Ure, Colin
Prime Ministers and the Media: issues of power and control
Oxford: Blackwell, 2003
270p. ISBN 0 631 16687 4
History of the changing relationship between British Prime Ministers and the media, including Harold Macmillan, Harold Wilson, Margaret Thatcher, John Major

OFF-AIR

and Tony Blair. A contemporary focus provides a closer look at the Blair premiership and the culture of spin. It examines the role of the Prime Minister and public communications, as well as the rise of the Downing Street Press Secretary and the influence of political rumour and satirical cartoons.

Tumber, Howard and Palmer, Jerry
The Media at War: The Iraq crisis
London: Sage Publications
192p. ISBN 1412901820
News and journalism scholars Tumber and Palmer focus on the reporting of journalists involved in the Iraq War, whether embedded or not.

Wilson, David and O'Sullivan, Sean
Images of Incarceration: Representations of prison in film & television drama
Winchester: Waterside Press
192p ISBN 1904380 085
Serious studies on UK social issues and television are rare. This volume is the result of the work of The Prison Film Project – the first major national initiative devoted to examining the portrayal of prison in film and television drama. It seeks to ask how (un)/realistic fictional portrayals are and touches on major TV examples, notably *Bad Girls*.

Wolff, Michael
Autumn of the Moguls
London: Flamingo, 2003.
381p. ISBN 0 00 717881 6
Entertaining and perceptive anecdotes about encounters with global television industry moguls, including Rupert Murdoch and Disney's Michael Eisner amongst others by the media columnist of *New York* magazine and *The Guardian*.

Wyatt, Will
The Fun Factory: a life in the BBC
London: Aurum Press, 2003
372p. ISBN 18554109154
Will Wyatt started his BBC career in radio as a news sub-editor in 1965, transferring to television and rising through presentation (producer on *Late Night Line Up*) and documentary features, eventually becoming Managing Director,

Television in 1991, and Chief Executive, Broadcast in 1996, before retiring in 1999. His frank, detailed account of 34 years in the BBC chronicles the John Birt era, and the contest for Director General in 1999. A staunch advocate of public service broadcasting, Wyatt believes in the responsibility of the BBC to enhance the quality of life in the UK.

Mainstream Publishing

Bentley, Chris
The Complete Book of Gerry Anderson's UFO
Surrey: Reynolds and Hearn, 2003
176p. illus (b&w). ISBN 190311165X
£12.99
Chapter and verse overview of Anderson's first foray into live-action adult science-fiction TV, originally aired in 1970. Production info is admirably detailed and similarly no stone is left unturned to provide five regional ITV transmission orders and a definitive merchandise guide. Weak point is a dry episode guide forgoing insight or comment in favour of synopses and trivia. Cast profiles are exhaustive for this kind of book and should prove a boon to biography researchers. The blessing of copyright holder Carlton provides a wealth of beautifully reproduced photos to produce a very attractive, keenly-priced package.

Bentley, Chris (foreword. Gerry Anderson)
The Complete Gerry Anderson
Surrey: Reynolds and Hearn, 2003
318p. illus (b&w, some colour). ISBN 1903111412 £15.99
Useful all-in-one guide to the TV output of Gerry Anderson, including everything from *Torchy the Battery Boy* to *Lavender Castle*. Material on biggest hit series *Thunderbirds* and *Captain Scarlet* will be familiar to those who have read Bentley's previous single-title publications on those series. Very much a factual reference work, detailed episode synopses and production data are present and correct as are some nice snippets of trivia – comment and review are deemed less important.

Lewisohn, Mark (contrib. ed. Dick Fiddy)
Radio Times Guide to TV Comedy (2nd edition)
London: BBC Worldwide, 2003
961p. illus (b&w). ISBN 0 563 48755 0
£19.99
Definitive, exhaustive and entertaining work on the history of TV comedy, revised to include the last five years' TV output, including modern classics such as *The Office* and *Phoenix Nights*. Essential.

McCabe, Bob with the Python team
The Pythons – Autobiography by the Pythons
London: Orion, 2003
360p. illus (colour). ISBN 0752852930
£30
Coffee table book, superbly illustrated with hundreds of pictures including snapshots and ephemera from the Pythons' own collections. The text details the lives and work of the Python team – John Cleese, Michael Palin, Terry Jones, Eric Idle, Terry Gilliam and the late Graham Chapman – via extensive interviews conducted with McCabe.

Richards, Justin
Doctor Who: the Legend – 40 Years of Time Travel
London: BBC Books, 2003
400p. illus (colour). ISBN 0563486023
£40
Now sold out from distributors, this weighty and lavish coffee table book marked the 40th anniversary of the sci-fi series. Production values are excellent but the design is not likely to be to everyone's taste – silver inks and lurid colour schemes are used with abandon and some beautiful archive photos are thrown away by being overprinted with text or used at small sizes. The text, a story-by-story guide with some short contextual pieces throughout, is effective and accurate but not revelatory – the less lavish *The Television Companion* (Howe and Walker) probably remains the best single reference volume on the series.

Journals

Emma Smart

Academic

Cahiers du Comite D'histoire de la Television
1 issue p.a.
Publisher: Comité d'Histoire de la Télévision
4, avenue de l'Europe
94366 Bry-Sur-Marne Cedex
France
Country: FR
Language: French

Classic Images
12 issues p.a.
Publisher: Muscatine Journal
301 East Third Street
Muscatine
IA 52761
USA
Country: US
Language: English

Dox - Documentary Film Quarterly
4 issues p.a.
Publisher: European Documentary Network
Skindergade 29A, #4
1159 Copenhagen K
Denmark
Country: DK
Language: English

European Journal of Communication
4 issues p.a.
Publisher: Sage Publications
1 Oliver's Yard
London EC1Y 1SP
Country: UK
Language: English

Generation Series
4 issues p.a.
Publisher: Gimmick Press
3, rue Buirette
51100 Reims
France
Country: FR
Language: French

Historical Journal of Film, Radio & Television
3 issues p.a.
Publisher: Carfax Publishing
Taylor & Francis
PO Box 25
Abingdon
Oxfordshire OX14 3UE
Country: UK
Language: English

Index on Censorship
6 issues p.a.
Publisher: Writers & Scholars International
Lancaster House
33 Islington High Street
London N1 9LH
Country: UK
Language: English

Journal of Broadcasting & Electronic Media
4 issues p.a.
Publisher: Broadcast Education Association
1771 N Street, NW
Washington
DC 20036
USA
Country: US
Language: English

Journal of Communication
4 issues p.a.
Publisher: Oxford University Press
2001 Evans Road
Cary
NC 27513
USA
Country: US
Language: English

Journal of Popular Film and Television
4 issues p.a.
Publisher: Heldref Publications
1319 Eighteenth St, NW
Washington
D.C. 20036-1802
USA
Country: US
Language: English

New Review of Film and Television
2 issues p.a.
Publisher: Routledge Journals
Taylor & Francis Ltd
4 Park Square
Milton Park
Abingdon
Oxfordshire OX14 4RN
Country: UK
Language: English

Screen
4 issues p.a.
Publisher: Oxford University Press
(on behalf of John Logie Baird Centre)
Great Clarendon Street
Oxford OX2 6DP
Country: UK
Language: English

Spectator
2 issues p.a.
Publisher: University of Southern California
School of Cinema-Television
University Park
Los Angeles
CA 90089-2211
USA
Country: US
Language: English

Television and New Media
4 issues p.a.
Publisher: Sage Publications
1 Olive's Yard
55 City Road
London EC1Y 1SP
Country: UK
Language: English

Business

Ariel

52 issues p.a.
Publisher: BBC
Room 123, Henry Wood House
3&6 Langham Place
London W1A 1AA
Country: UK
Language: English

Broadcast

52 issues p.a.
Publisher: EMAP Media
33-39 Bowling Green Lane
London EC1R ODA
Country: UK
Language: English

Broadcasting and Cable

52 issues p.a.
Publisher: Reed Business Information
360 Park Ave South
New York
NY 10010
USA
Country: US
Language: English

Cable & Satellite Europe

12 issues p.a.
Publisher: Informa Media Group
Mortimer House
37-41 Mortimer Street
London W1T 3JH
Country: UK
Language: English

Cineinforme

12 issues p.a.
Publisher: ExportFilm
Gran Via 64
28013 Madrid
Spain
Country: ES
Language: Spanish

Commonwealth Broadcaster

4 issues p.a.
Publisher: Commonwealth Broadcasting
Association
17 Fleet St
London EC4Y 1AA
Country: UK
Language: English

Creation

12 issues p.a.
Publisher: Hardware Creations Limited
48 The Broadway
Maidenhead
Berkshire SL6 1PW
Country: UK
Language: English

Documentary Box

2 issues p.a.
Publisher: Yamagata International
Documentary Film Festival
Tokyo Office
ID Kawadecho Bldg., 3rd Floor
7-6 Kawadacho
Shinjuko-ku
Tokyo 162-0054
Japan
Country: JP
Language: English

Euromedia

12 issues p.a.
Publisher: Kagan World Media
524 Fulham Road
London SW6 5NR
Country: UK
Language: English

Free Press

6 issues p.a.
Publisher: Campaign for Press and
Broadcasting Freedom
2nd Floor, Vi & Garner Smith House
23 Orford Road
London E17 9NL
Country: UK
Language: English

Hollywood Reporter

365 issues p.a.
Publisher: VNU Business Publications
5055 Wilshire Blvd
Los Angeles
CA 90036-4396
USA
Country: US
Language: English

In Camera

(irregular) issues p.a.
Publisher: Kodak
Kodak House
PO Box 66

Hemel Hempstead
Herts HP1 1JU
Country: UK
Language: English

Intermedia

5 issues p.a.
Publisher: International Institute of
Communications
Regent House Business Centre
24-25 Nutford Place
London W1H 5YN
Country: UK
Language: English

International Documentary

12 issues p.a.
Publisher: International Documentary
Association
1201 West 5th Street
Suite M320
Los Angeles
CA 90017-1461
USA
Country: US
Language: English

Iris

10 issues p.a.
Publisher: European Audiovisual
Observatory
76, allée de la Robertsau
67000 Strasbourg
France
Country: FR
Language: English

Licensing Today Worldwide

4 issues p.a.
Publisher: A4 Publications
Thornleigh
35 Hagley Rd
Stourbridge
West Midlands DY8 1QR
Country: UK
Language: English

Media Asia

4 issues p.a.
Publisher: Asian Media, Information and
Communication Centre
School of Communication Studies Building
Nanyang Technological University
Jurong Point
PO Box 360

Singapore 916412
Singapore
Country: SG
Language: English

Media Week

52 issues p.a.
Publisher: Quantum Publishing
Quantum House
19 Scarbrook Rd
Croydon CR9 1LX
Country: UK
Language: English

Pact Magazine

12 issues p.a.
Publisher: Producers Alliance for Cinema
and Television
45 Mortimer Street
London W1W 8HJ
Country: UK
Language: English

Playback

25 issues p.a.
Publisher: Brunico Communications
366 Adelaide Street West, Suite 500
Toronto
Ontario M5V 1R9
Canada
Country: CA
Language: English

Programme News

6 issues p.a.
Publisher: Profile Group
27-29 Macklin Street
London WC2B 5LX
Country: UK
Language: English

Promo

12 issues p.a.
Publisher: United Business Media
8th Floor, Ludgate House
245 Blackfriars Road
London SE1 9UR
Country: UK
Language: English

Screen Digest

12 issues p.a.
Publisher: Screen Digest
Lymehouse Studios
38 Georgiana Street
London NW1 0EB
Country: UK
Language: English

Stage Screen And Radio

12 issues p.a.
Publisher: Broadcasting Entertainment
Cinematograph and Theatre Union
111 Wardour Street
London W1F 0AY
Country: UK
Language: English

Television

6 issues p.a.
Publisher: Royal Television Society
Holborn Hall
100 Gray's Inn Road
London WC1X 8AL
Country: UK
Language: English

Television Business International (TBI)

10 issues p.a.
Publisher: Informa Media Group
Mortimer House
37-41 Mortimer Street
London W1T 3JH
Country: UK
Language: English

Televisual

12 issues p.a.
Publisher: Televisual Magazine
St. Giles House
50 Poland Street
London W1V 4AX
Country: UK
Language: English

Variety

52 issues p.a.
Publisher: Cahners Publishing
5700 Wilshire Blvd, Suite 120
Los Angeles
CA 90036
USA
Country: US
Language: English

Popular

Action TV

c. 3 issues p.a.
Publisher: Michael Richardson
PO Box 1265
Huddersfield
HD5 7WZ
Country: UK
Language: English
Coverage of retro and cult action, crime,
spy and sci-fi TV series.

Cult Times

12 issues p.a.
Publisher: Visual Imagination
See *TV Zone*
Country: UK
Language: English
Listings info specialising in sci-fi and cult
TV shows – sister title to *TV Zone*.

Doctor Who Magazine

12 issues p.a. plus occasional specials
Publisher: Panini Publishing Ltd
Panini House
Coach and Horses Passage
The Pantiles
Tunbridge Wells
Kent TN2 5UJ
Country: UK
Language: (ENG)
Advertising Sales: 0207 321 0701 or
01372 802 800
Subscriptions: 01858 414712
The magazine dedicated to all aspects of
the cult sci-fi series celebrated its own
25th anniversary in 2004 and also the
announcement of the TV series' return.

Emmy

6 issues p.a.
Publisher: Academy of Television Arts
and Sciences
5220 Lankershim Blvd
North Hollywood
CA 91601-3109
USA
Country: US
Language: English

OFF-AIR

Entertainment Weekly

52 issues p.a.
Publisher: Entertainment Weekly Inc
1675 Broadway
New York
NY 10019
USA
Country: US
Language: English

Radio Times

52 issues p.a.
Publisher: BBC Worldwide
80 Wood Lane
London W12 OTT
Country: UK
Language: English

Starburst

16 issues p.a.
Publisher: Visual Imagination
Coverage of sci-fi and fantasy film and
television. See *TV Zone*

Telerama

52 issues p.a.
Publisher: Télérama
163, bd Malesherbes
75859 Paris Cedex 17
France
Country: FR
Language: French

TV Guide

52 issues p.a.
Publisher: TV Guide Magazine Group
1211 Avenue of the Americas
New York
NY 10036
USA
Country: US
Language: English

TV Times

52 issues p.a.
Publisher: IPC Magazines
King's Reach Tower
Stamford St
London SE1 9LS
Country: UK
Language: English

TV Zone

16 issues p.a.
Publisher: Visual Imagination
9 Blades Court
Deodar Rd
London SW15 2NU
Country: UK
Language: English
Coverage of cult TV series; usually
specialising in fantasy and sci-fi.

Fan Publishing

Alistair D. McGown

What constitutes genuine fan-publishing today is a tricky question. Fans have for many years now accepted professional publishing commissions and others, such as Surrey outfit Reynolds and Hearn, have built their own mini-empires from the kitchen table. The power of the web meanwhile has undoubtedly revolutionised TV fandom since the mid-90s, delivering previously undreamt of audiences and feedback to the passionate and talented TV fan. The paper fanzine is the only casualty – the often scurrilous and frequently hilarious underground publications of the 80s and 90s (published mainly in areas of sci-fi and fantasy TV) shrank from view as fandom went resolutely overground.

Among those benefiting from increased exposure are the core members of TV Cream – this site began as an A-Z of hazy telly reminiscences, drawing an audience of millions of students and office workers wanting to know how the theme to *Little House on the Prairie* went or how many *Animal Kwackers* there were. In recent years it's expanded its mailout digest activity and moved into in-depth, accurate features sections based upon digest material. It's resisted the overtly commercial advances its vast hit rate inevitably brings. TVC's Graham Kibble-White insists there will be no sell-out: 'TVC would lose all of its charm if it started offering mobile ring tones for three-quid a pop'. He feels simply that it 'is there for our own amusement. There's no policy. Because we're a non-commercial outfit we write about what we like, and if other people enjoy it, that's great. If they don't, that's great too. We just don't really care!'

The power of the web has undoubtedly revolutionised TV fandom since the mid-90s ... the paper fanzine is the only casualty.

Nonetheless TV Cream and Kibble-White's other site, Off The Telly, have brought him, and others like him, considerable career benefits that paper fanzines rarely provided. After a stint as a web journalist for Mersey TV, he is now Deputy TV journalist at the Press Association: 'I have to confess, my writing career has come about solely due to the online platform I've built for myself ... if you're putting good stuff out there you'll earn a reputation you can trade upon – it doesn't matter whether it's part of a commercial operation, or simply a bit of fun knocked up to amuse yourself and your mates'.

Networking opportunities undreamt of in the photocopy and staples era abound, although today's universal access does bring problems. TV Cream and OTT articles have reappeared thinly disguised in national newspapers. 'If you put all this info online, people are going to use it, whether they credit you or not. 'The flipside is that industry people are becoming more likely to try securing our services on a professional level. They realise there's more to gain if they use the brains behind these sites to come up with bespoke material rather than just cherry-pick material already available free to everyone.'

Graham's brother Jack was employed as consultant on Channel 4 documentary *Who Killed Saturday Night TV?* after his series of articles on OTT attracted the programme-makers' attention. Long may this profitable cross-pollination continue (and please, do speak to my agent) – for too long TV companies regarded fans as nerdy loonies, rather than recognising the knowledge some might possess.

Since 1999, Graham's OTT has published lengthy, in-depth analysis and review of TV shows, both current and archive, by a variety of writers – a formula that's surprisingly unique. 'OTT flagrantly under uses the potential of the web – it's simply reams of text and nothing else. The web's great for media clips, episode guides and info about those programmes with strong fan followings but I could never find any solid chunks of writing about television *per se* online.'

This seems as true today as in 1999. The medium's nature more readily lends itself to data capsules than to lengthy review and in-depth articles (try my own site at www.starmaidens.co.uk for a stab at merging the two approaches). Foremost among such episode guide collections are Action TV and Cult TV. The episode guide is the dominant fan form at present – the best are the result of many hours transcribing data and articles from library copies of *Radio Times* and *TV Times* (episode titles, writers, cast lists). The Mausoleum Club goes further than the rest, digging into the BBC's Infax database and Written Archive Centre, perusing PasB sheets to present arcane data such as film inserts used, music cues and VTR numbers. While it takes a certain mindset to appreciate such digging, there is no doubting its use as an accessible desktop source for academia and the

Action TV is now virtually the only printed fan magazine widely available (left). The Mausoleum Club's data files are published only in electronic form (right). Meanwhile, Kaleidoscope have issued the lavish coffee-table guide to *Out of the Unknown* (centre).

television industry itself. For the most part, 'data sites' provide little in the way of critique or review, bar basic overviews of series' format.

Steve Rogers runs the Mausoleum, a collection of episode guide data, engaging archive TV forums and news reports of the latest DVD releases (in this regard it is only surpassed by Julian Knott's scoops at Zeta Minor). Steve has gone a step further by selling his own printed fanzine ('It's always nice to have something tangible and say that you own it,' feels Steve) but recently faced a dilemma over formats. *The Gazette*, previously a simply printed collection of TV info, is now electronic – essentially a website on a disc. Steve explains the reasoning behind this; 'For readers outside of the UK it was costing more to post an issue than to buy the issue itself. Putting this material directly on the web is not always an option – there are some heavy images that would crucify dial-up people. Also, I pay for the webspace out of my own pocket and the forum traffic can regularly exceed what I am paying for.' Steve specialises in 'gubbins that no one remembers or cares about,' and 'avoids covering mainstream sci-fi as much as possible'.

OFF-AIR

Compared with the ease of access and low cost of electronic media, print seems an increasingly expensive option.

There's still plenty of free material on Steve's site in printable PDF and an index to every *Play For Today* is steadily building there.

Compared with the ease of access and low cost of electronic media, print seems an increasingly expensive option. Kaleidoscope, a fan organisation whose printed guides to TV archive holdings became a godsend to industry researchers in the last decade, are now wrestling with this format quandary. A hugely expanded revision of their Drama Guide, due soon, is likely to extend to eight paper volumes and cost £270. Freed from the constraints of mainstream publishing, they have also published Mark Ward's truly definitive 500-page guide to 60s/70s BBC fantasy anthology *Out of the Unknown* at a coffee table price of £45.

The only genuine, semi-regular TV fanzine joining the (fantasy) pro zines such as *TV Zone* and *Dreamwatch* on the shelves of better bookshops these days is Mike Richardson's *TV Action*. Focusing on all kinds of action series (crime, sci-fi, spy) it largely sticks with tried and trusted favourites like *The Avengers* and *The Champions*, – its coverage of the more obscure likes of *Strange Report* is much appreciated. It does take a slightly drier approach and, like the web, tends to major in episode guides and production data rather than enthuse or analyse (Andrew Screen oversees an episode guide-dominated online companion). Design has been vastly improved by the recent addition of Jaz Wiseman's talents – Wiseman has

his own fanzines, the subscription-only *Nuisance Value* and *The Morning After*, beautifully produced A5 fanzines devoted to *The Persuaders!* and other ITC's 60s and 70s action series.

Whether electronically or in print, the fans continue to indulge their passions but there's no denying it's the web which has made their devoted work far more accessible to wider, appreciative audiences.

Web Addresses
URLs for the mentioned sites

Action TV
http://www.action-tv.org.uk

Cult TV
http://www.cult-tv.org.uk

Kaleidoscope Publications
http://www.kalpublish.org.uk

The Mausoleum Club
http://the-mausoleum-club.org.uk

The Morning After (ITC fanclub)
http://www.itc-classics.com

Off The Telly
http://www.offthetelly.co.uk

TV Cream
http://tv.cream.org

Zeta Minor
http://www.zetaminor.com

Immensely popular TV nostalgia site TV Cream has diversified from its original A-Z reminiscences into features

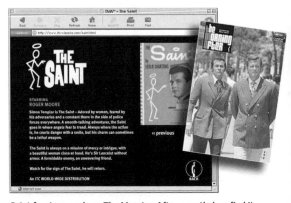

Print fanzines, such as *The Morning After*, nonetheless find it useful to maintain a web presence

TV on DVD

Alistair D. McGown

Several articles in this first BFI TV Handbook have, in an attempt to provide some kind of context, harked back to events the last time any kind of TV Yearbook was published (Dick Fiddy's *Virgin TV Yearbook* in 1985). Suffice to say that Kieran Prenderville was smearing new fangled CDs, never mind DVDs, with jam on *Tomorrow's World* back then and Betamax was still a serious contender in home video.

DVD has virtually obliterated the sell through and rental markets for VHS in the past four years. TV on DVD has flourished alongside the blockbuster movie market – not only are most successful current series (both UK and US) available in full on DVD as a matter of course but the last few years have seen more archive TV released via shiny disc than in the previous twenty years of home video.

In early 2002 BBC Learning issued three Special Interests DVDs, limited edition discs with a literary connection and a semi-educational remit, selling for £20 each; 1977's *Dracula*, 1976's *The Picture of Dorian Gray* and Peter Cushing as Sherlock Holmes in *The Hound of the Baskervilles* from 1968. These titles were not intended for mainstream distribution and thought to have a viable if very limited cult appeal – they were also obviously something of an attempt to test the water. It's perhaps the clearest measure of how far the market has matured and expanded that in the Summer of 2004 all five existing Cushing Sherlock Holmes adventures are available to buy in high street megastores as a £25 box set. DVD, with its potential for high picture quality and easily accessible extra features, is of course a perfect format for TV collectors but not even the most optimistic TV fan could have predicted the explosion of hundreds of titles it would usher in.

The *bfi* was, inevitably, another to pioneer classic television on DVD – its releases of landmark productions from *The Stone Tape* to *Cathy Come Home* widened the range of material available from 2001 onwards. The *bfi*'s releases have educational aims in mind with an emphasis on quality –the extras concentrating on interviews with key crew and production paperwork. Until recently the *bfi* releases were the only outlet for titles outside of populist, mainstream series work but in 2004 they are just part of a market that takes

The last few years have seen more archive TV released via shiny disc than in the previous twenty years of home video

in every kind of archive TV strand, from series to plays, classics to curiosities, in every kind of genre.

2003 saw the BBC begin to release many of its own recognised classics, now with no perceived need for the Special Interests rubric, beginning with conspiracy thriller *Edge of Darkness* and Alan Bleasdale's tales of 80s Liverpool *Boys From the Blackstuff*. 2004 has seen the strand build to encompass several key works from Dennis Potter; *The Singing Detective*, *Pennies From Heaven*, *Brimstone and Treacle* and *Casanova*. Perhaps the strongest exploitation of the format is still seen in the BBC's regular *Doctor Who* releases, which regularly include entertaining documentaries and

OFF-AIR

The *bfi* has released a wide range of landmark television on DVD, from 1966's docudrama *Cathy Come Home* to 1992's hoax reality horror show *Ghostwatch*

VHS-only issues a thing of the past. This label tends to specialise in period drama – John Duttine's 1981 serial *To Serve Them All My Days* is a recent addition to their range. Acorn also specialise in spiffing period crime and the adventures of heroes such as cracksman *Raffles* (starring Anthony Valentine from 1977) and Victorian detective *Cribb* (Alan Dobie in the 1980 Granada series) are available from this label. Granada Visual subsidiary Cinema Club have also been active in period drama, with titles such as *Lillie* (the story of Lillie Langtry, mistress to the Prince of Wales) and rural melodrama *Flambards* seeing release in early January, luxuriously packaged if low on extras.

An independent label previously specialising in military and transport documentary, DD Video has in the last year or two moved into TV Drama – predictably so with the wonderful 1968 BBC adaptation of *The Railway Children* or 1972 RAF drama *The Pathfinders* but less predictably with a digipak set of Season 1 of Terry Nation's dark sci-fi series *Survivors* (hopefully the next two seasons will follow).

Although Network had always been a worthwhile label, issuing both classic and curious material on VHS since 1997 (French film serial *Robinson Crusoe* was their first release), 2003-4 saw it mature from a small concern to become the most respected DVD label among archive TV fans. 2002's extras-laden box sets of HTV's *Robin of Sherwood* were landmark titles, and such quality releases have opened doors with the very biggest of television rights holders, as Managing Director, Tim Beddows explains: 'Our work has given us the credibility with companies like Fremantle and Granada. Acquiring a jewel like *The Sweeney* wasn't easy but we had a great plan for the show, which included restoration and a wealth of extras. Fremantle approved it wholeheartedly and now we have a trusted, working relationship.' The *Sweeney* box sets have included cast and crew interviews, isolated soundtracks and 5.1 mixes and have been

obscure snippets of related clips from series such as *Blue Peter*. The VidFIRE treatment that restores the original, crisp, fluid videotape look to smeary old monochrome film recordings is seen to its best effect on 60s William Hartnell and Patrick Troughton episodes of the sci-fi series and a bumper collection of restored black and white episodes is due Christmas 2004. The VidFIRE process ought to be used on every black and white DVD release sourced from telerecordings but industry ignorance means this is rarely the case.

Several key players have expanded their archive TV output in the last twelve months to become market leaders. Universal/Playback have continued to issue popular BBC sitcoms under licence from BBC Worldwide (Worldwide themselves prefer to retain DVD rights to recent hits like *The Office* and *The Day Today*) and in 2004 titles have included Ronnie Corbett's *Sorry!*, John Sullivan's under-rated class-war romcom *Just Good Friends* and continuing volumes of *Hi-De-Hi* and *Keeping Up Appearances*. These are complemented by some big TV drama hits, including several volumes of *A Touch of Frost*.

Acorn have been slow to embrace DVD but finally seem to have grasped the nettle, with their enthusiastically praised by fans.

DVD's meteoric rise has taken the video industry by surprise and a small label like Network took time to adjust: 'I don't know anyone within the industry who has not been taken aback by the speed at which the format in general has exploded. The television market has been one of the fastest growing areas and, as a result, I think all the distributors are taking more commercial care over what they are prepared to licence out to third party labels. You can't blame them, after all this is new territory for all of us.'

Why has the format been such a success? 'It's a clean, convenient and efficient format which the world would have cried out for sooner or later. VHS seems such hard work now. The actual format isn't necessarily easier to work on; technically it is faster, less labour intensive and takes up less space both on the factory and shop floor but there is a huge amount of pre-production work, particularly when extras are involved.'

Network's attention to remastering and extras are what sets them apart from their rivals. ITC's *Strange Report* for example has just been issued with original incidental scores (complete with orchestra chatter) and hundreds of unpublished photos taken for the series title sequence among a myriad of goodies. Beddows is aware that word on a TV release – good or bad – spreads quickly among devotees, so taking such care is important. 'I read a post on one web forum from someone who was going to purchase *Strange Report*, never having seen the series, because of a recommendation he'd read elsewhere on the web and because it was on Network. That is very gratifying and that kind of real feedback was almost unimaginable in the video days.'

Strange Report (Anthony Quayle heading a trio of crime-fighters investigating off-beat cases) is not among ITC's most famous output – how do Network strike a balance when selecting releases? 'Obviously, commerciality is the major

The Goodies and colour episodes of *Till Death Us Do Part* are among a wealth of archive TV releases from Network

consideration,' says Beddows, 'but that doesn't mean we always have to sell thousands of discs of any given title to turn in decent figures. Every single release is unique in terms of acquisition costs, remastering and marketing and this will ultimately be reflected in the final price and sales potential. We don't do any great marketing research because we know our market extremely well now. This experience dictates whether extras and involved work will actually result in higher sales but it does tend to be the older series that attract interest for that kind of material. They're the most fun to work on too.'

In a major development, 2004-5 will see Network release key ITC properties, taking over the mantle from rights holder Carlton's own issues – Beddows is currently overseeing restoration of *Man In a Suitcase*, *Department S* and *Jason King*. He expects that Network will release a staggering ten releases or more for each of ten months of the year in late 2004 into 2005 – on the slate are more *Goodies*, more of children's comedy drama *Press Gang*, Fay Weldon's *The Life and Loves of a She Devil*, 80s space police procedural *Star Cops* and Michael Palin's *Boys' Own* period pastiche *Ripping Yarns* as well as a good few shows Beddows is keeping under wraps.

No doubt 2005, thanks to Network and others, will see many more classics and curiosities making their way to DVD. Archive TV fans have never had it so good.

> **'I don't know anyone within the industry who has not been taken aback by the speed at which the DVD format has exploded'**
> **Tim Beddows, MD, Network**

OFF-AIR

Obituaries

Barrie MacDonald

Obituaries for the period 1 July 2003 – 30 June 2004

Obituary notices for figures from the television industry, or those who have made a contribution to television in front of and behind the camera. While some figures may have had careers extending to theatre and film, we will concentrate here primarily on their television work.

Robert ADDIE. b. 10 February 1960, d. 20 November 2003. Actor.
Sir Guy of Gisburne in *Robin of Sherwood*, *Red Dwarf* Series 3.

Anthony AINLEY. b. circa 20 August 1932, d. 3 May 2004. Actor.
Elizabeth R (BBC, 1971), Reverend Emilius in *The Pallisers* (BBC, 1974), and The Master (from 1981-89) in *Doctor Who*.

Ben ARIS. b. 16 March 1937, d. 4 September 2003. Actor.
Julian Dalrymple-Sykes in *Hi-De-Hi!*, and *To The Manor Born*.

Dennis BARDENS. b. 19 July 1911, d. 7 February 2004. Journalist.
First Editor of *Panorama* (from 1953-54).

Gillian BARGE. b. 27 May 1940, d. 19 November 2003. Actor.
Goneril in Jonathan Miller's *King Lear* (BBC, 1982), Princess Shcherbatskya in *Anna Karenina* (Channel 4, 2000), and *Armadillo* (BBC, 2001).

Sir Alan BATES. b. 17 February 1934, d. 27 December 2003. Actor.
The Mayor of Casterbridge (BBC, 1978), *A Voyage Round My Father* (Thames/ITV, 1982), as Guy Burgess in *An Englishman Abroad* (BBC, 1983), *Love in a Cold Climate* (BBC, 2001) and as George V in *Bertie and Elizabeth* (Carlton/ITV, 2002). CBE, 1995; Knighted, 2003.

Polly BIDE. b. 25 August 1949, d. 9 July 2003. TV Executive/ Film-maker.
Granada Television: *Granada Reports*,

Thames Television: *Mothers Behind Bars* (1990); Freelance: *Great Ormond Street* (BBC, 1995); BBC: Chief Adviser, Editorial Policy, 1998-99; Carlton Television: Controller of Factual Programmes, 1999-2003.

Lyndon BROOK. b. 10 April 1926, d. 9 January 2004. Actor.
I Claudius (BBC, 1976), George VI in *Churchill and the Generals* (BBC, 1979).

Robert BROWN. b. 23 July 1921, d. 11 November 2003. Actor.
Ivanhoe, King of the River, guest appearances in *The Saint, Danger UXB*.

Tony CAPSTICK. b. 27 July 1944, d. 23 October 2003. Actor/ Comedian.
Capstick's Capers, brewery manager Harvey Nuttall in *Coronation Street*, and policeman Fred Allen in *Last of the Summer Wine*.

Art CARNEY. b. 4 November 1918, d. 9 November 2003. Actor (USA).
The Honeymooners, The Snoop Sisters.

Alistair COOKE. b. 20 November 1908, d. 30 March 2004. Journalist.
America (Time-Life/BBC, 1972-73); *Masterpiece Theatre*.

Simon CUMBERS. b. 23 January 1968, d. 6 June 2004. Reporter/ Cameraman.
Freelancer who worked for the BBC, Associated Press Television News (APTN), ITN and Sky Television. Killed in Saudi Arabia on BBC assignment.

Sheila DUNN. d. 3 March 2004. Actor.
Dennis Potter's *Stand Up, Nigel Barton* (BBC, 1965); *The Lost Prince* (BBC, 2003).

Buddy EBSEN. b. 2 April 1908, d. 6 July 2003. Actor (USA).
Jed Clampett in *The Beverly Hillbillies, Barnaby Jones* and *Matt Houston*.

Harry ELTON. b. 5 January 1930, d. 16 May 2004. Television Producer.
Granada Television, 1957-63: commissioned *Coronation Street* from Tony Warren.

A(rthur) A(dolf) ENGLANDER. d. 29 January 2004. TV Cameraman.
BBC Television: *Quatermass and the Pit*, Kenneth Clark's *Civilisation, Colditz*.

Don ESTELLE. b. 22 May 1933, d. 2 August 2003. Actor/Singer.
Gunner 'Lofty' Sugden in *It Ain't Half Hot Mum*.

Dai FRANCIS. b. 23 February 1928, d. 27 November 2003. Entertainer.
The Black and White Minstrel Show.

Rikki FULTON. b. 15.April 1924, d. 28 January 2004. Actor/Comedian.
The Rikki Fulton Show, The Rikki Fulton Hour, Rob Roy (BBC, 1977) and *Scotch and Wry*. Autobiography: *Is It That Time Already?* (1998).

Brian GIBSON. b. 22 September 1944, d. 4 January 2004. Director.
Horizon, an adaptation of Thomas Keneally's *Gossip From The Forest* (Granada/ ITV, 1979), Dennis Potter's *Blue Remembered Hills* (BBC, 1979).

Stuart GOLLAND. b. 3 August 1945, d. 11 September 2003. Actor.
Pub landlord George Ward in *Heartbeat* and Ernie Wagstaff in *Coronation Street*.

Nick GORDON. b. 9 May 1952, d. 25 April 2004. Wildlife Film-maker.
Anglia Television's *Survival* series including *Tarantula* (ITV, 1991), *Web of the Spider Monkey* (ITV, 1996), *Jaguar – Eater of Souls* (ITV, 2001).

Bob GRANT. b. 14 April 1932, d. 8 November 2003. Actor.
Bus conductor Jack Harper in *On The Buses*.

Max HARRIS. b. 15 September 1918, d. 13 March 2004. Composer.
Theme music for *The Strange World of Gurney Slade, Doomwatch, Porridge* and *Open All Hours*.

Keith HATFIELD. b. 18 January 1943, d. 20 May 2004. Reporter.
Anglia Television; ITN, 1967-91: notably covered Northern Ireland, 1969; Israel-Egypt War, 1973; Turkish invasion of Cyprus, 1974.

John HAWKESWORTH. b. 7 December 1920, d. 30 September 2003. TV Producer. *Upstairs, Downstairs, The Duchess of Duke Street, Danger UXB, The Flame Trees of Thika* and *The Return of Sherlock Holmes*.

David HEMMINGS. b. 18 November 1941, d. 3 December 2003). Actor/ Producer/ Director. Samuel Taylor Coleridge in *Clouds of Glory* (Granada/ ITV, 1978), P. D. James' *A Mind to Murder* (Anglia/ITV, 1995); directed episodes of *Follyfoot, The A-Team, Magnum P.I.* and *Murder, She Wrote*.

Harry HERBERT (Earl of Pembroke). b. 19 May 1939, d. 7 October 2003. Producer/ Director. Episodes of *Bergerac, Shoestring, By The Sword Divided*.

Rose HILL. b. 5 June 1914, d. 22 December 2003. Actor.
Fanny (Fifi) Lafanne in *'Allo, 'Allo, Nicholas Nickleby* (Primetime/Channel 4, 1982).

Gregory HINES. b. 14 February 1946, d. 9 August 2003. Actor/ Dancer (USA).
Gregory Hines Show, Bojangles (Showtime, 2001), Ben Doucette in *Will & Grace*.

Bob HOPE. b. 29 May 1903, d. 27 July 2003. Actor/ Comedian (USA).
The Bob Hope Show (BBC, 1961); many *Royal Variety Performances, Miss World* etc.
CBE (Hon), 1976; KBE (Hon), 1998.

Vernon HOWE. b. 18 January 1943, d. 27 November 2003. Advertising Executive.
Award-winning director of TV commercials including Campari with Lorraine Chase ('Were you truly wafted here from paradise?' – 'No, Luton Airport'), and Heineken ('Refreshes the parts other beers cannot reach').

Russell HUNTER. b. 18 February 1925, d. 26 Febuary 2004. Actor.
Lonely in *Callan, The School for Scandal* (BBC, 1975), *Rule Britannia, The Gaffer*.

Walter JEFFERIES. b. 12 August 1921, d. 21 July 2003. Designer (USA)
The Untouchables, Dallas and creator of the starship USS Enterprise in *Star Trek*.

Godfrey JENNISON. d. 14 October 2003. Producer/Director
Film Partnership: *Passport* (first TV travel series).

Penry JONES. b. 18 August 1922, d. 25 January 2004. Producer/Regulator.
ABC Television, 1959-64: *The Sunday Break*; ITA: Religious Programmes Officer, 1964-67; BBC: Head of Religious Broadcasting, 1967-71; IBA: Chief Assistant, Television (formerly Deputy Head of Programme Services), 1971-82.

Philip JONES. b. 7 December 1927, d. 7 May 2004. Producer.
Tyne Tees Television, 1955-60; ABC Television, 1960-68; Thames Television, Head of Light Entertainment, 1968-88: *Love Thy Neighbour, Man About The House, Give us a Clue, The Kenny Everett Video Show* and *Shelley*. BBC, Executive producer: *As Time Goes By*. OBE, 1978.

Michael KAMEN. b. 15 April 1948, d. 18 November 2003. Composer (USA)
Wrote the music for Troy Kennedy Martin's *Edge of Darkness* (BBC, 1986)

Alexis KANNER. b. 2 May 1942, d. 13 December 2003. Actor.
DC Stone in *Softly, Softly* and 'The Kid' in *The Prisoner*.

M(ary) M(argaret) KAYE. b. 21 August 1908, d. 29 January 2004. Writer.
The Far Pavilions (Goldcrest/ Channel 4, 1984).

Caron KEATING. b. 5 October 1962, d. 13 April 2004. Presenter.
Blue Peter (from 1986 to 1990), with her mother Gloria Hunniford in *Family Affairs, London Tonight, This Morning* and *Rich and Famous*.

Natasha KROLL. b. 20 May 1914, d. 2 April 2004. Production Designer.
BBC Television, 1955-66: *Monitor*, Ken Russell's television documentaries.

Dinsdale LANDEN. b. 4 September 1932, d. 29 December 2003. Actor
Mickey Dunne (BBC, 1967), *Plaintiffs and Defendants* (*Play for Today*) (BBC, 1975), *The Buccaneers* (BBC, 1995) and *The Wingless Bird* (Tyne Tees/ITV, 1997)

Richard LEECH. b. 24 November 1922, d. 24 March 2004. Actor.
Interpol Calling, Mr Rochester in *Jane Eyre* (BBC, 1963), *The Doctors* and *A Woman of Substance* (Portman/Channel 4, 1985).

Harry LITTLEWOOD. b. 1921, d. 26 December 2003. Actor/ Scriptwriter.
Ours is a Nice House and *Mind Your Language*.

Philip LOCKE. b. 29 March 1928, d. 19 April 2004. Actor.
Codename Icarus (BBC, 1981), *She Fell Among Thieves* (BBC, 1982), *Ivanhoe* (CBS, 1982), *Jekyll & Hyde* (LWT/ITV, 1990), *Doctor Who*, Sir Roderick Glossop in *Jeeves and Wooster*.

David LODGE. b. 19 August 1921, d. 18 October 2003. Actor
United! (BBC, 1965-67); guest appearances in *The Saint, The Sweeney* and *Minder*. Autobiography: *Up the Ladder to Obscurity* (1986).

Alfred LYNCH. b. 26 January 1931, d. 16 December 2003. Actor.
Alun Owen's *No Trams To Lime Street* (*Armchair Theatre*) (ABC/ITV, 1959), *Hereward The Wake* (BBC, 1965), *The Gold Robbers* (LWT/ ITV, 1969) and *Manhunt* (LWT/ ITV, 1970); guest appearances in *Bergerac* and *Lovejoy*.

OFF-AIR

Obituaries

Midge MACKENZIE. b. 6 March 1938, d. 28 January 2004. Film-maker.
Formed Mowhawk Films (with Frank Cvitanovich); *Shoulder to Shoulder* (BBC, 1975).

Norris McWHIRTER. b. 12 August 1925, d. 20 April 2004. Author/Broadcaster.
Co-host *Record Breakers* (BBC, 1974-85). In 1984 took out an unsuccessful summons against the IBA over the use of subliminal images in *Spitting Image*.

Richard MARNER. b. 27 March 1921, d. 18 March 2004. Actor.
Colonel Von Strohm in *'Allo 'Allo*. Also *P. D. James' Shroud for a Nightingale* (Anglia/ ITV, 1984).

Joan MARSDEN. b. 20 May 1919, d. 3 March 2004. TV Floor-Manager.
BBC Television, -1979: Lime Grove Studios, including *Panorama*. MBE.

Bob MONKHOUSE. b. 1 June 1928, d. 29 December 2003. Comedian/Presenter.
Compered *Candid Camera*, *The Golden Shot*, *Celebrity Squares*, *Family Fortunes* and *Bob Says Opportunity Knocks*. OBE, 1993. Autobiography: *Crying with Laughter* (1988).

Julia Trevelyan OMAN. b. 11 July 1930, d. 10 October 2003. Designer.
BBC Television, 1955-67; Jonathan Miller's *Alice in Wonderland* (BBC, 1966). CBE, 1986.

Jack PAAR. b. 1 May 1918, d. 27 January 2004. Broadcaster (USA)
Talk-show host: *The Tonight Show* (renamed *The Jack Paar Tonight Show* in 1959) (NBC, 1957-62) and *The Jack Paar Program* (NBC, 1962-65).

Anthony PRAGNELL. b. 15 February 1921, d. 17 June 2004. Administrator.
ITA/ IBA: Deputy Director-General, 1961-83; Channel 4 Television: Director, 1983-88; European Institute for the Media: Visiting Fellow 1983-97. CBE, 1982.

Denis QUILLEY. b. 26 December 1927, d. 5 October 2003. Actor.
Traynor in *Timeslip* (ATV/ITV, 1970-1), *In*

This House of Brede (CBS, 1975), *The Crucible* (BBC, 1980), as Gladstone in *Number 10* (YTV/ITV, 1982) and as Lord Curzon in *A Dangerous Man: Lawrence after Arabia* (Anglia/ITV, 1990).

John RAMSDEN. d. 28 October 2003. TV Sound Engineer.
Rediffusion, 1967-68; Thames Television, 1968-92; freelance: *Family Affairs* (Five).

Tony RANDALL. b. 26 February 1920, d. 17 May 2004. Actor (USA).
The Odd Couple and *The Tony Randall Show*.

John RANDOLPH. b. 1 June 1915, d. 24 February 2004. Actor (USA)
Arthur Miller's *The American Clock* (Amblin/ Turner Network, 1993) and Roseanne's father in *Roseanne*.

Andrew RAY. b. 31 May 1939, d. 20 August 2003. Actor.
King George VI in *Crown Matrimonial* (LWT/ITV, 1974) and *Edward and Mrs Simpson* (Thames/ITV, 1978); P. D. James' *Death of an Expert Witness* (Anglia/ITV, 1983) and as Dr John Reginald in *Peak Practice*.

Gordon REID. b. 6 September 1939, d. 26 November 2003. Actor.
Angus Livingstone in *Doctor Finlay*, guest appearances in *Taggart*, *Lovejoy*, *Poirot*.

Ted RHODES. b. 9 May 1934, d. 16 December 2003. Scriptwriter.
All Creatures Great and Small and *Triangle*.

Alun RICHARDS. b. 27 November 1929, d. 2 June 2004. Writer.
Hear the Tiger, See the Bay (*Armchair Theatre*) (ABC/ITV, 1962), *The Onedin Line*.

Roy ROBERTS. b. 14 May 1935, d. 27 April 2004. Television Producer.
Granada Television, 1963-89: *The Mallens* (ITV, 1979-80), *All for Love* series (ITV, 1982-84), *December Flower* (ITV, 1985), John Fowles' *The Ebony Tower* (ITV, 1986) and *A Wreath of Roses* (ITV, 1987).

Guy ROLFE. b. 27 December 1911, d. 19 October 2003. Actor.
The Avengers, *Space:1999* and *Secret Army*.

George ROPER. b. 15 May 1934, d. 1 July 2003. Comedian.
The Comedians.

Jack ROSENTHAL. b. 8 September 1931, d. 29 May 2004. Writer.
Coronation Street (129 episodes from 1961-69; also producer c.1967), *The Dustbinmen* (Granada/ITV, 1969-70), *The Lovers* (first series Granada/ITV, 1970; also producer), *Bar Mitzvah Boy* (BBC, 1976), *Ready When You Are, Mr McGill* (Granada/ ITV, 1976), *Spend, Spend, Spend* (BBC, 1977), *The Knowledge* (Thames/ITV, 1979), *P'tang, Yang, Kipperbang* (Goldcrest/Channel 4, 1982), *London's Burning* (LWT/ITV, 1986), *Eskimo Day* (BBC, 1996) and *Cold Enough for Snow* (BBC, 1997). CBE, 1994.

Mario ROSSETTI. b. 1 February 1920, d. 15 January 2004. Cameraman.
ITN cameraman from 1955.

William SARGENT. b. 1927, d. 19 October 2003. Engineer/Producer (USA).
Started pay-per-view television in the USA in 1962 with Home Entertainment Company screening of Muhammad Ali – George Logan boxing match, and invented Electronovision – a video-to-film transfer process – in 1964.

John SCHLESINGER. b. 16 February 1926, d. 25 July 2003. Director.
BBC, 1957-60: *Monitor*, *An Englishman Abroad* (BBC, 1983), *A Question of Attribution* (BBC, 1991) and *Cold Comfort Farm* (BBC, 1995). CBE, 1970.

Tony SHRYANE. b. 20 January 1919, d. 22 September 2003. Producer.
BBC Television: *My Word*, *My Music*. As radio producer of *The Archers* he devised the spoiling tactic of killing Grace Archer to upstage the opening night of ITV on 22 September 1955.

Milton SHULMAN. b. 30 August 1913, d. 21 May 2004. Writer/Critic.
Granada Television, Executive Producer, 1958-62: *Animal Story* (ITV, 1960-62), *Challenge* (Granada/ ITV, 1961); Associated-Rediffusion, 1962-64: *Here and Now* (ITV, 1962-3); *Evening Standard*, TV Critic, 1964-73. Publication: *The Least Worst Television in the World* (1973).

Bill STRUTTON. b. 23 February 1918, d. 23 November 2003. Scriptwriter.
Wrote episodes of *Ivanhoe, The Avengers, The Saint* and *Doctor Who.*

Shaun SUTTON. b. 14 October 1919, d. 14 May 2004. Producer.
BBC Television, 1952-89: BBC children's drama producer 1952-61. Director: *Z Cars, Softly, Softly, Detective* (BBC, 1964), *Kipling* (BBC, 1964); Head of Drama Serials, 1966-69: *The Troubleshooters, The Forsyte Saga* (BBC, 1967); Head of Drama Group, 1969-81; Executive Producer, BBC Television Shakespeare series, 1981-84. Publication: *The Largest Theatre in the World: thirty years of television drama* (1982). OBE, 1979.

Don TAYLOR. b. 30 June 1936, d. 11 November 2003. Director/Writer.
Directed David Mercer's trilogy *Where the Difference Begins, A Climate of Fear* and *The Birth of a Private Man* (BBC, 1961-63), *A Suitable Case for Treatment* (BBC, 1962) and his new verse translation of Sophocles' *The Theban Plays* (BBC, 1984).

Alan TILVERN. b. 5 November 1918, d. 17 December 2003. Actor.
Appearances in *Poldark* and *Dad's Army.*

Zena WALKER. b. 7 March 1934, d. 24 August 2003. Actor.
The Adventures of Sir Lancelot, Man at the Top, Albert and Victoria and *The One and Only Buster Barnes* (ATV/ITV, 1978).

Kent WALTON. b. 22 August 1917, d. 24 August 2003. Sport Commentator.
Presenter, *Cool for Cats;* wrestling commentator on *World of Sport.*

David WEBSTER. b. 11 January 1931, d. 6 August 2003. TV Producer/ Executive.
BBC: *Panorama.* Producer, 1959-64, Deputy Editor, 1966, Editor, 1967-69; BBC Representative in the USA, 1971-76; Controller of Information Services, 1976-77; Director, Public Affairs, 1977-80; Director, US, BBC, 1981-85.

Peter WEST. b. 12 August 1920, d. 2 September 2003. Broadcaster.
BBC: Sports commentator; and presenter of *Guess My Story, Come Dancing* (from 1957-72). HTV: *Facing West* (HTV/ITV, 1986-88). Autobiography: *Flannelled Fool and Muddied Oaf* (1986).

Accountants

AGN Shipleys
10 Orange Street
Haymarket
London WC2H 7DQ
Tel: 020 7312 0000
Fax: 020 7312 0022
Web: www.agnshipleys.com

Baker Tilly
2 Bloomsbury Street
London WC1B 3ST
Tel: 020 7413 5100
Fax: 020 7413 5101
Web: www.bakertilly.co.uk

Clayman & Co.
189 Bickenhall Mansions
Bickenhall Street
London W1U 6BX
Tel: 020 7935 0847
Fax: 020 7224 2216
Email: info@claymans.co.uk

David Hurwich & Co
8 Parkview Court
8 Roehampton Vale
London SW15 3RY
Tel/Fax: 020 8780 2589
Web: www.davidhurwich.co.uk

Deloitte
Stonecutter Court
1 Stonecutter Street
London EC4A 4TR
Tel: 020 7936 3000
Fax: 020 7583 1198
Web: www.deloitte.com

The Fisher Organisation
Acre House
11/15 William Road
London NW1 3ER
Tel: 020 7388 7000
Fax: 020 7380 4900
Web: www. hwfisher.co.uk

Henry Bach & Co
15 Broad Court
Covent Garden
London WC2B 5QN
Tel: 020 7240 2834
Fax: 020 7240 2813.

Ivan Sopher & Co
5 Elstree Gate
Elstree Way
Borehamwood
Hertfordshire WD6 1JD
Tel: 020 8207 0602
Fax: 020 8207 6758
Web: www.ivansopher.co.uk

Lubbock Fine
Russell Bedford House
City Forum
250 City Road
London EC1V 2QQ
Tel: 020 7490 7766
Fax: 020 7490 5102
Web: www.lubbockfine.co.uk

MacCorkindale Alonso & Holton
1-2 Langham Place, PO BOX 2398
London W1A 2RT
Tel: 020 7636 1888
Fax: 020 7636 2888
Web: www.mahibm.com

McDermott & Co
39 Bucharest Road
London SW18 3AS
Tel: 020 8871 0153.
Fax: 020 8877 9786.

Monitor Bookeeping
PO Box 1573
Ilford
Essex IG1 4AY
Tel: 020 8491 8663
Fax: 020 8491 8303
Web: www.monitorbookkeeping.co.uk

MWM
6 Berkeley Crescent
Clifton
Bristol BS8 1HA
Tel: 0117 929 2393
Fax: 0117 929 2696
email: office@mwmuk.com

Nyman Lisbon Paul
Regina House
124 Finchley Road
London NW3 5JS
Tel: 020 7433 2400
Fax: 020 7433 2401
Web: www.nymanlibsonpaul.co.uk

The Phillip Hills Partnership
2a Whitehill Street
Musselburgh EH21 8RA
Tel: 0131 657 5757
Fax: 0131 657 3737
Web: www.philliphills.com

Potter & Co
10 The Square
Dinas Powys
Vale of Glamorgan CF64 4YR
Tel: 029 2051 4732
Fax: 029 2051 4732
email: howard@potterco.demon.co.uk

Pricewaterhouse Coopers
1 Embankment Place
London WC2N 6RH
Tel: 020 7212 4516
Fax: 029 2051 4732
Web: www.pwc.com

R & R Media Advisory Services
198 Edgwarebury Lane
Edgware
Middlesex HA8 8QW
Tel: 020 8905 3600
Fax: 020 8905 3600
email: rrfilmmedia@aol.com

Agents & Managers

Silver Levene
37 Warren Street
London W1T 6AD
Tel: 020 7383 3200
Fax: 020 7383 4165
Web: www.silverlevene.co.uk

Willott Kingston Smith
Quadrant House (Air Street Entrance)
80-82 Regent Street
London W1B 5RP
Tel: 020 7304 4646
Fax: 020 7304 4647
Web: www.kingstonsmith.co.uk

The Agency
24 Pottery Lane
London W11 4LZ
Tel: 020 7727 1346
Fax: 020 7727 9037
email: info@theagency.co.uk

Artists Independent Network
32 Tavistock Street
London WC2E 7PB
Tel: 020 7257 8727
Fax: 020 7240 9029
email: mail@artsindependent.com

Artists Management Group
9465 Wilshire Blvd
Beverly Hills
Ca 90212
USA
Tel: 001 310 860 8000
Fax: 001 310 860 8100

Artmedia
20 avenue Rapp
75007 Paris
France
Tel: 33 1 43 17 33 00
Fax: 33 1 44 18 34 60
email: info@artmedia.fr
Web: www.artmedia.fr

Casarotto Ramsey & Associates
National House
60-66 Wardour Street
London W1V 4ND
Tel: 020 7287 4450
Fax: 020 7287 5644
email: agents@casarotto.uk.com

Chatto & Linnit
123A Kings Road
London SW3 4PL
Tel: 020 7352 7722
Fax: 020 7352 3450
email: chattolinnit@kingsrdsw3.demon.co.uk

Conway Van Gelder
18-21 Jermyn Street
London SW1Y 6HP
Tel: 020 7287 0077
Fax: 020 7287 1940

Creative Artists Agency
9830 Wilshire Blvd.
Beverly Hills
CA 90212-1825
USA
Tel: 001 310 288 4545
Fax: 001 310 288 4800

Curtis Brown
Haymarket House
28-29 Haymarket
London SW1Y 4SP
Tel: 020 7396 6600
Fax: 020 7396 0110
email: cb@curtisbrown.co.uk

Diamond Management
31 Percy Street
London W1T 2DD
Tel: 020 7631 0400
Fax: 020 7631 0500
email: agents@diman.co.uk

ICM
Oxford House
76 Oxford Street
London W1N 0AX
Tel: 020 7636 6565
Fax: 020 7323 0101
US Office
8942 Wilshire Blvd
Beverly Hills, CA 90211
USA
Tel: 001 310 550 4000
Fax: 001 310 550 4100

Jonathan Altaras Associates
13 Short's Gardens
London WC2H 9AT
Tel: 020 7836 8722
Fax: 020 7836 6066

Judy Daish Associates
2 St. Charles Place
London W10 6EG
Tel: 020 8964 8811
Fax: 020 8964 8966

DIRECTORY

Julian Belfrage Associates
46 Albermarle Street
London
W1X 4PP
Tel: 020 7491 4400
Fax: 020 7493 5460

Ken McReddie
91 Regent Street
London W1R 7TB
Tel: 020 7439 1456
Fax: 020 7734 6530

Markham & Froggatt
Julian House
4 Windmill Street
London W1P 1HF
Tel: 020 7636 4412
Fax: 020 7637 5233
email: markham@online.rednet.co.uk

PFD
Drury House
34-43 Russell Street
London WC2B 5HA
Tel: 020 7344 1010
Fax: 020 7836 9544
email: postmaster@pfd.co.uk
Web: www.pfd.co.uk

Richard Stone Partnership
2 Henrietta Street
London WC2E 8PS
Tel: 020 7497 0849
Fax: 020 7497 0869

William Morris Agency
52-53 Poland Street
London
W1F 7LX
Tel: 020 7534 6800
Fax: 020 7534 6900
Web: www.wma.com
US Office
1 William Morris Place
Beverly Hills
CA 90212
USA
Tel: 001 310 859 4000
Fax: 001 310 859 4462

Archives/Footage

Archives and Footage Libraries

4 Clip Sales
c/o ITN Archive
200 Gray's Inn Road
London WC1X 8XZ
Tel: 020 7430 4480
Fax: 020 7430 4453
email: sales@itnarchive.com
Web: www.4clipsales.com
Clip sales from the Channel 4 programme archive.

APTN Library
(Associated Press Television News Library)
The Interchange
Oval Road
Camden Lock
London NW1 7DZ
Tel: 020 7482 7482
Fax: 020 7413 8327
email: info@aptnlibrary.com
Web: www.aptnlibrary.com
Holdings cover international news, entertainment, features and sport.

BBC Worldwide Library Sales
Room E251 Woodlands
80 Wood Lane
London W12 0TT
Tel: 020 8433 2861
Fax: 020 8433 2939
email: uk@bbclibrarysales.com
Web: www.bbclibrarysales.com
Footage suppliers for the BBC television archives and sales agent for CBS News footage.

bfi Archival Footage Sales
21 Stephen Street
London W1T 1LN
Tel: 020 7957 4842
Fax: 020 7436 4014
email: footage.films@bfi.org.uk
Web: www.bfi.org.uk/collections/afs
Access to the materials held in the *bfi*'s National Film and Television Archive. Footage available ranges from the earliest films to documentaries, fiction, home movies, animation and classic and contemporary television. Core collections include British Transport Films, the National Coal Board, ETV and the silent newsreel, Topical Budget.

British Defence Film Library
Chalfont Grove
Narcot Lane
Chalfont St Peter
Gerrard's Cross
Bucks SL9 8TN
Tel: 01494 874 461
Fax: 01494 872 982
Web: www.ssvc.com
Armed forces audio visual training materials.

British Movietonews
Denham Media Park
North Orbital Road
Denham
Middlesex UB9 5HQ
Tel: 01895 833071
Fax: 01895 834893
email: library@mtone.co.uk
Web: www.movietone.com
Includes newsreel archive covering 1929-79.

British Pathe Ltd
c/o ITN Archive
200 Gray's Inn Road
London WC1X 8XZ
Tel: 020 7430 4480
Fax: 020 7430 4453
email: sales@itnarchive.com
Web: www.itnarchive.com
Newsreel archive spanning 1896-1970. The British Pathe archive has been remastered and digitised in its entirety, and can be viewed online.

Canal + Image UK Ltd
Pinewood Studios
Pinewood Road
Iver
Bucks SLO ONH
Tel: 01753 631111
Fax: 01753 655813
British television and feature film catalogue and stock footage library.

Carlton International
(see Granada International below)

Clips & Footage
2nd floor
80A Dean Street
London W1D 3SN
Tel: 020 7287 7287
Fax: 020 7439 4886
email: clipsetc@easynet.co.uk
Web: www.clipsandfootage.com
Stock footage library with research
facilities.

COI Footage File
c/o Film Images
2 The Quadrant
135 Salusbury Road
London NW6 6RJ
Tel: 020 7624 3388
Fax: 020 7624 3377
email: research@film-images.com
Web: www.film-images.com
Films produced by the Central Office of
Information (COI).

Contemporary Films
24 Southwood Lawn Road
London N6 5SF
Tel: 020 8340 5715
Fax: 020 8348 1238
email: inquiries@contemporaryfilms.com
Web: www.contemporaryfilms.com
Archive includes cultural and political
documentary from around the world.

Film Images
2 The Quadrant
135 Salusbury Road
London NW6 6RJ
Tel: 020 7624 3388
Fax: 020 7624 3377
email: research@film-images.com
Web: www.film-images.com
Including films produced by the Central
Office of Information (COI).

Footage Farm Ltd
22 Newman Street
London W1T 1PH
Tel: 020 7631 3773
Fax: 020 7631 3774
email: info@footagefarm.co.uk
Web: www.footagefarm.co.uk
Specialises in US public domain footage.

FremantleMedia Archive Sales
1 Stephen Street
London W1T 1AL
Tel: 020 7691 6733
Fax: 020 7691 6080
email: archive@fremantlemedia.com
Web: www.fremantlemedia.com
Large television archive including Thames
Television.

FRPS
(Film Research & Production Services)
PO Box 28045
London SE27 9WZ
Tel: 020 8670 2959
Fax: 020 8670 1793
email: frps@aol.com
Web: www.filmresearch.co.uk
Contemporary and archival footage and
stills.

Getty Images
17 Conway Street
London W1T 6EE
Tel: 0800 279 9255
email: motion.sales@gettyimages.com
Web: www.gettyimages.com
Incorporating Image Bank Film and
Archive Films as well as royalty-free
collections.

Granada International
c/o ITN Archive
200 Gray's Inn Road
London WC1X 8XZ
Tel: 020 7396 6000
Fax: 020 7430 4453
email: sales@itnarchive.com
Web: www.itnarchive.com
Incorporates the former Granada Visual
and Carlton Television catalogues. Other
former Carlton International collections –
including the ITC, ATV and Rank
collections – are handled directly by
Granada International (Tel: 020 7389
8664, Fax: 020 7389 8745) and not via
ITN Archives.

Huntley Film Archives
191 Wardour Street
London W1F 8ZE
Tel: 020 7287 8000
Fax: 020 7287 8001
email: films@huntleyarchives.com
Web: www.huntleyarchives.com

**Imperial War Museum Film and
Video Archive**
Lambeth Road
London SE1 6HZ
Tel: 020 7416 5291
Fax: 020 7416 5299
email: filmcommercial@iwm.org.uk
Web: www.iwm.org.uk

Index Stock Shots
33 Greenwood Place
London NW5 1LD
Tel: 020 7482 1953
Fax: 020 7482 1967
email: info@indexstockshots.com
Web: www.indexstockshots.com
Stock footage library.

ITN Archive
200 Gray's Inn Road
London WC1X 8XZ
Tel: 020 7430 4480
Fax: 020 7430 4453
email: sales@itnarchive.com
Web: www.itnarchive.com
In addition to ITN's news and feature
output, ITN Archive also handles the
Reuters Television Archive and footage
sales for the Granada Visual archive,
British Pathe and the Channel 4 archive.

Moving Image
Maidstone Studios
Vinters Park
Maidstone
Kent ME14 5NZ
Tel: 01622 684 569
Fax: 01622 687 444
email: mail@milibrary.com
Web: www.milibrary.com
Historical and contemporary, including
British Tourist Authority archives.

OSF
(Oxford Scientific Films)
Network House
Station Yard
Thame, Oxfordshire OX9 3UH
Tel: 01844 262 370
Fax: 01844 262 380
email: film.library@osf.uk.com
Web: www.osf.uk.com
Subsidiary of Southern Star. Stock
footage of wildlife, the natural world,
medicine and science.

DIRECTORY

Reuters
c/o ITN Archive
200 Gray's Inn Road
London WC1X 8XZ
Tel: 020 7430 4480
Fax: 020 7430 4453
email: sales@itnarchive.com
Web: www.itnarchive.com
Newsreel and television news and feature
footage dating from 1896.

Ronald Grant Archive
The Masters House
The Old Workhouse
2 Dugard Way
off Renfrew Road
London SE11 4TH
Tel: 020 7840 2200
Fax: 020 7840 2299
email: pixdesk@rgapix.com
Documentary and fiction film dating from
1896. Large stills archive also.

S4C
Parc Ty Glas
Llanishen
Cardiff
CF4 5DU
Tel: 029 2074 7444
Fax: 029 2027 5444
Web: www.s4c.co.uk
Extract sales of S4C library.

Sky News Library Sales
6 Centaurs Business Park
Grant Way
Isleworth
Middlesex TW7 5QD
Tel: 020 7705 3132
Fax: 020 7705 3201
email: libsales@bskyb.com
Web: www.sky.com

TWI Archive
McCormack House
3 Burlington Lane
London W4 2TH
Tel: 020 8233 5500
Fax: 020 8233 6476
email: twiarchive@imgworld.com
Web: www.twiarchive.com
Archive includes large international sports
collections.

Awards

For British awards ceremonies, all
nominations are given where possible –
winners are listed first and in bold. For
overseas awards, British-based winners
only have been indicated.

**British Academy Television Awards
(BAFTA)**
Awarded 18/4/04, Grosvenor House
Hotel, London
Sponsored by *Radio Times*
TV transmission ITV1 19/4/04; Dir:
Russell Norman, Pr: Rachel Ashdown

Best Actor: Bill Nighy (*State of Play*),
Jim Broadbent (*The Young Visiters*),
Christopher Eccleston (*The Second
Coming*), David Morrissey (*State of Play*)

Best Actress: Julie Walters (*Canterbury
Tales* – 'The Wife of Bath'), Gina McKee
(*The Lost Prince*), Helen Mirren (*Prime
Suspect 6*), Miranda Richardson (*The Lost
Prince*)

Single Drama: *The Deal, Danielle Cable:
Eyewitness, This Little Life, Canterbury
Tales* – 'The Wife of Bath'

**Drama Serial: *Charles II – The Power
and the Passion**, Prime Suspect 6, The
Second Coming, State of Play*

Drama Series: *Buried, Clocking Off,
Foyle's War, William and Mary*

Continuing Drama: *Coronation Street,
The Bill, Casualty, Holby City*

**Comedy Programme or Series: *Little
Britain**, Bo' Selecta!, Creature Comforts –
'Cats or Dogs?', Double Take*

**Situation Comedy: *The Office Christmas
Specials**, Hardware, Marion and Geoff,
Peep Show*

Comedy Performance: Ricky Gervais
(*The Office Christmas Specials*), Martin
Freeman (*The Office Christmas Specials*),

Matt Lucas (*Little Britain*), David
Walliams (*Little Britain*)

**Lew Grade Award for Entertainment
Series or Programme: *Friday Night with
Jonathan Ross**, Ant & Dec's Saturday
Night Takeaway, Have I Got News For
You, Pop Idol*

**Entertainment Performance: Jonathan
Ross** (*Friday Night with Jonathan Ross*),
Stephen Fry (*QI*), Boris Johnson (*Have I
Got News For You*), Paul Merton (*Have I
Got News For You*)

Features: *Wife Swap, Grand Designs,
That'll Teach 'Em, Top Gear*

**Flaherty Documentary Award: *ONE Life*
– 'Lager, Mum and Me'**, *Pompeii – The
Last Day, My Family and Autism, Real Life
– 'Being Terri'*

**Huw Wheldon Award for Factual Series
or Strand: *The National Trust**, Leonardo,
Operatunity, Seven Wonders of the
Industrial World*

News Coverage: *Channel 4 News –* The
Fall of Saddam, *BBC 10 O'Clock News,
Newsnight, Sky News –* The Fall of
Baghdad

Current Affairs: *The Secret Policeman,
Breaking the Silence: Truth & Lies in the
War on Terror* – A Special Report by
John Pilger, *The Fall of Milosevic, Terror
in Moscow*

Sport: Rugby World Cup Final (ITV),
Channel 4 at the Races – Cheltenham
Gold Cup Day, *London Marathon* (BBC),
Test Cricket (Sunset and Vine/C4)

***Radio Times* Audience Award: *Only
Fools and Horses**. Nominations included:
A Touch of Frost, Cold Feet*

**The Alan Clarke Award for Creative
Contribution to Television:** Beryl Vertue

The Dennis Potter Award for Outstanding Writing Within Television: Paul Abbott

The Richard Dimbleby Award for Personal Contribution in Factual: Andrew Marr

The Academy Fellowship: Roger Graef

BAFTA Television Craft Awards

Awarded 16/5/04, The Dorchester Hotel, London

Costume Design: Mike O'Neill (*Charles II: The Power and the Passion*), Lyn Avery (*The Mayor of Casterbridge*), Annie Hardinge (*Little Britain*), Sammy Sheldon (*Canterbury Tales* – 'The Wife of Bath')

Editing Factual: Sean Mackenzie (*Arena* – 'The Many Lives of Richard Attenborough'), Mark Gravil (*Ancient Egyptians* – 'The Battle of Megiddo'), Chris King (*Days That Shook The World* – 'Hiroshima'), Steve Stevenson (*George Orwell: A Life In Pictures*)

Editing Fiction/Entertainment: Mark Day (*State Of Play*), Clare Douglas (*The Lost Prince*), St John O'Rorke (*Prime Suspect*), Paul Knight (*Spooks*)

Graphic Design: Tim Varlow (*Restoration*), Christine Buttner (*Cambridge Spies*), David Freeman, Will Skinner (*Natural World*), Tim Varlow (*Film 2003*),

Make Up & Hair Design: Lisa Cavalli-Green (*Little Britain*), Kate Benton, Diane Chenery-Wickens (*Dead Ringers*), Karen Hartley-Thomas (*Charles II: The Power and the Passion*), Liz Tagg (*The Lost Prince*)

New Director Factual: Oli Barry (*The Nine Lives of Alice Martineau*), Will Anderson (*Surviving Extremes* – 'The Swamp'), Paul Berczeller (*ALT TV* – 'This Is A True Story'), Jamie Jay Johnson (*ALT TV* – 'Holiday Around My Bedroom')

New Director Fiction: Sarah Gavron (*This Little Life*), Andrew Lincoln (*Teachers*), Gabriel Range (*The Day Britain Stopped*), Tim Supple (*Twelfth Night*)

New Writer: Rosemary Kay (*This Little Life*), Helen Blakeman (*Pleasureland*) Terry Cafolla (*Holy Cross*), Jack Lothian (*Teachers*)

Original Television Music: Nicholas Hooper (*The Young Visiters*), Geoffrey Burgon (*The Forsyte Saga*), Nicholas Hooper (*State Of Play*), Adrian Johnston (*The Lost Prince*)

Photography Factual: Peter Greenhalgh (*Ancient Egyptians* – 'The Battle of Megiddo'), Jeff Baynes (*George Orwell: A Life In Pictures*), Peter Greenhalgh (*Colosseum*), Mike Spragg (*Seven Wonders of the Industrial World* – 'Hoover Dam')

Photography & Lighting Fiction/Entertainment: Ryszard Lenczewski (*Charles II: The Power and the Passion*), Barry Ackroyd (*The Lost Prince*), David Higgs (*Cambridge Spies*), Chris Seager (*State Of Play*)

Production Design: John-Paul Kelly (*The Lost Prince*), Sarah Greenwood (*Charles II: The Power and the Passion*), Mike Gunn (*Cambridge Spies*), Stephen Fineren (*The Forsyte Saga*)

Sound factual: Trevor Hotz, Paul Parsons, Graham Haines (*Operatunity*), Paul Hamblin, Tim Owens, Max Bygrave (*Ancient Egyptians* – 'The Battle of Megiddo'), Peter Davies, Paul Cowgill, Paul Cooper (*Elephants: Spy In the Herd*), Samantha Handy, Zubin Sarosh, Dion Stuart (*Living With Michael Jackson*)

Sound Fiction/Entertainment: Simon Okin, Stuart Hilliker, Jamie McPhee, Pat Boxshall (*State Of Play*), Richard Manton, Bernard O'Reilly, André Schmidt, Hugh Johnson (*Cambridge Spies*), John Taylor, Paul Hamblin, Catherine Hodgson, Lee Critchlow (*Charles II: The Power and the*

Passion), Simon Okin, Ben Baird, Nick Roberts (*Prime Suspect*)

Visual Effects: Max Tyrie, Tim Greenwood, Jez Gibson-Harris, Jamie Campbell (*Sea Monsters – A Walking With Dinosaurs Trilogy*), Grahame Andrew, Rob Harvey, Julian Parry, Abbie Tucker-Williams (*Ancient Egyptians* – 'The Battle of Megiddo'), Aidan Farrell, Barney Jordan (*George Orwell: A Life In Pictures*), Max Tyrie, George Roper, Jez Gibson-Harris, Jamie Campbell (*Land of the Giants – A Walking With Dinosaurs Special*)

Special Award: Adrian Wood – Film Researcher/Archivist

8th BAFTA Children's Film and Television Awards

Awarded 30/11/03, London Hilton Hotel In association with the LEGO company (only Television Awards listed)

Animation: *Bob the Builder Special - A Christmas to Remember* (Jackie Cockle, Sarah Ball; HOT Animation/HIT Entertainment/BBC), *Albie*, *Bounty Hamster*, *Pongwiffy*

Drama: *Bootleg* (The Production Team/Burberry Productions/CBBC/BBC1), *Behind Closed Doors*, *My Parents are Aliens*, *The Story of Tracy Beaker*

Entertainment: *The Raven* (Colin Nobbs, Bob Harvey, Brian Ross; CBBC Scotland/CBBC), *Globo Loco*, *Rule the School*, *You Can Do Magic*

Factual: *Blue Peter* – launch of the Tanzania Water Appeal (Steve Hocking, Richard Marson, Kez Margrie; CBBC/BBC1), *Get the Skinny*, *Rad and the Grommets Tour*, *The Really Wild Show*

Presenter: Matt Baker (*Blue Peter*, BBC), Angelica Bell (CBBC), Christian Stevenson (*Rad and the Grommets Tour*), Reggie Yates (*Smile*)

Pre-school animation: *Hilltop Hospital* (Pascal Le Notre, Robin Lyons; Siriol/CITV), *Boo, Tiny Planets, Yoko! Jakamoko! Toto!*

Pre-school live action: *Ripley and Scuff* (Robert Howes, Tim Scott, Neil MacLennan; The Children's Company/CITV), *Balamory, Boohbah, Fimbles*

Schools Drama: *Lion Mountain* (Hilary Durman, Ray Harrison Graham; BBC/Resource Base), *Extra: Une Étoile est Née, Stopping Distance, Twelfth Night*

Schools Factual – Primary: *Let's Write a Story: Writing Academy* (Sarah Miller, Patrick Reams; CBBC Education/BBC2), *New Kid in Class, Primary Geography: Water, Primary History: Saxons and Vikings*

Schools Factual – Secondary: *The English Programme: Film Focus: Animation – Food Commercials* (Ingrid Falck; Channel Four/Double Exposure), *Cool Keys, Curriculum Bites: English, Curriculum Bites: Interpretations*

International: *Arthur* (Lesley Taylor, Pierre Valette, Greg Bailey; BBC/WGBH Educational Foundation/Cinar), *Don't Blame the Koalas, Eight Simple Rules For Dating My Teenage Daughter, That's So Raven*

Best Writer: Alex Williams for *Sir Gadabout: The Worst Knight in the Land*, Tony Collingwood (*Yoko! Jakamoko! Toto!*), Mary Morris (*The Story of Tracy Beaker*), Carol Noble (*Girls in Love*)

Outstanding creative contribution to children's programming: Christopher Grace

Broadcasting Press Guild Television Awards 2003
Awarded 26/3/04, Theatre Royal, Drury Lane

Best Single Drama: *The Lost Prince* (Talkback/WGBH for BBC 1)

Best Drama Series/Serial: *State of Play* (Endor for BBC1)

Best Documentary Series: *Wife Swap* (RDF Media for Channel 4)

Best Single Documentary: *The Kennedy Assassination: Beyond Conspiracy* (P J Productions for BBC 2)

Best Entertainment: *Little Britain* (BBC 3 for BBC 2)

Best Actor: Bill Nighy (*State of Play, The Young Visiters, The Lost Prince*)

Best Actress: Julie Walters (*Canterbury Tales* – 'The Wife of Bath', *The Return*)

Best Performer (Non-Acting): Paul Merton (*Have I Got News for You, Room 101*)

Writer's Award: Paul Abbott (*State of Play*)

Multichannel Award: *Reporters At War: Dying To Tell The Story* (Discovery Channel)

Harvey Lee Award for Outstanding Contribution to Broadcasting: Greg Dyke

61st Golden Globe Awards
Awarded 25/1/04, Beverly Hilton, Beverly Hills, Los Angeles by the Hollywood Foreign Press Association

Best Television Series – Musical Or Comedy: *The Office*

Best Performance by an Actor in a Television Series – Musical or Comedy: Ricky Gervais (*The Office*) (This was the first time a British TV comedy series has ever won a Golden Globe)

44th Golden Rose of Montreux
Awarded 17/4/04
Eleven awards to British productions/ talent

Best Comedy: *Creature Comforts* (Aardman Animations)

Best Game Show: *My New Best Friend* (Tiger Aspect/C4)

Best Reality Show: *Wife Swap* (RDF)

Best Sitcom: *Peep Show* (C4)

Best Variety: *Ant and Dec's Saturday Night Takeaway* (Granada)

Press Prize: *Little Britain* (BBC)

Best Male Comedy Performance: Harry Hill (*Harry Hill's TV Burp*)

Best Male Sitcom Performance: Martin Freeman (*Hardware*)

Best Male Soap Performance: Shane Richie (*EastEnders*)

Best Game Show Performance: Ant McPartlin and Declan Donnelly (*Ant and Dec's Saturday Night Takeaway*)

Best Pilot: *Fur TV* (BBC)

44th Monte Carlo Television Festival
Awarded 28/6/04 – 3/7/04, The Grimaldi Forum

European TV Producer Award: Company Pictures (for past two years' output including *Shameless, White Teeth, Sons and Lovers*)

Outstanding European Drama Producer: Company Pictures (George Faber, Charlie Pattinson, Paul Abbott, Matthew Jones for *Shameless*)

Television Films Gold Nymphs
Best Performance by an Actor: Benedict Cumberbatch (*Hawking*)

Mini-Series Gold Nymphs
Best Script: Paul Abbott (*State of Play*)

Drama Gold Nymphs
Outstanding Actress: Anne-Marie Duff (*Shameless*)

Format Gold Nymphs
Best Reality Format: *Wife Swap* (RDF)
Best Gameshow Format: *Who Wants to be a Millionaire?* (Celador)
Best Scripted Format: *Love Bugs* (Distraction)

Best 24-hour News Programme: BBC News 24 Holy Festival bombings, March 2004 (Director: Simon Waldman)

Prix Amade: *Orphans of Nkandla* (True Vision Productions)

Monaco Red Cross Prize: *Orphans of Nkandla* (True Vision Productions)

Royal Television Society Awards

RTS Programme Awards 2003
Awarded 16/3/04

Actor Female: Kate Ashfield (*This Little Life*, BBC Films & The Film Council/

Common Features/Northern Production Fund/Yorkshire Media Production Agency/Studio of the North for BBC 2), Bronagh Gallagher (*Holy Cross*, BBC NI/RTÉ for BBC 1), Joanne Froggatt (*Danielle Cable: Eyewitness*, Granada for ITV1)

Actor Male: David Morrissey (*The Deal*, Granada for Channel 4), Antony Sher (*Home*, BBC Fictionlab for BBC 4), Bill Nighy (*State of Play*, Endor for BBC 1)

Arts: *Operatunity* (Diverse for Channel 4), *George Orwell: A Life in Pictures* (Wall to Wall for BBC 2), *Jump London* (Optomen for Channel 4)

Children's Drama: *Girls in Love* (Granada Kids for CITV), *The Illustrated Mum* (Granada Kids for Channel 4), *Bus Life: Bad Hair Day* (Disney Channel)

Comedy Performance: David Walliams & Matt Lucas (*Little Britain*, BBC New Comedy for BBC 3), Jocelyn Jee Esien (*3 Non Blondes*, Brown Eyed Boy for BBC 3), Ricky Gervais (*The Office Christmas Specials*, BBC for BBC 1)

Daytime Programme: *Britain's Secret Shame* (BBC Daytime/BBC Current Affairs for BBC 1), *Trisha* (Anglia for ITV1), *Richard & Judy* (Cactus for Channel 4)

Documentary Series – General: *The Last Peasants* (October for Channel 4), *National Trust* (Oxford Film & Television for BBC 4), *Surviving Extremes* (Keo Films.com/AAC FACT for Channel 4)

Drama Serial: *State of Play* (Endor for BBC 1), *The Lost Prince* (Talkback/BBC Films/WGBH Boston for BBC 1), *The Second Coming* (Red for ITV1)

Drama Series: *Spooks* (Kudos for BBC 1), *At Home with the Braithwaites* series 4 (Yorkshire for ITV1), *Teachers* series 3 (Tiger Aspect for Channel 4)

Entertainment: *Little Britain* (BBC New Comedy for BBC 3), *Ant & Dec's Saturday Night Takeaway* (Granada for ITV1), *Bo' Selecta!* (TalkbackTHAMES for Channel 4)

Entertainment Performance: Jonathan Ross (*Friday Night With Jonathan Ross*, Open Mike for BBC 1), Ant & Dec (*Ant & Dec's Saturday Night Takeaway/ I'm A Celebrity ... Get Me Out Of Here!/ Pop Idol*), Mark Steel (*Mark Steel Lectures*, BBC New Comedy for BBC 4)

Event: Comic Relief 2003: *The Big Hair Do* (BBC Entertainment for BBC 1)

History: *Georgian Underworld: Invitation to a Hanging* (Juniper for Channel 4), *Killing Hitler* (Diverse for BBC 2), *Colosseum* (BBC Specialist Factual for BBC 1)

Judges' Award: Greg Dyke

Network Newcomer – Behind The Screen: Sarah Gavron, Director (*This Little Life*, BBC Films/The Film Council/Common Features/Northern Production Fund/Yorkshire Media Production Agency/Studio of the North for BBC 2), Helen Blakeman, Writer (*Pleasureland*, Kudos for Channel 4), Avie Luthra, Writer (*Canterbury Tales:* The Sea Captain's Tale', Ziji Productions for BBC 1)

Network Newcomer – On Screen: Katie Lyon (*Pleasureland*, Kudos for Channel 4), Marc Wootton (*My New Best Friend*, Tiger Aspect for Channel 4), Harry Eden (*Real Men*, BBC Scotland for BBC 2)

Presenter (Factual): Melvyn Bragg (*The Adventure of English/The South Bank Show*), Nigel Marven (*Sea Monsters & Land of Giants*, Impossible Pictures for BBC 1), Ben Lewis (*Art Safari*, Bergmann Pictures for BBC 4)

Regional Presenter: Gerry Anderson (*Anderson In ...*, Green Inc. for BBC 1 NI), Lucinda Lambton (*Sublime Suburbia*, Clementine/Carlton London), Michele Newman (*It's Your Shout/ Pulling Power*, Carlton Central)

Regional Programme: *Christine's Children* (Double Band Films for BBC 1 NI), *Chancers* (Tern for BBC 1 Scotland)

Science & Natural History: *Motherland – A Genetic Journey* (Takeaway Media for BBC 2), *Seven Wonders of the Industrial World* (BBC Specialist Factual for BBC 2), *DNA* (Windfall for Channel 4)

Single Documentary – General: *The Secret Policeman* (BBC Documentaries & Contemporary Factual for BBC 1), *ONE Life – 'Size Doesn't Matter'* (BBC Documentaries & Contemporary Factual for BBC 1), *Living with Michael Jackson* (Granada for ITV1)

Single Drama: *This Little Life* (BBC Films/The Film Council/Common Features/Northern Production Fund/Yorkshire Media Production Agency/Studio of the North for BBC 2), *Larkin: Love Again* (World Productions for BBC 2), *The Deal* (Granada for Channel 4)

Situation Comedy and Comedy Drama: *The Office Christmas Specials* (BBC Entertainment for BBC 1), *Marion & Geoff* (Baby Cow for BBC 2), *Peep Show* (Objective for Channel 4)

Soap: *Coronation Street* (Granada for ITV), *Doctors* (BBC Birmingham for BBC 1), *EastEnders* (BBC 1)

Writer: Paul Abbott (*State of Play*, Endor for BBC1), Terry Cafolla (*Holy Cross*, BBC NI/RTÉ for BBC 1), Russell T. Davies (*The Second Coming*, Red for ITV1)

Features and Factual Entertainment: *Holiday Showdown* (RDF Media for ITV1), *Wife Swap* (RDF Media for Channel 4), *How Clean Is Your House?* (TalkbackTHAMES for Channel 4)

Children's Programme: *UP2U* (WisedUp for CITV), *Dick & Dom in Da Bungalow* (CBBC for the CBBC/BBC 1), *Jungle Run* (Granada Kids for CITV)

RTS International Award: *24* Season 2 (Real Time/Imagine/Twentieth Century Fox Television), *Six Feet Under* (HBO), *Sex and the City* (HBO)

RTS Craft & Design Awards 2002-3

Awarded 17/11/03, Le Meridien Grosvenor House, London

Costume Design – Drama: Odile Dicks-Mireaux (*The Lost Prince*, Talkback/BBC Films/WGBH Boston for BBC 1), Michael Johnson (*Cutting It*, BBC Drama Serials for BBC 1), Mike O'Neill (*Daniel Deronda*, BBC/WGBH Boston for BBC 1)

Costume Design – Entertainment & Non Drama: Annie Hardinge (*Little Britain*, BBC New Comedy for BBC 3), Stephen Adnitt (*Gladiator: Benn v Eubank*, Zig Zag Productions for Five), Annie Hardinge (*The Boosh* (pilot), Baby Cow for BBC 3)

Design & Craft Innovation: John Downer, Michael W Richards, Geoffrey Bell & Stuart Napier (*Elephants: Spy in the Herd*, John Downer Productions for BBC 1), Mark Brownlow & Andrew Sneath (*Wildlife Special: Smart Sharks – Swimming with Roboshark*, BBC Natural History Unit for BBC1), *Channel 4 News* Production Team (ITN for Channel 4)

Graphic Design – Programme Content Sequences: Rob Hifle & Jason Mullings, Burrell Durrant Hifle (*Smash Hits Awards*, Done and Dusted for Channel 4), BBC Post Production Design Bristol (*Collision Course*, BBC Factual & Learning), BBC Post Production Design Bristol (*Monsters We Met*, BBC Natural History Unit)

Graphic Design – Titles: Dimitri Kevgas (*What the World Thinks of America*, BBC 2), Paul Tigwell at Burrell Durrant Hifle (*Great Britons*, BBC 2), Tim Varlow at Liquid TV (*Restoration*, Endemol UK for BBC 2)

Graphic Design – Trails & Packaging: Brand Identity Team, Lambie Nairn (BBC 3 Brand Identity), Brand Identity Team, Lambie Nairn (BBC 2 Brand Identity)

Judges' Award: *I'm A Celebrity ...Get Me Out Of Here!* team

Lifetime Achievement: Brian Pearce

Lighting, Photography & Camera – Lighting for Multicamera: Darryl Noad (*Re:Covered*, Blaze for BBC 3), Martin Kempton (*I'm Alan Partridge*, Talkback for BBC 2), Geoff Stafford (*Songs of Praise: Salisbury Christmas*, BBC Religion and Ethics for BBC 1)

Lighting, Photography & Camera – Multicamera Work: Camera Team *The Abyss – Live* (BBC Natural History Unit), Chris Howe, Ben Frewin, Jim Parsons & Rachel Squire (*Re:Covered*, Blaze for BBC 3), Production and Camera Team (*Wild in Your Garden*, BBC Natural History Unit)

Lighting, Photography & Camera – Photography Documentary & Factual & Non Drama Production: Roger Chapman (*The Last Peasants*, October Films for Channel 4), Charlie Hamilton-James & Jamie McPherson (*Natural World: My Halcyon River*, BBC Natural History Unit), Camera Team *Fighting the War* (BBC Documentaries and Contemporary Factual for BBC 2)

Lighting, Photography & Camera – Photography Drama: Chris Seager (*State of Play*, Endor for BBC 1), Alan Almond BSC (*Messiah 2: Vengeance is Mine*, BBC NI/Paramount International Television/Vengeance Films for BBC1), Blasco Giurato & Chris Plevin (*Dr Zhivago*, Granada for ITV1)

Make Up Design – Drama: Jessica Taylor (*Cutting It*, BBC 1), David Myers (*The Forsyte Saga II*, Granada for ITV1), Jan Sewell (*Messiah 2: Vengeance is Mine*, BBC 1)

Make Up Design – Entertainment & Non Drama: Lisa Cavalli-Green (*Little Britain*, BBC 3), Helen Barrett (*Bremner, Bird & Fortune* Series 4, Vera for Channel 4), Leigh Francis and the team (*Bo' Selecta!*, Talkback for Channel 4)

Music – Original Score: Rob Lane (*Daniel Deronda*, BBC/WGBH for BBC 1), Murray Gold (*The Second Coming*, Red for ITV1), *Dextrous – Feltham Sings* (Century/Films of Record for Channel 4)

Music - Original Title Music: Chris Elliott (*The British Empire in Colour*, TWI/Carlton for ITV1), Norman Cook (*Fatboy Slim: Musical Hooligan*, BBC Sport for BBC 3), Rob Lane (*Hearts of Gold*, BBC Wales for BBC 1)

Production Design – Drama: Don Taylor (*Daniel Deronda*, BBC/WGBH for BBC 1), Rob Harris (*Hornblower*, Meridian/A&E for ITV), Donal Woods (*State of Play*, Endor for BBC 1)

Production Design – Entertainment & Non Drama Productions: Peter Gordon (*The Day Britain Stopped*, Wall to Wall for BBC 2), Derek Brown & Michael Mosley (*Leonardo: The Man Who Wanted to Know Everything*, BBC Specialist Factual for BBC 1), Xiang Hai Ming (*Fight School*, Granada for Sky One)

Sound – Drama: Ian Richardson (*Tomorrow La Scala!*, Home Movies/BBC Films/the Film Council), Simon Okin, Stuart Hilliker, Jamie McPhee & Pat Boxshall (*State of Play*, Endor for BBC 1), Sound Team, *Dr Zhivago* (Granada for ITV

Sound – Entertainment & Non Drama Productions: Sound Team *Fighting the War* (BBC Documentaries and Contemporary Factual for BBC 2), Bob Jackson & Viorel Ghiocel (*The Last Peasants*, October Films for Channel 4), Owen Newman, Lucy Rutherford & Andrew Wilson (*Natural World: Cats under Serengeti Stars*, BBC Natural History Unit for BBC 2)

Tape & Film Editing – Documentary & Factual: Ollie Huddleston (*The Last Peasants*, October for Channel 4), Mitch Baker (*The Nine Lives of Alice Martineau*, Thames for BBC 3)

Tape & Film Editing – Drama: Tony Cranstoun (*The Second Coming* and *Danielle Cable: Eyewitness*), Mark Day (*State of Play*, Endor for BBC 1), Andrew Hulme (*White Teeth*, Company Pictures for Channel 4), Pete Drinkwater (*Peter Cook - At a Slight Angle to the Universe*, BBC 2)

Tape & Film Editing – Entertainment & Situation Comedy: Pete Hallworth (*Phoenix Nights II*, Ovation for Channel 4), Tony Cranstoun (*Early Doors*, Ovation for BBC 2), Graham Hodson (*Marion & Geoff* Series 2, Baby Cow for BBC 2)

Team Prize: Angus Macqueen, Roger Chapman, Claudia Murg & Iris Maor (*The Last Peasants*, October Films for Channel 4), *Channel 4 News* Production Team (ITN), Craft & Design Team, *The Lost Prince* (Talkback/BBC Films/WGBH for BBC 1)

Picture Enhancement: Gerry Gedge, Phil Moss & Steve Moore (*The British Empire in Colour*, TWI/Carlton for ITV1), Jonathon Prosser & Adrian Woodward, BBC Post Production Design Bristol (*Monsters We Met*, BBC Natural History Unit/Discovery/Animal Planet for BBC), Aidan Farrell, The Farm (*Darwin's Daughter*, Tiger Aspect for Channel 4)

Visual Effects – Special Effects: Tom Harris, Any Effects (*Hornblower*, Meridian/A&E for ITV1), Simon Frame & Simon Carr (Men From Mars) and Pavel Sagner (Flash Barendorf) (*Dr Zhivago*, Granada for ITV1), Alex Gurucharri, Any Effects (*The Day Britain Stopped*, Wall to Wall for BBC 2)

Visual Effects – Digital Effects: The Framestore CFC Team (*Walking With Dinosaurs Special*, Impossible Pictures for BBC 1), Shane Warden, Pepper (*Trouble in Tahiti*, BBC Wales), Shane Warden & Simon Giblin, Pepper (*Tipping the Velvet*, Sally Head Productions for BBC 2)

The RTS Television Journalism Awards 2002-3
Awarded 24/2/04

Camera Operator of the Year: Darren Conway (BBC 4/BBC 1), Rob Bowles (ITV1), Fred Scott (BBC 1/BBC 4)

Current Affairs – Home: *Cot Death - Real Story with Fiona Bruce* (BBC 1), *ID Snatchers - Kenyon Confronts* (BBC 1),

Seroxat: Emails from the Edge – Panorama (BBC 1)

Current Affairs – International: *In The Line of Fire – Panorama* (BBC 1), *Breaking the Silence – Truth and Lies in the War on Terror* (Carlton/ITV1), *The Killing Zone – Dispatches* (Channel 4)

Innovation: *Reporting the Courts* – Sky News, CNN's Digital Newsgathering, APTN Direct, Associated Press Television News

Judges Award
This year the award is dedicated to the memory of and to show our respect for all those who died working in Iraq in the pursuit of the high quality television news (read by Will Wyatt CBE, President, RTS)

News – Home: Ulster Racism (BBC 1), Chatroom Dangers (BBC 1), Dodgy Dossier – *Channel 4 News*

News – International: Welcome To Baghdad – *ITV News*, Friendly Fire – *BBC Ten O'Clock News*, Liberia – James Brabazon for *Newsnight* (BBC 2)

News Channel of the Year: Sky News

News Event: Iraq War – Channel Four, The Iraq War – BBC 1, War In Iraq – Sky News

Presenter of the Year: John Stapleton (GMTV), Mark Austin (ITV1), Jon Snow (Channel 4)

Programme of the Year: *Living with Michael Jackson* (Granada)

Regional Current Affairs: *Loyalists at War - Spotlight* (BBC Northern Ireland), *Rough Sleepers – Crimefighters* (Chameleon/Yorkshire Television), *A Tale of Torture – Frontline Scotland* (BBC1 Scotland)

Regional Daily News Magazine: *Scotland Today* (Scottish TV), *BBC London News* (BBC London)

Specialist Journalism: Hilary Andersson (BBC 1/BBC 4), Tim Marshall (Sky News), Rageh Omaar (BBC 1)

Television Journalist of the Year: John Irvine (ITV1), Lindsey Hilsum (Channel 4), James Mates (ITV1)

Young Journalist of the Year: Mark Daly for *The Secret Policeman* (Documentaries and Contemporary Factual BBC 1), Ben Anderson (BBC 2), Ben D'Arcy (Central News South)

Regional Daily News Magazine: *Meridian Tonight* (South)

News Programme of the Year: *ITV Evening News*, *BBC Ten O'Clock News*, *Channel 4 News*

RTS Technical Innovation Awards 2003
Awarded 3/11/03, Bafta, 195 Piccadilly, London

Innovative Applications: QScript advanced autocue system

Advanced Engineering Technniques: VISTA – EPG with speech recognition/synthesis capability for visually-impaired users
British Sky Broadcasting Limited, City University London, University of East Anglia, The Victoria University of Manchester, Televirtual Limited and Sensory Inc. for the Independent Television Commission

Judges' Award: The Pace Development Team 1994-2002, for their contribution to the advancement of digital broadcasting, early recognition of digital broadcasting and innovative approaches to technological design.

RTS Student Television Awards 2003

Sponsored by JVC Professional
Awarded 7/5/04 at The Magic Circle, Centre for the Magic Arts, 12 Stephenson Way, London

Undergraduate Animation: *The Birds and The Bees* by Gemma Manger, Southampton Institute

Postgraduate animation: *Coming Home* by Gemma Carrington, Tora Young, Sarah Bartles-Smith, Angela Feeney & Jake Roberts, National Film & Television School

Undergraduate Factual: *High Flyers* by Jean Devlin & Shona Mullen, Dublin Institute of Technology

Postgraduate Factual: *Riles* by Ditsi Carolino, Sadhana Buxani, Valerio Bonelli, Peter Marquez, Martin Jensen & Bradley Miles, National Film and Television School

Undergraduate Non-Factual: *Rocket Boy Roger* by Russell Holliss & James Robinson, Hull School of Art & Design

Postgraduate Non-Factual: *Little Scars* by Jan Bauer, Teresa Mulqueen, Tanja Koop, Helle le Fevre & David Schweitzer, National Film & Television School

RTS Television Sports Awards 2003

Awarded 24/5/04, London Hilton Hotel, London W1

Creative Sports Sequence : *Rugby World Cup Final: Happy The Man* (ISN/Granada Sport for ITV Sport), *Six Nations Grandstand: Whisper It Softly* (BBC TV Sport), *The Premiership: The Premiership Titles* (Carlton/ISN for ITV Sport)

Judges' Award: Martin Hopkins

Lifetime Achievement Award: Richie Benaud OBE

Live Outside Broadcast Coverage of the Year: Channel 4 Cricket 2003 (Sunset + Vine), Rugby World Cup Final

(ISN/Granada Sport for ITV Sport), UEFA Champions League: Manchester United v Real Madrid (Carlton/ISN for ITV Sport)

Regional Sports Actuality Programme: *The Championship* (BBC Northern Ireland), *NatWest Island Games 2003* (Channel Television), *Soccer Sunday* (Granada Television, Manchester)

Regional Sports Presenter or Commentator: Alistair Mann (Granada Television, Manchester), Roger Johnson (BBC South Today), Stephen Watson (BBC Northern Ireland)

Regional Sports Programme: *Big Six* (BBC Northern Ireland), *George Reynolds – Playing By His Own Rules* (BBC North East and Cumbria for BBC 1), *Kicking It Around – Christmas Special* (Carlton Television for ITV Central)

Sports Commentator: Steve Cram (BBC TV Sport), Clive Tyldesley (ITV Sport), Eddie Butler (BBC TV Sport)

Sports Documentary: *The Real John Curry* (Granada Television for Channel 4), *Bare Knuckle Boxer* (Juniper for Channel 4), *Inside the Mind of Paul Gascoigne* (Seek for Channel 4)

Sports Feature: *Grand National: Johnny Vegas – Super Jockey* (BBC TV Sport), *Jonathan Pearce's Football Night* – Leeds Feature (Sunset + Vine for five), *On The Ball* – Notts County (Carlton/ISN for ITV Sport)

Sports Innovation: *Sunday Grandstand – Silverstone Flying Lap* (BBC TV Sport), UEFA Champions League Final 2003 – Wire-Cam (Carlton/ISN for ITV Sport), Wales Rally GB – WRC Live (Chrysalis Television for Channel 4)

Sports News Reporter: Sue Turton (ITN for Channel 4 News), Adam Parsons (BBC News for BBC 1), James Pearce (BBC News 24)

Sports Presenter: Clare Balding (BBC TV Sport), Steve Rider (BBC TV Sport), Jim Rosenthal (ITV Sport)

Sports Programme of the Year: *Rugby World Cup Final* (ISN/Granada Sport for ITV Sport), Channel 4 Cricket 2003 (Sunset + Vine for Channel 4), *Channel 4 Racing* – Cheltenham Gold Cup (Highflyer Productions for Channel 4)

Sports Pundit: Michael Johnson (BBC TV Sport), François Pienaar (ITV Sport), Andy Townsend (ITV Sport)

Sports Show or Series: *Grand National Preview: The Night Before the National* (BBC TV Sport), *The Premiership On Monday* (Carlton/ISN for ITV Sport), Channel 4 Cricket 2003: *The Cricket Show* (Sunset + Vine for Channel 4)

Television and Radio Industries Club (TRIC) Awards

Awarded 9/3/04, Grosvenor House Hotel, London

Satellite/Digital TV Personality: Jeremy Thompson
Radio/Digital Radio Personality: Jonathan Ross
TV Personality: Jonathan Ross
Sports Presenter/Reporter: Gabby Logan
Newscaster/Reporter: Mary Nightingale
Weather Presenter: Michael Fish
New TV Talent: Christopher Parker (Spencer Moon, *EastEnders*)
TV Music and Arts Programme: *The Big Read*
Satellite/Digital TV Programme: *Soccer AM*
Radio/Digital Radio Programme: *Woman's Hour*
TV Comedy Programme: *Absolutely Fabulous*
TV Drama Programme: *Charles II: the Power and the Passion*
TV Morning/Daytime Programme: *BBC Breakfast*
TV Entertainment Programme: *Relocation, Relocation*
TV Soap of the Year: *Coronation Street*
TRIC Special Award: Alan Titchmarsh

Awards section compiled by Alistair McGown

Careers

Information about careers in the media industries is available from a number of sources and we have provided details of some of these in this section, but you should note no-one is likely to provide individually-tailored information. The most exciting development for young people hoping to get into the industry is the emergence of the skillsformedia helpline and website (see below).

Many people are attracted to the media industries because they seem glamorous, but they can be difficult to get into. Anyone wanting to work in these industries should anticipate the need to update their skills regularly, and offering a range of skills rather than just one may be to an applicant's benefit. It is important that anyone considering working in the industry takes care to investigate what courses are available (see Courses section for a selection of courses currently on offer) and if possible, although this is rarely easy, talk to someone already doing the kind of job they want. You may discover that they managed to 'get a foot in the door' and then using initiative and skill worked their way towards the job they now have: this may indicate that formal qualifications are only part of the picture, but you can be fairly certain that such people have had to work and train hard, possibly for little reward, and that this kind of opportunity is becoming less common.

Sources for company contacts

It is still a common practice for prospective employees to solicit work through mailing their CV. There are online sources (visit the Contacts section at www.bfi.org.uk/gateway) but these are not as comprehensive as those in the standard directories for the UK film, television and video industries.

These sources include:

BFI Film Handbook
Kay's UK Production Manual
Kemp's Film and TV Yearbook
The Knowledge
Pact Directory
Production Guide

Although the Pact directory contains a modest amount of companies, its listings are very thorough and detailed. They include company personnel and production credits both past and projected. It also contains very handy indexes including one of production company by programme type (eg comedy, documentary etc). It is also a good deal cheaper than its peers but remains steadfastly in hard copy and its contents are not available on the web, unlike some others (eg www.theknowledgeonline.com)

Sources for jobs

Newspapers and Journals
Saturday and Monday edition of the Guardian contain a Creative, Media and Sales Jobs section in its Media supplement, which is well worth consulting. The trades press such as *Broadcast* also contain job adverts, but these tend to be aimed at people already in the industry.

The next step is to consult the specialist subscription listings. However, they tend to be expensive. Below are the two main listings which are available from the bfi National Library.

PCR (Production and Casting Report)
PCR
PO Box 100
Broadstairs
Kent
CTO IUJ
Tel: 01843 860885
Fax: 01843 866538
Web: www.pcrnewsletter.com
Weekly detailed listing for upcoming film, television and theatre productions seeking cast. Back page lists casting directors for ongoing feature productions and upcoming/long-running TV programmes. May need to be used in conjunction with Who's Where directory available from PCR

Programme News (Bulletin)
Profile Group (as above)
Tel: 020 7440 8558
email: info@programmenews.co.uk
Web: www.programmenews.co.uk
Listing of upcoming television programmes and reported stage of development. Contains contact details

Useful Bibliography

A Careers Handbook for TV, Radio, Film, Video & Interactive Media
Llewellyn, Shiona
A&C Black, 2000
ISBN 0713656981

Getting Into Films & Television
Angell, Robert
How To Books, 7th ed. 2002
ISBN 1857037715

Lights, Camera, Action! Careers in Film, Television, Video
Langham, Josephine
BFI, 2nd ed. 1997
ISBN 0851705731

Research for Media Production
Chater, Kathy
Focal Press, 2nd ed. 2002
ISBN 02405 16486

Training Organisations

4 Skills
c/o 4th Floor Warwick House
9 Warwick Street
London W1R SLY
Tel: 020 7734 5141
Fax: 020 787 9899
email: ft2@ft2.org.uk
Web: www.ft2.org.uk Sharon Goode
Managed by ft2, this is Channel 4's
biennial training programme for people
from ethnic minority backgrounds wishing
to train as new entrants in junior
production grades

ARTTS Skillcentre
Highfield Grange
Bubwith
North Yorkshire YO8 6DP
Tel: 01757 288088
Fax: 01757 288253
email: admin@artts.co.uk
Web: www.artts.co.uk
ARTTS Skillcenter offers a fully
residential, one-year training course for
Theatre, Film, Television and Radio.
Trainees have the opportunity to
specialise in Acting, Directing or
Production Operations. The courses are
100 per cent practical and hands-on.
Courses commence in April and October
each year

Cyfle (& Media Skill Wales)
Gronant, Penrallt Isaf
Caemarfon
Gwynedd LL55 INS
Tel: 01286 671000
Fax: 01286 678831
email: post@cyfle.co.uk
Web: www.cyHe.co.uk
This organisation supports the training

needs of the Welsh film and television
industry..

FT2 - Film & Television Freelance Training
4th Floor
Warwick House
9 Warwick Street
London W1R SLY
Tel: 020 7734 5141
Fax: 020 787 9899
email: ft2@ft2.org.uk
Web: www.ft2.org.uk
FT2 is the only UK-wide provider of new
entrant training for young people wishing
to enter the freelance sector of the
industry in the junior construction,
production and technical grades. Funded
by the Skillset Investment Funds,
European Social Fund and Channel 4, FT2
is the largest industry managed training
provider in its field and has a 100 per
cent record of people graduating from the
scheme and entering the industry. FT2 is
also an approved Assessment Centre and
offers assessment to industry
practitioners for the Skillset Professional
Qualifications

Gaelic Television Training Trust
Sabhal Mor Ostaig
An Teanga
IsleofSkye IV448RQ
Tel: 01471 888 000
Fax: 01471 888 001
Web: www.smo.uhi.ac.uk

Lighthouse
9-12 Middle Street
Brighton BN1 1AL
Tel: 01273 384222
Fax: 01273 384233
email: info@lighthouse.org.uk
Web: www.lighthouse.org.uk
Training and production centre providing
courses, facilities, and production advice.
Bursaries offered 3 times a year

Northern Film and Media
Central Square
Forth Street
Newcastle-upon-Tyne NE1 3PT
Tel: 0191 269 9200
Fax: 0191 269 9213
email: training@noithernmedia.org

Web: www.northernmedia.org Annie
Wood

Northern Ireland Film and Television Commission (NIFTC)
3rd Floor Alfred House
21 Alfred Street
Belfast BT2 8ED
Tel: 01232 232444
Fax: 01232 239918
email: info@niftc.co.uk
Web: www.niftc.co.uk

Skillset
Prospect House
80-110 New Oxford Street
London WC1A 1HB
Tel: 020 7520 5757
Fax: 020 7520 5758
email: info@skfllset.org
Web: www.skillset.org
Skillset is the sector skills council for
broadcast film and video.

Skillsformedia.com
Tel: 08080 300 900
This is the UK's only specialist media
advise service and is the joint initiative of
Skillset, the Sector Skills Council and
BECTU, the industry trades union. It is
available to anyone wanting to get in or
get on in the media. The website has case
studies, a useful glossary of job titles and
descriptions, and resources to investigate.
Telephone 08081 008 094 for industry
careers advice

The Regional Training Consortium for the South West
59 Prince Street
Bristol BS1 4QH
Tel: 0117 925 4011
Fax: 0117 925 3511
email: info@swscreenco.uk
Web: www.skillnetsouthwest.com

Paying Your Way

It is important to be clear on the cost of any course you embark on and sources of grants or other funding. Generally speaking, short courses do not attract grants but your local authority or careers office may be able to advise on this. Check directories of sources for grants at your local library. The main ones are the Directory of Grant-Making Trusts, Directory of Small Grant-Making Trusts, Charities Action Foundation.

Learn Direct may also be able to advise. They are on 0800 100 900 with a (multilingual) website at www.learndirect.co.uk. (Learn Direct, PO Box 900, Manchester M60 3LE)

Commissioners & Controllers

The resignation of Greg Dyke as BBC DG and the restructuring of ITV post-merger has led to a round of more executive changes than is usual in 2003-4. The ripples of these events are still being felt and as a result one or two posts were still vacant at time of going to press 31/8/04.

BBC TV

Director-General: Mark Thompson
Deputy Director-General: Mark Byford
Director of Television: Jana Bennett
Business and Finance: Bal Samra
Director, Television BBC Independent Executive: Elaine Bedell

Director of New Media and Technology: Ashley Highfield
Head of Interactive: Emma Somerville
Head of Fictionlab and New Media: Richard Fell

Controller BBC 1: Lorraine Heggessey
Controller BBC 2: Roly Keating
Controller BBC 3: Stuart Murphy
Controller BBC 4: Janice Hadlow
Controller of Daytime: Alison Sharman
Commissioning Executive (Daytime, Factual): Dominic Vallely
Commissioning Executive (Daytime, Entertainment): Gilly Hall

Senior Commissioning Executive (BBC 4): Richard Klein
Senior Commissioning Editor (BBC 3): Celia Taylor

BBC Creative Director, Director of Drama, Entertainment and Children's Television: Alan Yentob

Drama

Controller Commissioning, Drama: Jane Tranter

Head of Genre Management and Business Affairs, Drama: Felicity Milton
Controller, Drama Series and Serials: Mal Young
Head of Drama Serials: Laura Mackie
Head of Drama, Independents Commissioning: Gareth Neame
Head of Films and Single Drama: David Thompson
BBC Films Executive Producer and Head of Development: Tracey Scoffield
Controller, Innovation and Factual Drama: Susan Spindler
Creative Director, New Writing: Kate Rowland
BBC Scotland, Head of Drama: Barbara McKissack
Executive in Charge of Production, Scotland: Christine MacLean
BBC Wales, Head of Drama: Julie Gardner
BBC Northern Ireland, Head of Drama: Patrick Spence

Entertainment

Head of Entertainment Group: Wayne Garvie
Controller Commissioning, Entertainment: Jane Lush
Head Of Genre Management & Business Affairs, Entertainment: Claire Evans
Proposals Co-ordinator, Peak Time Entertainment: Beth Hurran
Creative Head of Entertainment Events: Bea Ballard
Head of Comedy: Sophie Clark Jervoise
Head of Comedy Entertainment: Jon Plowman
BBC Scotland, Head of Comedy and Entertainment: Mike Bolland
BBC Northern Ireland, Head of Events, Entertainment and Sport: Mike Edgar
Commissioning Editor Independents, Wales: Martyn Ingram
BBC Manchester, Managing Editor Entertainment: Helen Bullough

Children's Television

Controller, CBBC: Dorothy Prior
Head of Pre-School: Clare Elstow
Head of Entertainment: Anne Gilchrist
Head of News and Factual: Roy Milani
Head of Drama: Elaine Sperber
Development Executive: Amanda Gabbitas
Programme Finance Manager: Sally Carroll
Head of Legal and Business Affairs: Tim Morley
Head of CBBC Scotland: Donalda MacKinnon
Head of Acquisitions: Michael Carrington

Factual and Learning

Director of Factual and Learning: John Willis
Controller of Factual TV: Glenwyn Benson
Head of Genre Management And Business Affairs: Anne Sullivan

Controller of Learning and Interactive, Commissioner New Media: Liz Cleaver
Controller, Children's Education: Frank Flynn
Project Leader, Digital Curriculum: Anne Eastgate
Creative Director for Learning: Nick Ware
Executive Editor, Children's Television: Karen Johnson
Editor, Education, Scotland: Moira Scott
Editor, Learning, Northern Ireland: Kieran Hegarty
Head of Education and Learning, Wales: Eleri Wyn Lewis

Controller of Documentaries and Contemporary Factual: Anne Morrison
Head of Independent Commissioning, Documentaries and Contemporary Factual: Jo Clinton-Davis
Head of Documentaries: Alan Hayling
Commissioner, Documentaries and Contemporary Factual: Tom Archer
Commissioning Executives: Maxine Watson, Helena Appio
Creative Director, Factual Entertainment: Vicki Barrass

Creative Director, Homes and Gardens: Owen Gay
Development Executive: Nicky Colton/Sara Brailsford
Commissioning Editor (ONE Life): Todd Austin
Commissioning Editor (Storyville): Nick Fraser
Head of Independent Commissioning, Specialist Factual, Current Affairs and Arts: Adam Kemp
Commissioner, Specialist Factual: Emma Swain
Creative Director of History: Laurence Rees
Creative Director of Science: John Lynch
Head of Religion and Ethics: Alan Bookbinder

Commissioner, Arts and Culture: Franny Moyle
Arts and Culture, Executive Editor: Jacquie Hughes
Head of TV Classical Music and Performance: Peter Maniura
Creative Director of Arts: Mark Harrison
Head of Topical Arts Unit: George Entwistle

Head of BBC Natural History Unit: Neil Nightingale
Creative Director of General Documentaries (Manchester): Ruth Pitt
Head of General Factual Programmes (Bristol): Mark Hill
Head of Programmes (Birmingham): Tessa Finch
Creative Directors, Factual Entertainment: David Mortimer, Andy Batten-Foster
Head and Commissioner of Current Affairs and Investigations: Peter Horrocks
Senior Commissioning Executive, Current Affairs: Lucy Hetherington
Creative Director Investigations: Alex Holmes
Creative Director, Events: Nick Vaughan-Barrett

Commissioner, Lifeskills: Seetha Kumar

Head of Factual Programmes, Scotland: Andrea Miller

Head of Factual Programmes, Wales: Adrian Davies
Head of Arts, Wales: Paul Islwyn Thomas
Head of Music (Outside London) and Entertainment, Wales: David Jackson
Head of Factual Programmes, Northern Ireland: Fiona Campbell
Head of Arts, Northern Ireland: Declan McGovern

Nations and Regions

Director, Nations and Regions: Pat Loughrey
Controller, Scotland: Ken MacQuarrie
Controller, Wales: Menna Richards
Controller, English Regions: Andy Griffee
Controller, Northern Ireland: Anna Carragher
Controller Network Development, Nations and Regions: Colin Cameron
Head of Production, Scotland: Nancy Braid
Commissioning Editor, Television, Scotland: Ewan Angus
Head of Programmes in English, Wales: Clare Hudson
Head of Broadcast, Northern Ireland: Peter Johnston
Head of Production Operations, Scotland: Nick Hawkins
Business and Finance Manager, Northern Ireland: Peter Morrow
Programme Finance Manager, Wales: Pauline Sandford

Sport

Director of Sport: Peter Salmon
Head of New Media, Sports News and Development: Andrew Thompson
Head of Sports Programmes and Planning: Pat Younge

Programme Acquisitions

Controller, Programme Acquisitions: George McGhee
Head of Films: Steve Jenkins
Head of Series: Sue Deeks
Business Development Manager: Paul Egginton

News

Director of News: Helen Boaden
Deputy Director of News: Mark Damazer
Head of TV News: Roger Mosey
Director of World Service and Global
News: Richard Sambrook

Worldwide

Director of Worldwide: Vacant (Rupert
Gavin resigned July 2004)
Independents Unit Director:
Helen Jackson
Independents Unit Commercial
Manager: Aine Doherty
Independents Unit Senior Legal and
Business Manager: Lisa Cfas
Business Development Manager,
Broadband and Interactive:
Sian Teesdale

ITV

Chief Executive: Charles Allan
Chief Executive, ITV Broadcasting:
Mick Desmond

Director of Programmes: Nigel Pickard
Head of Programme Strategy: David
Bergg
Controller of Drama: Nick Elliott
Head of Drama: Jenny Reeks
Head of Continuing Series: Corinne
Hollingsworth
Controller of Entertainment: Claudia
Rosencrantz
Head of Entertainment: Tony Everden

Controller of Factual: Bridget Boseley
Controller of Commissioned
Programmes, ITV2 and Factual
Editor, ITV1: Daniela Neuman
Controller of Comedy: Sioned Wiliam
Controller of Off-Peak Programming
And Children's Programming:
Steven Andrew
Deputy Controller of Children's
Programming/Editor CITV:
Estelle Hughes
Controller of Off-Peak Programme
Strategy: Stephen Price

Editor of Daytime: Nick Thorogood
Controller of Night-Time: Carol Groves
Controller of Current Affairs, Arts and
Religion: Steve Anderson
Controller of Sport: Brian Barwick
Controller of Network Acquisitions:
Jeremy Boulton
Channel Editor ITV2: Zai Bennett
Head of Regional Programmes:
Ian Squires
Managing Director, London:
Christy Swords

Channel 4

Chief Executive: Andy Duncan
Deputy Chief Executive: David Scott
Sales Director: Andy Barnes
Controller of Acquisitions:
June Drumgoole
Head of Acquired Programming:
Jay Kandola
Head of Nations and Regions:
Stuart Cosgrove
Head of 4-Learning: Heather Rabatts

Director of Television: Kevin Lygo

Managing Editor, Commissioning:
Janey Walker
Manager, Commissioning:
Helen Robertson
Producer, Talent Development:
Charlotte Black
Editorial Manager, Cultural Diversity:
Mary Fitzpatrick

Head of Comedy: Caroline Leddy
Commissioning Editor, Comedy: Vacant
(Iain Morris leaves August 2004)

Head of Entertainment: Andrew Newman
Commissioning Editor, Entertainment:
Kate Taylor

Head of Documentaries: Peter Dale
Commissioning Editor, Documentaries:
Hilary Bell
Commissioning Editor, Documentaries
and Cutting Edge: Danny Cohen
Deputy Commissioning editor,
Documentaries: Sam Bickley
Head of Science and Education:
Simon Andrae

Editor, Independent Film and Video:
Jess Search
Head of Drama: John Yorke
Commissioning Editor, Drama:
Lucy Richer
Editor, Drama: Hannah Weaver
Head of Film: Tessa Ross

Head of Factual Entertainment:
Julian Bellamy
Editor, Factual Entertainment:
Sharon Powers
Editor, Factual Entertainment:
Nav Raman
Editor, Factual Entertainment:
Andrew MacKenzie
Editor, Cross-platform Development:
Debbie Searle

Head of Features: Sue Murphy
Commissioning Editor, Features:
Liam Humphreys
Head of Daytime: Adam MacDonald
Editor, Daytime: Mark Downie
Deputy Commissioning Editor, Daytime,
Features and Documentaries:
Bridget Bakokodie

Head of News and Current Affairs:
Dorothy Byrne
Editor, Investigations: Kevin Sutcliffe
Editor, News and Current Affairs: Mark
Rubens

Head of History and Religion: Hamish
Mykura
Editor, History: Ralph Lee
Editor, Religion: Aaquil Ahmed

Commissioning Editor, Arts and
Performance: Jan Younghusband
Commissioning Editor, Schools and
Youth: Deborah Ward
Editor, Education: Simon Dickson

Head of Sport: Dave Kerr
Deputy Editor, Sport: Deborah Poulton

Head of T4 and Scheduling:
Jules Oldroyd
Editor, Music and Youth: Neil McCallum

Head of E4: Murray Boland
Commissioning Editor, E4:
Deborah O'Connor

five

Chief Executive: Jane Lighting
Director of Programmes: Dan Chambers
Managing Editor and Director of Acquisitions: Jeff Ford
Factual Acquisitions Executive: Bethan Corney
Head of Co-productions: Lilla Hurst

Senior Controller, News, Current Affairs and Documentaries: Chris Shaw
Deputy Controller, News, Current Affairs and Documentaries: Ian Russell
Head of Documentaries: Nick Godwin
Controller, Features and Entertainment: Ben Frow
Head of Comedy (in collaboration with Paramount comedy channel): Graham Smith
Deputy Controller, Features and Entertainment: Angela Jain
Head of Factual Entertainment: Steve Gowans
Commissioning Editor, Factual Entertainment: Vacant
Deputy Commissioning Editor, Factual Entertainment: Ian Dunkley
Controller of Arts, Daytime and Religion: Kim Peat
Controller of History: Alex Sutherland
Controller of Science: Justine Kershaw
Controller of Special Events and Pop Features: Sham Sandhu
Controller of Children's TV: Nick Wilson
Controller of Sport: Robert Charles

S4C

Director of Programmes: Iona Jones
Head of Factual: Cenwyn Edwards
Head of Light Entertainment: Huw Chiswell
Head of Drama: Angharad Jones
Commissioning Editor, Children's Programmes: Siwan Jobbins
Director of International Business: Huw Walters

Multichannel

Sky

Chief Executive: James Murdoch
Chief Operating Officer: Richard Freudenstein
Managing Director, Sky Networks: Dawn Airey
Deputy Head of Networks and Director of Film Channels and Acquisitions: Sophie Turner Laing
Head of Sky Sports: Vic Wakeling
Controller, Sky One: James Baker
Director of Original Programming, Sky One: Jo Wallace
Sky One, Head of Factual: Matthew Paice
Sky One, Commissioning Editor Factual Entertainment: Paul Crompton
Head of History and Biography Channels: Richard Melman
Managing Director, Artsworld: John Hambley

Discovery Channel UK

Director of Programmes: Vacant
Deputy Channel Commissioner: Hannah Barnes

Flextech

Managing Director: Lisa Opie
Head of Living TV, Director of Programmes Bravo TV: Richard Woolfe
Head of Challenge TV and Trouble: Jonathan Webb
Commissioning Editor, Challenge TV and Trouble: Louise Lynch
Controller, UKTV: John Keeling
Head of Factual, UKTV: Charlotte Ashton
Head of Entertainment and Drama, UKTV: Matt Tombs
Head of Lifestyle, UKTV: Vacant

Sci-Fi Channel Europe

Director of Programmes: Vlad Lodzinski

Cartoon Network

Head of Channels: Richard Kilgariff

Nickelodeon

Director of Programming: Howard Litton

MTV

Vice-President of Programming and Development: Chris Sice

Paramount Comedy Channel

Managing Director: Tony Orsten
Director of Programming: Heather Jones
Paramount Head of Programming: Sarah Mahoney

Courses

The courses listed below represent a small selection of those which are available in the UK. The listing focuses on full-time undergraduate and postgraduate level courses although there are many short courses and further education courses on offer. The selection also focuses on those courses which have a higher practical component than academic or theoretical.

Details of courses can be found at www.bfi.org.uk/education/courses/mediacourses which also gives further information about entrance requirements as well as an indication in percentage terms of the practical component of each course.

Undergraduate

The Bournemouth Media School
Bournemouth University
Talbot Campus
Fern Barrow
Poole, Dorset
BH12 5BB
Contact: The Programme Administrator
Tel: 01202 595351
Fax: 01202 595099
email: bmsugrad@bournemouth.ac.uk
Web: media.bournemouth.ac.uk
Course: BA (Hons) Television Production

University of Central England in Birmingham
Perry Barr
Birmingham
B42 2SU
Contact: Dr D.C. Paton
Tel: 0121 331 5460
email: Dan.Paton@uce.ac.uk
Web: www.uce.ac.uk
Course: BSc (Hons) Television Technology and Production (run in association with Sandwell College)

University of Central Lancashire
Department of Technology
Preston
PR1 2HE
Contact: Dr Martyn Shaw
Tel: 01772 893249
Fax: 01772 892915
email: mjshaw@uclan.ac.uk
Web: www.uclan.ac.uk
Course: BSc (Hons) Television Production

University of Derby
Kedleston Road
Derby
DE22 1GB
Contact: Admissions Office
Tel: 01332 591167
Fax: 01332 597754, 01332 597749
email: admissions@derby.ac.uk
Web: www.derby.ac.uk
Course: BA (Hons) Film and Television

Edinburgh College of Art
School of Visual Communication
74 Lauriston Place
Edinburgh
EH3 9DF
Contact: Noè Mendelle
Tel: 0131 221 6114
Fax: 0131 221 6100
email: viscom@eca.ac.uk
Web: www.eca.ac.uk
Course: BA (Hons) Visual Communication (Film and Television)

University of Huddersfield
School of Music and Humanities
Queensgate
Huddersfield
West Yorkshire
HD1 3DH
Contact: Chris Prior
Tel: 01484 422288
Fax: 01484 478428
email: mediaadmissions@hud.ac.uk
Web: www.hud.ac.uk
Course: BA (Hons) Media and Television Production

International Film School Wales
University of Wales College, Newport
School of Art, Media and Design
Caerleon Campus
PO Box 179
Newport
NP18 1YG
Contact: Humphry Trevelyan
Tel: 01633 432 954
Fax: 01633 432 885
email: humphry.trevelyan@newport.ac.uk
Web: http://www.ifsw.newport.ac.uk
Course: BA (Hons) Documentary Video and Television

University of Lincoln
Faculty of Art, Architecture and Design
Brayford Pool
Lincoln
LN6 7TS
Contact: Jane Bird
Tel: 01522 837 171
Fax: 01522 837 135
email: jbird@lincoln.ac.uk
Web: www.lincoln.ac.uk
Course: BA (Hons) Digital and Interactive Television (run at Hull)

London College of Music and Media
Thames Valley University
St Mary's Road
Ealing
London
W5 5RF
Contact: Tony Nandi
Tel: 020 8231 2638
Fax: 020 8231 2546
email: photography@tvu.ac.uk
Web: mercury.tvu.ac.uk/photoimaging
Course: BA (Hons) Film and Television Studies (with additional options such as Video Production, Advertising etc)

University of Luton
Department of Media Arts
75 Castle Street
Luton
Beds
LU1 3AJ
Tel: 01582 734111
Fax: 01582 489014

DIRECTORY

Web: www.luton.ac.uk/MediaArts/
Course: BA (Hons) Television Production

Middlesex University
Television Department
School of Arts
Trent Park
Bramley Road
London
N14 4YZ
Contact: Professor Alan Fountain
Tel: 07767 371 478
email: alan5@mdx.ac.uk
Web: www.mdx.ac.uk
Course: BA (Hons) Television Production

University of Reading
Department of Film, Theatre and
Television
Bulmershe Court
Woodlands Avenue
Earley
Reading
RG6 1HY
Contact: Teresa Murjas, Alastair Phillips
Tel: 0118 931 8878
Fax: 0118 931 8873
email: e.a.silvester@reading.ac.uk
Web: www.rdg.ac.uk/FD
Course: BA (Hons) Film and Theatre,
and Television Studies

**Royal Scottish Academy of Music
and Drama**
100 Renfrew Street
Glasgow
G2 3DB
Contact: Russell Boyce
Tel: 0141 332 4101
Fax: 0141 270 8351
Course: BA (Hons) Digital Film and
Television

St Helens College
College of Arts
Town Centre Campus
Brook Street
St Helens
Merseyside
WA10 1PZ
Contact: Millard Parkinson
Tel: 01744 623218
Fax: 01744 623400
email: mparkinson@sthelens.ac.uk
Web: www.sthelens.ac.uk

Course: BA (Hons) Television and Video
Production

University of Salford
Faculty of Arts, Media and Social Sciences
School of Media, Music and Performance
Adelphi, Peru Street
Salford
Manchester
M3 6EQ
Contact: Admissions
Tel: 0161 295 6026
Fax: 0161 295 6023
email: r.humphrey@salford.ac.uk
Web: www.salford.ac.uk
Course: BA (Hons) Television and Radio

Sandwell College
Lakeside Studios
Crocketts Lane
Smethwick
B66 3BU
Contact: George Kingsnorth
Tel: 0121 331 7440
email: george.kingsnorth@tic.ac.uk
Web: www.sandwell.ac.uk
Course: BSc (Hons) Television
Technology and Production

University of Surrey Roehampton
Erasmus House
Roehampton Lane
London
SW15 5PU
Contact: Enquiries Office
Tel: 020 8392 3232
Fax: 020 8392 3148
email: enquiries@roehampton.ac.uk
Web: www.roehampton.ac.uk
Course: BA and BSc (Hons) Television
Studies

Technology Innovation Centre
Millennium Point
Curzon Street
Birmingham
B4 7XG
Contact: Stephen Gordon
Tel: 0121 331 7436
Fax: 0121 331 5401
email: stephen.gordon@tic.ac.uk
Web: www.tic.ac.uk
Course: BSc (Hons) Television
Technology and Production

University of Teesside
School of Arts and Media
Middlesbrough
Tees Valley
TS1 3BA
Contact: Admissions
Tel: 01642 384019
Fax: 01642 384099
email: arts@tees.ac.uk
Web: www.tees.ac.uk
Course: BA (Hons) Television Production
Professional Practice

University of Westminster
School of Media, Arts and Design
Harrow Campus
Watford Road
Northwick Park
Harrow
HA1 3TP
Contact: Admissions Office
Tel: 020 7911 5903
Fax: 020 7911 5955
email: harrow-admissions@wmin.ac.uk
Web: www.wmin.ac.uk/harrow
Course: BA (Hons) Film and Television
Production

York St John
College of the University of Leeds
Lord Mayor's Walk
York
YO31 7EX
Contact: Dr Robert Edgar-Hunt
Tel: 01904 716672
Fax: 01904 716931
email: r.edgar@yorksj.ac.uk
Web: www.yorksj.ac.uk
Course: BA (Hons) Film and Television
Production

Design Your Future

P C A D
MADE IN PLYMOUTH

BIPP Professional Qualifying Exam
Photography, Film and Television

BA (Hons)
PhotoMedia and Design Communication
Environmental Visual Communications

Foundation Degree
Animation and Creative Media
Moving Image Production
Multimedia
Photography and Electronic Imaging

BTEC National Diploma
Audio
Moving Image
Photography

City and Guilds
Photography (6924 and 6923)

For more information contact

Plymouth College of Art and Design
01752 203434
enquiries@pcad.ac.uk
www.pcad.ac.uk

PROFESSIONAL FILM TRAINING FROM SCRIPT TO SCREEN TAUGHT BY FILMMAKERS

The LFA is "a much needed addition to training for an industry that needs all the talent and skills it can get"
Lord Puttnam

"The LFA provides students with a solid grounding in all areas of film-making. An appreciation of the workings of each department is crucial to be successful in any role in film"
Stewart Le Maréchal
(Associate producer "Wondrous Oblivion")

LFA COURSES:

FILM-MAKING DIPLOMA
(1 year, Sep & Feb intakes)

INTRO TO FILM-MAKING CERTIFICATE
(4 wks, full-time or 8 wks part-time)

SHORT COURSES IN FILM-MAKING
(incl. AVID Xpress DV, Short Film Production)

London Film Aacademy is a non profit making trust.

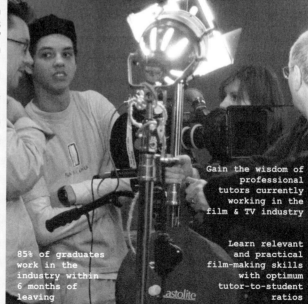

Gain the wisdom of professional tutors currently working in the film & TV industry

Learn relevant and practical film-making skills with optimum tutor-to-student ratios

85% of graduates work in the industry within 6 months of leaving

LONDONFILMACADEMY.COM   T. 020 7386 7711
THE OLD CHURCH, 52A WALHAM GROVE, LONDON SW6 1QR   E. INFO@LONDONFILMACADEMY.COM

DIRECTORY

Postgraduate

National Film and Television School
Beaconsfield Studios
Station Road
Beaconsfield
Bucks
HP9 1LG
Contact: The Registry
Tel: 01494 731425/731413
Fax: 01494 674042
email: admin@nftsfilm-tv.ac.uk
Web: www.nftsfilm-tv.ac.uk
Course: Offer various options for postgraduate MA in Film and Television (eg. Producing, Editing, Scriptwriting)

The Bournemouth Media School
Bournemouth University
Talbot Campus
Fern Barrow
Poole, Dorset
BH12 5BB
Contact: Jacki Simmons
Tel: 01202 595745
Fax: 01202 595530
email: bmspgrad@bournemouth.ac.uk
Web: media.bournemouth.ac.uk
Course: MA in Television Production

Brighton – University of Brighton
School of Computing, Mathematical and Information Sciences
Watts Building
Lewes Road
Brighton
BN2 4GJ
Contact: Richard Griffiths
Tel: 01273 642 477
Fax: 01273 642 405
email: r.n.griffiths@brighton.ac.uk
Web: www.brighton.ac.uk/interactive/courses/postgrad/aboutmsc.htm
Course: MSc in Digital Television Management and Production

Falmouth College of Arts
Woodlane
Falmouth
Cornwall
TR11 4RH
Contact: Admissions
Tel: 01326 211 077
Fax: 01326 213 880
email: admissions@falmouth.ac.uk
Web: www.falmouth.ac.uk
Course: PgDip in Television Production

Goldsmiths College
University of London
New Cross
London
SE14 6NW
Contact: Admissions Office
Tel: 020 7919 7060 (PG Enquiries)
email: admissions@gold.ac.uk
Web: www.goldsmiths.ac.uk
Course: MA in Television Documentary; MA in Television Drama

Royal Holloway
University of London
Department of Media Arts
Egham
Surrey
TW20 0EX
Contact: Susanna Capon
Tel: 01784 443734
Fax: 01784 443832
email: s.capon@rhul.ac.uk
Web: www.rhul.ac.uk/media-arts
Course: MA in Producing Film and Television

Salford – University of Salford
Faculty of Arts, Media and Social Sciences
School of Media, Music and Performance
Adelphi, Peru Street
Salford
Manchester
M3 6EQ
Contact: Admissions
Tel: 0161 295 6026
Fax: 0161 295 6023
email: r.humphrey@salford.ac.uk
Web: www.salford.ac.uk
Course: MA and PgDip in Television Features and Documentary Production

Sunderland – University of Sunderland
School of Arts, Design and Media
Ashburne House
Backhouse Park
Ryhope Road
Sunderland
SR2 7EF
Contact: Media Admissions
Tel: 0191 515 3593
Fax: 0191 515 2132
email: student-helpline@sunderland.ac.uk
Web: http://www.sunderland.ac.uk
Course: MA in Media Production (Television and Video)

"Knowing how a process works liberates the imagination. Progress in filmmaking is inconceivable to me without a formal education in cinema – for me it was two years at LFS"

MICHAEL MANN

LFS graduate
1967

The LFS
two-year six-film
MA FILMMAKING
programme
starts in
September,
January
and May

MA validated by

LONDON
metropolitan
university

lfs.org.uk
+44 (0)20 7836 9642

THE LONDON FILM SCHOOL

The Society for Cinema and Media Studies

SCMS

2005 Conference Announcement

The Institute of Education
University of London
Bedford Way

Thursday, 31 March 2005
through
Sunday, 3 April 2005

Our 2005 conference aims to promote dialogue and communication among colleagues across national borders. In addition to panels and workshops focusing on film, television, video and electronic media and a *Screen* sponsored panel on European Cinema 2000-2005, three special plenaries will examine the current state of theory and criticism, the issues of nationalism, inter-nationalism and transnationalism, and television and new media. Among the speakers for the special plenaries are Richard Dyer, Thomas Elsaesser, Gertrud Koch and Laura Mulvey.

For more information on the conference or to register to attend:
www. cmstudies.org or

e-mail inquiry to:
office@cmstudies.org

DIRECTORY

Events

Banff Television Festival

1350 Railway Avenue
Canmore
Alberta
Canada
T1W 3E3
Tel: 001 403 678 9260
Fax: 001 403 678 9269
Web: www.btvf.com
International event for programme makers and content creators in television and new media.
Dates: June

BAFTA Television Awards

British Academy of Film and Television Arts
195 Piccadilly
London
W1J 9LN
Tel: 020 7734 0022
Fax: 020 7734 1792
Web: www.bafta.org.
Dates: April and May (Craft Awards).

British Television Advertising Awards

3rd Floor, 37 Berwick Street
London
W1V 3RF
Tel: 020 7734 6962
Fax: 020 7437 0748
Web: www.btaa.co.uk
Dates: March

British Television Advertising Craft Awards

3rd Floor, 37 Berwick Street
London
W1V 3RF
Tel: 020 7734 6962
Fax: 020 7437 0748
Web: www.btaa.co.uk
Dates: 2004 1 November

Broadcast Production Show

EMAP Media
33-39 Bowling Green Lane
London
EC1R 0DA
Tel: 020 7505 8329.
Fax: 020 7505 8335.

Web: www.productionshow.com
Dates: Earls Court 2, 1-3 June 2005

International Emmy Awards

International Academy of Television Arts and Sciences
142 West 57th Street, 16th Floor
New York
NY 10019
USA
Tel: 001 212 489 6969.
Fax: 001 212 489 6557.
Web: www.iemmys.tv
The 32nd International Emmy Awards Gala will take place in New York City on 22 November 2004.

Media Guardian Edinburgh International TV Festival

1st Floor
17-21 Emerald Street
London
WC1N 3QN
Tel: 020 7430 1333.
Fax: 020 7430 2299.
Web: www.mgeitf.co.uk
Dates: last weekend in August

MILIA (Cannes)

c/o Reed Midem Organisation UK
Walmer House
295 Regent Street
London
W1B 3AB
Tel: 020 7528 0086.
Fax: 020 7895 0949.
Web: www.milia.com
World interactive content forum.

MIPCOM (Cannes)

c/o Reed Midem Organisation UK
Walmer House
295 Regent Street
London
W1B 3AB
Tel: 020 7528 0086
Fax: 020 7895 0949
Web: www.mipcom.com
International marketplace for entertainment content.
Dates: 4-8 October 2004

MIPCOM – Junior (Cannes),

c/o Reed Midem Organisation UK
Walmer House
295 Regent Street
London
W1B 3AB
Tel: 020 7528 0086.
Fax: 020 7895 0949.
Web: www.mipcomjunior.com
Mipcom children and youth event.
Dates: 2-3 October 2004

MIP-DOC (Cannes)

c/o Reed Midem Organisation UK
Walmer House
295 Regent Street
London
W1B 3AB
Tel: 020 7528 0086.
Fax: 020 7895 0949.
Web: www.mipdoc.com
Mipcom documentary event.
Dates: 9-10 April 2005

MIP-TV (Cannes)

c/o Reed Midem Organisation UK
Walmer House
295 Regent Street
London
W1B 3AB
Tel: 020 7528 0086
Fax: 020 7895 0949
Web: www.miptv.com
International television programme market
Dates: 11-15 April 2005

Monte Carlo Television Festival

4 Boulevard du jardin Exotiqute
MC 98000
Monaco
Tel: 00337 93 104060
Fax: 00337 93 507014
Web: www.tvfestival.com
Festival and Golden Nymph Awards.
Dates: June/July

Film Distributors

NATPE

2425 Olympic Boulevard, Suite 600E
Santa Monica
California 90404
USA
Tel: 001 310 453 4440
Fax: 001 310 453 5258
Web: www.natpe.org
Annual conference and exhibition from
the leading association for content
professionals.
Dates: NATPE 2005, January 25-27,
Tuesday-Thursday, Mandalay Bay Resort,
Las Vegas

Rose D'Or Festival

(Golden Rose of Montreux)
P.O. Box 5511
CH - 3001 Bern
Switzerland
Tel: 0041 31 318 3737
Fax: 0041 31 318 3736
Web: www.rosedor.com
Festival for entertainment television
programming and annual awards.
Dates: April

Royal Television Society Programme Awards

Holborn Hall
100 Gray's Inn Road
London
WC1X 8AL
Tel: 020 7430 1000.
Fax: 020 7430 0924.
Web: www.rts.org.uk.
Dates: March

Arrow Film Distributors

18 Watford Road
Radlett
Herts WD7 8LE
Tel: 01923 858306
Fax: 01923 859673
email: info@arrowfilms.co.uk
Web: www.arrowfilms.co.uk

Artificial Eye Film Company

14 King Street
London WC2E 8HR
Tel: 020 7240 5353
Fax: 020 7240 5242
email: info@artificial-eye.com
Web: www.artificial-eye.com

Axiom Films

12 D'Arblay Street
London W1V 3FP
Tel: 020 7287 7720
Fax: 020 7287 7740
email: mail@axiomfilms.co.uk
Web: www.axiomfilms.co.uk

bfi Distribution

21 Stephen Street
London W1T 1LN
Tel: 020 7957 8935
Fax: 020 7580 5830
email: bookings.films@bfi.org.uk
Web: www.bfi.org.uk

Blue Dolphin

40 Langham Street
London W1W 7AS
Tel: 020 7255 2494
Fax: 020 7580 7670
email: info@bluedolphinfilms.com
Web: www.bluedolphinfilms.com

Buena Vista International

3 Queen Caroline Street
London W6 9PE
Tel: 020 8222 1000
Fax: 020 8222 2795
Web: www.bvimovies.com

Cinéfrance

12 Sunbury Place
Edinburgh EH4 3BY
Tel: 0131 225 6191
Fax: 0131 225 6971
email: info@cinefrance.co.uk
Web: www.cinefrance.co.uk

Columbia TriStar Films (UK)

Europe House
25 Golden Square
London W1R 6LU
Tel: 020 7533 1111
Fax: 020 7533 1105
Web: www.sonypictures.co.uk

Entertainment Film Distributors

Eagle House
108-110 Jermyn Street
London SW1Y 6HB
Tel: 020 7930 7744
Fax: 020 7930 9399

Eros International

Unit 23, Sovereign Park
Coronation Road
London NW10 7QP
Tel: 020 8963 8700
Fax: 020 8963 0154
email: eros@erosintl.co.uk
Web: www.erosentertainment.com

Gala

26 Danbury Street
London
N1 8JU
Tel: 020 7226 5085
Fax: 020 7226 5897

Guerilla Films

35 Thornbury Road
Isleworth
TW7 4LQ
Middlesex
Tel: 020 8758 1716
Fax: 020 8758 9364
email: info@guerilla-films.com
Web: www.guerilla-films.com

DIRECTORY

ICA Projects
12 Carlton House Terrace
The Mall
London SW1Y 5AH
Tel: 020 7766 1416
Fax: 020 7306 0122
Web: www.ica.org.uk

Icon Film Distributors
The Quadrangle
4th Floor
180 Wardour Street
London W1F 8FX
Tel: 020 7494 8100
Fax: 020 7494 8151
Web: www.iconmovies.co.uk

Metrodome Distribution
33 Charlotte Street
London W1T 1RR
Tel: 020 7153 4421
Fax: 020 7153 4401
Web: www.metrodomegroup.com

Millivres Multimedia
Unit M
32-34 Spectrum House
London NW5 1LP
Tel: 020 7424 7461
Fax: 020 7424 7401
email: info@millivres.co.uk
Web: www.millivresmultimedia.co.uk

Miracle Communications
38 Broadhurst Avenue
Edgware
Middlesex HA8 8TS
Tel: 020 8958 8512
Fax: 020 8958 5112
email: martin@miracle63.freeserve.co.uk

Momentum Pictures
2nd Floor 184-192 Drummond Street
London NW1 3HP
Tel: 020 7388 1100
Fax: 020 7383 0404
Web: www.momentumpictures.co.uk

Optimum Releasing
9 Rathbone Place
London W1T 1HW
Tel: 020 7637 5403
Fax: 020 7637 5408
email: info@optimumreleasing.com
Web: www.optimumreleasing.com

Palm Pictures
8 Kensington Park Road
London W11 3BU
Tel: 020 7229 3000
Fax: 020 7229 0897
Web: www.palmpictures.com

Parasol Peccadillo
34 Hoxton Works
128 Hoxton Street
London N1 6SH
Tel: 020 7012 1770
Fax: 020 7012 1771
email: info@pprfilm.com
Web: www.pprfilm.com
Incorporates Peccadillo Pictures and PPR
(Parasol Peccadillo Releasing).

Pathé Distribution
Kent House
14-17 Market Place
Great Titchfield Street
London W1W 8AR
Tel: 020 7323 5151
Fax: 020 7631 3568
Web: www.pathe.co.uk

Redbus Film Distribution
Ariel House
74a Charlotte Street
London W1T 4QT
Tel: 020 7299 8800
Fax: 020 7299 8801
Web: www.helkon-sk.com

Soda Pictures
3 Rupert Court
London W1D 6DX
Tel: 020 7287 7100
Fax: 020 7287 7077
email: info@sodapictures.com
Web: www.sodapictures.com

Tartan Films
Atlantic House
5 Wardour Street
London W1D 6PB
Tel: 020 7494 1400
Fax: 020 7439 1922
Web: www.tartanvideo.com

Twentieth Century Fox Film Co.
31-32 Soho Square
London W1V 6AP
Tel: 020 7437 7766

Fax: 020 7439 3187
Web: www.fox.co.uk

UGC Films UK
34 Bloomsbury Street
London WC1B 3QJ
Tel: 020 7631 4683
Fax: 020 7323 9817
email: info@ugcfilms.co.uk

UIP
(United International Pictures UK)
12 Golden Square
London W1A 2JL
Tel: 020 7534 5200
Fax: 020 7636 4118
Web: www.uip.co.uk

Verve Pictures
2nd Floor
Kenilworth House
79/80 Margaret Street
London W1D 2JH
Tel: 020 7436 8001
Fax: 020 7436 8002
email: giorgia@vervepics.com
Web: www.vervepics.com

Warner Bros.
98 Theobalds Road
London WC1X 8WB
Tel: 020 7984 5000
Fax: 020 7984 5211
Web: www.warnerbros.co.uk

Winchester Film Distribution
19 Heddon Street
London W1B 4BG
Tel: 020 7851 6500
Fax: 020 7851 6506
email: mail@winchesterent.co.uk
Web: www.winchesterent.com/
uk_distribution/

Yash Raj Films International Ltd (UK)
Wembley Point
1 Harrow Road
Wembley
Middlesex HA9 6DE
Tel: 0870 739 7345
Fax: 0870 739 7346
email: ukoffice@yashrajfilms.com
Web: www.yashrajfilms.com

International Sales

All3Media International
87-91 Newman Street
London W1T 3EY
Tel: 020 7907 0150
Fax: 020 7907 0160
email: international@all3media.com
Web: www.all3media.com
Represents the production companies of the All3Media group and third-party producers.

APTN Associated Press Television News
The Interchange
Oval Road
Camden Lock
London NW1 7DZ
Tel: 020 7482 7400
Fax: 020 7413 8327
Web: www.aptn.com
The international television arm of The Associated Press.

BBC Worldwide
Woodlands
80 Wood Lane
London
W12 0TT
Tel: 020 8433 2000
Fax: 020 8749 0538
Web: www.bbcworldwide.com

Beyond Television
22 Newman Street
London WIT 1PH
Tel: 020 7636 9611
Fax: 020 7636 9622
Web: www.beyond.com.au
UK office of Australian production, sales and distribution company.

bfi Achival Footage Sales
21 Stephen Street
London W1T 1LN
Tel: 020 7957 4842
Fax: 020 7580 4014
email: footage.films@bfi.org.uk
Web: www.bfi.org.uk/collections/afs
Access to the materials held in the bfi's National Film and Television Archive. Footage available ranges from the earliest films to documentaries, fiction, home movies, animation and classic and contemporary television. Core collections include British Transport Films, the National Coal Board, ETV and the silent newsreel, Topical Budget.

British Film Institute
Film Sales
21 Stephen Street
London W1T 1LN
Tel: 020 7957 8909
Fax: 020 7436 4014
email: sales.films@bfi.org.uk
Web: www.bfi.org.uk
Sales of bfi-produced features, shorts and documentaries, and other acquired titles.

Carlton International
(see Granada International below)

Channel Four International
124 Horseferry Road
London SW1P 2TX
Tel: 020 7396 4444
Fax: 020 7306 8363
Web: www.c4i.tv
Represents rights for Channel 4 commissioned programmes and the FilmFour library.

Columbia TriStar International Television
Europe House
25 Golden Square
London W1R 6LU
Tel: 020 7533 1000
Fax: 020 7533 1246
Web: www.sonypictures.co.uk

Cumulus Distribution
Sanctuary House
45-53 Sinclair Road
London W14 0NS
Tel: 020 7300 6624
Fax: 020 7300 6529
Web: www.entercloud9.com
A subsidiary of the Cloud 9 Screen Entertainment Group, specialising in family drama programming.

DLT Entertainment UK Ltd
10 Bedford Square
London WC1B 3RA
Tel: 020 7631 1184
Fax: 020 7636 4571
email: info@dltentertainment.com
Web: www.dltentertainment.com
Specialising in comedy and drama.

Documedia International Films Ltd
19 Widegate Street
London E1 7HP
Tel: 020 7625 6200
Fax: 020 7625 7887
Distributors of drama and documentary programming.

Endemol UK
Shepherds Building Central
Charecroft Way
London W14 0EE
Tel: 0870 333 1700
Web: www.endemoluk.com
Licensing and distribution of Endemol programming and formats.

Fremantle International Distribution
1 Stephen Street
London W1T 1AL
Tel: 020 7691 6000
Fax: 020 7691 6060
email: fidsales@fremantlemedia.com
Web: www.fremantlemedia.com
Television distribution arm of FremantleMedia, whose library includes Thames TV and Talkback Productions among others.

Granada International
48 Leicester Square
London WC2H 7FB
Tel: 020 7491 1441
Fax: 020 7493 7677
email: int.info@granadamedia.com
Web: www.int.granadamedia.com
A division of ITV plc, merging the existing Granada International and Carlton International operations. Also incorporates the former Action Time brand.

DIRECTORY

Indigo Film & Television

116 Great Portland Street
London W1W 6PJ
Tel: 020 7612 1700
Fax: 020 7612 1705
email: info@indigofilm.com
Web: www.indigofilm.com
Distributor and co-producer of films,
drama series, documentaries and
children's programming.

NBD TV

Unit 2 Royalty Studios
105 Lancaster Road
London W11 1QF
Tel: 020 7243 3646
Fax: 020 7243 3656
email: distribution@nbdtv.com
Web: www.nbdtv.com
Specialising in music and light
entertainment programming.

Paramount Television

49 Charles Street
London W1J 5EW
Tel: 020 7318 6400
Fax: 020 7491 2086
Web: www.paramount.com

Park Entertainment

4th floor
50-51 Conduit Street
London W1S 2YT
Tel: 020 7434 4176
Fax: 020 7434 4179
email: sales@parkentertainment.com
Web: www.parkentertainment.com
Financier, distributor and sales agent for
independently produced
television programming and film.

Portman Film and Television

21-25 St. Anne's Court
London W1F 0BJ
Tel: 020 7494 8024
Fax: 020 7494 8046
email: sales@portmanfilm.com
Web: www.portmanfilm.com
International distributor of television
drama and feature films.

RM Associates

Shepherds West
Rockley Road
London W14 0DA
Tel: 020 7605 6600
Fax: 020 7605 6610
email: rma@rmassociates.co.uk
Web: www.rmassociates.co.uk
Distributor of music and arts
documentary and performance
programming.

S4C International

50 Lambourne Crescent
Llanishen
Cardiff CF4 5DU
Tel: 029 2074 1440
Fax: 029 2075 4444
email: international@s4c.co.uk
Web: www.s4ci.com
International sales arm of the Welsh
broadcaster S4C.

Screen Ventures

49 Goodge Street
London W1T 1TE
Tel: 020 7580 7448
Fax: 020 7631 1265
email: info@screenventures.com
Web: www.screenventures.com
TV distribution catalogue includes
documentary, live performance and music
programming.

SMG

3 Waterhouse Square
138-142 Holborn
London EC1N 2NY
Tel: 020 7882 1000
Fax: 020 7882 1020
Web: www.smg.plc.uk
The Television division of SMG
incorporates Scottish TV, Grampian TV,
SMG TV Productions and Ginger
Television.

Southern Star

45-49 Mortimer Street
London W1W 8HJ
Tel: 020 7636 9421
Fax: 020 7436 7426
Web: www.southernstargroup.com
Catalogue includes drama, children's and
family entertainment, wildlife
and documentary programming.

Target Entertainment

Drury House
34-43 Russell Street
London WC2B 5HA
Tel: 020 7344 1950
Fax: 020 7344 1951
Web: www.target-entertainment.com
Distribution and licensing of drama,
comedy and entertainment formats.

Twentieth Century Fox Television

31-32 Soho Square
London W1V 6AP
Tel: 020 7437 7766
Fax: 020 7439 1806
Web: www.fox.co.uk

TWI

McCormack House
3 Burlington Lane
London W4 2TH
Tel: 020 8233 5300
Fax: 020 8233 5301
Web: www.imgworld.com
TWI is the television arm of IMG,
specialising in the distribution and
production of sports programming.

Walt Disney Television International

3 Queen Caroline Street
London W6 9PA
Tel: 020 8222 1000
Fax: 020 8222 2795
Web: www.disney.co.uk

Warner Bros International Television

98 Theobalds Road
London WC1X 8WB
Tel: 020 7494 3710
Fax: 020 7287 9086
Web: www.wbitv.com

Winchester Television

19 Heddon Street
London W1B 4BG
Tel: 020 7851 6500
Fax: 020 7851 6506
email: mail@winchesterent.co.uk
Web: www.winchesterent.com/tv
Television sales and licensing agency
focusing on intellectual properties for the
international pre-school and children's
entertainment market.

Legal Services

Bates, Wells & Braithwaite
138 Cheapside
London
N1 1EN
Tel: 020 7551 7796
Fax: 020 7551 7800
Web: www.bateswells.co.uk

Bird & Bird
90 Fetter Lane
London
EC4A 1JP
Tel: 020 7415 6000
Fax: 020 7415 6111
Web: www.twobirds.com

Davenport Lyons
1 Old Burlington Street
London
W1S 3NL
Tel: 020 7468 2600
Fax: 020 7437 8216
Web: www.davenportlyons.com

David Wineman
Craven House
121 Kingsway
London
WC2B 6NX
Tel: 020 7400 7800
Fax: 020 7400 7890
Web: www.davidwineman.co.uk

Denton Wilde Sapte
5 Chancery Lane
Clifford's Inn
London
EC4A 1BU
Tel: 020 7320 6557
Fax: 020 7404 0087
Web: www.dentonwildesapte.com

Gersten & Nixon
National House
60-66 Wardour Street
London
W1F 0TA
Tel: 020 7439 3961
Fax: 020 7734 2479
Web: www.gernix.oc.uk

Hammonds
7 Devonshire Square
Cutlers Gardens
London
EC2M 4YH
Tel: 0870 839 1000
Fax: 0870 839 1001
Web: www.hammonds.com

Harbottle & Lewis
Hanover House
14 Hanover Square
London
W1S 1HP
Tel: 020 7667 5000
Fax: 020 7667 5100
Web: www.harbottle.com

Harrison Curtis
8 Jockey's Fields
London
WC1 4BP
Tel: 020 7611 1720
Web: www.harrisoncurtis.co.uk

Howard Kennedy
Harcourt House
19 Cavendish Square
London
W1A 2AW
Tel: 020 7546 8976
Fax: 020 7491 2899
Web: www.howardkenndy.com

Lee & Thompson
Greengarden House
15-22 St Christophers Place
London
W1U 1NL
Tel: 020 7935 4665
Fax: 020 7563 4949
Web: www.leandthompson.com

Marriot Harrison
12 Great James Street
London
WC1N 3DR
Tel: 020 7209 2000
Fax: 020 7209 2001
Web: www.marriotharrison.com

Matthew Arnold & Baldwin
21 Station Road
Watford
Hertfordshire
WD17 1HT
Tel: 01923 202020
Fax: 01923 215050
Web: www.mablaw.co.uk

Olswang
90 High Holburn
London
WC1V 6XX
Tel: 020 7067 3000
Fax: 020 7208 8800
Web: www.olswang.com

Richards Butler
Beaufort House
St Botolph Street
London
EC3A 7EE
Tel: 020 7247 6555
Fax: 020 7247 5091
Web: www.richardsbutler.com

The Simkins Partnership
41-51 Whitfield Street
London
W1T 4HB
Tel: 020 7907 3011
Fax: 020 7907 3111
Web: www.simkins.com

Tods Murray
66 Queens Street
Edinburgh
EH2 4NE
Tel: 0131 226 4771
Fax: 0131 225 3676
Web: www.todsmurray.com

DIRECTORY

Legislation & Regulation Barrie MacDonald

Legislation and Regulation of UK Television

This section of the Handbook has a twofold purpose; first, to provide a brief history of the legislation relating to the television industry in the UK and, second, to provide a short summary of the current principal instruments of legislation. This section has been compiled by Barrie MacDonald.

Milestones in the Legislative History of UK Television

Early History

1904 *Wireless Telegraphy Act*: the origins of broadcasting in Britain, it gave Government wide powers of control and regulation of wireless telegraphy.
1923 *Licence and Agreement*: first licence issued to the newly established British Broadcasting Company.
1923 *The Broadcasting Committee Report* (Chairman: Sir Frederick Sykes): first government committee of inquiry into broadcasting recommended continued Government control of broadcasting with funding by a receiving licence fee.

1927 *Wireless Broadcasting*: the first Royal Charter for the renamed British Broadcasting *Corporation*.

1934 *Report of the Television Committee, 1934-5* (Chairman: Lord Selsdon): first inquiry on the development of television recommended a trial of the Marconi-EMI 405-line electronic system and Baird's 240-line mechanical process.

1954 *Television Act 1954*: broke the BBC monopoly by establishing commercial television (Independent Television - ITV), set up and regulated by a public body (Independent Television Authority - ITA) responsible to Parliament.

1962 *Report of the Committee on Broadcasting, 1960* (Chairman: Sir Harry Pilkington): criticised ITV and recommended a second BBC television channel on the new 625-line UHF standard.

1972 *Sound Broadcasting Act 1972*: renamed the ITA the Independent *Broadcasting* Authority (IBA) to set up and regulate local commercial radio.

1977 *Report of the Committee on the Future of Broadcasting* (Chairman: Lord Annan): recommended a fourth television channel, and an independent Broadcasting Complaints Commission.

1980 *Broadcasting Act 1980*: provided for the establishment of the fourth channel (Channel 4) in England, Scotland and Northern Ireland by the IBA, and a separate independent Welsh-language fourth channel (S4C) in Wales.

1984 *Cable and Broadcasting Act 1984*: provided for the expansion of broadband cable television regulated by the Cable Authority, and for satellite television.

1986 *Report of the Committee on Financing the BBC* (Chairman: Professor Alan Peacock): recommended a radical shake-up and deregulation of British television, including putting ITV franchises out to competitive tender, and Channel 4 ceasing to be a subsidiary of the IBA and sell its own airtime.

1990 *Broadcasting Act 1990*: radically changed television regulation by abolishing the IBA and Cable Authority, replacing them with the Independent Television Commission to regulate terrestrial, cable or satellite television, and changing the television licensing process with competitive tendering for franchises.

1991 Council of the European Communities Directive 89/552/EEC (known as *Television without frontiers*): came into force in the UK, and required removal of all restrictions on the retransmission of programme services within the EU.

1996 *Broadcasting Act 1996*: provided for digital broadcasting, changes in media ownership rules, and merger of the Broadcasting Complaints Commission and the Broadcasting Standards Council as a Broadcasting Standards Commission.

2003 *Communications Act 2003*. See below.

Current Legislation and Regulations Affecting Television Broadcasting

Office of Communications Act 2002

Paving legislation that established Ofcom, preparatory to receiving its full duties from the *Communications Act*, and giving the existing regulators a duty to assist Ofcom.

Communications Act 2003

It established a new framework for the communications sector, and a new unified independent regulator, Ofcom, to replace five former regulators – the Independent Television Commission, Radio Authority, Broadcasting Standards Commission, Oftel and the Radiocommunications Agency.

Specific provisions related to television include:
• the development of the current system of regulating television to reflect technology change, the switchover from analogue to digital, and to rationalise the regulation of the public service broadcasters
• the establishment of a Content Board to ensure representation of the public interest in the nature and quality of programmes, and promote media literacy

- the establishment of a Consumer Panel, to advise and assist Ofcom, and represent and protect consumer interests, and other advisory committees
- granting Ofcom concurrent powers under the *Competition Act 1998* and *Enterprise Act 2002* with those of the Office of Fair Trading in promoting effective competition in the whole communications services sector
- an overhaul of the rules governing media ownership, principally scrapping those rules preventing single ownership of ITV subject to Competition Commission approval, and removing ownership rules for Channel 5
- protection for independent producers by provision of the 25% quota of qualifying programmes, and for programme rights to remain with production companies (not the broadcasters) unless negotiated otherwise.

Selected Statutory Instruments (subordinate legislation)

The Communications Act 2003 (Commencement No.1) Order 2003 (SI 2003/ 1900)

Bringing into force on 25 July 2003 the provisions in Schedule 1 of the Act, and Schedule 2 on 18 September, and enabling the Secretary of State and Director General of Telecommunications to exercise the functions of Ofcom for a transitional period.

The Advanced Television Services Regulations 2003 (SI 2003/ 1901)

Measures relating to wide-screen television services, scrambling, and inter-operability of analogue and digital television sets.

The Wireless Telegraphy (Limitation of Number of Licences) Order 2003 (SI 2003/ 1902)

Specifies the uses and number of frequencies for which the Secretary of State will grant only a limited number of licences, and the criteria to determine the number.

The Dissolution of the Independent Broadcasting Authority Order 2003 (SI 2003/ 2554)

Tidying-up order finally dissolving the IBA, whose property, rights and liabilities had been divided between the ITC, Radio Authority and NTL.

The Office of Communications Act 2002 (Commencement No. 3) and Communications Act 2003 (Commencement No. 2) Order 2003 (SI 2003/ 3142)

There are nine other statutes for Ofcom to follow, the unconsolidated parts of:
- *Broadcasting Acts 1990/ 1996*
- *Competition Act 1998*
- *Enterprise Act 2002*
- *Marine (Etc) Broadcasting (Offences) Act 1967*
- *Telecommunications Act 1984*
- *Wireless Telegraphy Acts 1949/ 1967/1998*

Selected UK legislation affecting television broadcasters

The Cinematograph Films (Animals) Act 1937

Prohibits showing of any scene that involved actual cruelty to animals.

Contempt of Court Act 1981

Prohibits any publication that might prejudice a defendant's right to fair trial in a court case, and permits injunction, even prosecution over prejudicial publication.

Copyright Designs and Patents Act 1988

Primary legislation for copyright protection includes films, broadcasts and cable programmes.
The Duration of Copyright and Rights Protection in Performances Regulations 1995 (SI 1995/ 3297) implements *European Directive 93/ 98/ EEC*, and establishes the term of protection for broadcasts and cable programmes as 50 years after originally made or a recording was released.
The Copyright and Related Rights Regulations 1996 (SI 1996/ 2967) covered broadcasts, satellite broadcasts, and cable re-transmission, and performers rights.
The Copyright and Related Rights Regulations 2003 (SI 2003/ 2498) implement *European Directive 2001/ 29/ EC* on the use of copyright material in public communications (electronic transmission, including digital broadcasting and 'on-demand' services), and redefines 'broadcast'.

Criminal Justice Act 1988

Gives the media special rights of appeal to the Court of Appeal against gag orders or decisions to exclude them from any part of a trial.

DA – Defence Advisory Notices (formerly known as D-Notices)

Voluntary and informal, but not strictly legal, system of Government advice to the media on reporting military and security matters.

Data Protection Act 1998

Comprehensive regulation of personal data systems, regulating of the processing of information relating to individuals, including the obtaining, holding, use or disclosure of such information. Implements the *European Directive 95/46/EC* that aimed at harmonising data protection across Europe. Users of personal data must obtain necessary consents before supplying it or using it in broadcasts. Exemptions for journalism, literature and arts, and for research, history or statistical purposes.

Defamation Act 1996

Makes it an offence to publish any defamation or malicious falsehood likely to make reasonable and respectable people think less of the claimant. Broadcasters of live programmes in which they have no effective control over the maker of the defamatory statement are exempt. Courts have to reconcile the right to free speech with the right to reputation.

Freedom of Information Act 2000

Guarantees citizens legal right of access to information held by public authorities, except for the security services, documents filed with courts or covered by Parliamentary privilege, personal information, where it would result in breach of confidence or punishable for contempt of court, or prejudicial to commercial interests. 'Public authorities' include Ofcom, and the BBC and Channel 4, though only those held in respect of purposes other than journalism, art or literature – an exception which protects them divulging commercially-sensitive programme information.

Human Rights Act 1998

Incorporates the *European Convention on Human Rights*. Guarantees freedom of expression, subject only to exceptions of public interest, competing individual rights or the authority of judges. Courts must take particular regard to this right in actions against the media. Public authorities required to comply include Ofcom. ITC/Ofcom programme codes have been reviewed to take account of human rights provisions.

Obscene Publications Acts 1959/ 1964

Applied to broadcasters by the *Broadcasting Act 1990*, they enable prosecution in England and Wales of any published material that tends to 'deprave and corrupt'.

Official Secrets Acts 1911/ 1989

Protects secret or classified information on security, intelligence, defence and international relations matters. Government employees have a duty of secrecy under the Act. Gives police powers of search and arrest. The *Public Interest Disclosure Act 1998* gives protection for 'whistle-blowers' who disclose 'official secrets' they consider in the public interest or can be proved to already be in the public domain.

Political Parties, Elections and Referendums Act 2000

Requires industry regulators to draw up rules on broadcasting constituency reports, with regard to the views of the Electoral Commission. Ofcom announced a consultation on 24 June 2004 on the rules for party political and referendum broadcasts, and will issue its own regulations in due course. The *Representation of the People Act 2000* banned publication of exit polls before the close of poll.

Protection of Children Act 1978

Makes it illegal to take, distribute or show any indecent or pseudo indecent photographs of children under the age of 16, and to publish any advertisement likely to be understood as conveying that the advertiser distributes or shows such indecent photos. Equivalent provisions for Scotland: *Civic Government (Scotland) Act 1982*.

Public Order Act 1986

Makes an offence of publishing inflammatory material likely to incite racial hatred, extended to broadcasting by *Broadcasting Act 1990*, and enables prosecution of the BBC, TV companies, programme producers or persons.

Terrorism Act 2000

Makes it a duty to disclose information or assistance to police on terrorists and any payment or assistance to them may amount to an offence.

Tribunals of Enquiry (Evidence) Act 1921

Enables broadcasters right to televise proceedings of tribunals of inquiry. Precedent established by CNN in 2002 in exercising the right to film the Harold Shipman inquiry, though Scottish courts refused BBC application for the Lockerbie inquiry.

Wireless Telegraphy Act 1949

Provides for the licensing of wireless telegraphy and makes it an offence to use a wireless receiver to intercept police messages, or to publish information about messages intercepted without authority.

Principle European Union regulations

European Convention on Trans-Frontier Television

Ratified by the UK law. It endorses freedom of expression and applies to all broadcasting formats – terrestrial, cable and satellite – received in any country party to the convention. It restrains broadcasters transmitting pornography, incitement to violence or racial hatred and requires a right of reply.

European Directive 89/ 552/EEC (as amended by 97/ 36/EC) (Television Without Frontiers).

Enforceable throughout the European Union, it sets out to remove barriers to transfrontier broadcasting between Member States and lays down certain minimum standards relating to programmes and advertising and measures to protect minors from pornography and violent programmes. Each Member State has jurisdiction over broadcasters established (as their main centre of activity) in that country. The right to take unilateral action against broadcasts from other EU countries, if they involve pornography or gratuitous violence, has been exercised by the UK, which 'proscribed' such pornographic satellite channels as Red Hot Television. It is a criminal offence to supply programmes or equipment to, or advertise on 'proscribed' channels.

Libraries & Research Facilities

This section contains contact details for the main centres of research resources relating to television and broadcasting based in the UK. These institutions hold special and in some cases unique collections which will be of particular interest to those researching all aspects of television and, in some cases, film and other media. Academic institutions will usually have their own libraries and those that run specialist media courses will have the largest relevant collections – see the COURSES section for more information.

bfi National Library

21 Stephen Street
London WIT 1LN
Tel: 020 7255 1444
020 7436 0165 (Information)
Fax: 020 7436 2338

The bfi National Library offers access to the world's largest collection of information on film and television. As a major national research collection the main priority is to provide comprehensive coverage of British film and television, but the collection itself is international in scope.

Books

Over 46,000 books covering all aspect of film and television ranging from reference books and biographies to published scripts, academic texts and broadcasting policy studies.

Periodicals

There are over 5,000 indexed periodical titles in the collection and over 400 are received every year from 45 countries.

Newspaper Cuttings

Scripts

Over 20,000 unpublished scripts, including production and post-production, and a number of television scripts. Translations used for earphone commentaries at the National Film Theatre are also held.

Publicity Materials

A wide range of materials is available from press releases to campaign books from the turn of the century, and festival catalogues dating back to the 1934 Venice Film Festival.

Audio Tapes

The Library offers three main collections; 200 interviews from on-stage events at the National Film Theatre from 1962 onwards; the Denis Gifford Collection; and a major Oral History Project organized by BECTU.

CD-ROMs

Along with other indexes and CD-ROMs the bfi's CD-ROM film Index International provides filmographic data and periodical references relating to over 100,000 feature films from around the world.

SIFT (Summary of Information on Film and Television) Database.

The Reading Room

All of the collections are available for reference only in the Reading Room. Access to the Reading Room is available to either Day Pass holders or holders of the Library Annual Pass. The Majority of materials are stored in stacks, which are not open to users, but most can be consulted in the Reading Room. The book catalogue can be browsed in advance at www.bfi.org.uk/library/olib. Certain categories of material can only be consulted in the Special Collection study room. Staff are on hand and full details are available in the Reading Room to support users and help them get the best out of the collections.

Special Collections Unit

If you wish to consult unpublished materials or originals of press book publicity then this must be done in the Special Collections Unit at Stephen Street. It is necessary to book an appointment in advance, please ring 020 7957 4772 or email speccoll@bfi.org.uk.

Information Services

Collection information and providing answers to enquiries and research requests is an important part of the work of the bfi National Library. Further details can be found at www.bfi.org.uk/library/services. Charges are applicable for many requests.

Reading Room opening hours
Monday 10.30 a.m. - 5.30 p.m.
Tuesday 10.30 a.m. - 8.00 p.m.
Wednesday 1.00 p.m. - 8.00 p.m.
Thursday 10.30 a.m. - 8.00 p.m.
Friday 10.30 a.m. - 5.30 p.m.
Closed at weekends

Institutional pass: £50.00
Annual Library pass: £35.00
NFT Members pass: £28.00
Annual Discount passes: £22.00*
Weekly pass: £15.00
Day pass: £6.00**
*Available to Senior Citizens, Registered Disabled and Unemployed upon proof of eligibility. Students may also apply for a discounted library pass.
**Available to anyone. Spaces may be reserved by giving 48 hours notice.
For more information on Institutional and Annual membership and to subscribe please call 020 7815 1374.

Enquiry Lines

The Enquiry Line is available for short enquiries. Frequent callers subscribe to an information service. The line is open from 10.00 a.m. – 1 p.m. and 2.00 p.m. – 5.00 p.m. Monday to Friday on 020 7255 1444

DIRECTORY

BBC Written Archives Centre

Caversham Park
Reading RG4 8T2
Tel: 0118 948 6281
Fax: 0118 946 1145
email: heritage@bbc.co.uk
Web: www.bbc.co.uk/heritage/research/
wac_home.shtml
Resources: The Centre holds thousands of
files (including PasB records and internal
BBC production memoranda) and scripts
from as far back as the BBC's formation
in 1922, together with information about
past programmes and the history of
broadcasting. The WAC conserves for the
future the documents which have formed
the BBC's written history –
correspondence, memoranda, contracts,
scripts and many publications. Academics
and accredited researchers can visit the
Centre and study these written archives.

The reading room is open Wednesdays
to Fridays 9.45 a.m. to 5 p.m. Visits are by
appointment only. Access is only available
to those:
• working on academic research or
  courses accredited by their institution
• commissioned to write a book or article
• undertaking research for a commercial
  project

Bristol – University of Bristol Theatre Collection

Department of Drama
Cantocks Close
Bristol BS8 1UP
Tel: 0117 928 7836
Fax: 0117 928 7832
email: theatre-collection@bristol.ac.uk
Web: www.bristol.ac.uk/theatrecollection
Contact: Jo Elsworth

British Universities Film & Video Council Library

77 Wells Street
London W1T 3QJ
Tel: 020 7393 1500
Fax: 020 7393 1555
email: library@bufvc.ac.uk
Web: www.bufvc.ac.uk
Contact: Luke McKernan, Head of
Information
Resources: Scientific Film Association
papers, BKSTS book collection, Slade Film

History Register, Reuters Television
newsreel documents

East Anglian Film Archive

University of East Anglia
Norwich NR4 7TJ
Tel: 01603 592664
Fax: 01603 458553
email: eafa@uel.ac.uk
Web: www.uea.ac.uk/eafa
Contact: Assistant Archivist

Leicester Reference and Information Library

Bishop Street
Leicester LE1 6AA
Tel: 0116 2995401
email: central.reference@leicester.gov.uk
Contact: Librarian
Resources: Burchell Collection of books,
journals and memorabilia on British films
from the 1920's to the late 1960's.

Leicester – University of Leicester Library

PO Box 248
University Road
Leicester LE1 9QD
Tel: 0116 252 2055
Fax: 0116 252 2066
email: bem1@le.ac.uk
Web: www.le.ac.uk/library
Contact: Brian Marshall, Information
Librarian
Resources: Collection supporting Mass
communication studies

Manchester Arts Library

Central Library
St Peters Square
Manchester M2 5PD
Tel: 0161 234 1974
Fax: 0116 1234 1961
Web: www.manchester.gov.uk/libraries/
central/arts/index.htm
email: arts@libraries.manchester.gov.uk
Contact: Arts Librarian

National Museum of Photography, Film and Television

The Education Department
Bradford BD1 1NQ
Tel: 01274 202040
Fax: 01274 772325

email: education.nmpft@nmsi.org.uk
Web: www.nmpft.org.uk/television/
Contact: Enquiries
Resources: The TV Heaven section of the
museum is home to a collection of more
than 900 British television programmes,
which are available to view free of charge
– the full catalogue can be searched at
the website. The museum also houses a
huge historical collection of TV
technology and hardware, from receivers
to cameras and technical literature.

North West Film Archive

Manchester Metropolitan University
Minshull House
47-49 Chorlton Street
Manchester M1 3EU
Tel: 0161 247 3097
Fax: 0161 247 3098
email: n.w.filmarchive@mmu.ac.uk
Web: www.nwfa.mmu.ac.uk
Contact: Enquiries
Resources: Moving image archive. Part of
the Manchester Metropolitan University
Library Service.

Northern Ireland Film and Television Commission (Digital Film Archive)

3rd Floor Alfred House
21 Alfred Street
Belfast BT2 8ED
Tel: 44 28 902 32 444
Fax: 44 28 902 39 918
email: info@NIFTC.co.uk
Web: www.nifc.co.uk
Contact: Information Officer
Resources: Archive of moving images
about Northern Ireland 1897-2000.
There is also a digital film archive of
selected materials that can be viewed at
various sites in Northern Ireland.

Nova Film and Videotape Library

62 Ascot Avenue, Cantley
Doncaster DN4 6HE
Tel: 0870 765 1094
email: info@novaonline.co.uk
Web: www.novaonline.co.uk
Contact: Gareth Atherton
Resources: Non-fiction and archive film
and contemporary videos.

BRADFORD FILM FESTIVAL CALL FOR PAPERS

CRASH CINEMA
The Symposium that annually explores issues of Representation In Film

CRASH CINEMA 4
WEDNESDAY 16 MARCH 2005
CUBBY BROCCOLI CINEMA
NATIONAL MUSEUM OF PHOTOGRAPHY, FILM & TELEVISION
Building on three successful annual symposia, Crash Cinema 4 continues to explore issues of representation within film and videographic media. Synopses are invited that engage with the mainstream (Hollywood / Bollywood), fine art, cult and the edges of popular culture. All papers will be published in Vol. 4 of *Crash Cinema: The Proceedings*

Send 200 word synopses by **Friday 31 December 2004**
to Patrick Eyres, MA Representation in Film,
The Bradford School of Art, Great Horton Road,
Bradford, BD7 1AY
Tel: (+0044)1274 433104
Email: patricke@bilk.ac.uk

experience film

NATIONAL
MUSEUM
PHOTOGRAPHY
FILM & TELEVISION

The Literary Consultancy

script assessment and editorial advice for theatre, TV, film and radio

"This is just what writers need – a quality script-reading service to help them look carefully at the real potential of their work."

Tessa Ross, Head of FilmFour

www.literaryconsultancy.co.uk

The Literary Consultancy Ltd,
Diorama Arts, 34 Osnaburgh St,
London NW1 3ND
Tel/Fax: 020 78134330

ARTS COUNCIL ENGLAND

intellect Journals

e-mail: orders@intellectbooks.com | www.intellectbooks.com

www.intellectbooks.com

New Cinemas: Journal of Contemporary Film

New Cinemas aims to challenge hegemonic value judgement about Cinema from around the world to explore approaches that posit the egalitarian value of Cinema, with a focus on what is happening now. The tendency to focus upon issues of 'otherness' and 'marginality' – ignoring the specificities of the films – is challenged head-on with a focus on the evaluation of the Cinema.

ISSN 1474–2756
3 nos/vol (Vol. 2, 2004)
avail. in print & on-line

For a print sample issue for just £10, or a free electronic sample copy contact: Intellect. PO Box 862. Bristol BS99 1DE, UK Fax: 0117 958 9911

Studies in European Cinema

Studies in European Cinema provides a forum for high-quality research being carried out on European Film, European Film culture, and the changing nature of film output in Europe. The Journal is distinctive as it places the debates within both a cultural and an historical context. Unique in its willingness to engage with all the Cinemas of Europe, the Journal provides a pre-eminent international platform for discussion.

ISSN 1741–1548
3 nos/vol (Vol. 1, 2004)
avail. in print & on-line

For a print sample issue for just £10, or a free electronic sample copy contact: Intellect. PO Box 862. Bristol BS99 1DE, UK Fax: 0117 958 9911

Studies in Hispanic Cinemas

Studies in Hispanic Cinemas is set to be the primary scholarly journal on Spanish-speaking Cinemas in English. The Journal has a broad range, publishing work in Film as text, representation, history, theory, modes of production, as well as reception. The different Hispanic Cinemas – in relation to Alternative, Third, Independent, Avant-garde forms, as well as regional and local film practices – are covered in the same diverse way.

ISSN 1478–0488
3 nos/vol (Vol. 1, 2004)
avail. in print & on-line

For a print sample issue for just £10, or a free electronic sample copy contact: Intellect. PO Box 862. Bristol BS99 1DE, UK Fax: 0117 958 9911

intellect | PUBLISHERS OF ORIGINAL THINKING.

DIRECTORY

Royal Scottish Academy of Music and Drama

The Whittaker Library
100 Renfrew Street
Glasgow G2 3DB
Tel: 0141 270 8268
Fax: 0141 270 8353
email: library@rsamd.ac.uk
Web: www.rsamd.ac.uk/library/index.html
Resources: The Whittaker Library contains comprehensive collections of learning materials for music and drama to support Academy staff and students and is open to the public for reference purposes. Extra-mural membership on payment of an annual fee is available to graduates of the RSAMD. The RSAMD is a member library of the British Universities Film and Video Council which allows it access to post-1995 off-air TV material. It also has its own collection of older VHS material.

Scottish Screen Information Service

1 Bowmont Gardens
Glasgow G12 9LR
Tel: 0141 302 1730
Fax: 0141 302 1778
email: info@scottishscreen.com
Web: www.scottishscreen.com
Contact: Isabella Edgar, Information Manager
Resources: Production information, press cuttings and journals. They also provide a research service. Access to the Shiach Script library with over 100 feature and short film scripts.

Surrey Performing Arts Library

Denbies Wine Estate
London Road
Dorking
Surrey RH5 6AA
Tel: 01306 875453
email: performing.arts@surreycc.gov.uk
Web: www.surreycc.gov.uk/libraries
Resources: Wide-ranging collection on cinema, including scripts and soundtracks.

Vivid - Birmingham's Centre for Media Arts

Unit 311F, The Big Peg
120 Vyse Street
Birmingham B18 6ND
Tel: 0121 233 4061
Fax: 0121 212 1784
email: info@vivid.org.uk
Web: www.vivid.org.uk
Contact: Marian Hall, Facilities Manager
Resources: With a focus on new media, a small archive and facilities for use by practitioners.

VLV - Voice of the Listener and Viewer Ltd

101 King's Drive
Gravesend
Kent DA12 5BQ
Tel: 01474 352835
Fax: 01474 351112
email: info@vlv.org
Web: www.vlv.org.uk
Contact: VLV Librarian
Resources: VLV holds archives of the former Broadcasting Research Unit (1980-90) and British Action for Children's Television (1988-95). Access to these and VLV's own archive, which includes all VLV responses to government and public consultations and transcripts of most VLV conferences since 1984 is increasingly on their website, but please contact them for further information on accessing them.

Westminster Reference Library

35 St Martins Street
London WC2H 7HP
Tel: 020 7641 4606
Fax: 020 7641 4640
email: reference@librarywc2@westminster.gov.uk
Web: www.westminster.gov.uk/libraries/special/perform.cfm
Contact: Arts Librarian

York St John College

Fountains Learning Centre
Lord Mayors Walk
York YO31 7EX
Tel: 01904 716699
Fax: 01904 612512
email: f.ware@yorksj.ac.uk
Web: www.yorksj.ac.uk/
Contact: Fiona Ware, Academic Support Librarian
Resources: Holds the Yorkshire Film Archive

CAMBRIDGE

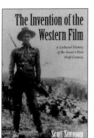

The Invention of the Western Film
A Cultural History of the Genre's First Half Century
Scott Simmon
An in-depth exploration of the early Western.
£65.00 | HB | 0 521 55473 X | 410pp
£22.95 | PB | 0 521 55581 7

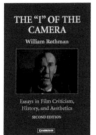

The 'I' of the Camera
Essays in Film Criticism, History, and Aesthetics
Second edition
William Rothman
This second edition of William Rothman's classic includes fourteen new essays and a new foreword.
Cambridge Studies in Film
£55.00 | HB | 0 521 82022 7 | 424pp
£19.99 | PB | 0 521 52724 4

Roberto Rossellini's *Rome Open City*
Sidney Gottlieb
This volume is an accessible introduction to Rossellini's *Rome Open City*.
Cambridge Film Handbooks
£40.00 | HB | 0 521 83664 6 | 206pp
£13.99 | PB | 0 521 54519 6

British Film
Jim Leach
This book explores British cinema in relation to its social political and cultural contexts.
National Film Traditions
£40.00 | HB | 0 521 65276 6 | 304pp
£16.99 | PB | 0 521 65419 X

Horror Film and Psychoanalysis
Edited by Steven Schneider
This volume explores the subject of psychoanalysis and film.

'Who can resist a volume which, apropos the most popular movie genre - horror, stages the debate between the main orientations of contemporary psychoanalytic film theory? And why should we resist a unique combination of top theory and fascinating topic? Everyone in cinema and cultural studies should just grab this collection, sit down and learn!'
Slavoj Zizek (University of Ljubljana, Slovenia)

'This superb collection offers its readers a roller-coaster ride through contemporary film theory and the question of horror. Psychoanalysis is the central issue for many contributors, with essays exploring not only its place in relation to the Gothic Imagination at the heart of horror but also its consequent role in both forming and analysing the horror film. Sparks fly across the pages as the philosophical and epistemological premises of theories of horror are themselves subjected to analysis and evaluation as well as, in some cases, rejection. All the while the horror film, in all its gory glory, both uncanny and irrepressible, remains centre stage throughout the wide-ranging discussions and analyses of films from Nosferatu to Scream. The essays in The Horror Film and Psychoanalysis: Freud's Worst Nightmares are exemplary philosophical and aesthetic discussions, their complex and subtle arguments are both challenging and thought-provoking.'
Elizabeth Cowie, University of Kent, Canterbury
Cambridge Studies in Film
£45.00 | HB | 0 521 82521 0 | 320pp

www.cambridge.org  CAMBRIDGE UNIVERSITY PRESS

DIRECTORY

Multichannel

The current overcrowded multichanel market is one typified by cycles of rapid start up and closure – many channels, particularly those that sprang up to serve the ONdigital/ITV Digital platform, have closed their doors in recent years. It was predicted many years ago that television channels would become more like printed magazines, with many new titles springing up with great regularity and just as many folding soon after. Channels will inevitably close and restructure come 2005 but we have endeavoured to select only major companies to list below in the hope that contact information will remain valid in the year.

Channel numbers are given for Sky Digital channels, all Freeview channels (including those available from Top-Up TV by subscription) and selected NTL and Telewest cable services and were accurate at 29/7/04

Source: BFI Information Services/Ofcom/Television Business International with additional assistance from Alistair McGown

18 Plus Movies
6 Centaurs Business Park
Grant Way
Isleworth TW7 5QD
Tel: 020 7705 3000
Ownership: British Sky Broadcasing
Sky EPG: 763-769
Programming: Adult pay per view programming

Abu Dhabi Television Satellite Channel
PO Box 63
Abu Dhabi
United Arab Emirates
Tel: 971 2 4430000
Fax: 971 2 4435000
Ownership: Emirates Media Inc
Sky EPG: 824
Programming: general entertainment, news programming

The Adult Channel
Aquis House
Station Rd
Hayes UB3 4DX
Tel: 020 8581 7000
Fax: 020 8581 7007
email: adultch@spicecos.com
Web: www.theadultchannel.co.uk
Ownership: Home Video Channel [see MSP above]Playboy TV UK Ltd
Service start: Feb 1992
Sky EPG: 967
Programming: adult entertainment (premiumsubscription)

Adventure One
NGC-UK Partnership
Grant Way
Isleworth
Middlesex TW7 5QD
Tel: 020 7941 5073
Fax: 020 7941 5103
email: george.jeffrey@bskyb.com
Web: www.nationalgeographic .co.uk
Ownership: National Geographic 50%, British Sky Broadcasting [see MSP above] 50%
Satellite: Astra 2 North
Sky EPG: 560
Programming: documentaries on exploration and adventure

Alpha ETC Punjabi
Units 7-9
Belvue Business Centre
Belvue Road
Northolt UB5 5QQ
Tel: 020 8839 4000
Fax: 020 8841 9950
Ownership: Asia TV Ltd.
Sky EPG: 818
Programming: General entertainment

Amateur Babes
117-121 Salusbury Rd.
London NW6 6RG
Tel: 020 7328 8808
Fax: 020 7328 8858
Ownership: Broadcasting (Gaia) Ltd.
Sky EPG: 991
Programming: adult entertainment

Amore TV
Stonehills Complex
Shields Road
Gateshead
Tyne & Wear NE10 0HW
Tel: 0191 483 5585
Fax: 0191 483 6967
Due to launch February 2005

The Amp
British Sky Broadcasting
Grant Way
Isleworth
Middlesex
Tel: 0870 240 3000
Fax: 0870 240 3060
Ownership: BSkyB
Web: www.theamp.tv
Sky EPG: 469
Programming: indie/alternative rock promos and magazines e.g. The Xfm Show

Animal Planet
160 Great Portland St
London W1W 5TB
Tel: 020 7462 3600
Web: www.animal.discovery. com
Ownership: BBC Worldwide, Discovery Communications [see MSP above]
Service start: Sep 1998
Satellite: Hot Bird 1 (PAL/encrypted)2 South
Sky EPG: 570 (+1 service on 571)
NTL: 503/136
Telewest: 215
Programming: natural history documentaries

Arab News Network
14-17 Wells Mews
London W1P 3FL
Tel: 020 7323 9920
Ownership: Linkchain LTD
Programming: current affairs in Arabic

ARY Digital
AML House
12 Cumberland Ave
Park Royal NW10 7QL
Tel: 020 8961 4911
Fax: 020 7493 1333
Ownership: Pakistani Channel Ltd.
Sky EPG: 812
Programming: general entertainment

Artsworld
Artsworld Channels Ltd.
80 Silverthorne Road
London SW8 3XA
Tel: 020 7819 1160
Fax: 020 7819 1161
email: tv@artsworld.com
Web: www.artsworld.com
Ownership: BSkyB 50%
Service start: 2 Dec 2000
Satellite: Astra 2 North
Sky EPG: 157
Programming: arts (premium)

Asian Music Channel
Vis Television Media International
Fountain House
140 Dudley Port
Tipton
West Midlands DY4 7RE
Tel: 08700 110020
Fax: 08700 110030
email: info@vismediaint.com
Web: vismediaint.com
Programming: Material for Asian, African and UK broadcasters. Currently off-air but due to relaunch later in 2004.

Asianet
PO Box 38
Greenford
Middlesex UB6 7SB
Tel: 020 8566 9000
Fax: 020 8810 5555
Web: www.asianet-tv.com
Cable only from videotape
Programming: movies and entertainment in Hindi, Punjabi and other languages

Attheraces
Tel: 0870 787 1000
email: team@attheraces.co.uk
Web: www.attheraces.co.uk
Ownership: Arena Leisure 50%, British Sky Broadcasting [see MSP above] 50%. Channel 4 previously owned 33% but withdrew their investment in March 2004.
Service start: 1 May 2002
Satellite: Eurobird
Sky EPG: 415
Programming: horse races, interactive betting

Auctionworld
Elena House
Unit 6, I/O Centre
Lea Riad
Waltham Cross
Herfordshire EN8 7PG
Tel: 0870 122 6510
Fax: 01992 760888
email: info@auction-world.tv
Web: www.auction-world.tv
Ownership: Auctionworld Ltd
Service start: 1 Nov 2001
Satellite: Eurobird
Sky EPG: 651
Programming: teleshopping

Avago
Unit 6-7
Princes Court
Wapping Lane
London EC1W 2DA
Tel: 020 7942 7942
Fax: 0207942 7943
email: customercare@avago.tv
Web: www.avago.tv
Ownership: Digital Television Production Company Ltd
Service start: 5 Jul 2002
Sky EPG: 181
Programming: light entertainment, interactive game shows

B4U
19 Heather Park Drive
Wembley HA0 1SS
Tel: 020 8795 7171
Fax: 020 8795 7181
email: b4utv@b4unetwork.comtv.com
Web: www.b4utv.com
Ownership: Bollywood Eros Network

Service start: 26 Aug 1999
Programming: mainstream Hindi feature films (subscription)

The Bangla Channel
Prestige House
Clifford Rd
Walthamstow
London E17 4JW
Tel: 020 8523 4555
Fax: 020 8523 4888
email: postbox@balnglatv.co.uk
Web: www.banglatv.co.uk
Service start: 17 Nov 1999
Satellite: Eurobird, Hot Bird 3
Programming: light entertainment [subscription]

Bangla TV
Warton House
150 High St
Stratford
London E15 2NE
Tel: 020 8519 3200
Fax: 020 8519 2229
Web: www.banglatv.co.uk
Sky EPG: 811

BBC 3
BBC Television Centre
London
W12 7RJ
Tel: 020 8743 8000
email: info@bbc.co.uk
Web: www.bbc.co.uk/bbcthree
Service start: 9 Feb 2003
Freeview: 7
Sky EPG: 115
NTL: 126/11
Telewest: 106
Programming: general entertainment, primarily aimed at 25-34 age group. Cutting edge comedy: *Little Britain*, *Nighty Night*, *The Mighty Boosh*, *Three Non-Blondes*, *The Smoking Room*. Drama series includes *Bodies* and *Burn It*. Entertaining semi-educational series: *Body Hits*, *Sex, Warts and All*. Key series often shown soon after on BBC 2. Set up on two year licence granted by the DCMS.

BBC 4

BBC Television Centre
London W12 7RJ
Tel: 020 8743 8000
email: info@bbc.co.uk
Web: www.bbc.co.uk/bbcfour
Service start: 2 Mar 2002
Satellite: Astra 2 South
Freeview: 10
Sky EPG: 116
NTL: 127/12
Telewest: 107
Programming: arts (classical music, rock, jazz, world cinema) and documentary. Archive TV retrospectives (such as *Summer in the 60s, Missing Believed Wiped*). Key shows: Archive social history strand *Time Shift, The Alan Clark Diaries, The National Trust, The Proms.*

BBC News 24

Woodlands
80 Wood Lane
London W12 0TT
Tel: 020 8433 2000
Fax: 020 8749 0538
email: info@bbc.co.uk
Web: www.bbc.co.uk/news24
Ownership: BBC Worldwide [See MSP above]
Satellite: Astra 2A, 2B
Freeview: 40
Sky EPG: 507
Programming: rolling news

BBC Parliament

BBC Westminster
4 Millbank
London SW1P 3JA
Tel: 020 7973 6048
Fax: 020 07973 6049
email: info@bbc.co.uk
Web: www.bbc.co.uk/bbcparliament
Ownership: British Broadcasting Corporation
Satellite: Astra 2A
Freeview: 40 (quarter screen only)
Sky EPG: 508
Programming: live daily coverage of Parliamentary proceedings

Best Direct TV

167 Imperial Drive
Harrow
HA2 7SP
Tel: 020 8868 4355
Fax: 020 8868 5024
email: customerservices@bestdirect.co.uk
Web: www.bestdirect.tv
Ownership: Best Direct (International) Ltd
Satellite: Eurobird
Sky EPG: 640
Programming: home shopping

Bid-up.tv/Screenshop

50 Lambourne Crescent
Llanishen
Cardiff
Wales CF14 5GG
Tel: 029 2074 1440
Fax: 029 20755 4444
email: info@bid-up.tv
Web: www.bid-up.tv
Ownership: sit-up Ltd
Service start: 2 Nov 2000
Satellite: Astra 2B
Freeview: 23
Sky EPG: 647
Programming: shopping – live auctions

The Biography Channel

Grant Way
Isleworth
Middlesex TW7 5QD
Tel: 0870 240 3000
Fax: 020 7705 3030
Ownership: Arts & Entertainment Television Network 5%, British Sky Broadcasting [see MSP above] 50%
Service start: 1 Oct 2000
Satellite: Astra 2 South
Sky EPG: 229
NTL: 802
Programming: historical and biographical programmes (mostly US-originated)

Bloomberg Television

City Gate House
39-45 Finsbury Square
London EC2A 1PQ
Tel: 020 7330 7500
Fax: 020 7661 57487256 5326
email: ukfeedback@bloomberg.net
Web: www.bloomberg.co.uk
Service start: 1 Nov 1995
Satellite: Astra 1E, Eutelsat II-F1Eurobird
Freeview: 44 (via Top-Up TV subscription)
Sky EPG: 504
Programming: business and finance news and information

Boomerang (see also Cartoon Network)

Turner House
16 Great Marlborough St
London
W1F 7HS
Tel: 020 7693 1000
Fax: 020 7693 1001
Web: www.cartoonnetwork.co.uk
Ownership: Turner Broadcasting
Service start: 27 May 2000
Freeview: 33 (via Top-Up TV subscription)
Sky EPG: 603
Programming: classic cartoons, with extensive use of Hanna-Barbera archive (e.g. *Hong Kong Phooey, Flintstones, Josie and the Pussycats*).

The Box

Mappin House
4 Winsley Street
London W1W 8HF
Tel: 020 7436 1515
Fax: 020 7312 8227
Web: www.thebox.com
Ownership: Emap
Service start: 2 March 1992
Sky EPG: 449
Programming: interactive pop music jukebox

Bravo

160 Great Portland Street
London W1W 5QA
Tel: 020 7299 5000
Fax: 020 7299 6000
email: enquiriesenquiries@bravo.co.uk
Web: www.bravo.co.uk
Ownership: Flextech Television
Service start: Sept 1985
Satellite: Astra 2A
Sky EPG: 124 (+1 service on 125)
NTL: 406/104
Telewest: 138
Programming: general entertainment for young men. Much in the way of 'extreme' US TV e.g. police video shows. Retro movies and television programmes (*Knight Rider, ChiPs*). Some UK originations, e.g. *Street Hypnosis, Tasteful TV*

Bright Entertainment Network (BEN)
3 Central Hall
Archway
London N19 3TD
Tel: 07050 202 460
Ownership: African Broadcasting Corp.
Sky EPG: 184
Programming: general entertainment, with an African focus

British Eurosport see Eurosport

Cartoon Network
Turner House
16 Great Marlborough St
London W1V 1AFF 7HS???
Tel: 020 7693 1000
Fax: 020 7693 1001
email: toon.pressoffice@turner.com
Web: www.cartoon-network.co.uk
Ownership: Turner Broadcasting Systems (TBS) Inc, an AOL Time Warner Company
Service start: 17 Sept 1993
Satellite: Astra 2A, 2B
Freeview: 32 (via Top-Up TV subscription)
Sky EPG: 601
Programming: edgier US animation for older children – *The Cramp Twins, Powerpuff Girls, Dexter's Laboratory*

CBBC
BBC Television Centre
Wood Lane
London
W12 7RJ
Tel: 020 8752 8000
email: cbbc.online@bbc.co.uk
Web: www.bbc.co.uk/cbbc
Ownership: BBC Worldwide [see MSP above]
Service start: 11 February 2002
Satellite: Astra 2A
Freeview: 30
Sky EPG: 616
NTL: 598/67
Telewest: 701
Programming: children's, for 6-13s. Most shows are reruns from BBC 1, others are originated here and may run later on BBC 1 and BBC 2. Key shows: *Dick and Dom in Da Bungalow* (Sunday edition), *Blue Peter, UK Top 40, Newsround* (bulletins throughout the day), *Xchange, Cave Girl, Basil Brush Show, Story of Tracy Beaker.*

CBeebies
see above
email: cbeebies@bbc.co.uk
Web: www.bbc.co.uk/cbeebies
Service start: 11 February 2002
Satellite: Astra 2A
Freeview: 31
Sky EPG: 617
NTL: 599/68
Telewest: 702
Programming: for children under six. Key shows: *Teletubbies, Tweenies, Balamory, Fimbles, Bedtime Hour.*

Celtic TV
See Setanta Television.
Sky EPG: 430
Programming: news from Celtic FC

Challenge TV
160 Great Portland Street
London W1W 5QA
Tel: 020 7299 5000
Fax: 020 7299 6000
email: challengetv_enquiries@flextech.co.uk or enquiries@challengetv.co.uk
Web: www.challengetv.co.uk
Ownership: Flextech [see MSP above]
Service start: 3 February 1997
Satellite: Astra 2A
Sky EPG: 121
Programming: general entertainment, game and quiz shows and live interactive competitions. Key shows: *Takeshi's Castle, Fort Boyard.* Originations include new *Telly Addicts, Celebrity Addicts, Celebrity Poker Club, House of Games.* Archive game shows including *Blankety Blank, Bullseye, 3-2-1.*

Channel U
18 Soho Square
London W1D 3QL
Tel: 020 7025 8088
Fax: 020 7025 8188
Sky EPG: 467
Programming: interactive urban and R&B music videos

Chart Show TV
37 Harwood Road
London SW6 4QP
Tel: 020 7384 2243
Fax: 020 7384 2026
Web: www.chartshow.com

Sky EPG: 455
Programming: music videos in themed collections e.g. The Dance Chart etc

Chelsea TV
Stamford Bridge
Fulham Road
London
SW6 1HS
Tel: 020 7915 1951
Fax: 020 7381 4831
email: chelseatv@chelseavillage.com
Web: www.chelseafc.com
Ownership: Chelsea Digital Media Ltd
Service start: Aug 2001
Satellite: Astra 2A
Sky EPG: 421
Programming: football coverage and news

CNBC Europe
10 Fleet Place
London EC4M 7QS
Tel: 0181 653 9300020 7653 9300
Fax: 020 7653 9333
email: feedback@cnbceurope.com
Web: www.cnbceurope.com
Ownership: International General Electrics
Service start: 11 Mar 1996
Satellite: Astra 1E2B
Sky EPG: 510
Programming: business news

CNN International
CNN House
19-22 Rathbone Place
London W1P 1DF
Tel: 020 7637 6921 and 020 7637 6700
Fax: 020 7637 6868738
email: cnni@turnercnn.com
Web: www.europe.cnn.com and www.cnn.com
Ownership: Turner Broadcasting Systems (TBS) Inc, an AOL Time Warner Inc Company
Service start: Oct 1985
Satellite: Astra 2A
Sky EPG: 513
Programming: international rolling news

The Community Channel
3-7 Euston Centre
Regents Place
London NW1 3JG
Tel: 020 7874 7626
Fax: 020 7874 7644
email: info@communitychannel.org
Web: www.communitychannel.org.uk
Ownership: The Media Trust
Service start: 18 September 2000
Satellite: Astra 2B
Freeview: 46 (airs between 0245-0545)
Sky EPG: 585 (airs 24 hours)
Programming: community affairs and social action programmes.

Create and Craft With Ideal World
Ideal Home House
Newark Road
Peterborough PE1 5WG
Tel: 0870 777 002
Fax: 0870 777003
Web: www.createandcraft.tv
Ownership: Ideal Shopping Direct plc.
Sky EPG: 695
Programming: home shopping

The Dating Channel
124-128 City Road
London EC1V 2NJ
Tel: 020 7748 1500
Fax: 020 7748 1501
email: info@thedatingchannel.com
Web: www.thedatingchannel.co.uk
Ownership: Euro Digital Corporation Ltd
Satellite: Eurobird
Sky EPG: 685
Programming: interactive dating service

The Discovery Channel
160 Great Portland Street
London W1N 5TB
Tel: 020 7462 3600
Fax: 020 7462 3700
email: comments_uk@discovery.com
Web: www.discovery.com
Ownership: Discovery Communications Europe
Service start: Apr 1989
Satellite: Hot Bird 1 (PAL/encrypted)2A
Freeview: 27 (via Top-Up Tv subscription)
Sky EPG: 551
NTL: 500/130
Telewest: 212
Programming: documentaries

Discovery Civilization
see above
Sky EPG: 554
Programming: ancient history

Discovery Health
see above
Sky EPG: 154
Programming: health. Mostly operations footage, plastic surgery documentaries from the US.

Discovery Home & Leisure
See above
Web: www.homeandleisure.co.uk
Satellite: Eurobird, Astra 2A
Freeview: 28 (via Top-Up TV subscription)
Sky EPG: 133
NTL: 304/133
Telewest: 271
Programming: lifestyle

Discovery Kids
see above
Sky EPG: 615
Programming: children's

Discovery Science
see above
Sky EPG: 555

Discovery Travel & Adventure
see above
Sky EPG: 553

Discovery Wings
see above
Sky EPG: 556
Programming: aviation

The Disney Channel UK
3 Queen Caroline St
Hammersmith
London W6 9PE
Tel: 020 8222 1000
Web: www.disneychannel.co.uk
Ownership: Walt Disney Company Ltd
Satellite: Astra 2D
Sky EPG: 611
NTL: 700/63
Telewest: 724
Programming: family entertainment; children's includes cartoons *Men in Black*, *The Little Mermaid*, *Aladdin*. Bonus with Sky Premier and Moviemax (premium).

E4
124 Horseferry Road
London SW1P 2TX
Tel: 020 7396 4444
Web: www.channel4.com/entertainment
Ownership: 4 Ventures Ltd
Service start: 19 Jan 2001
Satellite: Astra 2 North
Freeview: 14 (via Top-Up Tv subscription)
Sky EPG: 163 (+1 service on 164)
NTL: 144
Telewest: 144
Programming: general youth entertainment, swapping runs with Channel 4, especially in field of US acquisitions e.g. *Friends, ER, Six Feet Under, Sopranos, The West Wing, Ally McBeal*. Runs almost uninterrupted coverage of *Big Brother* in summer months – related originations include *Big Brother's Little Brother* and *Big Brother's Efourum*. Other originations have included celebrity magazine *What Sadie Did Next*.

Eurosport
84 Theobalds Road
London WC1X 8RW
Tel: 020 7468 7777
Fax: 020 7468 0024
email: network@eurosport.co.uk
Web: www.eurosport.com
Ownership: ESO Ltd = TF1 34%, Canal Plus 33%, ESPN 33%
Service start: Feb 1989
Satellite: Hot Bird 1 (PAL/clear), Astra 2A
Sky EPG: 410 (Eurosport News on 411)
NTL: 112/43
Telewest: 521
Programming: sport

Extreme Sports Channel
The Media Centre
131-151 Great Titchfield Street
London W1W 5BB
Tel: 020 7244 1000
Fax: 020 7244 0101
email: info@extreme.com
Web: www.extreme.com
Ownership: United Pan-Europe Communications and The Extreme Group
Satellite: 13 Oct 2000
Sky EPG: 419
Programming: youth orientated sports and lifestyle programs

FilmFour

124 Horseferry Road
London SW1P 2TX
Tel: 020 7396 4444
Fax: 020 7306 8366
email: generalfilmenquiries@filmfour.com
Web: www.filmfour.com
Ownership: Channel 4 Television; 4
Ventures Ltd
Sky EPG: 323
NTL: 701/50
Telewest: 444
Programming: feature and short films
(premium)

FilmFour Weekly

see above
Sky EPG: 325
NTL: 715/47
Programming: extreme and challenging
movies (premium)

Flaunt

(see The Amp)
Web: www.theamp.tv
Sky EPG: 473
Programming: music videos, aimed at
young women

Fox Kids (FK) UK

338 Euston Road
London NW1 3AZ
Tel: 020 7554 9000
Fax: 020 7554 9005
email: webmaster@foxkids.co.uk
Web: www.foxkids.co.uk
Ownership: Fox Television 50%, Saban
50%
Satellite: Astra 2B
Sky EPG: 609 (+1 service on 610)
Programming: children's, with a boys
angle. Mainly action series e.g. *Hulk, Mask,
Power Rangers.*

Friendly TV

Interxion Building
11 Hanbury Street
London E1 6QR
Tel: 020 7247 8544
Fax: 020 7247 0135
Web: www.friendlytv.com
Sky EPG: 208

Programming: Hollywood and celebrity
news, interactive text programming and
quizzes; erotic late night interactive show
for adults only, Babecast.

Ftn

160 Great Portland Street
London W1W 5QA
Tel: 020 7299 5203
Fax: 020 7299 6366
Web: www.ftn.tv
email: richard_woolfe@flextech.co.uk
Ownership: Flextech Television Ltd
Freeview: 20
Sky EPG: 199
NTL: 914
Telewest: 123
Programming: general entertainment,
showcasing other Flextech-owned channel
output. *Dilbert, Kath and Kim.* People/Talk
shows e.g. *6ixth Sense with Colin Fry,
Ricki Lake, Jay Leno*

FX

Fox International Channels
Grant Way
Isleworth
Middlesex TW7 5QD
Tel: 020 7705 8000.
Web: www.fxtv.co.uk
Ownership: Fox Television
Sky EPG: 289
Programming: male-skewed US action
series (*The X-Files, JAG, The Shield*)

Golf TV

First Floor
1 Kingsgate
Bradford Business Park
Bradford BD1 4SJ
Tel: 01274 725909
Sky EPG: 699
Programming: golf programmes and
home shopping

Granada Men & Motors see Men &
Motors

Granada Plus see Plus

The Hallmark Channel
Entertainment Network

3-5 Bateman Street
London W1V 5TT
Tel: 020 7368 91007439 0633
Fax: 020 7368 91017439 0644
Web: www.hallmarkchannelint.com.uk
Service start: 1 Nov 2001
Satellite: Astra 2D
Sky EPG: 190
NTL: 190
Telewest: 190
Programming: family drama and movies

The History Channel

6 Centaurs Business Park
Grant Way
Isleworth
Middlesex TW7 5QD
Tel: 020 7705 3000
Fax: 020 7705 3030
email: feedback@thehistorychannel.co.uk
Web: www.thehistorychannel.co.uk
Ownership: BSkyB 50%, Arts
&Entertainment Television Networks 50%,
British Sky Broadcasting 50%
Service start: 1 Nov 1995
Sky EPG: 561 (+1 service on 562)
NTL: 504/138
Telewest: 234
Programming: historical and biographical
documentaries

The Hits

Mappin House
4 Winsley Street
London W1W 8HF
Tel: 020 7436 1515
Fax: 020 7376 1313
Ownership: Emap
Freeview: 18
Sky EPG: 458
Programming: chart music promo jukebox

The Horror Channel

50 Riverside
South Church
Bishop Auckland
County Durham DL14 6XT
Tel: 01388 601361
email: info@thehorrorchannel.tv
Web: www.horrorchannel.co.uk
Sky EPG: 330
Programming: films and entertainment
with horror genre focus

DIRECTORY

Ideal World Home Shopping
Ideal Home House
Newark Road
Peterborough PE1 5WG
Tel: 01733 777 305
Fax: 01733 777 315
email: Web@idealshoppingdirect.co.uk
Web: www.idealworldtv.co.uk
Ownership: Ideal Shopping Direct plc
Service start: 17 Apr 2000
Satellite: Astra 2B
Sky EPG: 635
Programming: home shopping

The Islam Channel
72 New Bond Street
London W1S 1RR
Fax: 020 7374 4602
Email: info@islamchannel.tv
Web: www.islamchannel.tv
Sky EPG: 836

ITV News Channel
200 Gray's Inn Road
London WC1X 8XZZ
Tel: 020 7833 3000
Fax: 020 7430 47004868
email: contact@itn.co.uk
Web: www.itv.co.uk and www.itn.co.uk
Satellite: Astra 2B
Freeview: 41
Sky EPG: 525
Programming: news

ITV1
200 Gray's Inn Road
London WC1X 8HF
Tel: 020 7843 8000
Fax: 020 7843 8443
email: dutyoffice@itv.co.uk
Web: www.itv.co.uk
Ownership: ITV companies
Satellite: Astra 2D
Freeview: 3
Sky EPG: 103
Also on cable

ITV2
see above
Freeview: 6
Sky EPG: 175
NTL: 117/6
Telewest: 113

ITV3
See above
Due to launch 1 November 2004
(Freeview first). Drama and entertainment
programming from recent ITV archive,
aimed at 30+ viewers e.g. *Cold Feet,
Inspector Morse, A Touch of Frost.*

JML Direct
JML House
Regis Rd
London NW5 3EG
Telephone: 020 7691 3800
Fax: 020 7691 3878
Web Site: www.jmldirect.com
Sky EPG: 664
Programming: Home Shopping

Kerrang!
Mappin House
4 Winsley Street
London W1W 8HF
Tel: 020 7436 1515
Fax: 020 7312 8227
email: lee.thompson@emap.com
Web: www.kerrang.com
Ownership: Emap
Service start: 5 Dec 2001
Satellite: Eurobird
Sky EPG: 454
Programming: interactive music video
programming; rock and metal genres

Kiss TV
Mappin House
4 Winsley Street
London W1W 8HF
Tel: 020 7436 1515
Web: www.kissonline.co.uk
Ownership: Emap
Sky EPG: 450
Programming: urban, R&B music promos

Life TV
Westbrooke House
18 Albion Place
Maidstone
Kent ME14 5DZ
Tel: 01622 776776
Fax: 01622 678080
Web:
www.christiantelevisionbroadcasting.com
Sky EPG: 160
Programming: American-owned religious
pledge channel

L!ve TV
Telford House
Corner Hall
Hemel Hempstead
Tel: 08701 107108
Web: www.livetv.co.uk
Ownership: Eckoh Technologies (UK) Ltd.
Programming: Entertainment, mostly
lads' erotic and comedy. All shows from
the archive of the formerly active station.

Live XXX TV
Units 6 & & Princes Court
Wapping Lane
London E1 9DA
Tel: 020 7942 7942
Fax: 020 7942 7943
Ownership: Digital Television Production
Company
Sky EPG: 995
Programming: Adult Entertainment

Living TV
160 Great Portland St
London W1N 5TB
Tel: 020 7299 5000
Fax: 020 7299 6000
Web: www.livingtv.co.uk
Ownership: Flextech [see MSP above]
Service start: Sept 1993
Satellite: Astra 2A
Sky EPG: 112 (+1 service on 113)
NTL: 401/111
Telewest: 129
Programming: daytime lifestyle, evening
general entertainment, particularly aimed
at women. Also some series aimed at gay
demographic e.g. *Will and Grace, Queer
Eye For the Straight Guy.* Other key series
include *Most Haunted* and other
'paranormal' entertainment shows.

Magic
Mappin House
4 Winsley Street
London W1W 8HF
Tel: 020 7436 1515
Fax: 020 7436 1313
Web: www.magictv.co.uk
Ownership: Emap
Service start: 5 Dec 2001
Satellite: Eurobird
Sky EPG: 452
Programming: interactive 'golden oldie'
music videos

MBC (Middle East Broadcasting Centre)

80 Silverthorne Road
Battersea
London SW8 3XA
Tel: 020 7501 1111
Fax: 020 7501 1110
email: info@mbc1.tv
Web: www.mbc-tv.com
Service start: 18 Sep 91
Satellite: Hotbird 5
Sky EPG: 822
Programming: general entertainment and news in Arabic

Men & Motors

Franciscan Court
16 Hatfields
London SE1 8DJ
Tel: 020 7578 4040
Fax: 020 7578 4176
email: men@gsb.co.uk
Web: www.menandmotors.co.uk
Ownership: Granada Sky Broadcasting Ltd
Satellite: Astra 2A
Sky EPG: 136
Programming: male-oriented, motoring and softcore adult viewing

MTV

180 Oxford Street
London W1N 0DS
Tel: 020 7478 6000
Web: www.mtv.co.uk
Ownership: Viacom
Service start: Aug 87
Sky EPG: 440
Programming: youth channel; still some music videos but much of schedule now taken up with US 'extreme' and reality formats e.g. *Jackass, Dirty Sanchez, The Osbournes, MTV Cribs, Newlyweds.*

MTV2

see above
email: ViewerFeedback@mtveuropean.com
Web: www.mtv2europe.com
Sky EPG: 442
Programming: music videos, with accent on alternative rock

MTV Base

180 Oxford Street
London W1N 0DS
Tel: 020 7284 7777

Fax: 020 7284 7788
email: info@mtv.co.uk
Web: www.mtv.co.uk/base.asp
Ownership: MTV Networks Europe
Satellite: Astra 2A
Sky EPG: 443
Programming: urban, R&B and dance music promos

MTV Dance

see above
Service start: 20 Apr 2001
Web: www.mtv.co.uk/dance
Sky EPG: 444
Programming: music videos

MTV Hits

see above
Web: www.mtv.co.uk/hits
Sky EPG: 441
Programming: general chart pop music videos/teen market.

Music Box Channel

33 New Cavendish Street
London W1G 9TS
Tel: 020 7224 5504
Fax: 020 7224 5506
Ownership: Eclipse Sat Ltd.

Music Choice

Fleet House
57-61 Clerkenwell Road
London EC1M 5LA
Tel: 020 7014 8700
Fax: 020 7534 2144
Web: www.musicchoice.co.uk
Ownership: Sony 8%, Warner 16%, MCE 13%, private investors 27%, BSkyB 36%
Sky EPG: 480
Programming: music (interactive)

Muslim TV Ahmadiyyah

16 Gressenhall Road
London SW18 5QL
Tel: 020 8870 09228517 ext 210
Fax: 020 8870 0684
Web: www.alislam.org/mta
Ownership: Al-Shirkatul Islamiyyah
Service start: Jan 1994
Satellite: Intelsat 601Eurobird
Sky EPG: 807
Programming: spiritual, and educational, training programmes for the Muslim community

MUTV

Manchester United Television
274 Deansgate
Manchester M3 4SB
Tel: 0161 930 1968834 1111
Fax: 0161 876 5502
email: mutv@manutd.com
Web: www.manutd.com/mutv
Ownership: Manchester United FC 33.3%, Granada 33.3%, BSkyB 33.3%
Satellite: Astra 2B
Sky EPG: 406
Programming: Reports, news and match highlights from Manchester United FC (premium)

NASN

52 Haymarket
London SW1Y 4RP
Tel: 020 7389 0771
Fax: 020 7925 0580
Sky EPG: 417
Programming: Sport

Nation 217 (was Nation 277 at launch)

Web: www.nation217tv
Sky EPG: 217
Programming: interactive games and entertainment. Key show – *Flipside TV.*

National Geographic Channel

6 Centaurs Business Park
Grant Way,
Isleworth
Middlesex TW7 5QD
Tel: 020 7941 5068/ 020 7805 2293
Fax: 020 7 805 2295
Ownership: National Geographic 50%, British Sky Broadcasting 50%, National Geographic
email: natgeoweb@bskyb.com
Web: www.nationalgeographic.co.uk
Service start: 1997
Sky EPG: 558 (National Geographic + on 559)
NTL: 505/139
Telewest: 230
Programming: natural history documentaries

Nickelodeon
15-18 Rathbone Place
London W1P 1DF
Tel: 0171 462 1000/0800 801 801/
020 7462 1000
Fax: 0171 462 1030/0800 802 802/
020 7462 1030
Web: www.nicktv.co.uk
Ownership: British Sky Broadcasting
50%, MTV NetworksViacom 50%, British
Sky Broadcasting 50%
Service start: 1 September 93
Satellite: Astra 2B
Sky EPG: 604 (Nicktoons, cartoon
material only, on 606)
Programming: children's; American
cartoons and sitcom. Key shows: *Sabrina,
Saved by the Bell, Kenan and Kel,
Spongebob Squarepants, Fairly Odd
Parents.*

Nick Jr
See Nickelodeon above
Web: www.nickjr.co.uk
Sky EPG: 618
Programming: pre-school slant on the
above

NSAT Ltd
12 Sheet Street
Windsor SL4 1BG
Tel: 01733 349413
Sky EPG: 837
Web: www.nsat.tv

OBE TV
391 City Rd
2nd Floor
Angel
London EC1V 1NE
Tel: 020 7837 8377
Fax: 020 7837 8388
Sky EPG: 223
Programming: general entertainment for
African audiences

Open Access
2-4 Hoxton Square
London N1 6NU
Tel: 0870 744 2041
Fax: 0870 054 2891
Ownership: Definition Consultants Ltd
Sky EPG: 687
Programming: light entertainment

Overload-Showcase
Westbrook House
18/20 Albion Place
Maidstone
Kent ME14 5DZ
Tel: 01622 776 776
Fax: 01622 678 080
Sky EPG: 166
Ownership: Channel 208 Ltd.
Programming: London TV, with news and
reports from London, airs on this EPG
number in daytime, with lads' TV after 11
p.m.

The Paramount Comedy Channel
3-5 Rathbone Place
London W1P 1DA
Tel: 020 7399 7700
Fax: 020 7399 7730
Web: www.paramountcomedy.co.uk
Ownership: Viacom 75%, BSkyB 25%
Service start: 1 Nov 1995
Satellite: Astra 2A
Sky EPG: 127 (Paramount Comedy 2 on
128; 936 on NTL and 133 on Telewest)
NTL: 400/105
Telewest: 132
Programming: comedy series. A mix of
classics and new shows from the US (*Two
and a Half Men, Ally McBeal, Seinfeld*)
and UK (*Monthy Python's Flying Circus,
The New Statesman, Minder*)

Performance: The Arts Channel
60 Charlotte Street
London W1T 2NU
Tel: 020 7307 6202
Fax: 020 7636 4338
email: info@performancetv.co.uk
Web: www.performancetv.co.uk
Ownership: Arts & Entertainment Ltd
Service start: Oct 1992
Satellite: Telstar 11
Sky EPG: 202
Telewest: 312
Programming: opera, jazz and classical
concerts, drama, performing arts

Playboy TV
2nd floor, Aquis House
Station Road
Hayes
Middlesex UB3 4DX
Tel: 020 8581 7000
Fax: 020 8581 7007

Web: www.playboytv.co.uk
Ownership: Flextech 51%, BSkyB, Playboy
Service start: 1 Nov 1995
Satellite: Astra 2B
Sky EPG: 966
Programming: erotic (premium) adult
entertainment

Playhouse Disney
Building 12
566 Chiswick High Road
London W4 5AN
Tel: 020 8222 1000
Fax: 020 8222 2565
email: guest.mail@online.disney.com
Web: www.disney.co.uk/disneychannel/
playhouse
Ownership: The Walt Disney Company Ltd
Satellite: Astra 2D
Sky EPG: 614
Programming: pre-school children's
entertainment incuding *Bear in the Big
Blue House* [premium]

Plus (was Granada Plus)
Franciscan Court
16 Hatfields
London SE1 8DJ
Tel: 020 7578 4040
Fax: 020 7578 4176
email: plus@gsb.co.uk
Web: www.gplus.co.uk
Ownership: Granada 50.5 %, BSkyB 49.5%
Satellite: Astra 2 North
Sky EPG: 118
NTL: 301/101
Telewest: 128
Programming: classic TV drama and
comedy, from ITV archives (*Taggart,
Cracker, The Sweeney, Poirot, The Saint,
Rising Damp*), BBC (*Two Ronnies*) and the
US (*Kojak, Columbo, Dukes of Hazzard*).

Price-drop.tv
4 Warple Way
London W3 0EU
Tel: 020 8600 9700
Fax: 020 8746 2811
Web: www.sit-up.tv
Freeview: 35
Sky EPG: 636
Programming: teleshopping auctions

Prime TV
AMC House
12 Cumberland Ave
Park Royal
London NW10 7QL
Tel: 020 8961 4911
Fax: 020 8961 4913
email: info@primetv.freeserve.co.uk
Web: www.primetv.freeserve.co.uk
Ownership: Pak Television Ltd
Service start: Nov 1998
Satellite: Intelsat 707, Astra 2B
Sky EPG: 815
Programming: family programming aimed at the Pakistani community (subscription).

Private Blue
email: info@privatebroadcasting.nl
Web: www.privateblue.com
Service start: 2 Mar 2001
Satellite: Astra 2 South
Sky EPG: 988
Programming: erotic

Private Girls
see above
Satellite: Astra 2 North
Sky EPG: 989
Programming: adult entertainment

Q
Mappin House
4 Winsley Street
London W1W 8HF
Tel: 020 7436 1515
Fax: 020 7376 1313
email: qtv@q4music.com
Web: www.q4music.com
Ownership: Emap
Service start: 2000
Satellite: Astra 2B
Sky EPG: 453
Programming: music promos – not an exact match to the character of its parent magazine, with slightly more mainstream feel.

QVC: The Shopping Channel
Marco Polo House, Chelsea Bridge
346 Queenstown Road
London SW8 4NQ
Tel: 020 7705 5600
Fax: 020 7705 56021
Web: www.qvcuk.com

Ownership: QVC (= Comcast, TCI) 80%, BSkyB 20%
Satellite: Astra 2B
Freeview: 16
Sky EPG: 630
Service start: Oct 1993
Programming: home shopping

Rangers TV
See Setanta
Sky EPG: 431
Programming: news from Glasgow Rangers FC

Rapture TV
43 Parkhead Loan
Edinburgh EH11 4SJ
Tel: 0131 443 4642
Ownership: Power TV Ltd
Sky EPG: 205
Programming: light entertainment aimed at teenage market. NB was off air temporarily in July 2004.

Reality TV
Zone Broadcasting
Queen's Studios
117-121 Salisbury Road
London NW6 6RG
Tel: 020 7328 8808
Fax: 020 7328 8858
email: pobox@zonevision.com
Web: www.zonevision.com
Sky EPG: 187
Programming: documentaries/fly-on-the-wall programmes. Mostly of the 'extreme weather' variety from the US. Some UK programmes e.g. *The Real Bad Girls.*

Red Hot All Girl
Suite 14
Burlington House
St Saviour's Road
St Helier
Jersey JE2 4LA
Tel: 01534 703 720
Fax: 01534 703 760
Web: www.redhottv.co.uk
Ownership: RHF Productions Ltd
Sky EPG: Red Hot channels run from 976-983
Programming: adult entertainment (subscription)

Red Hot Amateur
see above
Programming: adult films

Red Hot Euro
see above
Programming: adult entertainment

Red Hot Films
see above
Programming: adult films

Sci-Fi Channel (Europe)
5-7 Mandeville Place
London W1M 5LB
Tel: 020 7535 3500
Fax: 020 7535 3585
Web: www.scifi.com
Ownership: Sci-Fi Channel Europe
Service start: 1 Nov 1995
Satellites: Hot Bird 1 (PAL/encrypted), Astra 2A
Sky EPG: 130
NTL: 402/102
Telewest: 135
Programming: science fiction, fantasy, horror, some US science documentary. Key shows: *Millennium, Farscape.*

Screenshop
4 Warple Way
London W3 0UE
Tel: 020 8600 9700
Fax: 020 8746 0299
email: screenshop_enquiries@screenshop.co.uk
Web: www.screenshop.co.uk
Ownership: Sit-Up, Flextech
Service start: 30 Sep 1999
Satellite: Astra 2A
Sky EPG: 647
Programming: home shopping

Scuzz
See The Amp
Web: www.scuzz.tv
Sky EPG: 471
Programming: rock/metal music video

Setanta Television

Broadcasting House
3a South Prince's Street
Dublin 2
Eire
Tel: 00 353 1 677 6705
Fax: 00 353 1 671 6671
email:
setanta.uktvproduction@setanta.com
Web: www.setanta.com
Ownership: Setanta Sport Ltd
Service start: 1999
Sky EPG: 429
Programming: Gaelic sports for pubs
Gaelic soccer and rugby. See also SPL TV.

S4C2

Sianel Pedwar Cymru
Parc Ty-Glas
Llanisihen
Cardiff
Wales CF4 5DU
Tel: 029 2074 7444
Fax: 020 2075 4444
email: s4c@s4c.co.uk
Web: www.s4c..co.uk
Service start: 15 Sep 1999
Satellite: Astra 2A
Sky EPG: 519
Programming: coverage of the Welsh
Assembly in session initially, news and
general entertainment in Welsh and
English

Shop America

1st floor
1 Kingsgate
Bradford Business Park
Canal Road
Bradford BD1 4SJ
Tel: 0800 0821 821
email: info@shopamerica.co.uk
Web: www.shopamerica.co.uk
Ownership: Shop America (Australasia)
Ltd
Satellite: Astra 2 South
Sky EPG: 637
Programming: home shopping

Shop Smart

Unit 24 Metro Centre
Britania Way
Park Royal
London NW10 7PA
Tel: 0870 124 5656

email: enquiries@shopsmart.tv
Web: www.shopsmart.tv
Ownership: Shop Smart Television Ltd
Satellite: Eurobird
Sky EPG: 656
Programming: home shopping

Simply Home

See below
Sky EPG: 641

Simply Ideas

See below
Sky EPG: 642

Simply Shopping

150 Great Portland Street
London W1W 6QD
Tel: 020 7758 3100
Fax: 020 7758 3101
email: feedback@simplyshoppingtv.co.uk
Web: www.simplyshoppingtv.co.uk
Ownership: Invest TV Ltd
Sky EPG: 639
Programming: home shopping

Sky Box Office

6 Centaurs Business Park
Grant Way
Syon Lane
Isleworth
Middlesex TW7 5QD
Tel: 0870 240 3000020 7705 3000
Fax: 020 7705 3030
email: feedback@sky.co.uk
Web: www.sky.co.uk
Ownership: British Sky Broadcasting
Service start: 1 Dec 97
Satellite: Eurobird, Astra 2A, 2B, 2D1E
Programming: movies, concerts, events
(pay-per-view)

Sky Movies Cinema

see above
Ownership: British Sky Broadcasting
Service start: Oct 92
Satellite: Astra 2B
Programming: movies (premium)

Sky Movies Max

Ownership: British Sky Broadcasting (see
above)
Service start: Feb 1989
Satellite: Astra 2A, 2B
Programming: movies (premium)

Sky Movies Premier

see above
Web: www1.sky.com/movies/premier
Satellite: Astra 2A, 2B
Programming: movies (premium)

Sky News

Ownership: BSkyB (see above)
Web: www.sky.com/skynews
Service start: Feb 1989
Satellite: Astra 2AB (Sky News
International airs on Astra 1E)
Freeview: 42
Sky EPG: 501
Programming: rolling news

Sky One

Ownership: British Sky Broadcasting (see
above)
Web: www.skyone.co.uk
Service start: Feb 1989
Satellite: Astra 2B, 2A
Sky EPG: 106 (Sky One Mix with
alternative schedule on 107; 930 on NTL)
NTL: 140/30
Telewest: 120
Programming: general entertainment,
mainly US acquisitions such as *The
Simpsons, 24, Malcolm in the Middle, Tru
Calling, Futurama, Buffy, Angel,* various
Star Trek series. Originated UK dramas
aimed at young adults include *Mile High*
and *Dream Team.* Specialises in 'noisy'
event, tabloid TV – Rebecca Loos
interview, *How Gay Are You?, There's
Something About Miriam.*

Sky Pub Channel

BSkyB
Grant Way
Isleworth
Middlesex TW7 5QD
Tel: 020 7941 5572
Fax: 020 7941 5123
email: generalenquiries@pubchannel.com
Web: www.pubchannel.com
Ownership: British Sky Broadcasting
Satellite: Astra 2B
Sky EPG: 846
Programming: food, drink. entertainment
programmes for the licensing trade (Mon-
Fri; subscription)

Sky Sports 1

Ownership: BSkyB (see above)
Web: www.skysports.com
Service start: Apr 1991
Satellite: Astra 2A, 2B
Sky EPG: 401
NTL: 721/40
Telewest: 511
Programming: sport (premium)

Sky Sports 2

Ownership: BSkyB (see above)
Service start: Aug 1994
Satellite: Astra 2A, 2B
Sky EPG: 402
NTL: 722/41
Telewest: 512
Programming: sport (premium)

Sky Sports 3

Ownership: BSkyB (see above)
Service start: Aug 1994
Sky EPG: 403
NTL: 723/42
Telewest: 513
Programming: sport (premium)

Sky Sports News

see above
Satellite: Astra 2A
Freeview: 43
Sky EPG: 408
Programming: sports news

Sky Sports Xtra

Ownership: BSkyB (see above)
Service start: Aug 1999
Satellite: Astra 2A, 2D
Sky EPG: 404
NTL: 950
Telewest: 514
Programming: sports (bonus with premium channels)

Sky Travel

Ownership: BSkyB (see above)
Web: www.skytravel.co.uk
Satellite: Astra 2D
Freeview: 11
Sky EPG: 139
NTL: 931
Programming: travel documentaries, e.g. *Airline*, *24 Hours in Soho*

Smash Hits!

Mappin House
4 Winsley Street
London W1W 8HF
Tel: 020 7436 1515
Fax: 020 7312 8246
email: feedback@smashhits.net
Web: www.smashhits.net
Ownership: Emap
Service start: 5 Dec 2001
Satellite: Eurobird
Sky EPG: 451
Programming: teen pop music videos and information (interactive)

Snatch It

Unit 2d
Eagle Road
Moons MOAt North Industrial Estate
Redditch B98 9HF
Tel: 01527 406100
Fax: 01527 406112
Sky EPG: 646
Programming: teleshopping auctions

Sony Entertainment Television Asia

Molinare
34 Fouberts Place
London W1B 2BH
Tel: 020 7534 7575
Fax: 020 7534 7585
Web: www.setindia.com
Ownership: Sony Pictures Entertainment Inc
Service start: 26 Aug 1999
Satellite: Astra 2 South
Sky EPG: 802
Programming: general entertainment (subscription)

South For You

MPK House
233 Belgrave Gate
Leicester LE1 3HT
Tel: 0116 253 2288
Fax: 0116 253 8900
Web: www.ceeitv.tv
Sky EPG: 817
Programming: Asian entertainment

Spice

Aquis House
Station Road
Hayes
Middlesex UB3 4DX
Tel: 020 8581 7000
Fax: 020 8581 4090
email: enquiry@spicexxx.co.uk
Web: www.spicexxx.co.uk
Ownership: Playboy TV UK Ltd
Service start: 2 Mar 2001
Satellite: Astra 2A, Hot Bird 1
Sky EPG: 987
Programming: adult entertainment

SPL TV

52 Haymarket
London SW1Y 4RP
Tel: 020 7930 8926
Fax: 020 7930 2059
Ownership: Setanta Sport Ltd
Programming: Live Scottish Premier League football available in the UK via subscription packages on Setanta PPV channels. Also airs without subscription in Ireland. SPL rights owned for four years to 2008.

SportTV

6-7 Princes Court
Wapping Lane
London E1 9DA
Tel: 020 7942 7942
Fax: 020 7942 7943
Ownership: Digital Television Production Company Ltd.
Programming: adult

SportXXXTantalise

See above
Sky EPG: 993

SportXXXGirls

See above
Sky EPG: 994

STAR News

8th floor
1 Harbourfront
18 Tak Fung Street
Hungkom
Kowloon
Hong Kong
Tel: 00 852 2621 8888
Fax: 00 852 2621 8000

DIRECTORY

Web: www.startv.com
Ownership: STAR Group, a subsidiary of News Corporation
Service start: Jan 2001
Satellite: Astra 2 South
Sky EPG: 803
Programming: news and analysis in English and Hindi (premium)

STAR Plus
see above
Service start: Jan 2001
Sky EPG: 804
Programming: Asian general entertainment (premium)

TCM (Turner Classic Movies)
Turner House
16 Great Marlborough Street
London W1F 7HS
Tel: 020 7693 1000
Fax: 020 7693 1001
email: tcmeurope@turner.com
Web: www.tcmonline.co.uk
Ownership: Turner Broadcasting
Service start: Sept 93
Freeview: 25 (via Top-Up TV subscription)
Sky EPG: 327
NTL: 403/103
Telewest: 419
Programming: movies

Tel Sell
Unit 5
The Robert Eliot Centre
1 Old Nichol Street
London E2 7HR
Web: www.telsell.com
Ownership: Tel Sell UK Ltd
Satellite: Eurobird
Sky EPG: 649
Programming: home shopping

Teletext
Building 10 Chiswick Park
566 Chiswick Hight Road
London W4 5TS
Tel: 0870 731 3000
Freeview: 9

Television:X (The Fantasy Channel)
Suite 14
Burlington House
St. Saviour's Road
St. Helier
Jersey JE2 4LA
Tel: 01534 703720
Fax: 01534 703760
Ownership: Portland Enterprises
Freeview: 60 (via Top-Up TV premium subscription)
Sky EPG: 969
Programming: adult

Television:X 2 and 3
See above

Thane Direct
35-37 Fitzroy Square
London W1T 6DX
Tel: 0870 444 2252
Fax: 020 7323 0396
Web: www.thanedirect.co.uk
Ownership: Thane International Inc
Satellite: Eurobird
Sky EPG: 655
Programming: informercials and home shopping

Thane Stop and Shop
52 Amerland Road
London SW18 1PX
Tel: 020 8870 2404
Ownership: Thane Direct UK Ltd.
Sky EPG: 660
Programming: teleshopping

Thomas Cook TV
8 Park Place
Lawn Lane
Vauxhall
London SW8 1UD
Tel: 020 7840 7163
Fax: 020 7820 4471
Web: www.thomascooktv.com
Ownership: Thomas Cook Ltd
Service start: Nov 2001
Satellite: Eurobird
Sky EPG: 648
Programming: travel

TMF (The Music Factory)
180 Oxford Street
London W1N 1DS
Tel: 020 7284 7777
Fax: 020 7478 6007
Ownership: MTV Networks
Freeview: 21
Sky EPG: 448
Programming: chart music videos

Toon Disney
Building 12
566 Chiswick High Road
London W4 5AN
Tel: 020 8222 1000
Fax: 020 8222 2565
Web: www.disney.co.uk
Ownership: The Walt Disney Company Ltd
Satellite: Astra 2D
Sky EPG: 613
Programming: children's entertainment (premium)

Toonami
Turner House
16 Great Marlborough Street
London W1F 7HS
Tel: 020 7693 0779
Fax: 020 7693 0780
Web: www.toonami.co.uk
Ownership: Turner Entertainment Networks Inc.
Sky EPG: 621
Programming: animation and children's shows – boys' action slant with key shows X-Men, He-Man, Dragonball

The Travel Channel
66 Newman Street
London W1P 3LAW1T 3EQ
Tel: 020 7636 5401
Fax: 020 7636 6424
email: enquiries@travelchannel.co.uk
Web: www.travelchannel.co.uk
Ownership: Landmark Communications
Service start: 1 February 1994
Sky EPG: 148 (Travel Channel 2 on 149)
Programming: travel

Trouble

160 Great Portland Street
London W1N 5TB
Tel: 020 7299 5000
Fax: 020 7299 6000
email: webmaster@trouble.co.uk
Web: www.trouble.co.uk
Ownership: Flextech Television
Service start: February 1997
Satellite: Astra 2 South
Sky EPG: 607
Programming: tween/teen fare, mostly from US. *Clueless, That 70s Show, The Fresh Prince of Bel Air.*

Turner Classic Movies (see TCM)

TV Travel Shop

1 Stephen Street
London W1T 7AL
Tel: 020 7691 6132
Fax: 020 7691 6392
email: admin@tvtravelshop.ltd.uk
Web: www.tvtravelshop.com
Service start: 4 Apr 1998
Satellite: Astra 2A
Freeview: 24
Sky EPG: 631
Programming: holiday and travel home shopping

TV Travel Shop 2

see above
Service start: 2000
Satellite: Astra 2A
Sky EPG: 632
Programming: holiday and travel home shopping

TV Warehouse

Chalfont Grove
Narcot Lane
Chalfont St Peter
Buckinghamshire SL9 8TW
Tel: 0800 052 0300
Fax: 01494 878076
email: info@tv-warehouse.co.uk
Web: www.tv-warehouse.co.uk
Ownership: Sirius Television Ltd
Satellite: Astra 2B
Sky EPG: 644
Programming: home shopping

UKTV Bright Ideas

160 Great Portland Street
London W1W 5QA
Tel: 020 7299 5000
Fax: 01483 750901
Web: www.uktv.co.uk/uktvBrightIdeas/
Ownership: UKTV New Ventures Ltd
Freeview: 19
Sky EPG: 196
NTL: 913
Telewest: 263
Programming: lifestyle; gardening and some food

UKTV Documentary

160 Great Portland Street
London W1W 5QA
Tel: 020 7299 5000
Fax: 020 7765 2416
Web: www.uktv.co.uk/uktvDocumentary/
Ownership: UK Channel Management Ltd
Sky EPG: 564 (+1 service on 565)
NTL: 506/137
Telewest: 225
Programming: rerun factual entertainment and documentaries, e.g. Louis Theroux, Michael Palin travel shows, *Have I Got News For You?*

UKTV Drama

4th floor
160 Great Portland Street
London W1W 5QA
Tel: 020 7299 5000
Fax: 020 7625 2179
Web: www.uktv.co.uk/uktvDrama/
Ownership: UKTV = BBC Worldwide, Flextech
Service start: 31 March 2000
Satellite: Astra 2A
Sky EPG: 146
NTL: 305/110
Telewest: 147
Programming: classic British drama series and serials. Mostly post-90s and very recent fare (e.g. *State of Play*) but some archive including *Upstairs Downstairs, The Jewel in the Crown*. Airs from 9 p. m. only.

UKTV Food

see above
email: info@ukfood.tv
Web: www.ukfood.tv
Service start: 5 Nov 2001

Satellite: Astra 2A
Freeview: 29 (via Top-Up TV subscription)
Sky EPG: 144 (+1 service on 145)
NTL: 808
Telewest: 260
Programming: food (known as BBC Food in some territories)

UKTV Gold

160 Great Portland Street
London W1W 5QA
Tel: 020 7299 5000
Web: www.uktv.co.uk/uktvGold/
Ownership: UKTV = BBC Worldwide, Flextech
Service start: Nov 1992
Satellite: Astra 2A
Freeview: 17 (via Top-Up TV subscription)
Sky EPG: 109 (+1 service on 110)
NTL: 300/31
Telewest: 124
Programming: archive comedy and drama, mainly drawn from the BBC archives. Staples include *My Family, The Royle Family, Jonathan Creek, Fawlty Towers, The Good Life, Are You Being Served?, Doctor Who.*

UKTV G2 (was UK Gold 2)

See above
Web: www.uktv.co.uk/uktvG2/
Sky EPG: 111
NTL: 830/32
Telewest: 125
Programming: UKTV G2 focuses on a younger 20-30s audience than its parent channel, with modern comedy hits such as *Men Behaving Badly, They Think It's All Over, Absolutely Fabulous, I'm Alan Partridge, The League of Gentlemen.*

UKTV History

See UKTV Bright Ideas
Web: www.uktv.co.uk/uktvHistory/
Sky EPG: 582 (+1 service on 583)
Freeview: 12
NTL: 607/100
Telewest: 203
Programming: History documentary: *Timewatch, Meet the Ancestors*

UKTV People

See above
Web: www.uktv.co.uk/uktvPeople/
Sky EPG: 566
Programming: light factual e.g. *Robot Wars*

UKTV Style

See above
Web: www.uktv.co.uk/uktvStyle/
Freeview: 26 (via Top-Up TV subscription)
Sky EPG: 142 (+1 service on 143)
NTL: 407/112
Telewest: 265
Programming: lifestyle; homes, interiors, makeovers, gardening e.g. *Changing Rooms, Ground Force, Trading Up, Ready Steady Cook, Big Strong Boys.*

The Vault

37 Harwood Road
London SW6 4QP
Tel: 020 7384 2243
Fax: 020 7384 2026
Web: www.chartshow.com
Sky EPG: 456
Programming: golden oldie music videos, mostly 80s and 90s.

Vectone

58 March Lane
London E14 9TP
Tel: 020 7170 0400
Fax: 020 7170 0419
Web: www.vectone.com
Programming: Vectone Bolly shows Bollywood films (Sky EPG 831); Vectone Tamil is 832 and Vectone Bangla is 833

VH-1

180 Oxford Street
London W1N 0DS
Tel: 020 7284 7777
Fax: 020 7284 7788
Web: www.vh1online.co.uk

Ownership: MTV Networks = Viacom (100%)
Satellite: Astra 2A
Sky EPG: 445
Programming: adult-orientated rock music

VH-2

See above
Sky EPG: 446
Programming: music video, with an alternative rock and indie playlist.

VH1 Classic

see above
Satellite: Astra 2A
Sky EPG: 447
Programming: music video, with a classic rock playlist.

The Wrestling Channel

Welby House
96 Wilton Road
London SW1V 1DW
Tel: 020 7599 8904
Fax: 020 7599 8965
Web: www.thewrestlingchannel.tv
Sky EPG: 427
Programming: wrestling and related features

Xplicit XXX

Units 6 & 7 Princes Court
Wapping Lane
London E1 9DA
Tel: 020 7942 7942
Fax: 020 7942 7943
Ownership: Digital Television Production Company Ltd
Sky EPG: 984
Programming: adult

XXX Television

117-121 Salusbury Road
London NW1 6RG
Tel: 020 7328 8808

Ownership: Broadcasting Gaia Ltd
Sky EPG: 990
Programming: adult

You TV

1st Floor
1 Kingsgate
Bradford Business Park
Canal Road
Bradford BD1 4SJ
Sky EPG: 178
Programming: US-led shopping channel

Zee Cinema

Unit 7-9
Belvue Business Centre
Belvue Road
Northolt
Middlesex UB5 5QQ
Tel: 020 8839 4012
Fax: 020 8841 9550
email: uk@zeetelevision.com
Web: www.zeetelevision.com and www.zeetv.co.uk
Ownership: Asia TV Ltd
Satellite: Astra 2A, 2B
Sky EPG: 810
Programming: feature films (subscription)

Zee Music

see above
Sky EPG: 809
Programming: music (subscription)

Zee TV Europe

See above
Sky EPG: 808

News Agencies

AFX News
Finsbury Tower
103-105 Bunhill Row
London EC1Y 8LZ
Tel: 020 7422 4800
Fax: 020 7422 4993
Web: www.afxnews.com
Financial news agency

Agence France Presse
78 Fleet Street
London EC4Y 1NB
Tel: 020 7353 7461
Fax: 020 7353 8359
Web: www.afp.com

ANSA
Essex House
12-13 Essex Street
London WC2R 3AA
Tel: 020 7240 5514
Fax: 020 7240 5518
Web: www.ansa.it
Italian news agency

Australian Associated Press
12 Norwich Street
London EC4A 1QJ
Tel: 020 7353 0153
Fax: 020 7583 3563
email: news.london@aap.com.au
Web: www.aap.com.au

Bloomberg News
City Gate House
39-45 Finsbury Square
London EC2A 1PQ
Tel: 020 7330 7500
Fax: 020 7392 6666
email: newsalert@bloomberg.net
Web: www.bloomberg.com/uk
Financial, economic and corporate news.

Deutsche Presse Agentur
30 Old Queen Street
London SW1H 9HP
Tel: 020 7233 2888
Fax: 020 7233 3534
email: london@dpa.com
Web: www.dpa.com

Dow Jones Newswires
10 Fleet Place
Limeburner Lane
London EC4M 7RB
Tel: 020 7842 9900
Fax: 020 7842 9361
Web: www.dowjonesnews.com

Government News Network (GNN)
Hercules House
Hercules Road
London SE1 7DU
Tel: 020 7261 8527
email: nds@gnn.gsi.gov.uk
Web: www.gnn.gov.uk

Islamic Republic News Agency (IRNA)
3rd Floor
390 High Road
Wembley
Middlesex HA9 6AS
Tel: 020 8903 1630
Fax: 020 8900 0705
email: falahati.irna@btconnect.com
Web: www.irna.com

Jiji Press
International Press Centre
76 Shoe Lane
London EC4A 3JB
Tel: 020 7936 2847
Fax: 020 7583 8353
email: edit@jiji.co.uk
Web: www.jiji.co.jp
Japanese news agency.

Parliamentary & EU News Service
19 Douglas Street
London SW1P 4PA
Tel: 020 7233 8283
Fax: 020 7821 9352
email: info@parliamentary-monitoring.co.uk
Web: www.parliamentary-monitoring.co.uk

Press Association (PA) HQ
292 Vauxhall Bridge Road
London SW1V 1AE
Tel: 020 7963 7000
Fax: 020 7963 7192
Web: www.pressassociation.press.net

RTÉ News (Radio Telefís Éireann)
4 Millbank
London SW1P 3JA
Tel: 020 7233 3384
Fax: 020 7233 3383
Web: www.rte.ie

Reuters
85 Fleet Street
London EC4P 4AJ
Tel: 020 7250 1122
Web: www.reuters.com

Spanish News Agency (EFE)
299 Oxford Street
London W1C 2DZ
Tel: 020 7493 7313
Fax: 020 7493 7314
Web: www.efe.es

Tass/Itar
320 Regent Street
London W1R 3BD
Tel: 020 7580 5543
Fax: 020 7580 5547
Web: www.itar-tass.com
Russian news agency.

United Press International (UPI) UK
Empire House
Empire Way
Middlesex HA9 0EW
Tel: 020 8970 2604
Fax: 020 8970 2613
Web: www.upi.com

Wales News Service
Market Chambers
5-7 St. Mary Street
Cardiff CF10 1AT
Tel: 029 2066 6366
Fax: 029 2066 4181
email: news@walesnews.com

Xinhua News Agency of China
8 Swiss Terrace, Belsize Road
London NW6 4RR
Tel: 020 7586 8437
Fax: 020 7722 8512
email: xinhua@easynet.co.uk
Web: www.xinhuanet.com

DIRECTORY

Organisations

BAFTA
(British Academy of the Film and Television Arts)
195 Piccadilly
London W1V 0LN
Tel: 020 7734 0022
Fax: 020 7734 1792
Web: www.bafta.org
BAFTA is the UK's leading membership led organisation promoting and rewarding excellence in film, television and interactive media. Formed in 1947, BAFTA is a charity, involved in education and training, and provides facilities for screenings and conferences. Membership is available to those with three years' professional experience in television or other media industries. Its award ceremonies for television and film are televised annually.

BARB
(Broadcasters' Audience Research Board)
2nd Floor
181 Dering Street
London W1R 9AF
Tel: 020 7529 5531
Fax: 020 7529 5530
Web: www.barb.co.uk
Set up in 1981 to 'provide the industry standard audience measurement service for television broadcasters and the advertising industry', BARB represents and is owned by the major UK broadcasters and the Institute of Practitioners in Advertising. It is the main source for television audience research in the UK.

BECTU
(Broadcasting Entertainment Cinematograph and Theatre Union)
373-377 Clapham Road
London SW9 9BT
Tel: 020 7346 0900
Fax. 020 7346 0901
email: info@bectu.org.uk
Web: www.bectu.org.uk
BECTU is the independent union for those working in broadcasting, film, interactive media and allied areas in the UK, and offers a wide range of services to its members. Affiliated to the TUC and founded in 1991 after a series of mergers between separate unions during the 1980s.

BKSTS – The Moving Image Society
Suite 104, G Block
Pinewood Studios
Iver Heath
Buckinghamshire SL0 0NH
Tel: 01753 656656
Fax: 01753 657016
email: info@bksts.com
Web: www.bksts.com
The Society aims to educate, train and represent those involved creatively and technically within the moving image industry. An independent organization, founded in 1931, BKSTS also focuses on developments in film technology, organises events and conferences and has regional branches throughout the UK. Funded by members and sponsors.

British Amateur Television Club
(BATC)
The Villa
Plas Panteidal
Aberdyfi
Gwynedd LL35 0RF
Tel: 01654 767702
email: memsec@batc.org.uk
Web: www.batc.org.uk
Founded in 1949 to encourage and co-ordinate the activities of 'amateurs involved in all aspects of television as a hobby', this non profit making organisation is run by volunteers. Members' interests cover transmitting and receiving TV images and the technology behind video and programme productions. Enthusiasts include teachers, business personnel and private individuals. BATC produces a mainly technical quarterly magazine CQ-TV and maintains a library. Material, including videos, is available for loan to members.

British Film Institute
21 Stephen Street
London W1T 1LN
Tel: 020 7255 1444
Fax: 020 7436 7950
Web: www.bfi.org.uk
The National Film, TV and Video Archive (NFTVA) at the *bfi* is the largest archive of moving image material in the world and in 2004 included 210,000 TV programmes, dating from the 1950s onwards. Details of TV holdings are catalogued and held in the *bfi* database SIFT and information can be found via the *bfi* Web at Screenonline. This useful, educational site provides an historical overview of TV in the UK and holds essays on TV genres, the industry and audiences. Viewing copies of many TV programmes are held in the archive, whilst reviews, research and information on UK broadcasting can be accessed via the *bfi* national library. Preservation of TV is included in the remit of the *bfi* archive and through its publishing department, TV is continually seen as a subject for indepth analysis and research.

British Universities Film and Video Council (BUFVC)
77 Wells Street
London W1T 3QJ
Tel: 020 7393 1500
Fax. 020 7393 1555
email: ask@bufvc.ac.uk
Web: www.bufvc.ac.uk
A representative body promoting the production, study and use of film and related media in higher and further education and research. Founded in 1948 as the British Universities Film Council. The Council receives core grant support from the Joint Information Systems Committee (JISC) of the Higher Education Funding Councils via the Open University. The BUFVC currently employs around 17 staff and has an annual turnover of approximately £700,000. Around 30% of total revenue is raised through income from subscriptions, conferences, publishing, grants and sponsorship.

Campaign for Press and Broadcasting Freedom

(CPBF)
2nd Floor
Vi & Garner Smith House
23 Orford Road
Walthamstow
London E17 9NL
Tel: 020 8521 5932
email: freepress@cpbf.org.uk
Web: www.cpbf.org.uk
The Campaign for Press and Broadcasting Freedom is an independent voice for media reform and works to promote policies for a diverse, democratic and accountable media. Membership includes national trade unions, local trade union and Labour Party branches as well as media, cultural and educational organisations. The organisation initiates debate, and continually lobbies on media ownership, censorship, broadcasting deregulation and the future of public service broadcasting. Activities include research, publishing and relevant political and cultural events.

Children's Film and Television Foundation

(CFTF)
The John Maxwell Building
Elstree Film and Television Studios
Shenley Road
Borehamwood
Herts. WD6 1JG
Tel: 020 8953 0844
Fax: 020 8207 0860
email: annahome@cftf.onyxnet.co.uk
Originating as the Children's Film Foundation in the 1950s, the CFTF finances script development for children's and family films and television projects. Provides funding on a loan basis and films are available for hire on 35mm, 16mm and video format.

Cinema and Television Benevolent Fund

22 Golden Square
London W1F 9AD
Tel: 020 7437 6567
Fax: 020 7439 4550
Web: www.ctbf.co.uk

The British trade charity of film, cinema and the commercial television industries. Provides practical and financial assistance, assisting costs of mortgages, bills, debt counselling and TV Licences to anyone who has worked in the industry for two years or more. Membership is free. The charity also provides conference facilities, runs its own residential/convalescent home and helps with nursing fees and regular grants to those in need.

Deaf Broadcasting Council

70 Blacketts Wood Drive
Chorleywood
Rickmansworth
Herts WD3 5QQ
Tel: 01923 284538
Fax: 01923 283127
email: rmyers@waitrose.com
Web: www.deafbroadcastingcouncil.org.uk
Founded in 1980 as the Deaf Broadcasting Campaign, the registered charity monitors full access to television via the quality of subtitles/signed programmes. Also alerts broadcasters to the needs of deaf people and responds to Government/industry discussion papers. Other campaigns include furthering employment opportunities for the deaf in the media, and encouraging positive representation in TV programmes, dramas etc.

Defence Press and Broadcasting Advisory Committee

Room G27
Ministry of Defence
Metropole Building
Northumberland Avenue
London WC2N 5BP
Tel: 020 7218 2206
Fax: 020 7218 5857
Web: www.dnotice.org.uk
The Committee 'oversees a voluntary code which operates between those Government department which have responsibilities for national security and the media, using as a vehicle the DA Notice system'. Members of the Committee include senior officials from the Ministry of Defence, the home office and representatives of the media. DA

Notices – Defence Advisory Notices – do not possess any legal authority. The system is based on the 'shared belief' that a voluntary, advisory basis is the preferable approach to the issue of security and media regulation.

Focal International Ltd

(Federation of commercial audio-visual libraries)
Pentax house
South Hill Avenue
South Harrow HA2 0DU
Tel: 020 8423 5853
Fax: 020 8933 4826
email: info@focalint.org
Web: www.focalint.org
Founded in 1985 as a professional trade association, Focal International represents a wide range of film, audiovisual and still libraries. Membership includes over 300 international archives, researchers and related services. Established as one of the 'leading voices of the industry', the association provides a free searching service allowing users to locate clips, archives, footage, stockshots and stills from over 100 audiovisual libraries. Response time from individual libraries to initial request is usually within 48 hours.

Guild of Television Cameramen

1 Churchill Road
Whitchurch
Tavistock
Devon PL19 9BU
Tel: 01822 614405
Fax: 01822 615785
Web: www.gtc.org.uk
The GTC, formed in 1972 and with over 1,000 members, is an 'authoritative source of advice and information' on the craft of camerawork in television. Acting as a representative for camera technicians, the organisation is both independent and international. Sponsored by major manufacturers and suppliers within the industry, it provides awards for best work and achievement, publishes regular magazines and newsletters, and holds workshops and seminars for its members.

DIRECTORY

Guild Of Vision Mixers

147 Ship Lane
Farnborough
Hampshire
England GU14 8BJ
Tel: 01252 514953
Fax: 01252 656756
email: peter.turl@dtn.ntl.com
Web: www.guildofvisionmixers.org.uk
Established in 1984 and representing the interests of Vision Mixers working in TV production in UK and Ireland, the Guild aims to advance the status and skill of its members and maintain professional standards. Services to members include providing news, tax advice and an on-line magazine.

Intellect

Russell Square House
10-12 Russell Square
London WC1B 5EE
Tel: 020 7331 2000
Fax: 020 7331 2040
email: info@intellectuk.org
Web: www.intellectuk.org
Operating as the trade-body for the UK based information technology, telecommunications and electronics industry, Intellect aims to promote the business to government and the private sector. Responds to Government papers and producers press releases on topics such as Digital TV, telecommunications and consumer electronics. Also raises media awareness, promotes the business interests of members and establishes standards in the industry.

IABM

(International Association of Broadcasting Manufacturers)
PO Box 2264
Reading
Berkshire RG31 6WA
Tel: 01189 418 620
Fax: 01189 418 630
email: secretariat@theiabm.org
Web: www.theiabm.org/
Founded in 1976, the IABM aims to be the leading trade association representing internationally the broadcasting manufacturing industry. Members include service providers, consultants and manufacturing companies. Promoting the interests of exhibitors and providing publications, training and news of events, the Association influences the establishment of recommended practices, standards and legislation.

IIC

(International Institute of Communications)
Regent House
24-25 Nutford Place
London W1H 5YN
Tel: 020 7323 9622
Fax: 020 7323 9623
email: enquiries@iicom.org
Web: www.iicom.org
Acting as a forum for industry, government and academia, the IIC debates and analyses trends in communication, producing alliances and links between sectors, organisations and countries. Aiming to 'promote access to communications for all people of the world', the Institute publishes 'Intermedia', provides a research programme on key issues, maintains a library and liases with I.G.O.'s and N.G.O.'s. The Broadcasting Forum facilitates senior decision-makers, and commentators and academics on broadcasting, to network and address the major issues of the industry.

Mediawatch-uk

3 Willow House
Kennington Road
Ashford
Kent TN24 0NR
Tel: 01233 633936
Web: www.mediawatchuk.org.
The National Viewers' and Listeners' Association was founded in 1965 by Mary Whitehouse CBE and her associates, following the huge public support for the Clean Up TV Campaign launched in 1964. Mary Whitehouse passed away in November 2001. Part of her legacy is the continuing work of mediawatch-uk.

Mental Health Media

356 Holloway Road
London N7 6PA
Phone: +44 (0) 20 7700 8171
Fax: +44 (0) 20 7686 0959
email: info@mhmedia.com
Web: www.mhmedia.com
Organisation which aims to promote via all media information on mental distress and 'challenge the discrimination' which individuals experience. MHM works with journalists and broadcasters, provides media skills, training and support to both users and professionals. Also runs the annual 'Mental Health Media Awards'.

NAHEMI

(National Association for Higher Education in the Moving Image)
City Campus
Central House
59-63 Whitechapel High Street
London E1 7PH
Tel: +44 020 8840 2815
email: yossibal@aol.com
A forum for debate on all aspects of film, video and animation production in Higher Education. The Association has links with industry and government bodies and represents courses in the UK and Eire that offer a major study in film, video, television, animation and new media practice.

Ofcom - Office of Communication

Contact Centre
Riverside House
2a Southwark Bridge Road
London SE1 9HA
Tel: 0845 456 3000 or 020 7981 3040
Fax: 0845 456 3333
email: contact@ofcom.org.uk
Web: www.ofcom.org.uk
'Ofcom is the regulator for the UK communications industries, with responsibilities across television, radio telecommunications and wireless communication services.' In 2004 it replaced five existing regulators, including the Broadcasting Standards Commission and the ITC. Aiming to further the interests of 'citizen consumers', Ofcom promotes choice, competition and cultural diversity. Its codes of policy on broadcasting relate to programmes, advertising, sponsorship, subtitling and access for the deaf and partially sighted. Ofcom also encourages viewers/ consumers to make a complaint and submit enquiries concerning broadcasting and other communication industries.

Pact

(Producers Alliance for Cinema and Television)

45 Mortimer Street
London W1W 8HJ
Tel: 020 7331 6000
Fax: 020 7331 6700
email: enquiries@pact.co.uk
Web: www.pact.co.uk
Pact is the UK trade association that 'represents and promotes the commercial interests of independent feature films, television, animation and interactive media companies'. Based in London and Scotland, Pact is also a lobbying organisation and acts as a regulator/opinion former on issues affection its members and the media industry. In addition, involved in encouraging financial investment in the UK independent sector, EU policy and agreements with union and guilds.

The Production Managers Association

Ealing Studios
Ealing Green
Ealing
London W5 5EP
Tel: 020 8758 8699
email: pma@pma.org.uk
Web: www.pma.org.uk
Providing a network for freelance and permanent Production Managers in the Film, TV and multi-media industries, the Association also producers 'invaluable information and support for its members'. This includes regular social events, workshops and training courses, plus details of employment opportunities. Affiliated to Pact, the PMA publishes a directory of members, is involved in sponsorship and promotion, offers an online forum and CV service to prospective employers and producers a newsletter aiding its networking activities.

The Research Centre

227 West George Street
Glasgow G2 2ND
Tel: 0141 568 7113
Fax: 0141 568 7114
Web: www.researchcentre.co.uk
The Research Centre operates as a knowledge bank, ideas factory, business and training centre and also undertakes keynote industry research.

Royal Television Society

Holborn Hall
100 Grays Inn Road
London WC1X 8AL
Tel: 020 7430 1000
Fax: 020 7430 0924
email: info@art.org.uk
Web: www.rts.org.uk
The Royal Television Society is the 'leading forum for discussion and debate on all aspects of the television industry' and offers unrivalled opportunities for networking and learning for people 'at all levels and across every sector'. Individuals can join via e-membership and enjoy priority booking of events and receive the RTS's monthly magazine *Television*. Through its Awards, the Society rewards/recognizes excellence and also holds conferences, lectures and various social events. Its archive, dating back to the foundation of the Society in 1927, is both open to Members and also to academic researchers.

Seirbheis nam Meadhanan Gàidhlig

Gaelic Media Service
4 Harbour View
Cromwell Street
Stornoway
Isle of Lewis HS1 2DF
Tel: 01851 705550
Fax: 01851 706432
email: admin@ccg.org.uk
Web: www.ccg.org.uk

Evolved from the Gaelic television committee, established in 1990, the GMS provides funding for Gaelic programme production, training and audience research. The service aims to 'deploy a substantial proportion of its production and development funds in the independent sector'. Past projects include documentaries, children's programmes and current affairs.

A Voice of the Listener and Viewer

VLV Librarian
101 King's Drive
Gravesend
Kent DA12 5BQ
Tel: 01474 352835
Fax: 01474 351112
email: vlv@btinternet.com
Web: www.vlv.org.uk
VLV represents the 'citizens and consumer interest in broadcasting and works for quality and diversity in British broadcasting'. Founded in 1983, VLV is an independent organisation and addresses on behalf of its members the structures, regulation and funding of broadcasting. It aims to preserve the impartiality of the BBC, the public service remit of Channel 4 and secure the funding of the BBC World Service. Through lectures, conferences and lobbying, the VLV makes its views known to MPs, the BBC, ITC and relevant bodies worldwide.

DIRECTORY

255

Production Companies

12 Yard Productions
10 Livonia Street
London W1F 8AF
Tel: +44 020 7432 2929
Fax: +44 020 7439 2037
email: contact@12yard.com
Web: www.12yard.com/index.php

19 Television
16 Ransomes Dock
35-37 Parkgate Road
London SW11 4NP
Tel: +44 020 7801 1919
Fax: +44 020 7223 1864
email: jane@19.co.uk
Web: www.19.co.uk

3BM Television
63 Gee Street
London EC1V 3RS
Tel: +44 020 7251 2512
Fax: +44 020 7251 2514
email: 3bmtv@3bmtv.co.uk
Web: www.3bmtv.co.uk
Part of Ten Alps Communications PLC

Aardman Animations
Gasferry Road
Bristol BS1 6UN
Tel: +44 0117 984 8485
Fax: +44 0117 984 8486
email: mail@aardman.com
Web: www.aardman.com

All3Media
87-91 Newman Street
London W1T 3EY
Tel: +44 020 7907 0177
Fax: +44 020 7907 0199
email: information@all3media.com
Web: www.all3media.com
Formed following the acquisition of
Chrysalis Group's Television division.
Covers six production companies from the
UK, Netherlands, and New
Zealand; as well as an international
distribution company.

Assembly
Riverside Studios
Crisp Road
London W6 9RL
Tel: +44 020 8237 1075
Fax: +44 020 8237 1071
email: judithmurrell@riversidestudios.co.uk
Web: www.all3media.com
Part of the All3Media group

At It Productions
Unit 314, Westbourne Studios
242 Acklam Road
London W10 5YG
Tel: +44 020 8964 2122
Fax: +44 020 8964 2133
email: enquiries@atitproductions.com
Web: www.atitproductions.com

Atlantic Productions
3rd Floor
Shepherds Central
Charecroft Way
Shepherds Bush
London W14 0EH
Tel: +44 020 7371 3200
Fax: +44 020 7371 3222
email: info@atlanticproductions.co.uk
Web: www.atlanticproductions.tv

Avalon Television
4a Exmoor Street
London W10 6BD
Tel: +44 020 7598 7280
Fax: +44 020 7598 7281
email: leet@avalonuk.com
Web: www.avalonuk.com

Baby Cow Productions
77 Oxford Street
London W1D 2ES
Tel: +44 020 7399 1267
Fax: +44 020 7399 1262
email: info@babycow.co.uk
Web: www.babycow.co.uk

Bentley Productions
Pinewood Studios
Pinewood Road
Iver
Buckinghamshire SL0 0NH

Tel: +44 01753 656594
Fax: +44 01753 652638
Web: www.all3media.com
Part of the All3Media group

Big Bear Films
36 Courtnell Street
London W2 5BX
Tel: +44 020 7229 5982
Fax: +44 020 7221 0676
email: office@bigbearfilms.co.uk
Web: www.bigbearfilms.co.uk

Blakeway Productions
32 Woodstock Grove
London W12 8LE
Tel: +44 020 8743 2040
Fax: +44 020 8743 2141
email: admin@blakeway.co.uk
Web: www.blakeway.co.uk

Blast! Films
Unit C, Imperial Works
Perren Street
London NW5 3ED
Tel: +44 020 7267 4260
Fax: +44 020 7485 2340
email: blast@blastfilms.co.uk
Web: www.blastfilms.co.uk

Box TV
Enterprise House
59-65 Upper Ground
London SE1 9PQ
Tel: +44 020 7593 0440
Fax: +44 020 7593 0449
email: asquire@box-tv.co.uk
Web: www.box-tv.co.uk

Brian Waddell Productions
Strand Studios
5/7 Shore Road
Holywood
County Down BT18 9HX
Tel: +44 028 9042 7646
Fax: +44 028 9042 7922
email: strand@bwpltv.co.uk
Web: www.bwpltv.co.uk

Brighter Pictures

Shepherds Building Central
Charecroft Way
Shepherds Bush
London W14 0EE
Tel: +44 020 8222 4100
Fax: +44 020 8222 4186
email: info@brighter.co.uk
Web: www.brighter.co.uk
Part of the Endemol UK group

Brook Lapping

6 Anglers Lane
Kentish Town
London NW5 3DG
Tel: +44 020 7428 3100
Fax: +44 020 7284 0626
email: info@tenalps.com
Web: www.tenalps.com/brooklapping
Part of Ten Alps Communications PLC

CactusTV

373 Kennington Road
London SE11 4PS
Tel: +44 020 7091 4900
Fax: +44 020 7091 4901
email: touch.us@cactustv.co.uk
Web: www.cactustv.co.uk
Part of the All3Media group

Cardinal

15a Clive Road
Caerdydd
Cardiff CF5 1HF
Tel: +44 029 2022 8807
Fax: +44 029 2022 8925
email: post@cardinal-tv.co.uk
Web: www.cardinal-tv.co.uk

Carnival Films

12 Raddington Road
London W10 5TG
Tel: +44 020 8968 0968
Fax: +44 020 8968 0177
email: info@carnival-films.co.uk
Web: www.carnival-films.co.uk

Celador Productions

39 Long Acre
London WC2E 9LG
Tel: +44 020 7240 8101
Fax: +44 020 7836 1117
email: tvhits@celador.co.uk
Web: www.celador.co.uk

Chameleon Television

Great Minster House
Lister Hill
Horsforth
Leeds LS18 5DL
Tel: +44 0113 205 0040
Fax: +44 0113 281 9454

Channel X

2nd Floor
Highgate Business Centre
33 Greenwood Place
London NW5 1LB
Tel: +44 020 7428 3999
Fax: +44 020 7428 3998
email: info@chxp.co.uk
Web: www.chxp.co.uk

Coastal Productions

25b Broad Chare
Quayside
Newcastle upon Tyne NE1 3DQ
Tel: +44 0191 222 3160
Fax: +44 0191 222 3169
email: coastalproductions@msn.com

The Comedy Unit

Glasgow Media Park
Craigmont Street
Glasgow G20 9BT
Tel: +44 0141 305 6666
Fax: +44 0141 305 6600
email: general@comedyunit.co.uk
Web: www.comedyunit.co.uk

Company Pictures

Suffolk House
1/8 Whitfield Place
London W1T 5JU
Tel: +44 020 7380 3900
Fax: +44 020 7380 1166
email: enquiries@companypictures.co.uk
Web: www.companypictures.co.uk

CTVC

Hillside
Merry Hill Road
Bushey
Hertfordshire WD23 1DR
Tel: +44 020 8950 4426
Fax: +44 020 8950 6694
email: prods@ctvc.co.uk
Web: www.ctvc.co.uk

Darlow Smithson Productions

4th Floor
Highgate Business Centre
33 Greenwood Place
London NW5 1LB
Tel: +44 020 7482 7027
Fax: +44 020 7482 7039
email: mail@darlowsmithson.com
Web: www.darlowsmithson.com

Darrall Macqueen

17 Park Street
Borough Market
London SE1 9AB
Tel: +44 020 7407 2322
Fax: +44 020 7407 2323
email: info@darrallmacqueen.com
Web: www.darrallmacqueen.com

Denham Productions

Quay West Studios
Old Newnham
Plymouth PL7 5BH
Tel: +44 01752 345444
Fax: +44 01752 345448
email: info@denham-productions.co.uk
Web: www.denham-productions.co.uk

Diverse

Gorleston Street
London W14 8XS
Tel: +44 020 7603 4567
Fax: +44 020 7603 2148
email: info@diverse.tv
Web: www.diverse.tv

DLT Entertainment UK

10 Bedford Square
London WC1B 3RA
Tel: +44 020 7631 1184
Fax: +44 020 7636 4571
email: jbartlett@dltentertainment.com
Web: www.dltentertainment.com

Done and Dusted

87 Lancaster Road
Notting Hill
London W11 1QQ
Tel: +44 020 7229 4100
Fax: +44 020 7229 1794
Web: www.doneanddusted.com

DIRECTORY

Ecosse Films
Brigade House
8 Parsons Green
London SW6 4TN
Tel: +44 020 7371 0290
Fax: +44 020 7736 3436
email: info@ecossefilms.com
Web: www.ecossefilms.com

Endemol UK Productions
Shepherds Building Central
Charecroft Way
Shepherds Bush
London W14 0EE
Tel: +44 0870 333 1700
Fax: +44 0870 333 1800
email: info@endemoluk.com
Web: www.endemoluk.com
Part of the Endemol UK group - contact
as above

Flashback Bristol
1-2 Fitzroy Terrace
Lower Redland Road
Bristol BS6 6TF
Tel: +44 0117 973 8755
Fax: +44 0117 317 1710
email: bristol@flashbacktv.co.uk
Web: www.flashbacktv.co.uk

Flashback Television
9-11 Bowling Green Lane
London EC1 0BG
Tel: +44 020 7490 8996
Fax: +44 020 7490 5610
email: mailbox@flashbacktv.co.uk
Web: www.flashbacktv.co.uk

Folio
43 Whitfield Street
London W1T 4HA
Tel: +44 020 7258 6800
Fax: +44 020 7691 1988
email: folio@mentorn.co.uk
Web: www.mentorn.co.uk
Part of the Television Corporation

Folio Scotland
Part of the Television Corporation - for
contact information see Mentorn
Scotland

Freeform Productions
Unit 302-304
Greenheath Business Centre
London E2 6JB
Tel: +44 020 7739 9234
Fax: +44 020 7729 6374

FremantleMedia Ltd
1 Stephen Street
London W1T 1AL
United Kingdom
Tel: +44 (0)20 7691 6000
Fax: +44 (0)20 7691 6100
Web: www.fremantlemedia.com

FulcrumTV
3rd Floor
Bramah House
65-71 Bermondsey Street
London SE1 3XF
Tel: +44 020 7939 3160
Fax: +44 020 7403 2260
email: info@Fulcrumtv.com
Web: www.fulcrumtv.com

Granada Television
Quay Street
Manchester
Lancashire M60 9E4
Tel: +44 0161 832 7211
Fax: +44 0161 827 2029
Web: www.granadamedia.com

Greenlit Productions
3rd Floor
14-15 D'Arblay Street
London W1F 8DZ
Tel: +44 020 7287 3545
Fax: +44 020 7439 6767
email: info@greenlit.co.uk
Web: www.greenlit.co.uk

Hanrahan Media
P.O. Box 163
Stratford-Upon-Avon
Warwickshire CV37 8NG
Tel: +44 01789 450182
Fax: +44 01789 450143
email: info@hanrahanmedia.com
Web: www.hanrahanmedia.tv

Hat Trick Productions
10 Livonia Street
London W1F 8AF
Tel: +44 020 7434 2451

Fax: +44 020 7287 9791
email: info@hattrick.com
Web: www.hattrick.com

Hewland International
The Old Lab
3 Mills Studios
London E3 3DU
Tel: +44 020 8215 3345
email: abrook@hewland.co.uk

Hit Entertainment
5th Floor
Maple House
149 Tottenham Court Road
London W1T 7NF
Tel: +44 020 7554 2500
Fax: +44 020 7388 9321

Hotbed Media
The Hothouse
16 Regent Place
Birmingham B1 3NJ
Tel: +44 0121 248 3900
Fax: +44 0121 248 4900
email: mail@hotbedmedia.co.uk
Web: www.hotbedmedia.co.uk

Imago Productions
5th Floor
Grosvenor House
Norwich NR1 1NS
Tel: +44 01603 727600
Fax: +44 01603 727626
email: mail@imagoproductions.tv
Web: www.imagoproductions.tv

Independent Television News (ITN)
200 Gray's Inn Road
London WC1X 8XZ
Tel: +44 020 7833 3000
Fax: +44 020 7430 4868
email: editor@itn.co.uk
Web: www.itn.co.uk

Initial
Shepherds Building Central
Charecroft Way
Shepherds Bush
London W14 0EE
Tel: +44 0870 330 1700
Fax: +44 0870 330 1800
email: info@endemoluk.com
Web: www.endemoluk.com
Part of the Endemol UK group

Want to find out about sound design schools?

Do a credit check.

VFS

For immediate information, call Vancouver Film School
1-800-661-4101
www.vfs.com/credits

Robert Grieve
Head of Department
Sound Design for Visual Media

Taking Lives

Body Heat

The Big Chill

Silverado

The Big Easy

Broadcast News

Zoolander

Pretty in Pink

The Accidental Tourist

Robin Hood
Prince Of Thieves

The Changeling

Wolfen and Wyatt Earp

Dreamcatcher

61*

METROPOLITAN
FILM SCHOOL

Take your story to the screen!

Our courses include:

Three-day Intensive Filmmaking
From Story to Screen – 8 weeks, 4 weeks and evening options
Complete Script Development – for shorts and features
Young Filmmakers Workshop

0845 658 4400 | metfilmschool.co.uk

DIRECTORY

IWC Media (Glasgow)
St George's Studio
93-97 St George's Road
Glasgow G3 6JA
Tel: +44 0141 353 3222
Fax: +44 0141 353 3221
email: mailglasgow@iwcmedia.co.uk
Web: www.iwcmedia.co.uk
Was Ideal World Productions (Glasgow),
now incorporates Wark Clements.

IWC Media (London)
3-6 Kenrick Place
London W1U 6HD
Tel: 020 7317 2230
Fax: +44 020 7684 1441
email: maillondon@iwcmedia.co.uk
Web: www.iwcmedia.co.uk

Juniper Communications
47-49 Borough High Street
London SE1 1NB
Tel: +44 020 7407 9292
Fax: +44 020 7407 3940
email: juniper@junipertv.co.uk
Web: www.junipertv.co.uk

Kilroy Television Company
South Block
Teddington Studios
Broom Road
Teddington TW11 9NT
Middlesex
Tel: +44 020 7893 7900
Fax: +44 020 7893 7950
email: info@kilroy.co.uk

Kudos Film and Television
12-14 Amwell Street
London EC1R 1UQ
Tel: +44 020 7580 8686
Fax: +44 020 7580 8787
email: reception@kudosproductions.co.uk
Web: www.kudosproductions.co.uk

Lion Television
Lion House
26 Paddenswick Road
London W6 0UB
Tel: +44 020 8846 2000
Fax: +44 020 8846 2001
email: firstname.surname@liontv.co.uk
Web: www.liontv.co.uk

Maverick Television
(Birmingham)
Progress Works
The Custard Factory
Heath Mill Lane
Birmingham B9 4DY
Tel: +44 0121 771 1812
Fax: +44 0121 771 1550
email: mail@mavericktv.co.uk
Web: www.mavericktv.co.uk

Maverick Television (London)
4th Floor
15 Berners Street
London W1T 3LJ
Tel: +44 020 7631 1062
Fax: +44 020 7436 3900
email: mail@mavericktv.co.uk
Web: www.mavericktv.co.uk

Mentorn
43 Whitfield Street
London W1T 4HA
Tel: +44 020 7258 6800
Fax: +44 020 7258 6888
email: mentorn@mentorn.co.uk
Web: www.mentorn.co.uk
Part of The Television Corporation

Mentorn Oxford
The Old Iron Works
35a Great Clarendon Street
Oxford OX2 6AT
Tel: +44 01865 318450
Fax: +44 0186 5318451
email: oxford@mentorn.co.uk
Web: www.mentorn.co.uk
Part of The Television Corporation

Mentorn Scotland
Riverside House
260 Clyde Street
Glasgow G1 4JH
Tel: +44 0141 204 6600
Fax: +44 0141 204 6666
email: lcummings@mentorn.co.uk
Web: www.mentorn.co.uk
Part of The Television Corporation

The Mersey Television Company
Campus Manor
Childwall Abbey Road
Childwall
Liverpool L16 0JP
Tel: +44 0151 722 9122
Fax: +44 0151 722 1969
Web: www.merseytv.com

Monkey
Biscuit Building
10 Redchurch Street
London E2 7DD
Tel: +44 020 7749 3110
email: info@monkeykingdom.com
Web: www.monkeykingdom.com

Music Box
Part of The Television Corporation - for
contact information see Mentorn
Scotland

North One Television
Mayward House
46-52 Pentonville Road
London N1 3HF
Tel: +44 020 7502 6000
Fax: +44 020 7502 5600
Web: www.all3media.com
Formerly known as Chrysalis Television;
now part of the All3Media group

Objective Productions
314 King Street
London W6 0RR
Tel: +44 020 8846 3950
Fax: +44 020 8846 3951
email: info@objectiveproductions.net

October Films
Spring House
10 Spring Place
London NW5 3BH
Tel: +44 020 7284 6868
Fax: +44 020 7284 6869
email: info@octoberfilms.co.uk
Web: www.octoberfilms.co.uk

Optomen Television
1 Valentine Place
London SE1 8QH
Tel: +44 020 7967 1234
Fax: +44 020 7967 1233
email: otv@optomen.com
Web: www.optomen.com

Oxford Film and Television

6 Erskine Road
London NW3 3AJ
Tel: +44 020 7483 3637
Fax: +44 020 7483 3567
email: email:@oftv.co.uk
Web: www.oftv.co.uk

Pilot Film & Television

Productions
The Old Studio
18 Middle Row
London W10 5AT
Tel: +44 020 8960 2771
Fax: +44 020 8960 2721
email: info@pilotguides.com
Web: www.pilotguides.com

Pioneer Productions

Voyager House
32 Galena Road
London W6 0LT
Tel: +44 020 8748 0888
Fax: +44 020 8748 7888
email: pioneer@pioneertv.com
Web: www.pioneertv.com

Princess Productions

Princess Studios
3rd Floor, Unit 316
Whiteley Centre
151 Queensway
London W2 4SB
Tel: +44 020 7985 1985
Fax: +44 020 7985 1986
email: reception@princesstv.com
Web: www.princesstv.com

Principal Films

Picture House
65 Hopton Street
London SE1 9LR
Tel: +44 020 7928 9287
Fax: +44 020 7928 9886
email: films@principalmedia.com
Web: www.principalmedia.com

Prism Entertainment

1-2 Grand Union Centre
West Row Courtyard
London W10 5AS
Tel: +44 020 8969 1212
Fax: +44 020 8969 1012
email: info@prism-e.com
Web: www.prismentertainment.co.uk

Prospect Pictures

Wandsworth Plain
London SW18 1ET
Tel: +44 020 7636 1234
Fax: +44 020 7636 1236
email: info@prospect-uk.com
Web: www.prospect-uk.com

Ragdoll

Timothy's Bridge Road
Stratford-Upon-Avon
Warks CV37 9NQ
Tel: +44 01789 404100
Fax: +44 01789 404136
email: info@ragdoll.co.uk
Web: www.ragdoll.co.uk

RDF Media

Gloucester Building
Kensington Village
Avonmore Road
London W14 8RF
Tel: +44 020 7013 4000
Fax: +44 020 7013 4001
email: contactus@rdfmedia.com
Web: www.rdfmedia.com

Real Life Media Productions

Chapel Allerton House
114 Harrogate Road
Leeds LS7 4NY
Tel: +44 0113 237 1005
Fax: +44 0113 288 8523
email: info@reallife.co.uk
Web: www.reallife.co.uk

Red Production Company

c/o Granada TV
Quay Street
Manchester M60 9EA
Tel: +44 0161 827 2530
Fax: +44 0161 827 2518
email: info@redlimited.co.uk
Web: www.redproductioncompany.com

Ricochet Films

Cairo Studios
4 Nile Street
London N1 7RF
Tel: +44 020 7251 6966
Fax: +44 020 7490 8394
email: mail@ricochet.co.uk
Web: www.ricochet.co.uk

Ricochet South

Brighton Media Centre
21-22 Old Steine
Brighton BN1 1EL
Tel: +44 01273 648 396
Fax: +44 01273 648 391
email: mail@ricochetsouth.co.uk
Web: www.ricochet.co.uk

Rollem Production Company

20 Hustlers Row
Meanwood
Leeds LS6 4QH
Tel: +44 0113 275 1830
Fax: +44 0113 275 4779
email: rollemproductions@aol.com
Web: www.rollem.com

Sally Head Productions

Twickenham Film Studios
The Barons
St Margarets
Twickenham
Middlesex TW1 2AW
Tel: +44 020 8607 8730
Fax: +44 020 8607 8964
email: admin@shpl.demon.co.uk

Scream Films

Lamb House
Church Street
Chiswick
London W4 2PD
Tel: +44 020 8995 8255
Fax: +44 020 8995 8456
email: info@screamfilms.com
Web: www.screamfilms.com

September Films

Glen House
22 Glenthorne Road
London W6 0NG
Tel: +44 020 8563 9393
Fax: +44 020 8741 7214
email: september@septemberfilms.com
Web: www.septemberfilms.com

Seventh Art Productions

63 Ship Street
Brighton BN1 1AE
Tel: +44 01273 777678
Fax: +44 01273 323777
email: info@seventh-art.com
Web: www.seventh-art.com

DIRECTORY

Shed Productions

Customs House
Three Mills Studios
Three Mill Lane
London E3 3DU
Tel: +44 020 8215 3387
Fax: +44 020 8709 8646
email: shed@shedproductions.com
Web: www.shedproductions.com

Shine

108 Palace Gardens Terrace
London W8 7RT
Tel: +44 020 7313 8000
Fax: +44 020 7313 8041
email: info@shinelimited.com
Web: www.shinelimited.com

So Television

18 Hatfields
London SE1 8GN
Tel: +44 020 7960 2000
Fax: +44 020 7960 2095
email: info@sotelevision.co.uk
Web: www.sotelevision.co.uk

Somethin' Else

Units 1-4
1a Old Nichol Street
London E2 7HR
Tel: +44 020 7613 3211
Fax: +44 020 7739 9799
email: info@somethin-else.com
Web: www.somethin-else.com

Sunset+Vine

30 Sackville Street
London W1S 3DY
Tel: +44 020 7478 7300
Fax: +44 020 7478 7407
email: reception@sunsetvine.co.uk
Web: www.sunsetvine.co.uk
Part of The Television Corporation

Sunset+Vine North

Rushmere Lodge
Arthington Lane
Pool-in-Wharfedale
Leeds LS21 1JZ
Tel: +44 0113 284 2400
email: nicklord@sunsetvine.co.uk
Part of The Television Corporation

Talent TV

Lion House
72-75 Red Lion Street
London WC1R 4NA
Tel: +44 020 7421 7800
Fax: +44 020 7421 7811
email: entertainment@talenttv.com
Web: www.talenttv.com

talkbackTHAMES

20-21 Newman Street
London W1T 1PG
Tel: +44 020 7861 8000
Fax: +44 020 7861 8001
email: reception@talkbackthames.tv
Web: www.talkbackTHAMES.tv
UK production arm of Fremantle Media.

Teledu Telesgop

22 Crescent Road
Llandeilo
Carmarthenshire SA19 6HN
Tel: +44 01558 823828
Fax: +44 01558 823011
email: Telesgop@Tel:esgop.co.uk
Web: www.Telesgop.co.uk

Telemagination

Royalty House
72-74 Dean Street
London W1D 3SG
Tel: +44 020 7434 1551
Fax: +44 020 7434 3344
email: mail@tmation.co.uk
Web: www.telemagination.co.uk

The Television Corporation

30 Sackville Street
London W1S 3DY
Tel: +44 020 7478 7300
Fax: +44 020 7478 7415
email: tvcorp@tvcorp.co.uk
Web: www.tvcorp.co.uk
The Television Corporation comprises of
Mentorn, Sunset+Vine, Folio,
Music Box and VTV.

Tell-Tale Productions

Elstree Film Studios
Shenley Road
Borehamwood
Hertfordshire WD6 1JG
Tel: +44 020 8324 2308
Fax: +44 020 8324 2696

email: info@Tell-tale.co.uk
Web: www.Tell-tale.co.uk

Ten Alps Broadcasting

6 Anglers Lane
London NW5 3DG
Tel: +44 020 7428 3100
Fax: +44 020 7284 0626
email: info@tenalps.com
Web: www.tenalps.com
Part of Ten Alps Communications PLC

Tern Television Productions

73 Crown Street
Aberdeen AB11 6EX
Tel: +44 01224 211123
Fax: +44 01224 211199
email: office@terntv.com
Web: www.terntv.com

Tiger Aspect Productions

7 Soho Street
London W1D 3DQ
Tel: +44 020 7434 6700
Fax: +44 020 7434 1798
email: general@tigeraspect.co.uk
Web: www.tigeraspect.co.uk

Tigress Productions

5 Soho Square
London W1V 5DE
Tel: +44 020 7434 4411
Fax: +44 020 7287 1448
email: general@tigressproductions.co.uk
Web: www.tigressproductions.co.uk

Tigress Productions (Bristol)

2 St. Paul's Road
Bristol BS8 1LT
Tel: +44 0117 933 5600
Fax: +44 0117 933 5666
email: general@tigressbristol.co.uk
Web: www.tigressproductions.co.uk

Tinopolis

Park Street
Llanelli
Carmarthenshire SA15 3YE
Tel: +44 01554 880880
Fax: +44 01554 880881
email: info@tinopolis.com
Web: www.tinopolis.com

Are you passionate about film?

With writing from the world's most influential directors, screenwriters and academics Sight & Sound is the only film magazine that matters.

To subscribe call 01858 438848 or visit www.bfi.org.uk

New subscribers annual rate: £35.75 (UK), £44.75 (overseas)

 British Film Institute

DIRECTORY

Topical Television

TV Centre
Radcliffe Rd
Southampton SO14 0PZ
Tel: +44 023 8071 2233
Fax: +44 023 8033 9835
Web: www.topical.co.uk

Twenty Twenty Television

20 Kentish Town Road
London NW1 9NX
Tel: +44 020 7284 2020
Fax: +44 020 7284 1810
email: mail@twentytwenty.tv
Web: www.twentytwenty.tv

TWI

McCormack House
Burlington Lane
Chiswick
London W4 2TH
Tel: +44 020 8233 5300
Fax: +44 020 8233 5301

Two Four Productions

Quay West Studios
Old Newham
Plymouth
Devon PL7 5BH
Tel: +44 01752 333900
Fax: +44 01752 344224
email: enq@twofour.co.uk
Web: www.twofour.co.uk

UMTV

Clearwater Yard
35 Inverness Street
Camden
London NW1 7HB
Tel: +44 020 7278 3021
Fax: +44 020 7713 9551
email: enquiries@umtv.tv
Web: www.umtv.tv

Unique Communications Group

Laser House
Waterfront Quay
Salford Quays M50 3XW
Tel: +44 0161 874 5700
Fax: +44 0161 888 2242
email: factuals@uniquecomms.com
Web: www.uniquecomms.com

VTV

30 Sackville Street
London W1S 3DY
Tel: +44 020 7478 7300
Fax: +44 020 7478 7415
email: vtv@venner.tv
Web: www.venner.tv
Part of The Television Corporation

Wall to Wall

8-9 Spring Place
London NW5 3ER
Tel: +44 020 7485 7424
Fax: +44 020 7267 5292
email: mail@walltowall.co.uk
Web: www.walltowall.co.uk

Wark Clements & Co

Studio 7
The Tollgate
19 Marine Crescent
Glasgow G51 1HD
Tel: +44 0141 429 1750
Fax: +44 0141 429 1751
email: info@warkclements.co.uk
Web: www.warkclements.com

Wild Rover Productions

112-114 Lisburn Road
Belfast BT9 6AH
Tel: +44 028 9050 0980
Fax: +44 028 9050 0970
email: enquiries@wild-rover.com
Web: www.wild-rover.com

Windfall Films

1 Underwood Row
London N1 7LZ
Tel: +44 020 7251 7676
Fax: +44 020 7253 8468
email: enquiries@windfallfilms.com
Web: www.windfallfilms.com

World of Wonder

40 Chelsea Wharf
Lots Road
London SW10 0QJ
Tel: +44 020 7349 9000
Fax: +44 020 7349 9777
email: wow@worldofwonder.net
Web: www.worldofwonder.net

World's End Productions

35 Harwood Road
Fulham
London SW6 4QP
Tel: +44 020 7751 9880
Fax: +44 020 7731 0406
email: info@worldsendproductions.com
Web: www.worldsendproductions.com

Zeal Television

1 Burston Road
London SW15 6AR
Tel: +44 020 8780 4600
Fax: +44 020 8780 4601
email: firstname.lastname@zealtv.net
Web: www.zealtv.net

Zenith Entertainment

43-45 Dorset Street
London W1U 7NA
Tel: +44 7224 2440
Fax: +44 7224 1027
email: general@zenith-entertainment.co.uk
Web: www.zenith-entertainment.co.uk

Zeppotron

Shepherds Building Central
Charecroft Way
Shepherds Bush
London W14 0EE
Tel: +44 0870 330 1700
Fax: +44 0870 330 1800
email: contact@zeppotron.com
Web: www.zeppotron.com
Part of the Endemol UK group

Zig Zag Productions

13 Great Sutton St
London EC1V 0BX
Tel: +44 020 7017 8755
email: production@zigzag.uk.com
Web: www.zigzagproductions.tv

Studios

3 Mills Studios

Three Mill Lane
London E3 3DU
Tel: 020 7363 3336
Fax: 020 8215 3499
email: candice.macdonald@3mills.com
Web: www.3mills.com
Contact: Candice McDonald
(Bookings/PR Manager)
Stages: 16 Stages, 6 Rehearsal Rooms,
Production Offices, Restaurant/Bar
Recent television: *Bad Girls, Footballers'
Wives, NY-LON, 15 Storeys High, The
Mighty Boosh, Dream Team, Mile High,
24 Hour Quiz*

BBC Television Centre Studios

Wood Lane
London W12 7RJ
Tel: 020 8700 100 883
email: bbcresources.co.uk
Web: bbcresources.com
Contact: National Call Centre
Studios: 8 full-facility television studios:
TC1 10,250 sq ft; TC3 8,000 sq ft; TC4
and TC8 8,000 sq ft (digital and
widescreen capable); TC6 8,000 sq ft
(digital); TC2, TC5 and TC7 3,500 sq ft

Bray Studios

Down Place
Water Oakley
Windsor Road
Windsor SL4 5UG
Tel: 01628 622111
Fax: 01628 770381
email: b.earl@tiscali.co.uk
Studio manager: Beryl Earl
Stages: 1 (sound) 955 sq metres; 2
(sound) 948 sq metres; 3 (sound) 238 sq
metres; 4 (sound) 167 sq metres
Recent Television: *Born and Bred* series
2 and 3, *Fimbles* series 1 and 2

De Lane Lea Dean Street Studio

75 Dean Street
London W1V 5HA
Tel: 020 7432 3800
Fax: 020 7432 3838
email: info@delanelea.com
Web: www.delanelea.com
Contact: Huw Penallt-Jones, Chief
Operating Officer

Ealing Studios

Ealing Green
London W5 5EP
Tel: 020 8567 6655
Fax: 020 8758 8658
email: info@ealingstudios.com
Web: www.ealingstudios.com
Contact: Bookings Office
Stages: 1 (silent) = area 232m2; 2
(sound) = 864m2; 3A (sound) = 530m2;
3B (sound) = 530m2; 3A/B combined =
1,080m2; 4 (model stage silent) =
390m2; 5 (sound) = 90m2;
Recent Television: *Rodger Rodger,
Spooks, Red Cap, The Royle Family*

Halliford Studios

Manygate Lane
Shepperton
Middx TW17 9EG
Tel: 01932 226341
Fax: 01932 246336
email: sales@hallifordstudios.com
Web: www.hallifordfilmstudios.com
Contact: Callum Andrews/Studio manager
Stages: A stage 60'x60' (18.27x18.27m)
334sq metres, 18'6" high (5.63m);
B stage 60'x40' (18.27x12.18m) 223sq
metres, 18'6" high (5.63m)

Holborn Studios

49/50 Eagle Wharf Road
London N1 7ED
Tel: 020 7490 4099
Fax: 020 7253 8120
email: reception@holborn-studios.co.uk
Web: www.holbornstudios.com

Contact: Ian Barker, Studio manager
Stages: 4 2,470 sq ft; 6 2,940 sq ft; 7
2,660 sq ft; 18 roomsets 3,125 sq ft
Also eight fashion studios, set building, E6
lab, b/w labs, Calumet in house, canal-side
restaurant and bar.

Lamb Studios

Lamb House
Church Street
Chiswick
London W4 2PD
Tel: 020 89969961
Fax: 020 89969966
Web: www.bell.com

Leavesden Studios

PO Box 3000
Leavesden
Herts WD2 7LT
Tel: 01923 685 060
Fax: 01923 685 061
Studio Manager: Daniel Dark
Stages: A 32,076sq ft; B 28,116 sq ft; C
11,285 sq ft; D 11,808 sq ft; F 15,427 sq
ft; G 14,036 sq ft; Flight Shed 1 35,776;
Effects 15,367 sq feet
Back Lot 100 acres. 180 degrees of clear
and uninterrupted horizon. Further
200,000 sq ft of covered space available

Magic Eye Film Studios

20 Lydden Road
London SW18 4LR
Tel: 020 8877 0800
Fax: 020 8874 7274
email: info@magiceye.co.uk
Web: www.magiceye.co.uk
Magic Eye offers five fully operational
stages, ranging from 900 to 4,500
square feet. They all include production
offices and make-up rooms. Several of the
stages are also fully covered.

DIRECTORY

265

Millennium Studios

Elstree Way
Herts WD6 1SF
Tel: 020 8236 1400
Fax: 020 8236 1444
Web: www.elstree-online.co.uk
Contact: Ronan Willson
'X' Stage: 327 sq metres sound stage with
flying grid and cyc. Camera room,
construction workshop, wardrobe,
dressing rooms, edit rooms, hospitality
suite and production offices are also on
site. Recent productions: Carnival Films
Bugs series

Pinewood Studios

Pinewood Road
Iver Heath
Bucks SL0 0NH
Tel: 01753 651700
Fax: 01753 656844
Web: www.pinewood-studios.co.uk
Managing Director: Steve Jaggs
Stages: A 1,685 sq m (Tank: 12.2m x
9.2m x 2.5m); B 827 sq m; C 827 sq m; D
1,685 sq m (Tank: 12.2m x 9.2m x 2.5m);
E 1,685 sq m (Tank: 12.2m x 9.2m x
2.5m); F 698 sq m (Tank: 6.1m x 6.1m x
2.5m); G 247 sq m; H 300 sq m; J 824 sq
m - dedicated TV Studio; K 824 sq m; L
880 sq m; M 880 sq m; N/P 767 sq
metres; R 1,780 sq m; S 1,789 sq m;
South Dock (silent) 1,547 sq m; Albert R
Broccoli 007 (silent) 4,223 sq m (Tank:
90.5m x 22.3m x 2.7m Reservoir: 15.3m x
28.7m x 2.7m); Large Process 454 sq m;
Exterior Lot 50 acres, comprising formal
gardens and lake, woods, fields, concrete
service roads and squares; Exterior Tank
67.4m narrowing to 32m wide, 60.4 long,
1.06m deep. Capacity 764,000 gallons.
Inner Tank: 15.5m x 12.2m x 2.7m.
Backing 73.2m x 18.3m. Largest outdoor
tank in Europe
Recent Television: *Dinotopia, Jack and
the Beanstalk – the Real Story, Wit,
Hornblower, Thursday the 12th, Sam's
Game, My Family*

Riverside Studios

Crisp Road
Hammersmith
London W6 9RL
Tel: 020 8237 1000
Fax: 020 8237 1011
email: jonfawcett@riversidestudios.co.uk
Web: www.riversidestudios.co.uk
Contact: Jon Fawcett
Stages: Studio 1 529 sq m; Studio 2 378
sq m; Studio 3 130 sq m
Plus preview cinema, various dressing
rooms, offices, café
Recent Television: *T.F.I. Friday, Collins' &
Maconie's Movie Club, Channel 4 Sitcom
Festival, This Morning with Richard Not
Judy, Top of the Pops* (2001)

Rotherhithe Studios/Sands Films Studios

119 Rotherhithe Street
London SE16 4NF
Tel: 020 7231 2209
Fax: 020 7231 2119
email: ostockman@sands.films.co.uk
Web: sandsfilms.co.uk
Contacts: O. Stockman, C. Goodwin
Stages: 1 Rotherhithe 180 sq metres
Pre-production, construction, post-
production facilities, period costume
making, props

Shepperton Studios

Studio Road
Shepperton
Middx TW17 0QD
Tel: 01932 562 611
Fax: 01932 568 989
email: admin@sheppertonstudios.co.uk
Web: www.sheppertonstudios.co.uk
Contact: Paul Olliver
Stages: A 1,668 sq metres; B 1,115 sq
metres; C 1,668 sq metres; D 1,115 sq
metres; E 294 sq metres; F 294 sq
metres; G 629 sq metres; H 2,660 sq
metres; I 657 sq metres; J 1,394 sq
metres; K 1,114 sq metres; L 604 sq
metres; M 259 sq metres; T 261 sq
metres; R 948 sq metres; S 929 sq
metres

South West Film Studios

St Agnes
Cornwall TR5 0LA
Tel: (0)1872 554131
Fax: (0)1872 552880
email: info@southwestfilmstudios.com
Web: www.southwestfilmstudios.com
Kate Hughes
South West Film Studios is a new
purpose built studio facility, located on
the stunning north coast of Cornwall. It
offers a complete package for film
productions, including sound stages,
water stage, workshop and office spaces,
all set in beautiful landscaped gardens.
South West Film Studios offers a flexible
approach, whether you require a
production base for a location shoot or
fully sound proofed stage facilities.
Stages: 1A - 24m x 18m x 12m; 1B - 24m
x 18m x 12m including water tank 3 x 3 x
2.5m; 1A/B combined 36m x 24m x 12m;
Stage 2 - 21m x 21m x 11.5m

Stonehills Studios

Shields Road
Gateshead
Tyne and Wear NE10 0HW
Tel: 0191 495 2244
Fax: 0191 495 2266
Studio Manager: Nick Walker
Stages: 1 1,433 sq ft; 2 750 sq ft
The North's largest independent television
facility comprising of Digital Betacam Edit
Suite with the BVE 9100 Edit Controller
and Abekas ASWR 8100 mixer, A57 DVE
and four machine editing, including two
DVW 500s. Also three Avid off-line suites,
2D Matador and 3D Alias graphics and a
Sound Studio comprising a Soundtracs
6800 24-track 32 channel desk and
Soundscape 8-track digital editing
machine
Recent Television: *Germ Genie, The
Spark, Come Snow Come Blow*

Teddington Studios

Broom Road
Teddington
Middlesex TW11 9NT

Tel: 020 8977 3252
Fax: 020 8943 4050
email: sales@teddington.co.uk
Web: www.teddington.co.uk
Contact: Sales and Client Liaison
Studios: 1 653 sq m; 2 372 sq m; 3 120 sq m
Recent Television: *This is Your Life, Today with Des and Mel, Harry Hill's TV Burp, Brian Conley Show, Alistair McGowan, My Hero, Beast, Coupling*

Twickenham Film Studios

St Margaret's
Twickenham
Middx TW1 2AW
Tel: 020 8607 8888
Fax: 020 8607 8889
Web: www.twickenhamstudios.com
Gerry Humphreys, Caroline Tipple (Stages)
Stages: 1 702 sq m with tank 37 sq m x 2.6m deep; 2 186 sq m; 3 516 sq m
2 x dubbing theatres; 1 x ADR/Foley theatre; 40 x cutting rooms; Lightworks, Avid 35/16mm

Westway Studios

8 Olaf Street
London W11 4BE
Tel: 020 7221 9041
Fax: 020 7221 9399
Contacts: Steve/Kathy
Stages: 1 502 sq m (Sound Stage); 2 475 sq m; 3 169 sq m; 4 261 sq m

Terrestrial TV Companies

British Broadcasting Corporation (BBC)

Television Centre
Wood Lane
Shepherds Bush
London W12 7RJ
Tel: 020 8743 8000

BBC Broadcasting House
Portland Place
London W1A 1AA
Tel: 020 7580 4468

Web: www.bbc.co.uk

Chairman: Michael Grade
Director General: Mark Thompson
Other executive posts detailed in COMMISSIONERS & CONTROLLERS
History: Started broadcasting television to the London area on 2 November 1936, with coverage extended to the Midlands in 1949, and Scotland, South Wales and West in 1952. Operates under a Royal Charter of Incorporation (first granted in 1927) and a licence from the Home Secretary. Financed by the Licence Fee.

BBC Drama
Television Centre
Wood Lane
London W12 7RJ
Tel: 020 8743 8000
Tel: 020 85761 1861 (publicity dept)

BBC Resources
Television Centre
Wood Lane
London W12 7RJ
Tel: 08700 100 883
Fax: 08700 100 884
Web: www.bbcresources.co.uk

BBC Worldwide
Woodlands
80 Wood Lane
London W12 0TT
Tel: 020 8433 2000

Fax: 020 8749 0538
Web: www.bbcworldwide.com
Catalogue: www.bbcworldwidetv.com

BBC Broadcast Programme Acquisition
BBC TV Centre
Wood Lane
London W12 7RJ
Tel: 020 8225 6721
Fax: 020 8749 0893

BBC North West
New Broadcasting House
Oxford Road
Manchester M60 1SJ
Tel: 0161 200 2020
Fax: 0164 236 1005
Head of Regional & Local Programmes: Leo Devine
Also produces for Entertainment and Features.

BBC West
Broadcasting House
Whiteladies Road
Bristol BS8 2LR
Tel: 0117 973 2211
Head of Regional & Local Programmes: Andrew Wilson
Only commissioning centre outside London including natural history programmmes.

BBC West Midlands
The Mailbox
Royal Mail Street
Birmingham B1 1XL
Tel: 0121 567 6767
Tel: 0121 432 8888
Head of Regional & Local Progs: David Holdsworthy
Also produces multicultural programmes.

BBC Northern Ireland
Broadcasting House
Ormeau Avenue
Belfast BT2 8HQ
Tel: 028 9033 8000
Fax: 028 9033 8800
Controller: Anna Carragher

DIRECTORY

BBC Scotland
Broadcasting House
Queen Margaret Drive
Glasgow G12 8DG
Tel: 0141 338 2000
Fax: 0141 334 0614
Controller: Ken MacQuarrie
Edinburgh Office Tel: 0131 225 3131
Aberdeen Office Tel: 01224 625233

BBC Wales/Cymru
Broadcasting House
Llandaff
Cardiff CF5 2YQ
Tel: 029 2032 2000
Controller: Meena Richards

Channel Four Television

124 Horseferry Road
London SW1P 2TX
Tel: 020 7396 4444
Fax: 020 7306 8353
Web: www.channel4.com
Chairman: Luke Johnson
Chief Executive: Andy Duncan
Director of Programmes: Kevin Lygo.
See COMMISSIONERS & CONTROLLERS
History: On-air 2 November 1982.
Channel 4 is a national service set up by
Act of Parliament in 1982 as a non profit
making corporation, funded principally by
its revenue from advertising. Its remit is
to: have a distinctive character of its own,
and cater for interests not served by
other channels. With a handful of
exceptions, C4 does not make
programmes itself – it both commissions
new material from production companies
and buys in already completed
programmes.

Channel Television

Television Centre
La Pouquelaye Road
St Helier
Jersey JE1 3ZD
Tel: 01534 816816
Fax: 01534 816817
Web: www.channeltv.co.uk.

and
Television House
Bulwer Avenue
St Sampson
Guernsey GY2 4LA
Tel: 01481 241888
Fax: 01481 241866
Chief Executive: Huw Davies
Managing Director: Michael Lucas
Director of Resources and Transmission:
Kevin Banner
Group Finance Director: David Jenkins
Director of Sales: Gordon de Ste Croix
**Director of Business Development &
Compliance:** Rowan O'Sullivan
Director of Finance and Administration:
Amanda Trotman
History: On-air 1 September 1962.
Covering the Channel Islands (principally
the Islands of Jersey, Guernsey, Alderney,
Herm and Sark) with a population of
150,000. Channel Television produces
regional programming and the station's
main studios are based in Jersey with
additional studios in Guernsey. Smallest
ITV company, that was originally founded
by leading Jersey citizens Senator George
Troy and Senator Wilfred Krichefski
(President, Jersey Tourist Committee),
Guernsey Star, Jersey Evening Post, and
Harold Fielding (theatre impresario).
Acquired by Iliffe News & Media in 2001.

London Office
Unit 16A, 3rd floor
Enterprise House
59-65 Upper Ground
London SE1 9PQ
Tel: 020 7633 9902
Fax: 020 7401 8982

Five

22 Long Acre
London WC2E 9LY
Tel: 020 7550 5555
Fax: 020 7550 5554
Web: www.five.tv
Chief Executive: Jane Lighting
**Deputy Chief Executive and Director of
Sales:** Nick Milligan
Director of Programmes: Dan Chambers.
Director of Finance: Grant Murray
Director of Legal and Business Affairs:
Colin Campbell

Director of Marketing: David Pullan
Director of Broadcasting: Ashley Hill
Director of Acquisitions: Jeff Ford
History: Channel 5 launched on 30 March
1997, as the UK's fifth terrestrial
broadcaster. Before broadcasting could
begin it was faced with the Herculean
task of retuning 9 million homes across
the UK. Coverage has now extended to
86.6% of homes. Channel 5 is owned by
two shareholders, RTL Group 64.625%
and United Business Media 35.375%. In
2002 Channel 5 changed its name to five.

GMTV

London Television Centre
Upper Ground
London SE1 9TT
Tel: 020 7827 7000.
Fax: 020 7827 7001
Web: www.gm.tv.
Chairman: Charles Allen CBE
Managing Director: Paul Corley
Director of Programmes: Peter McHugh
Managing Editor: John Scammell
Editor: Martin Frizell
Head of Press: Nicki Johnceline
History: On-air 1 January 1993. Original
consortium, Sunrise Television, comprised
Carlton, Guardian Media Group, LWT,
Scottish Television, and Walt Disney. ITV
plc owns 75% of the shares after buying
SMG stake in 2004. GMTV broadcasts
nationally news and magazine
programming, with features on life style
and show business, on the ITV network
from 6.00 a. m. to 9.25 a. m.

Grampian Television

The Television Centre
Craigshaw Business Park
West Tullos
Aberdeen AB12 3QH
Tel: 01224 848848.
Web: www.grampiantv.co.uk.
Managing Director: Derrick Thomson
Chairman: Dr Calum A MacLeod CBE
History: On-air 30 September 1961.
Covering the North of Scotland, including
Aberdeen, Dundee and Inverness. Original
History: North of Scotland TV consortium
comprised Sir Alexander King (Caledonian
Associated Cinemas), Lord Forbes, Captain

Iain Tennant, and Dr T. J. Honeyman (former ITA Member), with Thomas Johnston and Neil Patterson co-opted from rival Caledonian TV. Taken over by Scottish Television in 1997. Part of the Scottish Media Group.

Independent Television News (ITN)

200 Gray's Inn Road
London WC1X 8XZ
Tel: 020 7833 3000
Fax: 020 7430 4868
Web: www.itn.co.uk
Chief Executive: Mark Wood
History: ITN is the news provider nominated by the Independent Television Commission to supply news programme for the ITV network. Subject to review, this licence is for a ten year period from 1993. ITN also provides news for Channel 4 and for the Independent Radio News (IRN) network but lost its contract with Five to Sky News in 2004. ITN is recognised as one of the world's leading news organisation whose programmes and reports are seen in every corner of the globe. In addition to its base in London, ITN has permanent bureaux in Washington, Moscow, South Africa, the Middle East, Hong Kong, and Brussels as well as at Westminster and eight other locations around the UK. Other business concerns are ITN Archive (libraries acquired include Granada, Reuters, British Pathe), ITN Factual and ITN International.

ITV plc

Board
Chairman: Sir Peter Burt
Deputy Chairman: Sir George Russell CBE
Chief Executive: Charles Allen CBE
Finance Director: Henry Staunton
Non-Executive Members: David Chance, James Crosby, John McGrath, Sir Brian Pitman
Company Secretary: James Tibbitts

The London Television Centre (Production)
Upper Ground
London SE1 9LT
Tel: 020 7620 1620

ITV Network Centre (Commisioning)
200 Gray's Inn Road
London WC1X 8HF
Tel: 020 7843 8000
Fax: 020 7843 8158
Web: www.itv.com and www.itvplc.com
History: ITV is a federation of regional broadcasters. National coverage is achieved by 15 licensees, broadcasting in 14 regional areas: Anglia, Border, Carlton London, Carlton Central, Carlton West Country, Channel, Grampian, Granada, HTV, LWT, Meridian, Scottish Television, Ulster Television, Tyne Tees, Yorkshire. (London had two licensees, one for the weekday – Carlton – and one for the weekend – LWT). In May 2002 the ITV licensees agreed a Charter for the Nations and the Regions with its regulator, the ITC. In autumn 2002 ITV1 was adopted as the lead channel brand in most ITV regions. At least 25% of programmes shown on ITV1 each year come from independent producers. Regional programmes are commissioned by each regional company. ITV2 launched on 7 December 1998 and is ITV's younger entertainment channel. It is available on Freeview (digital terrestrial), Sky Digital and Cable (analogue and digital) throughout the UK. In October the merger of Granada and Carlton was approved and since February 2004 they have traded as ITV plc.

Chief Executive, ITV Broadcasting: Mick Desmond
Director of Programmes: Nigel Pickard
Director of Programme Strategy: David Bergg
For more executives see COMMISSIONERS & CONTROLLERS
For more on regional ITV production history see A Corporate History of ITV on p.62

The following companies make up ITV plc:

ITV Anglia

Anglia House
Norwich
Norfolk NR1 3JG
Tel: 01603 615151.
Fax: 01603 631032.

Chairman: David McCall
Managing Director: Graham Creelman
Regional Programme Executive: Mike Talbot
Broadcast and Regional Affairs Executive: Jim Woodrow
Director of Broadcasting: Bob Ledwidge
Head of Network Factual Programmes: Andrea Cornes
History: Taken over by MAI (United News & Media) in 1994, by Granada Media Group in 2000, and now part of ITV plc since February 2004.
Regional Offices: Cambridge, Chelmsford, Ipswich, Luton, Milton Keynes, Northampton, Peterborough,

ITV Border

The Television Centre
Carlisle
Cumbria CA1 3NT
Tel: 01228 525 101
Chairman: James L. Graham
Managing Director: Douglas Merrall
Director of Programmes: Neil Robinson
Head of News: Ian Proniewicz
History: Covering 288,000 homes in Cumbria, Border Television's broadcast coverage extends from Peebles in the North, down to Seascale in the south and includes the Isle of Man. Taken over by Capital Radio Group in 2000, sold to Granada in 2001, and now part of ITV plc since February 2004.

Carlton

See ITV plc

ITV Central

Central Court
Gas Street
Birmingham B1 2JT
Tel: 0121 643 9898
Fax: 0121 643 4897
Managing Director: Ian Squires

ITV Granada

Quay Street
Manchester M60 9EA
Tel: 0161 832 7211
Fax: 0161 827 2029
Managing Director, Granada Television: Susan Woodward
History: The ITV franchise for North West England also has offices in

DIRECTORY

Liverpool, Blackburn, Chester and Lancaster. Granada took over LWT in 1994, Yorkshire/Tyne Tees in 1997, Anglia in 2000, Border and Meridian in 2001, and merged with Carlton to form ITV plc from February 2004.

The Granada name is still used for the production of content and is the main supplier to the ITV Network. They are based at London TV Centre head offices.

Chief Executive, Granada: Simon Shaps

Chief Operating Officer, Granada: John Cresswell

Controller, Arts & Features, Granada: Melvyn Bragg

Controller of Regional Programmes: Kieran Collins

Director of Factual, Entertainment and Sport, Granada: Jim Allen

ITV London

London Television Centre
Upper Ground
London SE1 9LT.
Tel: 020 7620 1620
Fax: 020 7827 7500
Managing Director: Christy Swords
On-air: 2 August 1968.
History: LWT was taken over by Granada in 1994 and the LWT identity dropped in 2003 – ITV London is now part of ITV plc (since February 2004). The London Franchise for the weekend, beginning 17.15 on Fridays and ending 06.00 Mondays.

ITV Meridian

Television Centre
Northam Road
Southampton
Hants SO14 0PZ
Tel: 023 8022 2555
Fax: 023 8033 5050
Managing Director, Meridian: Lindsay Charlton
Controller of Regional Programmes: Mark Southgate
Director of News: Andy Cooper
Director of Commercial and Regional Affairs: Martin Morrall
General Manager: Jan Beal
Controller of Personnel: Peter Ashwood
Finance Controller: Sian Harvey
History: Taken over by Granada in 1994, and part of ITV plc since February 2004.

ITV Tyne Tees

Television Centre
City Road
Newcastle Upon Tyne NE1 2AL
Tel: 0191 261 0181
Fax: 0191 261 2302
Managing Director: Margaret Fay
Controller of Programmes: Graeme Thompson
Engineering Manager: Dixon Marshall
Head of Operations: Howard Beebe
Head of Regional Affairs: Norma Hope
History: TyneTees a transmission area stretching from Berwick in the North to Selby in the South and across to Alston in the West. Operating from studios and offices in Newcastle, Sunderland, Billingham, York, and Westminster. Taken over by Yorkshire in 1992, by Granada in 1997, now part of ITV plc since February 2004.

ITV Wales

Television Centre
Culverhouse Cross
Cardiff CF5 6XJ
Tel: 02920 59059
History: HTV Wales taken over in 2001 by Granada, who sold it on to Carlton, and now part of ITV plc since February 2004.

ITV West

Television Centre
Bath Road
Bristol BS4 3HG
Tel: 0117 972 2722
History: HTV West taken over in 2001 by Granada, who sold it on to Carlton, and now part of ITV plc since February 2004.

ITV West Country

Western Wood Way
Langage Science Park
Plymouth PL7 5BQ
Tel: 01752 333333
Fax: 01752 333444
Managing Director: Mark Haskell
Controller, Technical Operations: Mark Chaplin
Controller of Business Affairs: Peter Gregory
History: Owned by Carlton, West Country Television has a network of seven regional studios together with the main studio and headquarters in Plymouth and broadcasts

to Cornwall and Devon and much of Dorset and Somerset. Now part of ITV plc since February 2004.

ITV Yorkshire

The Television Centre
Kirkstall Road
Leeds LS3 1JS
Tel: 0113 243 8283
Fax: 0113 242 3867
Managing Director: David Croft
Director of Programmes: John Whiston
Director of Business Affairs Granada Content North: Filip Cieslik
Head of Site Services: Peter Fox
Head of Media Relations North: Sallie Ryle
Head of Regional Affairs: Sallie Ryle
Head of Engineering: John Nichol
Head of Business Affairs: Justine Rhodes
Head of Sales and Planning: Jim Richardson
Director of Finance, Granada Content North: Ian Roe
General Manager: John Surtees
Head of Personnel: Sue Slee
History: On-air 29 July 1968. Covering Yorkshire, Humberside and Lincolnshire, Yorkshire Television broadcasts to a population of 5.7 million. The main studio complex is in Leeds but there are regional offices in Sheffield, Hull, Grimsby, Lincoln, and York. Created in 1968 (new region). The original consortium, Telefusion Yorkshire, led by Sir Richard Graham (former High Sheriff of Yorkshire) and Sir Geoffrey Cox (ITN), backed by newspaper groups, including the Yorkshire Post. In 1970 set up Trident Television, a joint holding company with neighbouring Tyne Tees Television, to maximise advertising potential, but disbanded it in 1980 at the IBA's request. Took over Tyne Tees in 1992, then was taken over by Granada in 1997, and is now part of ITV plc since February 2004.

NB: Channel Television, Grampian, Scottish Television and UTV are independent companies and are not a part of ITV plc

Scottish Television

200 Renfield Street
Glasgow G2 3PR
Tel: 0141 300 3000
Fax: 0141 300 3030
Web: www.scottishtv.co.uk.
Chief Executive, SMG: Andrew Flanagan
**Divisional Chief Executive, SMG
Television:** Donald Emslie
Managing Director, Scottish TV:
Sandy Ross
Head of News and Current Affairs:
Paul McKinney
**Managing Director SMG Television
Productions/Ginger Television:** Elizabeth
Partyka
On-air: 31 August 1957.
History: Scottish has held the ITV licence
for Central Scotland since commercial
television started in 1957. Original
successful bid by Roy Thomson (Scotsman
Publications), with Howard & Wyndham
Theatres, backed by the Royal Bank of
Scotland. Took over Grampian Television
in 1997, and formed Scottish Media Group.

S4C

Parc Ty Glas
Llanishen
Cardiff CF14 5DU
Tel: 029 2074 7444
Fax: 029 2075 4444
and
Lôn Ddewi
Caernarfon
LL55 1ER
Tel: 01286 674622
Web: www.s4c.co.uk
Chairman: Elan Closs Stephens
Chief Executive: Huw Jones
Director of Programmes: Iona Jones
Managing Director, S4C Masnachol:
Wyn Innes
Director of Channel Management:
Emlyn Penny Jones
Director of Corporate Affairs:
Alun Davies
**Director of Finance and Human
Resources:** Kathryn Morris
Director of Engineering and IT:
Arshad Rasul
History: S4C (Sianel Pedwar Cymru –
Channel 4 Wales) was established under
the Broadcasting Act, 1980 and is
responsible for providing a service of
Welsh and English programmes on the
Fourth Channel in Wales, with a remit
that the majority of programmes shown
between 18.30 and 22.00 should be in
Welsh. Since 1993 S4C has been directly
funded by the Treasury and is responsible
for selling its own advertising. In
November 1998 S4C Digital was
launched.

Ulster Television: see UTV below

UTV

Havelock House
Ormeau Road
Belfast BT7 1EB
Tel: 02890 328122.
Fax: 028 90246695
Web: www.utv.co.uk
Chairman: John B McGuckian
Group Chief Executive: John McCann
Director of Television: A. Bremner
Group Finance Director: J. R. Downey
Head of Press and Public Relations:
Orla McKibbin
Head of News: Rob Morrison
History: Ulster on-air 31 October 1959.
Covering Northern Ireland. Original
consortium led by the Earl of Antrim,
included Laurence Olivier, Betty Box
(Beaconsfield Films) and Commander
Oscar Henderson (Belfast Newsletter). It
is still an independent company with no
single large shareholding. It recently
rebranded and now Ulster television is
known as UTV.

DIRECTORY

Video/DVD Distributors

Abbey Home Media
435-437 Edgware Road
London W2 1TH
Tel: 020 7563 3910
Fax: 020 7563 3911
Web: www.abbeyhomemedia.com

Acorn Media
10 Smith's Yard
Summerley Street
London SW18 4HR
Tel: 020 8879 7000
Fax: 020 8879 1616
Web: www.acornmediauk.com

BBC Worldwide Publishing
Woodlands
80 Wood Lane
London W12 0TT
Tel: 020 8433 2000
Fax: 020 8749 0538
Web: www.bbcworldwide.com

bfi Video Publishing
21 Stephen Street
London W1T 1LN
Tel: 020 7957 8960
Fax: 020 7957 8968
email: video.films@bfi.org.uk
Web: www.bfi.org.uk/video

Buena Vista Home Entertainment
3 Queen Caroline Street
Hammersmith
London W6 9PE
Tel: 020 8222 1000
Fax: 020 8222 2795

Carlton Visual Entertainment
See Granada Ventures

Channel 4 Video
124 Horseferry Road
London SW1P 2TX
Tel: 020 020 7396 4444
Fax: 020 7306 8350
Web: www.channel4.co.uk

Cinema Club
See Video Collection International

Clear Vision
36 Queensway
Ponders End
Enfield
Middlesex EN3 4SA
Tel: 020 8805 1354
Fax: 020 8805 9987
email: info@clearvision.co.uk
Web: www.clearvision.co.uk

Columbia Tri-Star Home Video
25 Golden Square
London W1R 6LU
Tel: 020 7533 1200
Fax: 020 7533 1015

Contender Entertainment Group
48 Margaret Street
London W1W 8SE
Tel: 020 7907 3773
Fax: 020 7907 3777
Web: www.contendergroup.com

Elstree Hill Entertainment
C/o Pickwick Group Ltd
230 Centennial Park
Elstree Hill South
Elstree
Borehamwood WD6 3SN
Tel: 020 8236 7065
Fax: 020 8236 2312

FremantleMedia
1 Stephen Street
London W1T 1AL
Tel: 020 7691 6000
Fax: 20 7691 6100
email: videodvd@fremantlemedia.com
Web: www.fremantlemedia.com

Granada Media
See Granada Ventures

Granada Ventures
Communications Building
4th Floor
48 Leicester Square
London WC2H 7FB
Tel: 020 7389 8555
Fax: 020 7389 8799
Web: www.itv.com

HIT Entertainment
5th Floor
Maple House
141-150 Tottenham Court Road
London W1P 9LL
Tel: 020 7554 2500
Fax: 020 7388 9321
Web: www.hitentertainment.com

Kult-TV
See Contender Entertainment Group

MGM Home Entertainment
(Europe)
5 Kew Road
Richmond TW9 2PR
Tel: 020 8939 9300
Fax: 020 8939 9411
Web: www.mgm.com

Momentum Pictures Home
Entertainment
2nd Floor
184-192 Drummond Street
London NW1 3HP
Tel: 020 7391 6900
Fax: 020 7383 0404
Web: www.momentumpictures.co.uk

Network
Unit 2
Phase 2
The Birches Industrial Estate
East Grinstead
West Sussex RH19 1UB
Tel: 01342 310100
Fax: 01342 326122
Web: www.networkvideos.co.uk

Paramount Home Entertainment
45 Beadon Road
Hammersmith
London W6 0EG
Tel: 020 8741 9333
Fax: 020 8741 5690
Web: www.paramount.com

Playback
See Universal Pictures Video

Revelation
CarbonCo Ltd
Stratford Workshops
Burford Road
Stratford E15 2SP
Tel: 020 8866 7145
Fax: 020 8426 2788
email: info@revfilms.co.uk
Web: www.revfilms.com

20th Century Fox
Home Entertainment
Twentieth Century House
31-32 Soho Square
London W1V 6AP
Tel: 020 7753 8686
Fax: 020 7437 1625
Web: www.foxuk.com

Universal Pictures Video
Prospect House
3rd Floor
80-110 New Oxford Street
London WC1A 1HB
Tel: 020 7079 6000
Fax: 020 7079 6524

Video Collection International
76 Dean Street
London W1D 3SQ
Tel: 020 7396 8888
Fax: 020 7396 8996/7
Web: www.vci.co.uk

VVL (Vision Video Ltd)
See Universal Pictures Video

Warner Home Video
Warner House
98 Theobald's Road
London WC1X 8WB
Tel: 020 7984 6400
Fax: 020 7984 5001
Web: www.warnerbros.co.uk

Warner Vision International
35-38 Portman Square
London W1H 6LR
Tel: 020 7467 2566
Fax: 020 7467 2564

Worldwide Media Companies

British Sky Broadcasting
The Cromwell Centre
Grant Way
Isleworth
Middlesex TW7 5QD
Tel: 0870 240 3000
Web: www.sky.com
Chief Executive Officer: James Murdoch

Cablevision NY Group
1111 Stewart Avenue
Bethpage
NY 117143581 USA
Tel: 001 536 803 2300
Web: www.cablevision.com
Chairman, President and CEO:
James L Dolan

Charter Communications
12405 Powerscourt Drive
St Louis
MO 631313660 USA
Tel: 001 314 965 0555
Web: www.charter.com
President, Director and CEO:
Carl E. Vogel

Comcast
1500 Market Street
Philadelphia
PA 191022148 USA
Tel: 001 215 665 1700
Web: www.comcast.com
President and Chief Executive Officer:
Brian L Roberts

Cox Communications
1400 Lake Hearn Drive NE
Atlanta
GA 30319 USA
Tel: 001 404 843 5000
Web: www.cox.com
President and Chief Executive Officer:
James O Robbins

EchoStar Commununications
5701 South Santa Fe Drive
Littleton
CO 80120 USA
Tel: 001 303 723 1000
Web: www.echostar.com
Founder, Chairman, &CEO:
Charles W. Ergen

Fuji Television Network
2-4-8 Daiba
Minato-ku, Tokyo 137-8088
Japan
Tel: 0081 3 5500 8888
Web: www.fujitv.co.jp
President: Hisashi Hieda

Grupo Televisa
Avenida Vasco de Quiroga 2000
Colonia Sante Fe
01210 Mexico City DF
Mexico
Tel: 0052 555 261 2000
Web: www.televisa.com.mx
Chairman, President & Chief Executive
Officer: Emilio Fernando Azcarraga Jean

ITV
3-7 Upper Ray Street
Upper Ground
London EC1R 3DR
Tel: 020 7239 9857
Web: www.itv.com
Chief Executive Officer: Charles Allen

Lagardère SCA
121 avenue Malakoff
75216 Paris Cedex 16
France
Tel: 0033 1 4069 1600
Web: www.lagardere.com
Managing Partner: Arnaud Lagardère

DIRECTORY

Liberty Media
12300 Liberty Boulevard
Englewood
CO 80112 USA
Tel: 001 720 875 5400
Web: www.libertymedia.com
President and CEO: Robert R Bennett

M6-Metropole Television
89 avenue Charles de Gaulle
92575 Neuilly sur Seine
France
Tel: 0033 1 4192 6666
Web: www.m6.fr
Chairman: Nicolas de Tavernost

Mediaset
Via Paleocapa 3
20121 Milan
Italy
Tel: 0039 2 25141
Web: www.mediaset.it
Chief Executive Officer: Giuliano Adreamo

Metro-Goldwyn-Mayer
10250 Constellation Boulevard
Santa Monica
CA 90067 USA
Tel: 001 310 449 3000
Web: www.mgm.com
Chairman and CEO: Alex Yemenidjian

News Corp
2 Holt Street
Sydney NSW 2010
Australia
Tel: 0061 2 9288 3000
Web: www.newscorp.com
Chief Exec Officer: Keith Murdoch

Nippon TV Network
1-6-1 Higashi-Shinbashi
Minato-ku, Tokyo 105-7444
Japan
Tel: 0081 813 6215 1111
Web: www.ntv.co.jp
President: Seiichiro Ujiie

Pixar
1200 Park Avenue
Emeryville
CA 94608 USA
Tel: 001 310 510 752 3000
Web: www.pixar.com
Chief Executive Officer: Steven P. Jobs

Publicis Groupe
133 avenue des Champs Elysées
75380 Paris Cedex 08
France
Tel: 0033 1 4443 7000
Web: www.publicis.com
Chairman: Maurice Lévy

Publishing & Broadcasting
2nd Floor, 54 Park Street
Sydney NSW 1028
Australia
Tel: 0061 29282 8000
Web: www.pbl.com.au
Managing Director & CEO: Peter Wilson Yates

Quebecor
612 Saint-Jacques Street
Montreal, Quebec H3C 4M8
Canada
Tel: 001 514 380 1999
Web: www.quebecor.com
Chief Executive Officer: Pierre Karl Péladeau

Regal Entertainment Group
9110 East Nichols Avenue
Suite 200, Centennial
CO 80112 USA
Tel: 001 303 792 3600
Web: www.regalcinemas.com
Co-Chairman & Co-Chief Executive Officer: Michael L Campbell

Reuters Group
85 Fleet Street
London EC4P 4AJ
Tel: 020 7250 1122
Web: www.reuters.com
Chief Executive Officer: Thomas H Glocer

Shaw Communications
630 - 3rd Avenue Southwest
Suite 900
Calgary T2P 4L4
Canada
Tel: 001 403 750 4500
Web: www.shaw.ca
Chief Executive Officer: James R Shaw

Sogecable
Avenida de los Artesanos, 6
28760 Tres Cantos, Madrid
Spain
Tel: 0034 91 736 7000
Web: www.sogecable.es
Chief Executive Officer: Javier Dmez de Polanco

Time Warner
75 Rockefeller Plaza
New York
NY, 100196908 USA
Tel: 001 212 484 8000
Web: www.timewarner.com
Chairman and Chief Executive Officer: Richard D Parsons

Tokyo Broadcasting System
3-6 Akasaka 5-Chome
Minato-Ku, Tokyo 107-8006
Japan
Tel: 0081 3 3746 1111
Web: www.tbs.co.jp
Chairman: Yukio Sunahara

Univision Communications
1999 Avenue of the Stars
Los Angeles
CA 90067 USA
Tel: 001 310 556 7676
Web: www.univision.net
Chairman and Chief Executive Officer: A Jerrold Perenchio

Viacom
1515 Broadway
NY 10036 USA
Tel: 001 212 258 6000
Web: www.viacom.com
Chairman & Chief Executive: Sumner M. Redstone

Vivendi Universal
42 avenue de Friedland
75380 Paris Cedex 08
France
Tel: 0033 1 7171 1000
Web: www.vivendiuniversal.com
Chief Executive Officer: Jean-René Fourtou

Walt Disney Company
500 South Buena Vista Street
Burbank CA 91521 USA
Tel: 001 818 560 1000
Web: www.disney.go.com
Chief Executive Officer: Michael D. Eisner

Index

Illustration Acknowledgments

Thanks to www.bbcpictures.com for all BBC images, to the Press Association website (as was) for ITV and Five images and to www.image.net for all multichannel photos. We apologise in advance for any omissions either in relation to copyright holders or to other credits and any of these brought to our attention will be remedied in future printings. Where the photographer is known, their name is given first in the credits listings below.

p.10 *EastEnders*. Images © BBC. p.11 *Coronation Street*. Image © Granada; Michael Green – Carlton/ITV; *Derren Brown Plays Russian Roulette Live*. Image © Objective Productions. p.12 *There's Something About Miriam* – Brighter Pictures/Sky One; Brookside. Image © Mersey Television; *The Alan Clark Diaries* – Mike Hogan/BBC. p.13 Images © News 24. p.14 *I'm A Celebrity ... Get Me Out of Here!*. Image © LWT/Granada; Jane Root in *Happy Birthday BBC2*. Image © BBC; Michael Grade – Julian Wyth/BBC. p.15 *Derren Brown: Séance*. Image © Objective Productions. p. 16 *Big Brother*. Images © Endemol UK/Channel 4; The Sun newspaper © News International. p.17 Michael Grade and Mark Thompson – Jeff Overs/BBC. p.18 BBC brochures © BBC. p.19 *Doctor Who Magazine* – Panini Publishing Ltd; *North and South* – Mike Hogan/BBC. p.20 *Radio Times: The X Factor* – Jason Bell/Syco/talkbackTHAMES & BBC Publications. p.21 *Green Wing* – Talkback Productions/Channel 4. p.46 *Hustle* – Amanda Searle/BBC. *Charles II* – BBC. p.47 *Strictly Come Dancing* – Abi Wyles/BBC. p.48 Roly Keating – Richard Kendal/BBC; *Coupling* – Trevor Leighton/Hartswood/BBC. p.49 *Radio Times* © BBC Publications; *Hawking* – Laurence Cendrowicz/BBC; *Restoration* – Stuart Wood/Endemol UK/BBC Scotland. p.50 *The Mighty Boosh* – BBC; *Nighty Night* – Toby Jacobs/Babycow/BBC. p.51 *Date Rape: Sex and Lies* – Laurence Cendrowicz/Blast! Films/BBC; *The Smoking Room* – Simon Leigh/BBC. p.53 *Summer in the 60s* identity © BBC4; *The Alan Clark Diaries* – Mike Hogan/BBC. p.54 *Prime Suspect* – Granada; *Life Begins* – Granada. p.55 *Ant and Dec's Saturday Night Takeaway* – Granada. p.56 *I'm A Celebrity ... Get Me Out of Here!* – LWT/Granada; *Foyle's War* – Greenlit Productions/ITV. p.57 *Ramsay's Kitchen Nightmares* – Optomen/Channel 4. p.58 *Derren Brown: Séance*. Image © Objective Productions; *Brookside*. Image © Mersey Television; *Frasier* © Paramount/Channel 4. p.59 *Back to Reality* – Princess Productions/Five. p.60 *Dream Holiday Home* – RDF Media/Five. p.68 *Belonging* – BBC Wales. p.70 *Radio Times: Still Game* – The Comedy Unit/BBC Scotland & BBC Publications; *River City* – BBC Scotland. p.71 *Pulling Moves*

– BBC Northern Ireland. p.77 *There's Something About Miriam* – Brighter Pictures/Sky One. p.78 *War Women* – Eagle Media Productions/UKTV History; *Most Haunted* – Antix/Living TV. p.79 *Inside Clyde* – Talent Television/Disney; *Fort Boyard* – Challenge TV. p.80 *Street Hypnosis* – The Comedy Unit/Bravo. p.91 Image © BBC Parliament. p.95 *Take My Mother-In-Law* – Mentorn Scotland/ITV. p.97 BBC Freeview monkeys – Richard Kendal/BBC. p.100 Images © ITN. p.101 Fiona Bruce, BBC News – Chris Capstick/BBC. p.102-103 Images © BBC News 24. p.106 *Every Picture Tells a Story* – Five. p.107 *The Big Read* – BBC. p.108 *The Secret Policeman* – BBC. p.109 *Dunkirk* – Rolf Marriott/BBC. p.110 *The Crouches* – BBC. p.112 *Today With Des and Mel* – Mike Owen/Carlton/ITV. p.113 *Doctors* – Stuart Wood/BBC Birmingham. p.114 *Kath and Kim* – Ftn. p.115 *CSI: Crime Scene Investigation* – Five/Living TV. p.118 *Time Shift: Missing Believed Wiped*. Images © BBC Bristol/BBC4. p.120 *Time Shift: Fantasy Sixties*. Images © BBC Bristol/BBC4. p.121 *EastEnders* – Nicky Johnson/BBC. p.122 *Coronation Street* – Granada. p.124 *Footballers' Wives* – Shed Productions/ITV. p.125 *Shameless* – Company Pictures/Channel 4. p.126 *May 33rd* – BBC; *England Expects* – Mike Hogan/BBC; *Canterbury Tales* – Ziji Productions/BBC. p.127 *Passer By* – Liam Daniel/BBC; *Bella and the Boys* – Century Films/BBC. p.128 *New Tricks* – Mike Hogan/BBC. p.129 *Murder in Suburbia* – Carlton; *Waking the Dead* – Justin Canning/BBC. p.130 *Derren Brown: Séance*. Image © Objective Productions. *Most Haunted* – Antix/Living TV. p.131 *Sea of Souls* – Alan Peebles/BBC Scotland. p.132 *Charles II* – BBC. p.134 *Wall of Silence* – Granada/ITV. p.136 *The Office Christmas Specials* – Ray Burmiston/BBC. p.137 *Little Britain* – Stephen Gill/BBC. p.138 *Mad About Alice* – Simon Fowler/BBC. p.139 *Britain's Best Sitcom* – Ricky Kelehar/BBC; *Harry Hill's TV Burp* – Avalon/Carlton. p.140 *The Sack Race* – Danielle Horn/BBC. p.141 *24-Hour Quiz*. Images © Endemol UK/ITV; *Didn't They Do Well?* – Gary Moyes/BBC. p.142 *House Doctor* – talkbackTHAMES/Five. p.143 *Queer Eye UK* – Living TV. p.145 *Big Brother*. Images © Endemol UK/Channel 4. p.146 *Top of the Pops Saturday* – Simon Duncan/BBC. p.148 *Live At Johnny's* – Ian Derry/World's End/BBC. p.149 *6ixth Sense With Colin Fry* – Living TV; *Parkinson* – Alan Olley/BBC. p.150 *Dick and Dom in Da Bungalow* – Richard Kendal/BBC. p.151 *Feather Boy* – Gary Moyes/Childsplay/BBC; *Powers* – Will Sweet/BBC. p.153 *Ministry of Mayhem* – The Foundation/Carlton; *My Parents are Aliens* – Helen Turton/Granada Kids/Yorkshire; *Chinese Breakaway* – Here's One I Made Earlier/Five. p.154 *Blue Peter* – Chris Capstick/BBC. p.155 *Pleasureland*. Images © Kudos/Channel 4. p.157 *Match of the Day: Euro 2004* – Richard Kendal/BBC. p.159 *Radio Times* © BBC Publications